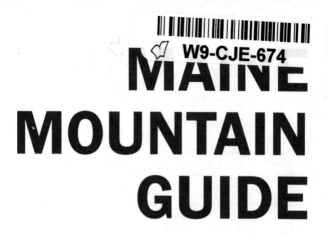

MAINE MOUNTAIN GUIDE

11TH EDITION

**AMC'S QUINTESSENTIAL TRAIL GUIDE
TO THE MOUNTAINS OF MAINE**

FEATURING BAXTER STATE PARK AND ACADIA NATIONAL PARK

Compiled and edited by
Carey Michael Kish

Appalachian Mountain Club Books
Boston, Massachusetts

AMC is a nonprofit organization, and sales of AMC Books fund our mission of protecting the Northeast outdoors. If you appreciate our efforts and would like to become a member or make a donation to AMC, visit outdoors.org, call 800-372-1758, or contact us at Appalachian Mountain Club, 10 City Square, Boston, MA 02129.

outdoors.org/books-maps

Distributed by National Book Network

Front cover photograph of Katahdin © Chris Bennett
Back cover photograph of Mt. Abraham © Chris Bennett
Cartography by Larry Garland, © Appalachian Mountain Club
Cover design by Kim Thornton
Interior design by Abigail Coyle

ISBN 978-1-62842-097-5

ISSN 1544-3604

The paper used in this publication meets the minimum requirements of the American National Standard for Information Sciences-Permanence of Paper for Printed Library Materials, ANSI Z39.48-1984. ∞

Interior pages and cover are printed on responsibly harvested paper stock certified by The Forest Stewardship Council®, an independent auditor of responsible forestry practices. Printed in the United States of America, using vegetable-based inks.

FSC
www.fsc.org
MIX
Paper from
responsible sources
FSC® C005010

5 4 3 2 1   18 19 20 21 22

EDITIONS OF THE MAINE MOUNTAIN GUIDE

First Edition	1961
Second Edition	1968
Third Edition	1971
Fourth Edition	1976
Fifth Edition	1985
Sixth Edition	1988
Seventh Edition	1993
Eighth Edition	1999
Ninth Edition	2005
Tenth Edition	2012
Eleventh Edition	2018

KEY TO LOCATOR MAPS

The numbers in the boxes below and on the locator maps at the beginning of each section indicate which pull-out map or maps cover that section. Trail descriptions are listed by the section in which the trailhead is located; parts of a trail may lie in another section or sections.

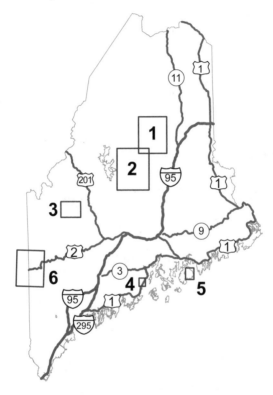

Map 1: Baxter State Park–Katahdin

Map 2: Maine Woods

Map 3: Bigelow Range

Map 4: Camden Hills

Map 5: Eastern Mt. Desert Island

Map 6: Mahoosuc Range–Evans Notch

CONTENTS

MAP INDEX

KEY TO HIKING ICONS

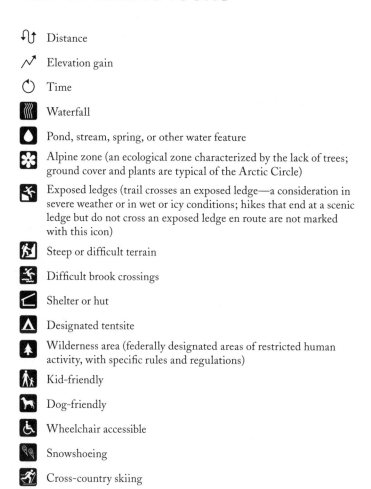

↧↥ Distance

↗ Elevation gain

◯ Time

Waterfall

Pond, stream, spring, or other water feature

Alpine zone (an ecological zone characterized by the lack of trees; ground cover and plants are typical of the Arctic Circle)

Exposed ledges (trail crosses an exposed ledge—a consideration in severe weather or in wet or icy conditions; hikes that end at a scenic ledge but do not cross an exposed ledge en route are not marked with this icon)

Steep or difficult terrain

Difficult brook crossings

Shelter or hut

Designated tentsite

Wilderness area (federally designated areas of restricted human activity, with specific rules and regulations)

Kid-friendly

Dog-friendly

Wheelchair accessible

Snowshoeing

Cross-country skiing

Scenic views

Fire tower (although some are more stable than others, all fire towers should be considered climb-at-your-own-risk)

KEY TO MAP ICONS

Conservation land (fee)

Conservation easement

🛉 Entrance or ranger station

🏠 Lodge, hut, cabin

🅰 Campground

🆑 Shelter

🔺 Tentsite

🅿 Parking

▲ Summit

❭ Gate

🗼 Observation/fire tower

🕯 Lighthouse

═ Highway

═ Improved road

== Unimproved road

— Trail

⋯ Mountain bike trail

Ⓐ Appalachian Trail

ABBREVIATIONS AND ACRONYMS

The following abbreviations and acronyms are used in this book.

100MW	100-Mile Wilderness	FR	Forest Route
AMC	Appalachian Mountain Club	FSHT	Francis Small Heritage Trust
ANP	Acadia National Park	ft.	foot, feet
AT	Appalachian Trail	GHP	Georges Highland Path
ATC	Appalachian Trail Conservancy	GIS	Geographic Information Systems
Ave.	Avenue		
AWW	Allagash Wilderness Waterway	GLWMA	Gene Letourneau Wildlife Management Area (Frye Mtn.)
BHHT	Blue Hill Heritage Trust	GPMCT	Great Pond Mountain Conservation Trust
BKP	Bingham's Kennebec Purchase		
BPP	Bingham's Penobscot Purchase	GPS	Global Positioning System
BRCA	Belgrade Regional Conservation Alliance	GRLT	Georges River Land Trust
		GWRLT	Great Works Regional Land Trust
BSP	Baxter State Park	HA	Hebron Academy
CC	City of Calais	HMLT	Hedgehog Mtn. Land Trust
CG	Campground	HPA	High Peaks Alliance
CMLT	Coastal Mountains Land Trust	IAT	International Appalachian Trail
CMP	Central Maine Power		
CTA	Chatham Trails Association	IHT	Island Heritage Trust
DCC	Downeast Coastal Conservancy	ITS	Interconnected Trail System
		jct.	junction
Dept.	Department	KELT	Kennebec Estuary Land Trust
DIFW	Maine Dept. of Inland Fisheries and Wildlife	KLT	Kennebec Land Trust
DLLT	Downeast Lakes Land Trust	KWWNM	Katahdin Woods and Waters National Monument
Dr.	Drive		
ED	Eastern Division	LELT	Loon Echo Land Trust
FBC	Frenchman Bay Conservancy	LGP	Land & Garden Preserve
FCT	Freeport Conservation Trust	LHFT	Libby Hill Forest Trails
FOBMM	Friends of Burnt Meadow Mountain	Ln.	Lane
		LP	loop

X ABBREVIATIONS AND ACRONYMS

MA	Maine Audubon	R	Range
MACR	Mt. Agamenticus Conservation Region	Rd.	Road
MATC	Maine Appalachian Trail Club	RRCT	Royal River Conservation Trust
MBPL	Maine Bureau of Parks and Lands	RT	round-trip
MCC	Midcoast Conservancy	RWD	Rumford Water District
MCHT	Maine Coast Heritage Trust	SD	Southern Division
MCPT	Mt. Cutler Preservation Trust	SFMA	Scientific Forest Management Area
MD	Middle Division	SIA	Sentier International des Appalaches
ME	Maine	SMSR	Sugarloaf Mtn. Ski Resort
MFS	Maine Forest Service	St.	Street
MHT	Maine Huts & Trails	T	Township
mi.	mile(s)	TCH	Town of Castle Hill
min.	minute	TOF	Town of Freeport
MLT	Mahoosuc Land Trust	TOL	Town of Leeds
MNWR	Moosehorn National Wildlife Refuge	TNC	The Nature Conservancy
mph	miles per hour	TOS	Town of Sebago
Mt.	Mount	U.S.	United States
MTF	Maine Trail Finder	USFS	United States Forest Service
Mtn.	Mountain	USGS	United States Geological Survey
MWI	Maine Woods Initiative	WBPC	West Branch Pond Camps
ND	Northern Division	WCC	Woodstock Conservation Commission
NFTM	No formal trail maintainer	WCTC	Waldo County Trails Coalition
NH	New Hampshire	WELS	West of the Easterly Line of the State
NHVIS	Northeast Harbor Village Improvement Society	WKR	West of Kennebec River
NMW	North Maine Woods	WMNF	White Mountain National Forest
NPS	National Park Service	yd.	yard(s)
NWP	North of Waldo Patent		
OW	one way		
PL	Public Land(s)		

FOREWORD

This hiker has been tramping the woods and mountains of Maine for going on five decades, since moving to the state in 1971 at the age of 13.

As a kid, I had a curiosity for any patch of woods, whether behind a neighbor's house or out back beyond the ball field fence. Blazing trails into those dark and mysterious woods always meant great adventure, and my friends and I would emerge hours later, dirty from head to toe with cuts and scratches and insect bites and smiles a mile wide. Living in Maine, where big woods were seemingly everywhere, certainly changed the scale of these childhood explorations. When we had thoroughly covered and mentally mapped the forests and trails around Bangor as far as our feet and bikes could take us, my adventurous group of pals moved on to hitchhiking to the hills east of town then south to the mountains of Acadia. And when my dad finally took me up to Baxter State Park and I climbed Katahdin, I might as well have been standing atop Mt. Everest, such was the elation. I was irrevocably hooked on hiking.

I bought my first *Maine Mountain Guide* in 1976 and, with that, realized the amazing wealth of mountains and trails across the state. I knew I had to hike them all. I was so inspired I decided to hike the entire Appalachian Trail, from Springer Mtn. in Georgia to Katahdin, a life-changing trek I completed in 1977 (and again in 2015). Ever since then, I've been seeking out the forested trails and craggy summits of our beautiful state of Maine, still striving to hike all of the trails in the guide. Given the explosion of trail building across the state in recent years, that task certainly has gotten a lot tougher.

The eleventh edition of this book captures and describes a whole host of these new trails and summits for your hiking pleasure, plus all of the old favorites. Open it wide, thumb through the pages, scribble some notes, pore over the maps, dream a little, and plan your next adventure or two. So many wild and scenic natural places in Maine await your footsteps, your eyes and ears, and the company of family and friends. Start your journey with this guide then go enjoy and savor time well spent in the Maine woods. Hope to see you on the trail!

Carey Michael Kish
Mt. Desert Island, Maine
March 1, 2018

ACKNOWLEDGMENTS

The *Maine Mountain Guide* is the product of the hard work and dedication of many people, including those who contributed in so many ways, large and small, to the ten previous editions of the book since its inception in 1961. You helped build the foundation for this guide, and as editor for the last two editions, I cannot thank you all enough. I am honored to follow in your footsteps and proud to carry on with this important outdoor tradition.

Huge thanks go to my wife and favorite trail companion, Fran Leyman, for accompanying me on nearly every one of the hundreds of trails that required hiking over the last two years; for putting up with my incessant note taking, GPS fiddling, and picture taking; for hiking a few of the trails and collecting notes on her own when I could not break away from my computer screen; and for looking the other way from the enormous mess I made of our house during the research and writing of this book. Fran, you're an angel, and I love you.

Sincere thanks are due the great staff at AMC Books. Shannon Smith, books editor, provided a wealth of advice, guidance, and support throughout the lengthy writing and editing process; Jennifer Wehunt, editorial director, offered an ear and good counsel when it was most needed; and Abigail Coyle, production manager, helped shepherd the book through the production process. Much appreciation goes to Larry Garland, AMC's cartographer, for the outstanding color and black-and-white maps that accompany this guide; they are not only eminently useful but a work of art, in my humble opinion. Thanks also to Bec Rollins, chief communications officer, and to her predecessor, Kevin Breunig, vice president of communications and marketing. Rob Burbank, AMC's public affairs director, got me started on this guidebook adventure back in 2011; thanks always, my friend.

Steve Smith is the editor extraordinaire of AMC's *White Mountain Guide*. I adapted Section 5: Mahoosuc Range and Grafton Notch and Section 6: White Mountain National Forest and Evans Notch from that venerable guidebook. Many thanks, Steve, for your sage advice and support. Thanks also to fellow AMC guidebook authors Peter Kick (*Catskill Mountain Guide*), John Burk (*Massachusetts Trail Guide*), Jerry and Marcy Monkman (*Outdoor Adventures: Acadia National Park*) and Matt Heid (*AMC's Best Backpacking in New England*); you've set a high bar and I'm pleased to be in your good company.

A plethora of heartfelt thanks goes out to so many people across Maine, all of those dedicated and caring individuals who provided much needed assistance in the shaping of this guide, from carefully reviewing trail descriptions and other sections of the text and providing valuable comment; to identifying new trails for inclusion, providing maps, and drafting new trail descriptions; to hitting the trail in earnest and gathering firsthand information in the field. This guide could not have been improved and expanded without your help and encouragement.

From the Maine Dept. of Agriculture, Conservation and Forestry, Bureau of Parks and Lands: Rex Turner, outdoor recreation planner, provided a great amount of information on Maine's public lands, state parks, and trail-building efforts; Vern Labbe, Northern Public Lands Office; Scott Thompson, Aroostook State Park; Chuck Simpson and Benjamin Clark, Eastern Public Lands Office; Bruce Farnham, Mt. Blue State Park; Matt LaRoche, Allagash Wilderness Waterway; Charles Cannon, Holbrook Island Sanctuary; Chris Silsbee and C. Ben Woodard, Bradbury Mtn. State Park. Jensen Bissell, park director, Baxter State Park, provided a comprehensive update of Baxter trails. From the Maine Forest Service: Ken Laustsen and Kevin Doran. From the Maine Dept. of Inland Fisheries and Wildlife: Sarah Spencer. From the U.S. Dept. of the Interior, National Park Service: Charlie Jacobi, Gary Stellpflug, and John Kelly of Acadia National Park; Tim Hudson, superintendent of the new Katahdin Woods and Waters National Monument.

From Maine's incredible community of land trusts, conservation organizations, environmental agencies, trail clubs, trail advocates, outdoor recreation groups, and other good friends of Maine trails: Chris Stevenson, Land & Garden Preserve; George Fields and Eileen Mielenhausen, Blue Hill Heritage Trust; Toni Bingel Pied, Belgrade Regional Conservation Alliance; Jackie Stratton, Coastal Mountains Land Trust; Rich Bard, Downeast Coastal Conservancy; Colin Brown, Downeast Lakes Land Trust; Aaron Dority, Frenchman Bay Conservancy; Katrina Van Dusen and Guy Blanchard, Freeport Conservation Trust; Steve McPike, Friends of Libby Hill; Dick Jarrett and Kathy Chaiklin, Francis Small Heritage Trust; Tom Henderson, Greater Lovell Land Trust; Cheri Domina, Great Pond Mtn. Land Trust; Brent West and David Elliott, George River Land Trust; Patti Mitchem, Great Works Regional Land Trust; Mike Little and Marissa Hutchinson, Island Heritage Trust; Jean-Luc Theriault, Kennebec Land Trust; Thom Perkins and Jon Evans, Loon Echo Land Trust; Robin Kerr and Darin Radatz, Mt. Agamenticus Conservation Program;

Simon Rucker, Maine Appalachian Trail Land Trust; Jean Bass, Mahoosuc Trust; Hannah Chamberlain, Midcoast Conservancy; Dan Hester, Mt. Cutler Preservation Trust; Shelby Rousseau, Tracy Clinch, and Amanda Laliberte, Rangeley Lakes Heritage Trust; Alan Stearns and Kyle Warren, Royal River Conservation Trust; Jeff Romano and Jane Arbuckle, Maine Coast Heritage Trust (special thanks to Jeff for the updated info on Maine's public and private lands); Bill Patterson, Dan Grenier, Jonathan Bailey, Nancy Sferra, Mathew Markot, Timothy Paul, and Matt Scaccia, The Nature Conservancy, Maine field office; Erica Kaufman, Kristen Hoffman, and Alan Hutchinson, Forest Society of Maine; Lester Kenway, Dave Field, Doug Dolan, Ron Dobra, Craig Dickstein, Don Miskill, Tom Giggey, Tom Gorrill, Mike Ewing, Laura Flight, Janice Clain, Patty Harding, Ray Ronan, Elsa Sanborn, Tim Akers, Carrington Rhodes, and Rick Ste. Croix, Maine Appalachian Trail Club; Ben Godsoe, High Peaks Alliance; Judy Berk, Natural Resources Council of Maine; Sherry Huber, Maine Tree Foundation; Bryan Wentzell, Maine Mountain Collaborative; Lucas St. Clair, Susan Adams, Megan Bremermann, Elliotsville Plantation Inc.; Ben Townsend, Clifton Climbers Alliance; Dan Rinard, Steve Tatko, Jared Coyne, Jenny Ward, AMC Maine Woods Initiative; Kaitlyn Bernard, AMC Maine Conservation Policy office; Peter Roderick, John Mullens, Jeff Pengel, Dave McCarthy, Gerry Sawyer, AMC Maine Chapter; Stephanie Clement, Friends of Acadia (special thanks for the great review of Acadia trails); Doug Ofiara, Friends of Burnt Meadow Mtn.; Jessie Perkins, Bethel Conservation Commission; Donna Larson, Town of Freeport; Beth Ward, Camden Parks & Recreation Dept.; Don Hudson, International Appalachian Trail; Bill Cobb, Maine Chapter, Forest Fire Lookout Association (special thanks for the fire tower blurb); Cayce Frigon, Sue Davis, Kate Boehmer, and Savannah Steele, Maine Huts & Trails; Buck O'Herin and Cloe Chunn, Waldo County Trails Coalition; Victor Borko, Trails for Rangeley Area Coalition; Ethan Austin, Sugarloaf; Christina Howe and Dana Black, Spencer Pond Camps. Thanks also to Angela Arno and Skye Lavigne, Moosehead Lake Chamber of Commerce; Robin Zinchuk, Bethel Area Chamber of Commerce; Theresa Fowler, Central Aroostook Chamber of Commerce; Holly Roberts, Greater York Chamber of Commerce; Lloyd Irland, the Irland Group; Laurie Boynton Cormier, Big Moose Inn; Bryant Davis, Maine Quest Adventures; Sarah Medina, Seven Islands Land Company; Kevin McGlauflin, Prentiss & Carlisle; Phyllis Jalbert, Willard Jalbert Camps; Mark Leathers, J.W. Sewall Company.

Many individual members of Maine's hiking community made important contributions to this guide. My thanks for all the trail miles and field notes from Keith Malone, Tim Terranova, Emily Terranova, Gregg Alexis, Emily Zimmermann, Jim Logan, Bill Geller, Tom Jamrog, Mike Zimmermann, Ryan Linn, Judith Foster, Wanda Greatorex, Lucy Johnston, Gary Dick, Aislinn Sarnacki, Don and Rae Cousins, Bruce Stone, Zach Porter, Chris Keene, Jake Skaff, Tedd Davis, Curtis and Lori Burley, Deanna Burtchell. Thanks also to Marvin Swartz, Eric and Elaine Hendrickson, Christina Perkins, Rick Sargent, Rick Hesslein, Carol Bourque, Abigail Bliss, Brian and Kathy Kaczor, Jim and Harriet Connors, Jacki and Chris Leighton, Jane and Jay Baxter, Ann Schneider, Mark Weisendanger, Cheri Neumayer, Josh Cheney, Leigh Dunkelberger, Bonnie Brown, Lydia Berman, Greg Pargellis, Jeff Toothaker, Billy Bowker, Lewis Dow, Paul Corrigan, and Tony Nunzo.

Carl Eppich, Bruce Hyman, Dana Thurston, Janet Thurston, Earl Brechlin, John Wilson, Melie Guzek: you were great trail companions; let's go hiking again real soon. Steve Spencer: your name and Maine trails will always appear together in my mind's eye. Thank you.

References consulted in preparing and revising the introductory text include *A Geography of Maine* (Eldred Rolfe), *Forest Trees of Maine* (Maine Forest Service), *Surficial Geologic History of Maine* (Maine Geological Survey), and *Bedrock Geologic History of Maine* (Maine Geological Survey).

This 11th edition is dedicated to Alan Hutchinson, a tireless conservationist and good friend of AMC, who passed away on August 27, 2017. In his twenty years as the executive director of the Forest Society of Maine, Alan helped conserve more than 1 million acres of working forestland in Maine's North Woods, including the 360,000-acre Moosehead Region Conservation Easement, a landmark project completed in 2012, in partnership with AMC and The Nature Conservancy. We miss you, Alan.

HOW TO USE THIS BOOK

This book aims to provide complete coverage of hiking trails in Maine's mountains, which are scattered across a large and geographically diverse area, ranging from the rockbound coast to the inland hills to the remote mountains of the northern interior. Trails on more than 300 mountains and hills are described, from Mt. Agamenticus in the southwestern corner of the state to Deboullie Mtn. and Black Mtn. in northern Aroostook County, and from Aziscohos Mtn. in northwestern Maine near the New Hampshire border to Klondike Mtn. in Lubec, not far from the easternmost point in Maine and the international border with New Brunswick, Canada.

The trails are segmented into twelve geographic regions. Four sections—Southwestern Maine, Midcoast, Acadia National Park, and Downeast—describe mountains in proximity to the coast, as well as some of the inland hills. The Southwestern Maine section includes all of York County and Cumberland County and the southern part of Oxford County. The Midcoast section includes the entirety of Waldo County, Knox County, Lincoln County, and Sagadahoc County. The Acadia National Park section covers Mt. Desert Island and Schoodic Peninsula in Hancock County and Isle au Haut in Knox County. The Downeast section covers all of Hancock County (except for Acadia National Park) and Washington County.

In the southern interior of Maine, the Oxford Hills section stretches westward from the Androscoggin River to the Maine portion of the White Mountain National Forest near the New Hampshire border, in the vicinity of Evans Notch. To the north, the rugged summits of the Mahoosuc Range encompass the deep valley of Grafton Notch. Ranging northeast from there are the high peaks of the Longfellow Mountains and the Appalachian Trail (AT) corridor, which are described in Western Lakes and Mountains, as well as in the section on the 100-Mile Wilderness and Moosehead Lake. This mountainous chain culminates in Katahdin and a jumble of wilderness summits within the boundaries of Baxter State Park. North and east of the park are the vast forestland and scattered mountains of Aroostook County. The mountain character of the Kennebec River valley and Moose River valley ranges from scattered low hills in the south to remote high peaks near the Canadian border in the north.

Each section begins with a listing of the major mountains in that region, as well as any significant public or private land preserves. Next an introduction describes the geography of the region, its boundaries, the dominant natural features, and the general location of the mountains covered. An overview of the major roads follows, describing in general terms the access to the various trailheads. Each introduction also includes options for public and private roadside and backcountry camping.

SUGGESTED HIKES

At the beginning of each section is a list of suggested hikes, selected to provide hikers with a number of options for easy, moderate, and strenuous routes within the given region. Criteria can vary from trail to trail, but in general, an easy hike may have little to no elevation gain, covers a relatively short distance, and can be completed in several hours or less. A moderate hike can take as long as half a day and covers a longer distance, often with more elevation gain. A strenuous hike requires a full day of six to eight hours, with significant mileage or elevation gain. The icons refer to features of note that hikers will encounter (see Key to Hiking Icons, p. vii). The numbers that follow indicate total distance, elevation gain, and time required. When choosing a trail, hikers should consider mileage, elevation gain, time required, available daylight, and difficulty of the terrain, as well as the experience, physical fitness, goals, and size of the group. For more information on planning a group trip, see *AMC's Mountain Skills Manual,* by Christian Bisson and Jamie Hannon (AMC Books, 2017).

TRAIL DESCRIPTIONS

Trail descriptions are segmented by the mountains on which the trails are found, although some trails are not associated with a mountain. Each trail is described individually, in the most commonly traveled direction—usually ascending. When a hike uses a combination of trails, readers may need to consult several descriptions. In the parenthetical next to the trail name, the acronym for the organization maintaining the trail (where known) appears first, followed by a reference to the map or maps that correspond to the trail. This list of maps may name the AMC in-text map or pull-out map, a U.S. Geological Survey (NFTM; USGS) quad, *Maine Atlas & Gazetteer* road map(s), Maine Appalachian Trail Club (MATC) map, a land management agency map available in print or online, or any combination thereof that best covers that particular trail.

A typical trail description first provides an overview of the trail(s), including its origin and destination and, if notable, its general character (gradient, roughness, etc.), and perhaps the view to be seen from the summit. From there, we cover driving directions to the trailhead, where appropriate. This is followed by concise, turn-by-turn directions for hiking the trail. The description notes important features, such as trail junctions, stream crossings, viewpoints, summits, and any significant difficulties. *Always check AMC's books updates page online for the most recent trail closures, reroutings, and other changes before you head out: outdoors.org/ books-maps.*

DISTANCES, TIMES, AND ELEVATIONS

The summary table above the trail description lists the distances, times, and elevation gains for the trail(s), which are cumulative from the starting point at the head of the table.

Most of the trails in this guide have been measured using GPS or a surveyor's wheel. Minor inconsistencies sometimes occur when measured distances are rounded, and the distances given may differ from posted trail signs and land management maps.

Elevations, when they are precisely known, are indicated. Otherwise, elevations are estimated to the nearest 50-ft. contour. In some places, such as where several minor ups and downs occur, these figures are only roughly accurate. USGS maps are the basis for these calculations.

There is no reliable method for predicting how much time a particular hiker or group of hikers will take to complete a hike on a specific day, because many factors influence the speed of an individual hiker or hiking group. To give hikers a basis for planning, estimated times have been calculated in this book using the formula of 30 min. for each mile of distance and 30 min. for each 1,000 ft. of climbing. These are known as "book times." These estimated time allowances do not include snack or lunch stops, scenery appreciation, or rest breaks. Some parties may require more time, and others may need less. Special factors, such as stream crossings, steep slopes, rough footing, heavy packs, fatigue, and weather conditions, can affect trail times. For example, a 6-mi. hike on easy terrain will require less effort, though perhaps more time, than a 3-mi. hike over rough trail with 1,500 ft. of elevation gain. The given times have not been adjusted for the difficulties of specific trails, so hikers should plan accordingly, always leaving a good margin for safety. Average descent times can vary even more, based on such factors as agility and the condition of a hiker's knees. In winter, times can be even less predictable; on a packed trail, travel may be faster than in summer, while in deep, untracked snow with heavy backpacks, the time may double or triple the summer estimate.

The following examples demonstrate how to read the information in the summary tables at the beginning of each trail description.

CADILLAC NORTH RIDGE TRAIL (NPS; MAP 5: D7)			
From Park Loop Rd. (400 ft.) to:	⮫⮨	⬈	⟳
Cadillac Mtn. summit (1,528 ft.)	2.2 mi.	1,125 ft.	1:40
elevation	*distance*	*elevation gain (reverse elevation gain)*	*time*

For Cadillac North Ridge Trail, refer to Map 5 included with this guide. To locate the trail, use the grid references on the left (letters) and top (numbers) edges of the map. This trail is found at the intersection of D and 7. The starting point is Park Loop Rd. at an elevation of 400 ft. The distance covered to the Cadillac Mtn. summit at 1,528 ft. is 2.2 mi., the elevation gain between trailhead and summit is 1,125 ft., and the hike will take an estimated time of 1 hour and 40 minutes. (*Note:* NPS in this example refers to the National Park Service, which is the trail maintaining agency for this particular trail.)

When no AMC map reference is listed in the table, the trail is not covered by any of the maps provided with this guide. In such cases, please refer to the summary table for the name of the appropriate maps for the trail, as in this example:

STONE MTN. TRAIL (FOBMM; USGS BROWNFIELD QUAD, GAZETTEER MAP 4, FOBMM BURNT MEADOW MTN. TRAIL MAP)			
From Twin Brook Trail (1,160 ft.) to:	⮫⮨	⬈	⟳
Stone Mtn. summit (1,624 ft.)	0.7 mi.	460 ft.	0:35
elevation	*distance*	*elevation gain (reverse elevation gain)*	*time*

Because there is no AMC map for Stone Mtn. Trail, hikers should obtain the USGS Brownfield quad (quadrangle map), and Map 4 of *The Maine Atlas and Gazetteer*, and/or the Burnt Meadow Mtn. Trail Map, produced by Friends of Burnt Meadow Mtn. (FOBMM).

MAPS AND NAVIGATION

This guide features two folded map sheets that contain six full-color maps covering many of Maine's popular hiking areas, including Map 1: Baxter State Park–Katahdin; Map 2: Maine Woods; Map 3: Bigelow Range; Map 4: Camden Hills; Map 5: Eastern Mt. Desert Island; and Map 6: Mahoosuc Range–Evans Notch. These high-quality maps, produced using GPS and GIS technology, indicate a range of data useful to the hiker, including trails, trail segment mileage, tentsites, shelters and campsites, campgrounds, public land ownership, parking areas, visitor centers and ranger stations, fire towers, ecological zones, boat launches, and picnic areas. Each map uses a contour interval of 100 ft. The scales vary from map to map, as does the magnetic declination, which in Maine ranges from 14.5 to 17 degrees west of true north. Latitude and longitude coordinates and Universal Transverse Mercator grid coordinates are included on the maps and allow their use with a handheld GPS unit. Contact information pertinent to the maps is also included.

A series of black-and-white maps covering a variety of trail networks are also provided within the text of this guide. Please refer to the Map Index on p. vi for a complete list of these handy maps.

Given the geographic distribution of mountains and hiking trails in Maine, not every trail described appears on the maps provided. For the areas not covered, please refer to the USGS 7.5-minute quadrangle map listed in the trail summary. Although the topographic quality of these maps is excellent, be aware that some trails may not be accurately depicted or may not appear at all. USGS maps are available from local retailers and outdoor shops or directly from the USGS (USGS.gov or 888-ASK-USGS). Index maps showing the available USGS quads in any state and the informative pamphlet *Topographic Maps* are available from USGS and are free by request.

Many state parks, land trusts, and other conservation and recreation organizations have useful trail maps available online and/or in print at trailheads. Where such maps are available, they are mentioned in the trail description. You may also refer to Appendix A: Helpful Information and Contacts on p. 564 for more information on land management and other agencies.

References to the appropriate *Maine Atlas and Gazetteer* map are included with each trail description, except for those trails covered by the maps included in the guide. The atlas is a useful (and sometimes indispensable) tool for trip planning and navigation to the trailhead, indicating back roads, dirt roads, some trails and trailheads, elevation contours, lakes and streams, public lands, land use cover, and boat ramps. Garmin, the Swiss GPS firm, purchased the atlas's publisher, DeLorme, in 2016 and has indicated it will continue to produce the venerable publication. The Gazetteer is available at many retail and online locations, including garmin.com/en-US/maps.

This book describes many of the mountain peaks along the AT in Maine, and readers may find *The Official Appalachian Trail Guide to Maine* (Maine Appalachian Trail Club) to be a helpful companion guide. The guide contains seven topographic and profile maps that cover the 282-mi. trail route from Katahdin to the New Hampshire state line, plus numerous side trails. The guidebook and maps are available at outdoor retailers and many bookstores or by contacting MATC at matc.org or P.O. Box 283, Augusta, ME 04332-0283.

In addition to the maps in this guide, other useful AMC maps for Maine hikers include the new *100-Mile Wilderness Map & Guide* (coming spring 2018); *Acadia National Park Map* for hiking, biking, and paddling; and waterproof Tyvek versions of the *Maine Mountains Trail Maps*, included in this book as paper maps. These may be purchased online at outdoors.org/amcstore, at most AMC lodges and visitor centers, and at many bookstores and outdoor equipment retailers. National Geographic also publishes several Trails Illustrated maps for Maine hiking locales: *Acadia National Park, White Mountain National Forest East: Presidential Range, Gorham*; *Baxter State Park: Mt. Katahdin/Katahdin Iron Works*; *Appalachian Trail: Mount Carlo to Pleasant Pond*; and *Appalachian Trail: Pleasant Pond to Katahdin*.

Hikers should always have a map and compass (and know how to use both) and carefully keep track of their approximate location on the map. We recommend carrying this guide, and/or a photocopy or photo of the sections pertaining to the intended hike, with you. Saving maps and trail descriptions on your smart phone is a useful trick, but it's best to always carry a paper backup should your cell battery run out. Snap a photo of the trailhead kiosk map, too, and obtain a copy of the land management agency's map and brochure for the intended hike, if available.

A baseplate compass—a circular, liquid-filled compass that turns on a rectangular base made of clear plastic—is well suited for hiking use. You can easily set such a compass to the bearing you want to follow, and then it's a simple matter of keeping the compass needle aligned north and following the arrow on the base. In Maine, there is deviation—known as *declination*—of between 14.5 degrees and 17 degrees between true north and magnetic north. This means true north will be anywhere from 14.5 degrees to 17 degrees to the right of (clockwise from) the north needle of the compass. (Declination changes over time; each AMC map and USGS quad map indicates the current declination for that particular map on its legend.) When taking a bearing from a map, you will need to add between 14.5 degrees and 17 degrees to the bearing when you set the compass. On the pull-out maps included with this guide, the black lines that run from bottom to top are aligned with true north.

GPS units are increasingly popular with many hikers. When used in conjunction with a map and compass, a GPS unit can be a very useful tool in the woods, but it is not a substitute for a map and compass. GPS reception can be spotty, and units are subject to damage or battery failure. Extra batteries are a must. Hikers should practice with the GPS unit and become familiar with its operation and features before starting out on a trip. There are now a number of quality GPS apps for smartphones, which function at a high standard and can serve as a useful substitute for a GPS unit in many cases.

For an excellent primer on map and compass use, GPS use, and other navigation skills, consult *AMC's Mountain Skills Manual* by Christian Bisson and Jamie Hannon (2017).

LIDAR DATA

Maps 3–5 summit elevations are based on recently acquired Light Detection and Ranging (LiDAR) data, a new technology accurate to about 18 cm. These elevations may vary from older sources—generally by 10 feet or less, although some elevations may vary up to 30 ft. The elevations, distances, and hiking times listed in this guide are based on data calculated before LiDAR was available.

INTRODUCTION

For this edition, the 11th Maine Mountain Guide, we have revised, updated, and expanded many existing trail descriptions, and we have added more than 175 new trails on 50 "new" mountains, thereby increasing the already wide variety of hiking possibilities available for every interest and ability level. In all, more than 625 trails are described on 300 mountains, a hiking bounty totaling close to 1,500 mi. and ranging from easy woodland walks to moderate hill climbs to strenuous mountain traverses. A series of detailed topographic pull-out maps highlighting seven popular hiking destinations as well as 22 topographic, in-text maps complement the hike descriptions. It is our hope that readers will find the guide and maps to be a helpful companion, leading to many days of outdoor pleasure and healthful exercise on the trails through the scenic woods and mountains of Maine.

MAINE'S PUBLIC AND PRIVATE LANDS

The forestland of Maine covers about 17.7 million acres, or 78 percent of the state, making it the most heavily forested state in the United States. Large tracts of undeveloped forestland, much of it commercial timberland, are found in northern, western, and eastern Maine. In other parts of the United States, particularly in the west, such large blocks of land are usually publicly owned and managed by the federal government—primarily the U.S. Forest Service (USFS) or Bureau of Land Management. In Maine, however, just 7 percent of the forestland, or about 1.3 million acres, is owned by the public, and the remaining 93 percent, or about 16.4 million acres, is privately owned.

The state of Maine owns more than 1 million acres of land. This includes 36 state parks totaling 67,000 acres, 156 public lands totaling 630,000 acres, and fifteen historic sites totaling 276 acres. These state lands are managed by the Maine Dept. of Agriculture, Conservation, and Forestry, Bureau of Parks and Lands. The 210,000-acre Baxter State Park (BSP) is administered as a separate entity by the BSP Authority, which consists of the Maine attorney general, the director of the Maine Forest Service (MFS), and the commissioner of the Maine Dept. of Inland Fisheries and Wildlife (DIFW). DIFW manages 100,000 acres of land as Wildlife Management Areas.

The federal government owns about 275,000 acres of land. This includes a 50,000-acre section of the White Mountain National Forest (WMNF) in and around Evans Notch in western Maine; 37,700 acres in

Acadia National Park (ANP) on Mt. Desert Island, Schoodic Peninsula, Isle au Haut, and eighteen other islands; ten National Wildlife Refuges totaling 64,600 acres, including Moosehorn, the largest in the state; 87,500 acres in Katahdin Woods and Waters National Monument; and the 31,800-acre Appalachian Trail (AT) corridor administered by the Appalachian Trail Conservancy (ATC) under the guidance of the National Park Service (NPS).

Large timberland owner groups, including the forest industry, corporate investors, families, and miscellaneous private parties, own more than 15 million acres. American Indian tribal landowners own about 184,000 acres.

Maine has a robust network of more than 80 land trusts and conservation organizations, including the Appalachian Mountain Club (AMC), that together own more than 600,000 acres. The Maine Chapter of The Nature Conservancy (TNC) owns the largest parcel, about 180,000 acres along the St. John River in Aroostook County in northwestern Maine.

Land trusts and conservation organizations have protected an additional 2.2 million acres through conservation easements. Public and private conservation land in Maine, in fee ownership and conservation easements, now totals 4.1 million acres, or about 21 percent of the state's land area.

The Land for Maine's Future Program (LMF) is an important source of conservation funding in Maine. LMF was established in 1987 when Maine citizens voted to fund $35 million to purchase lands of statewide importance. Voters approved five additional bond issues between 1999 and 2012. In three decades, the program has conserved more than 600,000 acres of land in Maine, including Mt. Kineo, the Cutler Coast, Tumbledown Mtn., Rumford Whitecap, and Mt. Abraham.

TRAIL COURTESY

The many hundreds of miles of trails on Maine's public and private lands exist due to the generosity of landowners and the stewardship of many organizations and individuals. On all public lands and some private lands, agreements—some formal and some not—exist to allow for foot trails and their public use. Some trails cross private land with no formal permission from the landowner. In such cases, these trails exist by virtue of a long tradition of public use.

Regardless of whether a trail is on public or private land, hikers should exercise care to observe all regulations that have been designed to protect the land itself and the rights of the landowners. Despite a history of public use and enjoyment, trails—especially those on private land—are subject to closure at the will of the landowner. Therefore, it is imperative that hikers treat all trails and property with great respect, as if the land were their own. This might require cleaning up after others less mindful.

Hikers should be aware they will sometimes share designated trails with other users, such as ATV riders, mountain bikers, and horseback riders. There is room for enjoyment for all in the Maine outdoors, so please be courteous.

Dog owners should have their pets under control at all times, whether by leash or voice command. Dogs are not allowed in BSP and on some land trust properties. In ANP, dogs are allowed on leash. Please check with the land management agency in advance for particular rules regarding dogs.

APPALACHIAN TRAIL

With the passage of the National Trails System Act (NTSA) by Congress in 1968, the AT became the first federally protected footpath in the United States and was officially designated the Appalachian National Scenic Trail. In 1978, amendments to the NTSA authorized funds and directed NPS and USFS to acquire lands to protect the AT corridor. In 1984, the Dept. of the Interior delegated the bulk of the responsibilities for managing the trail to the Appalachian Trail Conference, which changed its name to the Appalachian Trail Conservancy (ATC) in 2005 to better reflect its role. Today, ATC works to maintain and protect the AT in conjunction with a host of organizations—including the Maine Appalachian Trail Club (MATC)—in the fourteen states through which the trail passes.

The 2,190-mi. route of the AT enters Maine at the Maine–New Hampshire border in the Mahoosuc Range, negotiates the difficult mile-long stretch of Mahoosuc Notch, and proceeds to climb over a long series of high peaks—many exceeding 4,000 ft.—that make up the Longfellow Mountains. After traversing Bigelow Range, the AT crosses the wide and swift Kennebec River at Caratunk on its way to Monson, the last outpost of civilization before the 100-Mile Wilderness. Rugged mountains, lakes, ponds, waterfalls, and deep forests characterize this final leg of the trail to BSP. The northern terminus of the AT, and its 282-mi. route through Maine, is atop the lofty alpine summit of Katahdin, the highest mountain in the state. Most of the mountains along the AT in Maine are described in this guide.

INTERNATIONAL APPALACHIAN TRAIL

The brainchild of Dick Anderson of Freeport, Maine, the International Appalachian Trail (IAT) was first proposed to the public in 1994. Anderson "visualized a trail that would connect two countries and cultures, link a state and two provinces and traverse two major watersheds—the Gulf of

Maine and the Gulf of St. Lawrence." Today, the IAT extends across northern Maine, from just east of Katahdin and BSP in the new Katahdin Woods and Waters National Monument, through New Brunswick and Quebec, to Crow Head on the northernmost tip of Newfoundland, also the northernmost point of the Appalachian Mountains in the Western Hemisphere, a distance of more than 1,900 mi. Parts of the IAT route in North America have been extended to Prince Edward Island and Nova Scotia.

In Maine, the IAT crosses the summits of Deasey Mtn. and Lunksoos Mtn. Just west of the Canadian border, it climbs Mars Hill for a final view across Aroostook County before entering New Brunswick. This guide describes each of these three peaks.

NORTH MAINE WOODS

North Maine Woods (NMW) is a nonprofit corporation comprising a variety of public and private landowners. The consortium manages recreational access to 3.5 million acres of working forestland in northern Maine, ranging roughly from the Canadian border east to BSP and north through Aroostook County, including all of Allagash Wilderness Waterway (AWW) and the upper reaches of the St. John River. NMW also manages access to the 175,000-acre KI Jo-Mary Multiple Use Forest located between Millinocket, Greenville, and Brownville, which includes Gulf Hagas and a portion of the 100-Mile Wilderness.

Hikers entering NMW-managed lands must pass through a checkpoint and pay a fee for day use and camping. These fees help maintain hundreds of miles of roads and more than 560 campsites. Travel through NMW lands is on active industrial logging roads. For safety, visitors should always yield the right of way to trucks; avoid stopping on bridges, curves, and main roads; and drive attentively and prudently.

NMW lands are very remote. Services are few and far between and should not be counted on. Carry a cell phone, but be aware that service may be spotty or nonexistent in many places. Be sure to leave a trip plan with family or friends at home. In your vehicle, carry extra fuel, spare tire and jack, winch or come-along, fire-making materials, shovel, and extra food and water in case of delay or the unexpected need to spend the night out.

GEOGRAPHY

Maine is the easternmost state in the United States. It is bordered by New Hampshire, the Canadian provinces of Quebec and New Brunswick, and the Atlantic Ocean. At more than 35,000 sq. mi., Maine is nearly as large as the other five New England states combined. Maine is 39th in size among all states and roughly 320 mi. long from south to north and 210 mi. wide from west to east at its greatest extents. Maine's latitude ranges from 43° 4' N to 47° 28' N, and its longitude ranges from 66° 57' W to 71° 7' W. The geographic center of Maine is located in Piscataquis County, 18.0 mi. north of Dover-Foxcroft.

Maine's mountains extend from the coast to the northern interior and feature more than 100 summits greater than 3,000 ft. in elevation, with the highest peak on Katahdin at 5,268 ft., the northern terminus of the Appalachian Trail. The expansive landscape is home to 6,000 lakes and ponds, 32,000 mi. of rivers and streams, more than 17 million acres of forestland, and an abundance of wildlife. The state's coastline covers a geographic expanse of 230 mi. as the crow flies, but 3,500 mi. when every nook and cranny and some 3,000 islands are measured on the undulating margin from Kittery to Lubec.

To the south, Maine is bounded by the Atlantic Ocean from the Piscataqua River at Kittery to Passamaquoddy Bay at Lubec. The eastern boundary is a meridian line between Canada to the east and the United States to the west and extends from Hamlin to Pole Hill east of North Amity. The international boundary then follows Mountain Brook to North Lake, Grand Lake, and on to Spednik Lake. The St. Croix River forms the state boundary from Vanceboro to Passamaquoddy Bay. To the west, a meridian line separates Maine and New Hampshire from the jct. of the Maine, New Hampshire, and Quebec borders west of Bowman Hill south to Grand East Lake in Acton. From that point to Portsmouth Harbor and the Atlantic Ocean, the Salmon Falls River and then the Piscataqua River are the boundaries. The northern boundary is the most complex. From Bowman Hill in Bowmantown Township, the boundary follows the mountainous height-of-land separating the St. Lawrence River watershed from the Kennebec and Penobscot river watersheds. From Little St. John Lake, the Southwest Branch of the St. John River is the border as far as a point just west of Hardwood Mtn. in T9 R18 WELS. From there, a straight line runs to Lac Frontiere; then another line angles northeast to the Crown Monument at Estcourt. The St. Francis River flows east from there to empty into the St. John River near the village of St. Francis. The St. John River is the border as far as Hamlin just west of Grand Falls, Canada.

REGIONS

Maine can be divided into four distinct physical regions based on the general landforms found therein: the coastal lowlands, the hilly interior belt, the western mountains, and the dissected uplands.

The coastal lowlands include the sandy beaches from York to Casco Bay. Between Casco Bay and Penobscot Bay is the peninsula coast, characterized by long arms of land reaching out into the ocean. Farther north between Rockland and Schoodic Point is a region of big bays, wide peninsulas, and large islands, including Penobscot Bay, Blue Hill Bay, and Frenchman Bay. The area between Frenchman Bay and Passamaquoddy Bay is known as Downeast, where the wide bays are more exposed to the ocean and the peninsulas are broader, with fewer and smaller islands. The coastal lowlands are interrupted by a stretch of interior hills that extends from Unity to the Camden Hills on the coast. The mountains of Mt. Desert Island and ANP are also part of the hilly interior that reaches south to the ocean. This physical region includes some of the mountains in the Southwestern Maine, Midcoast, and Downeast sections, and all of the ANP section.

Inland from the coast is the hilly interior belt, a region of rolling hills, woods, farmland, lakes, ponds, and rivers that crosses the state from the New Hampshire border to Bangor and on to the New Brunswick border. The hills are mostly scattered and range from a few hundred feet to about 2,000 ft. in elevation. Included are the mountains in the White Mountain National Forest and Evans Notch section, as well as the Oxford Hills section; many of the trails in the Southwestern Maine, Midcoast, and Downeast sections; and some of the trails in the Kennebec and Moose River Valleys section.

The western mountains extend from the White Mountains east along the New Hampshire border and north across the state to Katahdin and the cluster of mountains nearby. This heavily forested region is characterized by the chain of high peaks known as the Longfellow Mountains—more than 75 peaks exceed 3,000 ft. and a handful exceed 4,000 ft.—and a series of large lakes, from Umbagog and Flagstaff to Moosehead and Grand Lake Seboeis. The western mountains encompass the entire Maine portion of the Appalachian Trail, BSP, and a variety of large conservation lands, including the Appalachian Mountain Club's Maine Woods recreation and conservation area. This expanse covers the following sections: Mahoosuc Range and Grafton Notch, Western Lakes and Mountains, 100-Mile Wilderness and Moosehead Lake, and BSP and Katahdin. It is also part of the northernmost mountains in the Kennebec and Moose River Valleys section.

The dissected uplands in northern Maine comprise all of Aroostook County and the far northern parts of Somerset, Piscataquis, and Penobscot counties. Forestland and farmland, scattered low mountains as high as 2,000 ft. in elevation, the Allagash Wilderness Waterway, and the valley of the St. John River characterize this region, which includes all of the mountains in the Aroostook County section.

GEOLOGY

The bedrock geology of Maine is the result of a series of complex natural forces—primarily sedimentation, and volcanic and mountain-building activities—from as early as the Late Proterozoic era, about 650 million years ago, to the Mesozoic era, about 66 million years ago. The continental rift between the combined European and African plates and the North American plate in the Late Mesozoic era led to continued uplift, erosion, faulting, and fracturing of the bedrock of the Appalachian Mountains of western Maine during the Tertiary period of the Cenozoic era about 1.6 million years ago.

Glaciation events of the Pleistocene epoch shaped much of the natural landscape we see today in Maine. Starting about 35,000 years ago, the Laurentide Ice Sheet spread across southern Quebec and New England. The ice sheet was as thick as 10,000 ft. and covered the highest mountains in the state, including Katahdin. The sheer mass of the ice sheet depressed the land many hundreds of feet. The movement of the glacial ice scoured the mountains and valleys, eroding the rock and carving enormous basins out of the mountainsides, moving great quantities of sand and gravel southward.

Due to climatic warming, the glaciers began to retreat about 21,000 years ago. The melting waters flooded as far as 75 mi. inland, creating the long peninsulas and islands that exist today. The retreating ice sheet dramatically changed the coastline, changed the mountain landscape, left behind more than 6,000 lakes and ponds, and changed the courses of the major rivers. The glaciers disappeared altogether about 11,000 years ago.

CLIMATE AND VEGETATION

Given Maine's geographic location on the eastern edge of the North American continent, its climate is influenced primarily by continental air masses flowing across the land on the westerly winds. This can be cold, dry air from Canada or warm, moist air from the Gulf of Mexico. The climate is affected to a lesser degree by cool, moist air from the Atlantic Ocean, which moderates the temperatures along the coast. Maine's location between the latitudes 43 degrees north and 47.5 degrees north reduces the sun's influence, making for generally mild summers and cold winters. The higher elevations in the mountains are usually cooler in the summer and much colder in winter. The mean January temperature ranges from 20 degrees Fahrenheit along the coast to 15 degrees inland to 10 degrees in the far north. The mean July temperature ranges from 65 degrees along the coast and in the far north to 67 degrees inland. Annual rainfall ranges from around 50 in. along the coast to 36 in. in the north, although the western mountains receive significant precipitation due to the effect of the cooler air at higher elevations. Snowfall totals range from as much as 80 in. along the coast to 81 to 100 in. inland to more than 110 in. in the western mountains and northern interior.

Maine occupies a transition zone between predominantly deciduous forests to the south and predominantly coniferous forests to the north. Within this zone, the broad mix of forest cover types is influenced to some degree by latitude, although soil variation and local climate also play a role. Along the coast from Casco Bay east to Passamaquoddy Bay, and in the western mountains and into the dissected uplands, the dominant tree species are spruce, fir, cedar, and larch. In southwestern Maine and in the western section of the hilly interior belt, the dominant species are oak, white pine, and hemlock. The northern hardwood mix of beech, maple, and birch dominates in a band stretching east from the western mountains to Washington County in the hilly interior and north in a band east of BSP to Canada and down along the St. John Valley of eastern Aroostook County.

FIRE TOWERS

In 1905, Maine erected its first fire lookout on Squaw Mtn. near Moosehead Lake. The tower proved the effectiveness of mountaintop fire detection, so the Maine Forestry Dept. (MFS historic name) began a program to erect as many such towers as possible in the coming years. By 1950, MFS was staffing more than 100 fire towers statewide. By the beginning of the 1960s, however, use of fire towers began to decline as the use of aircraft for fire detection grew in popularity and was ultimately found to be more economical. The decline continued, with only critical fire towers being staffed, until 1991, when the state closed the remaining towers. This ended an era of fire detection history that included the building of 144 fire towers overall.

Aside from fire protection, the era of fire towers opened many remote mountains to hiking opportunities. Fire warden trails and related phone line trails provided maintained systems for hikers, and many were also incorporated into trail systems, such as the AT. With the abandonment, degradation, and removal of fire towers over the years, many of these trails have been lost. But through the determined efforts of some volunteer groups, including the Maine Chapter of the Forest Fire Lookout Association, some fire towers continue to be maintained, restored, and even staffed. Given Maine's rich history of working forests and lumbering, the historical value of fire towers is recognized, and the towers continue to be a well-known symbol of fire detection. More than 60 of these fire tower trails are described in this guide.

TRIP PLANNING, WEATHER, AND SAFETY

The traditional hiking season in Maine extends from Memorial Day to Columbus Day, although an increasing number of hikers have come to know the joy of empty trails in the shoulder months of early spring and late fall. Trail conditions in Maine vary by geography. Coastal trails and those just inland will be snow-free much earlier than those farther north, along the mountains of the AT corridor, and will remain so longer, into fall and possibly even early winter. In some years, ice or snow drifts can linger at higher elevations into late May or early June, possibly later in some major cirques and bowls on north-facing slopes and high ridges, as well as in some sheltered areas, such as Mahoosuc Notch. Such conditions vary greatly from year to year and place to place. When snow or ice is present, trails may be more difficult to follow and more hazardous to hike. If icy trail conditions are expected, it is prudent to bring some type of traction footgear.

Even if it feels like summertime in the lower elevations, it can be like winter on the high ridges and summits. In fact, winter conditions can occur in the higher mountains in any month of the year. Keep in mind that air temperatures will drop 3 to 5 degrees Fahrenheit with each 1,000 ft. of elevation gain, without factoring in the impact of wind chill. As a result, even on sunny days in midsummer, hikers venturing to the exposed summits should always be prepared for cold weather with a minimum of a synthetic fleece jacket or wool sweater, hat, gloves, and a wind parka, all of which will provide comfort and protection against sudden storms. The often windy, wet, and foggy conditions along the Maine coast demand similar precautions.

Plan your trip schedule with safety in mind. Consider the strength of your party and the strenuousness of the trip: the overall distance, the amount of climbing, and the roughness of the terrain. Get a weather report, but be aware that a forecast may not apply to the mountain regions.

The National Weather Service provides detailed local weather forecasts on its website at weather.gov/gyx and on NOAA Weather Radio; check the website for a list of broadcast stations serving Maine. You can also get a recorded forecast by calling 207-688-3210. Frequent weather updates are also available on weather.com and smartphone weather apps.

Plan to finish your hike with daylight to spare and remember that days grow shorter rapidly in late summer and fall. Hiking after dark, even with flashlights or headlamps (which frequently fail), makes finding trails more difficult and crossing streams hazardous. Let someone know where you will be hiking and don't allow people to become separated from the group, especially those who are inexperienced.

Many unpaved roads may not be passable until Memorial Day or after. Take extra precautions to ensure your vehicle has a full gas tank and a usable spare tire, and that you have extra food, water, and clothing before driving into Maine's remote regions. Please check with the specific land management agency for road conditions and closures before you go.

Consider bringing your children or those of friends on appropriate hikes, as introducing young people to the outdoors has many benefits. Kids who are exposed to frequent, unstructured outdoor play are healthier, do better in school, have higher self-esteem, feel more connected to nature, and are more likely to be tomorrow's conservation leaders. AMC is committed to helping kids build strong connections to the outdoor world, including protection of the environment. Bringing children into the outdoors teaches them the need to take care of the world around them.

HIKESAFE HIKER RESPONSIBILITY CODE

The Hiker Responsibility Code was developed and is endorsed by the WMNF and New Hampshire Fish and Game, and is supported by BSP. For more information, visit hikesafe.com.

You are responsible for yourself, so be prepared:

1. **With knowledge and gear.** Become self-reliant by learning about the terrain, conditions, local weather, and your equipment before you start.

2. **To leave your plans.** Tell someone where you are going, the trails you are hiking, when you will return, and your emergency plans.

3. **To stay together.** When you start as a group, hike as a group and end as a group. Pace your hike to the slowest person.

4. **To turn back.** Weather changes quickly in the mountains. Fatigue and unexpected conditions can also affect your hike. Know your limitations and when to postpone your hike. The mountains will be there another day.

5. **For emergencies.** Even if you are headed out for just an hour, an injury, severe weather, or a wrong turn could become life threatening. Don't assume you will be rescued; know how to rescue yourself.

6. **To share the hiker code with others.** HikeSafe: It's Your Responsibility.

FOLLOWING TRAILS

In general, trails are maintained to provide a clear pathway while protecting the environment by minimizing erosion and other damage. Some may offer rough and difficult passage. Many hiking trails are marked with paint blazes on trees or rocks, with signs marking the trailhead and intermediate points en route. The AT in Maine is marked with white 2-by-6-in. vertical paint blazes. Side trails off the AT are usually marked with blue paint blazes. Trails may be marked in a variety of colors, and some will exhibit colored flagging (plastic tape) along the way. Some trails lack any signs or markers whatsoever. Above treeline, on open ridges and ledge areas, cairns (piles of rocks) usually mark the trails.

Below treeline, the treadway is usually visible except when covered by snow or fallen leaves. In winter, snow often covers signs at trailheads and intersections and blazes. Trails following or crossing woods roads require taking special care at intersections to distinguish the trail from diverging roads, particularly because blazing may be sporadic or nonexistent while the trail follows the road. Around shelters or campsites, beaten paths may lead in all directions, so look for signs and paint blazes.

Hikers should be aware that some trails in this book (as noted in descriptions) are less easy to follow than others. The presence of signs and blazes varies, and some trails are too new to have a well-defined footway; others have received very little use and are overgrown and becoming obscure. Trails may not be cleared of fallen trees and brush until late summer, and not all trails are cleared every year. Inexperienced hikers should avoid trails described as being difficult to follow, and all trail users should observe and follow trail markings carefully.

Although trails vary greatly in the amount of use they receive and the ease with which they can usually be followed, almost any trail might close unexpectedly or suddenly become obscure or hazardous under certain conditions. Landowners can reroute, abandon, or close trails. Trail signs are stolen or fall from their posts. Storms may cause blowdowns or landslides, which can obliterate a trail for an entire hiking season or longer. Logging operations can cover trails with debris and add a bewildering network of new roads. Development and road construction can obliterate trails.

Momentary inattention to trail markers—particularly arrows at sharp turns or signs at junctions, or misinterpretation of signs or guidebook descriptions—can cause hikers to become separated from all but the most heavily traveled paths. At a minimum, it can lead them into what may be a much longer or more difficult route. Please remember that this book is an aid to planning, not a substitute for observation and judgment. All of the trail maintaining organizations, including AMC, reserve the right to discontinue any trail without notice and expressly disclaim any legal responsibility for the condition of any trail.

A number of online sites post hiker reports on trails and mountain peaks in Maine and around New England, and when available for your particular hike, this information that can help you better plan and prepare. *Always check AMC's books updates page online for the most recent trail closures, reroutings, and other changes before you head out: outdoors.org/books-maps.*

IF YOU'RE LOST

Keeping track of where you are at all times and how long ago you observed the last trail marker is the best way to avoid becoming lost. In the event you wander off the trail and are no longer sure where you are, stop and briefly assess the situation. Often just by looking side to side, you can find the trail. If not, try backtracking a short distance to the last known trail marker.

If you are not with your hiking companions, yell or blow a whistle. They or others are likely nearby. If you still cannot find the trail and no one answers your calls, try to remain calm. Many situations where a person has become lost for any length of time involve panic and aimless wandering, so it is important to stop and take a break, make an inventory of useful information, decide on a course of action, and stick to it. (The caution against allowing inexperienced persons to become separated from a group should be emphasized here, as they are most likely to panic and wander. Also make sure all group members are familiar with the route of the trip and the names of the trails so that, if they do become separated, they will have some prospect of rejoining the group.)

Even when you cannot immediately find the trail, the situation is concerning but not necessarily serious. If you have kept track of your location on the map, some careful forays from your current position should help you relocate the trail. Should this effort fail, you can usually find a nearby stream, trail, or road to which you can set a compass course to follow. In many areas, distances are short enough (except in the North Maine Woods in Aroostook County, the northern reaches of Somerset County and Piscataquis County, and along the Canadian border) that it is possible, in the absence of alternatives, to reach a road in half a day, or at most in a whole day, simply by hiking downhill until you come upon a river or brook. Follow it downstream, and it should lead to civilization.

BUSHWHACKING

This guide deals only with mountains in Maine that have recognized foot trails, with one new exception. Mt. Redington is one of Maine's fourteen 4,000-ft. peaks, and the unofficial herd path from the top of South Crocker Mtn. that has been used by bushwhackers for years is now included. All other trailless peaks in Maine are excluded. Bushwhacking should only be attempted by hikers who are highly experienced in backcountry navigation with map and compass and/or GPS units under difficult field conditions. Many trailless peaks in Maine are on private property, and as such, hikers should seek advance permission from the landowner. Bushwhackers should not mark their routes, as leaving flagging tape and building cairns may confuse the next hikers who come along and goes against Leave No Trace principles.

SKI AREAS

Although not described, the ski trails at Maine's downhill skiing areas and resorts offer hiking routes that, due to their width and zigzag course over steep slopes, often make for good summer climbing. In the skiing offseason, factors to consider include lack of shade, rough footing, and wet areas. In winter, ski mountains and their ready-made packed trails allow for straightforward snow travel, and wide-open ascent routes offer continuous views. Ski areas are private property, and summer or winter, hikers should ask about the uphill access policy and request permission.

WHAT TO CARRY AND WEAR

Adequate equipment for a hike in the mountains of Maine varies greatly according to the time of year, the geographic location, the length of the trip, the potential terrain hazards, and the difficulty of getting to the nearest trailhead if a problem arises.

Good things to have in your pack for an ordinary day hike in spring, summer, and fall in the Maine mountains include:

- guidebook and maps
- compass
- minimum of 2 quarts of water
- pocketknife
- rain/wind gear
- synthetic or wool jacket/sweater(s)
- long pants (preferably convertible to shorts)
- warm hat
- sun hat
- sunglasses
- gloves or mittens
- extra shirt(s)
- extra socks
- watch
- lunch and high-energy snacks
- bandana
- personal medications
- first-aid kit
- repair kit
- nylon cord
- trash bag for garbage
- toilet paper (and small plastic bag to pack out used TP)
- wet wipes and hand sanitizer
- sunscreen
- insect repellent
- whistle
- cell phone
- space blanket or bivouac sack
- headlamp or flashlight (with extra batteries and spare bulb)
- lighter or waterproof matches
- notebook and pen or pencil

Wear comfortable, broken-in hiking boots. Lightweight to medium-weight boots provide the needed ankle support on rough and rocky trails. Two pairs of socks are recommended: a lightweight inner pair and a heavier outer pair that are both at least partly wool. Adjustable trekking poles offer many advantages to hikers, especially on descents, traverses, and stream crossings.

Jeans, sweatshirts, and other cotton clothing are not recommended because, once they become wet, they dry very slowly. In adverse weather conditions, they can quickly drain a cold and tired hiker's heat reserves; thus, the hiker maxim, "Cotton kills." Synthetics and wool are superior materials for outdoor apparel, especially for hikers intending to travel in adverse conditions, to remote places, or above treeline. Synthetics and wool retain much of their insulating value even when wet and are indispensable for hikers wanting to explore remote places from which return to the trailhead might require substantial time and effort if conditions turn bad. Multiple layers of clothing are best, from wicking undergarments to insulating down and/or fleece to a wind and rain shell. Extra clothing is always a smart choice. Hats, gloves, and other similar gear provide an extra margin of safety in adverse conditions, and they allow hikers to enjoy the summits in comfort on those crisp, clear days when the views are particularly fine. A camera, binoculars, nature identification guides, altimeter, book for leisure reading, and GPS unit are extras to consider. For more on essential clothing and gear, refer to *AMC's Mountain Skills Manual* by Christian Bisson and Jamie Hannon (2017).

CAMPING

Trailside camping is available on a first-come, first-served basis at established lean-tos and tentsites along the AT corridor, from Carlo Col Shelter in the Mahoosuc Range just north of the New Hampshire border to Abol Pines Campsite on the Penobscot River at Abol Bridge just south of BSP. Where caretakers (AMC or MATC) are in place, a fee may be charged. Backcountry campsites are also available at a number of Maine's public lands units, including Amherst Community Forest, Bigelow Preserve, Days Academy, Deboullie, Donnell Pond, Little Moose, Machias River Corridor, the Mahoosucs, Moosehead Lake, Mt. Abraham, Nahmakanta, Round Pond, Scraggly Lake, Scopan, Tumbledown, and others. The Bureau of Parks and Lands (MBPL) allows dispersed camping on most public lands, provided backpackers practice Leave No Trace principles. Lean-tos and tentsites in remote areas of BSP are available with advanced reservations only. Five lean-tos along the IAT, four in Katahdin Woods and Waters National Monument, and one on Mars Hill west of the Canadian border are available to hikers. Overnight camping is permitted in nearly all of the WMNF backcountry in Maine, although campers should check with USFS on the latest Forest Protection Area rules, if any, for the areas they wish to visit. ANP has five remote shelters at Duck Harbor CG on Isle au Haut.

Roadside camping is available at a variety of public campgrounds, including Blackwoods, Seawall, and Schoodic Woods campgrounds in ANP; eight drive-in campgrounds in BSP; and five WMNF campgrounds in the Evans Notch area (Cold River, Basin, Wild River, Hastings, and Crocker Pond). Eleven state parks feature vehicle-accessible camping: Aroostook, Bradbury Mtn., Camden Hills, Cobscook Bay, Lake St. George, Lamoine, Lily Bay, Mt. Blue, Peaks-Kenny, Rangeley Lake, and Sebago Lake. More than 500 primitive campsites are available within the boundaries of NMW, and more than 60 campsites are within the KI Jo-Mary Multiple Use Forest. Close to 200 privately owned and operated campgrounds throughout Maine offer a wide variety of facilities and amenities.

See Appendix A: Helpful Information and Contacts on p. 564 for information on campground locations and reservations.

FIRE REGULATIONS

Campfire permits are required for some remote campsites in the unorganized townships. Permits are site specific and valid only for a short time frame. In organized towns, landowner permission must be obtained and a permit issued by the town forest fire warden. Most Maine maps, including *The Maine Atlas and Gazetteer*, distinguish between campsites that require a permit (permit sites) and those that do not (authorized sites). If unsure, contact the nearest MFS office; see Appendix A: Helpful Information and Contacts. Campfire permits are not required when the ground is covered by snow. Permits are free.

In BSP, ANP, and Maine public lands and state parks, fires are allowed only at designated sites. Along the AT, fires are allowed only at designated shelters and tentsites. Use of backpacker stoves is strongly encouraged on the AT and elsewhere to help minimize environmental impact and campsite degradation. Fires are allowed in the backcountry of the WMNF in Maine except where prohibited by the specific rules of Forest Protection Areas.

The Maine legislature has banned the transport of all firewood from outside the state to help control the spread of potentially devastating insect pests, such as the emerald ash borer and Asian long-horned beetle. If firewood is transported, it must be completely burned within 24 hours. Campers are urged to leave all firewood at home and buy it locally where it will be used.

WINTER CONSIDERATIONS

This book describes trails in the snowless season, which can vary considerably from year to year. Higher elevations have much shorter snow-free seasons. Because snowshoeing and winter hiking in the woods and mountains of Maine are popular, however, a few general considerations are provided here.

As more hikers have discovered the beauty of the woods in winter, advances in clothing and equipment have made it possible for experienced winter travelers to enjoy greater levels of comfort and safety. Although travel on lower elevation trails in average conditions can be relatively safe, much more experience is required to recognize and avoid dangerous situations in winter than in summer. Summer hiking boots are inadequate;

regular headlamp batteries fail quickly; and drinking water freezes unless carried in an insulated container. The winter hiker should be in good physical condition and should dress carefully to avoid overheating and excessive perspiration, which soaks clothing and soon leads to chilling. Hikers should avoid cotton clothes in winter; only synthetic fabrics and wool retain their insulating values when wet. Multiple layers of clothing are best, from wicking undergarments to insulating down and/or fleece to a wind and rain shell. Extra clothing is always a smart choice. Hikers should increase fluid intake, as dehydration can be a serious problem in the cold and dry winter air. Larger packs are necessary to carry the extra clothing and gear required in winter.

Snow, ice, and weather conditions are constantly changing, and a relatively trivial error in judgment may have serious, even lethal, consequences. Conditions can vary greatly from day to day and from trail to trail. Days are very short, particularly in early winter when darkness falls around 4 P.M. Trails are frequently difficult or impossible to follow in deep snow, and navigation skills may be hard to apply in adverse weather conditions. (Thus, out-and-back hikes—where one retraces one's tracks—are often preferable to loop hikes, where unknown conditions ahead could make completing the trip much more difficult than anticipated.) Brook crossings can be difficult and potentially dangerous if the water is not adequately frozen.

Deep snow requires snowshoes or skis and the skill to use them efficiently (although some popular trails may be packed out through most of winter). Breaking trail on snowshoes through new snow can be strenuous and exhausting work. Trail courtesy suggests that winter hikers wear snowshoes when trails are not solidly packed out. Post-holing, or plunging one's legs into and out of deep snow, is unnecessarily tiring and creates unpleasant and potentially hazardous trail conditions for those who follow.

When ice is present on trails, as it often is in late fall, early spring, and after winter freeze-thaw cycles, mountains with steep, open slopes or ledges are particularly dangerous. If you expect icy trail conditions, bring traction footgear, such as crampons (full or instep) or some type of ice cleats or spikes. In spring, deep snowdrifts may remain on northern slopes and wooded ridgelines, even at lower elevations, after snow has melted on southern exposures.

It is important to note that some trails, such as those on Katahdin, pass through areas that may pose a danger of avalanches. Basin walls, ravines, and open slopes are especially prone to avalanches, though slides can also occur below treeline. These areas should be regarded as technical terrain and strictly avoided unless party members have been trained in avalanche safety.

Above timberline, conditions often require specialized equipment and skills, as well as experience of a different magnitude. The conditions on Katahdin, the Bigelows, Saddleback, and other high and exposed alpine summits can be severe, and only the most experienced and well-equipped climbers should attempt hikes. Severe storms can develop suddenly and unexpectedly, but perhaps the most dangerous aspect of winter in the higher elevations of the Maine mountains is the variability of the weather. It is not unusual for a cold, penetrating, wind-driven rain to be followed within a few hours by a cold front that brings below-zero temperatures and high winds.

No book can begin to impart all of the knowledge necessary to cope safely with the potential for such serious conditions, but those interested in learning more about winter hiking should consult the *AMC Guide to Winter Hiking & Camping,* by Lucas St. Clair and Yemaya Maurer (2008). Hikers who are interested in extending their activities into the winter season, especially at higher elevations, are strongly advised to seek out organized parties with leaders who have extensive winter experience. AMC's Maine Chapter sponsors numerous evening and weekend workshops, in addition to introductory winter hikes and regular winter treks on which participants can gain experience. Information on these activities can be found at amcmaine.org and outdoors.org/activities.

No attempt is made to cover any kind of skiing in this guide, although a number of the hiking trails described are well suited to cross-country and backcountry skiing. For more on these activities, see AMC Books' *Best Backcountry Skiing in the Northeast*, by David Goodman (2010).

BACKCOUNTRY HAZARDS

Safe hiking means knowing how to avoid potentially dangerous situations, as well as being prepared to deal with problems when they do occur. AMC and many other outdoor organizations offer courses that teach the principles of backcountry safety, wilderness first aid, and incident management. Dozens of helpful books are available on these subjects. Some of the common hazards encountered in the Maine outdoors and how to approach them are outlined here.

Falls and Injuries

Injuries on the trail are always a serious matter, but more so with increasing distance from the trailhead. Be alert for places where the footing may be poor, especially in rainy weather and on steep, rough, or wet sections of trail. In autumn, wet leaves and hidden ice are particular hazards. Remember that carrying a heavy pack can affect your balance. Another potential cause of injury in mountainous areas is rockfall from ledges that rise above the trail.

In case of serious injury, apply first aid and keep the injured person warm and comfortable. Then take a minute to assess the situation before going or calling for help. Backcountry evacuation can take many hours, so don't rush. Write down your location, the condition of the injured person, and any other pertinent facts. If cell phone service is not available, at least one person should stay with the injured hiker while two others go for help. (Hence the maxim that it is safest to hike in the backcountry in groups of four or more.)

Hypothermia

Hypothermia, the most serious danger to hikers in the Maine woods and mountains, is the loss of ability to preserve body heat and may be caused by injury, exhaustion, lack of sufficient food, and inadequate or wet clothing. This often occurs on wet, windy days at between 32 and 50 degrees Fahrenheit.

Symptoms of moderate hypothermia include uncontrolled shivering, impaired speech and movement, lowered body temperature, and drowsiness. Be on the lookout for what current hypothermia education programs refer to as the umbles—stumbles, mumbles, and bumbles—which amount to a loss of agility, an inability to speak clearly, difficulty with knots and zippers, and similar issues that indicate loss of normal muscular and mental functions. An affected hiker should be put in dry clothing and a sleeping bag, if available, then given quick-energy food to eat and something warm (not hot) to drink.

In cases of severe hypothermia, which occurs when a body's temperature has reached a point below 90 degrees Fahrenheit, shivering ceases, but the affected suffers an obvious lack of coordination to the point that walking becomes impossible. Sure indicators are slurred speech, mental confusion, irrational behavior, disorientation, and unconsciousness. Only prompt evacuation to a hospital offers reasonable hope for recovery. Extreme care must be used in attempting to transport such a person to a trailhead, because even a slight jar can bring on heart failure. The victim should be protected from further heat loss as much as possible and handled with extreme gentleness. Call trained rescue personnel for immediate assistance.

Successful rescue of a profoundly hypothermic person from the backcountry is difficult, so the need for prevention or early detection is essential. The advent of hypothermia is usually fairly slow, and in cold or wet weather all members of a hiking group must be aware of the signs of developing hypothermia and pay constant attention to the first appearance of such signs—which may be fairly subtle—in all fellow group members.

Heat Exhaustion

Excessive heat can also be a serious problem in the mountains, particularly in midsummer on hot, humid days. Heat exhaustion, usually in a mild form, is quite common. The hiker feels tired, perhaps light-headed or nauseous, and may have cramps in large muscles. The principal cause is dehydration and loss of electrolytes (mostly salt) through perspiration, often combined with overexertion. On a hot day, a hiker can be well on the way to serious dehydration before feeling any thirst. To prevent heat exhaustion, hikers should carry plenty of water (and the means to treat or filter it) and drink copiously before thirst is evident. Wearing a hat to block sun is another preventive measure.

The treatment for heat exhaustion is to provide adequate water and possibly salt (salt without adequate water will make the situation worse), to help the victim cool down (especially the head and torso) by moving him or her into the shade, and to minimize further physical exertion. Heat exhaustion must be taken seriously because it can progress to life-threatening cardiac problems or to heatstroke, a medical emergency in which irreversible damage to the brain and other vital organs can quickly occur. This condition requires immediate cooling of the victim.

Lightning

Lightning is another serious hazard on any open ridge or summit; avoid these dangerous places when thunderstorms are likely. Look for shelter in thick woods as quickly as possible if an unexpected "thumper" is detected. Most thunderstorms occur when a cold front moves through or on very warm days. Storms produced by cold fronts are typically more sudden and violent. Weather forecasts that mention cold fronts or predict temperatures much above 80 degrees Fahrenheit in the lowlands and valleys should arouse concern.

Wildlife

In recent years, there have been hundreds of collisions between automobiles and moose, most occurring in spring and early summer, although the hazard exists year-round. Motorists need to be aware of the seriousness of the problem, particularly at night when these large, dark-colored animals are both active and very difficult to see. Instinct often causes moose to face an auto rather than to run from it, and they are apt to cross the road unpredictably as a car approaches. Be aware that where one moose crosses, there may well be another coming right behind it. Moose typically constitute little threat to hikers on foot, although it would be wise to give a wide berth to a cow with young or to a bull during the fall mating season.

Bears are common but tend to keep well out of sight. The black bear is a large and unpredictable animal that must be treated with respect. Deliberately feeding bears or allowing a dog to harass them may unnecessarily provoke an attack. No animal in the wild should be approached, startled, or fed. Bears are omnivorous opportunists, especially fond of nuts and berries, and sometimes hikers' food bags. They have become a nuisance and even a hazard at some popular campsites, because any bear that has lost its natural fear of humans—and has gotten used to living off hiker leftovers—is potentially very dangerous. Hikers confronted by a bear should attempt to appear neither threatened nor frightened and should back off slowly. Never run. Food should not be abandoned unless the bear appears overly aggressive. A loud noise, such as that made by a whistle or by banging metal pots, is often useful.

Careful protection of food and scented items, such as toothpaste, at campsites is essential. Food bags should never be kept overnight in a tent but rather hung between trees well off the ground—at least 10 ft. high and 4 ft. away from the tree trunk. This helps keep other curious critters out of the larder as well. Bear canisters are effective and less work, and thereby increasingly popular. Where there is a metal bear box, please use it.

There are no known poisonous snakes in Maine.

Insect Pests

Mosquitoes and blackflies are the woodland residents that hikers most frequently encounter in Maine. Mosquitoes are worst throughout the summer in low, wet areas, and blackflies are most bloodthirsty in late May, June, and early July. Head nets of fine nylon mesh can be useful. The most effective repellents for mosquitoes and blackflies, as well as gnats, no-see-ums, deer flies, and chiggers, are based on the active chemical ingredient N,N-diethyl-meta-toluamide, commonly known as DEET.

These repellents are available in a variety of forms, including aerosols, pump sprays, lotions, and wipes and in different concentrations, from 100 percent DEET to lesser mixtures with more inert ingredients. There are some questions about the safety of using DEET, so hikers should apply such repellents to clothing, rather than directly on the skin, where possible; avoid use on small children. Alternatives to DEET include picaridin, which is odor-free and not oily like DEET, and repellents using natural or synthesized plant oils.

Ticks are most common along the coast and in the woods and fields of southern and central Maine, but are spreading to other areas of the state. More than a dozen species of ticks reside in the Maine woods, but the deer tick, *Ixodes scapularis*, is the most troublesome. This tick can transmit the bacterium that causes Lyme disease. In the early stages, flu-like symptoms may appear, as well as an expanding or bull's-eye-shaped rash around the site of the tick bite. Detected early, Lyme disease can be treated with antibiotics. Left untreated, this serious disease can spread to joints, the heart, and the nervous system, leading to chronic health issues.

Countermeasures against ticks include using insect repellent on shoes, socks, and pant legs; wearing light-colored long pants tucked into socks; and frequently checking clothing and skin. Ticks wander for several hours before settling on a spot to bite, so they can be removed easily if found promptly. Once a tick is embedded, take care to remove it in its entirety, as the head detaches easily and may remain in the skin, possibly producing infection. Use tweezers or a special notched spoon or remover.

Bee stings may be painful, and for some individuals with allergies, they can cause potentially deadly anaphylactic reactions. Hikers with known allergies should carry Benadryl tablets and a prescription epinephrine pen.

Poison Ivy

Two types of poisonous plants are common in Maine: poison ivy and poison sumac. Poison ivy is found throughout the state, but poison sumac is much less common, found mostly in the southern part. Poison ivy generally has three dark green leaves that shine in the sun but are dull in the shade.

Direct contact with the oil (urushiol, an allergen) from the leaves, roots, stems, flowers, or fruit of these plants, or indirect contact with an object that has touched the plant, may result in an allergic skin rash. Symptoms include itchy skin and a red area or red streaks where the oil or contaminated object touched the skin, small bumps or larger raised areas, and blisters with fluid that may leak out and cause the rash to spread. The rash usually appears between eight and 48 hours after contact. Early treatment involves thoroughly washing the contact area with soap and water. The next step is the use of a topical cortisone cream. In severe cases, antibiotics may be necessary.

Stream Crossings

Hikers often cross streams, brooks, and rivers without bridges, stepping from rock to rock. Trekking poles, a hiking staff, or a stout stick can be a great aid to balance in these cases. Use caution, however, because serious injuries or worse can result from a fall on slippery rocks, especially in the middle of a stream. If you need to wade across a stream, it is recommended that you wear your boots (but not necessarily socks). If you know in advance that wading may be required, a good option is to carry lightweight sandals or other water footwear and change into them before crossing, keeping your boots dry. Unbuckle backpack straps so you can shrug out of the pack if necessary in a fall.

Many water crossings that may be only a nuisance in summer can be a serious obstacle in cold weather, when feet and boots must be kept dry. Another type of hazard can occur in late fall, when cold nights may cause exposed rocks to be coated with a treacherous thin layer of ice. Higher waters can turn innocuous brooks into raging torrents in the spring, as snow melts, or after heavy rainstorms, particularly in fall when trees drop their leaves and take up less water. Avoid trails with potentially dangerous stream crossings during these high-water periods. If you are cut off from roads by swollen streams, it is better to make a long detour, even if you need to wait and spend a night in the woods. Rushing currents can make wading extremely hazardous and not worth the risk. Floodwaters may subside within a few hours, especially in small brooks. It is particularly important not to camp on the far side of a brook en route to your exit point if the crossing is difficult and heavy rain is predicted.

Hunting Seasons

Deer-hunting season (with firearms) in Maine generally starts on the Monday of the first week of November and lasts through the Saturday after Thanksgiving. A youth deer-hunting day is usually held the third Saturday in October, and a Maine resident day is held the fourth Saturday in October. Archery season is generally from late September through late October, and muzzleloader season is usually late November through early to mid-December. The start and duration of moose-hunting season varies by region, generally from late September to late November. The start and duration of wild turkey hunting in spring varies by region, usually from late April to early June; in fall, the season is generally from early to late October.

Most hunters stay fairly close to roads, so, in general, the harder it would be to haul a deer out of a given area, the lower the probability a hiker will encounter hunters there. In any case, avoid wearing brown or anything that might give a hunter the impression of the white flash of a white-tailed deer running away. Wearing at least two pieces of bright orange clothing, the same as required of hunters, is strongly recommended.

For the specific dates of Maine hunting seasons, visit mefishwildlife.com or call 207-287-8000. Hunting is not allowed on Sundays in Maine.

Drinking Water

The presence of microscopic cysts of the intestinal parasite *Giardia lamblia* in water sources in Maine is thought to be common, if difficult to prove. *Cryptosporidium* is another similar parasite of concern. It is impossible to be sure whether a given source is safe, no matter how clear the water seems or how remote the location. The safest course is for hikers to carry their own water from home. For those who source water in the woods, always purify the water before drinking it.

Water purification methods include boiling, chemical treatment (tablets or drops), ultraviolet treatment, and water filters. When boiling water, bring it to a rolling boil and boil for at least five minutes. The downside to boiling is the increased consumption of fuel. Water can be treated with an iodine-based disinfectant. Allow extra contact time and use twice as many tablets if the water is very cold. Chlorine-based products are ineffective in water that contains organic impurities, and all water-purification chemicals tend to deteriorate quickly. Sterilizer pens using ultraviolet light are relatively new and apparently very effective. Inserting the pen into the water for a few minutes kills viruses, bacteria, and protozoa. The water must be filtered before sterilizing, and hikers will need to carry extra batteries. Various types of pump filters remove impurities, often making the water look and taste better; several new gravity filters eliminate hand pumping and allow for water storage.

The symptoms of giardiasis and cryptosporidiosis are similar and include severe intestinal distress and diarrhea. But such discomforts can have many other causes, making the diseases difficult to diagnose accurately. The principal cause of the spread of these noxious ailments in the woods is probably careless disposal of human waste (see "Sanitation," below).

Sanitation
Keep human waste at least 200 ft. away from water sources. Use a toilet where one is available. If no toilets are nearby, dig a hole 6 to 8 in. deep (but not below the organic layer of the soil) for a latrine and cover the hole completely after use. The bacteria in the organic layer of the soil will then decompose the waste naturally. Be scrupulous about washing hands or using a hand sanitizer after answering calls of nature. Put used toilet tissue and wet wipes in a plastic bag and pack it out to minimize impact.

Theft
Cars parked at trailheads are frequently targets of break-ins, so never leave valuables or expensive equipment inside your vehicle while you are hiking, particularly overnight.

Search and Rescue
In emergencies, call 911 or any of the Maine State Police regional communications centers:

Gray   207-657-3030
Augusta   207-624-7076
Bangor   207-973-3700
Houlton   207-532-5400

Hikers should be aware that cell phone coverage in Maine's backcountry, both along the coast and in the mountains, can be very unreliable, particularly in deep valleys but also on some summits, and there is absolutely no assurance that a cell phone call will get through to authorities in an emergency. Both phones and their batteries can fail, often at inconvenient times. Sometimes a text message will get through when a call will not, but hikers should not rely on cell reception.

By state law, the Maine Warden Service of DIFW is responsible for search-and-rescue operations in the Maine outdoors. Whenever the commissioner receives notification that any person has gone into the woodlands or onto the inland waters of the state and has become lost or stranded, the commissioner will take reasonable steps to ensure the safe and timely recovery of that person. The commissioner reserves the right to end a search-and-rescue operation by members of the department when all reasonable efforts have been exhausted. The person for whom the search and rescue was conducted may be responsible for all directly related costs.

Search-and-rescue operations are serious matters. Time is required to organize rescue parties, which typically require a minimum of eighteen people for litter carries and can endanger the rescuers. In addition, an unnecessary rescue mission may leave no resources if a real emergency occurs. Please make sure there really is an emergency before you call or go for help.

STEWARDSHIP AND CONSERVATION

Trails don't just happen. The trails we use and enjoy are the product of the dedication and hard work of local, state, and federal agencies, many public and private nonprofit organizations, and a host of volunteers. A significant number of trails in Maine are on private property and are open for public use through the generosity of the various landowners. Many trails, particularly on private property, are cared for by one dedicated person or a small group. Funds for trail work are scarce, and unless hikers contribute both time and money to maintenance, the diversity of trails available to the public may be threatened. Every hiker can make some contribution to trail improvement, if nothing more than pushing a blowdown off the path rather than walking around it. But a more formal commitment, even if it is just one day or one weekend each year, is welcomed. Many hands do make light work, and working together for the betterment of our trails is a fun and satisfying way to give something back.

Volunteer trail maintenance opportunities abound in Maine through public and private agencies such as AMC, MATC, BSP, MBPL, ANP, and WMNF. The primary mission of the MATC is to oversee the 282 mi. of the AT, its many shelters and campsites, and miles of side trails. AMC's Maine Chapter is active in building and maintaining trails. And dozens of local and regional land trusts, conservation commissions, and recreation departments can use your assistance. Many of these organizations are listed in Appendix A: Helpful Information and Contacts on p. 564.

LEAVE NO TRACE

AMC is a national educational partner of Leave No Trace, a nonprofit organization dedicated to promoting and inspiring responsible outdoor recreation through education, research, and partnerships. The Leave No Trace program seeks to develop wild land ethics: ways in which people think and act in the outdoors to minimize their impact on the areas they visit and to protect natural resources for future enjoyment. Leave No Trace unites four federal land management agencies—USFS, NPS, Bureau of Land Management, and U.S. Fish and Wildlife Service—with manufacturers, outdoor retailers, user groups, educators, organizations such as AMC, and individuals.

The Leave No Trace ethic is guided by these seven principles:

- Plan ahead and prepare.
- Travel and camp on durable surfaces.
- Dispose of waste properly.
- Leave what you find.
- Minimize campfire impacts.
- Respect wildlife.
- Be considerate of other visitors.

AMC is a national provider of the Leave No Trace Master Educator course. AMC offers this five-day course, designed especially for outdoor professionals and land managers, as well as the shorter two-day Leave No Trace Trainer course, at locations throughout the Northeast.

For Leave No Trace information and materials, contact the Leave No Trace Center for Outdoor Ethics, P.O. Box 997, Boulder, CO 80306; 800-332-4100 or 302-442-8222; or lnt.org. For a schedule of AMC Leave No Trace courses, see outdoors.org/education/lnt.

SECTION 1

BAXTER STATE PARK AND KATAHDIN

Pull-Out Map
Map 1: Baxter State Park–Katahdin

SEC
1

INTRODUCTION

This section, on Baxter State Park (BSP) and the Katahdin region, provides comprehensive coverage of the hiking trails in BSP, while also describing trails in the new Katahdin Woods and Waters National Monument (KWWNM), which abuts the park to the east, and a handful of other peaks in the general neighborhood east and north of BSP. Featured are trails to the high mountain peaks, as well as a wide variety of hikes along streams and rivers and to remote ponds and lakes. Included are the six major summits of the Katahdin massif: Pamola, Chimney, South, Baxter, Hamlin, and Howe. To the west are the Owl, Mt. OJI, Mt. Coe, North and South Brother, and Doubletop Mtn. Sentinel Mtn. is in the southwest corner of the park. South Turner Mtn. lies east of Katahdin. In the northern part of the park are the mountains surrounding the South Branch ponds: to the east are North Traveler Mtn., Traveler, and Center Ridge; to the west are South Branch and Black Cat mountains. Burnt Mtn. is farther west. Close to Matagamon Gate are Horse Mtn. and Trout Brook Mtn. Wadleigh Mtn. is the northernmost summit in the park. East of Katahdin Lake and the BSP boundary, along the route of the International Appalachian Trail (IAT), are Bernard Mtn., Deasey Mtn., and Lunksoos Mtn., all in KWWNM. East of Matagamon Gate are Sugarloaf Mtn. and Mt. Chase; Owl's Head and Norway Bluff are farther north. In all, this section describes 76 trails on 31 mountains.

GEOGRAPHY

BSP is a vast wilderness area located in the northern reaches of Piscataquis County. A portion of the park near Grand Lake Matagamon and around Katahdin Lake spills over into neighboring Penobscot County. Katahdin is the predominant natural feature of BSP and is Maine's highest mountain, an irregular-shaped mass of rock that rises abruptly from comparatively flat terrain to a gently sloping plateau above the treeline. The massif culminates on its southeastern margin in a series of low summits, of which the southern two are the highest. These peaks are 0.3 mi. apart, and Baxter Peak (5,268 ft.) to the northwest is the higher of the two. From the southeastern South Peak (5,240 ft.), a serrated ridge of vertically fractured granite, known as Knife Edge, curves away to the east and northeast, culminating in a rock spire called Chimney Peak (4,910 ft.). Immediately beyond Chimney Peak, separated from it by a sharp cleft, is the broader summit of Pamola (4,919 ft.), named for the spirit that inhabits the mountain, according to Penobscot mythology. West and north of Baxter Peak is the Tableland, a broad, open plateau of alpine terrain ranging from Baxter Peak to Thoreau Spring and the Gateway north to the Saddle. North of the Saddle, the wide mass of Hamlin Peak (4,756 ft.) rises above the Tableland, which extends to Howe Peak (4,750 ft.) and the Northwest Plateau.

The Tableland is nearly 4 mi. long and drops away abruptly by 1,000 to 2,000 ft. on all sides. After that, the slope becomes gentler. Great ridges extend out and around to encompass a series of glacial cirques, or basins. Great Basin and its branch, North Basin, are the best known. At the base of Great Basin, at an elevation of 2,914 ft., Chimney Pond lies flanked by impressive cliffs and bordered by dense spruce and fir forest. The pond is about 8 acres in size and is a base for many and varied mountain climbs. The compact basin immediately beyond (southwest of) Chimney Pond is known as South Basin. North of Great Basin, but still on the eastern side of the mountain, is North Basin, at an elevation of 3,100 ft., where high mountain walls surround a barren, boulder-strewn floor. Nearby Little North Basin is trailless and sees few visitors. On the western side of the Tableland, remote Northwest Basin lies at about 2,800 ft., and farther south is a broad valley known as the Klondike. Klondike Pond rests in a small glacial arm of this valley, just below the plateau, at 3,435 ft. The pond is 0.3 mi. long, deep, narrow, and remarkably beautiful. From the peaks at its northern and southern ends, the Tableland slopes gradually toward the center, known as the Saddle. The land falls off gently from the eastern escarpment of the Saddle toward the dense scrub that carpets the northwestern edge. Many avalanches have scored the walls of the Tableland, but only one of these scorings is still a trail: Saddle Slide at the western end of Great Basin. Abol Trail on Abol Slide, on the southwestern flank of the mountain, was rerouted in 2014–15 after significant landslides made the trail too dangerous.

The isolated location of Katahdin allows for exceptional views that take in dozens of lakes and ponds, including Moosehead Lake, the many windings of the Penobscot River, and, to the south, the peaks of Mt. Desert Island and the Camden Hills on the coast. To the southwest is the 100MW and the mountains along the AT corridor. White Cap, the Bigelows, and Mt. Abraham are among the peaks visible. Katahdin is the northern terminus of the 2,190-mi. AT, which follows Hunt Trail on Katahdin itself.

The Owl (3,670 ft.) lies west of Katahdin, across the Klondike, where trailless Barren Mtn. (3,696 ft.), Mt. OJI (3,434 ft.), Mt. Coe (3,795 ft.), South Brother (3,970 ft.), North Brother (4,151 ft.), and Fort Mtn. (3,867 ft.) are also located. On the west side of Nesowadnehunk Stream is the twin-peaked Doubletop Mtn. (the higher summit is 3,489 ft.). Sentinel Mtn. (1,842 ft.) is in close proximity to a host of wild and beautiful ponds. Trailless Mullen Mtn. (3,463 ft.) and Wassataquoik Mtn. (2,981 ft.) lie in the remote area between Fort Mtn. and Wassataquoik Lake. To the east are Wassataquoik Stream and Russell Pond, in the heart of the park's interior. Wadleigh Mtn. (1,259 ft.) sits alone amid the sprawling woods of the Scientific Forest Management Area on the park's northern edge. Trout Brook Mtn. (1,767 ft.) and Horse Mtn. (1,589 ft.) are south of Grand Lake Matagamon in the Fowler Ponds area. Traveler Mtn., the principal mountain in the northern section of the park, is crowned by three high summits: the Traveler (3,550 ft.), Center Ridge (3,254 ft.), and North Traveler (3,152 ft.). The South Branch ponds lie at the western base of Traveler Mtn. Rising steeply west of South Branch Pond are South Branch Mtn. (2,630 ft.) and Black Cat Mtn. (2,611 ft.). South Turner Mtn. (3,110 ft.) is to the northeast of Katahdin and offers fantastic views; trailless North Turner Mtn. (3,325 ft.) is nearby. The magnificent Katahdin Lake sprawls at the base of the Katahdin massif a few miles to the east.

Bordering BSP to the east is the new Katahdin Woods and Waters National Monument, its eastern boundary a wild and beautiful stretch of the East Branch of the Penobscot River. Wassataquoik Stream slices through the southern half of the heavily forested monument to empty into the East Branch near Lunksoos. Seven mountains ranging between 1,000 and 2,000 ft. in elevation dot the landscape; three have trails that lead to spectacular views of Katahdin and the mountainous skyline of Baxter. Barnard Mtn. (1,558 ft.) is the most easily accessed; it looks out over Katahdin Lake. North of Wassataquoik Stream are Lunksoos Mtn. (1,762 ft.) and Deasey Mtn. (1,942 ft.), the latter with a fire tower cab.

Between Shin Pond and the Seboeis River is the steep and shapely peak of Sugarloaf Mtn., while just north of Patten, Mt. Chase (2,440 ft.) rises prominently from a low range of summits. Isolated Norway Bluff (2,285 ft.) looms above Munsungan Lake north of BSP while the bump of Owl's Head (930 ft.) looks out over Scraggly Lake.

BAXTER STATE PARK

BSP was created as a gift from the former governor Percival P. Baxter in 1931 when he donated Katahdin and 6,000 surrounding acres to the state of Maine to be kept "forever wild." Over the next three decades, Governor Baxter continued to purchase additional lands and add them to the park in deeds of trust, a total of 28 donations in all; his last, in 1962, brought the extent of BSP to more than 200,000 acres. Governor Baxter died in 1969. As a condition Baxter's gift the area (BSP): "shall forever be left in its natural wild state, forever be kept as a sanctuary for wild beasts and birds, and forever be used for public forest, public park, and public recreational purposes." BSP has continued to expand in recent years, adding more than 8,000 acres through purchase or gift, including 4,100 acres around iconic Katahdin Lake in 2006. The current park size is now 209,644 deeded acres and features 215 mi. of hiking trails and 337 campsites.

About 75 percent of BSP is managed as a wildlife sanctuary, while 14 percent of the park (in its northwest corner) is managed as a Scientific Forest Management Area, where timber harvesting is allowed. About 25 percent of the park is open to hunting (though not for moose) and trapping. BSP is not part of Maine's state park system; the park is operated through user fees, income from trust funds provided by Governor Baxter, and revenue from timber sales. Governance of the park is the sole responsibility of the BSP Authority, which consists of Maine's attorney general, the commissioner of the Maine Dept. of Inland Fisheries and Wildlife, and the director of the Maine Forest Service.

BSP Regulations

Persons planning to camp, hike, and use the facilities in the park should be familiar with the rules and regulations, which are revised periodically. A complete list can be found at baxterstatepark.org. The salient points for hikers and campers are summarized as follows:

- Camping is permitted by reservation only, and only at authorized campgrounds and campsites, between May 15 and October 22, and from December 1 through March 31.
- All persons entering the park by road or trail must register at the first opportunity at a staffed gatehouse or a self-registration station. Prior registration is required for groups of twelve or more.
- Hiking or mountain climbing may be restricted at the discretion of the park director.
- Hunting and trapping are prohibited, except in specifically designated areas. Maine fishing laws apply within the park.
- Pets and other domestic animals are not allowed in the park. Do not bait, feed, or disturb any animal in the park.
- Fires and cooking or heating devices are permitted only at designated campsites or picnic areas.
- Anything carried into the park must be carried out; for example, trash and gear.

- No person may use electronic devices in any way that impairs others' enjoyment of the park.
- No person may disturb or remove natural objects, plants, or animals.
- Single vehicles more than 9 ft. high, 7 ft. wide, or 22 ft. long—or 44 ft. long for combined units—are prohibited. Motorcycles, ATVs, and motorized trail bikes are prohibited. Bicycles are allowed only on park roads.
- Aircraft are generally prohibited in the park. The possession of a drone on any trail or waterway is prohibited.
- All groups of five or more persons under the age of 16 must be accompanied by an adult.

BSP Hiking Considerations

The trails on many BSP routes are among the steepest and most difficult in New England. Hikers planning to go to higher and more distant elevations should take plenty of food, water, and warm clothing and should be in good physical condition. Others may want to limit their activities accordingly. Do not leave the trails, particularly on Katahdin or during severe weather or limited visibility.

Caution: Severe injuries and deaths have occurred in the park over the years. Visitors must be responsible for their own safety and that of their group. The upper summits are very rugged and exposed above the timberline. Weather and trail conditions can change quickly, even in summer. The weather on Katahdin is similar to that of Mt. Washington, but longer access routes can make conditions even more dangerous.

The alpine environment above treeline on Katahdin is home to many rare and unusual plants and animals. Please help care for these fragile ecosystems by staying on marked trails. Observe all wildlife from a safe distance.

The staff of BSP and volunteers maintain all of the more than 200 mi. of park trails. All trails are blazed with blue paint; the only exception is the white-blazed AT.

BSP Road Access

The south entrance of BSP at Togue Pond Gate is reached by traveling on I-95 to Exit 244 at Medway. From there, travel west on ME 157 and then ME 157/11 through East Millinocket to Millinocket and finally on Baxter Park Rd. to reach the park. It is about 18 mi. from Millinocket to the gate. The north entrance of the park at Matagamon Gate is reached by traveling on I-95 to Exit 264 at Sherman. From there, go north on ME 11 to Patten, then northeast on ME 159 to Shin Pond. Take Grand Lake Rd. west to the park. It is about 26 mi. from Patten to the gate.

All park visitors must stop at the entrance gate to register and obtain a park pass. Rangers can also assist with directions and information about hiking trails and camping. Hikers entering the park via the AT must register at the trail kiosk at the park boundary near Abol Bridge. Most visitors enter the park at Togue Pond Gate. An entrance fee is charged for non-Maine-licensed vehicles. Just beyond the gate, the road forks. The right fork is Roaring Brook Rd., which leads 8.1 mi. to Roaring Brook CG. To the left is Park Tote Rd., leading 41.1 mi. to the north entrance at Matagamon Gate.

In accordance with the terms of Governor Baxter's deeds of trust, park roads are unpaved and relatively unimproved. Park Tote Rd. and Roaring Brook Rd. are very narrow and winding dirt and gravel roads. Dense foliage along the roads restricts views to the immediate corridor for much of the way, but there are occasional viewpoints. From Togue Pond Gate, Park Tote Rd. first leads northwest and then generally north. It skirts the southern and western flanks of Katahdin. During the first five or so miles of the drive, the mountain is briefly visible a few times. After passing Abol and Katahdin Stream campgrounds, the road reaches Foster Field, where you can see Doubletop Mtn., Mt. OJI, and other mountains in the range west of Katahdin. After that, the views are very restricted much of the way to the Matagamon Gatehouse. Most of Park Tote Rd. follows the routes of old logging roads.

Park Tote Rd. from Togue Pond Gate to:

Roaring Brook Rd.	100 ft.
Abol CG	5.7 mi.
Katahdin Stream CG	7.7 mi.
Daicey Pond access road (1.1 mi. to Daicey Pond from Park Tote Rd.)	10.0 mi.
Kidney Pond access road (1.4 mi. to Kidney Pond from Park Tote Rd.)	10.3 mi.
Foster Field	10.3 mi.
Nesowadnehunk CG	16.8 mi.
Trout Brook Crossing	33.8 mi.
South Branch Pond CG via access road from Trout Brook Crossing	36.1 mi.
Trout Brook CG	38.5 mi.
Matagamon Gate	41.1 mi.

Roaring Brook Rd. diverges right from Park Tote Rd. 100 ft. beyond Togue Pond Gate. Katahdin is immediately visible on the left across Helon

Taylor and Rum ponds. Roaring Brook Rd. then proceeds through the woods, following along the base of the mountain to the east, passing Rum Brook Day Use Site, Bear Brook Group Site, and Avalanche Field before reaching its terminus at Roaring Brook CG.

SEC 1

Roaring Brook Rd. from Togue Pond Gate to:

Rum Brook Day Use Site	1.3 mi.
Bear Brook Group Site	5.2 mi.
Avalanche Field	6.6 mi.
Roaring Brook CG	8.1 mi.

The park is open to the public twelve months a year, although access is often limited during the spring thaw, from April to mid-May. Roads are unplowed during the winter months and are available for cross-country skiing and snowmobiling.

BSP headquarters is located at 64 Balsam Dr. in Millinocket. The park operates a seasonal visitor center at Togue Pond, a short distance before the Togue Pond Gate.

BSP Day-Use Parking and Camping Reservations

Day-use visitors desiring to climb Katahdin are strongly urged to use the Day Use Parking Reservation (DUPR) system. This service is available for hikers wanting to climb Katahdin from Roaring Brook, Abol, or Katahdin Stream campgrounds. DUPRs can be made by phone at 207-723-3877 or online at baxterstatepark.org.

Camping reservations are mandatory and can be made through a rolling reservation system. Reservations may be made online, by mail (check), or in person (cash or check) at park headquarters in Millinocket up to four months in advance of the desired trip date. Reservations are limited to seven days at any one site and fourteen days total for any one visit to the park. Last-minute reservations may be made by phone fourteen days or less before the desired arrival date. Reservations made by phone must be paid by credit card. To get a printable camping reservation form, to view campsite availability, or to make a camping reservation for as many as seven days at a single campsite, go to baxterstatepark.org or call the reservation office at 207-723-5140. Mailing address is 64 Balsam Dr., Millinocket, ME 04462; physical address for in-person reservations is the same.

BSP Camping

The park offers a wide variety of camping opportunities at ten campgrounds, from drive-in campsites, walk-in tentsites, cabins, and bunkhouses to remote backcountry lean-tos and tentsites. Camping is permitted by reservation only, and only at authorized campgrounds and campsites, between May 15 and October 22, and from December 1 through March 31.

Seven campgrounds are located along Park Tote Rd.: Abol, Katahdin Stream, Nesowadnehunk, Kidney Pond, Daicey Pond, South Branch Pond, and Trout Brook. Group camping sites are also available at Foster Field, Nesowadnehunk, and Trout Brook. Located on Roaring Brook Rd. are Roaring Brook CG and Bear Brook Group Site. Backcountry campgrounds, accessible only on foot, are located at Chimney Pond and Russell Pond. Gain access to Chimney Pond by trail from Roaring Brook CG. Russell Pond may be reached by trails from Roaring Brook, Nesowadnehunk, and South Branch Pond campgrounds.

All campgrounds have lean-tos (except Daicey Pond and Kidney Pond) and tentsites (except Chimney Pond, Daicey Pond, and Kidney Pond). Daicey Pond and Kidney Pond have cabins only. There are bunkhouses at Roaring Brook, Nesowadnehunk, South Branch Pond, Russell Pond, Chimney Pond, and Trout Brook. All of these sites offer only the most basic facilities. No hot showers, grocery stores, or gas stations are available in the park. Water is available but is untreated throughout the park, so some method for purifying is essential. Campers and visitors must supply their own camping gear, food, and cooking utensils. Fires are permitted only at designated sites. Firewood is available for purchase.

Backcountry campsites (which may be lean-tos or tentsites) are available at Davis Pond, Katahdin Lake, Martin Ponds, Wassataquoik Stream, Wassataquoik Lake, Little Wassataquoik Lake, Center Pond, Pogy Pond, Upper South Branch Pond, Lower and Middle Fowler ponds, Long Pond, Billfish Pond, Frost Pond, Hudson Pond, Webster Lake, Webster Stream, KP Dam, and First and Second Matagamon lakes. A number of water-access-only campsites are also available. Canoes, paddles, and personal flotation devices are available for rent at many campgrounds and select backcountry sites. Check with a ranger for more information.

Abol CG

This campground is situated on Abol Stream, at the foot of Abol Slide on the southwest flank of Katahdin, 5.7 mi. north of Togue Pond Gate. Visitor facilities include a day-use area with picnic tables and toilet, and camping at twelve lean-tos and nine tentsites. Abol Trail (see p. 22) leaves from the campground and climbs more than 3,300 ft. to reach a vast alpine plateau called the Tableland below the summit of Katahdin, merging with Hunt Trail at Thoreau Spring for the final ascent to Baxter Peak. A side trail to Little Abol Falls from the campground offers a pleasant short walk.

Katahdin Stream CG

This campground is situated on Katahdin Stream, at the base of Katahdin's southwestern flank, 7.7 mi. from Togue Pond Gate. Facilities include picnic shelters and toilets, plus twelve lean-tos and ten tentsites. Nearby Foster Field Group Area (2.6 mi. north) has a capacity of 50 people. The AT enters Katahdin Stream CG and merges with Hunt Trail on its way to the summit of Katahdin. A variety of other day hikes are possible from this location: to Katahdin Stream Falls; the Owl; Tracy, Elbow, Daicey, and Grassy ponds; and Blueberry Ledges.

Roaring Brook CG

This campground is on the southern bank of Roaring Brook at the terminus of Roaring Brook Rd., 8.1 mi. from Togue Pond Gate. Facilities include nine lean-tos, ten tentsites, and a ten-person bunkhouse. Nearby Bear Brook Group Site has three group campsites with a capacity of 42 persons. Roaring Brook CG is the base for ascending Katahdin from the east and for backpacking into the southern interior of the park. Trails to Pamola, Chimney Pond, and Russell Pond start here. Close by is Sandy Stream Pond, where hikers can often see moose and other wildlife, and South Turner Mtn.

Chimney Pond CG

This campground, the oldest in the park, is in a spectacular setting near the north shore of Chimney Pond in Katahdin's Great Basin, where the walls of the mountain rise more than 2,000 ft. to the high summits of Baxter Peak and Pamola. The campground is accessible only via a 3.2-mi. hike from Roaring Brook CG. Facilities include nine lean-tos and a ten-person bunkhouse. Open fires are not allowed at Chimney Pond, so campers must bring a lightweight backpacking stove for cooking.

Saddle, Cathedral, and Dudley trails leave from Chimney Pond and ascend to the high summits and ridges of Katahdin: Baxter Peak, Knife Edge, South Peak, and Pamola. Nearby Hamlin Ridge Trail leads to Hamlin Peak and Howe Peak, and North Basin Trail leads to North Basin and Blueberry Knoll.

Russell Pond CG

Located along the western shore of Russell Pond, in the heart of the wilderness north of Katahdin, this hike-in-only campground makes a convenient base for exploring the central interior of the park. The wildlife in this remote area is especially intriguing. Facilities include three tentsites, five lean-tos, and an eight-person bunkhouse in the woods along the west shore of Russell Pond. Little Wassataquoik Campsite, Island Campsite on Wassataquoik Lake, and Wassataquoik Stream and Pogy Pond campsites are easily reached from Russell Pond. Short trails nearby lead to Caverly Lookout, Grand Falls, Six Ponds, and Wassataquoik Lake.

Daicey Pond CG

This campground is situated on Daicey Pond, 11.1 mi. north of Togue Pond Gate via Park Tote Rd. and the Daicey Pond access road. Established as a sporting camp in the early 1900s and operated as York's Twin Pine Camps until 1971, the scenic Daicey Pond CG offers outstanding views of the west side of Katahdin and, from a canoe on the pond, fine views of Doubletop Mtn. and other nearby peaks. The campground features ten self-service cabins, a library, canoe and kayak rentals, and trailhead parking. Day-use parking is available in a clearing on the Daicey Pond access road, 1.0 mi. south of Park Tote Rd. and 0.1 mi. north of Daicey Pond CG.

The AT passes close to the campground and follows the north shore of the pond for a 0.4 mi. South of the pond, the AT passes Toll Dam on Nesowadnehunk Stream, Little Niagara Falls, and then Big Niagara Falls. All are worth seeing and within an easy walk of the campground. Daicey Pond is also a good alternate starting point for access to Sentinel Mtn. and Kidney Pond, although Sentinel Mtn. Trail from this direction does require fording Nesowadnehunk Stream. Beautiful Tracy, Elbow, and Grassy ponds are also within easy reach. Inquire at the Daicey Pond ranger cabin about other short pond hikes not described here.

Kidney Pond CG

This campground is situated on Kidney Pond, 11.8 mi. north of Togue Pond Gate via Togue Pond Gate and the Kidney Pond access road. The cabins at Kidney Pond were established as a sporting camp in 1899 and operated as a private camp until 1988. Kidney Pond CG now serves as a central hub for hiking, as well as for fishing and canoeing on Kidney Pond and the surrounding ponds, including Rocky, Celia, Jackson, and Lily Pad. The campground features twelve self-service cabins, a library, canoe and kayak rentals, and trailhead parking. Kidney Pond is a good base for hikes to Sentinel and Doubletop mountains, as well as to many pretty outlying ponds.

Nesowadnehunk CG

This beautiful campground, 16.8 mi. north of Togue Pond Gate via Park Loop Rd., is along the eastern bank of Nesowadnehunk Stream.

Nesowadnehunk is the base for the approach to Doubletop Mtn. from the north and for trails to Center Pond, Wassataquoik Lake, and Russell Pond to the northeast. The campground features nine tentsites, eleven lean-tos, and a four-person bunkhouse. Two group areas accommodate as many as 48 people.

South Branch Pond CG

The South Branch ponds, consisting of an upper and a lower pond situated in a deep valley between Traveler Mtn. to the east and South Branch and Black Cat mountains to the west, have one of the most spectacular surroundings anywhere in Maine. The campground, located at the north end of Lower South Branch Pond, is a base for hiking the peaks of Traveler Mtn.

From the ponds, visitors are rewarded with choice views of the peaks and ridges of Traveler Mtn., rising south and east, and of the bulk of South Branch Mtn., rising to the south and west. The campground features 21 tentsites, twelve lean-tos, an eight-person bunkhouse, two walk-in/canoe-in sites on Lower South Branch Pond, one walk-in/canoe-in site on Upper South Branch Pond, a picnic area, canoe and kayak rentals, and trailhead parking.

Trout Brook CG

Trout Brook CG is on the site of a farm dating to 1837 that once supported logging operations. The campground is on the north side of Park Tote Rd., about 27 mi. west of Patten, 2.6 mi. west of Matagamon Gate, and 4.7 mi. east of Trout Brook Crossing Day Use Site, where the road to South Branch Pond CG leads south. The campground features fourteen tentsites, one walk-in lean-to along Trout Brook, four group sites, canoe rentals, and trailhead parking.

The campground is a good starting point for a variety of explorations in this region of the park, including hikes on Freezeout Trail to the north and the network of trails in the Fowler Ponds area to the south. The trail to Trout Brook Mtn. leaves just across the road from the campground. Trout Brook CG is also a good base for canoe trips on the brook and nearby Grand Lake Matagamon.

KATAHDIN WOODS AND WATERS NATIONAL MONUMENT

The new Katahdin Woods and Waters National Monument preserves 87,500 acres of craggy mountain peaks, deep woods, and free-flowing rivers and streams in the Maine woods east of BSP, an area long recognized for its ecological, recreational, and cultural importance. Using the authority granted by the Antiquities Act of 1906, President Barack Obama established the monument with a proclamation on August 24, 2016.

KWWNM is the latest addition to a diverse matrix of public and private conservation lands in Maine's North Woods that range southwest across the 100MW to Moosehead Lake and then west to the Canadian border. The lands that compose the new monument were assembled by the privately held Elliotsville Plantation Inc. between 2001 and 2014 and then donated to the federal government. Along with the land, the foundation donated $20 million to establish an endowment for the monument and pledged to raise an additional $20 million in the future.

The National Park Service manages the monument and is working through an initial three-year process to develop a management plan that will guide future activities on the land, where, as of 2017, there was little infrastructure. That may change soon: AMC received a $25,000 grant from The Conservation Alliance for work in 2018 to create an advocacy campaign focused on protecting and promoting KWWNM. Immediate plans include familiarization trips to the monument for AMC chapters and engaging outdoor lovers in the management-planning process. For updates and to learn more, visit outdoors.org/kwwnm.

KWWNM is open year-round for a variety of recreational activities, including hiking and backpacking, canoeing and kayaking, mountain biking and fishing, bird and wildlife watching, cross-country skiing, and horseback riding. Drive-in camping is available but limited. The Katahdin Loop Rd. is a gravel road that traces a 17-mi. route through the southern section of KWWNM, offering visitors a good introduction by touching on the most popular hikes, walks, and viewpoints available at this time. A fire permit from the Maine Forest Service is required for all campsites within KWWNM, and a parking permit is required for vehicles left overnight at trailheads.

Two KWWNM welcome centers in neighboring communities offer visitor information and orientation (Memorial Day through Columbus Day): one in downtown Millinocket, at 200 Penobscot Ave., and the other in Patten, at the Patten Lumberman's Museum on ME 159.

KWWNM Road Access

There are two main access points for KWWNM.

Directions to the southern section of the monument: From I-95, Exit 264 at Sherman, drive west on ME 158 for 0.6 mi. to the jct. of ME 11, turn south on ME 11 (ME 11 bears sharply left), and drive 5.0 mi. to Swift Brook Rd. For an alternate route from I-95, take Exit 244 at Medway, drive west on ME 157 for 0.75 mi., turn north on ME 11, and proceed 20.0 mi. to Swift Brook Rd. on the left.

From either of the options above, turn onto Swift Brook Rd., which quickly becomes a gravel road. (*Note:* There is active logging traffic on this road; please yield to trucks.) At a jct. 5.2 mi. from ME 11, turn left for Katahdin Loop Rd. and, in another 1.7 mi., reach Whetstone Bridge over the East Branch of the Penobscot River. Pass Roberts Rd. on the left then Stacyville Rd. on the left on the way to Sandbank Stream Campsite, which is 2.9 mi. from Whetstone Bridge. Located at this old gravel pit are an information kiosk and three car-camping sites with picnic tables, fire pits, and a vault toilet. This is the official start of Katahdin Loop Rd. The main jct. of the road is 2.2 mi. ahead; visitors desiring to drive the entire loop should turn left at that point to travel in the recommended clockwise direction (several steep, narrow sections after Mile 7 are one-way). Visitors planning to hike Barnard Mtn. and the IAT should proceed right from the main jct.

Directions to the northern end of the monument: From I-95, Exit 264 at Sherman and drive west on ME 158 for 0.6 mi. to the jct. of ME 11. Bear right on ME 11 for 9.3 mi. to the northerly jct. of ME 159 and ME 11 in Patten. Turn left on ME 159 and drive 24.2 mi. (ME 159 becomes Grand Lake Rd. after Shin Pond) to Messer Pond Rd., which is on the left, just after the bridge over the East Branch of the Penobscot River and Matagamon Wilderness CG. The northern entrance to KWWNM is 0.7 mi. south on Messer Pond Rd.

KWWNM Camping

At KWWNM, there is currently one primitive drive-in camping area with two sites. Four trailside shelters are found along the IAT through KWWNM. There are at least eight privately operated campgrounds ringing the outskirts of BSP and KWWNM.

SUGGESTED HIKES

■ Easy

LITTLE ABOL FALLS

	⇅	↗	○
RT via Little Abol Falls Trail	1.6 mi.	250 ft.	0:55

This short, scenic hike leads easily from Abol CG to a series of falls on Abol Stream, with possible views of Katahdin en route. See Little Abol Falls Trail, p. 23.

KATAHDIN STREAM FALLS

	⇅	↗	○
RT via Hunt Trail	2.4 mi.	500 ft.	1:25

From Katahdin Stream CG, hike to the pretty Katahdin Stream Falls, an 80-ft. series of cascades in a mossy canyon. See Hunt Trail, p. 23.

BLUEBERRY KNOLL

	⇅	↗	○
RT via North Basin Trail	2.0 mi.	140 ft.	1:15

Enjoy sweeping views of Katahdin's North Basin and Great Basin from this high and open spot. South Turner Mtn. and Katahdin Lake are in full view to the east. See North Basin Trail, p. 29.

CAVERLY LOOKOUT

	⇅	↗	○
RT via Pogy Notch Trail, Grand Falls Trail, and Caverly Lookout Trail	2.6 mi.	400 ft.	1:40

This short hike from Russell Pond leads to a panoramic view of the vast interior of the park. To begin, see Pogy Notch Trail, p. 42.

BIG AND LITTLE NIAGARA FALLS

	⇅	↗	○
RT via AT Southbound from Daicey Pond trailhead	2.4 mi.	200 ft.	1:15

This easy jaunt from Daicey Pond leads to three thundering waterfalls: Toll Dam, Little Niagara Falls, and Big Niagara Falls. See AT Southbound from Daicey Pond trailhead, p. 45.

DAICEY POND, GRASSY POND, AND ELBOW POND

	⮏	↗	⟳
LP via AT Northbound from Daicey Pond trailhead	2.9 mi.	250 ft.	1:35

Enjoy grand Katahdin views and watch for moose and other wildlife on this lovely loop through spruce woods in the vicinity of three idyllic ponds. See AT Northbound from Daicey Pond trailhead, p. 46.

LEDGES NORTH OF SOUTH BRANCH POND

	⮏	↗	⟳
LP via Ledges Trail	1.2 mi.	100 ft.	0:40

This short loop hike leads to open ledges with good views south across the steep-walled valley that contains Lower and Upper South Branch ponds. See Ledges Trail, p. 51.

OWL'S HEAD

	⮏	↗	⟳
RT via Owl's Head Trail	3.4 mi.	250 ft.	1:50

The long drive to get here is worth it when you hike to the ledges high on Owl's Head. Enjoy the fine view over pristine Scraggly Lake, to high summits of BSP and many other peaks. See Owl's Head Trail, p. 64.

■ Moderate
CHIMNEY POND

	⮏	↗	⟳
RT via Chimney Pond Trail	6.0 mi.	1,425 ft.	4:00

Hike from Roaring Brook CG to Chimney Pond, dramatically located at the base of the towering walls of South Basin. Baxter Peak, Knife Edge, and Pamola loom above. See Chimney Pond Trail, p. 25.

HAMLIN PEAK AND HOWE PEAK

	⮏	↗	⟳
RT via Chimney Pond Trail, North Basin Trail, Hamlin Ridge Trail, North Peaks Trail, Hamlin Peak Cutoff, and Northwest Basin Trail	5.3 mi.	1,950 ft.	4:15

From Chimney Pond, combine the first three trails listed above to scale Hamlin Peak. Then explore Howe Peak, parts of Northwest Plateau, and Caribou Spring via the last three trails. To begin, see Chimney Pond Trail, p. 25.

SEC 1

SOUTH TURNER MTN.

RT via South Turner Mtn. Trail	4.4 mi.	1,633 ft.	3:00

Visit scenic Sandy Stream Pond on the way to panoramic Katahdin views from the upper slopes of South Turner Mtn. See South Turner Mtn. Trail, p. 32.

KATAHDIN LAKE

LP via Katahdin Lake Trail and Martin Ponds Trail	7.4 mi.	250 ft.	4:00

Hike to iconic Katahdin Lake for lunch then return by way of Martin Ponds Trail and get a brilliant view of Katahdin from the campsite there. See Katahdin Lake Trail, p. 34.

HOWE BROOK

RT via Pogy Notch Trail and Howe Brook Trail	5.8 mi.	700 ft.	3:20

From South Branch Pond CG, follow Pogy Notch Trail south along the pond then turn east and climb Howe Brook Trail to enjoy pools, potholes, slides, chutes, and a beautiful waterfall at trail's end. To begin, see Pogy Notch Trail, p. 42.

CRANBERRY POND, KETTLE POND, AND ABOL POND

RT via Cranberry Pond Trail and Kettle Pond Trail	6.2 mi.	100 ft.	3:10

From near Togue Pond Gate, hike to Abol Beach Day Use Site for a picnic and a swim. To begin, see Cranberry Pond Trail, p. 44.

BLUEBERRY LEDGES

OW via Blueberry Ledges Trail	4.9 mi.	250 ft.	2:35

This wonderful hike leads through an area that was burned in a forest fire in the summer of 1977. Lush growth has all but erased signs of the burn, but hints are still noticeable if you look close. Cool off in Katahdin Stream along the way and pick blueberries in season. See Blueberry Ledges Trail, p. 47.

SENTINEL MTN.

	↥↧	↗	◷
RT via Sentinel Link Trail and Sentinel Mtn. Trail	6.2 mi.	791 ft.	3:30

This fun hike leaves from Kidney Pond and reaches viewpoints overlooking the West Branch of the Penobscot River. To begin, see Sentinel Link Trail, p. 48.

FIVE PONDS

	↥↧	↗	◷
LP via Five Ponds Trail	6.0 mi.	500 ft.	3:30

This nice loop around the base of Trout Brook Mtn. passes five scenic ponds: Long, High, Round, Billfish, and Littlefield. See Five Ponds Trail, p. 58.

TROUT BROOK MTN.

	↥↧	↗	◷
LP via Trout Brook Mtn. Trail and Five Ponds Trail	3.5 mi.	1,070 ft.	2:30

This nice circuit hike leads to fine views of the Traveler Mtn. massif and the many beautiful ponds around the mountain's base. To begin, see Trout Brook Mtn. Trail, p. 59.

BARNARD MTN.

	↥↧	↗	◷
RT via IAT and Barnard Mtn. Trail	4.4 mi.	750 ft.	2:40

From Katahdin Loop Rd. at Mile 12 in the new KWWNM, hike the IAT and Barnard Mtn. Trail to the large ledge atop Barnard. You'll be rewarded with a grand view of Katahdin Lake and majestic Katahdin. See Barnard Mtn. Trail, p. 63.

■ Strenuous
BAXTER PEAK VIA ABOL

	↥↧	↗	◷
RT via Abol Trail and Hunt Trail (the AT)	8.4 mi.	4,000 ft.	6:10

Hike the rerouted Abol Trail to the Tableland then follow the last mile of Hunt Trail to the summit of Katahdin at Baxter Peak, the northern terminus of the AT. To begin, see Abol Trail, p. 22.

PAMOLA

	⤵	↗	◔
RT via Helon Taylor Trail	7.2 mi.	3,430 ft.	6:20

For sustained views of Katahdin and Knife Edge, climb Pamola from the east on the exposed Keep Ridge. See Helon Taylor Trail, p. 24.

KATAHDIN CIRCUIT

	⤵	↗	◔
LP via Dudley Trail and Saddle Trail	6.0 mi.	2,358 ft.	5:00

This exciting loop hike starts and ends at Chimney Pond. Climb Pamola via Dudley Trail, traverse the airy crest of Knife Edge to Baxter Peak, and descend by way of Saddle Trail. To begin, see Dudley Trail, p. 25.

MT. COE AND SOUTH BROTHER

	⤵	↗	◔
LP via Mt. Coe Trail and Marston Trail	9.4 mi.	3,500 ft.	6:00

This loop hike reaches two high peaks that both provide excellent views over the Klondike to Katahdin. To begin, see Mt. Coe Trail, p. 37.

ROARING BROOK TO SOUTH BRANCH POND

	⤵	↗	◔
OW via Russell Pond Trail and Pogy Notch Trail	15.8 mi.	450 ft.	8:25

Traverse the wild central interior of BSP on a two-day backpacking trip. Camp overnight in a lean-to at remote Russell Pond. To begin, see Russell Pond Trail, p. 39.

TRAVELER CIRCUIT

	⤵	↗	◔
LP via Pogy Notch Trail, Center Ridge Trail, Traveler Mtn. Trail, and North Traveler Mtn. Trail	11.1 mi.	3,675 ft.	7:30

This demanding loop hike over Center Ridge, Traveler, and North Traveler Mtn. rewards hikers with outstanding views from the high and craggy alpine ridges and summits en route. To begin, see Pogy Notch Trail, p. 42.

DOUBLETOP MTN.

OW via Doubletop Mtn. Trail	8.2 mi.	2,425 ft.	5:20

This outstanding hike from Kidney Pond to Nesowadnehunk Field climbs the craggy twin summits of Doubletop Mtn. for impressive views of Katahdin, South Brother, Mt. Coe, Mt. OJI, and Barren Mtn. See Doubletop Mtn. Trail, p. 50.

SCIENTIFIC FOREST MANAGEMENT AREA

RT via Freezeout Trail	28.2 mi.	100 ft.	14:00

Spend two or three days backpacking the wilds of the Scientific Forest Management Area in BSP's remote northern part. There are several tentsites and lean-tos along this route, from Trout Brook Farm to Webster Lake. See Freezeout Trail, p. 56.

DEASEY MTN. AND LUNKSOOS MTN.

RT via IAT Northbound	10.6 mi.	2,150 ft.	8:00

From the end of Orin Falls Rd. in KWWNM, hike into the IAT then follow it north to bag the rocky summits of Deasey Mtn. and Lunksoos Mtn., which both offer excellent views west to the BSP mountain skyline. See IAT Northbound, p. 61.

TRAIL DESCRIPTIONS

SEC 1

KATAHDIN AND VICINITY

■ KATAHDIN: BAXTER PEAK (5,268 FT.), PAMOLA (4,919 FT.), SOUTH PEAK (5,240 FT.), AND CHIMNEY PEAK (4,850 FT.)

At 5,268 ft., Katahdin is Maine's highest mountain and as wild and allur-ing as any mountain in the eastern United States. Rising majestically from the Maine woods just north of the West Branch of the Penobscot River, about 80 mi. north of Bangor, Katahdin is BSP's crown jewel. Its first recorded ascent was via the southwest ridge (once known as the Southwest Spur, this is today's Hunt Spur) in 1804 by a party of eleven, including Charles Turner Jr., who wrote an account of the trip. There may have been unrecorded ascents during the next fifteen years, but we do know that peo-ple climbed the mountain again in 1819 and 1820. After this date, ascents became more regular. Henry David Thoreau scaled the mountain in 1846 but did not reach the top. Katahdin has six major summits—Baxter Peak, Pamola, South Peak, Chimney Peak, Hamlin Peak, and Howe Peak—and features a network of sixteen trails that ascend the mountain from every major compass direction.

ABOL TRAIL (BSP; MAP 1: E3)

Cumulative from Abol CG (1,300 ft.) to:	�??↑	↗	○
Thoreau Spring and Hunt Trail (4,636 ft.)	3.4 mi.	3,336 ft.	3:30
Baxter Peak (5,268 ft.) via Hunt Trail	4.2 mi.	3,968 ft.	4:05

Abol Trail is the shortest route to Baxter Peak from a park road, and as such, it is the mountain's most popular ascent route. A huge avalanche created the obvious Abol Slide in 1816, making it a prominent landmark for Katahdin climbers ever since. The first recorded ascent of Abol Slide was in 1819 by a party of British surveyors led by Colin Campbell. The famous slide was an integral part of Abol Trail until 2013, when significant landslide activity moved untold tons of rocks, gravel, and other debris, leaving the unstable slope too dangerous for hiking and forcing its closure. Crews routed the trail away from Abol Slide to the ridge immediately west during the summers of 2014 and 2015; the trail was reopened in the summer of 2015. The rerouted Abol Trail is now 3.4 mi., or 0.6 mi. longer than it was previously.

The trail leaves Park Tote Rd. at Abol CG, passes through the camp-ground and, at 0.2 mi. between lean-tos 11 and 12, enters an old tote road to reach the southern bank of a tributary of Abol Stream. Abol Trail continues along the stream for 0.6 mi. before bearing sharply right (northeast), away from the brook. The trail reaches a gravel wash from the old Abol Slide and begins to steepen. Just above, in sight of the old Abol Slide, the trail diverges left onto the new footway. After a long rising traverse and multiple sets of rock steps, the trail switchbacks east and continues to climb steeply.

At treeline, the trail offers a fine panoramic vista over the 100MW and a nice view west to the Hunt Spur and the AT. Here, Abol Trail turns east again to reach the top of Abol Slide and offers a sweeping look down the former route. From here to the Tableland, the original rock scramble—600 ft. of strenuous climbing—remains. Upon reaching the Tableland, the trail leads 0.1 mi. to Thoreau Spring (unreliable water source) and the jct. with Hunt Trail at 3.2 mi. For Baxter Peak, turn right on Hunt Trail and continue northeast up gentler slopes for 1.0 mi. to the summit.

LITTLE ABOL FALLS TRAIL (BSP; MAP 1: E3)

From Abol CG (1,300 ft.) to:	↕	↗	↻
Little Abol Falls (1,550 ft.)	0.8 mi.	250 ft.	0:30

This short, scenic trail leads easily from Abol CG to a series of falls on a branch of Abol Stream. Views of Katahdin are possible en route.

HUNT TRAIL (BSP; MAP 1: E2–E3)

Cumulative from Katahdin Stream CG (1,099 ft.) to:	↕	↗	↻
Owl Trail (1,500 ft.)	1.1 mi.	400 ft.	0:45
Katahdin Stream Falls (1,600 ft.)	1.2 mi.	500 ft.	0:50
Thoreau Spring (4,636 ft.) at jct. of Abol Trail and Baxter Peak Cutoff	4.5 mi.	3,537 ft.	4:15
Baxter Peak (5,268 ft.)	5.5 mi.	4,169 ft.	5:00

The white-blazed Hunt Trail is the route of the AT up Katahdin and climbs the mountain from the southwest. The first recorded ascent of Katahdin was in 1804 by a surveyor named Charles Turner Jr., who is believed to have climbed the peak via the Southwest Spur, the route of today's Hunt Trail. Hunt Trail was first cut in 1900 by Irving O. Hunt, who operated a sporting camp on Nesowadnehunk Stream. Hunt Trail requires 4,169 ft. of elevation gain, the most of any route to Baxter Peak; from treeline to the Tableland, the trail is trail is long, steep, and rough.

From the day-use parking lot, follow the Hunt Trail north through the campground. Just past tentsite 16, the trail enters the woods to closely follow the northern side of Katahdin Stream. At 1.1 mi. from the campground, Hunt Trail passes the trail to the Owl on the left, then crosses Katahdin Stream. Soon after, a short spur trail leads left to Katahdin Stream Falls, an 80-ft. cascade in a mossy canyon. Hunt Trail steepens through the spruce and fir forest, ascending via rock staircases in places. The trail crosses O-Joy Brook, the last sure water, at 2.0 mi. At 2.8 mi., Hunt Trail reaches two large rocks that form a cave.

The trail passes through a growth of small spruce and fir and, in another 0.2 mi., emerges on Hunt Spur, a bare, steep crest on the southwest shoulder of the mountain. Here, cairns mark the trail, which winds among huge boulders. Steel rungs aid the ascent in places. The trail then traverses a broad shelf and climbs steeply for 0.5 mi. over broken rock to the Tableland at 3.6 mi., where two slabs of rock mark the "Gateway."

The trail continues east, following a worn path and paint blazes, until it reaches Thoreau Spring, an unreliable water source, at 4.2 mi. At the spring, Baxter Peak Cutoff Trail goes left and reaches Saddle Trail in 0.9 mi. To the right, Abol Trail descends 3.4 mi. to Abol CG. From the spring, Hunt Trail climbs moderately northeast for 1.0 mi. to the summit of Baxter Peak, with its commanding panoramas and outstanding views of Great Basin, Chimney Pond, and Knife Edge.

HELON TAYLOR TRAIL (BSP; MAP 1: E4)

Cumulative from Roaring Brook CG (1,489 ft.) to:	↧↥	↗	↻
Start of Helon Taylor Trail (1,550 ft.) via Chimney Pond Trail	0.1 mi.	60 ft.	0:05
Pamola summit (4,919 ft.) and jct. of Dudley Trail and Knife Edge	3.6 mi.	3,430 ft.	3:30
Baxter Peak (5,268 ft.) via Knife Edge	4.7 mi.	3,800 ft.	5:50

This trail offers a direct route from Roaring Brook CG to Pamola, following the exposed Keep Ridge. The trail provides the most sustained views of any trail on Katahdin, but hikers on this route are exposed to the elements for most of the climb. Consider avoiding this trail in bad weather, particularly if hiking plans include Baxter Peak via Knife Edge.

The route leaves left (south) from Chimney Pond Trail 0.1 mi. northwest of the ranger cabin at Roaring Brook CG. Helon Taylor Trail climbs 0.5 mi. through mixed growth to a ridge crest, then levels off for a short period, passing through scrub and a boulder field. After that, the trail climbs steeply through small birch, enters an old flat burn, and drops to the small Bear Brook (unreliable), one of the branches of Avalanche Brook and the only water on the trail.

Beyond, the trail ascends steeply through scrub, a fine stand of conifers, and a boulder field with wide views in all directions. The trail then climbs over and between boulders to Keep Ridge and along the open ridge with spectacular views ahead to Knife Edge, north to the Basin Ponds and South Turner Mtn., and east to Katahdin Lake. The trail reaches the summit of Pamola at 3.6 mi. and offers excellent views of Baxter Peak, Great Basin, Chimney Pond, and the high peaks of the Katahdin massif.

CHIMNEY POND TRAIL (BSP; MAP 1: D4–E4)

Cumulative from Roaring Brook CG (1,489 ft.) to:	↧↥	↗	○
Brook crossing (1,900 ft.)	1.0 mi.	410 ft.	0:35
North Basin Cutoff jct. (2,500 ft.)	2.1 mi.	1,010 ft.	1:30
North Basin Trail jct. (2,850 ft.)	2.8 mi.	1,360 ft.	2:20
Chimney Pond CG (2,914 ft.)	3.0 mi.	1,425 ft.	2:30

This trail begins at the ranger cabin at Roaring Brook CG. Just ahead, Russell Pond Trail (p. 39) leaves right (leads 6.6 mi. to Russell Pond), and at 0.1 mi., Helon Taylor Trail leaves left (leads 3.6 mi. to Pamola). Continuing on, Chimney Pond Trail climbs west along the south bank of Roaring Brook. After 0.6 mi., the trail bears gradually away from the brook and climbs more steeply. At 1.0 mi., the trail crosses a brook, the outlet of Pamola Pond.

The route reaches Lower Basin Pond at 1.9 mi., and a short side trail on the right leads to the pond, where there are excellent views of the northern summits, cirques, and ridges of Katahdin. At 2.0 mi., Chimney Pond Trail goes left, uphill into the woods. At 2.1 mi., North Basin Cutoff leaves to the right. Beyond this jct., pass a depression known as Dry Pond, which holds water in the spring and after heavy rains. At 2.8 mi., North Basin Trail to Hamlin Ridge and North Basin leaves to the right. At 3.0 mi., the trail enters a small clearing and a covered day shelter with benches on the left. Beyond, the trail proceeds gently downhill through Chimney Pond CG to the ranger cabin and, just ahead, Chimney Pond. From this vantage point are magnificent views of the Great Basin, formed by the sweeping rock walls of Katahdin, from Pamola and Chimney Peak to South Peak and Baxter Peak.

DUDLEY TRAIL (BSP; MAP 1: E4)

Cumulative from Chimney Pond CG (2,910 ft.) to:	↧↥	↗	○
Pamola summit (4,919 ft.) and jct. of Helon Taylor Trail and Knife Edge	2.4 mi.	2,009 ft.	2:30
Baxter Peak (5,268 ft.) via Knife Edge	3.5 mi.	2,358 ft.	3:30

This trail ascends from Chimney Pond to Pamola via its north ridge, also known as Dudley Ridge. (*Note:* In 2016, a rockslide on the lower portion of Dudley Trail at the jct. of the Pamola Caves side trail permanently interrupted the route, *temporarily closing the trail*. As of late summer of 2017, a new route had been located and cleared, but significant work remains. Park officials expect to open the rerouted Dudley Trail sometime in 2018.)

The trail starts from the ranger cabin at Chimney Pond and heads east to cross the outlet of the pond. The trail then continues eastward through a boulder field along the base of Dudley Ridge. After passing through a cleft in a large boulder, Dudley Trail ascends steeply up the wooded ridge. At treeline, the trail emerges on the open ridge. The ridge is steep and exposed from here to the Pamola summit. The trail passes to the right of Index Rock, a prominent fingerlike boulder, and continues at a more gradual angle to reach the top of Pamola and the jct. with Helon Taylor and Knife Edge trails. It is 1.1 mi. to Baxter Peak via Knife Edge.

KNIFE EDGE (BSP; MAP 1: E3–E4)

From Pamola summit (4,919 ft.), Helon Taylor Trail, and Dudley Trail to:	⇅	↗	⟳
Baxter Peak (5,268 ft.)	1.1 mi.	450 ft.	1:45

This long, narrow, serrated ridge tops the southern wall of Great Basin and connects South Peak with Pamola. Steep cliffs plummet more than 2,000 ft. into Great Basin to the north, and in places, the ridge is reduced to only 2 or 3 ft. in width. The dizzying height, sheer cliffs, and extreme exposure combine to make this one of the most spectacular mountain trails in the eastern United States.

From the summit of Pamola, the trail leads southwest (follow the cairns) before dropping abruptly into the sharp cleft at the top of the Chimney. The trail then climbs the equally steep rock tower of Chimney Peak (4,900 ft.) and has several steel bars as aids. Beyond, the trail takes an undulating route over a series of rocky knobs before descending to a low point on the ridge. It then climbs steeply to South Peak (5,240 ft.) and continues along the spine of the summit ridge to Baxter Peak, joining the Hunt and Saddle trails.

(*Note:* Knife Edge is completely exposed and can be hazardous in bad weather. Under no circumstances should hikers leave the trail, as there are no safe alternate routes. Over the years, a number of attempts at shortcuts down to Chimney Pond have had tragic results. Knife Edge is not recommended for persons with a fear of heights.)

CATHEDRAL TRAIL (BSP; MAP 1: E3–E4)

Cumulative from Chimney Pond CG (2,914 ft.) to:	⇅	◩	◔
Cathedral Cutoff (4,700 ft.)	1.5 mi.	1,790 ft.	2:20
Saddle Trail (5,150 ft.)	1.8 mi.	2,240 ft.	2:35
Baxter Peak (5,268 ft.) via Saddle Trail	2.0 mi.	2,354 ft.	2:45

This trail provides the shortest route to Baxter Peak from Chimney Pond, climbing past the three immense, columnar Cathedral Rocks on its way to the summit. From the ranger cabin at Chimney Pond, the trail climbs through thick forest to reach Cathedral Pool on the right at 0.3 mi. At 0.4 mi., by a large cairn, the trail turns right toward the Cathedrals, crosses a bridge of rock covered with low growth, climbs steeply through boulders to a high point and continues upward through low trees.

Blazes mark the way around to the right, then up the steep side of the first Cathedral (0.8 mi.). The second Cathedral offers spectacular views of the Chimney and Knife Edge. The route continues to the top of the third Cathedral. At 1.5 mi., the trail forks. The right (west) fork is Cathedral Cutoff (leads 0.3 mi. to Saddle Trail and Baxter Peak Cutoff). Cathedral Trail bears left (south), climbing over large boulders to join Saddle Trail, which leads a gradual 0.2 mi. left to Baxter Peak. **Cathedral Cutoff**, a 0.3-mi. connector trail, leaves the jct. of Saddle Trail and Cathedral Cutoff 1.5 mi. from Chimney Pond via Cathedral Trail. **Baxter Peak Cutoff** contours southwest over the Tableland along the base of Baxter Peak, ending at Thoreau Spring and the jct. of Hunt and Abol trails, making it possible to hike a loop over Baxter Peak. In addition, the cutoff provides an alternative path to a safer descent trail in case of bad weather.

SADDLE TRAIL (BSP; MAP 1: E3–E4)

Cumulative from Chimney Pond CG (2,914 ft.) to:	⇅	◩	◔
Saddle and Northwest Basin Trail (4,250 ft.)	1.4 mi.	1,340 ft.	1:25
Cathedral Cutoff and Baxter Peak Cutoff (4,700 ft.)	1.9 mi.	1,790 ft.	1:55
Baxter Peak (5,268 ft.)	2.5 mi.	2,354 ft.	2:30

Climbers have taken this general route out of Great Basin via Saddle Slide since an avalanche in the winter of 1898–99 enlarged an existing but smaller slide. Saddle Trail offers the most moderate route up Katahdin from Chimney Pond.

From the ranger cabin near the pond, the worn trail climbs a rocky path through dense softwoods. Beyond, the trail swings to the right (north) and becomes easier underfoot and more gradual. It crosses Saddle Brook at 0.8 mi. and then climbs steeply over large boulders. At 0.9 mi., the trail bears left up Saddle Slide and passes through stunted birches. At 1.0 mi., the trail emerges into the open and climbs for 0.2 mi. up the loose rocks and gravel of the slide.

At 1.4 mi., the trail reaches the top of the slide and gains the level, open ground of the Tableland of the Saddle between Baxter and Hamlin peaks and a trail jct. To the right (north), Northwest Basin Trail leads to Hamlin Ridge Trail, North Peaks Trail, Northwest Basin, and eventually to Russell Pond. To the left (south), Saddle Trail continues south over moderate slopes, and cairns mark the well-worn path. At 1.9 mi., the trail passes a large boulder and a jct. To the left (east), Cathedral Cutoff connects to Cathedral Trail in 0.3 mi. To the right (west), Baxter Peak Cutoff contours southwest along the base of the summit cone for 0.9 mi. to connect with Abol and Hunt trails at Thoreau Spring. Continuing on, Cathedral Trail from Chimney Pond enters on the left at 2.3 mi. Ahead, Saddle Trail climbs to Baxter Peak at 2.5 mi.

BAXTER PEAK CUTOFF (BSP; MAP 1: E3)

Cumulative from Chimney Pond CG (2,914 ft.) to:	↥↧	↗	⟳
Start of Baxter Peak Cutoff (4,700 ft.) via Saddle Trail	1.9 mi.	1,790 ft.	1:55
Start of Baxter Peak Cutoff (4,700 ft.)	1.9 mi.	1,790 ft.	1:55
Thoreau Spring (4,636 ft.) and jct. of Hunt Trail and Abol Trail	2.8 mi.	1,840 ft.	2:25

This 0.9-mi. trail leaves the jct. of Saddle Trail and Cathedral Cutoff 1.9 mi. from Chimney Pond via Saddle Trail. The Baxter Peak Cutoff contours southwest over the Tableland along the base of Baxter Peak, ending at Thoreau Spring and the jct. of Hunt and Abol trails, making it possible to hike a loop over Baxter Peak. In addition, the cutoff provides an alternative path to a safer descent in case of bad weather.

■ KATAHDIN: HAMLIN PEAK (4,756 FT.) AND HOWE PEAK (4,750 FT.)

Hamlin Peak is the second-highest summit in Maine. Rising prominently north of Baxter Peak and the Saddle, Hamlin is part of the extensive alpine area on Katahdin that includes the Tableland and six high peaks. Five trails cross the flanks of this mountain. Immediately north of Hamlin Peak is Howe Peak and its two summits, the North Peaks.

NORTH BASIN TRAIL (BSP; MAP 1: D4)

Cumulative from Chimney Pond CG (2,914 ft.) to:	⇅	↗	↻
Start of North Basin Trail (2,850 ft.) via Chimney Pond Trail	0.2 mi.	-65 ft.	0:10
North Basin Cutoff (3,000 ft.)	0.8 mi.	90 ft.	0:30
Blueberry Knoll (3,050 ft.)	1.0 mi.	140 ft.	0:45

From Chimney Pond, Chimney Pond Trail leads northeast toward the Basin Ponds. At 0.2 mi., North Basin Trail starts on the left (north) and runs through spruce-fir forest to a jct. with Hamlin Ridge Trail on the left (west) at 0.6 mi. It then passes across the foot of Hamlin Ridge to a jct. (signs, large cairn) with North Basin Cutoff at 0.8 mi. Ahead, North Basin Trail continues to the lip of North Basin and then reaches Blueberry Knoll at 1.0 mi., where there is a sweeping view of both the North and Great basins, as well as the landscape to the east, including South Turner Mtn., Katahdin Lake, and the forestland of KWWNM.

NORTH BASIN CUTOFF (BSP; MAP 1: D4)

Cumulative from Roaring Brook CG (1,489 ft.) to:	⇅	↗	↻
Start of North Basin Cutoff via Chimney Pond Trail (2,500 ft.)	2.1 mi.	1,000 ft.	1:30
North Basin Trail (3,000 ft.)	2.8 mi.	1,500 ft.	2:25
Blueberry Knoll (3,050 ft.) via North Basin Trail	3.0 mi.	1,550 ft.	2:35
Hamlin Ridge Trail (3,000 ft.) via North Basin Trail	3.2 mi.	1,500 ft.	2:25
Chimney Pond CG (2,914 ft.) via North Basin Trail and Chimney Pond Trail	3.8 mi.	1,500 ft.	2:55

This 0.7-mi. trail from the Basin Ponds to the base of Hamlin Ridge and North Basin forks right (sign) at a point 2.1 mi. from the Roaring Brook CG via Chimney Pond Trail. The cutoff traverses an area of second-growth softwoods, goes past several active beaver ponds, and then climbs steeply through old growth to a jct. with North Basin Trail at 0.7 mi.; to reach Hamlin Ridge, turn left (southwest). To reach Blueberry Knoll and North Basin, turn right (northeast).

HAMLIN RIDGE TRAIL (BSP; MAP 1: D3–D4)

Cumulative from Chimney Pond CG (2,914 ft.) to:	⇅	↗	⟳
Start of Hamlin Ridge Trail (2,850 ft.) via Chimney Pond Trail and North Basin Trail	0.6 mi.	-65 ft.	0:20
Hamlin Peak (4,756 ft.)	2.1 mi.	1,900 ft.	2:30
Caribou Spring (4,650 ft.)	2.3 mi.	1,900 ft.	2:40

This trail climbs largely in the open up Hamlin Ridge, which separates North Basin and Great Basin. The views are superb. From Chimney Pond CG, follow Chimney Pond Trail 0.2 mi. north to North Basin Trail. Follow this for 0.4 mi. to the start of Hamlin Ridge Trail. Hamlin Ridge Trail reaches treeline after about 20 min. of climbing. After a short stretch of boulder-strewn slope, the trail rises to the ridge proper, then ascends moderately, following the open ridge to Hamlin Peak (4,756 ft.) and a jct. with North Peaks Trail at 2.1 mi. (North Peaks Trail leads right [north] for 0.5 mi. to the summit of Howe Peak [4,750 ft.], and then on to Russell Pond in 6.9 mi.)

Beyond Hamlin Peak, Hamlin Ridge Trail descends gradually 0.2 mi. west across the Tableland and through a boulder field to Caribou Spring (unreliable) and another trail jct. at 2.3 mi. Bearing sharply right, Hamlin Peak Cutoff leads 0.2 mi. to North Peaks Trail, which leads along the headwall of North Basin to the summit of Howe Peak (4,750 ft.) in another 0.2 mi. To the left (south), Northwest Basin Trail leads 0.9 mi. to meet Saddle Trail; to the right, Northwest Basin Trail leads to Russell Pond in 7.6 mi.

Hamlin Peak Cutoff (BSP; Map 1: D3). Following a good path along a contour at about 4,650 ft., this 0.2-mi. connector trail links North Peaks Trail with Northwest Basin Trail at Caribou Spring.

NORTH PEAKS TRAIL (BSP; MAP 1: D3)

Cumulative from Hamlin Peak (4,756 ft.) to:	⇅	↗	⟳
Howe Peak, the southerly of the North Peaks (4,750 ft.)	0.5 mi.	50 ft.	0:15
Northwest Basin Trail (1,500 ft.)	5.7 mi.	100 ft.	2:00
Russell Pond CG via Northwest Basin Trail (1,333 ft.)	6.9 mi.	100 ft.	3:30

This trail extends from the summit of Hamlin Peak to Howe Peak and then north to Russell Pond. From the jct. of Hamlin Ridge Trail atop Hamlin Peak, North Peaks Trail descends gradually northwest along the edge of

North Basin to a shallow col, where Hamlin Peak Cutoff enters from the left. North Peaks Trail then climbs over broken rocks to reach Howe Peak at 0.5 mi. Hike over a knob on the ridge beyond to reach the northerly of the North Peaks at 1.0 mi. and then descend gradually, crossing two knobs. On the ridge beyond are good views north to the valley of Wassataquoik Stream and the peaks of Traveler Mtn. At 1.8 mi., scramble over the last rocky knob on the long and exposed ridge, then make a steady descent to the treeline and continue the moderate descent into the trees below. At 3.3 mi., the trail drops steeply into the deep valley between Russell Mtn. to the east and a shoulder of Tip-Top Mtn. to the west. It reaches Tracy Brook at 3.9 mi. and continues down through the narrow ravine along the cascading brook. In another 0.1 mi., the trail crosses Tracy Brook and continues along its bank at an easier grade. Following the ridge of an esker, the trail descends to the confluence of Tracy Brook and Wassataquoik Stream and then fords the latter at 5.4 mi. (*Caution:* This ford can be hazardous in high water.) Bearing away from the stream, the trail ends at the jct. with Northwest Basin Trail at 5.7 mi. Russell Pond CG is 1.2 mi. to the right on this trail.

NORTHWEST BASIN TRAIL (BSP; MAP 1: E3–D4)

Cumulative from Saddle Trail (4,350 ft.) to:	⇅	↗	↻
Caribou Spring (4,650 ft.), at jct. of Hamlin Ridge Trail and Hamlin Peak Cutoff	0.9 mi.	400 ft.	0:40
Davis Pond Lean-to (2,950 ft.)	3.3 mi.	400 ft.	1:55
Russell Pond CG (1,333 ft.) via Russell Pond Trail	8.5 mi.	450 ft.	4:30

This trail extends from the Saddle between Baxter Peak and Hamlin Peak to Russell Pond, taking in the extensive alpine terrain on the west side of Hamlin Peak and the Northwest Plateau, secluded Davis Pond and Lake Cowles high in the rugged Northwest Basin, and a good stretch of Wassataquoik Stream en route.

The trail starts at the jct. with Saddle Trail, 1.4 mi. above Chimney Pond and 1.1 mi. below the summit of Katahdin at Baxter Peak. Northwest Basin Trail descends gradually, then makes a steady ascent of Hamlin Peak. At 0.9 mi., the trail reaches Caribou Spring and a jct. Here, Hamlin Ridge Trail leads 0.2 mi. east to the summit of Hamlin Peak, while Hamlin Peak Cutoff leads 0.2 mi. northeast to North Peaks Trail.

From Caribou Spring, Northwest Basin Trail bears left and descends gradually north and then west to reach a large cairn on a high knob at 2.0 mi. on the western end of the Northwest Plateau, a level extension of the northern Tableland that separates Northwest Basin from the Klondike Pond ravine. From this point, the trail bears north and begins a steep descent. At treeline, the trail enters scrub growth. Farther below, the descent turns very steep for 0.3 mi. At the base, the trail soon reaches Davis Pond Lean-to at 3.3 mi. A short side trail leads left down to Davis Pond. The trail beyond climbs a heath-covered glacial sheepback rock, which provides excellent views of the entire Northwest Basin. Descending the far side of the sheepback, the trail reaches Lake Cowles and soon crosses its outlet. A knoll just beyond the lake offers more good views. From the large pile of stones nearby, the trail turns right and begins a steep descent out of the Northwest Basin. After the polished rock of a stream bed, the angle eases and the trail joins the route of an old tote road that parallels Northwest Basin Brook. At 4.8 mi., ford Wassataquoik Stream, then continue north on the old Wassataquoik Tote Rd. At 5.9 mi., the trail crosses Annis Brook. It eventually trends away from Wassataquoik Stream to cross the relatively level terrain in the area southwest of Russell Pond. At 7.2 mi., North Peaks Trail enters from the right. Continuing straight ahead, Northwest Basin Trail descends gradually on old tote roads to reach Turner Deadwater. Cross the outlet and soon reach the jct. with Russell Pond Trail at 8.4 mi. Russell Pond Trail leads left 0.1 mi. to the southern end of Russell Pond CG.

■ SOUTH TURNER MTN. (3,110 FT.)

This mountain northeast of Katahdin offers magnificent views of Katahdin's massif and sheer-walled basins. The approach to South Turner Mtn. is from Roaring Brook CG and involves a moderate climb up the mountain's southwestern slide.

SOUTH TURNER MTN. TRAIL (BSP; MAP 1: D4)

Cumulative from Roaring Brook CG (1,489 ft.) to:	↥↧	↗	↻
Start of trail (1,550 ft.) via Russell Pond Trail and Sandy Stream Pond Trail	0.7 mi.	60 ft.	0:20
South Turner Mtn. summit (3,122 ft.)	2.2 mi.	1,650 ft.	1:55

This trail leaves from Sandy Stream Pond Trail at a point 0.7 mi. from Roaring Brook CG. From the ranger cabin, follow the path north and quickly arrive at a jct. with Russell Pond Trail (p. 39). Turn right on Russell Pond Trail and cross the bridge over Roaring Brook. At 0.1 mi., where Russell Pond Trail heads left, bear right on Sandy Stream Pond Trail. Follow this around the south shore of the pond. En route, three side trails offer outstanding views of the Katahdin massif: the first is a loop along the pond, the second leads to the pond at Big Rock, and the third goes to the pond's outlet. At 0.7 mi., the trail reaches a jct. with South Turner Mtn. Trail, which leaves to the right. (Sandy Stream Pond Trail continues to the left toward, but not quite to, Whidden Ponds. It then loops back south, coinciding with Russell Pond Trail, to return to Roaring Brook, a complete circuit of 2.3 mi.)

Continue easily ahead on South Turner Mtn. Trail, then climb moderately up the south slope of the mountain. Ahead, the trail enters a small boulder field and is marked by cairns and paint blazes on the rocks. Beyond, the trail turns left, rises steeply, and soon passes a side trail right to a spring. Eventually, the trail leaves the scrub and climbs steeply over a rocky ridge to reach the alpine-like summit. The fine panoramic views range over Katahdin and the other high peaks and ridges to the west, east to sparkling Katahdin Lake and KWWNM, and north to the forestland and hills of Aroostook County.

■ THE OWL (3,670 FT.)

This is the first summit in the long, high range that runs west and north from Katahdin around the Klondike. The distinctive cliffs on its southern face overlooking the valley of Katahdin Stream are especially steep.

OWL TRAIL (BSP; MAP 1: E3)

Cumulative from Katahdin Stream CG (1,099 ft.) to:	⇕	↗	↻
Start of trail (1,500 ft.) via Hunt Trail	1.1 mi.	400 ft.	0:45
The Owl summit (3,670 ft.)	3.5 mi.	2,571 ft.	3:00

From Katahdin Stream CG, follow Hunt Trail for 1.1 mi. to a jct. Here, Owl Trail diverges left just before Katahdin Stream. The trail then follows the north bank of a tributary before turning sharply right (southeast) and crossing the tributary at 1.6 mi. (last source of water). The trail climbs gradually through dense spruce and fir and follows the western spur toward the summit. At 2.9 mi., the trail rises steeply through a ravine and then across the upper part of the Owl's prominent cliffs. At 3.4 mi., the trail reaches the first outlook. After a more gradual climb, it reaches the summit at 3.5 mi. Views in all directions are outstanding, especially those into the Klondike and Witherle Ravine.

■ KATAHDIN LAKE

In 2006, 4,119 acres to the east of Katahdin were gifted to BSP. The predominant feature of this parcel of land is the iconic 640-acre Katahdin Lake, which offers outstanding views of Katahdin, including Baxter Peak,

Knife Edge, Pamola, Hamlin Peak, and Howe Peak. Soon after, a pleasant network of trails was developed and opened for hikers, including three backcountry campsites. The private Katahdin Lake Wilderness Camps, a traditional sporting camp on the south shore of the lake, operates under a lease agreement with the park.

Trailhead access to the trails around Katahdin Lake is from Avalanche Field on Roaring Brook Rd., 6.6 mi. north of Togue Pond Gate and 1.5 mi. south of Roaring Brook CG.

KATAHDIN LAKE TRAIL (BSP; MAP 1: E4–E5)

Cumulative from Avalanche Field at Roaring Brook Rd. (1,250 ft.) to:	⥮	↗	○
Martin Ponds Trail, upper jct. (1,150 ft.)	1.7 mi.	50 ft.	0:55
Katahdin Lake Campsite and lower jct., Martin Ponds Trail (1,022 ft.)	3.0 mi.	75 ft.	1:30
Katahdin Lake Wilderness Camps (1,022 ft.)	3.3 mi.	75 ft.	1:40

This trail leaves Roaring Brook Rd. at Avalanche Field (parking, toilet, register box) and heads east on an old woods road (the former Katahdin Lake Tote Rd.), which the trail follows for much of its route to Katahdin Lake. The trail crosses a small stream at 0.1 mi. At 0.5 mi., it crosses Sandy Stream near the ruins of Hersey Dam, an old logging structure once used by river drivers. Beyond, the trail ascends gently to crest a low ridge before descending to cross the former park boundary. At 1.7 mi., Martin Ponds Trail diverges to the left (northwest). It leads 0.6 mi. to Martin Ponds and Martin Ponds Campsite (lean-to).

Continuing on, Katahdin Lake Trail crosses a wet area, then ascends gradually to reach the lower jct. of Martin Ponds Trail. To the left, it is 100 yd. to South Katahdin Lake Campsite (lean-to), 0.1 mi. to the Day Use Picnic Site, and 0.2 mi. to Katahdin Lake and the store of rental canoes. To the right, it is 0.3 mi. to Katahdin Lake Wilderness Camps (a private sporting camp open to the public).

MARTIN PONDS TRAIL (BSP; MAP 1: D5–E5)

Cumulative from Avalanche Field at Roaring Brook Rd. (1,250 ft.) to:	⥮	↗	○
Start of trail (1,150 ft.) via Katahdin Lake Trail	1.7 mi.	50 ft.	0:55
Martin Ponds Campsite (1,250 ft.)	2.3 mi.	100 ft.	1:10
North Katahdin Lake Trail (1,250 ft.)	2.6 mi.	100 ft.	1:20
South Katahdin Lake Campsite and Katahdin Lake Trail (1,022 ft.)	4.4 mi.	100 ft.	2:05

This trail diverges left (northwest) from Katahdin Lake Trail at a point 1.7 mi. from Avalanche Field. Martin Ponds Trail traverses a low ridge before skirting a beaver flowage and crossing the outlet of the northerly pond of the two Martin Ponds. At 2.3 mi., it reaches a jct. with a short side trail to Martin Ponds Campsite, where there is an excellent view of Katahdin. Ahead, the trail passes to the west and north of the southerly pond of the two Martin Ponds before descending to an outlook to the Turner mountains. The trail reaches a jct. with North Katahdin Lake Trail at 2.6 mi. Beyond, Martin Ponds Trail descends gradually to reach Katahdin Lake, crossing several streams en route. From there, the trail follows the east shore to an inlet and an old beaver dam. Cross this and bear left along the sandy beach of the lake to reach South Katahdin Lake Campsite and, just ahead, a jct. with Katahdin Lake Trail at 4.4 mi.

NORTH KATAHDIN LAKE TRAIL (BSP; MAP 1: D5)

Cumulative from Avalanche Field at Roaring Brook Rd. (1,250 ft.) to:	⇅	↗	↻
Start of North Katahdin Lake Trail (1,250 ft.) via Katahdin Lake Trail and Martin Ponds Trail	2.6 mi.	100 ft.	1:20
North Katahdin Lake Campsite (1,022 ft.)	4.4 mi.	100 ft.	2:15

This trail leaves from Martin Ponds Trail at a point 0.9 mi. from Katahdin Lake Trail and 2.6 mi. from Avalanche Field on Park Tote Rd. North Katahdin Lake Trail crosses a ridge to the north before descending toward Katahdin Lake, crossing several streams en route. The trail reaches North Katahdin Lake Campsite (lean-to) at 1.8 mi. Good views of the Katahdin massif are possible from the lakeshore.

WEST AND NORTHWEST OF KATAHDIN

■ MT. OJI (3,434 FT.)

Mt. OJI got its name from three slides on its southwestern slope that at one point in time formed the shapes of the three letters. After a major storm in 1932, however, the slides began to enlarge, and the letter shapes became distorted. A fourth large slide came down in 1954.

MT. OJI TRAIL (BSP; MAP 1: D2–E2)

Cumulative from Park Tote Rd. at Foster Field (1,050 ft.) to:	⇅	↗	↻
Old Jay Eye Rock (3,000 ft.)	3.5 mi.	1,950 ft.	2:45
Mt. OJI summit (3,434 ft.)	4.0 mi.	2,400 ft.	3:15
OJI Link Trail (3,200 ft.)	4.2 mi.	2,400 ft.	3:20

This trail leaves Park Tote Rd. at the Foster Field Group Site, 10.3 mi. north of Togue Pond Gate and directly opposite the access road to Kidney Pond. The trail passes a brook to the left, then goes through a cedar swamp. After a blowdown area and a grove of mature beech, the trail begins to climb at a moderate grade. Turning northwest, Mt. OJI Trail crosses a stream and then climbs to the saddle separating West Peak and OJI Ridge at 2.7 mi. At the jct. in the saddle, a spur trail leads left (southwest) 0.2 mi. to a fine viewpoint over the Nesowadnehunk Stream valley. Mt. OJI Trail continues to climb the northwestern ridge of the mountain. At 3.2 mi., the trail turns southeast and ascends steeply up the ridge, passing through a narrow cleft in the rock outcrop and reaching Old Jay Eye Rock at 3.5 mi. Here are excellent views over West Peak to Doubletop Mtn. The wooded summit of Mt. OJI is reached at 4.0 mi. In another 0.2 mi., the trail ends at OJI Link Trail, which descends north into the col between Mt. OJI and Mt. Coe.

Another approach to Mt. OJI is by climbing the Mt. Coe slide via Marston Trail and Mt. Coe Trail to OJI Link Trail, which leads 0.5 mi. from the Mt. Coe slide across the col to a jct. with Mt. OJI Trail 0.2 mi. from the summit.

■ NORTH BROTHER MTN. (4,151 FT.) AND SOUTH BROTHER MTN. (3,970 FT.)

North and South Brother mountains are open peaks that offer splendid views in all directions, especially of the Katahdin massif. (*Caution:* Early in the hiking season, sometimes through mid-June, hikers should expect to find deep snow at the higher elevations on these peaks, often starting about 1.5 mi. from the trailhead.)

MARSTON TRAIL (BSP; MAP 1: D2–D3)

Cumulative from Park Tote Rd. near Slide Dam (1,150 ft.) to:	↟↧	↗	↻
Mt. Coe Trail, lower jct. (2,150 ft.)	1.3 mi.	1,000 ft.	0:50
Mt. Coe Trail, upper jct. (3,450 ft.)	3.7 mi.	2,300 ft.	3:20
North Brother summit (4,151 ft.)	4.6 mi.	3,000 ft.	3:45
From Park Tote Rd. near Slide Dam (1,150 ft.) to:			
South Brother summit (3,970 ft.) via Mt. Coe Trail	4.6 mi.	2,800 ft.	3:45

This trail is the best approach for exploring the Brothers area. Trailhead parking is on the east side of Park Tote Rd. near Slide Dam Day Use Site, 5.7 mi. north of Katahdin Stream CG, and about 3.5 mi. south of Nesowadnehunk CG.

At 0.2 mi., the trail crosses a brook, then bears left and climbs over a slight rise into the drainage of a second brook. Climbing steadily, the trail follows this brook closely. At 0.8 mi., the trail crosses the brook. Several more crossings appear in the next 0.4 mi. before the trail reaches a jct. with Mt. Coe Trail at 1.3 mi. Here, Marston Trail leads to the left and climbs gradually through extensive blowdowns. Teardrop Pond is reached at 2.1 mi. Beyond the pond's outlet, the trail climbs steeply, passing several viewpoints. After leveling off, it reaches the upper jct. with Mt. Coe Trail at 3.6 mi. To the right, Mt. Coe Trail leads 0.9 mi. to South Brother via a side trail. To the left, it is 0.9 mi. to North Brother via Marston Trail.

Continuing on Marston Trail after crossing a fairly level area, the trail passes a spring and then climbs steeply. Ahead, the trail leaves the scrub and continues among open boulders, reaching the summit of North Brother at 4.5 mi. Here are fine views of the western slopes of Katahdin and, in the opposite direction, of the Nesowadnehunk Lake area and Little Nesowadnehunk Stream area. The long, flat ridgeline of trailless Fort Mtn. is immediately northeast.

■ MT. COE (3,795 FT.)

This peak, just north of Mt. OJI, has excellent views into the Klondike and is well worth the challenge of the climb. Mt. Coe's high summit ridge provides access to Mt. OJI and South Brother Mtn.

MT. COE TRAIL (BSP; MAP 1: D2–D3)

Cumulative from Park Tote Rd. near Slide Dam (1,150 ft.) to:	�)↑(	↗	↻
Start of Mt. Coe Trail (2,150 ft.) via Marston Trail	1.3 mi.	1,000 ft.	0:50
Mt. Coe summit (3,795 ft.)	3.2 mi.	2,650 ft.	3:00
South Brother Trail to South Brother summit (3,600 ft.)	4.5 mi.	3,150 ft.	4:00
South Brother summit (3,970 ft.) via South Brother Trail	4.8 mi.	3,500 ft.	4:15
Marston Trail (3,450 ft.)	5.7 mi.	3,500 ft.	4:40

Follow Marston Trail to a sign at 1.3 mi. from Park Tote Rd. Turn right here on Mt. Coe Trail to reach the bottom of the Mt. Coe slide (it follows a stream) at 1.5 mi. Beyond, the climb is steady, moderate at first, then steep. At 2.5 mi., the trail bears left and climbs the left center of a wide slide area on granite slabs and loose gravel. At 2.7 mi., it reaches the jct.

with OJI Link Trail (leads right 0.5 mi. to Mt. OJI Trail and 0.2 mi. farther to the summit of OJI).

At 3.1 mi., Mt. Coe Trail enters scrub growth; it reaches the summit at 3.3 mi. Continuing on, the trail descends the eastern ridge of Coe and proceeds toward South Brother. At 4.3 mi., it passes two clearings with fine views of Mt. Coe. At 4.5 mi., South Brother Trail leads right 0.3 mi. to the summit of South Brother. At 5.1 mi., Mt. Coe Trail reaches the jct. with Marston Trail. Ahead, it is 0.9 mi. to the summit of North Brother via Marston Trail. To the left, Marston Trail leads 3.7 mi. to Park Tote Rd. near Slide Dam.

■ BURNT MTN. (1,810 FT.)

The trail to Burnt Mtn. begins at Burnt Mtn. Day Use Site on Park Tote Rd., 13.7 mi. west of Matagamon Gate. The summit is the site of a former fire tower, removed in 2005.

BURNT MTN. TRAIL (BSP; MAP 1: B2)

From Burnt Mtn. Day Use Site (1,050 ft.) to:	�	↗	↺
Burnt Mtn. summit (1,810 ft.)	1.3 mi.	760 ft.	1:00

The trail climbs to the summit in 1.3 mi. Trees are gradually blocking what were once excellent views from the top of Burnt Mtn., but hikers can still get a good view from the ledges 0.1 mi. to the southeast of the old fire tower footings.

DWELLEY POND TRAIL (BSP; MAP 1: B2–C2)

Cumulative from Park Tote Rd. (1,500 ft.) north of Nesowadnehunk CG to:	�	↗	↺
Dwelley Pond (1,450 ft.)	1.6 mi.	-50 ft.	0:40
Park Tote Rd. south of Burnt Mtn. Day Use Site (1,350 ft.)	5.4 mi.	250 ft.	2:45

This easy trail starts from an old turnout on Park Tote Rd. at a point 5.7 mi. north of Nesowadnehunk CG; it follows the grown-in route of a former park road for its 3.2-mi. length, reaching Dwelley Pond and Dwelley Pond Day Use Site at 1.6 mi. Beyond, the trail swings east then north around the base of McCarty Mtn. Ahead, the trail follows the South Branch of Trout Brook before finally crossing it. The trail then bears northwest around Burnt Mtn. to end at Park Loop Rd. at 5.4 mi.

RUSSELL POND

RUSSELL POND TRAIL (BSP; MAP 1: D4)

SEC 1

Cumulative from Roaring Brook CG (1,489 ft.) to:	⇅	↗	○
Sandy Stream Pond Trail, upper jct. (1,550 ft.)	1.1 mi.	60 ft.	0:30
Wassataquoik Stream Trail (1,500 ft.)	3.1 mi.	60 ft.	1:40
Wassataquoik Tote Rd. (1,350 ft.)	6.3 mi.	60 ft.	3:10
Northwest Basin Trail (1,350 ft.)	6.7 mi.	300 ft.	3:40
Russell Pond CG (1,333 ft.)	6.8 mi.	300 ft.	3:45

This trail extends from Roaring Brook CG northward to Russell Pond CG through the valley of Wassataquoik Stream between Katahdin and Turner Mtn. The trail is the principal approach to the Russell Pond area deep in the park's interior.

Leaving from the ranger cabin at Roaring Brook CG, where Chimney Pond Trail turns left (west), Russell Pond Trail crosses a bridge over Roaring Brook. At 0.1 mi., the trail turns left (northwest). (To the right, Sandy Stream Pond Trail leads to Sandy Stream Pond and on to South Turner Mtn. via South Turner Trail.) In the next 0.5 mi., Russell Pond Trail crosses several brooks while gradually climbing to the low height-of-land between Sandy Stream Pond and Whidden Pond. The trail then descends and passes east (right) of Whidden Pond, where there is an extensive view of the basins and peaks on the east side of Katahdin.

At 1.1 mi., Sandy Stream Pond Trail joins from the right. Ahead, an open area yields good views. Beyond, Russell Pond Trail moves into denser forest and crosses several brooks, and at 3.1 mi., the trail reaches a jct. on the right with Wassataquoik Stream Trail (leads 2.3 mi. to Wassataquoik Stream Campsite and rejoins Russell Pond Trail in 3.6 mi.). Ahead, Russell Pond Trail crosses the South Branch of Wassataquoik Stream and soon crosses an unnamed a brook. (*Note:* No bridges are available here. The crossing is knee-deep in dry weather, and in wet weather, the high-water crossing can be hazardous.)

The trail, now on the west side of the valley, passes under an overhanging rock, a glacial erratic. Moving away from Wassataquoik Stream, the trail passes several brooks and springs and climbs gently for about 2 mi. before descending gradually to cross the main branch of Wassataquoik Stream at 6.3 mi. At 6.5 mi., Russell Pond Trail crosses the old Wassataquoik Tote Rd. and passes a clearing on the right. At a jct., Wassataquoik Stream Trail leads right (east) 1.3 mi. to Wassataquoik Stream Campsite. Immediately beyond the tote road, Russell Pond Trail crosses Turner

Brook. At 6.7 mi., Northwest Basin Trail to the Saddle leaves to the left (west). Soon after, Russell Pond Trail reaches Russell Pond and Russell Pond CG and the jct. with Pogy Notch Trail.

WASSATAQUOIK STREAM TRAIL (BSP; MAP 1: D4–D3)

Cumulative from Roaring Brook CG (1,489 ft.) to:	↧↥	↗	⟳
Start of Wassataquoik Stream Trail (1,500 ft.) via Russell Pond Trail	3.1 mi.	60 ft.	1:40
Wassataquoik Stream Campsite (1,250 ft.)	5.4 mi.	60 ft.	3:00
Russell Pond CG (1,333 ft.) via Russell Pond Trail	7.2 mi.	60 ft.	3:45

Formerly known as Tracy Horse Trail or Wassataquoik South Branch Trail, this trail runs from Russell Pond Trail along the South Branch of Wassataquoik Stream to the main branch of Wassataquoik Stream.

Wassataquoik Stream Trail leaves on the right (east) side of Russell Pond Trail 3.1 mi. north of Roaring Brook CG, just before that trail crosses the South Branch (*Caution:* hazardous during high water). Wassataquoik Stream Trail then leads 2.3 mi. to the jct. with the main branch and continues along its southern bank for about 100 yd. Wassataquoik Stream Campsite is located here.

Continuing to Russell Pond, the trail crosses to the north side of Wassataquoik Stream upstream from the campsite's lean-tos (ford, no bridge) and merges with the old Wassataquoik Tote Rd. at the jct. with Grand Falls Trail (leads 1.6 mi. to Inscription Rock, 2.0 mi. to Grand Falls, and 3.8 mi. to the north side of Russell Pond). Beyond this point, Wassataquoik Stream Trail reaches a jct. with Russell Pond Trail at 3.6 mi., just south of the Turner Brook crossing. Turn right on Russell Pond Trail to reach the south end of Russell Pond and Russell Pond CG at 4.1 mi.

GRAND FALLS TRAIL (BSP; MAP 1: C4–D4)

Cumulative from Russell Pond CG (1,333 ft.) to:	↧↥	↗	⟳
Caverly Lookout Trail (1,350 ft.) via Pogy Notch Trail	0.4 mi.	20 ft.	0:10
Side trail to Grand Falls (1,150 ft.) and Inscription Rock	2.2 mi.	20 ft.	1:05
Wassataquoik Stream Trail (1,250 ft.)	3.8 mi.	170 ft.	2:00

This trail leads east from the north end of Russell Pond CG to several interesting locations in Wassataquoik Valley, then returns west to near the south end of Russell Pond.

From the campground, follow Pogy Notch Trail around the west shore of the pond. Wassataquoik Lake Trail leaves to the left soon after the start of the route. Just ahead, at a jct. at 0.2 mi., Pogy Notch Trail continues north (left), and Grand Falls Trail heads right, passes the ranger station, and continues to the next jct. at 0.4 mi. Here, Caverly Lookout Trail leaves to the left (north) and leads 0.9 mi. to a viewpoint. To the right, Grand Falls Trail continues ahead through woods and over relatively level ground, passing Bell Pond.

At a jct. close to Wassataquoik Stream at 2.2 mi., a side trail leaves to the left (north) and follows the north side of the stream 0.4 mi. to Grand Falls, which drops steeply between high granite walls. The ruins of a logging dam lie just upstream. From this same jct., another side trail to the right leads 50 ft. to the bank of Wassataquoik Stream and Inscription Rock, a huge boulder inscribed with a historical 1883 notice about logging in the area.

Beyond, Grand Falls Trail follows the west bank of Wassataquoik Stream, passing Ledge Falls to meet Wassataquoik Stream Trail at the South Branch of Wassataquoik Stream at 3.8 mi. To the right, it is 0.4 mi. north to Russell Pond via Russell Pond Trail. (*Note:* A round-trip to Grand Falls via the side trail adds 0.8 mi. to the total hike distance.)

CAVERLY LOOKOUT TRAIL (BSP; MAP 1: C4–D4)

Cumulative from Russell Pond CG (1,333 ft.) to:	↕	↗	⟳
Start of Caverly Lookout Trail (1,350 ft.) via Grand Falls Trail	0.2 mi.	20 ft.	0:10
Caverly Lookout ledges (1,730 ft.)	1.3 mi.	400 ft.	0:50

This high outlook (1,730 ft.) offers views ranging from Traveler Mtn. to Katahdin and is easy to reach from the north end of Russell Pond CG. From the jct. of Pogy Notch Trail, follow Grand Falls Trail for 0.4 mi. and turn left at a jct. Caverly Lookout Trail climbs moderately and steadily to reach open ledges and fine views east and south.

WASSATAQUOIK LAKE TRAIL (BSP; MAP 1: D1, C3, D3)

Cumulative from Park Tote Rd. near Nesowadnehunk CG (1,300 ft.) to:	↕	↗	⟳
Center Pond Lean-to (1,650 ft.)	4.7 mi.	300 ft.	2:30
Little Wassataquoik Lake Campsite (1,600 ft.)	9.4 mi.	400 ft.	4:55
Side trail to Green Falls (1,350 ft.)	11.2 mi.	400 ft.	5:50
Side trail to Wassataquoik Lake (1,350 ft.)	12.4 mi.	400 ft.	6:25
Russell Pond CG (1,333 ft.)	14.3 mi.	400 ft.	7:20

This trail, one of the longest in the park, extends east from Nesowadnehunk CG to Center Pond and then Wassataquoik Lake to reach Russell Pond in the central interior of the park. The trail begins on Park Tote Rd. at a point just south of the bridge over Little Nesowadnehunk Stream and near the entrance road to Nesowadnehunk CG.

The trail follows the southern bank of Little Nesowadnehunk Stream, crosses the stream at 1.0 mi., then follows the north bank for a distance before trending away. At 4.6 mi., it reaches Center Pond and follows its westerly shore to a jct. 0.1 mi. ahead. Here, a side trail leads 0.1 mi. to Center Pond Lean-to. Well beyond Center Pond, Wassataquoik Lake Trail descends into the Trout Brook drainage, crosses the South Branch of Trout Brook, and then bears gradually away to join an old tote road.

At 8.0 mi., the trail turns sharply right onto another old tote road and, after a gradual ascent, reaches an old field, then ascends to a gap. Beyond the gap, the trail is a footpath and soon reaches a side trail leading left 175 yd. to Little Wassataquoik Lean-to next to a small stream. Ahead, the trail reaches Little Wassataquoik Lake and follows its western shore. After the lake, the trail skirts a beaver flowage, then makes a moderate descent to the west end of Wassataquoik Lake at 10.2 mi. The trail closely follows the lakeshore, and at 11.2 mi., a side trail on the right leads 0.1 mi. to the base of pretty Green Falls. At 12.4 mi., a side trail on the left leads 0.1 mi. to the east end of Wassataquoik Lake and the canoe landing for reaching Wassataquoik Lake Lean-to, which is 50 yd. across the lake on a small island. Continuing on, the trail crosses Turner Brook, and soon passes between two of the Six Ponds on a narrow esker. Pass a boggy flowage, cross a grassy flowage with a small stream and then a side trail leading left to Deep Pond. At 14.3 mi., enter a cleared area near the west shore of Russell Pond and the jct. with Pogy Notch Trail. Russell Pond CG is along the pond to the left and right.

POGY NOTCH TRAIL (BSP; MAP 1: B4, C4, D4)
Cumulative from South Branch Pond CG (981 ft.) to:

	↕	↗	○
North Traveler Trail (1,000 ft.)	0.1 mi.	20 ft.	0:05
Howe Brook Trail (1,050 ft.)	0.9 mi.	70 ft.	0:30
Center Ridge Trail (1,050 ft.)	1.4 mi.	120 ft.	0:45
South Branch Mtn. Trail (950 ft.)	1.9 mi.	120 ft.	1:00
Pogy Pond (1,150 ft.) and side trail to lean-to	5.6 mi.	350 ft.	3:00
Russell Pond (1,333 ft.)	8.8 mi.	350 ft.	4:30
Russell Pond CG (1,333 ft.)	9.0 mi.	350 ft.	4:40

This trail connects South Branch Pond CG with the trails on Traveler Mtn., then continues to Pogy Pond and finally to Russell Pond CG in the heart of BSP.

From the east end of South Branch Pond CG, opposite campsite 19, enter woods on the trail toward the eastern shore of the pond. North Traveler Trail diverges left at 0.1 mi. Passing between the pond on the right and cliffs on the left, at 0.9 mi., the trail reaches Howe Brook and Howe Brook Trail, which leaves to the left (east). Ahead, Pogy Notch Trail climbs over the end of the cliff between Lower and Upper South Branch ponds. Center Ridge Trail diverges left at 1.4 mi. Pogy Notch Trail descends, follows the east shore of Upper South Branch Pond, and reaches a jct. with South Branch Mtn. Trail at 1.9 mi. Upper South Branch Pond Campsite is a short distance west on this trail.

Pogy Notch Trail continues south, passing through an alder swamp and beaver works at 2.8 mi. The trail crosses several brooks and rises and falls moderately in the next 0.5 mi. At 3.3 mi., the trail forks. Turn right here, and climb gradually to pass through Pogy Notch. Bear left at 3.9 mi. into a sparsely grown old burn. The trail then crosses a beaver canal and descends into the Pogy Pond watershed. It crosses a brook several times while passing out of the notch area, then crosses several other brooks before reaching the head of Pogy Pond, where there are good views of the Traveler and Turner mountains, as well as Katahdin, from the shore of the pond.

The trail then bears right, uphill, and at 5.6 mi., a side trail to the left leads 0.2 mi. to Pogy Pond Campsite.

The main trail descends nearly to the pond, then bears right, away from the water. The trail rises gradually, then descends through an old burn, traverses a series of shallow rises, and bears right. Beyond, the trail drops into the gully of the western tributary of Pogy Brook, crosses it, and climbs the opposite slope. Then the trail runs through a swampy hollow, climbs a rocky rise, and descends gradually to cross another brook. Immediately after this second brook, the trail bears right and climbs gradually through sparse mixed growth. The trail crosses a beaver meadow, reaches a rough boulder field, and descends through it and toward Russell Pond. Just before the pond, the trail to Grand Falls and Caverly Lookout leaves to the left, and a short distance ahead, Wassataquoik Lake Trail leaves to the right. Russell Pond CG is reached at 8.8 mi. Pogy Notch Trail ends 0.2 mi. ahead near the southwest corner of Russell Pond CG at the jct. with Russell Pond Trail (p. 39).

SEC 1

ABOL POND–TOGUE POND

CRANBERRY POND TRAIL (BSP; MAP 1: E4–F4)

From Togue Pond Day Use Site (600 ft.) to:	⇅	↗	⟳
Park Tote Rd., upper jct. (650 ft.)	1.4 mi.	50 ft.	0:45

This trail departs from Togue Pond Day Use Site, just beyond the BSP Visitor Information Center and just south of Togue Pond Gate. The trail ambles southwest of the road past Togue, Cranberry, and Rocky ponds, ending at Park Tote Rd. at 1.4 mi., just across from the Kettle Pond trailhead.

KETTLE POND TRAIL (BSP; MAP 1: E3–E4)

Cumulative from Park Tote Rd. (650 ft.) to:	⇅	↗	⟳
Park Tote Rd., north jct. (650 ft.)	1.4 mi.	0 ft.	0:40
Abol Beach Day Use Site access road (500 ft.)	1.7 mi.	0 ft.	0:50

The southern trailhead for this short but scenic trail is on the right (north) side of Park Tote Rd., 1.0 mi. from Togue Pond Gate. In 200 yd., a short side trail leads right to Caverly Pond. At 0.1 mi., the trail forks. To the right, Rum Pond Trail leads 2.0 mi. past Rum Pond to Roaring Brook Rd. south of Rum Brook Day Use Site. Follow the left fork past several kettles (small ponds) to the intersection with Park Tote Rd. at 1.4 mi. Cross the road and hike an additional 0.3 mi. to the access road for Abol Pond. The beach at Abol Pond and a day-use area are 50 yd. south.

RUM POND TRAIL (BSP; MAP 1: E4)

Cumulative from Park Tote Rd. (650 ft.) to:	⇅	↗	⟳
Kettle Pond Trail and Rum Pond Trail (650 ft.)	0.1 mi.	50 ft.	0:05
Roaring Brook Rd. (650 ft.)	2.1 mi.	50 ft.	1:00

Rum Pond Trail forks right from Kettle Pond Trail, 0.1 mi. from its southern trailhead. This trail winds east around Caverly and Rum ponds to meet Roaring Brook Rd. at a point about 0.1 mi. south of Rum Brook Day Use Site. Togue Pond Gate is 1.0 mi. from either end of this trail.

ABOL POND TRAIL (BSP; MAP 1: E3)

From Blueberry Ledges Trail (650 ft.) to:	⇅	↗	⟳
Abol Beach Day Use Site access road (600 ft.)	1.7 mi.	150 ft.	0:55

To reach this trail, start from the Golden Rd. 0.2 mi. east of Abol Bridge and hike north on the AT. In 0.5 mi., Abol Stream Trail departs right. Ahead on the AT, at 0.7 mi., there is a jct. with Blueberry Ledges Trail at a BSP information kiosk. Turn north here to follow Blueberry Ledges Trail. In 0.2 mi., Abol Pond Trail departs to the right.

Abol Pond Trail proceeds over mild terrain. After several beaver ponds, the trail intersects several old woods roads. Bear left at the first, then sharply right at the second. Beyond, make a steep descent to Abol Stream. At a wide trail (old road), bear left to end at the access road to Abol Beach Day Use Site, which is 50 yd. south.

ABOL STREAM TRAIL (BSP; MAP 1: E3)

From AT jct. (550 ft.) to:	Distance	Elevation gain	Time
Abol Beach Day Use Site (600 ft.)	1.2 mi.	50 ft.	0:35

To reach this trail, start from the Golden Rd. 0.2 mi. east of Abol Bridge and hike north on the AT. In 0.5 mi., Abol Stream Trail departs right. The trail follows an old tote road. Cross an unnamed stream on a bridge, then continue along Abol Stream. Ahead, leave Abol Stream and climb over a low ridge. At the outlet of Abol Pond, cross a bridge to reach Abol Beach Day Use Site.

DAICEY POND–KIDNEY POND

AT SOUTHBOUND (BSP; MAP 1: E2–E3)

Cumulative from Daicey Pond trailhead (1,087 ft.) to:	Distance	Elevation gain	Time
Side trails to Toll Dam and Little Niagara Falls (1,050 ft.)	0.9 mi.	-40 ft.	0:25
Side trail to Big Niagara Falls (900 ft.)	1.2 mi.	-200 ft.	0:40
Abol Bridge (650 ft.)	7.5 mi.	550 ft.	3:45

From the Daicey Pond day-use parking area, follow the AT south. At 0.1 mi., Nature Trail leaves left to circumnavigate Daicey Pond. Ahead on the AT, a side trail on the right leads to Toll Dam on Nesowadnehunk Stream at 0.9 mi. Just ahead (about 100 yd.), another side trail leads right to Little Niagara Falls. At 1.2 mi., a side trail leads 200 ft. to Big Niagara Falls. The jct. with Foss and Knowlton Pond Trail is at 6.3 mi. (returns to Daicey Pond in 5.4 mi. via Lost Pond and Nature trails). Just ahead, at 6.5 mi., Blueberry Ledges Trail departs left (leads 4.2 mi. to Katahdin Stream CG). Abol Stream Trail is reached at 6.9 mi.; it leads to Abol Pond in 1.2 mi.

Continuing south, the AT reaches the Golden Rd. at 7.3 mi.; turn right (west) here. A store and campground are just ahead; walk past them to reach the West Branch of the Penobscot River at Abol Bridge at 7.5 mi.

AT NORTHBOUND (BSP; MAP 1: E2–E3)

Cumulative from Daicey Pond trailhead (1,087 ft.) to:	⮃	↗	⏱
Tracy and Elbow Ponds Trail (1,087 ft.)	0.4 mi.	20 ft.	0:10
Grassy Pond Trail (1,150 ft.)	1.1 mi.	100 ft.	0:30
Park Tote Rd. at Katahdin Stream CG (1,099 ft.)	2.1 mi.	100 ft.	1:00

From the Daicey Pond day-use parking area, follow the AT north. Climb over a knoll, then descend to the shore of Daicey Pond and follow the AT to a jct. Here, Tracy and Elbow Ponds Trail leaves left, leading 1.0 mi. to Park Tote Rd. Continuing north on the AT, the trail follows the pond to a jct. with Nature Trail at 0.6 mi. (leads 0.7 mi. along the south shore of the pond to the campground). The AT turns left here and makes its way through a pleasant mix of forest to a jct. with Grassy Pond Trail at 1.1 mi. (connects with Tracy and Elbow Ponds Trail in 0.8 mi.). Beyond, the AT skirts the south end of Grassy Pond, crosses the outlet, and ends at Park Tote Rd. at the entrance road to Katahdin Stream CG at 2.1 mi.

TRACY AND ELBOW PONDS TRAIL (BSP; MAP 1: E2)

Cumulative from Daicey Pond day-use parking area (1,087 ft.) to:	⮃	↗	⏱
Start of trail (1,087 ft.) via AT Northbound	0.4 mi.	20 ft.	0:10
Park Tote Rd. (1,050 ft.)	1.0 mi.	100 ft.	0:30

This trail departs left (north) from the AT 0.4 mi. from the Daicey Pond CG access road. The trail climbs over a low ridge before descending to follow the southeast shore of Elbow Pond. After a gradual climb, Grassy Pond Trail enters from the right. Ahead, Tracy and Elbow Ponds Trail crosses the outlet of Elbow Pond on a bridge, climbs a knoll, then descends to cross the outlet of Tracy Pond on a bridge. Beyond, the trail follows an esker to end at Park Loop Rd., at a point 0.6 mi. northwest of Katahdin Stream CG. There are nice views of Doubletop and OJI along this trail.

GRASSY POND TRAIL (BSP; MAP 1: E2)

This short 0.8-mi. trail connects Tracy and Elbow Ponds Trail and the AT and makes a good loop hike from Daicey Pond, climbing over a low ridge between the two ponds. Excellent Katahdin views are possible en route.

SEC 1

NATURE TRAIL (BSP; MAP 1: E2)

This pleasant 0.7-mi. trail explores the south and east sides of Daicey Pond; combine it with the AT for a nice loop hike. From the ranger cabin at Daicey Pond CG, follow a wide path south. Soon, the AT enters from the right and heads south. Turn left here onto a foot trail to reach the shore of Daicey Pond. In 0.5 mi., pass Lost Pond Trail on the right. Ahead, the trail merges with the AT. Continue south on the AT for 0.4 mi. to complete the loop on the Daicey Pond CG access road. Turn left on the access road to reach the campground in another 0.1 mi.

LOST POND TRAIL (BSP; MAP 1: E2)

This trail leaves from the south shore of Daicey Pond, 0.5 mi. from Daicey Pond CG via Nature Trail. Lost Pond Trail heads southeast over easy terrain to reach Lost Pond in another 0.9 mi., at the jct. with Foss and Knowlton Pond Trail.

FOSS AND KNOWLTON POND TRAIL (BSP; MAP 1: E2–E3)

Cumulative from Daicey Pond CG (1,087 ft.) to:	⇅	↗	↻
Start of trail via Nature Trail and Lost Pond Trail	1.4 mi.	1,150 ft.	0:40
AT jct. (650 ft.)	5.4 mi.	550 ft.	2:45

This trail heads south from Lost Pond at a point 1.4 mi. south of Daicey Pond via Nature and Lost Pond trails. Foss and Knowlton Pond Trail heads south to join the AT near the West Branch of the Penobscot River 1.2 mi. from Abol Bridge. Foss and Knowlton Pond Trail uses fire roads built to fight the BSP fire of 1977 and traverses the burned area that is now being reclaimed by the forest. After a side trail to the pond's north shore, the trail follows closely along the west shore.

BLUEBERRY LEDGES TRAIL (BSP; MAP 1: E3)

Cumulative from Katahdin Stream CG (1,099 ft.) to:	⇅	↗	↻
Abol Pond Trail (650 ft.)	4.0 mi.	250 ft.	2:10
AT jct. (650 ft.)	4.2 mi.	250 ft.	2:15
Golden Rd. at Abol Bridge (550 ft.)	4.9 mi.	250 ft.	2:35

From Katahdin Stream CG, this trail travels through a variety of forest types and offers many interesting landscapes before meeting up with the AT near the West Branch of the Penobscot River. Much of the trail goes through the area burned in the BSP fire of 1977. The trail's namesake ledges are located about midway through the route, along the tumbling waters of Katahdin Stream. The area features large expanses of exposed bedrock with views of Katahdin and other geologic features.

From Park Tote Rd., 0.3 mi. east of Katahdin Stream CG, head south on Blueberry Ledges Trail. In 200 ft., the Birches Campsite (lean-to and tentsite), for AT thru-hikers only, is on the right. Just beyond, cross a small brook, then begin a gradual ascent. Gain the top of a knob, then make a steep descent into the valley beyond. Cross two branches of a brook, then ascend a ridge that forms the east side of the valley that holds Katahdin Stream.

Ahead, descend off the ridge into the valley proper, emerging into an extensive area of open ledges of smooth granite. Follow these ledges for the next 0.5 mi. To the right, several side paths lead to Katahdin Stream and a series of cascades, sluice drops, and pools. Swimming holes abound, as do blueberries here in high summer. Descending over ledges, the trail reaches an old woods road and follows it to meet Abol Pond Trail, which merges from the left at 4.0 mi. Blueberry Ledges Trail ends just ahead at 4.2 mi. at a jct. with the AT. Follow the AT south to reach the Golden Road in 0.7 mi. and Abol Bridge in 0.9 mi.

■ SENTINEL MTN. (1,842 FT.)

This low mountain in the southwest corner of BSP rises above the north bank of the West Branch of the Penobscot River, offering fine views of the west side of Katahdin. Direct access to the mountain is from Kidney Pond CG via Sentinel Link Trail and Sentinel Mtn. Trail. Longer access to the mountain is also possible from the east at Daicey Pond via Daicey–Kidney Link Trail, although hiking from this direction requires fording Nesowadnehunk Stream.

SENTINEL LINK TRAIL AND SENTINEL MTN. TRAIL (BSP; MAP 1: E2)

Cumulative from Kidney Pond CG (1,051 ft.) to:	⮃	↗	⏱
Sentinel Landing (1,051 ft.) via Sentinel Link Trail	0.5 mi.	0 ft.	0:15
Sentinel Mtn. summit ledges (1,842 ft.) and loop	3.1 mi.	791 ft.	2:00

From the trailhead parking area at Kidney Pond CG at the end of the access rd., follow Sentinel Link Trail and skirt the west side of Kidney

Pond. In 0.5 mi., the trail reaches Sentinel Landing, a canoe landing on Kidney Pond, passing Celia and Jackson Ponds Trail en route. From the landing, the Daicey-Kidney Link Trail enters from the east. Here, turn right (south) on Sentinel Mtn. Trail.

In 0.8 mi. from Sentinel Landing, the Sentinel Mtn. Trail crosses a small stream near a beaver pond. At 1.2 mi., it crosses Beaver Brook on stepping stones. The trail climbs the northeast side of the mountain along a brook, which crosses the trail at 1.6 mi. The trail reaches a wooded saddle at 2.0 mi. On the left, a short spur leads to an outstanding view over the West Branch of the Penobscot River. Return to the main trail and climb to a fork at 2.1 mi. on the summit ledges. This is the start of an 0.5-mi. loop trail. Follow the ledges to the right (north) to reach the true summit and excellent views of Katahdin.

DAICEY–KIDNEY LINK TRAIL (BSP; MAP 1: E2)

Cumulative from Daicey Pond day-use parking area (1,078 ft.) to:	⇅	↗	○
Sentinel Landing (1,051 ft.), Sentinel Link Trail, and Sentinel Mtn. Trail	1.0 mi.	0 ft.	0:30
Sentinel Mtn. summit ledges (1,842 ft.) and loop	3.6 mi.	765 ft.	2:10

This trail leaves from the Daicey Pond access road at a small parking pullout next to Nesowadnehunk Stream, 0.9 mi. from Park Tote Rd. and 0.2 mi. from Daicey Pond CG. The trail immediately crosses Nesowadnehunk Stream and enters an alder swamp. A side trail to Kidney Pond is on the right, then Lily Pad Pond Trail on the left. At 1.0 mi. from Nesowadnehunk Stream, the trail ends at its jct. with Sentinel Link and Sentinel Mtn. trails. Turn left to climb Sentinel Mtn. in 2.6 mi., or continue ahead to reach Kidney Pond in 0.5 mi.

ROCKY PONDS TRAIL (BSP; MAP 1: E1–E2)

This trail leads 0.6 mi. from Kidney Pond CG to the south shore of Rocky Pond. The trail continues to its end at Little Rocky Pond at 1.2 mi.

CELIA AND JACKSON PONDS TRAIL (BSP; MAP 1: E1–E2)

From Kidney Pond CG, Sentinel Link Trail leads south around the pond to the jct. with Celia and Jackson Ponds Trail at 0.3 mi. Turn right (west) on Celia and Jackson Ponds Trail to reach the north shore of Celia Pond at 1.4 mi. Jackson Pond is 0.2 mi. farther west; Little Beaver Pond is an additional 0.6 mi.

LILY PAD POND TRAIL (BSP; MAP 1: E2)

The start of this trail is 0.9 mi. from Kidney Pond and is reached from Kidney Pond via Sentinel Link and Daicey-Kidney Link trails. Lily Pad Pond Trail heads south to reach Beaver Brook in 0.4 mi.

SLAUGHTER POND TRAIL (BSP; MAP 1: E1–E2)

Leading to Slaughter Pond, this trail begins on the Kidney Pond access road immediately beyond the bridge over Nesowadnehunk Stream 0.4 mi. west of Park Tote Rd. The trail follows an old tote road. Doubletop Mtn. Trail enters from the left at 0.7 mi. and coincides with Slaughter Pond Trail for the next 0.6 mi. Doubletop Mtn. Trail departs right, but Slaughter Pond Trail continues ahead to end at Slaughter Pond at 2.3 mi., just outside the BSP boundary.

■ DOUBLETOP MTN. (SOUTH PEAK, 3,455 FT.; NORTH PEAK, 3,489 FT.)

The steep, slide-scarred eastern slopes of Doubletop Mtn. make it easy to identify from many points in the Katahdin region. From the two peaks, the views of Katahdin, South Brother, Mt. Coe, Mt. OJI, and Barren Mtn. are impressive. Doubletop can be climbed from Kidney Pond in the south or from Nesowadnehunk CG in the north. The most popular route is from Kidney Pond, and as such, the Doubletop Mtn. Trail is described in that direction.

DOUBLETOP MTN. TRAIL (BSP; MAP 1: D2–E2)

Cumulative from Kidney Pond (1,051 ft.) to:	⮃	⭧	⟳
Slaughter Pond Trail, second jct. (1,150 ft.)	1.9 mi.	100 ft.	1:00
Doubletop Mtn., south peak (3,455 ft.)	4.6 mi.	2,400 ft.	3:30
Doubletop Mtn., north peak (3,489 ft.)	4.8 mi.	2,425 ft.	3:40
Nesowadnehunk CG (1,300 ft.)	8.2 mi.	2,425 ft.	5:20

DOUBLETOP MTN. TRAIL, IN REVERSE (BSP; MAP 1: D2–E2)

Cumulative from Nesowadnehunk CG (1,300 ft.) to:	⮃	⭧	⟳
Stream crossing (1,650 ft.)	1.4 mi.	350 ft.	0:50
Doubletop Mtn., north peak (3,489 ft.)	3.4 mi.	2,189 ft.	2:50
Doubletop Mtn., south peak (3,455 ft.)	3.6 mi.	2,200 ft.	3:00
Kidney Pond CG (1,051 ft.)	8.2 mi.	2,200 ft.	5:15

Doubletop Mtn. Trail starts at Kidney Pond CG. At 0.3 mi., a side trail leads 0.1 mi. to Draper Pond. Ahead, cross Slaughter Brook and skirt the south shore of Deer Pond. At 1.3 mi., Slaughter Pond Trail enters from the right. The two trails coincide for the next 0.6 mi. Bear left to follow an old woods road (the former Slaughter Pond Tote Rd.) to reach a jct. at 1.9 mi. Here Doubletop Mtn. Trail forks right (north), leaving the old Camp 3 clearing near its northwest corner. Straight ahead (west), Slaughter Pond Trail continues 1.0 mi. to Slaughter Pond. (Watch carefully: this jct. can be easy to miss.)

Doubletop Mtn. Trail follows an old woods road northwest up a valley, crossing a stream four times. The stream and trail run together for a while, which often makes the route wet and muddy. The trail passes close under the cliffs on Moose's Bosom, the peak west of Doubletop Mtn. Just after crossing a small stream, the trail reaches a thick stand of spruce and fir and passes a spring. Turning north again, the trail climbs to a saddle between Moose's Bosom and Doubletop.

Beyond, the trail angles up a very steep and rocky trail on the timbered slope on the west side of the mountain to reach the open summit of the south peak of Doubletop at 4.6 mi. Spectacular 360-degree views abound from this vantage point, one of the finest in BSP, which includes the Katahdin massif and the high peaks to the north, plus the vast 100MW to the south.

The trail continues on to reach the north peak of Doubletop at 4.8 mi. and a section of steel ladder from the former fire tower. From this peak, the trail descends steadily (steeply at times) to the north, eventually reaching a brook at about 6.5 mi. Beyond the brook, the descent becomes more gradual. The last mile follows a fairly level course, reaching Nesowadnehunk CG at 7.9 mi. At the picnic area, bear right to cross a bridge over Nesowadnehunk Stream. The ranger cabin and day-use parking is a short distance ahead on the left at 8.2 mi.

SOUTH BRANCH PONDS

LEDGES TRAIL (BSP; MAP 1: B4)

From South Branch Pond CG, walk north on the access road for 0.1 mi. Turn right onto Middle Fowler Trail, and climb a series of ledges to reach a jct. at 0.3 mi. Ledges Trail begins here and heads left (north) across open ledges with good views south across the steep-walled valley that contains Lower and Upper South Branch ponds. Beyond, the trail descends to end at the access road. At 0.7 mi., turn left and hike 0.5 mi. back to the campground.

■ SOUTH BRANCH MTN. (2,630 FT.) AND BLACK CAT MTN. (2,611 FT.)

South Branch and Black Cat mountains rise steeply above the western shores of Lower and Upper South Branch ponds and offer commanding views of Traveler Mtn. massif. The summits and ridges of Katahdin are in full view to the south.

SOUTH BRANCH MTN. TRAIL (BSP; MAP 1: B4–C4)

Cumulative from South Branch Pond CG (981 ft.) to:	⇅	↗	↻
South Branch Mtn. summit (2,630 ft.)	2.0 mi.	1,650 ft.	1:40
Black Cat Mtn. summit (2,611 ft.)	2.5 mi.	1,725 ft.	2:10
Pogy Notch Trail (950 ft.)	4.7 mi.	1,725 ft.	3:30
South Branch Pond CG (981 ft.) via Pogy Notch Trail	6.6 mi.	1,725 ft.	4:30

This trail extends from South Branch Pond CG over both summits and down to Pogy Notch Trail, which it joins at the southeastern corner of Upper South Branch Pond.

South Branch Mtn. Trail starts at the northwest corner of Lower South Branch Pond, just south of the ranger cabin and adjacent to the picnic and dock area. Head west to cross the outlet brook, then pass a side trail to several walk-in tentsites. The trail parallels the brook for a distance, then climbs a ridge to lookouts with vistas of the ponds and the peaks of Traveler Mtn. After a gradual ascent, the trail turns abruptly to the left and climbs more steeply to ledges, a rocky knob, and then more open ledges, with excellent views of the pond below and the mountain peaks to the east. The partially wooded summit of South Branch Mtn. is reached at 2.0 mi. Beyond, the trail makes a brief descent into a saddle.

Ahead, the trail climbs to the top of Black Cat Mtn., at 2.5 mi., where the reward is a 360-degree panorama. Continuing on, the trail descends through meadows and rocky fields to open ledges on the southern side of the mountain, then swings eastward and descends through mixed forests. After a brief climb, the trail continues down toward Upper South Branch Pond. A side trail on the left leads to Upper South Branch Campsite, and beyond it, crosses a brook with beaver works before joining Pogy Notch Trail at 4.7 mi. Turn left (north) here for South Branch Pond CG (in 1.9 mi.) or right (south) for Pogy Notch and Russell Pond CG (in 7.0 mi.).

■ TRAVELER MTN.—NORTH TRAVELER MTN. (3,152 FT.), TRAVELER (3,550 FT.), AND CENTER RIDGE (3,254 FT.)

This starfish-shaped mountain mass has four high ridges that sprawl out to the south, west, northwest, and north, with four shorter spurs between them. Fires have ravaged the mountain, the last one in 1902, so although its lower slopes support trees of some size, its upper reaches are mostly bare. This is the highest volcanic mountain in New England and possibly the highest on the East Coast. The mountain was formed by a volcanic eruption similar in nature to the violent explosion at Mount Saint Helens in Oregon in 1980.

Combining Pogy Notch, Center Ridge, Traveler Mtn., and North Traveler trails creates an excellent, if long and strenuous, loop hike. (*Note:* It is recommended that hikers attempting this loop make the ascent via Center Ridge Trail and descend by way of North Traveler Trail.)

NORTH TRAVELER TRAIL (BSP; MAP 1: B4)

Cumulative from South Branch Pond CG (981 ft.) to:	⇅	↗	↻
Start of trail (1,000 ft.) via Pogy Notch Trail	0.1 mi.	20 ft.	0:05
North Traveler summit (3,152 ft.) and Traveler Mtn. Trail	2.9 mi.	2,171 ft.	3:00

From the east end of South Branch Pond CG, across from campsite 19, follow Pogy Notch Trail (p. 42) for 0.1 mi. to North Traveler Trail, which diverges left. North Traveler Trail climbs through open woods to the crest of the north ridge, which it follows over bare rhyolite ledges in places, with spectacular views of the valley ponds and the peaks to the west. After a wooded stretch, the trail passes through pretty alpine meadows and fine old woods that alternate with steep ledges. At about 1.7 mi., in one of the wooded sections, a side trail leaves left to a spring. After emerging from the last section of woods, North Traveler Trail continues in the open up the ridge to the broad alpine summit of North Traveler at 2.9 mi. and the jct. with Traveler Mtn. Trail.

HOWE BROOK TRAIL (BSP; MAP 1: B4)

Cumulative from South Branch Pond CG (981 ft.) to:	⇅	↗	↻
Start of trail (1,050 ft.) via Pogy Notch Trail	0.9 mi.	70 ft.	0:30
Waterfall (1,700 ft.)	2.9 mi.	700 ft.	1:50

Howe Brook Trail begins at the southeastern corner of Lower South Branch Pond, where the rocky, fanlike delta of Howe Brook merges with the pond. This inlet is 0.9 mi. south along Pogy Notch Trail (p. 42) from

South Branch Pond CG. Leaving left (east), Howe Brook Trail follows the route of the brook to the first chutes and potholes. Howe Brook is noted for its many pools, potholes, slides, and chutes, which continue for quite a distance up the valley. The trail crosses the brook a number of times before ending at a beautiful waterfall.

CENTER RIDGE TRAIL (BSP; MAP 1: B4–C4)

Cumulative from South Branch Pond CG (981 ft.) to:	⇅	↗	○
Start of trail (1,050 ft.) via Pogy Notch Trail	1.4 mi.	120 ft.	0:45
Peak of the Ridges (3,254 ft.)	3.7 mi.	2,273 ft.	3:05

This route starts at the foot of Center Ridge at the northeastern corner of Upper South Branch Pond, at a point 1.4 mi. south on Pogy Notch Trail (p. 42) from South Branch Pond CG. Diverging left (east) from Pogy Notch Trail, Center Ridge Trail climbs steadily through woods before breaking out into the open. Excellent views of the South Branch ponds, Howe Brook Valley, and North Traveler can be seen en route. Follow the open ridge over ledges and slabs, boulders and scree, and numerous false summits to reach the summit of Center Ridge, known as Peak of the Ridges, at 3.7 mi., and a jct. with Traveler Mtn. Trail. From this vantage point, the summit of the Traveler looms ahead in the distance, and Katahdin is in view over the Wassataquoik Valley to the south.

TRAVELER MTN. TRAIL (BSP; MAP 1: B4–C4)

Cumulative from South Branch Pond CG (981 ft.) to:	⇅	↗	○
Center Ridge Trail (1,050 ft.) via Pogy Notch Trail	1.4 mi.	120 ft.	0:45
Peak of the Ridges on Center Ridge (3,254 ft.) and start of Traveler Mtn. Trail	3.7 mi.	2,273 ft.	3:05
Traveler summit (3,550 ft.)	5.2 mi.	2,975 ft.	4:05
North Traveler summit (3,152 ft.)	8.2 mi.	3,675 ft.	6:00
South Branch Pond CG (981 ft.) via North Traveler Trail and Pogy Notch Trail	11.1 mi.	3,675 ft.	7:30

Traveler Mtn. Trail starts from the Center Ridge summit, also known as Peak of the Ridges; this point is reached via Pogy Notch and Center Ridge trails. Traveler Mtn. Trail traverses across and down "Little Knife Edge," a vertical spine of columnar rhyolite rock. At the base of this formation, cross an alpine meadow and begin to climb through stunted coniferous forest and over several scree walls of stone to reach a huge talus field. Cairns lead diagonally up the mass of loose rock to the summit cone of the

Traveler, at 1.5 mi. from Center Ridge. Excellent views in all directions are possible from this fine vantage point.

Beyond, the trail traverses a long stretch of open terrain. (*Caution:* In bad weather, exercise particular care here; watch carefully for blazes and cairn route markers.) At a high point known as Traveler Ridge, the trail drops sharply through dwarf birch, mountain ash, and balsam fir to a col cloaked with stunted coniferous growth. Beyond, gain a ridge before descending to a saddle dominated by dwarf birch. Finally, the trail climbs to the peak of North Traveler and a jct. with North Traveler Trail, which leads an additional 2.9 mi. down to South Branch Pond CG.

SCIENTIFIC FOREST MANAGEMENT AREA

This 29,537-acre area comprises the northern tier of the park, from Matagamon Lake in the east to Webster Lake in the west and generally north of Park Tote Rd. This is the only area in the park where timber harvesting is allowed, thanks to Governor Baxter, who believed having such an area set aside was in the interest of good forestry science. The SFMA, established in the mid-1950s, was mandated to serve as "a show place for those interested in forestry, a place where a continuing timber crop can be cultivated, harvested, and sold—an example and inspiration to others," Baxter wrote in 1955. Hikers may pass through areas of active or recent timber harvesting and at times may hear harvesting equipment but most often will experience a true sense of the remoteness of this wild northern part of the park. Hunting is also allowed in this area. Freezeout, Wadleigh Brook, and Frost Pond trails pass through the SFMA.

WADLEIGH BROOK TRAIL (BSP; MAP 1: A2–B3)

Cumulative from Park Tote Rd. (750 ft.) to:	↿⇂	↗	↻
Frost Pond Trail (800 ft.)	1.4 mi.	50 ft.	0:40
Blunder Pond Day Use Site (1,050 ft.)	6.8 mi.	300 ft.	3:25
Hudson Pond Campsite (950 ft.)	7.8 mi.	300 ft.	4:00
Freezeout Trail (850 ft.)	9.8 mi.	300 ft.	5:00

This trail leaves Park Tote Rd. about 1 mi. west of the bridge over Trout Brook at Trout Brook Crossing Day Use Site. The trail follows Wadleigh Brook west for a short distance, then turns north. At 1.4 mi., Frost Pond Trail enters from the right. Beyond, Wadleigh Brook Trail returns to Wadleigh Brook, tracing a route along its eastern bank. The trail wends around the upper side of Wadleigh Bog, then crosses a brook draining Blunder

Pond. At 6.8 mi., Wadleigh Brook Trail crosses a gravel road at Blunder Pond Day Use Site. Ahead, the trail crosses the inlet of Hudson Pond and soon reaches the pond proper at 7.8 mi. Here, a short side trail leads uphill to Hudson Pond Campsite (lean-to). Beyond, the trail follows the north shore of the pond before turning to the northeast to reach Hudson Brook and, soon after, a jct. with Freezeout Trail at 9.9 mi., just east of Pine Knoll.

Via Freezeout Trail, to the left it is 2.4 mi. to Webster Lake and its campsite (lean-to and tentsite); to the right, it is 11.7 mi. to Trout Brook CG, passing two campsites en route.

FREEZEOUT TRAIL (BSP; MAP 1: A2–A4, B2)

Cumulative from Trout Brook CG (680 ft.) to:	⥮	↗	↻
Frost Pond Trail (654 ft.)	4.0 mi.	20 ft.	2:00
Northwest Cove Campsite (654 ft.)	5.0 mi.	20 ft.	2:30
Little East Campsite (654 ft.)	5.4 mi.	20 ft.	2:45
Side trail to Grand Pitch (660 ft.)	5.8 mi.	25 ft.	3:00
Wadleigh Brook Trail (850 ft.)	11.7 mi.	40 ft.	6:00
Webster Lake Campsite (891 ft.)	14.1 mi.	40 ft.	7:00

This trail starts from Trout Brook CG, at the end of the campground road that leads to Trout Brook, where there is parking. Immediately cross Trout Brook on a footbridge, and soon pass to the left of several backcountry campsites and a walk-in lean-to site. Continue on the wide, graded trail, formerly a woods road (Freezeout Road). Cross two branches of Boody Brook and then pass over several low ridges. Cross Frost Pond Brook, and at about 3.5 mi., reach a large sawdust pile (the remains of an old mill site) on the right on the shore of Grand Lake Matagamon. At 4.0 mi., Frost Pond Trail diverges left (south).

Ahead, cross Hinckley Brook and continue to parallel the lake. Pass by Northwest Cove Campsite at 5.0 mi. (campsite to right, spring to left), and soon reach a sharp left turn at 5.4 mi. A short walk straight ahead is Little East Campsite (lean-to), at the confluence of the East Branch of the Penobscot River and Webster Stream.

From this point west to Webster Lake, the trail follows the south bank of Webster Stream. At 5.8 mi., a side trail leads 0.2 mi. to Grand Pitch, a thunderous 35-ft. falls on Webster Stream that drops into a narrow slate canyon. This side trail loops to rejoin Freezeout Trail in 0.3 mi.

Ahead, continue easily for a long 5-mi. stretch, with little change in elevation or scenery. Soon after passing over Pine Knoll, the trail reaches the jct. with Wadleigh Brook Trail, which enters from the left at 11.7 mi. Ahead, follow sections of old corduroy road and cross Ice Wagon Field, an old log yard. With Webster Lake in sight, pass a privy on the left. A side trail on the right leads to Webster Lake Campsite (lean-to and tentsite) on the east end of the lake at 14.1 mi.

■ WADLEIGH MTN. (1,259 FT.)

This low mountain, the only one in the vast SFMA, is traversed by Frost Pond Trail.

FROST POND TRAIL (BSP; MAP 1: A4–B3)

Cumulative from Trout Brook CG (680 ft.) to:	⇅	↗	↻
Start of Frost Pond Trail (654 ft.) via Freezeout Trail	4.0 mi.	20 ft.	2:00
Frost Pond Campsite (850 ft.)	5.5 mi.	220 ft.	2:50
Wadleigh Mtn. summit (1,259 ft.)	9.3 mi.	675 ft.	5:00
Wadleigh Brook Trail (850 ft.)	10.3 mi.	675 ft.	5:30

This trail leaves left (west) from Freezeout Trail at a point 4.0 mi. from Trout Brook CG. Frost Pond Trail ascends gradually southwest for 1.5 mi. to reach Frost Pond Campsite (lean-to) at 5.5 mi. Beyond, the trail continues west, climbing to the long ridge of Wadleigh Mtn. (1,259 ft.), where there are good views of the peaks of Traveler Mtn. and South Branch Mtn. in the south. The trail descends to the west, then crosses a gravel road. At 10.3 mi., the trail ends at a jct. with Wadleigh Brook Trail, 1.4 mi. north of Park Tote Rd.

NORTHEAST BAXTER STATE PARK

■ FIVE PONDS

The scenic Five Ponds area (despite the name, there are seven in all) is located west of Horse Mtn., south of Trout Pond Mtn., and northeast of South Branch Pond CG in the northeast corner of BSP. From west to east, these are Lower and Middle Fowler ponds, High and Long ponds, Round and Billfish ponds, and Littlefield Pond. A system of trails connects the ponds and seven backcountry campsites, providing fine day and overnight hiking. Hikers can gain access to trails from Park Tote Rd. at several points and from South Branch CG.

FIVE PONDS TRAIL (BSP; MAP 1: B4–B5)

Cumulative from Park Tote Rd. (700 ft.) to:	↥↧	↗	◷
Lower Fowler Pond Trail (842 ft.)	2.0 mi.	350 ft.	1:10
Horse Mtn. Trail (950 ft.)	3.5 mi.	450 ft.	2:00
Complete Five Ponds Loop Trail	6.0 mi.	500 ft.	3:30

This trail makes a loop around the base of Trout Brook Mtn. and passes seven scenic ponds en route. The trail is described in a counterclockwise direction. From Park Tote Rd., the trail immediately forks. Follow the right fork and climb over the west shoulder of Trout Brook Mtn. to reach a jct. with Lower Fowler Pond Trail (leads to Middle Fowler Pond and Lower Fowler Pond). Five Ponds Trail continues to the left (east), climbing to an esker and following its crest to reach a side trail to Long Pond Outlet Campsite.

Ahead, the trail continues on the esker between High and Long ponds, passing a side trail to Long Pond Pines Campsite at the east end of Long Pond. The trail continues past Round Pond to Billfish Pond and a side trail to Billfish Pond Campsite. Just ahead, Horse Mtn. Trail merges from the right. Five Ponds Trail gradually ascends a valley between Horse Mtn. and Trout Brook Mtn. to pass Littlefield Pond; a side trail at its outlet leads to the pond. Swinging northwest and following Littlefield Brook for a distance, Trout Brook Mtn. Trail enters from the left. Close the loop at Park Tote Rd. at 6.0 mi. at Trout Brook CG.

FOWLER BROOK TRAIL (BSP; MAP 1: B4)

From Park Tote Rd. (650 ft.) to:	↥↧	↗	◷
Lower Fowler Pond (850 ft.)	1.2 mi.	200 ft.	0:40

Fowler Brook Trail leads south from Park Tote Rd. about 2 mi. west of Trout Brook CG. The trail generally follows the course of Fowler Brook, climbing over a low ridge, regaining the brook, and passing a pretty flume. The trail then leads to the north shore of Lower Fowler Pond, Lower Fowler Outlet Campsite, and the jct. with Lower Fowler Pond Trail.

LOWER FOWLER POND TRAIL (BSP; MAP 1: B4)

This short 0.7-mi. trail connects Five Ponds Trail with Lower Fowler Pond, Middle Fowler Pond, and Fowler Brook trails. Lower Fowler Pond Trail diverges south from Five Ponds Trail at a point 2.0 mi. from Park Tote Rd. at Trout Brook CG. The trail soon reaches a jct. with Middle Fowler Pond Trail. Continuing on, Lower Fowler Pond Trail reaches Lower Fowler Pond Campsite, then continues along the pond's shore to end at Lower Fowler Outlet Campsite at 0.7 mi. From here, it is 1.2 mi. north to Park Tote Rd. via Fowler Brook Trail.

MIDDLE FOWLER POND TRAIL (BSP; MAP 1: B4)

Cumulative from South Branch Pond CG (981 ft.) to:	⇅	↗	↺
Side trail to Barrell Ridge (1,800 ft.)	2.8 mi.	820 ft.	1:50
Middle Fowler Pond (950 ft.)	3.7 mi.	820 ft.	2:15
Lower Fowler Pond Trail (1,000 ft.)	5.2 mi.	870 ft.	3:00
Park Tote Rd. (650 ft.) via Middle Fowler Pond Trail and Fowler Brook Trail	6.7 mi.	870 ft.	3:45

From South Branch Pond CG, walk north on the access road for 0.1 mi. Here, Middle Fowler Trail departs right. At a jct. at 0.3 mi., Ledges Trail leaves left. Middle Fowler Pond Trail continues beyond the jct., climbing gradually and following a small brook to open ledges. From there, the trail proceeds through the gap between Big Peaked and Little Peaked mountains. It then traverses the north slope of Traveler Mtn., providing occasional views. At 2.8 mi., a side trail leads left (north) 0.3 mi. to the open summit of Barrell Ridge, where there are fine views of Traveler Mtn., Billfish Mtn., and the wildland to the north.

From this point, the trail descends and reaches Middle Fowler Pond. Turning left (north), the trail soon reaches Middle Fowler South Campsite. From there, the trail continues along the west shore of the pond to its outlet and Middle Fowler North Campsite. Beyond, the trail proceeds to a jct. with Lower Fowler Pond Trail, which leads left to Lower Fowler Pond and on to Park Tote Rd, while ahead the trail joins Five Ponds Trail to reach Trout Brook CG.

■ TROUT BROOK MTN. (1,767 FT.)

This low mountain rises to the south of Trout Brook CG and offers fine views of the Traveler Mtn. massif and the surrounding ponds from its summit ledges.

TROUT BROOK MTN. TRAIL (BSP; MAP 1: B4)

Cumulative from Park Tote Rd. (700 ft.) to:	⇅	↗	↺
Trout Brook Mtn. summit (1,767 ft.)	1.4 mi.	1,070 ft.	1:20
Complete loop via Five Ponds Trail	3.5 mi.	1,070 ft.	2:30

This trail starts from Park Tote Rd. directly opposite Trout Brook CG. The trail climbs through mixed growth and hardwoods to open ledges with views north to Trout Brook Farm and Grand Lake Matagamon.

Ahead, the trail continues over more ledges to the open summit of the mountain and a 360-degree panorama. Beyond the peak, the trail follows the ridge southwest before dropping steeply and then more moderately to the valley between Trout Brook and Horse mountains. The trail reaches a jct. with Five Ponds Trail at 2.5 mi. To the left (north), it is 1.0 mi. to the trailhead and the close of the loop via Five Ponds Trail.

■ HORSE MTN. (1,589 FT.)

This mountain rises steeply above the west shore of Grand Lake Matagamon in BSP's northwest corner and features sheer cliffs on its east face. An old fire tower on top, erected in 1913, was removed in 1999.

HORSE MTN. TRAIL (BSP; MAP 1: B5)

Cumulative from Park Tote Rd. (750 ft.) to:	↻↑	↗	◯
Side trail to viewpoint (1,450 ft.)	1.2 mi.	700 ft.	1:00
Five Ponds Trail (950 ft.)	3.0 mi.	700 ft.	2:00
Trout Brook CG (700 ft.) via Five Ponds Trail	5.5 mi.	800 ft.	3:10

The trail leaves the south side of Park Tote Rd. just west of Matagamon Gate. It rises gradually over the mountain's north flank to a jct. Here, a side trail leads left (east) 0.4 mi. to a viewpoint over the valley of the East Branch of the Penobscot River. Just ahead on the main trail, a side trail leaves right and goes 0.2 mi. to the true summit of Horse Mtn. Semi-open ledges offer limited but nice views ranging east and south. Ahead, Horse Mtn. Trail descends to the shore of Billfish Pond and follows the shoreline to merge with Five Ponds Trail at 3.0 mi. Via Five Ponds Trail, to the right, it is 2.5 mi. to Park Tote Rd.

KATAHDIN WOODS AND WATERS NATIONAL MONUMENT/ INTERNATIONAL APPALACHIAN TRAIL

The 1,900-mile IAT officially begins near Mile 12 on the Katahdin Loop Rd. and heads northeast across Maine's North Woods to the Canadian border just east of Mars Hill. From there, the IAT crosses New Brunswick and Quebec to its current North American terminus in Newfoundland at Belle Isle. Within KWWNM's boundaries, 47.3 mi. of the IAT threads south to north. Marked with 2-by-6-in. blue and white plastic blazes, the IAT crosses two scenic mountains, Deasey and Lunksoos, which offer outstanding views of Katahdin from their open summits. The side trail to

Barnard Mtn. comes early on in the IAT route; the summit ledges on Barnard offer additional fine views of Katahdin.

■ DEASEY MTN. (1,984 FT.)
AND LUNKSOOS MTN. (1,811 FT.)

The craggy summits of these two mountains reward hikers with excellent views west to Katahdin, including Baxter Peak, South Peak, Knife Edge, and Pamola, plus Hamlin Peak, South Turner and North Turner, the peaks of Traveler, and many more mountaintops on the eastern side of BSP. The IAT reaches both Deasey Mtn. and Lunksoos Mtn.

IAT NORTHBOUND (IAT; MAP 1: C6, D5–D7, AND E5)

Cumulative from Katahdin Loop Rd. at Mile 12 (1,050 ft.) to:	↥↧	↗	○
Katahdin Brook Lean-to (970 ft.)	0.3 mi.	0 ft.	0:10
Side trail to Barnard Mtn. (1,070 ft.)	1.4 mi.	200 ft.	0:45
Wassataquoik Lean-to (600 ft.)	4.1 mi.	200 ft.	2:10
Orin Falls Trail (650 ft.)	4.9 mi.	250 ft.	2:25
Wassataquoik Stream (590 ft.)	5.2 mi.	250 ft.	2:35
Deasey Mtn. summit (1,964 ft.)	9.6 mi.	1,650 ft.	5:40
Lunksoos Mtn. summit (1,811 ft.)	10.7 mi.	1,950 ft.	6:20
Lunksoos Lean-to (1,250 ft.)	11.8 mi.	1,950 ft.	6:55

From the main jct. of Katahdin Loop Rd., 2.2 mi. west of Sandbank Stream Campsite, proceed to the right (north) to Barnard Mtn. At 1.3 mi., pass Orin Falls Rd. on the right and stay left on Katahdin Loop Rd. (Orin Falls Rd. leads 2.5 mi. to a barrier and parking not far from Wassataquoik Stream and the start of Orin Falls Trail. The trail is a shorter alternative for hikers wanting to make a day trip to Deasey Mtn. and Lunksoos Mtn.) At 4.9 mi., there is a T intersection near Mile 12 on Katahdin Loop Rd. Turn right here, and in 100 ft., reach the trailhead for the IAT and Barnard Mtn. Trail. Parking for several cars is on the right.

Hike north on the old Gardner Rd. (the IAT) past a gate, then head downhill to cross a bridge over Katahdin Brook. Just past the bridge on the left is Katahdin Brook Lean-to at 0.3 mi. Beyond, climb a long grade to a jct. with an old logging road at 1.0 mi. Turn right (east) on this road and reach the jct. of Barnard Mtn. Trail on the right at 1.4 mi. (leads 0.8 mi. to top of Barnard Mtn.). Continue to follow the IAT around the north side of Barnard Mtn. to a jct. with the Old Wassataquoik Tote Rd. at 3.5 mi. Follow this to the right (south) to reach Wassataquoik Lean-to at 4.1 mi.

Beyond the campsite, continue on the tote road, cross Katahdin Brook, and follow an esker south. At 4.9 mi., there is a jct. Here, the IAT departs left (east) down to Wassataquoik Stream, while Orin Falls Trail continues straight ahead (leads 0.5 mi. to parking near the end of Orin Falls Rd.). On the IAT, ford Wassataquoik Stream (*Caution:* difficult crossing in high water) and follow along the east bank. Ahead at 5.2 mi., the IAT turns left, crosses a tributary stream with sandy banks, and follows a blue-flagged trail west to a beaver dam. Cross just below the dam on logs, then turn right and gradually climb a bank before turning left to join the route of the Old Keep Path. The IAT nears Wassataquoik Stream once more, crosses another small tributary, and then turns northeast.

At 6.1 mi., the IAT leaves the Old Keep Path, turns northeast, and ascends to the col between Deasey Mtn. and a small hill to the south. The trail skirts the nose of Deasey Mtn., passes the house-sized boulder dubbed Earl's Erratic at 6.3 mi., and then crosses Owen Brook at 7.0 mi. Beyond a mature forest of spruce, hemlock, pine, and birch, the IAT turns north and climbs the east ridge of Deasey Mtn. At 8.0 mi., a spur trail leads 50 ft. right to a view of the East Branch of the Penobscot River. The trail descends gradually to cross a stream, then reaches the old Deasey Mtn. fire warden cabin at 8.5 mi., now in ruins. It passes in front of the cabin, then turns left to steeply climb northwest. Just below the summit of Deasey Mtn. at 9.6 mi., the IAT turns sharply right (north). Here, a spur trail leads left 100 ft. to the summit of Deasey, where the recently restored historical cabin sits directly on the ground (as it has since 1929), and hikers can enjoy 360-degree panoramic views. Continuing north, the IAT drops into the col between Deasey Mtn. and Lunksoos Mtn. and crosses a wet area and brook. A steep, winding climb then leads to a series of open ledges on the ridge summit of Lunksoos Mtn. Cairns mark the route across the ledges. At 10.7 mi., reach the top of Lunksoos Mtn., where there are fine views of Sugarloaf Mtn., Mt. Chase, and the valley of the East Branch of the Penobscot River. The IAT descends to reach Lunksoos Lean-to at 11.8 mi.

From Lunksoos Lean-to, the IAT skirts the west side of Hathorn Mtn., then swings east across the north slopes of Little Spring Brook Mtn. to reach the East Branch of the Penobscot River and the old Telos Tote Rd. The trail follows this road, more or less, north along the river corridor to Grand Pitch Lean-to, Haskell Rock, and then Haskell Deadwater, before turning west to join Messer Pond Rd. The IAT follows Messer Pond Rd. north out of KWWNM to Grand Lake Rd., which it reaches at 29.9 mi. from its southern terminus at Mile 12.

Useful companions for hiking this and other sections of the IAT in Maine are the guide *International Appalachian Trail in Maine: Baxter State*

Park to the U.S.–Canadian Border, Fort Fairfield and the map *IAT Maine Section*; both are available at internationalatmaine.org.

ORIN FALLS TRAIL (NPS; KATAHDIN WOODS AND WATERS NATIONAL MONUMENT LOOP ROAD INTERPRETIVE MAP)

Cumulative from trailhead on Orin Falls Rd.
(650 ft.) to:

	⇅	↗	↻
IAT near Wassataquoik Stream ford (650 ft.)	0.5 mi.	40 ft.	0:15
Orin Falls (650 ft.)	3.0 mi.	75 ft.	1:30

This trail offers a shorter approach for hikers looking to make a day trip to Deasey Mtn. and Lunksoos Mtn. On its own, Orin Falls Trail is a nice hike along Wassataquoik Stream to a series of cascades over boulders. Driving from the main jct. of Katahdin Loop Rd., 2.2 mi. west of Sandbank Stream Campsite, proceed to the right. At 1.3 mi., reach Orin Falls Rd. on the right. Turn right here and drive 2.5 mi. to a barrier and parking.

Orin Falls Trail follows an old road north to an esker on the south side of Wassataquoik Stream and turns left to follow the Old Wassataquoik Tote Rd. In 0.5 mi., Orin Falls Trail joins the IAT just west of the Wassataquoik Stream ford. Continue north, cross Katahdin Brook on a bridge, and reach Katahdin Brook Lean-to. Beyond, where the IAT turns left, continue straight ahead on Orin Falls Trail, still following the old tote road. Nearing the falls, Orin Falls Trail leaves the old road and follows a narrow path to the cascades.

■ BARNARD MTN. (1,621 FT.)

This mountain rises just east of BSP and Katahdin Lake. A large ledge on the summit rewards hikers with excellent views west to the high peaks of Katahdin and southwest across the 100MW to Jo–Mary Mtn., the White Cap Range, and Baker Mtn.

BARNARD MTN. TRAIL (NPS; MAP 1: D5–D6 AND E5)

Cumulative from Katahdin Loop Rd. at Mile 12
(1,050 ft.) to:

	⇅	↗	↻
Side trail to Barnard Mtn. (1,070 ft.)	1.4 mi.	200 ft.	0:45
Barnard Mtn. summit and ledge view (1,621 ft.)	2.2 mi.	750 ft.	1:30

Barnard Mtn. Trail begins from the jct. with the IAT, 1.4 mi. north of the start of that trail near Mile 12 on Katahdin Loop Rd. From the IAT, Barnard Mtn. Trail ascends the southeast ridge of the mountain via switchbacks to a huge erratic. The trail swings around the glacial boulder, then passes through a large crevice in the rock. Beyond, the trail contours past mossy boulders, then climbs moderately via more switchbacks. The angle eases, the trail passes a cairn, and soon the path emerges on a large slab of granite on the west side of the summit, where there is a picnic table and a fine vista of Katahdin Lake and the Katahdin massif.

NORTH AND EAST OF BAXTER STATE PARK

■ OWL'S HEAD (930 FT.)

Scraggly Lake Public Land, a 9,000-acre preserve just northwest of BSP, features a climb to Owl's Head, a prominent rocky knob overlooking Scraggly Lake and the forestland north of the park. From the northern jct. of ME 11 and ME 159 in Patten, drive west on ME 159 for 10.1 mi. to the village of Shin Pond. Soon after Shin Pond, ME 159 becomes Grand Lake Rd. (same road). At 6.0 mi. beyond Shin Pond, cross the Seboeis River and 0.7 mi. ahead reach Scraggly Lake Rd. on the right. Turn right on Scraggly Lake Rd. and follow it 9.3 mi. to signed trailhead parking on the right just before Scraggly Brook.

OWL'S HEAD TRAIL (MBPL; USGS HAY LAKE QUAD, GAZETTEER MAP 57, MTF SCRAGGLY LAKE PL–OWL'S HEAD TRAIL)

Cumulative from parking near Scraggly Lake outlet (725 ft.) to:	⇅	↗	↺
Loop jct.	1.4 mi.	20 ft.	0:40
Owl's Head summit (870 ft.)	1.5 mi.	225 ft.	0:50
Complete loop	3.4 mi.	250 ft.	1:50

The trail enters the woods on the left side of the small parking area, meandering north over a knoll through spruce and cedar woods. At 0.45 mi., reach the outlet arm of Scraggly Lake. Bear right to follow along the shore. At 0.65 mi., views open up to a boat launch across the lake to the left and to the distinctive bump of Owl's Head to the right. At 1.1 mi., a 20-ft. spur on the left offers another look at Owl's Head. Ahead, cross the steep slope between lake and hill on a narrow path. An outcrop provides good viewing. At 1.3 mi., a spur on the left leads 50 ft. down to the lake; this is the old water-access trailhead. The loop jct. is ahead at 1.35 mi. Bear right to ascend to Owl's Head. Climb a short, steep, rocky pitch, level off, traverse left, then head right and up a moderate to steep section. Above, a spur to the left leads to a ledge and wonderful views over Scraggly Lake. The vista takes in the Traveler summits and other peaks in the northern reaches of BSP, the high summits of Katahdin, the craggy ridgelines of Deasey Mtn. and Lunksoos Mtn., and shapely Sugarloaf Mtn. Then climb the rocks of the final ledges. Atop Owl's Head, a spur leads left over a narrow rocky ridge to more views.

Descend steeply down the back side of Owl's Head on switchbacks and several sets of rock steps. Pass through an impressive grove of mature hemlock, then reach the shore of Scraggly Lake. Cross the slope above the lake, passing through more mature spruce, hemlock, red pine, and cedar woods. Reach the lakeshore again, then climb left and up to the loop jct. Bear right to return to the trailhead.

■ SUGARLOAF MTN. (1,868 FT.)

The mountain is located in T5 R7 WELS, west of Shin Pond and east of the Seboeis River. Panoramic views from its bare summit ledges include the peaks of the Katahdin massif north to Traveler Mtn. and beyond, as well as the summits and forestland of KWWNM, Mt. Chase, Mars Hill, and many others.

From the jct. of ME 159 and ME 11 in Patten, drive northwest on ME 159 for 5.7 mi. Turn left (west) on Grondin Rd. and reset your mileage counter. At 2.7 mi. from ME 159, pass Sucker Brook Rd. on the right. At 3.0 mi., pass American Thread Rd. on the left. Cross a bridge at 3.9 mi. At 5.8 mi., bear left at a fork (orange and black sign for Sugarloaf Trail, the snowmobile trail). Beyond this point, a high-clearance vehicle is recommended. At 6.6 mi., cross an old bridge. Immediately beyond the bridge is a small clearing and a four-way intersection; stay straight (sign: 64 Sugarloaf Trail). At the next four-way intersection, at 7.2 mi., turn left and proceed 150 yd. to a small parking area on the right. In the trees, a wooden board with red letters reads, "Sugarloaf Mtn."

SUGARLOAF MTN. TRAIL
(NFTM; USGS SHIN POND QUAD, GAZETTEER MAP 51)

From parking area (950 ft.) to:	⬇⬆	↗	○
Sugarloaf Mtn. summit (1,868 ft.)	0.9 mi.	920 ft.	1:00

Follow the wide grassy trail into the woods. In 400 ft., climb a steep pitch. Bits of colored flagging tape mark the distinct trail corridor. Continue up the south ridge at a moderate but steady grade. At 0.55 mi., reach the base of the summit cone. Beyond, the ridge narrows and the grade is moderate to steep. Pass a boulder with a small cave at its base at 0.65 mi. Ahead, reach a level shelf and continue easily for a short distance. The final stretch to the peak involves multiple pitches of steep scrambling over ledges. Reach the top of Sugarloaf at 0.9 mi. The 360-degree views from the summit include Katahdin and the peaks of BSP, White Cap Mtn., the Barren-Chairback

Range, Norway Bluff, Round Mtn., Haystack Mtn., and Mars Hill. Grand Pitch on the Seboeis River is visible in the valley below the peak to the west.

■ MT. CHASE (2,440 FT.)

This mountain in the Penobscot County town of Mt. Chase is the highest among a cluster of peaks extending in a northeast–southwest line a few miles north of Patten and just west of the Aroostook County line.

From the northernmost jct. of ME 11 and ME 159 in Patten, drive north on ME 11 for 6.4 mi. Turn left (west) on the gravel-surfaced Mountain Rd. At 1.7 mi. from ME 11, Mountain Rd. becomes rough, and a high-clearance vehicle is recommended. At 2.1 mi., enter a large clearing. Here, a branch road goes left; stay straight on Mountain Rd. and park immediately beyond the jct. on the right. In 2017, there was a picnic table next to the parking area.

MT. CHASE TRAIL
(NFTM; USGS MT. CHASE QUAD, GAZETTEER MAP 52)

Cumulative from Mountain Rd. parking (1,000 ft.) to:	↕	↗	○
Mt. Chase summit (2,440 ft.)	1.5 mi.	1,450 ft.	1:30

To find the start of the trail, *do not* follow the grassy jeep road that heads north from the parking area and picnic table, but rather go left along Mountain Rd. for 100 ft. Here, a jeep trail heads right into the woods. An obscure sign (wood with red trim) to the left of the jeep track reads "Mt. Trail." To the right of the jeep trail is a rock cairn with an arrow on it.

The jeep trail, a rocky old woods road, leads easily uphill. At 0.2 mi., it levels off briefly, then rises moderately to cross a grassy old woods road. Climb a rocky gully, avoid an obscure side trail on the right, then continue ahead and up over a ledge. Ascend a moderate but steady grade, then pass huge boulders on the right on a short, steep section. A sign here reads "Rolling Rock." In the level area beyond, continue straight ahead (avoiding the grassy trail on the right). After a brief descent, climb a rocky path and pass through a cutover area (the summit ridge is in view ahead).

At 1.2 mi., reach a small clearing and the old fire warden cabin on the right. Just beyond, cross a stream. A signpost on the left reads "Mt. Chase Summit 0.5 mi." Climb steeply and then more moderately on rough trail, following colored flagging tape markers. Pass a spring on the left, then negotiate more steep, rough treadway. At 1.6 mi., a spur trail leads left to the open ledges of Eagle Rock and excellent views. Beyond, reach a high shoulder, bear left, and soon emerge into the semi-open on the summit ridge. Continue on the rocky ridge to the summit of Mt. Chase and a small communications tower. The footings of an old fire tower are here; the tower was moved to the Patten Lumberman's Museum in 2001. Views are grand: Katahdin and Traveler Mtn. to the west, Rocky Brook Range to the north-northeast, Peaked Mtn. to the north, Haystack Mtn. to the north-east, and Mars Hill to the east.

■ NORWAY BLUFF (2,285 FT.)

Norway Bluff rises above Munsungan Lake north of BSP and west of ME 11 in T9 R10 WELS. A communications tower is located on this remote ridge; the summit fire tower was moved to the Ashland Logging Museum in 2012. From ME 11 in Ashland, drive west on American Realty Rd. to the Six Mile Checkpoint. Norway Bluff is within the boundaries of the North Maine Woods, a large block of forestland, most of which is privately owned and cooperatively managed to provide recreational opportunities to the public. Visitors must register at the checkpoint and pay a day-use and camping fee to enter the area. Just beyond the checkpoint, bear left on Pinkham Rd. and follow it to milepost 31, just west of Mooseleuk Stream, where Pell & Pell Rd. enters from the right (northwest). Turn right on Pell & Pell Rd. and follow it northwest 8.7 mi. to a side road. Turn left onto this side road and drive another 4.1 mi. to a small gravel pit and park.

NORWAY BLUFF TRAIL (NFTM; USGS MOOSELEUK QUAD AND GAZETTEER MAPS 56, 57, 63, 64)

From the gravel pit parking area (1,600 ft.) to:	↕	↗	↻
Norway Bluff summit (2,285 ft.)	1.0 mi.	685 ft.	1:00

The trail is an old ATV track used by workers to service the communications tower. Facing the ridgeline of Norway Bluff, look for a cairn on the left side of the gravel pit. Just beyond, trees are marked with colored flagging tape at the edge of the woods; this is the start of the trail. The trail route has been logged to either side, but the pathway itself, which runs through a corridor of large trees, is clearly discerned and well marked. The trail rises directly up the side of a ridge with two long switchbacks near its top. The ATV track ends at the communications tower on the middle of the ridge, where there are good views. Continue south along the ridge to the site of an old fire tower at 1.0 mi.

SECTION 2
100-MILE WILDERNESS AND MOOSEHEAD LAKE

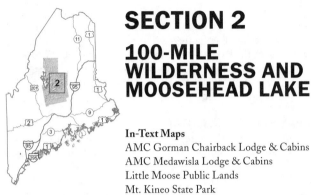

In-Text Maps

Pull-Out Map
Map 2: Maine Woods

SEC 2

SEC 2

INTRODUCTION

The region encompassing the 100-Mile Wilderness (100MW) and Moosehead Lake includes the southern half of sprawling Piscataquis County in north-central Maine, roughly 1.4 million acres. The second largest but least populous county in Maine, Piscataquis gets its name from the Abenaki word meaning "branch of the river" or "at the river branch." Five major rivers cross the county. The northern half of Piscataquis County features the wilds of BSP, a portion of the Allagash Wilderness Waterway (AWW), and an abundance of other lakes, rivers, hills, and mountains but no mountain trails, and as such is not described. The southern half of Piscataquis County is bounded on the north by BSP, the West Branch of the Penobscot River, and the Golden Rd. To the east, the section is more or less bounded by ME 11. To the south, ME 16/6 and ME 6 form an approximate boundary, while Moosehead Lake and ME 15/6 form the western boundary. This section describes 63 trails on 32 mountains.

GEOGRAPHY

Moosehead Lake is the largest lake in Maine; at 35 mi. long with an area of 120 sq. mi., it is the predominant natural feature in this region. The Moose River feeds into Moosehead Lake from the west, and the Roach River empties into the lake from the east. The Kennebec River flows from two outlets on the west side of the lake, emptying into the Atlantic Ocean 170 mi. downriver near Popham Beach. In the center of the region, the East Branch and West Branch of the Pleasant River flow eastward and join at Brownville Junction. From its source near the southwest corner of Moosehead Lake, the Piscataquis River flows south and then east across the county to merge with the Penobscot River at Howland. The Sebec River flows east from Sebec Lake to empty into the Piscataquis River at Milo.

The 100MW is the name given to the next-to-last section of the AT on its 2,190-mi. route from Springer Mtn. in Georgia to Katahdin in Baxter State Park (BSP). The name is credited to Stephen Clark, editor of the *The Official Appalachian Guide to Maine* from 1964 to 1982, who created the colorful label to alert AT thru-hikers that no resupply points existed along this remote 100-mi. stretch of trail, and that is still largely the case today. The moniker has long since come to refer to the entire 750,000-acre expanse of forests, mountains, lakes, ponds, rivers, and streams between the village of Monson, just south of Moosehead Lake, and Abol Bridge, which is on the West Branch of the Penobscot River on the Golden Rd., at the doorstep of BSP. Greenville in the west and Brownville Junction and Millinocket in the east further define the bounds of the 100MW.

Conservation lands abound in the 100MW, and when combined with the protected lands around Moosehead Lake, the total exceeds 2,000,000 acres of nearly contiguous conservation lands ranging west to the Canadian border and north into the watersheds of the St. John and Allagash rivers, thanks to the determined efforts of a host of public agencies and private conservation groups.

SEC
2

AMC established a presence in the 100MW in 2003 with the purchase of the Katahdin Iron Works Tract. AMC has since acquired three additional parcels, the Roach Pond Tract, Baker Mtn., and Silver Lake, bringing its total to 75,000 acres of conservation land. Trails from AMC's Little Lyford Lodge connect to a host of pristine ponds, to the West Branch of the Pleasant River and the spectacular slate canyon of Gulf Hagas, to craggy lookouts on Indian Mtn. (2,338 ft.), and to the AT. From Gorman Chairback Lodge on Long Pond, trails also lead to Gulf Hagas, as well as to the peaks on the eastern reaches of the Barren–Chairback Range via the AT, including Fourth Mtn. (2,383 ft.), Third Mtn. (2,061 ft.), Columbus Mtn. (2,326 ft.), and Chairback Mtn. (2,190 ft.). Barren Mtn. (2,670 ft.), the site of an old fire tower, ledges, and rock slides, anchors the range on the western end. Near Medawisla Lodge, paths explore the area around Second Roach Pond. South of the pond are Shaw Mtn. (2,499 ft.) and Hedgehog Mtn. (2,130 ft.).

East of AMC's land are the four high peaks of the White Cap Range, beginning with Gulf Hagas Mtn., which rises to 2,638 ft. east of the West Branch of the Pleasant River. From there, elevations increase along the AT across the range, with West Peak at 3,178 ft. and Hay Mtn. at 3,244 ft. The range culminates atop White Cap Mtn. (3,654 ft.). Topped with gnarled tree growth and scree fields, the White Cap summit provides panoramic views that are among the best in the state. Across from Barren Mtn. to the south, on the other side of Lake Onawa, is the twin-peaked Borestone Mtn., the higher peak topping out at 1,981 ft. Three pretty tarns are tucked into the high slopes of Borestone, which is distinctly visible from the sandy beach on Sebec Lake farther south. Here, a nice loop trail winds over the ledges on the northeast side of Birch Mtn.

Just west of Greenville, rising up from the southwest shore of Moosehead Lake, are the rugged mountain peaks encompassed by the 15,000-acre Little Moose Public Lands. Big Moose Mtn., the site of Maine's first fire tower, erected in 1905, reigns supreme at 3,194 ft. At the far end of the mountain's northwestern ridge is the airy pinnacle of Eagle Rock, which affords far-reaching views over Moosehead Lake to the east and the upper Kennebec River valley to the west. Situated midway up Moosehead Lake on a peninsula across from Rockwood is the iconic Mt. Kineo. The impressive 700-ft. wall of its southeast face is unmistakable from many vantage points in the region. On a peninsula on the eastern side of Moosehead Lake just north of Greenville is Burnt Jacket Mtn. (1,680 ft.). A few miles east, the remains of a crashed B-52 bomber lie scattered on the lower slopes of Elephant Mtn. (2,636 ft.). East of Lily Bay on Moosehead Lake and south of First Roach Pond is Number Four Mtn. (2,894 ft.). It is situated amid the 363,000-acre Moosehead Region Conservation Easement, which rings Moosehead Lake. Number Four Mtn. and the neighboring and formerly trailless Baker Mtn. (3,521 ft.) are sites of ambitious trail-building efforts by AMC and MBPL trail crews, as is neighboring Blue Ridge (2,350 ft.)

North of the Mt. Kineo peninsula and east of North Bay on Moosehead Lake is shapely Little Kineo Mtn. (1,927 ft.), where climbers must negotiate a rock chimney to gain the summit. Located between Spencer Pond and Ragged Lake, the long, flat-topped ridgelines of Little Spencer Mtn. (3,007 ft.) and Big Spencer Mtn. (3,206 ft.) dominate the landscape for miles around. Lobster Mtn. (2,318 ft.) rises south of Lobster Lake and is accessible only by water.

The state of Maine owns the 43,000-acre Nahmakanta Public Lands unit in the north-central section of the 100MW. The rugged Turtle Ridge and the ponds and ledges of the Debsconeag Backcountry are here. Rising steeply over the northern end of Nahmakanta Lake is Nesuntabunt Mtn. (1,550 ft.), where visitors will have fine views of Katahdin. Immediately to the east is a portion of the 210,000-acre Katahdin Forest Easement, which protects many miles of shoreline on Pemadumcook Lake, Jo-Mary Lake, the West Branch of the Penobscot River, and a number of other water bodies. Sprawling Potaywadjo Ridge (1,270 ft.) rises just west of Pemadumcook Lake and Lower Jo-Mary Lake. Abutting Nahmakanta Public Lands to the north is Debsconeag Lakes Wilderness Area, which contains the highest concentration of pristine lakes and ponds in New England, including Rainbow Lake. The AT threads a sinuous route through this area and leads to Rainbow Ledges (1,504 ft.) and Rainbow Mtn. (1,638 ft.).

Road Access

Running the length of the east side of the 100MW is ME 11, which connects Milo to Millinocket. Along the west side are ME 15/6, Lily Bay Rd., and Sias Hill Rd. To the south, ME 16/6 connects Milo to Dover-Foxcroft. To the west, ME 15/6 connects Dover-Foxcroft to Monson, Greenville, and Rockwood. From Millinocket on the northern end of the 100MW, Millinocket Lake Rd., Baxter State Park Rd., and Golden Rd. offer access to trails.

Once off these main roads and into the 100MW, visitors must travel on gravel logging roads. In the southern portion of the 100MW, KI Rd. is the major route from the east at Brownville Junction, while Greenville Rd. is the major road in from the west. From Kokadjo on Lily Bay Rd., French-town Rd. provides access. From ME 11 between Brownville Junction and Millinocket, Jo-Mary Rd. is the route into the northeastern interior of the 100MW. Lily Bay Rd. and Sias Hill Rd. connect Greenville to the Golden Rd. near Caribou Lake. The peaks northeast of Moosehead Lake can be accessed via this road.

SEC 2

Some of the mountains and trails in this section lie within the boundaries of North Maine Woods and the KI Jo-Mary Multiple Use Forest, two large blocks of forestland. Most of this forestland is privately owned and cooperatively managed for renewable resources while providing outdoor recreational opportunities for the public. Visitors must register at a checkpoint and pay camping and day-use fees to enter these areas. See p. xxvi for information about access to the lands managed by NMW.

Camping

Numerous primitive campsites throughout Nahmakanta PL allow for extended visits. Vehicle-accessible campsites are at Pollywog West, Wadleigh North End, Wadleigh South End, Nahmakanta South End, Musquash Stream, Musquash Field, and Leavitt Pond. East Side, West Side, and East Beach on Nahmakanta Lake can be reached by canoe or boat. Access to Leavitt Pond North, Tumbledown Dick Pond, and Pollywog Southeast is by foot trail only. Dispersed camping is possible in the Debsconeag Backcountry of Nahmakanta. Primitive backcountry campsites are available for backpackers at four ponds in Little Moose PL: Big Moose Pond, Little Moose Pond, Little Notch Pond, and Big Notch Pond.

Lily Bay State Park on Moosehead Lake just north of Greenville features 90 drive-in campsites, hot showers, restrooms, and other amenities, while Peaks–Kenny State Park on Sebec Lake in Dover-Foxcroft has 56 campsites and similar amenities.

Numerous primitive roadside campsites are within the boundaries of NMW, and 60 drive-in campsites are available within the KI Jo-Mary Multiple Use Forest. At least fourteen privately operated campgrounds throughout this region offer a variety of camping and lodging choices with amenities.

AMC's Maine Woods recreation and conservation area features three wilderness lodges with private cabins and shared bunkhouses, plus a growing number of drive-in, paddle-in, and walk-in campsites.

AMC'S MAINE WOODS INITIATIVE (MWI)

AMC's Maine Woods Initiative is one of the most important multiuse recreation and land conservation projects in the United States today, a landscape-scale project to conserve and protect land in a corridor of more than 1 million acres in the 100MW between Monson and BSP. This working model uses an innovative and thoughtful approach to conservation that combines recreation, natural resource protection, overnight lodging, responsible forest management, education, and local community partnerships to protect this beautiful region and preserve it for future generations.

AMC has permanently conserved 75,000 acres of forestland in the 100MW, including 27,000 acres of ecological reserve. Known as the Maine Woods recreation and conservation area, these lands include more than 115 sq. mi. of the Maine Woods, including 22 lakes and ponds, more than 20 mi. of the West Branch of the Pleasant River, countless miles of streams, 3,521-ft. Baker Mtn., Caribou Bog, Silver Lake, and multiple stands of late-successional forest, wetlands, and other critical wildlife habitats. To date, AMC has completed 28 fish passage projects and reopened 38 mi. of stream habitat with a goal of removing all barriers to fish passage on these lands by 2020.

AMC has been conserving land and building recreation infrastructure in the 100MW since 2003, when the club purchased the 37,000-acre Katahdin Iron Works Tract. In 2009, AMC added the abutting 29,500-acre Roach Ponds Tract. In 2015, AMC purchased 4,300 acres on wild and trailless Baker Mtn., the largest chunk of subalpine terrain outside of Katahdin. And in 2016, AMC gained 4,000 acres around Silver Lake. AMC's land is the southern anchor of a 63-mi.-long corridor of conserved land encompassing more than 500,000 acres, which includes properties owned by The Nature Conservancy, Maine Bureau of Parks and Lands, the National Park Service, and Elliotsville Plantation Inc. When adjacent working forest easement lands are included, the extent of conservation lands from Moosehead Lake to the northern end of BSP and east to the new Katahdin Woods and Waters National Monument exceeds 800,000 acres.

MWI has created a world-class destination for backcountry outdoor recreation. Three sporting camps in the Maine tradition have been opened to the public. These Maine Wilderness Lodges, Little Lyford near the Little Lyford Ponds, Gorman Chairback on Long Pond, and Medawisla on Second Roach Pond, offer visitors rustic charm, creature comforts, good food, and camaraderie amid spectacular natural surroundings. AMC has constructed more than 70 mi. of new trails, as well as more than a dozen backcountry campsites, and today maintains more than 130 mi. of meandering trails on the property for hiking, paddling, mountain biking, cross-country skiing and snowshoeing, fishing, wildlife watching, and camping.

AMC's Maine Woods property is located in the heart of the 100MW east of Greenville and west of ME 11 at Brownville Junction. A KI Jo-Mary Multiple Use Forest gate fee is charged from May through October for vehicle access to the southern half of AMC's lands, waved for overnight guests staying at the AMC lodges. Please note the access roads are not paved, and conditions can vary. Limit speed to 25 mph and yield to logging trucks. No fuel is available after leaving the state highways. Contact AMC in advance for road conditions during the spring and fall or when storms are expected.

For more information on MWI, visit outdoors.org/mwi. For information and reservations for AMC's Maine Wilderness Lodges, as well as outdoor recreation opportunities near each, visit outdoors.org/maine.

Gorman Chairback Lodge & Cabins

Built as a private camp in 1867, Gorman Chairback Lodge & Cabins is at the eastern end of beautiful Long Pond at the base of the rugged Barren–Chairback Range. The lodge can be reached by vehicle during summer and fall, and by ski, snowshoe, and dogsled in winter (though dogs are not allowed overnight). Refer to the driving directions for Little Lyford Lodge for driving directions to Gorman Chairback Lodge.

Accommodations include four private deluxe cabins, eight private shore-line cabins, and a shared bunkhouse. The central bathhouse in the main lodge has composting toilets and hot showers. It also has a wood-heated sauna in winter. Meals are provided in the main lodge, which has, in addition to the dining area, a fireplace, sitting area, library, cubbies for gear storage, game room, and small store.

A network of trails extends out from the lodge to reach Third Mtn., Indian Pond, Chairback Mtn., Gulf Hagas, and the AT. Even more trails are available in winter for cross-country skiing and snowshoeing. Several backcountry campsites are available.

Little Lyford Lodge & Cabins

The first of AMC's lodges in the 100MW, Little Lyford is adjacent to the Little Lyford Ponds on the site of a sporting camp that has been serving guests for more than 140 years. The lodge can be reached by vehicle during summer and fall, and by ski, snowshoe, and dogsled in winter. Little Lyford Lodge & Cabins is the only AMC-run property that allows dogs.

Accommodations include nine private log cabins and a shared bunk-house. Each cabin features a porch, a woodstove, gas lamps, and cold running water. A central bathhouse near the main lodge has composting toilets and hot showers, and a wood-heated sauna is available in winter. Meals are provided in the main lodge, which, in addition to the dining area, houses a fireplace, a sitting area, a library, and a small store.

A network of summer trails in the vicinity leads to the nearby Little Lyford Ponds, the West Branch of the Pleasant River, Gulf Hagas, the AT, a host of pristine ponds to the west, and outlooks high on Indian Mtn. In winter, even more trails are available for cross-country skiing and snowshoeing. A number of frontcountry and backcountry campsites are available.

Medawisla Lodge & Cabins

Rebuilt from the ground up and reopened in the summer of 2017, Medawisla (the Abenaki word for loon) is the newest of AMC's Maine Wilderness Lodges. Located at the confluence of Second Roach Pond and the Roach River, the area boasts a growing multiuse trail network for hikers and mountain bikers, plus bountiful opportunities for paddling, fishing, and camping. The lodge can be reached by vehicle year-round.

Accommodations include five private hilltop cabins with bath and shower, four waterfront cabins with bath and shower (these cabins also have a kitchenette), and two shared bunkhouses (one hilltop and one waterfront). Each cabin and bunkhouse has LED lighting and a wood-stove. Meals for guests staying in the full-service cabins are provided in the main lodge, which, in addition to the dining area, has a fireplace, sitting area, game room, conference space, library, and small store.

MWI Road Access

To Gorman and Little Lyford, from Greenville, to the west: From the blinking traffic light in the center of Greenville on ME 15/6, proceed north one block and turn right onto Pleasant St. (immediately after Northwoods Outfitters). Make a jog around the Greenville Municipal Airport. In 2.1 mi., the road becomes gravel. At 3.7 mi., cross a bridge over Big Wilson Stream. Beyond this point, the road is called KI Rd. At 10.4 mi., reach a large clearing area with parking; this is the winter trailhead and as far as you can drive in winter. Reach the Hedgehog Checkpoint at 12.1 (register and pay fee). At 1.8 mi. beyond the checkpoint, reach the jct. of KI Rd. and Upper Valley Rd. For Gorman Chairback Lodge & Cabins, turn right and drive 3.3 mi. to Chairback Mtn. Rd. on the right. Turn right on this road and drive 1.3 mi. to the entrance drive for Gorman Chairback, which leads directly to the facility. For Little Lyford Lodge, from the checkpoint on KI Rd., turn left on Upper Valley Rd. and drive 2.2 mi. to the entrance drive for Little Lyford Lodge & Cabins. Follow the blue squares with reflective arrows to the guest parking area a short distance from the lodge.

SEC 2

To Gorman and Little Lyford, from Brownville Junction, to the east: Approach KI Rd. on ME 11 either 26.0 mi. southbound from Millinocket or 5.5 mi. northbound from Brownville Junction. Look for signs for Katahdin Iron Works Historic Site (these may be missing, so check your mileage). Turn west onto KI Rd. The Katahdin Iron Works Checkpoint at the entrance to KI Jo-Mary Forest is 6.3 mi. from ME 11. Stop and register (fee charged). At 7.3 mi. from the gate, Chairback Mtn. Rd. is on the left; the entrance drive for Gorman Chairback Lodge & Cabins is 1.3 mi. west on this road. For Little Lyford Lodge, continue on KI Rd. for 3.3 mi. to the jct. of KI Rd. and Upper Valley Rd. Proceed straight ahead (north) on Upper Valley Rd. for 2.2 mi. to the entrance drive for Little Lyford Lodge & Cabins on the right. Follow the blue squares with reflective arrows to the guest parking area a short distance from the lodge.

To Medawisla: From the blinking light in the center of Greenville at the jct. of ME 15/6 and Lily Bay Rd., drive north on Lily Bay Rd. for 18.5 mi. to the small village of Kokadjo on First Roach Pond. Just beyond, at 18.8 mi., reach a fork (road turns to dirt here). North Shore Rd. goes right. Bear left on Sias Hill Rd. to continue on to Medawisla. At 20.3 mi., take a right on Smithtown Rd. Reach the entrance road to Medawisla Lodge & Cabins at 26.0 mi. from downtown Greenville. Follow the drive to the guest parking lot and the lodge.

GULF HAGAS

Popularly known as the Grand Canyon of Maine, Gulf Hagas is just west of the AT and the White Cap Range. This unique scenic area consists of a deep, narrow, slate canyon on the West Branch of the Pleasant River. The river drops about 400 ft. in about 4 mi., and in many places, the vertical walls of the canyon force the river into very narrow channels that form a series of waterfalls, rapids, chutes, and pools. The falls are particularly spectacular in late spring during peak runoff. In winter, ice builds up on the walls and, because the sun rarely reaches certain faces, often lasts into late June.

Gulf Hagas was designated a registered natural landmark in 1968, and 500 acres, including the entire canyon, were set aside for public enjoyment. In 1986, the National Park Service obtained nearly 2,000 acres, including the Gulf and the corridor along Gulf Hagas Brook, to permanently protect the unique natural beauty of this area. (*Note:* Camping and campfires are prohibited in Gulf Hagas.)

Much of the Gulf Hagas trail system runs near the rim of the canyon, with frequent side trails to viewpoints and falls. And by using the old Pleasant River Tote Rd. on the return trip, a loop hike is possible.

To reach the main Gulf Hagas trailhead (and the trailhead for the AT Southbound to Chairback Mtn.), drive north on ME 11 from Brownville Junction for 5.5 mi. Turn left (west) on Katahdin Iron Works Rd. and drive 6.8 mi. to the Katahdin Iron Works Checkpoint (register and pay fee). Beyond the gate, take the right fork. At 3.4 mi. from the gatehouse, the road reaches a second fork. Stay left, crossing the West Branch of the Pleasant River on a bridge. KI Rd. reaches the trailhead parking area on the right at 6.7 mi. from the gatehouse.

LITTLE MOOSE PUBLIC LANDS

This 15,000-acre unit of the Maine public lands system straddles the town lines of Big Moose Township and Moosehead Junction Township near the southwest corner of Moosehead Lake, just west of Greenville. The predominant natural feature is Big Moose Mtn., a sprawling mountain peak with a narrow summit that provides outstanding views of the Moosehead Lake region. This is also the site of the first fire tower in Maine. Nestled into the long ridge of Little Moose Mtn. are five scenic ponds known for wildlife watching and fishing. A system of trails wends through the preserve, connecting the ponds and leading to numerous outlooks, as well as climbing to the peak of Big Moose Mtn. A new trail leads north from the preserve to the pinnacle of Eagle Rock.

NAHMAKANTA PUBLIC LANDS

This remote 43,000-acre preserve, the largest in Maine's public lands system managed by MBPL, is in the unincorporated townships of T1 R12 WELS, T1 R11 WELS, and Rainbow Township, southwest of Katahdin and BSP and north of Katahdin Iron Works.

Pristine Nahmakanta Lake is the predominant natural feature among the 24 lakes and ponds, each more than than 10 acres in size, and a series of mountain peaks and ridges range as high as 2,524 ft. in elevation, offering fine views of the forested terrain. Nearly one-quarter of the preserve, or 11,802 acres, has been designated as an ecological reserve to ensure that environmentally sensitive plant life will remain in its natural condition and be periodically monitored. This includes the 9,200-acre roadless area known as the Debsconeag Backcountry.

More than 30 mi. of hiking trails are in Nahmakanta, including Turtle Ridge Loop, Tumbledown Dick Trail, and Debsconeag Backcountry Trail. A 9-mi. stretch of the AT traverses the preserve, entering in the east at Nahmakanta Stream and exiting in the north at Rainbow Stream. As of late 2017, MBPL was hard at work on a new backcountry trail connection over Wadleigh Mtn. west of Nahmakanta Lake, between Crescent Pond and Turtle Ridge Loop.

SEC 2

DEBSCONEAG LAKES WILDERNESS AREA

One of the crown jewels of conservation in Maine's North Woods is the Debsconeag Lakes Wilderness Area, a remote 46,271-acre tract of mature forests and pristine lakes and ponds rich with wildlife, situated at the far northern end of the 100MW, just south of the West Branch of the Penobscot River, BSP, and mile-high Katahdin. Acquired by The Nature Conservancy in 2002, DLWA is an ecological reserve that protects the highest concentration of remote ponds in New England as well as undisturbed stands of 300-year-old trees. (*Note:* Dogs are not allowed in DLWA. Backcountry camping is permitted at designated sites only.)

The AT meanders through the 100MW for about 15 mi., entering near Murphy Ponds and exiting on Golden Rd., just west of Abol Bridge. En route, the AT hugs the entire south shore of Rainbow Lake, the largest lake in the 100MW. A side trail climbs Rainbow Mtn. near the eastern end of the lake. Beyond, the trail climbs over Rainbow Ledges for outstanding views of Katahdin. Around 5 mi. of trails lead into the northern section of the 100MW from Golden Rd. at Horserace Brook. Horserace Pond Trail reaches the pond of the same name, where there are two primitive tentsites. Blue Trail diverges early on, leading past Clifford Pond and Woodman Pond to the north shore of Rainbow Lake. The Rainbow Loop Trail links these two trails for a nice circuit hike, which is known as the Rainbow Loop. The most popular hike is Ice Caves Trail, a short jaunt that leads to a cavernous hole beneath a jumble of boulders that often retains ice well into the summer and often the fall, not far from First Debsconeag Lake.

SUGGESTED HIKES

■ Easy

LITTLE LYFORD PONDS

	$\Downarrow\Uparrow$	$\nearrow$	$\circlearrowright$
LP via Pond Loop Trail	1.9 mi.	230 ft.	1:05

Make a nice circuit around these two ponds, where moose sightings are possible. See Pond Loop Trail, p. 90.

HENDERSON BROOK

	$\Downarrow\Uparrow$	$\nearrow$	$\circlearrowright$
RT via Henderson Brook Trail	2.2 mi.	325 ft.	1:15

Enjoy this winding path along the banks and through the gorge of Henderson Brook, just east of Long Pond. See Henderson Brook Trail, p. 93.

HINKLEY COVE

	$\Downarrow\Uparrow$	$\nearrow$	$\circlearrowright$
RT via Hinkley Cove Trail	1.6 mi.	60 ft.	0:50

From AMC's Medawisla Lodge, trace a route used by river drivers in the late 1800s to access the cove from the Second Roach Pond outlet dam. See Hinkley Cove Trail, p. 96.

BIRCH MTN.

	$\Downarrow\Uparrow$	$\nearrow$	$\circlearrowright$
LP via Birch Mtn. Ledge Trail	2.6 mi.	350 ft.	1:30

In Peaks–Kenny State Park, hike this pleasant loop then go for a swim at Sebec Lake. See Birch Mtn. Ledge Trail, p. 112.

BIG MOOSE POND AND LITTLE MOOSE POND

	$\Downarrow\Uparrow$	$\nearrow$	$\circlearrowright$
LP via Loop Trail	3.7 mi.	650 ft.	2:10

Wander through the wilds around these two scenic ponds then climb to the ridge beyond for a good look at Big Moose Mtn. See Loop Trail, p. 115.

ELEPHANT MTN.

	⮃	⌁	⏱
RT via Elephant Mtn. B-52 Memorial Crash Site Trail	0.5 mi.	70 ft.	0:20

Take a short hike on the lower slopes of Elephant Mtn. to a somber memorial at the 1963 crash site of a B-52 bomber. See B-52 Memorial Crash Site Trail, p. 124.

ICE CAVES

	⮃	⌁	⏱
RT via Ice Caves Trail	2.2 mi.	400 ft.	1:20

This short hike leads to a cavernous hole beneath a jumble of boulders that often retains ice well into the summer months. See Ice Caves Trail, p. 137.

◼ Moderate

INDIAN MTN.

	⮃	⌁	⏱
RT via Laurie's Ledge Trail	3.3 mi.	1,000 ft.	2:05

Hike to several great viewpoints on Indian Mtn. overlooking AMC's Maine Woods land. See Laurie's Ledge Trail, p. 87.

GORMAN LOOP

	⮃	⌁	⏱
LP via Gorman Loop Trail, Third Mtn. Trail, and Chairback Mtn. Rd.	5.4 mi.	800 ft.	3:00

Hike over the northern slopes of Columbus Mtn. and Third Mtn. To begin, see Gorman Loop Trail, p. 93.

SHAW MTN.

	⮃	⌁	⏱
RT via Shaw Mtn. Trail	3.4 mi.	970 ft.	2:10

Climb to the heights of Shaw Mtn. for a good look over Second Roach Pond toward Katahdin, well beyond. See Shaw Mtn. Trail, p. 95.

SEC 2

GULF HAGAS

🎋 🌢 🐾 ⛺ 🎣 ❄   ↺   ↗   ○

LP via AT, Rim Trail, and Pleasant River Tote Rd.	7.9 mi.	870 ft.	4:25

Get a good look at every waterfall in the spectacular slate canyon of Gulf Hagas on this scenic loop hike. Visit the stately pines of the Hermitage on the West Branch of the Pleasant River too. To begin, see Gulf Hagas Loop, p. 98.

BORESTONE MTN.

🌢 🚶 🎣 ❄   ↺   ↗   ○

RT via Base Trail and Summit Trail	4.0 mi.	1,200 ft.	2:35

Combine these two trails for a look at Sunrise Pond and its nature center then climb to the craggy peaks of Borestone Mtn. for excellent wilderness vistas. To begin, see Base Trail, p. 110.

BIG MOOSE MTN.

🌢 🐕 🎣 ❄ 🏕   ↺   ↗   ○

RT via Big Moose Mtn. Trail	4.2 mi.	1,850 ft.	3:00

Climb to the site of Maine's first fire tower (erected in 1905, removed in 2011) for panoramic views over Moosehead Lake to the jumble of peaks ranging as far north as Katahdin. See Big Moose Mtn. Trail, p. 117.

MT. KINEO

🌢 🚶 🐾 ❄ 🏕   ↺   ↗   ○

LP via Carriage Trail, Indian Trail, and Bridle Trail	3.4 mi.	800 ft.	2:05

Take a scenic ferryboat ride on Moosehead Lake to the Kineo Peninsula. Once there, tackle a great loop hike to the top of the 700-ft. cliffs on Mt. Kineo and its summit observation tower. To begin, see Carriage Trail, p. 121.

NUMBER FOUR MTN.

🌢 🐾 🎣 ❄ 🏕   ↺   ↗   ○

RT via Number Four Mtn. Trail	3.8 mi.	1,475 ft.	2:40

Enjoy great views of Baker Mtn., Lily Bay Mtn., Big Moose Mtn., and Moosehead Lake from the outlooks on Number Four Mtn. A summit bench makes a nice lunch spot. See Number Four Mtn. Trail, p. 125.

LITTLE SPENCER MTN.

		🔁	↗	⟳
RT via the Ram Trail		3.0 mi.	1,825 ft.	2:25

This challenging hike climbs through a narrow chimney and over steep terrain to the summit ledges of Little Spencer Mtn., with excellent views of the Moosehead Lake region. See the Ram Trail, p. 129.

SEC 2

BIG SPENCER MTN.

		🔁	↗	⟳
RT via Big Spencer Mtn. Trail		3.6 mi.	1,850 ft.	2:45

The hike to the north summit and old fire tower site on Big Spencer is steep and challenging, but the outstanding wilderness vistas are worth the effort. See Big Spencer Mtn. Trail, p. 130.

DEBSCONEAG WILDERNESS–RAINBOW LOOP

		🔁	↗	⟳
LP via Horserace Brook Trail, Blue Trail, and Rainbow Loop Trail		6.3 mi.	1,040 ft.	3:40

Combine these trails for a wonderful circuit through the wild and scenic Debsconeag Lakes Wilderness Area. To begin, see Horserace Pond Trail, p. 138.

■ Strenuous
WHITE CAP RANGE

		🔁	↗	⟳
OW via AT Northbound		14.3 mi.	3,900 ft.	9:05

Trek across all four peaks of the White Cap Range, from Gulf Hagas Mtn. and West Peak to Hay Mtn. and White Cap Mtn. via the AT in one long day or make it a multiday backpack. Three campsites en route offer overnight options. See AT Northbound, p. 103.

BARREN–CHAIRBACK RANGE

		🔁	↗	⟳
OW via AT Northbound		16.2 mi.	3,600 ft.	10:00

Hike across the rugged Barren–Chairback Range from the Otter Pond trailhead, tackling Barren Mtn., Fourth Mtn., Third Mtn., Columbus

Mtn., and Chairback Mtn. Three lean-tos en route make this a good two-to three-day backpacking trip. See AT Northbound, p. 104.

WHITE CAP MTN.

RT via AT Southbound	5.6 mi.	2,100 ft.	3:50

Climb the north side of White Cap Mtn. for outstanding views ranging far and wide over the 100MW, from Katahdin to Big Spencer Mtn. to the peaks of the Barren–Chairback Range. See AT Southbound, p. 105.

DEBSCONEAG BACKCOUNTRY

LP via Debsconeag Backcountry Trail	12.9 mi.	1,630 ft.	7:15

Make it a very full day or spread the mileage over a two-day backpack to enjoy the many remote ponds and scenic ridges east of Nahmakanta Lake. See Debsconeag Backcountry Trail, p. 134.

TRAIL DESCRIPTIONS

AMC'S MAINE WOODS INITIATIVE

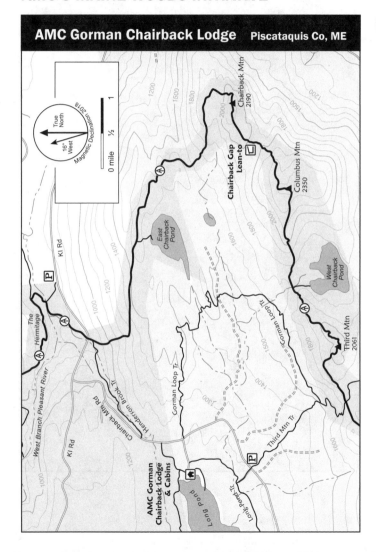

SEC 2

AMC Gorman Chairback Lodge   Piscataquis Co, ME

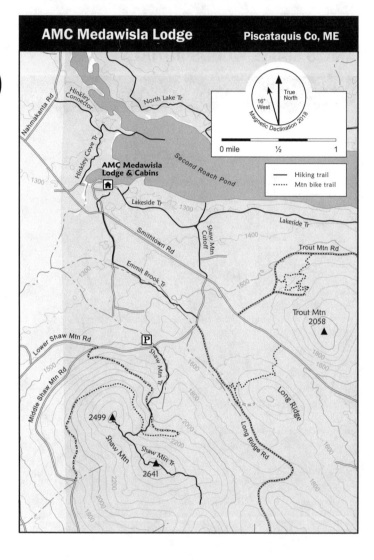

AMC Medawisla Lodge   Piscataquis Co, ME

True North

16° West

Magnetic Declination 2018

0 mile   ½   1

—— Hiking trail
········ Mtn bike trail

Nahmakanta Rd
Hinkley Connector
North Lake Tr
Hinkley Cove Tr
AMC Medawisla Lodge & Cabins
Second Roach Pond
1300
Lakeside Tr
1300
Shaw Mtn Cutoff
Lakeside Tr
1400
Smithtown Rd
Trout Mtn Rd
Emmit Brook Tr
1300
1500
Lower Shaw Mtn Rd
P
Trout Mtn 2058 ▲
Shaw Mtn Tr
1500
1600
1800
1800
Middle Shaw Mtn Rd
2499 ▲
2000
1800
Long Ridge
Shaw Mtn
2200
Shaw Mtn Tr
2641
Long Ridge Rd
1600
2200
2000
1800
1800

■ INDIAN MTN. (2,338 FT.)

Indian Mtn. rises prominently from the valley west of the West Branch of the Pleasant River. Its open summit ledges are reached via Laurie's Ledge Trail, which provides hikers with excellent views over AMC's Maine Woods lands to the many peaks and valleys beyond.

SEC 2

LAURIE'S LEDGE TRAIL (AMC; MAP 2: E2)

Cumulative from Upper Valley Rd. parking lot (1,300 ft.) to:	↕	↗	↻
Indian Mtn. Circuit, east jct. (1,500 ft.)	0.4 mi.	200 ft.	0:15
Indian Mtn. Circuit, west jct. (1,600 ft.)	0.7 mi.	300 ft.	0:30
Laurie's Ledge, westerly overlook (2,300 ft.)	1.6 mi.	1,000 ft.	1:20

Named for former AMC Board of Directors president Laurie Burt, the trail offers fine views to the north from its easterly overlook high on Indian Mtn. The summits of the White Cap Range are visible, and on a clear day, visitors can see Katahdin. From the westerly outlook, there are good views of Elephant Mtn., Prong Pond Mtn., and many of the area's ponds, including Horseshoe, Pearl, Mountain Brook, and Grassy. Parking for the trail is on the left side of Upper Valley Rd., 2.3 mi. north of the jct. of Greenville Rd. and KI Rd. (0.1 mi. after the entrance drive to Little Lyford Lodge & Cabins).

Follow the trail up the bank, then head left across a log bridge. The trail leads along the edge of a large boulder, where there is a view of Little Lyford Ponds, Elephant Mtn., and part of Baker Mtn. The trail then switchbacks to the left. After a gradual but steady ascent, it reaches a jct. with Indian Mtn. Circuit at 0.4 mi. The two trails share the same route, a grassy old logging road, for the next 0.3 mi. At 0.7 mi., where Indian Mtn. Circuit continues straight, Laurie's Ledge Trail turns left.

The trail ascends moderately, passing to the left of four huge boulders. Beyond, the trail climbs to the base of a large cliff band and runs along the lower part of this for 100 yd. It then turns right and climbs steeply to a narrow ledge with a fine view to the east and south. Ahead, a side trail on the right leads 50 yd. to the easterly overlook and views to Barren Mtn. and the other summits of that range. The main trail continues to climb steadily, steeply at times, for 0.4 mi. The angle finally eases and the trail leads over the upper slopes to reach the westerly overlook below the true summit of Indian Mtn.

INDIAN MTN. CIRCUIT (AMC; MAP 2: E2)

Cumulative from Upper Valley Rd. (1,300 ft.) to:	⇅	↗	↺
Laurie's Ledge Trail, east jct. (1,500 ft.)	0.4 mi.	200 ft.	0:20
Laurie's Ledge Trail, west jct. (1,600 ft.)	0.7 mi.	300 ft.	0:30
Gravel road (1,550 ft.)	1.7 mi.	400 ft.	1:05
Pearl Ponds Trail (1,500 ft.)	2.0 mi.	400 ft.	1:15
Horseshoe Pond (1,480 ft.) side trail	2.6 mi.	400 ft.	1:30
End of trail on gravel road (1,650 ft.)	3.1 mi.	570 ft.	1:45

This multiuse trail shared with mountain bikers extends across the northern flank of Indian Mtn., just west of Little Lyford Ponds. The trail starts on Upper Valley Rd., diagonally across from the entrance to Little Lyford Lodge & Cabins, at a point 2.2 mi. north of the jct. of Greenville Rd. and KI Rd. Parking is in a small lot at the trailhead.

The trail ascends gradually through the forest to the jct. with Laurie's Ledge Trail (sign) at 0.4 mi. The two trails share the same route for the next 0.3 mi. Ahead, where Laurie's Ledge Trail leaves to the left (south), Indian Mtn. Circuit continues its westerly course around the mountain, generally on a contour. At 1.7 mi., the trail crosses a logging road 100 yd. south of Baker Pond Rd. and continues directly across the road.

The wide, grassy forest path crosses four log bridges through a wet area to reach the jct. with Pearl Ponds Trail on the right at 2.0 mi. Continuing ahead on Indian Mtn. Circuit, the route follows a contour around the base of Indian Mtn. on an increasingly rough foot trail, crossing 29 bog bridges. Heading gradually downhill, the trail crosses a small stream just before a large wooden bridge. There is a view of Pearl Ponds to the right. The wide path climbs a small rise, then descends to a jct. just above the pond at 2.6 mi. A spur trail to the right leads 50 yd. to Horseshoe Pond Campsite and the pond, where a grassy clearing offers a beautiful view across the water to Elephant Mtn.

Continuing on, the path leads northeast, away from the pond, climbing gradually to its end on a logging road at 3.1 mi. To the left (north), this road may be followed for 0.8 mi. to the start of the trail just south of Baker Pond Rd., thus making a loop hike possible.

NATION'S NATURE TRAIL (AMC; MAP 2: E2)

Cumulative from Upper Valley Rd. parking lot (1,300 ft.) to:	⇅	↗	○
Start of trail (1,300 ft.)	0.2 mi.	-50 ft.	0:05
Complete loop	1.2 mi.	100 ft.	0:40
Complete loop from Upper Valley Rd.	1.4 mi.	150 ft.	0:45

SEC 2

Named for longtime AMC member and volunteer Peg Nation, this 1.2-mi. yellow-blazed loop trail circles the area around Little Lyford Lodge & Cabins, passing through woodlands and wetlands and reaching the Pinnacle and the West Branch of the Pleasant River. Park at the Laurie's Ledge Trail parking lot on Upper Valley Rd. 0.1 mi. north of the driveway into Little Lyford Pond Lodge & Cabins.

Cross Upper Valley Rd. to access a spur trail leading 0.2 mi. east to Nation's Nature Trail. The trail is over mostly easy ground except for one short, moderately steep climb up to the Pinnacle. Along the river, the trail coincides with Pleasant River Trail. Each area that the trail passes through has its own distinct ecological communities. Twelve interpretive stations en route offer more information, and a detailed trail brochure is available at Little Lyford Lodge & Cabins.

PLEASANT RIVER TRAIL (AMC; MAP 2: E2–F2)

From Little Lyford Lodge & Cabins (1,200 ft.) to:	⇅	↗	○
End of trail at woods road and bridge over West Branch of Pleasant River (1,155 ft.)	1.1 mi.	-45 ft.	0:30

This trail, an old logging tote road, extends along the West Branch of the Pleasant River. A portion of the trail from Little Lyford Lodge & Cabins south along the west bank of the river to a bridge crossing the river makes for a pleasant walk. This section of trail is also referred to as Lodge to Lodge Trail because it is a part of the winter ski route between Little Lyford and Gorman Chairback lodges.

The trail leaves from behind Mountain View Cabin in the Little Lyford Lodge & Cabins area. Start by crossing a wet area on bog bridges before reaching a jct. with a spur trail (leads to the Pleasant River at the site of an old dam). Just ahead, at 0.1 mi., Nation's Nature Trail diverges to the right.

Pleasant River Trail continues ahead at a moderate grade, following a ridge parallel to the river. Dropping down, it crosses a spot next to the river and then climbs gradually, crossing a minor drainage. The trail then continues south, bearing away from the river. Forrest's Folly, a winter ski trail, is on the right at 0.8 mi. Ahead, reach a woods road at 1.1 mi. A bridge crossing the West Branch of the Pleasant River is visible on the left. Cross the bridge to connect with Head of the Gulf Trail, which provides access to Gulf Hagas, or cross the woods road to continue on Head of the Gulf Trail to parking on Upper Valley Rd., in 0.5 mi.

POND LOOP TRAIL (AMC; MAP 2: E2)

Cumulative from Upper Valley Rd. (1,350 ft.) to:	⇅	↗	↻
Pond Loop Trail (1,200 ft.)	0.2 mi.	-150 ft.	0:05
Pleasant River Trail, south jct. (1,200 ft.)	0.9 mi.	40 ft.	0:25
Pleasant River Trail, north jct. (1,250 ft.)	1.4 mi.	80 ft.	0:45
Complete loop (via spur trail and Pleasant River Trail)	1.9 mi.	230 ft.	1:05

Using a portion of Pleasant River Trail, Pond Loop Trail circles the upper pond of Little Lyford Ponds. Numerous side trails provide opportunities for wildlife watching from vantage points along the shores of the upper and lower ponds. Trailhead parking is on Upper Valley Rd. at a point about 2.6 mi. north of the jct. of Greenville Rd. and KI Rd.

A short spur trail connects the road and parking with Pond Loop Trail in 0.2 mi. At the jct., turn right to circle the upper pond in a counterclockwise direction. There are views of the upper pond through the trees as the path winds over a few small rises. Shortly the trail crosses the upper pond's inlet on bog bridges. Climbing gradually uphill, it bears away from the pond to reach an old grassy road, which it follows through a clearing. Soon, the lower pond is visible through the trees on the right. Pass a large old stone chimney marked Gerry's Gazebo. Pryor's Path crosses the trail, leading left to a dock on the upper pond and right to a dock on the lower pond.

Pond Loop Trail continues to a jct. with Pleasant River Trail at 0.9 mi. The two trails share the route for the next 0.5 mi. Turn left and climb gradually. Follow a small brook before dropping down to the upper pond and views of Baker Mtn. through the trees. The trail descends the ridge and crosses a large wooden bridge, known as Kendall's Crossing, over the outlet of the upper pond. Beyond the bridge, the trail climbs again, bearing away from the pond. At a jct. at 1.4 mi., bear left off Pleasant River Trail to continue on Pond Loop Trail. There is a quick downhill before the trail levels off and winds through the forest, passing a side trail on the left to the upper pond. Cross a dozen bog bridges to reach a jct. at 1.7 mi. On the left is a clearing on the shore of the upper pond. Canoes are available there for use by AMC guests. Turn right (west) to return to the trailhead parking lot at 1.9 mi.

SEC 2

MOUNTAIN BROOK POND TRAIL (AMC; MAP 2: E2)

From parking lot on Upper Valley Rd. (1,550 ft.) to:	⇅	↗	↻
Mountain Brook Pond (1,530 ft.)	0.2 mi.	-20 ft.	0:50

This short walk leads to the south shore of pretty Mountain Brook Pond. Park on the left side of Baker Pond Rd. in a small parking lot, 1.2 mi. west of Upper Valley Rd. and 4.5 mi. north of the jct. of Greenville Rd. and KI Rd. (*Note:* From the same parking lot, Pearl Ponds Trail heads south.)

The trail to the pond (sign) leaves the road to the north about 20 ft. east of the lot. Cross the road and head north, down the bank on a wooded path, which leads into a small clearing just short of Mountain Brook Pond. Log bridges lead down to the shore. Canoes are available for use by AMC guests.

PEARL PONDS TRAIL (AMC; MAP 2: E2)

Cumulative from parking lot on Baker Pond Rd. (1,550 ft.) to:	⇅	↗	↻
Side trail to Pearl Ponds (1,500 ft.)	0.3 mi.	-50 ft.	0:10
End of trail at Baker Pond Rd. near Grassy Pond (1,500 ft.)	0.6 mi.	-50 ft.	0:20

Parking for this trail is the same as for Mountain Brook Trail. From the parking lot, the trail leads 0.2 mi. south to a jct. Here, a spur trail leads left (east) to join Indian Mtn. Circuit in 0.3 mi. Turn right (west) to continue on Pearl Ponds Trail. After crossing two small wooden bridges, the trail soon intersects with a short side trail on the left, which leads to Pearl Ponds. Continuing straight on wide and grassy Pearl Ponds Trail, bear left over a bridge, then reach a wooden bench with a view of the water. Ahead, the trail continues left and uphill to another jct. at 0.4 mi. To the right, a side trail leads to several Pearl Ponds roadside campsites. Straight ahead on the main trail is a jct. with Baker Pond Rd. at 0.6 mi. Grassy Pond Trail starts just across the road.

BAKER POND TRAIL (AMC; MAP 2: A1 AND E2)

Cumulative from parking lot on Baker Pond Rd. (1,550 ft.) to:	⇅	↗	↺
Start of trail via Baker Pond Rd. (1,550 ft.)	0.5 mi.	0 ft.	0:15
Baker Pond Trail and trail south to Mountain Brook Pond (1,600 ft.)	1.7 mi.	50 ft.	0:50
Baker Pond Campsite (1,650 ft.)	2.2 mi.	100 ft.	1:05
Mountain Brook Pond (1,530 ft.) via Mountain Brook Trail extension	2.5 mi.	100 ft.	1:15

Parking for this trail is the same as for Mountain Brook Trail. From the parking lot, walk 0.5 mi. west along Baker Pond Rd. Turn right and walk around the yellow gate, then up an old rocky roadbed. Shortly, where an older grown-in roadbed branches to the left, Baker Pond Trail heads to the right. The old road crests over three small hills, then straightens out. It then crosses a brook and bears to the right. The trail reaches a jct. where a sign indicates that Baker Pond is 0.5 mi. to the left and Mountain Brook Pond is straight ahead. Follow Baker Pond Trail north on a graded path, which soon bears to the left and crosses a wooden bridge. This lowland trail can often be wet and muddy. Ahead, the path narrows, and bog bridges are around the pond. The trail ends at Baker Pond Campsite. Just below the campsite is a nice view across the water.

From the jct., the trail to Mountain Brook Pond, an extension of Mountain Brook Trail, continues along the rocky roadbed. It quickly reaches a jct. with an old logging road. Here the trail turns right (sign). The road becomes overgrown and passes through a small clearing with good views of Baker Mtn. The trail turns into a grassy path as it heads down into the woods, descending to Mountain Brook Pond and a small clearing with pond views.

GRASSY POND TRAIL (AMC; MAP 2: A1 AND E2)

Cumulative from parking lot on Baker Pond Rd. (1,550 ft.) to:	⇅	↗	↺
Start of trail (1,500 ft.) via Baker Pond Rd. or Pearl Ponds Trail	0.6 mi.	-50 ft.	0:20
Grassy Pond (1,550 ft.)	0.8 mi.	50 ft.	0:25

Parking for this trail is the same as for Mountain Brook Trail and Pearl Ponds Trail. From the parking lot, walk 0.6 mi. west along Baker Pond Rd., past the start of Baker Pond Trail, to a grassy trail entrance on the right, immediately opposite the west end of Pearl Ponds Trail. A pleasant alternative is to follow Pearls Ponds Trail to Grassy Pond Trail.

Pass between three large boulders, following a wide path. The trail goes uphill briefly and then drops down a set of log stairs to the east shore of Grassy Pond.

HORSESHOE POND TRAIL (AMC; MAP 2: E2)

From parking lot at end of Baker Pond Rd. (1,500 ft.) to:	↥↧	↗	↻
Horseshoe Pond (1,462 ft.)	0.6 mi.	20 ft.	0:20

From the jct. of Greenville Rd. and KI Rd., drive 2.1 mi. north on Upper Valley Rd. to the jct. with Baker Pond Rd. Turn left onto Baker Pond Rd. and follow it to its end at a parking lot (sign) and Pearl Ponds campsite.

From the lot, follow the wide, graded trail. The route is flat and winding and leads gradually uphill and then down. The trail ends at a tiny inlet on the north shore of Horseshoe Pond. Wooden stairs lead down to the water.

HENDERSON BROOK TRAIL
(AMC; GORMAN CHAIRBACK LODGE, P. 85, AND MAP 2: F3)

From parking lot on Chairback Mtn. Rd. (1,100 ft.) to:	↥↧	↗	↻
AT and KI Rd. (776 ft.)	1.1 mi.	-325 ft.	0:35

This trail winds along the banks and through the gorge of Henderson Brook just east of Long Pond. To reach the trailhead, drive south from the jct. of Greenville Rd. and KI Rd. for 3.4 mi. Turn right (south) onto Chairback Mtn. Rd. and follow it for 0.9 mi. to a small parking lot on the right.

The trail starts across the road, heads northeast, and descends to the edge of Henderson Brook, which it follows down the valley past a series of pretty waterfalls and pools. The trail crosses and recrosses the brook several times. (*Note:* A rope strung across the brook in two places offers some assistance.) At 1.1 mi., the trail merges with the AT, which enters from the right. KI Rd. is 50 ft. beyond the jct.

GORMAN LOOP TRAIL
(AMC; GORMAN CHAIRBACK LODGE, P. 85, AND MAP 2: F3)

Cumulative from Chairback Mtn. Rd. (1,210 ft.) to:	↥↧	↗	↻
Third Mtn. Trail (1,500 ft.)	3.7 mi.	800 ft.	2:15
Chairback Mtn. Rd. (1,200 ft.)	4.6 mi.	800 ft.	2:40

This trail makes a nice circuit from the Gorman Chairback Lodge area, reaching a high point on the northern slopes of Columbus Mtn. and Third Mtn. A number of outlooks offer views along the Barren–Chairback

Range and to Blue Ridge, Elephant Mtn., Baker Mtn., Indian Mtn., and Long Pond. The trail meanders through a variety of ecological habitats, from northern hardwood ridges to montane spruce-fir forest, forested wetlands, and nonforested kettle bogs.

Gorman Loop Trail starts from Chairback Mtn. Rd., nearly opposite the entrance drive for Gorman Chairback Lodge. The trail climbs at a mostly moderate grade to a ridge, levels off, and passes through several bogs, one of which features a 250-ft. boardwalk and a bench—a nice spot for a break. The trail then drops into a drainage. Up and over the next low ridge, cross the outlet of East Chairback Pond. The trail switchbacks up the slope beyond to a narrow ridge and then winds down to cross a brook draining the west basin of Chairback Mtn. The path continues south, then turns west to cross the outlet stream of West Chairback Pond. Scramble up rocks to a high point beyond, where there is a viewpoint north. The trail then follows a contour for a stretch before angling across and down to meet Third Mtn. Trail on the north slope of Third Mtn., passing several more viewpoints en route. Turn left here to climb to the AT on the ridgeline above and then go on to the summit of Third Mtn. (reached in 2.0 mi.), or descend to the right on Third Mtn. Trail to return to Chairback Mtn. Rd. at a point 0.8 mi. west of the Gorman Loop Trail trailhead.

THIRD MTN. TRAIL
(AMC; GORMAN CHAIRBACK LODGE, P. 85, AND MAP 2: F3)

Cumulative from Chairback Mtn. Rd. (1,200 ft.) to:	⇅	↗	⟳
Gorman Loop Trail (1,500 ft.)	0.9 mi.	300 ft.	0:35
AT jct. west of Third Mtn. summit (1,880 ft.)	1.4 mi.	680 ft.	1:05
Indian Pond and campsites (1,060 ft.)	3.9 mi.	680 ft.	2:20

This trail climbs the north slope of Third Mtn. from the Gorman Chairback Lodge area to reach the AT (which provides access to the Third Mtn. summit), then descends to the south to end at a remote campsite on the north shore of Indian Pond. Park in the parking lot (on the left) just past the trailhead (sign) on Chairback Mtn. Rd. at a point 2.2 mi. from its jct. with KI Rd. and 0.8 mi. beyond the entrance drive for Gorman Chairback Lodge.

Leaving the Chairback Mtn. Rd., the trail makes a short, steep ascent through a stand of birch. Follow the blue blazes as the trail winds through the hardwood forest over the lower slopes of Third Mtn. Cross several small streams on wooden bridges and a wet area on bog bridges. Beyond, the trail begins to climb steadily on a number of long switchbacks. Follow it toward several large boulders before climbing several steep rock staircases and then a wooden ladder. Views begin to open up through the trees, and soon the angle eases and the trail reaches a jct. with the AT at 1.9 mi. at a height-of-land on the ridgeline. To the left (east), it is 0.5 mi. via the AT to grand views atop Monument Cliff on Third Mtn. To the right (west), it is 2.0 mi. via the AT to the wooded summit of Fourth Mtn., and 5.0 mi. to the abandoned fire tower atop Barren Mtn.

Beyond the AT jct., Third Mtn. Trail crosses the wide saddle between the peaks before making a mostly moderate descent. After crossing a stream, the trail levels out and joins the route of an old woods road. At 3.5 mi., the trail leaves the old road and turns sharply left. It ends at the pond, where there is an earthen tent pad, fire ring, and privy.

■ SHAW MTN. (NORTH PEAK, 2,499 FT.; SOUTH PEAK, 2,641 FT.)

The twin summits of Shaw Mtn. rise east of First Roach Pond and south of Second Roach Pond, offering good views over the 100MW as far north as Katahdin. To reach the trailhead, from the entrance road to Medawisla, continue east on Smithtown Rd. for 1.1 mi. Turn right on Lower Shaw Mtn. Rd. In another 0.4 mi., where Long Ridge Rd. forks left toward West Branch Pond Camps, stay right. Trailhead parking for Shaw Mtn. Trail is 0.4 mi. ahead. Parking is on the shoulder.

SHAW MTN. TRAIL
(AMC; MEDAWISLA LODGE, P. 86, AND MAP 2: D3)

Cumulative from Lower Shaw Mtn. Rd. (1,520 ft.) to:	⇅	↗	↺
Trail jct. in sag between north and south summits (2,410 ft.)	1.4 mi.	890 ft.	1:10
Shaw Mtn., north summit (2,499 ft.)	1.7 mi.	970 ft.	1:20

The trail climbs alongside a brook into the drainage between the twin peaks of Shaw Mtn. Ahead, it joins an old woods road and continues uphill to the left. The track narrows to a foot trail, then crosses an old skidder trail. At 0.7 mi., it joins an old haul road and turns sharply left. Beyond, with a view of the summit ridge in sight, bear right off the haul road onto a foot trail. Ascend steadily on a moderate grade to reach a bench on the right, where there is a fine view over Second Roach Pond all the way north to Katahdin and the peaks on the western side of BSP. Soon after the bench, bear right and climb steeply. Cross a grassy skidder trail, then a rock staircase. Reach a sag between the peaks and a jct.

To reach the north summit of Shaw Mtn., turn right. Easy walking on this spur trail along the ridge leads to a short climb to the flat, wooded summit.

From the sag jct., you can continue left toward the south summit; the trail currently (as of late 2017) ends in another 0.1 mi., with a view northeast to Second Roach Pond. AMC trail crews will be working over the next several years to extend the trail over the south summit of Shaw Mtn. and on to West Branch Pond Camps.

EMMIT BROOK TRAIL
(AMC; MEDAWISLA LODGE, P. 86, AND MAP 2: D3)

From Smithtown Rd. (1,283 ft.) to:	⇅	↗	⟳
Lower Shaw Mtn. Rd. (1,520 ft.)	1.3 mi.	240 ft.	0:45

This trail provides a convenient link between Medawisla Lodge and Shaw Mtn. Trail. From the Medawisla guest parking lot, walk the entrance road out to Smithtown Rd. Emmit Brook Trail begins immediately across the road from this jct.

Emmit Brook Trail follows the route of a 1950s logging road and has been graveled and graded for family biking and easy hiking. The trail meanders southeast along the course of Emmit Brook, reaching Lower Shaw Mtn. Rd. 0.5 mi. north of the start of Shaw Mtn. Trail.

HINKLEY COVE TRAIL
(AMC; MEDAWISLA LODGE, P. 86, AND MAP 2: D3)

From Medawisla guest parking lot (1,280 ft.) to:	⇅	↗	⟳
Point on Second Roach Pond (1,280 ft.)	0.8 mi.	30 ft.	0:25

Hinkley Cove Trail traces a route used by river drivers in late 1800s to access the cove from the Second Roach Pond outlet dam. Hinkley Cove was the site of many logjams due to slow moving water and foul winds. The trail leaves the Medawisla guest parking lot and leads west to a snowmobile trail bridge across the Roach River just west of Second Roach Pond. Beyond, the wide gravel trail wends through the woods around Hinkley Cove, passes the jct. with Hinkley Connector Trail at 0.6 mi., and arrives at the start of a long point that reaches east out into Second Roach Pond. Here is a small sand and gravel beach. Just north of this spot is a large gravel esker where there are great views of the Hinkley Cove wetlands complex, one of the most significant inland waterfowl wading environments in the Moosehead region.

NORTH LAKE TRAIL (AMC; MAP 2: C3)

From Nahmakanta Rd. (1,300 ft.) to:	⇅	↗	⟳
Remote campsite on north shore of Second Roach Pond (1,280 ft.)	4.1 mi.	120 ft.	2:05

SEC 2

This trail through the woods on the north side of Second Roach Pond was built for mountain biking and cross-country skiing, but it is equally suited for summer hiking. The trail starts on Nahmakanta Rd. From the jct. of Smithtown Rd. and the entrance drive to Medawisla, drive west on Smithtown Rd. for 0.9 mi. Turn right (north) on Nahmakanta Rd. and drive for 1.2 mi. Park on the side of the road by a gate at the start of the trail. The trail meanders east through the mildly rolling terrain. On the stretch along the lakeshore are fine views south to Shaw Mtn. and Trout Mtn. At 3.7 mi., the trail touches Nahmakanta Rd., then turns sharply south to end at a remote campsite on Second Roach Pond. This site can also be reached by canoe or kayak.

An alternative start to North Lake Trail is to hike part of Hinkley Cove Trail with Hinkley Connector Trail, then walk north on Nahmakanta Rd.

LAKESIDE TRAIL (AMC; MAP 2: C3)

From Medawisla guest parking lot (1,280 ft.) to:	⇅	↗	⟳
Campsite and boat launch on Second Roach Pond at end of Trout Pond Rd. (1,280 ft.)	2.6 mi.	150 ft.	1:25

This trail follows the route of the earliest road in Shawtown Township, the Yoke Pond Rd., which dates to the 1840s. This wide gravel trail is designed for mountain biking and cross-country skiing, but it is equally suited for hiking. From the Medawisla guest parking lot, stroll past the main lodge, then strike east on the trail. It rises gradually up the slope south of Second Roach Pond and reaches a jct. with Shaw Mtn. Cutoff on the right; this spur leads 0.5 mi. south to Smithtown Rd. at its jct. with Lower Shaw Mtn. Rd. Lakeside Trail continues east, more or less on a contour, to end at the boat launch and campsite on the pond at the end of Trout Pond Rd.

■ HEDGEHOG MTN. (2,130 FT.)

Hedgehog Mtn. is north of First West Branch Pond and Second West Branch Pond and south of Shaw Mtn. and Medawisla Lodge. The trail starts from Frenchtown Rd.

Directions from Greenville: From the blinking traffic light in the center of Greenville on ME 15/6, follow Lily Bay Rd. north 17.6 mi. to Frenchtown Rd., a wide dirt road on the right marked by both a street sign and a long row of mailboxes. Turn right onto Frenchtown Rd. and drive 10.0 mi. to the trailhead on the left. Parking is along the road. (*Note:* If you reach the driveway for West Branch Pond Camps, you've gone 0.2 mi. too far.)

Directions from Medawisla Lodge: From the jct. of the entrance road to the lodge and Smithtown Rd., drive southwest on Smithtown Rd. for 1.1 mi. Turn right (south) on Lower Shaw Mtn. Rd. and drive for 5.6 mi. then turn left on Frenchtown Rd. and proceed another 2.6 mi. to the trailhead on the left.

HEDGEHOG MTN. TRAIL (AMC; MAP 2: D3)

From Frenchtown Rd. (1,500 ft.) to:	⇅	↗	⟳
Hedgehog Mtn. summit (2,130 ft.)	1.75 mi.	630 ft.	1:10

This path dates back to the 1880s when West Branch Pond Camps was first founded as a sporting camp. The old trail was reclaimed and improved by AMC trail crews in 2017. From the road, the trail meanders north through mixed hardwood and softwood forests. The grade is gradual for the first 1.2 mi. The final 0.5 mi. is more challenging, climbing along a ridge to a flat, wooded summit. There are plans for AMC trail crews to continue the trail northward in the future, eventually connecting with Shaw Mtn.

■ GULF HAGAS
GULF HAGAS LOOP (MATC; MAP 2: F2–F3)

Cumulative from KI Rd. trailhead parking area (680 ft.) to:	⇅	↗	⟳
AT and West Branch of Pleasant River (658 ft.)	0.2 mi.	-20 ft.	0:05
Rim Trail and Pleasant River Tote Rd. via AT (920 ft.)	1.5 mi.	260 ft.	0:55
Gulf Hagas Cutoff via Rim Trail (1,000 ft.)	3.2 mi.	700 ft.	1:55
Head of the Gulf at Pleasant River Tote Rd. via Rim Trail (1,150 ft.)	4.3 mi.	850 ft.	2:35
AT via Pleasant River Tote Rd.	6.4 mi.	850 ft.	3:40
Complete Gulf Hagas Loop	7.9 mi.	870 ft.	4:25

This hike combines a section of the AT, Rim Trail, and Pleasant River Tote Rd. for a complete circuit through Gulf Hagas. From the KI Rd.

parking area, follow the spur trail downhill to a jct. with the AT at 0.2 mi. Turn right, and quickly reach the south bank of the West Branch of the Pleasant River. Ford the river (knee-deep in normal water conditions) to reach a jct. with Pleasant River Tote Rd. at 0.4 mi. Turn left (west) and walk through the Hermitage, a 35-acre preserve of old-growth white pines that is a National Natural Landmark protected by the Maine chapter of The Nature Conservancy. At 1.5 mi., the AT bears sharply right (north). To enter the Gulf Hagas area proper, proceed straight ahead and ford Gulf Hagas Brook (no bridge; use caution in high water).

Immediately after the crossing, the trail reaches a jct. Pleasant River Tote Rd. continues straight ahead for 2.2 mi. to the rocky island called Head of the Gulf. Most hikers use this trail for the return trip. Rim Trail leaves left and descends steeply along Gulf Hagas Brook past Screw Auger Falls and on to the rim of the canyon. The trail then continues west, and at 0.7 mi., a side trail leads left to Hammond Street Pitch, a point high above the canyon that offers a fine view of the gorge. Return to Rim Trail and turn left (at 0.9 mi., a short connector trail leads back to Pleasant River Rd.).

Continuing along Rim Trail, at 1.2 mi. from Pleasant River Rd., a series of side paths lead to views of the Jaws, where the river squeezes around a slate spur and narrows in many places. Back on Rim Trail, in another 0.5 mi., Gulf Hagas Cutoff diverges right, crosses Pleasant River Tote Rd. in 0.2 mi., and meets the AT in 1.2 mi. To the left, a spur trail leads to a viewpoint below Buttermilk Falls.

Beyond, the canyon gradually becomes shallower, and at times, the trail approaches the banks of the West Branch of the Pleasant River. At 2.5 mi. from Pleasant River Rd., the trail passes Billings Falls. At 2.6 mi., the trail reaches the ledge above Stair Falls, where the narrow river drops into a large pool. In another 0.1 mi., the trail bears sharply away from the river. (At this point, a short side trail leads left to the edge of the river near Head of the Gulf, where you can see some interesting logging artifacts.)

The trail reaches a jct. at 2.8 mi. from the AT and Pleasant River Rd. To the right (east), the Pleasant River Tote Rd. proceeds on a contour high above Gulf Hagas back to the jct. with the AT in 2.2 mi. Although it is often very marshy and wet, the road offers a quicker return than the Rim Trail. To the left, Head of the Gulf Trail leads 1.2 mi. to a bridge over the West Branch of the Pleasant River (an alternative route to Gulf Hagas during high-water conditions).

SEC 2

HEAD OF THE GULF TRAIL (AMC; MAP 2: F2–E2)

Cumulative from Upper Valley Rd. trailhead (1,150 ft.) to:	⮍	↗	⏱
Bridge over West Branch of Pleasant River (1,150 ft.)	0.5 mi.	0 ft.	0:15
Rim Trail and Pleasant River Tote Rd. (1,150 ft.)	1.7 mi.	0 ft.	0:50

This trail provides access to the Gulf Hagas area with the advantage of not requiring a ford of the West Branch of the Pleasant River. So, in high water conditions or with small children or otherwise, this trail is a good choice. The trail leaves the east side of Upper Valley Rd. at an information kiosk. This point is 0.9 mi. north of the jct. of KI Rd. and Greenville Rd. Trailhead parking is 50 ft. past (north) the trailhead on the left.

The trail starts out wide and flat. In 200 ft., bear left at a jct. At 0.2 mi., the trail crosses a bridge over a small brook, and in another 0.2 mi., it crosses a grassy floodplain on bog bridges. At 0.5 mi., the trail joins a gravel road and turns right to cross the West Branch of the Pleasant River on a bridge. It leaves the road to the right at 0.6 mi. and continues as a wide path. An unmarked angler's trail leaves left to Lloyd Pond at 0.9 mi., and just ahead, the trail crosses the rocky outlet of that pond. Following a stretch of rocky footing, the trail enters a balsam fir stand at 1.4 mi. After the trail crosses a brook and ascends briefly, a short spur to the right leads to views of the West Branch of the Pleasant River. The main trail makes a short descent before it takes a sharp right turn and enters NPS land (yellow sign). Beyond, the trail narrows and crosses a brook on a split-log bridge. At 1.7 mi., it reaches a jct. To the right, Rim Trail leads along the rim of Gulf Hagas canyon for 2.8 mi. to a jct. with the AT near Screw Auger Falls. Straight ahead, Pleasant River Tote Rd. follows an easier route high above the river canyon, reaching a jct. with the AT in 2.2 mi.

APPALACHIAN TRAIL CORRIDOR

■ BARREN MTN. (2,670 FT.)

The AT traverses Barren Mtn. in Elliotsville Township, the highest and most accessible of the five mountain peaks of the rugged Barren–Chairback Range. Barren Slide and Barren Ledges on the south side of the mountain offer excellent lookouts over Bodfish Intervale and Lake Onawa to Borestone Mtn. The abandoned fire tower (on the summit since 1951) is in disrepair. The AT on the west side of Barren Mtn. can be reached from Monson or Greenville.

AT NORTHBOUND, MONSON APPROACH
(MATC; MAP 2: G1–G2 AND F1–F2)

Cumulative from parking area near Otter Pond (690 ft.) to:	↕	↗	↺
AT east of Long Pond Stream Lean-to (950 ft.)	0.7 mi.	260 ft.	0:30
Side trail to Barren Slide (1,950 ft.)	1.8 mi.	1,260 ft.	1:30
Barren Ledges (2,000 ft.)	2.0 mi.	1,310 ft.	1:40
Barren Mtn. summit (2,670 ft.)	3.8 mi.	1,980 ft.	2:55

SEC
2

Directions from ME 15 in Monson: Drive north 0.5 mi. to Elliotsville Rd. Turn right and drive 7.7 mi. to a bridge over Big Wilson Stream. Cross the bridge and take an immediate left. Follow Bodfish Valley Rd. across the Central Maine & Quebec Railway tracks at 8.4 mi. Pass the trailhead for Borestone Mtn. Sanctuary at 8.5 mi. Just beyond, the road turns to gravel, levels off on the west shoulder of Borestone Mtn., and descends. At 10.5 mi., the road narrows and enters the site of the former Bodfish Farm. At 10.7 mi., bear left and cross a bridge over Long Pond Stream. Continue and turn left onto a dirt road at 11.3 mi. to reach a small cul-de-sac parking area at 12.0 mi.

An informal side trail leaves the rear of the parking area and goes north and then east for 0.7 mi. to a jct. with the AT just east of Long Pond Stream Lean-to. The trail is flagged most of the way and is easy to follow. Nearing the AT, the flagged trail bears right to avoid a muddy stretch. At the AT jct., bear right (east) to continue to Barren Mtn.

The AT climbs the northwestern slope of Barren Mtn., gradually at first, crossing an old woods road. The trail steepens and becomes rockier on its route through the spruce and fir. Beyond a small clearing, the trail bears left and becomes easier. On the crest of the ridge, the AT rises to a jct. on the right at 1.8 mi. Here, a blue-blazed side trail leads 250 ft. down to the head of Barren Slide, an interesting mass of boulders with a southerly vista. At 2.0 mi., the AT reaches the open Barren Ledges and another striking view. The old tower atop wooded Barren Mtn. is in sight to the east. The route bears left and winds along the northern slope of the range over rough terrain to the base of the summit cone at 3.0 mi. It then climbs steeply through boulders for a short distance to the summit at 3.8 mi.

The AT continues 12.0 mi. northeast over the remaining peaks of the range—Fourth Mtn., Third Mtn., Columbus Mtn., and Chairback Mtn.—to the KI Rd. in the valley of the West Branch of the Pleasant River. This hike is a backpacking trip of several days over rough terrain.

AT NORTHBOUND, GREENVILLE APPROACH
(MATC; MAP 2: G1–G2 AND F1–F2)

Cumulative from trailhead parking at AT crossing (700 ft.) to:	↕	↗	⟳
Long Pond Stream (650 ft.)	0.1 mi.	-50 ft.	0:03
Side trail to Long Pond Stream Lean-to (900 ft.)	0.9 mi.	250 ft.	0:35
Spur trail from parking area near Otter Pond (950 ft.)	1.0 mi.	300 ft.	0:40
Barren Mtn. summit (2,670 ft.)	4.1 mi.	2,000 ft.	3:05

Directions from ME 15 in the center of Greenville: Head east on Pleasant St. to where the road bears right around the airport. Continue on the gravel road and eventually cross Big Wilson Stream at the south end of Lower Wilson Pond. The road turns into KI Rd. (marked by a small blue street sign). Continue on it and pass access roads for Rum Ridge and Rum Pond. At 7.3 mi., turn right onto another gravel road just before Indian Pond (this road is known locally as Indian Pond Rd. but is not marked as such). After the turn, drive over the pond outlet. At 7.5 mi., turn left onto another gravel road. Continue on this road, making sure to stay straight at 9.2 mi. where other spur roads come in. At a fork at 11.3 mi., bear right. At about 13 mi., the AT crosses and the road leads right and goes down a hill. Park in the area of the AT sign.

The AT leaves the road and descends 0.1 mi. to cross Long Pond Stream at the normally knee-deep ford. A fixed guide rope is available for assistance in crossing. Beyond, the trail turns east, passing Slugundy Gorge. At 0.9 mi., the route reaches a blue-blazed side trail leading 150 yd. to Long Pond Stream Lean-to. Just ahead, the unmarked spur from the parking area north of Otter Pond enters from the right. See the prior Monson approach description for the AT route to the summit of Barren Mtn. from this point.

■ FOURTH MTN. (2,383 FT.), THIRD MTN. (2,061 FT.), AND COLUMBUS MTN. (2,326 FT.)

These three peaks, bookended by Barren Mtn. to the west and Chairback Mtn. to the east, form the heart of the Barren–Chairback Range. The AT connects the craggy summits of all three and passes by a number of fine viewpoints as well as two high ponds. The route is described northbound from the summit of Barren Mtn.

AT NORTHBOUND (MATC; MAP 2: F2–F3)

Cumulative from Barren Mtn. summit (2,670 ft.) to:	↿⇂	↗	○
Cloud Pond side trail to Cloud Pond Lean-to (2,490 ft.)	0.9 mi.	-180 ft.	0:25
Fourth Mtn. summit (2,383 ft.)	3.0 mi.	430 ft.	1:45
Third Mtn. Trail (1,800 ft.)	5.0 mi.	430 ft.	2:45
Monument Cliff on Third Mtn. (2,061 ft.)	5.5 mi.	750 ft.	3:10
West Chairback Pond outlet (1,760 ft.)	6.1 mi.	750 ft.	3:35
Columbus Mtn. (2,350 ft.)	7.4 mi.	1,350 ft.	4:25
Chairback Gap Lean-to (1,930 ft.)	7.8 mi.	1,350 ft.	4:40
Chairback Mtn. summit (2,190 ft.)	8.3 mi.	1,600 ft.	5:00

SEC 2

From the fire tower on the summit of Barren Mtn., the AT heads east along the high ridgeline through thick spruce and fir, trending easily down to the jct. with a side trail on the right that leads 0.3 mi. to Cloud Pond Lean-to on the pretty tarn, Cloud Pond. The trail is reasonably level for the next 0.5 mi., then drops abruptly and steeply, using rock stairs to reach the sag below. Cross a brook on the floor of the sag, then hike easily to Fourth Mtn. Bog and cross it on a long string of bog bridges. The hump of Fourth Mtn. can be seen ahead, and soon enough, the trail begins to steadily ascend the steep slope. On the summit plateau at 3.0 mi., there are good views of the surrounding peaks and valleys. Continuing on, the AT descends very steeply off the peak, then becomes steep to moderate before reaching the low point between Fourth Mtn. and Third Mtn. The next stretch is a strenuous one, with the trail leading into several gullies and climbing up and out to open ledges. After climbing over a knob, the trail descends, and Third Mtn. Trail crosses the AT at 5.0 mi.

The trail soon reaches the base of Third Mtn. summit cone and begins to climb. The steep ascent arrives at an open slab on top of Third Mtn., then continues along the craggy ridge to the long, flat ledge called Monument Cliff, where the wide-open view to the north, west, and east is one to behold. The scene includes all of the White Cap Range peaks, Baker Mtn., Elephant Mtn., Indian Mtn., Long Pond, and the valley of the West Branch of the Pleasant River. From the cliff, the AT continues along the ridge before descending into the sag at the base of Columbus Mtn., where it crosses the outlet stream of West Chairback Pond. The pond is a short distance uphill to the right and well worth a visit. The trail rises moderately at first, then more steeply. The angle eases at a viewpoint, and the going is more gradual to the open ledge on top of Columbus Mtn. at 7.4 mi. From the summit, the trail drops steeply to Chairback Gap Lean-to. Another drop next to the shelter leads to the actual gap, which is often wet and muddy. The trail bears right along a small stream, then begins to climb again, finally arriving at the open ledges on Chairback Mtn. at 8.3 mi. From there, it is 3.4 mi. down to the KI Rd.

■ CHAIRBACK MTN. (2,190 FT.)

This craggy peak in Bowdoin College East Grant Township rises south of the West Branch of the Pleasant River and forms the eastern end of the Barren–Chairback Range, which the AT traverses. To reach the trailhead parking, follow the driving directions for Gulf Hagas, which lead to the AT parking area on KI Rd.

CHAIRBACK MTN. VIA AT SOUTHBOUND (MATC; MAP 2: F3)

Cumulative from KI Rd. parking (680 ft.) to:	⇅	↗	↺
Side trail to East Chairback Pond (1,650 ft.)	1.9 mi.	970 ft.	1:30
Chairback Mtn. summit (2,190 ft.)	4.1 mi.	1,500 ft.	2:50

From the parking area, follow the spur trail downhill (north) to a jct. with the AT at 0.2 mi. Turn left (west) and hike uphill to cross KI Rd. at 0.7 mi. Beyond, the trail climbs moderately up the mountainside, passing a spring at 1.4 mi. Ahead at 1.9 mi., a side trail leads downhill off the ridge 0.2 mi. to East Chairback Pond. Proceeding south on the AT, continue climbing a moderate grade to reach the base of the peak at 3.0 mi. Then climb over steeper open ledges and up a talus slope to reach the summit of Chairback Mtn., with its outstanding views of the White Cap Range, Baker Mtn., and Elephant Mtn., at 4.1 mi.

Farther south on the AT, it is 0.5 mi. to Chairback Gap Lean-to, 0.9 mi. to the wooded summit of Columbus Mtn., 2.2 mi. to a short side trail leading to West Chairback Pond, 2.8 mi. to Monument Cliff on Third Mtn., and 3.3 mi. to the jct. with Third Mtn. Trail, which leads 1.4 mi. to Chairback Mtn. Rd.

■ WHITE CAP MTN. (3,654 FT.)

White Cap Mtn. in Bowdoin College Grant East Township is the highest point on the AT between Katahdin and Bigelow and the highest peak in the east–west range of mountains that includes Hay Mtn., West Peak, and Gulf Hagas Mtn. Rising north of the West Branch of the Pleasant River in the heart of the 100MW, White Cap Mtn. offers outstanding views from its high ridges and alpine summit. There are three approaches to White Cap Mtn.: from the north via the AT from Logan Brook Rd.; from the south via White Brook Trail and the AT; from the south and west via the AT across the peaks of the White Cap Range.

SEC 2

AT SOUTHBOUND (MATC; MAP 2: E4)

Cumulative from parking at gate on logging road (1,635 ft.) to:	↕	↗	○
AT (1,587 ft.)	0.4 mi.	-50 ft.	0:10
Logan Brook Lean-to (2,400 ft.)	1.9 mi.	810 ft.	1:20
White Cap Mtn. summit (3,654 ft.)	2.8 mi.	2,067 ft.	2:25

From the blinking traffic light in the center of Greenville on ME 15/6, follow Lily Bay Rd. north for 17.6 mi. to Frenchtown Rd., a wide dirt road on the right marked by both a street sign and a long row of mailboxes. Turn right onto Frenchtown Rd. and drive 10.3 mi. to the driveway of West Branch Pond Camps on the right. In 0.8 mi. beyond WBPC, Shaw Mtn. Rd. leaves to the left; bear right here. The road ahead gets increasingly narrow, wet, and rough and may not be passable by regular passenger cars. Bear right at a fork at 1.6 mi. beyond WBPC. In another 1.2 mi., the road, now called Logan Brook Rd., is gated. Park on either side of the road before the gate, but do not block the gate.

Walk east along Logan Brook Rd. for 0.4 mi. to its intersection with the AT (sign). There is a spring on the right 100 yd. farther along the road. The AT rises steadily up the north side of White Cap at a mostly moderate grade. At 0.8 mi., from Logan Brook Rd., cross a dry creek bed and join the route of an old tote road, which rises gradually up the ravine of Logan Brook. Logan Brook Lean-to is reached at 1.6 mi. The trail climbs at a moderate to steep grade on rough terrain to reach a contour and then, soon after, makes a sharp right on the ridge. After several more stepped rises, the trail arrives at a viewpoint on the right at 2.0 mi., where the northeast ridge of White Cap is in full view, plus Big Spencer Mtn. and Katahdin. The moderate ascent continues, and 0.3 mi. beyond the viewpoint, a long series of rock steps (dubbed the "stairway to heaven" by MATC maintainers) begins. Treeline is reached at 2.6 mi., and here the views north over the 100MW are unobstructed and grand, and now include Big and Little Boardman mountains and Jo-Mary Mtn. The AT rounds the ridge to the south side and continues to climb in the open. The scree fields of the exposed summit area soon lead to the top of White Cap at 3.0 mi. (sign).

Panoramic views from the summit include the long ridge of Saddleback to the east, Little Spruce Mtn. and Big Spruce Mtn. just to the southeast, Baker Mtn. and the other summits of the White Cap Range to the west, Big Moose Mtn. to the southwest, the rugged summits of the Barren–Chairback Range to the south, Big Spencer Mtn. to the northwest, and the vast lake country to the north, ranging all the way to Katahdin. The view is arguably one of the finest in the state.

WHITE BROOK TRAIL (MATC; MAP 2: E3–E4)

Cumulative from end of logging road (1,950 ft.) to:	↧↥	⤢	○
White Brook crossing (2,600 ft.)	1.4 mi.	650 ft.	1:00
AT (2,950 ft.)	1.9 mi.	1,000 ft.	1:25
White Cap Mtn. summit (3,654 ft.) via AT	3.0 mi.	1,700 ft.	2:20

To reach White Brook Trail (the former route of the AT, still maintained by MATC), turn left (northwest) off ME 11 5.5 mi. north of Brownville Junction. The sign for Katahdin Iron Works at the turnoff marks the start of a 6.8-mi. drive on KI Rd. from ME 11 to a gate at Katahdin Iron Works, an interesting state historical site with a blast furnace and a beehive charcoal burner. Register at the gate and pay a fee to enter the KI Jo-Mary Multiple Use Forest, a 175,000-acre block of privately owned commercial forestland between Greenville and Brownville.

Bear right after driving through the gate and cross the West Branch of the Pleasant River. At the 3.0-mi. mark, take the right fork. At about 5.8 mi. from Katahdin Iron Works, the road crosses the "High Bridge," a high, narrow bridge over White Brook. At the next jct., continue straight ahead up the west side of White Brook. (The left fork leads to Hay Brook and Gulf Hagas.) Follow the very rough gravel road (high-clearance vehicle necessary) for another 3.8 mi., taking the main branch at each fork, and park to the side of the road just south of where it crosses two brooks. (The culverts have been removed, and this is likely as far as you can drive, even with a four-wheel drive.)

The trail follows the old logging road uphill for 1.0 mi. to a large wood yard. The White Cap–Hay Mtn. sag is clearly visible from this yard. A blue-blazed trail leaves the left side of the yard at the end of the road and climbs the southern slope toward the sag through a heavily logged area. At 1.4 mi., the trail crosses White Brook near the ruins of the old fire warden's cabin. Just beyond is a jct. To the left, White Brook Trail climbs more steeply and reaches a jct. with the AT in another 0.5 mi. From this point, it is a 1.1-mi. hike along a high ridge to the open summit of White Cap Mtn. To the right, the very steep and eroded Fire Warden's Trail (not recommended) climbs 0.8 mi. to join the AT just 0.3 mi. west of the summit.

■ GULF HAGAS MTN. (2,683 FT.), WEST PEAK (3,178 FT.), AND HAY MTN. (3,244 FT.)

In addition to White Cap Mtn., three other high peaks make up the White Cap Range: Gulf Hagas Mtn., West Peak, and Hay Mtn. The AT traverses the range and offers some of the finest ridge walking in the state. Visitors can explore the range in a long day via a loop hike with considerable elevation gain and loss, ascending via the AT from the Pleasant River and returning via White Brook Trail and logging roads, but the trek is perhaps better done as a multiday backpacking trip. Several campsites are available along the AT.

To reach the trailhead parking for the AT, drive north on ME 11 from Brownville Junction for 5.5 mi. Turn left (west) on Katahdin Iron Works Rd. and drive 6.8 mi. to the Katahdin Iron Works Checkpoint (register and pay fee). Beyond the gate, take the right fork. At 3.4 mi. from the gatehouse, the road reaches a second fork. Stay left here, crossing the West Branch of the Pleasant River on a bridge. KI Rd. reaches the parking area on the right at 6.7 mi. from the gatehouse.

AT NORTHBOUND (MATC; MAP 2: F3 AND E3–E4)

Cumulative from KI Rd. trailhead parking area (680 ft.) to:	⇅	↗	↺
Gulf Hagas Mtn. summit (2,690 ft.)	6.6 mi.	2,000 ft.	4:20
West Peak summit (3,178 ft.)	8.2 mi.	2,750 ft.	5:30
Hay Mtn. summit (3,250 ft.)	9.8 mi.	3,250 ft.	6:30
White Cap Mtn. summit (3,654 ft.)	11.5 mi.	3,900 ft.	7:40

From the KI Rd. parking area, follow the spur trail downhill to a jct. with the AT at 0.2 mi. Turn right, and quickly reach the south bank of the West Branch of the Pleasant River. Ford the river (knee-deep in normal water conditions) to reach a jct. with Pleasant River Tote Rd. at 0.4 mi. Turn left (west) here and walk through the Hermitage, a 35-acre preserve of old-growth white pines that is a National Natural Landmark protected by the Maine chapter of TNC. At 1.5 mi., the AT bears sharply right (north).

The trail climbs steadily up the valley of Gulf Hagas Brook, passing Gulf Hagas Cutoff on the left early on. Nearing Gulf Hagas Mtn., the AT crosses Gulf Hagas Brook and reaches the Carl Newhall Lean-to on the left. Soon after the shelter, the trail begins to climb Gulf Hagas Mtn., moderately at first and then more steeply on switchbacks through the thick spruce and fir forest. Finally, the angle eases and the trail meanders along the summit ridge (6.6 mi.) through several semi-open clearings. With West Peak in view just ahead, the AT drops down into the gap between the peaks and arrives at a small clearing, Sidney Tappan Campsite.

The trail continues north on the course of an old skidder road, rising up the side of West Peak. The AT leaves the wide track to the right and ascends steeply and steadily through the dense woods on switchbacks and occasional rock staircases to the wooded summit of West Peak at 8.2 mi. Descending steeply off the northeast side of the mountain, the trail reaches the saddle below Hay Mtn. It climbs up and out to the west shoulder of Hay Mtn. and, after a brief easy stretch, ascends steadily to the broad summit plateau of Hay Mtn. at 9.8 mi.

Below in the next saddle, White Brook Trail enters from the right. This old AT route leads down the south side of the range to an old logging road, which then leads to the base of the mountains and the West Branch of the Pleasant River. Continuing the ascent, the AT reaches the White Cap summit ridge, where the angle eases briefly, then the steady ascent resumes. The old and very steep fire warden's trail enters from the right, and soon after, the trail breaks out of the trees on the summit of White Cap Mtn., where there is an extensive talus field and outstanding views south and east. A spur path from the summit leads a few yards north for a big view over the 100MW to Katahdin. Big Spencer Mtn. dominates the scene to the west.

The AT continues north from this point toward Logan Brook. It's worth the effort to follow the trail a short distance ahead over the rocky terrain for more excellent views to the north.

■ NESUNTABUNT MTN. (1,550 FT.)

This rugged mountain rises to the west of Nahmakanta Lake in T1 R11 WELS. Its summit offers excellent views of Katahdin as well as views over the wilderness region around Nahmakanta Lake. The AT traverses the mountain, and access is described via the AT Southbound.

The AT trailhead for Nesuntabunt Mtn. is on Wadleigh Pond Rd. in the northwest corner of Nahmakanta PL. To get there, follow driving directions for the north trailhead of Debsconeag Backcountry Trail on p. 136. The AT crosses en route.

AT SOUTHBOUND (MATC; MAP 2: B4–B5)

From AT crossing on Wadleigh Pond Rd.
(850 ft.) to:

	⇅	↗	↻
Nesuntabunt Mtn., north summit (1,550 ft.)	1.2 mi.	700 ft.	1:00

Follow the AT on a gradual climb southward. The grade becomes moderate for a stretch, and then the steep climbing via switchbacks begins. Ahead on the north summit of the mountain, reach a jct., where a 250-ft. side trail leads to splendid views.

SEC 2

■ POTAYWADJO RIDGE (1,270 FT.)

The open ledges atop this extensive ridgeline in T1 R10 WELS offer excellent views northeast over Pemadumcook Lake and Katahdin, east to Lower Jo-Mary Lake, and south to Jo-Mary Mtn. Potaywadjo Ridge is reached from the AT via a side trail. Make the trek as a long day hike or as a pleasant overnight trip. Two campsite options are possible.

From ME 11 in T4 R9 NWP, just south of the Piscataquis–Penobscot county line and about halfway between Brownville Junction and Millinocket, turn north on Jo-Mary Rd. and quickly reach the Jo-Mary Checkpoint. A fee is charged to pass through the gate. Drive 12 mi. on Jo-Mary Rd. to the AT crossing just after the bridge over Cooper Brook, where there is parking on the right.

AT NORTHBOUND AND POTAYWADJO RIDGE TRAIL (MATC; USGS NAHMAKANTA STREAM QUAD, GAZETTEER MAP 42, MATC MAP 2)

Cumulative from Jo-Mary Rd.
(608 ft.) to:

	⇅	↗	↻
Antler's Campsite (520 ft.)	4.4 mi.	50 ft.	2:10
Potaywadjo Ridge Trail at Lower Jo-Mary Lake (550 ft.)	5.7 mi.	50 ft.	2:50
Potaywadjo Ridge summit (1,270 ft.)	6.5 mi.	750 ft.	3:40

The AT heads north along the route of Cooper Brook before trending away. A side trail on the right at 1.3 mi. leads to Cooper Pond. At 2.6 mi., cross an old woods road next to a snowmobile bridge over Cooper Brook. Ahead, the trail soon crosses several outlet streams of Mud Pond, which is west of the trail at this point. Over the next rise, the AT wends west through the woods south of Lower Jo-Mary Lake, crossing an old logging road en route. At 4.4 mi., a side trail on the right leads to Antler's Campsite on a point cloaked in red pines near the west end of Lower Jo-Mary Lake.

Beyond, the trail winds around the head of the lake, crosses an inlet, and reaches the side trail to Potaywadjo Ridge at 5.7 mi. (a beautiful sand beach is just 0.2 mi. north, and Potaywadjo Lean-to is 2.0 mi. north). Potaywadjo Ridge Trail climbs steadily at a moderate to steep grade before easing off and wending north over ledges to end at a lookout with views southward to Jo-Mary Mtn. and Jo-Mary Lake.

BORESTONE MTN. AUDUBON SANCTUARY

■ BORESTONE MTN. (1,981 FT.)

This rugged mountain in Elliotsville Township is the central natural feature of the Borestone Mtn. Sanctuary, a 1,693-acre wildlife preserve owned and managed by Maine Audubon. Rising steeply above Lake Onawa, Borestone offers 360-degree views from its two craggy peaks. Three small ponds are found high on its southwestern slopes. Two trails, Base and Summit, combine to reach the top of the mountain, and the access road can be used to form a nice loop hike.

To reach the sanctuary, drive 0.5 mi. north on ME 15 from the center of Monson. Turn right on Elliotsville Rd. and drive 7.7 mi. to Big Wilson Stream. Cross the bridge and immediately turn left on Bodfish Valley Rd. and drive 0.6 mi. up the hill. Cross the tracks of the Central Maine & Quebec Railway and proceed another 0.1 mi. to the trailhead (sign) on the right. A parking area is on the left side of the road.

BASE TRAIL (MA; USGS BARREN MTN. WEST AND MONSON EAST QUADS, GAZETTEER MAP 41, MA BORESTONE MTN. AUDUBON MAP)

From Bodfish Valley Rd. (850 ft.) to:	⇅	↗	⏱
Sunrise Pond, visitor center, and Summit Trail (1,332 ft.)	1.0 mi.	480 ft.	0:45

Follow the access road through a gate. Just beyond is an information kiosk on the left and the start of Base Trail. A toilet is to the right. (*Note:* A small day-use fee is charged, and no dogs are allowed.) The trail, marked with green triangles, quickly reaches a rock staircase and continues upward through the forest at a moderate grade. In 0.5 mi., the angle eases, and soon the trail reaches the jct. with a side trail on the right, which leads 0.1 mi. to a nice viewpoint overlooking Little Greenwood Pond and Big Greenwood Pond. Base Trail continues easily ahead, then descends gradually to the access road at 0.9 mi. Turn left on the road and soon pass two privy stalls on the right. The road then winds around a corner to reach Sunrise

Pond and the Robert T. Moore Visitor Center at 1.0 mi. The center features wildlife displays and information about the interesting history of the mountain. A bench and picnic table make for a good rest spot and a place to enjoy the view of the upper reaches of Borestone, which rise steeply above the far shore of the pond. A short side trail, Peregrine Trail, leaves opposite the center and leads 0.4 mi. northwest to ledge viewpoints overlooking Midday Pond and Sunset Pond (stay right 0.2 mi. along this side trail; the left fork is for sanctuary staff only).

SEC 2

SUMMIT TRAIL (MA; USGS BARREN MTN. WEST AND MONSON EAST QUADS, GAZETTEER MAP 41, MA BORESTONE MTN. AUDUBON MAP)

Cumulative from Sunrise Pond and visitor center (1,332 ft.) to:	⇅	↗	↺
Borestone Mtn., west summit (1,970 ft.)	0.75 mi.	640 ft.	0:40
Borestone Mtn., east summit (1,981 ft.)	1.0 mi.	710 ft.	0:50

Leaving from the visitor center, Summit Trail follows the south shore of Sunrise Pond. Cross the pond outlet (*Caution:* lots of poison ivy), and immediately after, reach the jct. with Fox Pen Trail on the right, which makes a 0.3-mi. loop to some of the old pens of the former fox ranch that Robert T. Moore operated on the mountain in the early 1900s.

Bear left to continue on Summit Trail, which swings around the north shore of the pond. At 0.2 mi., begin a steep ascent away from the pond on a series of rock steps to attain the ridge proper. After a short level stretch, make a steep climb on rocks and roots. Ahead, the angle eases briefly, then there are more rocks and roots. Scramble over a steep bulge above to emerge from the trees. Two iron rungs and a handrail assist with the climb through the ledges beyond. More scrambling leads to a second handrail. At 0.75 mi., one more rung step and a low handrail lead up to the western summit of Borestone, a wide-open crag with outstanding views of Onawa Lake, the rugged ridgeline of Barren Mtn., Baker Mtn., Big Moose Mtn., Big Greenwood Pond, Sebec Lake, and more. Drop into a notch between the peaks, and then make a brief climb to the eastern and highest summit of Borestone at 1.0 mi. The iron bolts of the former fire tower (removed in 1950) remain. Views are spectacular in all directions.

PEAKS–KENNY STATE PARK

■ BIRCH MTN. (1,090 FT.)

Much of the northeastern quadrant of Birch Mtn. lies within Peaks–Kenny State Park in Dover-Foxcroft, an 839-acre park that features more than

1 mi. of shoreline on Sebec Lake. The park also has a 56-site campground and a sandy beach that offers great swimming, as well as fine views north to Borestone Mtn. and Barren Mtn. A trail makes a pleasant loop over the wooded slopes of Birch Mtn.

From downtown Dover-Foxcroft at the jct. of ME 16/6 and ME 153, drive north on ME 153 for 4.6 mi. Turn left on State Park Rd. (sign) and drive 1.1 mi. to the park entrance station (fee). Reach the large beach parking lot in another 0.5 mi. The grassy promenade and beach on Sebec Lake are just beyond. Restrooms are to the east of the parking lot (right as you are looking at the lake).

BIRCH MTN. LEDGE TRAIL (MBPL; USGS SEBEC LAKE, GAZETTEER MAP 32, MBPL PEAKS–KENNY STATE PARK MAP)

Cumulative from beach parking lot (330 ft.) to:	↕	↗	↻
Picnic table sculpture (650 ft.)	1.0 mi.	350 ft.	0:40
Complete loop	2.6 mi.	350 ft.	1:30

Find the start of the trail at the south end of the parking lot (away from the lake). Following blue blazes, meander through the hemlock woods in a shallow ravine. The lower end of Loop Trail (no sign) leaves to the left. Stay straight to reach the upper end of Loop Trail (sign). Birch Mtn. Ledge Trail continues easily ahead and soon crosses a brook on a footbridge. Cross a gravel park road (leads right, to the campground) at 0.4 mi. Beyond, the trail climbs gently into softwood forest with mossy ledges. At 0.8 mi., pass to the right of a large boulder. In another 0.1 mi., a mossy erratic is to the left. Follow the right side of a depression to a clearing and a large cairn and picnic table combination, one of twelve picnic table sculptures placed throughout the park that were created by artist Wade Kavanaugh through Maine's Per Cent for Art Act.

Beyond the sculpture, descend gradually through an impressive stand of white pines and hemlocks. Cross a brook and tread through sections of hemlock woods and mossy boulders. Soon after, the trail weaves through parklike groves of mature hardwood and softwood trees, some measuring more than 3 ft. in diameter. At 2.1 mi., reach a clearing and old road, with a pumphouse to the left. Bear right on the grassy gravel road. At a four-way jct. at 2.4 mi., go left to reach the beach. Pass through the picnic area, enter the grassy promenade, and cross a footbridge to the beach. At the lifeguard tower, turn right and follow the paved walkway to the parking lot.

LITTLE MOOSE PUBLIC LANDS

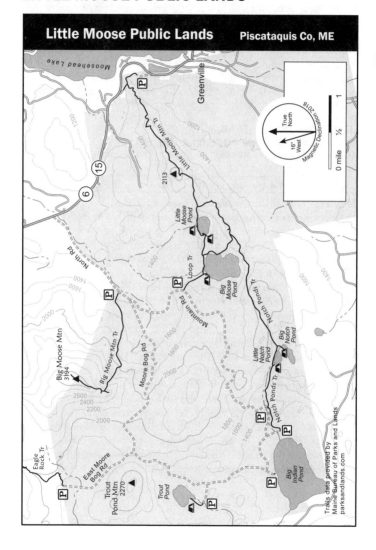

■ LITTLE MOOSE MTN. (2,126 FT.)

Little Moose Mtn. is a long and hilly ridgeline extending for more than 5 mi. from the northeast to the southwest, just west of the southern end of Moosehead Lake. This wooded mountain offers a surprising number of fine viewpoints, while primitive camping is available at four ponds along the mountain's length. The trail system on Little Moose Mtn. can be reached from three points in the unit: from ME 15/6 in the east, and from two trailheads on Mountain Rd., near Big Moose Pond and near Notch Ponds, in the west.

LITTLE MOOSE MTN. TRAIL
(MBPL; LITTLE MOOSE PUBLIC LANDS, P. 113)

From trailhead parking near ME 15 (1,100 ft.) to:	⇅	↗	○
Loop Trail near Little Moose Pond (1,620 ft.)	2.8 mi.	950 ft.	1:55

This trail starts at the northeastern base of Little Moose Mtn. and traverses a portion of the ridge to connect with Loop Trail near Little Moose Pond. From the blinking traffic light in the center of Greenville, drive north on ME 15/6 for 2.0 mi. Turn left (sign) and follow a gravel drive for 0.3 mi. to the trailhead parking lot at the end of the road.

The trail briefly follows the old roadbed (the former ME 15) for 200 ft., then turns left onto a foot trail, which soon reaches a vista and picnic table. The old trail from Moose Mountain Inn on ME 15 enters here. From this point, Little Moose Mtn. Trail ascends moderately to the southwest along the ridgeline of Little Moose Mtn. Frequent outlooks en route provide extensive views eastward to Borestone Mtn., the peaks of the Barren–Chairback Range, and Baker Mtn. north across Moosehead Lake, as well as wide views of Big Spencer Mtn., Little Spencer Mtn., and Mt. Kineo. Crest the eastern ridge of Little Moose Mtn. at 1.8 mi. Then descend steeply to Papoose Pond at 2.6 mi., and see Big Moose Mtn. rising impressively in the distance. At 2.8 mi., reach the jct. with Loop Trail. To the right, it is 1.5 mi. to the Mountain Rd. trailhead via Little Moose Pond and Big Moose Pond. To the left, it is 2.6 mi. over the west ridge of Little Moose Mtn. to Big Notch Pond and Little Notch Pond, and 3.5 mi. to the lower Notch Ponds trailhead on Mountain Rd.

LOOP TRAIL (MBPL; LITTLE MOOSE PUBLIC LANDS, P. 113)

Cumulative from Big Moose Pond trailhead (1,660 ft.) to:	↧↥	↗	↻
Greenwood Trail (1,620 ft.)	1.5 mi.	160 ft.	0:50
Notch Ponds Trail (1,770 ft.)	2.4 mi.	460 ft.	1:25
Close loop at Big Moose Pond	3.0 mi.	490 ft.	1:45
Complete loop	3.7 mi.	650 ft.	2:10

SEC 2

This trail leads to Big Moose Pond and Little Moose Pond, then makes a circuit over the central section of Little Moose Mtn. before returning to Big Moose Pond.

From the blinking traffic light in the center of Greenville, drive north on ME 15/6 for 5.0 mi. Turn left (west) on North Rd. and enter Little Moose Public Lands (sign). Pass the trailhead for Big Moose Mtn. on the right at 1.5 mi. and then reach a fork at 1.7 mi. Turn left at the fork and follow Mountain Rd. for another 1.0 mi. to the Big Moose Pond trailhead pullout on the left (kiosk).

At 0.15 mi., the trail descends a winding set of slate steps and then crosses a small brook on a curving footbridge. A bog is on the left just beyond. Reach a jct. at 0.4 mi., where a side trail leads south up over a low hump to several campsites on Big Moose Pond. Continue to the left on Loop Trail. A short distance ahead, cross the old concrete dam at the outlet of Big Moose Pond on a footbridge. At 0.7 mi., Loop Trail splits; go left to follow the circuit in a clockwise direction. Ahead, the easy trail goes over a low rise, then trends down to Little Moose Pond at 1.0 mi. A campsite and toilet are immediately to the right. The trail soon bears away from the pond and passes a toilet on the left and a spur to a campsite on the right. The narrow and sometimes rough route follows the pond margin and reaches a clearing with a campsite and toilet. The pond's outlet is just beyond. Leave the pond and climb a rise, pass to the right of a cliff wall, and cross the outlet of Papoose Pond before reaching the jct. of Little Moose Mtn. Trail at 1.5 mi.

Loop Trail bears right and climbs to the ridgeline of Little Moose Mtn. and a scenic outlook, where there is a nice view over the pond below. The trail continues southwest on the rugged, craggy ridge to the next outlook at a large outcrop, which provides a fine view over Big Moose Pond to Big Moose Mtn. At 2.4 mi., Loop Trail meets Notch Ponds Trail. Loop Trail heads right and descends to Big Moose Pond. Following the pond's west shore, the trail closes the loop near the northeast corner of the pond at 3.0 mi. Big Moose Pond trailhead on Mountain Rd. is 0.7 mi. to the left.

NOTCH PONDS TRAIL
(MBPL; LITTLE MOOSE PUBLIC LANDS, P. 113)

Cumulative from lower Notch Ponds parking lot (1,230 ft.) to:	⇅	↗	↺
Upper Notch Ponds parking lot (1,400 ft.)	0.4 mi.	170 ft.	0:15
Start of Loop Trail (1,770 ft.)	3.3 mi.	980 ft.	2:10

Notch Ponds Trail connects to Little Notch Pond and Big Notch Pond before climbing to the western ridgeline on Little Moose Mtn. to meet Loop Trail.

To reach the trailheads for Notch Ponds Trail, follow the driving directions for Loop Trail. From the Big Moose Pond trailhead, continue on Mountain Rd. In 2.8 mi., the upper trailhead parking lot for Notch Ponds Trail is on the right. The trail leaves immediately across the road. To reach the lower trailhead parking lot for Notch Ponds Trail, continue downhill on Mountain Rd. to a T intersection. Turn left to reach parking on the right at the end of the road. The trail starts just ahead at a kiosk and large boulder.

Notch Ponds Trail is described from the lower trailhead parking lot. From the kiosk and large boulder, proceed east to cross the footbridge over Notch Ponds Brook, the outlet of the two Notch ponds. At 40 ft. beyond the crossing, leave the wide, grassy woods road and enter the woods on the left (sign). Follow the brook uphill, eventually crossing it on a mossy footbridge. The trail emerges at an overflow parking spot on Mountain Rd. at 0.4 mi. Turn right and walk up Mountain Rd. Pass the upper trailhead parking area on the left and, just beyond, duck into the woods on the right. A kiosk is ahead.

On the trail, cross Notch Ponds Brook on a footbridge and follow the course of the brook eastward. Well beyond, the trail climbs a short, moderate pitch and soon reaches a jct. at 1.0 mi. Straight ahead, a spur leads 200 ft. to a campsite at Little Notch Pond. Turn left here and cross a bridge over the outlet brook. The trail follows an undulating route across a slope on the north side of the pond to reach a jct. at 1.4 mi. To the right, a spur leads 0.15 mi. to several campsites on Big Notch Pond.

From the jct., the trail rises steadily and then steeply to a notch high on the western ridgeline of Little Moose Mtn. Beyond, the trail follows the rugged heights across and then down to a notch south of Big Moose Pond. The trail then climbs steeply out to end at the jct. with Loop Trail at 3.3 mi.

■ BIG MOOSE MTN. (3,194 FT.)

Big Moose Mtn. dominates the landscape southwest of the lower section of Moosehead Lake. Located in Big Moose Township west of Greenville, the mountain is well known for its exceptional views of the Moosehead Lake region, Big Spencer Mtn. and Little Spencer Mtn., and Katahdin.

SEC 2

The 1919 steel fire tower (marking the site of Maine's first fire lookout, made of logs, established in 1905) was removed from the summit and reassembled next door to the Moosehead Lake Region Visitor Center on ME 15 on the way into Greenville from the south.

From the blinking traffic light in the center of Greenville, drive north on ME 15/6 for 5.0 mi. Turn left (west) on North Rd. and enter Little Moose Public Lands (sign). Proceed 1.5 mi. to trailhead parking on the right.

BIG MOOSE MTN. TRAIL
(MBPL; LITTLE MOOSE PUBLIC LANDS, P. 113)

Cumulative from North Rd. trailhead (1,350 ft.) to:	↟↡	↗	○
Old fire warden's cabin (2,260 ft.)	1.4 mi.	900 ft.	1:10
Big Moose Mtn. summit (3,194 ft.)	2.1 mi.	1,850 ft.	2:00

The well-marked trail leaves the rear of the parking lot to the right of a kiosk.

In 750 ft., the trail joins an old forest road and turns left to make a long, rising traverse to the west. It passes a spring at 0.9 mi. and climbs moderately. At 1.1 mi., the trail bears right and climbs parallel to a brook. Just ahead, it crosses a small brook on a footbridge. Continue to parallel the larger brook (which is to the left of the trail and not pictured on the USGS map). The old fire warden's cabin is on the right at 1.4 mi. Go 100 ft. beyond, meet the brook, turn right, and shortly after, cross the brook. Beyond this crossing, the trail begins a steady ascent via rock stairs and log stairs, climbing at a moderate to steep grade. Reach a level shelf on the south ridge of the mountain at 1.6 mi., where a spur on the left leads 0.1 mi. to several scenic overlooks. The first one on the right looks west to the Bigelows and the ski slopes of Sugarloaf, while the second looks north to the upper reaches of Big Moose Mtn. and east over Big Moose Pond and Little Moose Pond to a whole host of peaks beyond Moosehead Lake in the 100MW.

Continuing the steady ascent, the trail reaches the narrow crest of the high ridgeline and climbs the final distance to the open summit ledges at 2.1 mi., where there is a small communications tower and the footings of the old fire tower. The incredible vista now spans north all the way to Katahdin and the jumble of high mountains around it in BSP.

From the summit, a short trail leads north around a tower and solar array to a helipad and a ledge with a view down over Mirror Lake, an isolated pond on the northeastern spur of the mountain. Another trail continues north to the top of the Squaw Mtn. ski area.

■ EAGLE ROCK (2,367 FT.)

The long ridgeline of Big Moose Mtn. extends northwest several miles west toward Indian Pond and the Kennebec River, where it culminates at a large bald outcrop known as Eagle Rock, which offers a spectacular 360-degree view. To the north, across the length and breadth of Moosehead Lake, are the peaks of Mt. Kineo, Little Kineo Mtn., Big Spencer Mtn., Little Spencer Mtn., Number Four Mtn., Lily Bay Mtn., and Baker Mtn. The view ranges as far as Katahdin and the jumbled peaks of BSP, a distance of more than 50 mi. as the crow flies. To the west are the rugged and remote mountains reaching to Jackman and the Canadian border. To the south are summits of the Bigelow Range and the many peaks and ridges along the AT corridor. The mass of Big Moose Mtn. makes up much of the eastern view.

A portion of Eagle Rock lies within the Moosehead Region Conservation Easement. In 2015, the Maine Bureau of Parks and Lands completed the Eagle Rock Trail to the peak from the south in Little Moose Public Lands. An informal trail, referred to as Old Eagle Rock Trail, reaches Eagle Rock from the north.

EAGLE ROCK TRAIL (MBPL; USGS BIG SQUAW POND, MOOSEHEAD, AND INDIAN POND NORTH QUADS, GAZETTEER MAPS 41 AND 40, MTF EAGLE ROCK TRAIL MAP)

Cumulative from Moore Bog Rd. (1,780 ft.) to:	↕	↗	○
Raven Ledge (2,460 ft.)	2.5 mi.	975 ft.	1:45
Eagle Rock (2,367 ft.)	3.6 mi.	1,300 ft.	2:25

To reach the southern trailhead for Eagle Rock, follow the driving directions for Big Moose Mtn. From the Big Moose Mtn. trailhead, continue west on North Rd. for 0.2 mi. to a fork. To the left, Mountain Rd. continues to trailheads for Big Moose Pond and Notch Ponds. Proceed straight (right) on Moore Bog Rd. and drive 1.4 mi. to the end of the road (boulders and ditch) and trailhead parking on the right.

Eagle Rock Trail starts from the rear of the lot and heads east at first, following blue blazes. In 0.25 mi., it crosses an old gravel logging road, then traverses along a contour. Cross a small brook at 0.45 mi., then begin to climb out of the ravine along the brook's route. Above, cross the brook again, go up a rock staircase, cross the brook one more time, and climb to the northwest. Hike around a knob, then trend gradually down across a steep slope to reach the floor of a saddle. Climb up and around the next knob on a path that is moderate to steep. At 2.5 mi., reach a side trail on the left that leads 0.1 mi. to a fine lookout at Raven Ledge.

From the side trail jct., descend to a saddle and wind around the south side of the next knob to another saddle. Climb a moderate grade to a crest, then drop down over the next knob to a saddle at 3.5 mi. A small notch at 3.6 mi. marks the end of the official MBPL trail at the unmarked boundary of the conservation easement. The Old Eagle Rock Trail from the north side enters here; follow it left for a steep climb up the final slabs to the airy and spectacular pinnacle of Eagle Rock at 3.7 mi. with far-reaching views in every direction.

OLD EAGLE ROCK TRAIL
(NFTM; USGS INDIAN POND NORTH QUAD, GAZETTEER MAP 40)

From Burnham Pond Rd. (1,050 ft.) to:	↯↥	↗	↺
Eagle Rock (2,367 ft.)	1.5 mi.	1,300 ft.	1:25

From the blinking traffic light in the center of Greenville, drive north on ME 15/6 for 8.5 mi. Turn left (west) on Burnham Pond Rd., and go 3.7 mi. to a fork. Bear left at the fork, and drive 1.2 mi. to the trailhead on the left (marked by pink flagging and a handmade sign). Park just ahead along the road on the right.

The trail proceeds east for a distance at an easy grade before starting to climb in switchbacks. This is a well-used and well-marked path, but you will have to contend with occasional blowdowns. A wooden ladder and a rope aid in scrambling up a steep section. After leveling off for a time, the trail ascends steeply again, dips briefly, and then gains the huge open ledge at Eagle Rock with its panoramic views. Just before the final steep slabs to the pinnacle of Eagle Rock, Eagle Rock Trail from the southeast at Moose Bog Rd. enters from the left.

MT. KINEO STATE PARK

◼ MT. KINEO (1,800 FT.)

Mt. Kineo rises dramatically from a peninsula jutting out from the eastern shore of Moosehead Lake in Kineo Township, just north of Rockwood. The sheer 700-ft. southeastern face of this iconic mountain is visible from points throughout the region. In 1990, the state of Maine purchased 800 acres from the cliff face north to form Mt. Kineo State Park (the remainder of the peninsula is privately owned). Hikers to the summit ridge and fire tower are rewarded with remarkable views of the remote and beautiful woods and mountains around Moosehead Lake and far beyond. There is no road access to Kineo. The quickest and most scenic way to reach Kineo is by ferry from Rockwood.

From the blinking traffic light in the center of Greenville, travel north on ME 15/6 for 18.8 mi. to the village of Rockwood. Turn right on Village Rd.,

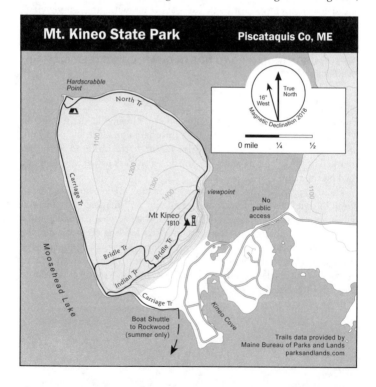

which is marked with signs for Rockwood Public Landing, where there is parking. From the landing, it is about a 10-min. boat ride to Mt. Kineo. The Kineo Shuttle is the sole provider of ferry services to Kineo for hikers, sightseers, and golfers. The shuttle operates from late May through early October and charges $12 per person (2017) round-trip, cash only and paid on the boat to the captain. In the high summer months of July and August, the shuttle runs hourly. In the shoulder months of May, June, September, and October, trips are less frequent. Call the Kineo Shuttle at 207-534-9012 for schedule information or check online: mooseheadlakegolf.wordpress.com.

Carriage Trail, North Trail, Bridle Trail, and Indian Trail can be used to climb the mountain and form hike loops of varying lengths.

CARRIAGE TRAIL (MBPL; MT. KINEO, P. 120)

Cumulative from Kineo public boat landing (1,030 ft.) to:	⇅	↗	⟳
Indian Trail (1,030 ft.)	0.6 mi.	0 ft.	0:20
Bridle Trail (1,030 ft.)	0.8 mi.	0 ft.	0:25
North Trail (1,030 ft.)	2.0 mi.	0 ft.	1:00
Hardscrabble Point (1,030 ft.)	2.1 mi.	0 ft.	1:05

From the dock and bench, turn left and proceed to the kiosk (day-use fee). To the right is Mt. Kineo Golf Course and its clubhouse, where sandwiches, snacks, and beverages are available to the public. Follow Carriage Trail north along the shore of Moosehead Lake, with great views of the Kineo cliff face. Pass by a talus slope with good views across the lake to Rockwood, the Moose River, and beyond to Misery Ridge. At the base of the cliff, the path narrows and reaches the jct. with Indian Trail at 0.6 mi. Just ahead, Carriage Trail passes a burned cabin on the right and a dock on the left. The trail continues easily along the west shore of the Kineo Peninsula to a jct. with North Trail on the right at 1.8 mi. Carriage Trail continues ahead another 0.1 mi. to its end at Hardscrabble Point, where there is a gravel beach and picnic tables. There are two designated campsites (picnic table, fire ring, privy) near the North Trail jct. and two more designated campsites at Hardscrabble Point.

INDIAN TRAIL (MBPL; MT. KINEO, P. 120)

Cumulative from Kineo public boat landing (1,030 ft.) to:	⇅	↗	⟳
Indian Trail (1,030 ft.) via Carriage Trail	0.6 mi.	0 ft.	0:20
Bridle Trail (1,680 ft.)	1.1 mi.	650 ft.	0:40
Mt. Kineo summit (1,800 ft.) via Bridle Trail	1.5 mi.	800 ft.	1:10

SEC
2

Indian Trail is the shortest route to the summit and observation tower and provides the most views. Indian Trail diverges right from Carriage Trail at 0.6 mi. from the public boat landing. A steep scramble over rocks and roots leads to ledges with fine views to the southeast and southwest. After a level stretch and another viewpoint, the trail turns left and up, climbing through the woods on the margin of the cliff face. The views over the golf course below and to the lake and beyond get bigger and better as you climb higher. Indian Trail ends at the jct. with Bridle Trail at 0.5 mi. Continue northeast on Bridle Trail to reach the top of the mountain and the observation tower, a former fire tower erected on the site in 1917.

BRIDLE TRAIL (MBPL; MT. KINEO, P. 120)

Cumulative from Kineo public boat landing (1,030 ft.) to:	⇅	↗	⟳
Indian Trail (1,030 ft.)	0.6 mi.	0 ft.	0:20
Start of Bridle Trail (1,030 ft.)	0.8 mi.	0 ft.	0:25
Indian Trail (1,680 ft.)	1.5 mi.	650 ft.	1:05
Mt. Kineo summit (1,800 ft.) via Bridle Trail	1.9 mi.	800 ft.	1:20

Bridle Trail is the original fire warden trail to the summit. It begins 0.2 mi. north of Indian Trail, or 0.8 mi. along Carriage Trail from the public boat landing. Bridle Trail is slightly longer than Indian Trail and has fewer views en route, but it does offer more moderate grades. Bridle Trail follows a wide, rocky, and eroded track at first before making a moderate climb and then easing off to meet Indian Trail. Here is an expansive view over the Mt. Kineo Golf Course and Kineo House, and far across Moosehead Lake to Lily Bay Mtn., Number Four Mtn., Baker Mtn., and many other peaks. Bridle Trail continues northeast up the mountain, crests a knob, then makes a short, steep drop. The meandering trail continues to the tower on the wooded summit, which is 1.9 mi. from the landing. Climb the tower for an outstanding 360-degree panorama, one of the finest anywhere in Maine.

NORTH TRAIL (MBPL; MT. KINEO, P. 120)

From Mt. Kineo summit (1,800 ft.) to:	⇅	↗	⟳
Carriage Trail near Hardscrabble Point (1,030 ft.)	2.0 mi.	50 ft.	1:00

North Trail connects the summit of Mt. Kineo with Hardscrabble Point at the northwest corner of the Kineo peninsula. From the summit observation tower, descend the north side of the mountain on a narrow path through spruce woods. The going is steep at first, levels off, and then drops steeply again. After a short side trail to a viewpoint on the right, the trail descends very steeply. It levels off on a shelf and continues down at a more moderate grade until it reaches the shore of Moosehead Lake at 0.7 mi. Shaw Mtn. is in view across the lake. Rough and wet in spots, North Trail heads northwest along a steep slope above the lake. The trail bears away from the lake at 1.8 mi. and soon bears sharply right (old trail to left). North Trail ends at the jct. with Carriage Trail at 2.0 mi., 0.1 mi. south of Hardscrabble Point and 2.0 mi. north of the public boat landing via Carriage Trail.

EAST OF MOOSEHEAD LAKE

■ BURNT JACKET MTN. (1,680 FT.)

This little mountain in Beaver Cove rises in the center of a peninsula on the southeastern side of Moosehead Lake, on private land amid a development named Burnt Jacket, which is owned by McPherson Timberlands. Hikers have access to Burnt Jacket Mtn. between June 1 and October 31.

From the blinking traffic light in the center of Greenville on ME 15/6, drive north on Lily Bay Rd. for 5.6 mi. Turn left on Burnt Jacket Rd. and proceed west on a good gravel road (passing Otter Slide Rd. and Pine Marten Rd. on the right en route). At 1.9 mi. from Lily Bay Rd., take a left on a lesser gravel road (the small sign for Burnt Jacket Mtn. may be obscured by shrubby growth). In another 0.2 mi., turn right and drive 0.3 mi. to a gravel pit. Proceed straight ahead past the pit to a parking area (watch for the sign) in the grassy meadow.

BURNT JACKET MTN. TRAIL
(NFTM; USGS LILY BAY QUAD, GAZETTEER MAP 41)

From grassy meadow parking (1,240 ft.) to:	⇅	↗	○
Burnt Jacket Mtn. summit (1,680 ft.)	0.7 mi.	440 ft.	0:35

Looking at the parking sign in the meadow, go right and follow the continuation of the old road around the base of the mountain. At 0.15 mi., leave the road and enter the woods on the right (there is a sign just into the woods nailed to a spruce tree). The trail is overgrown for much of its route lower down, but is well marked with red paint splotches and the footway is well defined. Cross several small clearings (old skidder trails). The trail then climbs a moderate pitch, levels off, and parallels an old, grassy skidder trail. Reenter the woods at a large sugar maple with a red paint dot on it. Ascend easily to an obvious rectangular rock in the trail; at the rock, bear right and up, again paralleling the old skidder trail. At 0.65 mi., Blue Trail enters from the left (there is a small network of color-coded trails on the mountain, but their maintenance and condition is reportedly variable, and there is no available map). Reach the summit ledges and a cairn at 0.7 mi. (Green Trail enters from the north at this point.) A plastic jar in the cairn contains a hiker logbook. Views are limited but nice, especially from the ledges ahead on Green Trail. Moosehead Lake, Big Moose Mtn., Little Moose Mtn., and even the cliff face of Mt. Kineo are all part of the scene.

■ ELEPHANT MTN. (2,636 FT.)

Unlike other mountains of the same name in Maine, this Elephant Mtn. actually does resemble an elephant's head, minus the tusks. The sloping southern face and the small ledge that appears as an eye are recognizable from many surrounding peaks. Though no foot trail reaches its summit, a short trail on its lower western slope leads hikers to the crash site of a B-52 bomber. On January 24, 1963, a U.S. Air Force Stratofortress bomber ran into severe turbulence and mechanical problems and crashed into the mountainside in subzero temperatures and blizzard conditions. Of the nine crew members, only the pilot and the navigator survived.

From the blinking traffic light in the center of Greenville on ME 15/6, drive north on Lily Bay Rd. for 7.0 mi. Turn right (east) on Prong Pond Rd. At 10.7 mi., bear left at a fork. At 12.4 mi., cross a wooden bridge then take the next left at 12.5 mi. Continue to the parking area and trailhead at 14.3 mi.

B-52 MEMORIAL CRASH SITE TRAIL
(NFTM; USGS NUMBER FOUR MTN. QUAD, GAZETTEER MAP 41)

From trailhead parking (1,630 ft.) to:	⇅	↗	⟳
Memorial site (1,700 ft.)	0.25 mi.	70 ft.	0:10

The trail begins opposite the parking area. The path to the crash site is an easy and very accessible 0.25 mi. Pieces of the wreckage line both sides of the trail route, which culminates at an information kiosk and a large slate memorial leaning against a big section of the cabin of the downed plane. Visitors have left a variety of flags and wreaths over time. It is a moving experience and a different kind of hike.

■ NUMBER FOUR MTN. (2,894 FT.)

Rising south of First Roach Pond in Frenchtown Township, Number Four Mtn. offers excellent views from the open ledges and the abandoned fire tower on its summit. The trail to the top of the mountain is part of an ambitious trail-building effort undertaken by MBPL through the

Moosehead Lake Region Concept Plan, on lands owned by Weyerhaeuser that are under the Moosehead Region Conservation Easement.

From the blinking traffic light in the center of Greenville on ME 15/6, drive north on Lily Bay Rd. for 17.7 mi. Turn right onto Frenchtown Rd. and follow it for 2.2 mi. Turn right onto Lagoon Brook Rd. and go 1.3 mi. then turn left onto Meadow Brook Rd. Follow this road south for 0.9 mi. to the signed trailhead on the left. The road passes over Lagoon Brook about 500 ft. before reaching the trailhead. There is ample parking along the road. (*Note:* A new trailhead parking area is planned for 2018.)

SEC 2

NUMBER FOUR MTN. TRAIL (MBPL; USGS NUMBER FOUR MTN. QUAD, GAZETTEER MAP 41, MTF NUMBER FOUR MTN. MAP)

From Meadow Brook Rd. (1,420 ft.) to:	⇅	↗	○
Number Four Mtn. summit (2,894 ft.)	1.9 mi.	1,475 ft.	1:40

The start of the blue-blazed trail is an old woods road. In 0.25 mi., bear right onto a foot path. Just ahead on the right are cabin ruins. Beyond, the trail picks up the route of another old road and climbs gently. For the next 0.5 mi., the route alternates between sections of old and eroded trail and switchbacks on recently built good foot trail. The steady grade turns from moderate to steep as the path follows an old fire warden's trail. Rock steps, log steps, and more switchbacks aid in the ascent. At 1.6 mi., the angle decreases and the going is easier on the narrowing ridgeline. A viewpoint is 50 ft. to the left at 1.8 mi. A level stretch and then a quick climb leads to the old fire tower (built in 1925), which no longer has a cab. The trail continues north a short distance to a lookout and bench, where the view includes Baker Mtn., Lily Bay Mtn., Big Moose Mtn., Little Moose Mtn., Moosehead Lake, Columbus Mtn., Chairback Mtn., and the White Cap Range. The new Baker Mtn. Trail proceeds south from this point (see Baker Mtn. Trail below).

■ BAKER MTN. (3,521 FT.)

This high and wild peak on the eastern side of the town Beaver Cove is south of Number Four Mtn. and southeast of Lily Bay Mtn. In 2015, AMC purchased 4,311 acres on Baker Mtn., which was surrounded by conservation lands but was unprotected until AMC's ownership. A new trail from the summit of Number Four Mtn., constructed by trail crews from the Maine Conservation Corps and AMC, now extends south to the summit of Baker Mtn. AMC plans to connect the trail to its existing system farther south.

BAKER MTN. TRAIL (AMC, MBPL; USGS NUMBER FOUR MTN. QUAD, GAZETTEER MAP 41, MTF NUMBER FOUR MTN. MAP)

Cumulative from Number Four Mtn. summit (2,894 ft.) to:	↻↑	↗	⟳
Snowmobile trail and planned campsite (2,700 ft.)	2.6 mi.	250 ft.	1:25
Baker Mtn. summit (3,521 ft.)	4.8 mi.	1,225 ft.	3:00

Southward along the ridge of Number Four Mtn., the new Baker Mtn. Trail winds its way along a mildly undulating ridge through fairly open forest stands, eventually entering thicker spruce and fir stands near the notch where the ridges of Number Four Mtn., Baker Mtn., and adjacent Lily Bay Mtn. come together. At this point, about 2.6 mi. from the Number Four summit area, the route crosses a snowmobile trail before beginning the moderate climb up Baker Mtn. After a modest amount of climbing, the trail reaches a small false summit before dropping back down. It then slowly rises on its way toward the true summit of Baker Mtn. Nearer the summit, open stands with low regrowth provide attractive views of the mountains and lakes ranging from Katahdin all the way to Moosehead Lake. From the snowmobile trail crossing to the summit area on Baker Mtn. is about 2.2 mi. (*Note:* A designated campsite is planned for a location north of the snowmobile trail crossing, but until that time, no camping is allowed on Baker Mtn. Trail.)

■ BLUE RIDGE (2,350 FT.)

This mountain ridgeline, situated between Greenville and AMC's Maine Woods conservation and recreation area, extends about 5 mi. in an east-west direction. Two small ponds, Cranberry and Notch, are found on the ridge, while Rum Pond is at its western base and Hedgehog Pond near it eastern edge.

Blue Ridge is the focus of recent trail building efforts by MBPL using Maine Conservation Corps trail crews, which is constructing the roughly 7.5-mi. Blue Ridge Trail system between Rum Pond and AMC's property line north of Hedgehog Pond. AMC trail crews have been working in concert with this effort to connect the trail with its existing trail system west of Indian Mtn. MBPL is also planning to build a trail between Rum Pond and the AT on the west end of Barren Mtn. through the Vaughan Stream valley. These projects are all part of the Moosehead Lake Region Concept Plan, a cooperative initiative to expand backcountry multiuse recreation opportunities for hikers, backpackers, trail runners, and mountain bikers in the area. Hikers should check with MBPL for updated information and trail maps pertaining to this exciting trail project.

RUM–CRANBERRY LOOP
(MBPL; USGS BARREN MTN. WEST QUAD)

SEC 2

Cumulative from Rum Pond parking (1,300 ft.) to:	⇅	↗	↻
Cranberry Pond (1,600 ft.)	1.5 mi.	475 ft.	1:00
Complete loop	3.0 mi.	475 ft.	1:45

The Blue Ridge Trail system is a work in progress, but as of late 2017, a short hiking circuit at the west end of the ridge, the Rum-Cranberry Loop, was nearly complete and is expected to be open to the public in 2018. This loop hike uses a portion of three trails: Blue Ridge Trail, Rum Brook Trail, and Headwaters Trail.

From Greenville at the jct. of Lily Bay Rd. and Pleasant St., turn onto Pleasant St. Drive east on Pleasant St., which becomes East Rd. as it heads to the Greenville Municipal Airport. Continue past the airport as the road becomes gravel-surfaced. Pass over Wilson Stream and continue east, where eventually becomes the Katahdin Iron Works Rd. Just over 7 mi. from Greenville, turn left (north) on Rum Pond Rd. The rather rough Rum Pond Rd. leads 1.1 mi. to the trailhead parking area.

From the parking, the trail heads towards Rum Pond then turns north and soon crosses a stream using a woods road bridge. The trail quickly veers back off the woods road and shortly reaches a jct. with yellow-blazed Rum Brook Trail—the eastern part of the loop and the route connecting to trail linkages southward. The main blue-marked Blue Ridge Trail continues generally northward and climbs a gentle slope above Rum Pond before descending to the shore of the pond in an open stand of mature softwood. Within 500 ft., the trail reaches a short spur to a proposed campsite on the shore of Rum Pond. The trail crosses the same woods road encountered at the start of the trail as the trail ascends away from the pond, passing through fairly recent timber harvesting while trending northwesterly at first before turning east. The trail follows the ridge to a high point, then descends to pretty Cranberry Pond. A campsite is proposed for the outlet of the pond just north. The trail turns and follows the south shore of Cranberry Pond. At the eastern end of the pond, Blue Ridge Trail reaches a jct. with the yellow-marked Rum Brook Trail. Turn south on Rum Brook Trail to return 1.4 mi. to the trailhead. (*Note:* At this jct., Blue Ridge Trail continues eastward and climbs through a wide gap in between two hills as it heads for Notch Pond and miles beyond. This full route is expected to be completed later in 2018.)

At about 0.5 mi. below Cranberry Pond on Rum Brook Trail, the red-marked Headwaters Trail enters from the east. This trail route, which at time of printing is complete from the jct. to an unnamed logging road to the south, leads roughly 2.2 mi. southward to a to-be-developed trailhead on the KI Rd. next to Vaughn Stream. Stay on Rum Brook Trail, descending gently through predominantly young forest stands. Cross a rapidly growing-in logging road several times before finally returning to the junction of Blue Ridge Trail. Turn south on Blue Ridge Trail to retrace the remaining 850 ft. of trail to the parking area.

■ LITTLE KINEO MTN. (1,927 FT.)

Rising prominently east of North Bay on Moosehead Lake and northeast of Mt. Kineo, Little Kineo Mtn., in Days Academy Grant Township, is part of the Days Academy Public Lands. The mountain is remote and takes some work to get to but rewards hikers for the effort with outstanding views from its summit ledges.

From the blinking traffic light in the center of Greenville on ME 15/6, drive north on Lily Bay Rd. for 18.8 mi. to the village of Kokadjo, on the west end of First Roach Pond. At 0.3 mi. beyond the village, the road turns to dirt and splits. Bear left at the fork onto Sias Hill Rd. and follow it for 1.1 mi. Turn left onto Spencer Bay Rd. At 8.2 mi., pass a sign for Spencer Pond Camps, and at 9.4 mi., cross a bridge over the outlet of Spencer Pond. At 11.2 mi., bear left at a fork, and at 15.0 mi., go right at a fork. The road comes to a T intersection at 17.8 mi. Turn left here and soon cross a bridge. At 18.0 mi., turn right (sign for Kelly Wharf). Go left at a fork at 18.7 mi., and soon the cliffs of Little Kineo Mtn. come into view. Reach the trailhead (sign) on the right at 20.2 mi. from Kokadjo. Park along either side of the road.

LITTLE KINEO MTN. TRAIL (MBPL; USGS MT. KINEO QUAD, GAZETTEER MAP 41, MBPL MOOSEHEAD SHORELINE PUBLIC LANDS MAP, MTF LITTLE KINEO MAP)

From trailhead parking (1,390 ft.) to:	⇅	↗	○
Little Kineo Mtn. summit (1,927 ft.)	1.0 mi.	540 ft.	0:45

The trail leaves the north side of the road and crosses a low area before beginning to climb northeast over the ledges composing the precipitous southeast face of the mountain. The trail is well marked with blazes, flagging, and rock cairns. It is steep in sections but overall is a moderate climb.

Views are good on the way up and get better with each step. The final 0.5 mi. along the summit ridgeline is superb, with vistas taking in the expanse of Moosehead Lake, Mt. Kineo, Big Moose Mtn., Big Spencer Mtn., Little Spencer Mtn., Katahdin, and countless more peaks in Maine's vast North Woods.

SEC 2

■ LITTLE SPENCER MTN. (3,007 FT.)

The elongated mass of Little Spencer Mtn. in East Middlesex Canal Township, with its steep flanks and rock faces, is a distinctive landmark in the Moosehead Lake region. The Little Spencer summit and nearby open ledges offer outstanding views.

From the blinking traffic light in the center of Greenville on ME 15/6, drive north on Lily Bay Rd. for 18.8 mi. to the village of Kokadjo at the west end of First Roach Pond. At 0.3 mi. beyond Kokadjo, turn left onto Sias Hill Rd. and follow it for 1.2 mi. then turn left onto Spencer Bay Rd. Follow it for 7.4 mi. Turn right at the sign for Spencer Pond Camps and continue 2.2 mi. to the Little Spencer trailhead on the right (sign).

THE RAM TRAIL
(NFTM; USGS LOBSTER MTN. QUAD, GAZETTEER MAP 49)

From Spencer Bay Rd. trailhead (1,180 ft.) to:	↕	↗	⏱
Little Spencer Mtn. summit (3,007 ft.)	1.5 mi.	1,825 ft.	1:40

A short distance into the woods is a commemorative plaque for the "Ram Trail." This is in honor of Richard Manson, who in the 1960s explored various routes to the summit from Spencer Pond Camps. The trail is well marked with flagging tape and sporadic blazes. (Occasional trail maintenance—though not of the ropes!—is done by the proprietors of Spencer Pond Camps.) The trail rises gently for 0.25 mi. then begins a very steep ascent. After passing a viewpoint over Spencer Pond and Moosehead Lake, the trail leads east to the south face of the mountain and soon begins to climb over ledges and rock slides to reach a 70-ft. chimney, a narrow, vertical crease in the cliff. The recommended approach for the chimney is one person at a time. Be careful not to dislodge any rocks. (*Caution:* Any fixed ropes found in the chimney for assistance have been placed there by anonymous members of the public. The reliability of these ropes cannot be guaranteed, so use at your own risk.) Further, due to the difficulty of the chimney, this hike may not be a good choice when the rocks are wet, or at any time with young children or dogs. After a third rock slide, the trail rises at an easier grade, wending through thick woods to reach the summit. The breathtaking vista takes in Katahdin, Big Spencer Mtn., Lobster

Mtn., Lobster Lake, Moosehead Lake, Lily Bay Mtn., Number Four Mtn., First Roach Pond, White Cap Mtn., Big Moose Mtn., and much more of the grand landscape.

SEC 2

■ BIG SPENCER MTN. (3,206 FT.)

Rising sharply from the countryside north of Kokadjo and First Roach Pond, Big Spencer Mtn., in the unorganized townships of T2 R13 WELS and TX R14 WELS, is a prominent landmark in the area northeast of Moosehead Lake. The remains of an old fire tower sit on the northeastern end of its long summit ridge. The true summit is 0.3 mi. southwest of the tower. Panoramic views are possible from both points. The mountain lies within the 4,244-acre Big Spencer Ecological Reserve managed by MBPL.

From the blinking traffic light in the center of Greenville on ME 15/6, drive north on Lily Bay Rd. for 18.8 mi. to the village of Kokadjo at the west end of First Roach Pond. At 0.3 mi. beyond Kokadjo, turn left onto Sias Hill Rd. Follow it for 7.8 mi. to a narrow one-lane bridge over Bear Pond Brook. After crossing the bridge, turn left on a road (no sign for the road but a sign for Big Spencer) and take this road 6.1 mi. to the trailhead parking lot (blue sign) on the left.

BIG SPENCER MTN. TRAIL
(MBPL; USGS BIG SPENCER MTN. QUAD,
GAZETTEER MAP 49, MTF BIG SPENCER PUBLIC LANDS MAP)

From Spencer Mtn. Rd. trailhead (1,356 ft.) to:	⇅	↗	○
Big Spencer Mtn. (3,206 ft.)	1.8 mi.	1,850 ft.	1:50

Pass by big rocks to start south up the old tote road, which rises gradually. In 0.5 mi., the grade turns to moderate. Cross a small brook at 0.7 mi. Beyond an eroded section of tote road, proceed on a contour, then cross a brook on a footbridge. Reach a small meadow and the site of the old fire warden's cabin at 1.0 mi., where there is a picnic table, a privy, and a wonderful view north to Katahdin and the many summits in BSP. The bulk of Big Spencer Mtn. rises precipitously south of the clearing.

Beyond the old cabin site, cross another brook on a footbridge and circle around a beaver pond. Just beyond, the trail is very steep, gaining more than 1,000 ft. of elevation over the final 0.7 mi. to the northern summit. Steep rock staircases and the first of several wooden ladders aid in the ascent at 1.25 mi. The eroded trail above is a steep scramble on rocks and roots. Scale a second wooden ladder at 1.35 mi. and a third at 1.45 mi. Climb several short rock walls, level off, then move up to scale a fourth and a fifth ladder. Treeline is just ahead at 1.7 mi. In another 0.1 mi., reach the old fire tower base, a helipad, and a small communications building on the northernmost peak on the long Big Spencer summit ridge. Hikers are asked to respect the privately owned communications infrastructure in view just ahead on the next summit, which is now the site of a huge solar array and a complex of communications towers.

SEC 2

■ LOBSTER MTN. (2,318 FT.)

This mountain in Lobster Township rises in a long, curving ridge south of Lobster Lake and east of the northern end of Moosehead Lake. Lobster Mtn. and Lobster Lake are central features in the wildest part of the Penobscot River Corridor, a vast assemblage of properties and easements between BSP and Seboomook Lake and Moosehead Lake, all managed by MBPL.

The trail to Lobster Mtn. can only be reached by canoe or kayak. The adventure starts at a put-in on Lobster Stream just south of the West Branch of the Penobscot River. To reach this access point requires considerable driving over active gravel logging roads, which visitors must share with heavy truck traffic (go slow and always yield). From the launch site, paddle downstream on Lobster Stream and then cross Lobster Lake to reach the trailhead. Due to the time and distances involved, this trip is perhaps best planned as an overnight journey. There are numerous primitive campsites on Lobster Lake (picnic table, fire ring, privy) available on a first-come, first-served basis. The boat launch on Lobster Stream may be reached from the south at Greenville or from the east at Millinocket.

Directions from Greenville: Drive north on Lily Bay Rd. to Kokadjo, then continue north on Sias Hill Rd. to the Golden Rd. at the south end of Caribou Lake, a distance of 33.0 mi. The directions from Millinocket join the route here.

Directions from Millinocket: At the jct. of ME 11 (south) and the end of ME 157 just past downtown, bear right and follow signs for BSP. The road has several names en route, including Millinocket Lake Rd., Baxter State Park Rd., and simply Lake Rd. Drive 8.6 mi. to Northwoods Trading Post and Big Moose Inn on the right. Bear left onto the parallel Golden Rd. and drive 10.1 mi. to Abol Bridge Campground and Store on the right. Just beyond, cross Abol Bridge over the West Branch of the Penobscot River. Continue on the Golden Rd. for another 19 mi. to the jct. of Sias Hill Rd.

Directions from the jct. of Sias Hill Rd. from Greenville and the Golden Rd. from Millinocket: Drive west on the Golden Rd. for 6.0 mi. to the North Maine Woods Caribou Checkpoint, where visitors must pay day-use and camping fees (cash only). From the gatehouse, continue west on the Golden Rd. for 9.2 mi. to an unmarked road on the left (this is Lobster Trip Rd.; signs for Raymond's Country Store and Northeast Carry). In another

3.4 mi., cross a bridge over Lobster Stream and reach the boat launch parking lot on the left (kiosk, toilet).

From the launch, paddle south on Lobster Stream for 1.8 mi. to Lobster Lake. Bear southeast across the lake to Ogden Point, a distance of 1.2 mi. Lobster Mtn. rises beyond, while the sprawling flat-topped bulk of Big Spencer Mtn. dominates the view to the left. From Ogden Point, make your way east around the point and then south into Jackson Cove to the Jackson Cove campsite on the south shore, about 0.8 mi. from Ogden Point. To the left of the campsite, at a gap in the thick shrubby shoreline growth, is a brown sign that reads "Lobster Mtn. 2 mi."

LOBSTER MTN. TRAIL (MBPL; USGS LOBSTER MTN. QUAD, GAZETTEER MAP 49, MBPL PENOBSCOT RIVER CORRIDOR & SEBOOMOOK PUBLIC LANDS MAP)

From Jackson Cove trailhead on Lobster Lake (965 ft.) to:	⇅	↗	↺
Overlook at trail's end (2,055 ft.)	2.0 mi.	1,100 ft.	1:30

The trail strikes off to the south on a gradual route through mixed forest. Blue blazes mark the way. A portion of the trail is eroded, and there are several steep sections of rocky terrain. The trail, after leading through woods of spruce and fir, ends at an overlook high on the north slope of the mountain, where there is a bench built by a Boy Scout troop from Connecticut. The view over Lobster Lake is lovely and well worth the significant effort to get there.

NAHMAKANTA PUBLIC LANDS

TURTLE RIDGE LOOP TRAIL (MBPL; MAP 2: C5)

Cumulative from west trailhead (1,260 ft.) to:	⇅	↗	↺
Sing Sing Pond outlet (1,270 ft.)	1.1 mi.	40 ft.	0:35
Hedgehog Pond via Turtle Ridge (1,350 ft.)	3.1 mi.	440 ft.	1:45
East trailhead via Turtle Ridge and Rabbit Pond (1,089 ft.)	4.7 mi.	440 ft.	2:35
Complete Turtle Ridge Loop via Henderson Pond	8.8 mi.	900 ft.	4:50

This scenic figure-eight loop hike on the southern boundary of the public lands unit traverses Turtle Ridge and passes by a series of remote mountain ponds. Hikers have excellent views of the surrounding countryside of this wild region southwest of Katahdin from various outlooks.

From ME 11 in T4 R9 NWP just south of the Piscataquis–Penobscot County line and about halfway between Brownville Junction and Millinocket, turn north on Jo-Mary Rd. and quickly reach the Jo-Mary checkpoint. A fee is charged to pass through the gate. Travel 16.0 mi. to the east trailhead and the parking lot at Rabbit Brook, where there is clear signage. Reach the west trailhead by continuing north and west on Jo-Mary Rd. for 3.8 mi. to a jct. Turn left (west) on Nahmakanta Stream Rd. and proceed 1.2 mi. to Long Pond Rd. Turn left (south) and drive 1.0 mi. to the parking lot and trailhead at the gate and bridge over Little Penobscot Stream.

SEC 2

The blue-blazed loop is described from the west trailhead. Walk easily 1.1 mi. east to a jct. near the southwest corner of Sing Sing Pond. Turn left (north) and cross the outlet of the pond on a footbridge.

After a short climb, the trail emerges at the west end of the Turtle Ridge cliffs and proceeds through semi-open spruce forest and across ledges to a cliff-top viewpoint overlooking the pond. The trail then descends to a jct. at the northeast corner of Hedgehog Pond. The trail to the right connects to the loop on the opposite side of the pond. Proceeding straight ahead, reach a jct. with the eastern half of the loop. Continue straight ahead to the outlet of Rabbit Pond and its large granite slabs. Cross the outlet and continue over open granite ledges and through some woods to the next jct. in an open ledge area. From there, it is 0.5 mi. to the east trailhead on Jo-Mary Rd.

Continuing to the right, the trail climbs the spine of a ridge to reach a series of cliffs with views to Katahdin and the many lakes to the north and east. Ahead, the loop follows the ridgeline to a side trail leading to a lookout over Henderson Pond. Beyond, the loop descends to the north shore of Henderson Pond before turning west and rising easily through semi-open forest to a height-of-land. The loop then drops down through mature forest to return to the loop jct. Turn left (west) to reach Hedgehog Pond, then continue along the south shore of Sing Sing Pond and farther on to the west trailhead and the completion of the loop.

TUMBLEDOWN DICK TRAIL (MBPL; MAP 2: C5–C6)

Cumulative from Jo-Mary Rd. trailhead (1,089 ft.) to:	⇅	↗	○
AT (690 ft.)	4.2 mi.	50 ft.	2:05
South end of Nahmakanta Lake, via AT (650 ft.)	5.2 mi.	50 ft.	2:35

This connector trail links Turtle Ridge Loop to the AT and Debsconeag Backcountry Trail and makes possible a number of overnight backpacking possibilities. The trail leaves Jo-Mary Rd. at a point 150 yd. north of the Turtle Ridge Loop east trailhead on Jo-Mary Rd.

Travel east, and Leavitt Pond is soon visible through the trees. A side trail leads to a viewpoint on its northwest shore. Ahead, the main trail follows the edge of the pond before bearing away to reach a jct. Here, a side trail leads right 175 yd. to a campsite and another viewpoint across the pond. Continuing through mostly cutover forest, the trail arrives at Tumbledown Dick Pond and a campsite set in the pines. The trail follows the west shore and, after crossing the pond's outlet, contours above Tumbledown Dick Stream through a pleasant forest.

Where the trail touches a logging road and bridge, it crosses the stream and immediately turns north to continue down the other side of the stream and soon reaches Tumbledown Dick Falls. From an open spot immediately northeast of the falls is a view of Katahdin. The falls is a wonderful narrow drop worthy of exploration. Just ahead, a side trail right leads to a pool at the base of the falls. Beyond is a gentle downhill walk to a jct. with the AT at a good swimming hole on a sharp 90-degree bend in Nahmakanta Stream, 100 yd. above the stream's second deadwater. To the left (upstream), it is 0.6 mi. to a campsite, hand-carry boat launch, and beach on the south shore of Nahmakanta Lake.

DEBSCONEAG BACKCOUNTRY TRAIL (MBPL; MAP 2: B5)

Cumulative from trailhead parking area (720 ft.) to:	�231↥	↗	◔
Loop jct. at Fifth Debsconeag Pond (800 ft.)	0.8 mi.	80 ft.	0:25
Connector trail to Sixth Debsconeag Pond (1,150 ft.)	4.9 mi.	975 ft.	2:55
Spur trail to north trailhead (850 ft.)	7.2 mi.	1,125 ft.	4:10
Sixth Debsconeag Pond via loop (950 ft.)	9.7 mi.	1,450 ft.	5:35
Loop jct. at Fifth Debsconeag Pond (800 ft.)	12.1 mi.	1,630 ft.	6:50
Complete Debsconeag Backcountry Trail loop	12.9 mi.	1,630 ft.	7:15

The outstanding Debsconeag Backcountry Trail covers more than a dozen scenic miles over a series of hills and ridges that hide at least a dozen pretty little ponds in the wild country east of Nahmakanta Lake. The trail wends through a large chunk of ecological reserve and roadless area. There are no developed campsites along the trail. Although there is evidence of overnight use here and there, it's best to find an out-of-the-way, low-impact tent spot. The loop can, of course, be hiked over the course of a long day.

From ME 11 in T4 R9 NWP just south of the Piscataquis–Penobscot county line and about halfway between Brownville Junction and Millinocket, turn north on Jo-Mary Rd. and quickly reach the Jo-Mary Checkpoint. A fee is charged to pass through the gate. Travel 21 mi. to the end of Jo-Mary Rd. at the major jct. with Nahmakanta Stream Rd. Turn right (north) and drive 2.0 mi. to a jct. where Wadleigh Pond Rd. continues straight ahead and Nahmakanta Stream Rd. makes a sharp right.

Directions to the south trailhead: Follow Nahmakanta Stream Rd. east, cross Nahmakanta Stream on a bridge at 3.5 mi. and continue 1.0 mi. to trailhead parking and a kiosk on the left.

Directions to the north trailhead: Continue north on Wadleigh Pond Rd. for about 6 mi. to a bridge over Pollywog Stream. (Cross the AT about 4 mi. north of the jct. of Wadleigh Pond Rd. and Nahmakanta Stream Rd. for access to Nesuntabunt Mtn.) After the bridge, take an immediate right onto the road into Nahmakanta Lake Camps. Proceed 0.25 mi. to a parking lot and kiosk on the right just before the gate.

From the south trailhead, the trail heads north through mixed woods and occasional sandy-soiled openings to a jct. just south of Fifth Debsconeag Pond at 0.9 mi. To the right, it is 0.5 mi. along a stream to Nahmakanta Stream Rd. and a parking area and boat landing on Fourth Debsconeag Pond. To the left, it is 2.0 mi. to the west side of Sixth Debsconeag Pond. Continue straight ahead to begin the loop.

Cross the outlet stream and continue along the east shore of Fifth Debsconeag Lake. Bear away from the lake, cross a stream, and climb alongside it to reach Stink Pond. Bear west and climb to the open granite ledges above the pond, where there are fine views of White Cap Mtn., before dropping into a shallow valley. Beyond, the trail climbs to the extensive open ledges above Seventh Debsconeag Pond, with views of Nesuntabunt Mtn., White Cap Mtn., Fifth Debsconeag Lake, and Pemadumcook Lake. Descending the ledges, arrive at a jct. at 4.4 mi. To the left, a section of the loop trail leads 1.0 mi. past Sixth Debsconeag Pond to the east shore of Nahmakanta Lake. Ahead, the trail crosses a stream and, on ledges, passes south of a pond, soon reaching Eighth Debsconeag Pond. Then the trail swings west and descends moderately to reach Gould Brook and a jct. at 6.9 mi. To the right, a spur leads 0.8 mi. to the north trailhead.

Following Gould Brook downhill, the trail reaches a small sand beach at the north end of Nahmakanta Lake. Nahmakanta Lake Camps can be seen a short distance west along the lake. The trail then parallels the shore for nearly half the length of the lake, until finally bearing east away from the water and rising through a small ravine. At 9.6 mi., the trail reaches a jct. at Sixth Debsconeag Pond. Straight ahead, the trail connects in 1.0 mi. to the loop above Seventh Debsconeag Pond. To the right, the trail contours along the south side of Sixth Debsconeag Pond and then Fifth Debsconeag Pond before arriving at the original trail jct. at 11.6 mi. Straight ahead, it is a

direct 0.8 mi. back to the trailhead parking area. To the left, the route leads
to Fourth Debsconeag Pond and a boat landing and parking.

DEBSCONEAG LAKES WILDERNESS AREA

SEC 2

Directions to DLWA: From I-95, Exit 244 in Medway, drive west on ME
157 through Medway and East Millinocket to downtown Millinocket at
11.6 mi. At the jct. of ME 11 (south) and the end of ME 157 just past
downtown at 11.8 mi., bear right and follow signs for BSP. The road has
several names en route, including Millinocket Lake Rd., Baxter State Park
Rd., and simply Lake Rd. Drive 8.6 mi. to Northwoods Trading Post and
Big Moose Inn on the right. Bear left onto the parallel Golden Rd. and
drive 10.1 mi. to Abol Bridge Campground and Store on the right. Just
beyond, cross Abol Bridge over the West Branch of the Penobscot River
(excellent view of Katahdin to the north).

Directions to Ice Caves Trail trailhead: Immediately beyond Abol Bridge,
turn left onto a gravel road and soon pass a DLWA information kiosk. At
3.1 mi., reach a fork. To the right is the Hurd Pond boater's access. For Ice
Caves Trail, continue straight ahead for another 0.7 mi. to parking on the
right (kiosk and red gate).

Directions for Horserace Brook, Rainbow Loop, and Blue trails: From Abol
Bridge, continue west on the Golden Rd. for 5.4 mi. to a narrow road on the
left (this left turn is at the top of a hill just past the state campsite at Rainbow
Deadwater; there's a small sign, but it's easy to miss). Turn here and follow
this partially paved road to its end in another 0.3 mi., where there is parking
and a kiosk (please parallel park along the side of the road, not in the turnaround area by the kiosk).

■ RAINBOW LEDGES (1,504 FT.) AND RAINBOW MTN. (1,638 FT.)

The extensive Rainbow Ledges are found east of Rainbow Lake and west
of Hurd Pond in the northeastern section of DLWA. From numerous
points atop the ledges, outstanding views are possible to Katahdin in the
north, and south over the vast 100MW as far as the White Cap Range and
Baker Range. Farther west, Rainbow Mtn. rises above the east end of
Rainbow Lake. Rainbow Ledges and Rainbow Mtn. are most easily
reached via the AT Southbound from Abol Bridge. (*Note:* A round-trip to
Rainbow Mtn. is a considerable distance and may be best done as an overnight with a camping stay at Hurd Brook Lean-to.)

For driving directions to the AT and Abol Bridge, refer to the introductory text for DWLA above. Just beyond the bridge, there is an AT trailhead parking area on the left, just off Golden Rd.

AT SOUTHBOUND AND RAINBOW MTN. TRAIL
(MATC; USGS ABOL POND AND RAINBOW LAKE EAST QUADS, GAZETTEER MAP 50, MATC MAP 1, TNC DEBSCONEAG LAKES WILDERNESS AREA VISITOR MAP)

Cumulative from Abol Bridge (588 ft.) to:	⇅	↗	○
Hurd Pond Lean-to (700 ft.)	3.5 mi.	500 ft.	2:00
Rainbow Ledges (1,520 ft.)	6.0 mi.	1,300 ft.	3:40
Rainbow Lake (1,050 ft.)	7.8 mi.	1,300 ft.	4:35
Rainbow Mtn. side trail (1,100 ft.)	9.5 mi.	1,300 ft.	5:25
Rainbow Mtn. summit (1,638 ft.)	10.3 mi.	1,800 ft.	6:00

SEC 2

From the AT parking lot, follow the AT west along Golden Rd. for 0.2 mi., then turn south into the woods. This is the start of the 100MW. The rolling route southwest climbs to a ridge, drops down to cross a stream just south of Pitman Pond, climbs a lower ridge, and then descends to Hurd Brook Lean-to, which is to the right of the trail at 3.5 mi. Just beyond, ford Hurd Brook, a crossing that can be difficult in high water. Then the trail ascends west, climbing to the high point on Rainbow Ledges in a series of steps. It weaves across semi-open ledges (the area burned in a large forest fire in 1923) before descending southwest to cross a stream and reaching the east end of Rainbow Lake just north of Little Beaver Pond. The AT continues on a contour along the southwest shore of Rainbow Lake to the jct. with Rainbow Mtn. on the left. Rainbow Mtn. Trail climbs 0.75 mi. to the open ledges on top, where there are panoramic views over DLWA and beyond.

ICE CAVES TRAIL
(TNC; USGS ABOL POND QUAD, GAZETTEER MAP 50, TNC DEBSCONEAG LAKES WILDERNESS AREA VISITOR MAP)

Cumulative from parking area at end of road near Hurd Pond Stream (564 ft.) to:	⇅	↗	○
Ice Caves (650 ft.)	1.1 mi.	200 ft.	0:40
First Debsconeag Lake (500 ft.)	1.5 mi.	200 ft.	0:50

Go around the red gate and cross the bridge over Hurd Pond Stream. Just ahead, turn left into the woods on a footpath. Following light blue blazes, weave a path through boulders covered with ferns and mosses. Beyond the boulder ins and outs, climb the hillside. Pass through two more huge rocks, then slab across the hillside. At 0.7 mi., the trail goes left on an old forest road, then quickly turns right off that road into the woods. Follow an undulating route to a jct. at 0.9 mi. To the right, a spur trail leads 0.1 mi. to a cliff-top view over First Debsconeag Lake to Jo-Mary Mtn.

For the Ice Caves and First Debsconeag Lake, continue left from the jct. Make a moderate descent to the next jct., where a spur to the right leads 0.2 mi. to a handrail and rungs leading down to the rocks below; these are the Ice Caves. Return to the jct. and make a moderate to steep descent. The trail passes under a rock roof, then drops down to the rocks along the north shore of First Debsconeag Lake, where it ends. (*Note:* Due to heavy use and to protect this sensitive area, it is important that visitors stay on the trail, especially at the Ice Caves entrance.)

HORSERACE POND TRAIL
(TNC; USGS RAINBOW LAKE EAST QUAD, GAZETTEER MAP 50, TNC DEBSCONEAG LAKES WILDERNESS AREA VISITOR MAP)

Cumulative from Horserace Brook trailhead (610 ft.) to:	↓↑	↗	○
Blue Trail (690 ft.)	0.6 mi.	80 ft.	0:20
Horserace Pond (1,056 ft.) and Rainbow Loop Trail	2.0 mi.	450 ft.	1:20

Start to the left of the kiosk and cross a footbridge over Horserace Brook. Following yellow blazes, the trail joins the route of an old forest road. Cross another footbridge and soon arrive at a jct. at 0.6 mi., where Blue Trail departs to the left. Bear right to stay on Horserace Brook Trail, which continues on a slippery trail of rocks and roots to meet Horserace Brook. The trail turns left to follow the brook, making a gentle climb west up the valley. Cross a small brook at 1.2 mi. Beyond, pass a huge boulder (with fading graffiti on it) on the left, make a quick up and down, then pass between more huge boulders to reach a small day-use area with a fire pit. Here, a side trail on the right leads 0.1 mi. to a campsite on the east side of Horserace Pond. The main trail continues to an overlook on the edge of Horserace Pond, then reaches the pond and a campsite at 2.0 mi.; Rainbow Loop Trail begins here.

BLUE TRAIL
(TNC; USGS ABOL POND QUAD, GAZETTEER MAP 50, TNC DEBSCONEAG LAKES WILDERNESS AREA VISITOR MAP)

Cumulative from Horserace Brook Trail (690 ft.) to:	↓↑	↗	○
Rainbow Loop Trail (1,330 ft.)	1.1 mi.	640 ft.	0:55
Rainbow Lake (1,050 ft.)	2.5 mi.	660 ft.	1:35

From its jct. with Horserace Brook Trail, Blue Trail climbs a slope of mature forest growth, then ascends along the right side of a ravine and up along the right side of a mossy cliff. The trail reaches a small saddle, then switchbacks up the slope beyond. It levels off, contours on the hillside, then ascends easily. After a good stretch of mostly level trail, reach the jct. with the new Rainbow Loop Trail on the right at 1.1 mi. Beyond, make a gradual descent to Clifford Pond, reaching a side trail to the pond on the right at 1.4 mi. In the next 0.25 mi., there are two more side trails to the pond. Ahead, Woodman Pond appears on the right at 2.1 mi. Beyond the pond, pass to the right of a huge prow-like boulder, then descend a gradual to moderate slope to the end of the trail on the north shore of Rainbow Lake. Across the pond is the private Rainbow Lake Camps, and rising above and beyond is Rainbow Mtn.

SEC 2

RAINBOW LOOP TRAIL
(TNC; USGS ABOL POND QUAD, GAZETTEER MAP 50, TNC
DEBSCONEAG LAKES WILDERNESS AREA VISITOR MAP)

From Blue Trail (1,330 ft.) to:	⇅	↗	↺
Horserace Pond (1,050 ft.)	2.5 mi.	400 ft.	1:30

This orange-blazed trail leaves Blue Trail at a point 1.7 mi. from the Horserace Brook trailhead via Horserace Brook Trail. Rainbow Loop Trail follows an undulating route through majestic stands of pine and spruce before climbing steadily to the first outlook, where there is a view over Woodman Pond. The minor ups and downs continue until the trail finally ascends a steep slope to a small beaver pond at the head of an outlet stream. After a sharp left uphill over some steep sections, the trail emerges on a flat area of open bedrock marked by a large cairn, where there is an expansive vista south to Rainbow Lake. Several hundred feet beyond, turn sharply downhill and back into the woods. The trail meanders through dense bracken ferns, then winds around a massive boulder to a viewpoint east over a high pond. From there, continue upslope to reach a long, narrow rock outcrop and a fine view of Katahdin. Continue up to the next outlook for an even finer view, then move along a level area of scrubby trees before descending through mature forest above Horserace Pond. Glimpses of the pond are possible as the trail drops down a short rock staircase to the water. After a viewpoint west down to the pond, follow the shoreline to a campsite and the jct. with Horserace Brook Trail, which leads out to the trailhead in 2.0 mi.

SECTION 3
KENNEBEC AND MOOSE RIVER VALLEYS

In-Text Maps

141

SEC
3

INTRODUCTION

This section, on Kennebec and Moose River Valleys, includes all of Kennebec County and most of Somerset County, as well as a small chunk of Franklin County northeast of Chain of Ponds. It encompasses an area ranging roughly from the capital city of Augusta and neighboring Gardiner north to the headwaters of the St. John River east of the Canadian border. The region is bordered by the coastal lowlands in the south and by Aroostook County and American Realty Rd. in the north. Along the eastern boundary with Piscataquis County are the interior hills and mountains, Moosehead Lake, and the forestland between the Allagash and St. John River watersheds. A portion of the Penobscot and Waldo county lines form the southerly part of the eastern boundary. To the west are the high peaks along the border with Quebec, Canada. From its source at Moosehead Lake, the Kennebec River flows south through the center of the region for 170 mi., emptying into the Gulf of Maine east of Popham Beach. The Moose River originates near the Canadian border and flows generally east to empty into Moosehead Lake at Rockwood. This section describes 28 trails on 20 mountains.

GEOGRAPHY

In the southern reaches of the Kennebec and Moose River valleys are numerous low hills and mountains less than 1,000 ft. in elevation, from Mt. Pisgah (809 ft.) and Monument Hill (606 ft.) in the vicinity of Androscoggin Lake to the Kennebec Highlands, where a small cluster of peaks dot the landscape of the 6,800-acre preserve around the Belgrade Lakes region. McGaffey Mtn. is the highest of these peaks at 1,288 ft. Nearby are Round Top Mtn. (1,133 ft.) and Sanders Hill (854 ft.). French Mtn. (716 ft.), Mt. Phillip (755 ft.), and auspiciously named The Mountain (665 ft.) are in the same neighborhood and sport numerous loop trails. East of Bingham, Kelly Mtn. rises to 1,675 ft. From Bingham north to The Forks, the mountains on both sides of the Kennebec River valley begin to exceed 2,000 ft. At Caratunk, the AT crosses the Kennebec River and leads to the craggy summits of Moxie Bald Mtn. (2,630 ft.) and Pleasant Pond Mtn. (2,447 ft.), which are separated by Moxie Pond. Lightly visited Mosquito Mtn. (2,215 ft.). rises above the northwest end of Moxie Pond. Northwest of the Kennebec River are the jumbled high peaks of the remote border region, many of which are more than 3,500 ft. in elevation. Lengthy travel over sometimes rough gravel roads is often required to reach these trailheads.

Coburn Mtn., southwest of Parlin Pond, is the highest in the section at 3,718 ft. Boundary Bald Mtn., near the Canadian border, reaches 3,686 ft. In the wildland of the Moose River valley west of Jackman are Sally Mtn. (2,221 ft.) and Burnt Jacket Mtn. (2,241 ft.). Number Five Mtn. tops out at 3,186 ft. The ridgeline of Williams Mtn. (2,410 ft.) is east of US 201 and south of Long Pond and the Moose River. West of beautiful Pittston Farm on Seboomook Lake is Green Mtn. (2,395 ft.). Kibby Mtn. (3,654 ft.) rises east of Chain of Ponds at the headwaters of the Moose River.

The AT traverses this section, extending 42 mi. from Flagstaff Lake at the foot of the Bigelows north to Bald Mtn. Pond just beyond Moxie Bald Mtn.

SEC 3

ROAD ACCESS

US 201 bisects the Kennebec and Moose River valleys region south to north, from Gardiner to Sandy Bay Township on the Canadian border; the highway is the primary travel route through the Kennebec Valley. ME 15/6 heads east from Jackman and follows the Moose River to Moosehead Lake. ME 27 leads to the heart of the Kennebec Highlands in the Belgrade Lakes region. Significant travel on gravel logging roads is required to reach some of the more remote trailheads. The roads that approach Green Mtn. are maintained by North Maine Woods, which collects a fee for their use at checkpoint gates (cash only).

CAMPING

Thirteen lean-tos and campsites along the AT in this region are available for trailside camping. There are no state parks or public lands available for either remote or drive-in camping. At least fourteen privately operated campgrounds, some run by commercial whitewater rafting companies, offer a variety of camping and lodging choices with amenities. There are approximately 30 authorized primitive roadside campsites available within the boundaries North Maine Woods in this region.

KENNEBEC HIGHLANDS

At 6,800 acres, the Kennebec Highlands constitutes the largest contiguous block of conservation land in central Maine, encompassing the highest mountains in Kennebec County, miles of streams, several wetlands areas, and five undeveloped ponds. Since 1998, the Belgrade Regional Conservation Alliance, in partnership with the Maine Bureau of Parks and Lands, has worked to protect the Kennebec Highlands, which range across the towns of Rome, Mt. Vernon, and Vienna in Kennebec County and New

Sharon in Franklin County. BRCA manages an additional 3,000 acres of conserved land in close proximity to the Kennebec Highlands. BRCA trails lead to Round Top Mtn., Sanders Hill, McGaffey Mtn., French Mtn., Mt. Phillip, and the Mountain.

SUGGESTED HIKES

SEC 3

■ **Easy**

SANDERS HILL

	⤵	⤢	○
LP via Sanders Hill Trail	2.9 mi.	450 ft.	1:40

This trail loops through the scenic northern part of the Kennebec Highlands, just west of Watson Pond. See Sanders Hill Trail, p. 150.

MT. PHILLIP

	⤵	⤢	○
LP via Mt. Phillip Trail	1.4 mi.	400 ft.	0:55

Enjoy views over Great Pond and the Kennebec Highlands to the west on this easy loop hike. See Mt. Phillip Trail, p. 151.

THE MOUNTAIN

	⤵	⤢	○
LP via The Mountain Trail and Long Pond Loop Trail	1.7 mi.	300 ft.	1:15

Rising between Long Pond and Great Pond, this loop hike offers fine views of the Kennebec Highlands. To begin, see The Mountain Trail, p. 152.

FRENCH MTN.

	⤵	⤢	○
LP via French Mtn. Trail	0.8 mi.	170 ft.	0:25

Walk this easy loop to steep cliffs and a lookout to Long Pond, Great Pond, The Mountain, and the village of Belgrade Lakes. See French Mtn. Trail, p. 153.

MT. PISGAH

LP via Tower Trail and Blueberry Trail	2.0 mi.	545 ft.	1:15

Combine these trails for a wonderful loop that leads over Mt. Pisgah, which is topped by a 60-ft. fire tower offering outstanding views. To begin, see Tower Trail, p. 154.

MONUMENT HILL

LP via Monument Hill Trails	1.0 mi.	210 ft.	0:40

A fun circuit hike to a Civil War monument and ledges offers pleasant views of Androscoggin Lake, as well as the farms and woodlands to the east. See Monument Hill Trails, p. 156.

■ **Moderate**

ROUND TOP MTN.

LP via Round Top Trail and Round Top Spur Trail	4.5 mi.	820 ft.	2:40

Follow this route for good views of the Kennebec Highlands and the beautiful Belgrade Lakes region. To begin, see Round Top Trail, p. 149.

PLEASANT POND MTN.

RT via AT Northbound	3.2 mi.	1,050 ft.	2:30

Hike to the craggy summit ledges of Pleasant Pond Mtn. for a panoramic view. A post-hike swim at Pleasant Pond is a nice bonus. See AT Northbound, p. 159.

MOSQUITO MTN.

RT via Mosquito Mtn. Trail	3.2 mi.	1,240 ft.	3:10

Enjoy panoramic views from the summit ledges of Mosquito Mtn., from Moxie Pond and the many peaks ringing Moosehead Lake to Katahdin and the Bigelows. See Mosquito Mtn. Trail, p. 160.

NUMBER FIVE MTN.

RT via Number Five Mtn. Trail	5.8 mi.	1,175 ft.	4:00

This long, gradual hike leads to a craggy summit topped with an old fire tower, where the reward is a 360-degree panorama of mountains and ponds. See Number Five Mtn. Trail, p. 162.

SALLY MTN.

RT via Sally Mtn. Trail	6.0 mi.	1,075 ft.	4:00

Hike along railroad tracks next to Attean Pond then head for the open ledges high on Sally Mtn., the site of the former fire tower, where the view ranges from Katahdin to the Bigelows. See Sally Mtn. Trail, p. 163.

BURNT JACKET MTN.

RT via Burnt Jacket Mtn. Trail	3.0 mi.	1,000 ft.	2:30

Enjoy excellent views of the Moose River valley and the peaks of the border region from this open summit west of Jackman. See Burnt Jacket Mtn. Trail, p. 164.

WILLIAMS MTN.

RT via Williams Mtn. Trail	3.0 mi.	610 ft.	2:30

Hike Williams Mtn.'s ridgeline to an old fire warden cabin and summit fire tower, which affords extensive views over the vast forestland west of Moosehead Lake. See Williams Mtn. Trail, p. 166.

KIBBY MTN.

RT via Kibby Mtn. Trail	4.0 mi.	1,100 ft.	3:00

Hike to the site of an old fire tower in a remote area for a wide vista that includes the wind turbines of Maine's largest wind farm. See Kibby Mtn. Trail, p. 168.

■ Strenuous
MOXIE BALD MTN.

⬤ 🏊 🎾 🥾		↻↑	↗	◔
RT via the AT Northbound		9.6 mi.	1,660 ft.	6:30

Hike the AT to the summit ledges on Moxie Bald Mtn., where extensive views include the peaks of Katahdin, Bigelow, Sugarloaf, Abraham, Coburn, and Boundary Bald. See AT Northbound, p. 157.

SEC 3

BOUNDARY BALD MTN.

🎾 🥾		↻↑	↗	◔
RT via Boundary Bald Mtn. Trail		4.8 mi.	1,800 ft.	4:20

Enjoy 360-degree views from the long, open summit ridge of Boundary Bald Mtn., including the lake country of northern Somerset County, the Moosehead Lake region, and southern Canada. See Boundary Bald Mtn. Trail, p. 165.

TRAIL DESCRIPTIONS

KENNEBEC HIGHLANDS

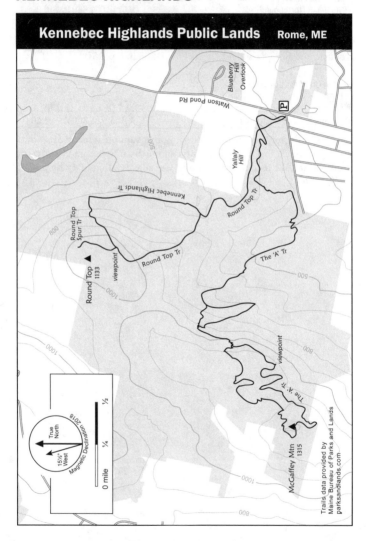

Kennebec Highlands Public Lands   Rome, ME

Blueberry Hill Overlook

Watson Pond Rd

Yallaly Hill

Kennebec Highlands Tr

Round Top Tr

Round Top Spur Tr

Round Top Tr

The 'A' Tr

viewpoint

Round Top 1133

viewpoint

The 'A' Tr

McGaffey Mtn 1315

True North

15½° West
Magnetic Declination
2018

0 mile   ¼   ½

Trails data provided by
Maine Bureau of Parks and Lands
parksandlands.com

■ ROUND TOP MTN. (1,133 FT.)

This mountain provides wonderful views over Long Pond and Great Pond, the village of Belgrade Lakes, and the surrounding hills. From the jct. of ME 27 and Watson Pond Rd., 4.4 mi. north of the village of Belgrade Lakes, turn left on Watson Pond Rd. and drive 4.0 mi. south to a parking lot at the corner of Wildflower Estates and Watson Pond Rd. Ascend Round Top Mtn. by combining Round Top Trail and Round Top Spur Trail.

ROUND TOP TRAIL (BRCA; KENNEBEC HIGHLANDS, P. 148)

SEC 3

Cumulative from Watson Pond Rd. trailhead (490 ft.) to:	↥↧	↗	↻
Round Top Spur Trail (1,090 ft.)	1.8 mi.	750 ft.	1:15
Complete loop via Kennebec Highlands Trail	3.9 mi.	750 ft.	2:20

Round Top Trail leaves the parking lot in a westerly direction, crossing the "A" Trail at 0.2 mi. After an initial rise, the trail briefly opens up for a view of Round Top Mtn. just before dropping to a well-signed jct. with Kennebec Highlands Trail at 1.0 mi. After crossing Kennebec Highlands Trail, Round Top Trail climbs steadily to the northwest. As the trail approaches the summit of Round Top Mtn., views open up to the east and south. Near the top, at 1.8 mi., Round Top Spur Trail departs to the left (see description below). The main Round Top Trail continues northeast, passing an overlook with views of Long Pond, the village of Belgrade Lakes, and Great Pond. The trail descends steeply and joins the Kennebec Highlands Trail at 2.2 mi. Turn right (south) onto this broad gravel trail. At 2.9 mi., bear right onto a narrower section. At 3.0 mi., Round Top Trail joins a snowmobile trail and soon comes to the signpost marking the initial jct. of Round Top Trail and Kennebec Highlands Trail. Turn left (east) and follow Round Top Trail back to the parking lot.

Round Top Spur Trail. This short 0.3-mi. spur leads from Round Top Trail to the north end of Round Top Mtn. (but does not go to the summit), gaining about 70 ft. of elevation en route. The first view looks north and east to Round Pond below and to French Mtn., Mt. Phillip, and Great Pond. The spur trail ends at a second overlook, where there are views of Watson Pond, Sanders Hill, and Vienna Mtn. (northwest through the trees).

■ McGAFFEY MTN. (1,288 FT.)

This twin-peaked mountain, immediately southwest of Round Top Mtn., is the highest in the Kennebec Highlands. The "A" Trail, designed as a multiuse trail to be shared by both hikers and mountain bikers, leads to the summit of McGaffey Mtn.

THE "A" TRAIL (BRCA; KENNEBEC HIGHLANDS, P. 148)

Cumulative from Watson Pond Rd. trailhead (490 ft.) to:	⬇︎⬆︎	↗	◷
Scenic lookout (1,125 ft.)	3.3 mi.	650 ft.	2:00
McGaffey Mtn. summit (1,288 ft.)	4.5 mi.	1,050 ft.	2:50

The "A" Trail starts at the northeast corner of the same parking lot as Round Top Trail (see directions on p. 149). The "A" Trail crosses Round Top Trail at 0.3 mi., continues west, and then turns south, crossing Goat Path at 1.0 mi. The trail next descends to intersect an old logging road at 1.3 mi., then follows the logging road to the right (northwest), crossing a stream and gradually narrowing to single-track as it climbs. At 2.1 mi., the "A" Trail turns left (south) on another grown-in logging road. (For hikers, a steeper, rockier option continues straight uphill, rejoining the bike trail in 0.2 mi.) The "A" Trail descends gradually until meeting another logging road at 2.4 mi., where it turns sharply to the right (north). From here, the trail follows the logging road, climbing to rejoin the hiking trail and then ascending in a series of short switchbacks. The trail beyond the 2.8-mi. point has been roughly cut but is not completed and has no signs. Proceed with caution. The trail turns southwest and steadily gains elevation until reaching an open area and a scenic lookout with views of Long Pond at 3.3 mi. From the lookout, the trail meanders along the ridgeline, ending at the summit of McGaffey Mtn. at 4.5 mi.

◼ SANDERS HILL (854 FT.)

This hill in Rome rises just west of Watson Pond in the scenic northern part of the Kennebec Highlands. From the jct. of ME 27 and Watson Pond Rd., 4.4 mi. north of the village of Belgrade Lakes, turn left onto Watson Pond Rd. and drive south 1.3 mi. to a small parking area on the right. Sanders Hill Trail, which makes a nice loop hike, is described counterclockwise.

SANDERS HILL TRAIL (BRCA; USGS BELGRADE LAKES QUAD, BRCA TRAIL MAP AND GUIDE TO KENNEBEC HIGHLANDS AND NEARBY AREAS)

Cumulative from Watson Pond Rd. (450 ft.) to:	⬇︎⬆︎	↗	◷
Sanders Hill summit (854 ft.)	1.2 mi.	450 ft.	0:45
Complete loop	2.9 mi.	450 ft.	1:40

Sanders Hill Trail leaves from the north side of the parking area, to the right of the trailhead kiosk, and soon reaches a large, flat rock affording views across Watson Pond. The trail bears right onto an old logging road and after several hundred feet turns left off the logging road, narrowing and climbing moderately to the west. The trail eventually turns right (north) and traverses through a rock field, where there are partial views to the east of Watson Pond, Mt. Phillip, and French Mtn. The trail cuts directly over and through some large granite slabs at 0.9 mi., then turns left (west) and climbs to the sparsely wooded summit area, which offers partial views to the east and south through the trees at 1.1 mi.

The trail continues northwest over the Sanders Hill summit (854 ft.), then descends to cross Kennebec Highlands Trail at 1.3 mi. After reentering the woods, the trail turns south and meanders along the bank of Beaver Brook. At 2.0 mi., the trail again crosses Kennebec Highlands Trail, continuing straight ahead. It swings east and then north, briefly following an old logging road before bearing left and then descending to a large boulder at 2.3 mi., where it crosses that same logging road. The trail continues east and then north over gently rolling terrain. At 2.8 mi., it intersects an old logging road at a wide, grassy jct. Turning right (east) onto the logging road. the trail leads back to the parking lot.

■ MT. PHILLIP (755 FT.)

This summit overlooking Great Pond in Rome provides good views of the Kennebec Highlands to the west. From the jct. of ME 27 and ME 225 at Rome Corner, travel east on ME 225 for 1.5 mi. to a parking lot on the north side of the road, directly across from Starbird Ln.

MT. PHILLIP TRAIL (BRCA; USGS BELGRADE LAKES QUAD, BRCA TRAIL MAP AND GUIDE TO KENNEBEC HIGHLANDS AND NEARBY AREAS)

Cumulative from ME 225 (350 ft.) to:	⇅	↗	◔
Mt. Phillip summit (755 ft.)	0.7 mi.	400 ft.	0:30
Complete loop	1.4 mi.	400 ft.	0:55

This loop trail can be followed in either direction; counterclockwise is described here. Mt. Phillip Trail leaves from the northeast corner of the parking lot and heads east. In less than 0.1 mi., the trail splits; bear right to follow it counterclockwise. The trail heads northwest up the eastern slope of Mt. Phillip, continues to a rocky ledge on the mountain's eastern side at 0.6 mi., and crosses a ledge westward to a partial summit clearing (755 ft.). Here there are views of Great Pond to the south and the Kennebec Highlands to the west. To continue the loop, descend to the west, make a sharp turn in a southerly direction, and follow the trail back to the jct. and the parking lot.

■ THE MOUNTAIN (665 FT.)

The Mountain in Rome is situated amid 207 acres owned and managed by BRCA and Belgrade Lakes Association. The Mountain rises between Long Pond and Great Pond, offering fine views of the Kennebec Highlands and the surrounding lakes and woods. From the village of Belgrade Lakes, drive 1.0 mi. north on ME 27. Turn right (east) onto Mountain Dr. and proceed 0.3 mi. to a parking area on the left (north) side of the road.

The trail network on The Mountain consists of a main trail 0.8 mi. long and three side trails that can be combined for loop hikes of up to 2.5 mi. The side trails can be hiked in either direction, but are described here from south to north.

THE MOUNTAIN TRAIL (BRCA; USGS BELGRADE LAKES QUAD, BRCA TRAIL MAP AND GUIDE TO KENNEBEC HIGHLANDS AND NEARBY AREAS)

From Mountain Dr. parking area (375 ft.) to:	⇅	↗	⟳
The Mountain high point (665 ft.) via the Mountain Trail	0.8 mi.	300 ft.	0:35
The Mountain high point (665 ft.) via the Mountain Trail and Great Pond Loop	0.8 mi.	300 ft.	0:35
The Mountain high point (665 ft.) via the Mountain Trail and Long Pond Loop	0.9 mi.	300 ft.	0:40

The Mountain Trail, an old logging road, heads north from the parking area. Great Pond Loop (marked by green arrows) leaves on the right (east) 0.4 mi. up the Mountain Trail. Long Pond Loop (white arrows) leaves the Mountain Trail on the left (west) at 0.5 mi. The Mountain Trail continues upward straight ahead and ends at a high point on the south ridge of the Mountain and a jct. with Great Pond Loop, which rejoins from the right. Long Pond Loop rejoins from the left.

Great Pond Loop. This loop, marked with green arrows, is 0.35 mi. long. From the parking area, follow the Mountain Trail. At 0.15 mi., Outer Loop (described on p. 153) leaves to the right. Ahead on the Mountain Trail, at 0.4 mi., Great Pond Loop departs to the right. Great Pond Loop climbs west to a small open area high on the Mountain, then turns north. Outer Loop rejoins from the right at 0.3 mi. Keeping left, Great Pond Loop descends steeply to its terminus at the jct. with the Mountain Trail and Long Pond Loop.

Long Pond Loop. This loop, 0.4 mi. long and marked with white arrows, leaves the Mountain Trail on the left (west), 0.5 mi. from the parking area. Long Pond Loop descends from the Mountain Trail, passing over a cliff with steep drop-offs and views of Long Pond and the Kennebec Highlands. The trail soon turns east and climbs to reach the jct. with the Mountain Trail and Great Pond Loop.

OUTER LOOP (BRCA; USGS BELGRADE LAKES QUAD, BRCA TRAIL MAP AND GUIDE TO KENNEBEC HIGHLANDS AND NEARBY AREAS)

From Great Pond Loop, lower jct. (580 ft.) to:	⮁	↗	⏱
Great Pond Loop, upper jct. (665 ft.)	1.1 mi.	200 ft.	0:40

Outer Loop is a 1.1-mile, blue-blazed trail that begins and ends on Great Pond Loop (described on p. 152). Outer Loop leaves to the right (north), 0.15 mi. from Great Pond Loop's lower jct. with the Mountain Trail, climbing through a rocky area before leveling out and proceeding northward. At 0.4 mi., Outer Loop passes two overlooks with views to Great Pond, both marked by "Steep Drop-Off" signs. Outer Loop then descends and turns west, crossing a snowmobile trail at 0.6 mi. The loop trail soon turns south through open woods, then climbs in several steps, crossing the snowmobile trail again at 1.0 mi., and ending at 1.1 mi. Here, Outer Loop rejoins Great Pond Loop just southeast of its upper jct. with the Mountain Trail.

■ FRENCH MTN. (716 FT.)

From this summit in Rome, there are good views of the Belgrade Lakes area, including Whittier Pond to the east, Mt. Phillip to the northeast, and Long Pond to the southeast. From the jct. of ME 27 and Watson Pond Rd., proceed south on Watson Pond Rd. for 0.7 mi. to a paved parking apron and a parking lot on the east side of the road.

FRENCH MTN. TRAIL (BRCA; USGS BELGRADE LAKES QUAD, BRCA TRAIL MAP AND GUIDE TO KENNEBEC HIGHLANDS AND NEARBY AREAS)

Cumulative from Watson Pond Rd. (550 ft.) to:	⮁	↗	⏱
French Mtn. summit (716 ft.) via right or left fork	0.4 mi.	170 ft.	0:15
Complete loop	0.8 mi.	170 ft.	0:25

French Mtn. Trail is a loop that can be followed in either direction; clockwise is described here. The trail leaves from the southeast corner of the parking lot, enters the woods, and heads east. It soon splits at a large signboard. Stay left for the most direct path to the summit. The trail climbs to the east, then swings south, following the ridge of French Mtn. (716 ft.) to reach a rocky precipice with views of Whittier Pond to the east and Long

Pond to the south. The trail continues along the open rocks, above steep cliffs overlooking the northern end of Long Pond. From here hikers can also see Great Pond, the Mountain, and Belgrade Lakes village. Just south of the summit, the trail turns west into the woods and descends several switchbacks before turning north and gradually descending back to the jct. and the parking lot.

SEC 3

ANDROSCOGGIN LAKE

■ MT. PISGAH (809 FT.)

The 950-acre Mt. Pisgah Conservation Area in Wayne and Winthrop is co-owned and co-managed by Kennebec Land Trust, the town of Winthrop, and a private landowner. Mt. Pisgah is the central feature of the land. A 60-ft. summit fire tower, in place since 1949, affords 360-degree views ranging from Mt. Washington and the Presidential Range in the west to the Camden Hills on the coast in the east.

From the jct. of US 202/ME 11/100 and ME 132 in Monmouth, proceed east on US 202/ME 11/100 for 0.5 mi. Turn left (north) onto North Main St. and drive 0.8 mi. to the crossroads in North Monmouth. Turn right onto Wilson Pond Rd. and go 0.2 mi. to Mt. Pisgah Rd. Turn left and drive 1.6 mi. to the trailhead on the right. Two trails, Tower Trail and Blueberry Trail, diverge from this common trailhead and combine for a nice hiking loop.

TOWER TRAIL (KLT; USGS WAYNE QUAD, GAZETTEER MAP 12, KLT MT. PISGAH CONSERVATION AREA MAP)

From Mt. Pisgah Rd. (450 ft.) to:	⇅	↗	↻
Mt. Pisgah summit (809 ft.)	0.7 mi.	360 ft.	0:30

Proceed left of the kiosk on the gravel tower access road, passing Blueberry Trail on the right, to a gate. Here, the blue-blazed Tower Trail departs left, up stone steps. The trail is easy at first, then climbs moderately through a forest of pines and hardwoods. Beyond a series of bog bridges and a jct. of stone walls, pass a large rock cairn to the left of the trail. Ledges Trail departs to the left at 0.5 mi. Climb the summit ledges to reach the fire tower in a small meadow. A cell tower and the gravel tower access road are just beyond.

BLUEBERRY TRAIL (KLT; USGS WAYNE QUAD, GAZETTEER MAP 12, KLT MT. PISGAH CONSERVATION AREA MAP)

From Mt. Pisgah summit (809 ft.) to:	⇅	↗	↻
Mt. Pisgah Rd. (450 ft.)	1.3 mi.	185 ft.	0:45

Blueberry Trail is commonly used as a descent route and is thus described from the summit of Mt. Pisgah to the trailhead. From the fire tower, cross the gravel tower access road and head downhill. A sign indicates that high-bush blueberry restoration is in progress. The trail passes through a forest of large white pines, maples, and oaks on its descent of the mountain's south slope. At the 550-ft. contour, the trail heads west, climbing to a knoll and crossing three small streams, the first two via footbridges and the third via rocks. After cresting the knoll, the trail descends along a stone wall, makes a traverse, then weaves through several stone walls to join an old woods road. Ahead, leave the old road to the right and follow a stone wall to the base of the mountain. Turn left on the gravel tower access road to return to the trailhead.

SEC 3

LEDGES TRAIL (KLT; USGS WAYNE QUAD, GAZETTEER MAP 12, KLT MT. PISGAH CONSERVATION AREA MAP)

From Tower Trail (740 ft.) to:	⇅	↗	⟳
Blueberry Trail (660 ft.)	1.4 mi.	170 ft.	0:45

The new Ledges Trail, opened in 2017, allows for a longer loop hike that connects Tower Trail with Blueberry Trail on a ridgeline north of the Pisgah summit. From the 740-ft. contour 0.5-mi. up Tower Trail from its base, turn left onto Ledges Trail and head northeast. The trail winds through a dense forest of hemlock and mixed hardwoods while descending to a point at 590 ft. on the northern ridgeline of Mt. Pisgah. Ledges Trail then heads south and crosses a small stream. Impressive ledges are to the west of the trail. A series of switchbacks crosses areas of exposed bedrock and then follows the contour to Blueberry Trail at 660 ft. Turn left to return to the parking area in 1.1 mi. following Blueberry Trail, or turn right on Blueberry Trail to return to the parking area in 1.1 mi. via the Pisgah summit and Tower Trail.

■ MONUMENT HILL (660 FT.)

Monument Hill, just west of Androscoggin Lake in Leeds, offers pleasant views of the surrounding farms, forests, and lakes. A granite obelisk on the summit is dedicated to Leeds soldiers and sailors of the Civil War. The monument is inscribed, "Peace was sure 1865." Community members of the town of Leeds maintain the trail.

MONUMENT HILL TRAILS (TOL; USGS TURNER CENTER QUAD, GAZETTEER MAP 12, MTF MONUMENT HILL)

From North Rd. (450 ft.) to:	⇅	↗	◌
Monument Hill summit (660 ft.) via left fork or right fork	0.5 mi.	210 ft.	0:20

To reach the trail from US 202 between Lewiston and Augusta, take ME 106 north for 6.2 mi. to Leeds. Take Church Hill Rd. left (west) for 0.9 mi. to North Rd. on the right. Take this for 0.9 mi. to the trailhead on the right (sign) and roadside parking.

Occasional wooden signs with black arrows mark the well-worn trail route. Follow a woods road easily uphill to an old log yard in a level area. Here, the trail forks. The left fork and right fork rise gently east and southeast, respectively, to join at the summit, where there is a viewpoint to the east just beyond the monument.

MOXIE POND

■ MOXIE BALD MTN. (2,630 FT.) AND MOXIE BALD, NORTH PEAK (2,350 FT.)

This mountain in Bald Mtn. Township features a long ridge extending north and south for about 4 mi. Its summit is alpine in nature, owing to the extensive area of open ledges. The views from the summit are excellent: Katahdin to the northeast; Bigelow, Sugarloaf, and Abraham to the west; Coburn and Boundary Bald to the north. The summit of Moxie Bald Mtn. is reached via the AT, which leaves from a point on Moxie Pond Rd. just south of Joe's Hole, the southernmost point on Moxie Pond. The side trail to North Peak, easy to reach from the AT 0.7 mi. north of the main summit, is worth exploring.

The Moxie Bald–AT trailhead can be reached from US 201 in The Forks in the north or from US 201 in Bingham in the south.

Directions from US 201 in The Forks: Just before US 201 crosses the Kennebec River, turn right on Lake Moxie Rd. Follow this paved road for 5.3 mi. to Lake Moxie Station and a T intersection. Turn right onto Troutdale Rd., a former railroad bed, and follow it along Moxie Pond. (*Note:* This road can be rough and narrow in places, and many camps are located on this shore of the lake, so drive carefully.) At 12.9 mi., reach a small parking area on the right side of the road. The sign for the AT and Moxie Bald Mtn. is on the left.

Directions from US 201 in Bingham: Turn east on ME 16 and drive 5.5 mi. Turn left (north) on Town Line Rd. Reset odometer. At 2.8 mi. from ME 16, turn right on Deadwater Rd. At 4.4 mi., cross an iron bridge; the road becomes Troutdale Rd. At 6.3 mi., there are power lines on the left. At 8.7 mi., pass under the power lines. At 9.7 mi., reach a four-way jct. Here, Baker Dimmock Rd. departs left and crosses a bridge. An unnamed road leaves to the right. To intersect the AT just north of Bald Mtn. Brook Lean-to and make for a shorter hike to the Moxie Bald Mtn. summit, take this unnamed road. (For a longer hike, continue north from this point on Troutdale Rd. for an additional 2.1 mi. to the AT crossing at Baker Stream at the south end of Moxie Pond.) Reset odometer. At 0.3 mi. from Troutdale Rd., pass under power lines. At 0.8 mi., turn left onto the AT Rd. Stay right at a fork at 1.7 mi. Cross a bridge over Bald Mtn. Brook at 3.8 mi. Park on the right at a small pullout. The AT crosses the gravel road just ahead.

AT NORTHBOUND (MATC; USGS MOXIE POND AND DIMMICK MTN. QUADS, GAZETTEER MAP 30, MATC MAP 4)

Cumulative from Troutdale Rd. (970 ft.) via AT to:	⇅	↗	⟳
Side trail to Bald Mtn. Brook Lean-to (1,350 ft.)	2.8 mi.	380 ft.	1:35
AT Rd. crossing (1,400 ft.)	3.0 mi.	430 ft.	1:40
Moxie Bald Mtn. summit (2,630 ft.)	4.8 mi.	1,660 ft.	3:15
Summit bypass trail, north jct. (2,450 ft.)	5.1 mi.	1,660 ft.	3:25
Moxie Bald, North Peak Trail (2,225 ft.)	5.8 mi.	1,660 ft.	3:45
Moxie Bald, North Peak (2,350 ft.)	6.5 mi.	1,785 ft.	4:10

The AT to Moxie Bald Mtn. leaves the east side of Troutdale Rd. and immediately crosses Baker Brook near the inlet to Moxie Pond. (*Note:* Even in times of moderate water levels, this crossing may be difficult.) At 0.5 mi., the trail crosses under a power line, and at 1.2 mi., it crosses Joe's Hole Brook. Ahead, the AT reaches Bald Mtn. Brook at 2.6 mi. Cross the brook, pass a campsite, and, at 2.8 mi., reach a side trail leading 0.1 mi. to Bald Mtn. Brook Lean-to. Just beyond the side trail to the lean-to, at 3.0 mi., cross a multiuse gravel road, the AT Rd. (see driving directions above to reach this crossing).

Continue climbing to reach a jct. with the blue-blazed summit bypass trail at 4.2 mi., a good option in bad weather. (*Note:* The bypass trail rejoins the AT in 0.5 mi. at a point just north of and below the Moxie Bald Mtn. summit.) Ahead on the AT, ascend more steeply over ledges before fully breaking out into the open. At 4.8 mi., reach the open summit of Moxie Bald Mtn., site of a fire tower from 1910 until 1994.

North Peak Trail (MATC). This short but very scenic side trail leaves the AT 0.7 mi. north of the Moxie Bald Mtn. summit. From the summit, descend via ledges to the north jct. of the summit bypass trail. Turn north here. Descend the north ridge of the mountain to a saddle and the jct. with North Peak Trail on the left. Follow North Peak Trail over the mostly open ridgeline of ledges to the wild and remote-feeling North Peak. Blueberries, when in season, are abundant on this side trail.

■ PLEASANT POND MTN. (2,447 FT.)

Located between Moxie Pond and the Kennebec River in The Forks, the long ridgeline of Pleasant Pond Mtn. has extensive open ledges that offer fine views in all directions. Hikers can reach the mountain via the AT from either the south or the north. The long and hilly north ridge of Pleasant Pond Mtn. features impressive forests of mature spruce and fir. A fire tower stood on the summit of Pleasant Mtn. from 1910 until 1951, when it was moved to Barren Mtn. in Elliotsville.

AT SOUTHBOUND (MATC; USGS THE FORKS AND MOXIE POND QUADS, GAZETTEER MAP 30, MATC MAP 4)

Cumulative from Troutdale Rd. (975 ft.) via AT Southbound to:	⇅	↗	○
Power line (1,000 ft.)	0.1 mi.	25 ft.	0:05
Brook crossing (1,050 ft.)	0.5 mi.	75 ft.	0:15
Pleasant Pond Mtn. summit (2,447 ft.)	4.9 mi.	1,500 ft.	3:15

To hike Pleasant Pond Mtn. from its north side, use the same approach by road as for Moxie Bald Mtn. (see above).

Walk north along Troutdale Rd. from the parking area for 0.2 mi. to where the AT heads west up the mountain from a spot near Joe's Hole at the southern end of Moxie Pond. At 0.1 mi., the trail crosses under a power line, then passes through a low area of beaver bogs. It crosses a brook at 0.5 mi. Beyond, the trail ascends to the long southerly ridge of the mountain and follows it over the middle summit until finally reaching the craggy ledges on the main summit at 4.9 mi.

AT NORTHBOUND (MATC; USGS FORKS AND MOXIE POND QUADS, GAZETTEER MAP 30, MATC MAP 4)

Cumulative from parking area (1,400 ft.) via AT Northbound to:	↥↧	↗	⟳
Side trail to Pleasant Pond Lean-to and beach (1,300 ft.)	0.3 mi.	-100 ft.	0:10
Pleasant Pond Mtn. summit (2,447 ft.)	1.6 mi.	1,050 ft.	1:15

The road approach for the hike from the south side of Pleasant Pond Mtn. starts at US 201 in the village of Caratunk at a point about 14 mi. north of the jct. of US 201 and ME 16 in Bingham. Leave US 201 to the right at a sign for Caratunk and Pleasant Pond. Proceed 0.8 mi. to Caratunk, then turn right and head uphill on Pleasant Pond Rd. At 3.9 mi., take the left fork onto North Shore Rd. At 4.2 mi. the pavement ends. At 5.3 mi., bear right where Boise Crossover Rd. bears left, and proceed straight into the woods on the parking lot driveway. Trailhead parking signs soon become evident as you approach a grassy opening and the AT at 5.5 mi.

The AT leaves the parking area and heads north toward Pleasant Pond Mtn. At 0.3 mi., reach a side trail leading 0.1 mi. to Pleasant Pond Lean-to. From the lean-to, a side trail leads an additional 0.2 mi. to a small sand beach on Pleasant Pond. Ahead on the AT, at 0.5 mi., another side trail leads 0.2 mi. to the aforementioned beach. Beyond, the rocky trail leads steeply uphill through dense woods. At 1.5 mi., the trail climbs over rock ledges and, shortly thereafter, at 1.6 mi., breaks out onto open ledges at the summit and the site of the former fire tower.

■ MOSQUITO MTN. (2,215 FT.)

Rising just west of Moxie Pond in The Forks, this mountain offers excellent views in all directions from its summit ledges, from the many peaks ringing Moosehead Lake to Katahdin and the Bigelows.

From US 201 in The Forks, just before the highway crosses the Kennebec River, turn right onto Lake Moxie Rd. Follow this paved road for 5.3 mi. to Lake Moxie Station and a T intersection. Turn right onto Troutdale Rd. and follow the old railroad bed along Moxie Pond. (*Note:* The road is narrow and can be rough in places, and many camps are located on this shore of the lake, so drive carefully.) At 1.9 mi., just beyond where the road bears left away from the power line and enters the woods, is a small parking area on the right, across from two camps. It is just large enough for several cars. (*Note:* Because Troutdale Rd. is narrow, avoid parking along it.) A red bear paw is painted on a rock at the trailhead.

SEC 3

MOSQUITO MTN. TRAIL
(NFTM; USGS MOXIE POND, GAZETTEER MAP 30)

From Troutdale Rd.
(975 ft.) to:

	⇅	↗	↻
Mosquito Mtn. summit (2,215 ft.)	1.6 mi.	1,240 ft.	1:35

At about 0.1 mi. from Troutdale Rd., the trail crosses under a power line and soon reaches an old woods road. Go left onto the woods road for 40 ft. before turning right onto the trail again. At a jct., turn left and follow the wide gravel road for 30 ft., then turn right uphill into the woods. Ahead, logging has reduced the forested trail corridor to a width of about 50 ft., and there are views north to Mt. Kineo. Beyond, the trail climbs steeply, passing a large boulder on the left, before leveling out for about 0.1 mi. After entering a stand of dense spruce, the eroded trail climbs steeply again, passing beneath a huge overhanging ledge to reach a long rock wall on the left. Follow this wall to its end, where a short side trail leads left onto ledges. The view of Moxie Pond is breathtaking. Big Moose Mtn. is in sight to the north, Moxie Bald Mtn. to the south. The main trail continues to climb steeply over rocks and ledges to the craggy open summit, which is reached at 1.6 mi.

US 201 CORRIDOR

■ KELLY MTN. (1,675 FT.)

This low mountain rises west of Bingham and the Kennebec River in Brighton Plantation. On the summit, the 1925 fire tower still stands and is accessible for good views of the area. The fire warden's trail once used to access the tower has become overgrown and more recently has been obliterated by logging. The current trail follows an ATV route from the southwest.

To reach the trail from US 201 in Bingham, turn east on ME 16 and drive 10.4 mi. to the jct. of ME 151 at Mayfield Corner. Proceed south on ME 151 for 4.2 mi. to the jct. of ME 151 and ME 154. From this jct., shown as Brighton on Gazetteer map 31, drive south on ME 151 for an additional 0.1 mi. Here, turn right (west) onto Stagecoach Rd. At 0.9 mi., bear left at the fork on the rise and go downhill, then bear right (northwest) at a T intersection at 1.3 mi. Continue to another T intersection at 2.3 mi. and turn left to cross a bridge. At 3.4 mi., at a four-corner intersection (the road left is more obscure than the other three), bear right, and at 3.5 mi., bear right again. At 5.3 mi., the road enters a grassy old log yard with parking on the left.

KELLY MTN. TRAIL
(NFTM; USGS KINGSBURY QUAD, GAZETTEER MAP 31)

From trailhead at old log yard (1,250 ft.) to:	↕	↗	◷
Kelly Mtn. summit (1,675 ft.)	0.6 mi.	425 ft.	0:30

The trail, an ATV track, exits the log yard to the north, passes through a ditch, and within 200 ft., turns up the mountain. Within 150 yd., the track turns right, and from this point to the top, it is marked with blue flagging. The track is well used and maintained, and leads directly uphill to the ridgeline and then follows it north to the tower at 0.6 mi. from the start. The views at the top can only be obtained by climbing the new, well-constructed (2017) observation platform.

SEC 3

■ COBURN MTN. (3,718 FT.)

This mountain, west of US 201 between The Forks and Jackman, straddles the Upper Enchanted Township and Johnson Mtn. Township boundaries. Coburn Mtn. is the highest peak in the region, with spectacular views rivaling the best in Maine. The top of the old fire tower (1938) has been replaced with an observation deck. MBPL owns a portion of the mountain, including the summit and southeastern slopes.

At a point 10.6 mi. north of the bridge over the Kennebec River in The Forks and 14.3 mi. south of the jct. of US 201 and ME 15/6 in Jackman, turn west off US 201 onto Enchanted Mtn. Rd. This rough gravel road is passable by passenger vehicle for just a short distance. A high-clearance vehicle is required to go the entire 2.1 mi. to the trailhead at base of the mountain, where there is a four-way intersection in a large clearing. (This is the site of the former base of the Enchanted Mtn. ski area, which operated on Coburn Mtn. from 1966 until about 1974.) Turn right and drive an additional 0.2 mi. to where the road bends to the right. Here, a jeep/snowmobile trail leaves left uphill; this is the start of the trail. Park on the left. There is no sign.

COBURN MTN. TRAIL (NFTM; USGS ENCHANTED POND AND JOHNSON MTN. QUADS, GAZETTEER MAP 40)

Cumulative from road/jeep trail jct. (2,475 ft.) to:	↕	↗	◷
First radio station and summit footpath (3,275 ft.)	0.5 mi.	600 ft.	0:35
Coburn Mtn. summit (3,718 ft.)	0.9 mi.	1,250 ft.	1:05

Follow the old jeep trail steeply uphill, with the route alternating between a footpath and a former ski trail. About 0.5 mi. from the trailhead, reach the first of two solar-powered radio repeating stations. A snowmobile trail leaves the station, coursing uphill to the summit. About 150 ft. along this trail, find the footpath exiting right, and proceed very steeply uphill on rough terrain. The trail exits the woods onto the summit ridge at about 1.1 mi., near a second solar-powered repeating station. The observation tower, what remains of the fire tower erected here in 1938, is just north (right) on the ridge. (The former fire warden's trail continues down the northeastern ridge but is in poor condition and not recommended.)

SEC 3

■ NUMBER FIVE MTN. (3,186 FT.)

This remote mountain west of US 201 at Parlin Pond is bisected by the town lines of T5 R7 BKP WKR and Appleton Township. An old fire tower (1933) still stands on the craggy ledges of the open summit. Number Five Mtn. is in the heart of Leuthold Forest Preserve, 16,934 acres of forestland owned by The Nature Conservancy just south of the Moose River. The preserve abuts a vast swath of other conservation lands, including Holeb Public Land (20,000 acres owned by MBPL), the Attean Pond conservation easement (20,000 acres held by Forest Society of Maine), and Moose River/Number Five Bog Conservation Land (5,000 acres owned by MBPL). The old fire warden's trail (reached by a 17-mi. drive on gravel logging roads) has been significantly improved by TNC trail crews.

From the jct. of US 201 and ME 15/6 in Jackman, drive south on US 201 for 11.5 mi. Opposite the boat launch on Parlin Pond, turn west on Spencer Rd. (aka Hardscrabble Rd. on the Gazetteer map). Reset odometer. At 5.3 mi. from US 201, bear right at a fork (street signs here are confusing). Reach the Spencer POW Camp Memorial on the left at 11.8 mi. At 14.4 mi., bear right at a fork. At 16.6 mi., at a small roadside cairn (may be missing) on the right, turn right on a minor double-track road and follow this to its end in a grassy meadow (an old wood yard) in 0.5 mi. Preserve guidelines and a map are posted on a signboard.

NUMBER FIVE MTN. TRAIL (TNC; USGS SPENCER LAKE, ATTEAN POND, HOLEB, AND TUMBLEDOWN MTN. QUADS, GAZETTEER MAPS 39 AND 40, TNC LEUTHOLD FOREST PRESERVE MAP)

From trailhead at end of gravel road (2,025 ft.) to:	↥↧	↗	○
Number Five Mtn. summit (3,186 ft.)	2.9 mi.	1,175 ft.	2:00

The trail starts up the grassy road left of the kiosk and soon climbs in and out of a gully. Continue on the grassy road, and at a fork just ahead (marked with a TNC yellow and green diamond), stay right. At 0.4 mi., cross onto TNC land (marked with red paint blazes), and in 100 ft., bear right onto a foot trail and follow light-blue paint blazes. For the next 1.75 mi., the trail rises at a pleasant grade, alternating between foot trail and old woods road corridors. The well-constructed trail features switchbacks, rock steps, stone water bars, wooden bog bridging, turnpikes, and contouring.

At 2.25 mi., cross a grassy, wet meadow on large log bog bridge sections. Beyond, the trail begins a moderate ascent through dense forest, past mossy boulders. Cross a small stream and pass remnants of old telephone line. Climb a short, steep, rocky pitch, then a more moderate stretch to open ledges, where the summit tower comes into view. Break into the open at 2.8 mi., with wonderful views south, east, and west, especially to Number Six Mtn. next door. Reach the fire tower on top at 2.9 mi. Views are excellent in every direction.

■ SALLY MTN. (2,221 FT.)

Sally Mtn. is located in Attean Township between Wood and Attean ponds. It has a long summit ridge extending northeast and southwest, with the highest point near its southwestern end. The mountain offers excellent views of the wild country of the upper Moose River valley. Local hikers maintain the Sally Mtn. Trail.

From US 201 in Jackman, 200 ft. south of its jct. with ME 15/6, turn west onto Attean Rd. Follow it for 1.4 mi., then park in the large lot on the right (north) side of the road.

SALLY MTN. TRAIL
(NFTM; USGS ATTEAN POND QUAD, GAZETTEER MAP 39)
Cumulative from Attean Rd.
(1,150 ft.) to:

	⇅	↗	⟳
Start of trail (1,200 ft.) via railroad tracks	1.8 mi.	50 ft.	0:50
Sally Mtn. summit (2,221 ft.)	3.0 mi.	1,050 ft.	2:00

Walk back 200 ft. on the road and turn left (north) on a gated camp road. Proceed 150 yd. to the railroad tracks of the Central Maine & Quebec Railway. Go left (west) along the tracks, cross the trestle over Moose River on the walkway, and proceed to a point 150 yd. beyond the railway's "mile 76" sign and 100 ft. before reaching a stack of old railroad ties on the left (south) side of the tracks. Here, a well-defined blue-blazed trail comes in from the left (south) from the beach and campsite on the shore of Attean Lake (trail sign here on shore). This trail from the lake crosses the tracks and continues right and on to the top of Sally Mtn.

From the tracks, the trail runs fairly level for a time before climbing steeply through the forest to the summit ridge. Among the rocks and scrub growth of the summit ridge, the trail becomes less distinct, but generally runs along the east-facing edge of the ridge on a gradual ascent toward the summit, passing the old fire warden's spring (sign) en route. At the summit, four pieces of steel bolted to the rocks mark the site of the former fire tower (erected in 1908 and abandoned in 1933). The views from the top are excellent, taking in several large ponds, and mountains ranging from Katahdin and Bigelow to the peaks along the Canadian border. (*Note:* An obscure blue-blazed trail leaves the summit and descends the far side of Sally Mtn. It is not recommended.)

A pleasant alternative to the start of the hike along the railroad tracks is to approach the trail by canoe. Drive to the end of Attean Pond Rd. and a boat launch on Attean Pond. (*Note:* This is the start of the Moose River Bow Trip.) Paddle along the north shore of the pond to reach the second established campsite in a small cove directly opposite Birch Island and Attean Lake Lodge. A trail leads through level forest for about 0.1 mi. to the railroad tracks and the start of the trail as described above.

■ BURNT JACKET MTN., EAST PEAK (2,119 FT.)

This sprawling, multisummited peak in Forsyth Township rises south and west of Little Big Wood Pond a few miles west of Jackman. From the bridge over the Moose River on US 201 in Jackman, continue north on the highway for 1.0 mi. Turn left (west) onto Sandy Stream Rd. and drive 0.3 mi. to a fork. Bear left onto Gander Brook Rd. and travel 4.2 mi. to a gated bridge over Wood Stream. Parking for several cars is available on the right side of the road.

BURNT JACKET MTN. TRAIL (NFTM; USGS JACKMAN, ATTEAN POND, AND STONY BROOK QUADS, GAZETTEER MAP 39)

From bridge over Wood Stream (1,250 ft.) to:	⇅	⟋	○
Burnt Jacket Mtn. summit (2,241 ft.)	1.5 mi.	1,000 ft.	1:15

Cross the bridge on foot, and in 200 ft. turn right and follow the grassy logging road about 100 yd., nearly to the top of the first rise. Look for a beaten path and flagging tape on the left (west). The colored tape and old blue blazes lead up a gravelly water runoff through hardwoods for about

0.5 mi. Then the path turns left, straight up through softwood trees. At the top of the first wooded ledge, the trail bears right and continues up a broad ridgeline to a large open ledge on a peak of the ridge at 1.1 mi. The best views are north to Boundary Bald Mtn., east to Katahdin, and then south.

The trail continues another 0.4 mi. to the next summit, which has some open ledges among the trees. From the first open ledges heading to the second summit, the trail drops through a rock chimney, which may hard for young children and dogs to negotiate. To follow this section of the trail takes great care, as it has no well-worn tread, brush and winter deadfall block the way in places, and the limited flagging and blue blazes are difficult to see.

SEC 3

■ BOUNDARY BALD MTN. (3,638 FT.)

This rocky summit is north-northeast of Jackman and about 8 mi. southwest of the Canadian border. The long open summit ridge of Boundary Bald Mtn. offers 360-degree views of the mountain and lake country of northern Somerset County, the Moosehead Lake region, and southern Canada. Reach the summit and a collapsed fire tower by a 1.2-mi. foot trail and a nearly equivalent-distance walk on gravel roads.

From the bridge on US 201 in Jackman, drive north toward Canada for 7.9 mi. to the start of Bald Mtn. Rd., which is on the right (east) side of the highway about 0.25 mi. above the Falls scenic area on the right. Hilton Timberlands, owner of the road, has posted directional signs for the Boundary Bald Mtn. Trail at the start of the road. Pass through the bright yellow gate and follow Bald Mtn. Rd signage for 4.5 mi. to the parking lot at the jct. of Notch Rd. and Trail Rd.

BOUNDARY BALD MTN. TRAIL (NFTM; USGS BOUNDARY BALD MTN. QUAD, GAZETTEER MAPS 39 AND 47)

Cumulative from parking area at jct. of Notch Rd. and Trail Rd. (1,850 ft.) to:	⇅	↗	⟳
Boundary Bald Mtn. trailhead (2,450 ft.)	1.4 mi.	600 ft.	1:00
Boundary Bald Mtn. summit (3,638 ft.)	2.4 mi.	1,800 ft.	2:10

From the parking area, hike up Trail Rd. for 1.4 mi. to the marked trailhead. The blue-blazed trail heads up a seasonal slate streambed. The trail is easily followed at a steady grade to the high summit ridge. Proceed across the airy ridge to a communications tower facility where excellent views await. Next to the tower lies the wreckage of the 1937 fire tower. (*Note:* Although the trail is easily discerned above treeline, pay particular attention on the return trip, where it drops down into the trees.)

■ WILLIAMS MTN. (2,410 FT.)

The long ridgeline of Williams Mtn. straddles the town lines of Misery Township and Parlin Pond Township amid the vast commercial timberland west of Moosehead Lake. The mountain lies on the western edge of the 363,000-acre Moosehead Region Conservation Easement, which is held by Forest Society of Maine. Weyerhaeuser owns the land. A steel fire tower, erected in 1914, still stands on the summit of Williams Mtn.

From the blinking light in downtown Greenville at the jct. of ME 15/6 and Lily Bay Rd., drive north on ME 15/6 for 34.1 mi., passing through Rockwood en route. With Demo Rd. to the right, turn left off the highway onto the gravel-surfaced Williams Mtn. Rd. In 0.9 mi., pass Smith Rd. on the right. At 3.6 mi. from ME 15/6, turn right on a minor double-track road and drive uphill for another 0.4 mi. to where the trail crosses the road. There is no parking lot here; drive ahead 100 yd. to a wide, grassy area to turn around and park.

WILLIAMS MTN. TRAIL (MBPL; USGS MISERY KNOB AND LONG POND QUADS, GAZETTEER MAP 40)

From gravel road (1,800 ft.) to:	⇅	↗	○
Williams Mtn. summit (2,410 ft.)	1.5 mi.	610 ft.	1:15

Editor's note: A new blue-blazed trail to the summit of Williams Mtn. was completed by the MBPL in 2017. At the time of printing, MBPL was working to acquire land at the base of the mountain for a trailhead parking lot, plus acreage on the summit to preserve both the fire tower and warden's cabin there. The driving directions above lead to a temporary parking area and a temporary trail start. Check with MBPL for updated details before venturing to Williams Mtn. for a hike.

From the grassy parking area, walk 100 yd. downhill to the trail. Turn left to begin the hike to Williams Mtn. The trail climbs easily west to reach the lower part of the northeast ridge of the mountain and a low granite knob just left of the trail at 0.3 mi. At 0.5 mi., the trail switchbacks left along the fairly narrow ridgeline, then reaches an old clear-cut clearing. Ahead, proceed along the now-wide ridge through semi-open forest, the remains of heavy timber harvesting. At 0.7 mi., reach the easternmost summit on the Williams Mtn. ridge, with a view ahead to the fire tower on top. Continue easily on the ridge to reach another clearing, where the summit cone and tower are in clear view.

At 1.2 mi., an old local trail enters from the right. From this point on, the new and old trails coincide, the way flagged with yellow tape. Cross a low wet area, then climb a moderate pitch up the summit cone and soon reach the old fire warden's cabin, still in surprisingly good condition. The fire tower is a short distance beyond. Here, a short 0.1-mi. loop leads right to several viewpoints before returning to the tower.

NORTHWEST OF MOOSEHEAD LAKE

■ GREEN MTN. (2,395 FT.)

An old fire tower (circa 1920) stands atop the southerly and highest summit of Green Mtn., which straddles the town lines of Hammond Township, Dole Brook Township, and Comstock Township in a remote area northwest of Seboomook Lake and Pittston Farm and northeast of Boundary Bald Mtn.

From ME 15/6, just west of the village of Rockwood, turn north on Northern Rd., immediately crossing Moose River. Turn right after the bridge and follow Northern Rd. for 19.8 mi. to the jct. with Seboomook Rd. Bear left here, and in another 0.5 mi., pass by Pittston Farm and cross the South Branch of the Penobscot River to reach the North Maine Woods Twenty Mile Checkpoint, where a fee is charged to pass through.

From the checkpoint gate, drive 1.9 mi. to a fork. Bear left here onto Cutoff Rd. (no sign) and drive 1.5 mi. to the jct. with South Branch Access Rd. Turn left here and follow South Branch Access Rd. west for 2.2 mi. Turn right (north) on Old Boundary Rd. and drive 3.2 mi. (passing two campsites on the left en route) to a small trailhead parking area on the right. A sign nailed to a tree here reads "GREEN" in green ink.

GREEN MTN. TRAIL (NFTM; USGS FOLEY POND QUAD, GAZETTEER MAP 48)

From Old Boundary Rd. trailhead (1,769 ft.) to:	↑↓	↗	○
Green Mtn. summit (2,395 ft.)	1.6 mi.	625 ft.	1:15

The trail starts immediately uphill on an old jeep track, then levels off and soon reaches a small clearing, the former site of an old fire warden's cabin. Push straight ahead through the brush to pick up the foot trail beyond, which is liberally marked with orange and pink flagging tape (and occasionally other colors). The treadway can be obscure in places, so go slow and follow the colored flagging closely. Ahead, the trail contours across the side of the mountain until it reaches a brook. Here, the trail turns uphill and crosses a wooded ridge before dropping into a slight depression and then rising again across the contours. It climbs the mountain in steps, following a series of old logging haul roads that are now heavily grown into corridors of brush and weeds and barely recognizable as any kind of road.

At 1.2 mi., bear sharply left and push through a short section of spruce blowdowns (as of 2017). Beyond, the path is again distinct. Cross a small brook and reach a small, disintegrating cabin (the old fire warden's lightning shelter) on the left at 1.5 mi. Continue an additional 0.1 mi. to the wooded summit and the tower standing tall in a small clearing. Get 360-degree views by climbing the tower ladder.

FAR NORTHERN FRANKLIN COUNTY

■ KIBBY MTN. (3,654 FT.)

This remote mountain in Skinner Township lies in the heart of the vast forestland northwest of Flagstaff Lake and east of the Canadian border and Chain of Ponds. From the ladder of the old fire tower on the summit are superb views of the jumble of mountain peaks in this region, as well as the many turbine towers of the Kibby Wind Farm to the south. (Owned by TransCanada, Kibby is New England's largest windpower facility.)

KIBBY MTN. TRAIL (NFTM; USGS KIBBY MTN. QUAD, GAZETTEER MAPS 28, 38, AND 39)

From parking area (2,550 ft.) to:	⥮	↗	↻
Kibby Mtn. summit (3,654 ft.)	2.0 mi.	1,100 ft.	1:30

From its jct. with ME 16 in Stratton, drive north on ME 27 for 16.8 mi. and turn right onto Gold Brook Rd. (sign for Kibby Wind Farm). Pass the Series B access road on the right at 3.6 mi., a road on the right at 6.0 mi., and Spencer Ball Rd. (Series A access road) on the right at 7.6 mi. Continue straight at a fork at 8.9 mi. Pass mile marker 9 (Beaudry Rd.) on the left, and reach the crest of a hill at 9.4 mi. Turn right onto a narrower gravel road with a wind turbine visible ahead. Drive 0.4 mi. to a parking clearing on the left. A double-track old road, the trail, heads into the woods at the east corner of the parking area.

Ascend gradually on the double-track. At 0.9 mi., bear right off the main track (flagging and a small cairn). Continue north up across the steep mountainside on a pleasantly shaded woods road that soon bends back to the south to follow the ridge to the summit at 2.0 mi. The debris that once littered the summit area (gas containers, aluminum piping, plastic sheeting) has been removed. The 12-ft. fire tower on top, built in 1926, is now an observation deck.

SECTION 4

WESTERN LAKES AND MOUNTAINS

In-Text Maps

Pull-Out Map
Map 3: Bigelow Range

SEC 4

INTRODUCTION

The Western Lakes and Mountains region includes, from west to east, all of the northern and most of the central areas of Oxford County, all of Franklin County, and the western part of Somerset County, roughly south of Flagstaff Lake and the Dead River. The relatively compact Mahoosuc Range, which spans west from the New Hampshire border to Andover, is described in Section 5. The international border with Quebec, Canada, forms the northern boundary of all three counties, and the New Hampshire border forms the western boundary of Oxford County. To the south, the region is bounded by the Androscoggin River and US 2 as far east as Sandy Stream, which forms much of the eastern boundary. This section describes 64 trails on 37 mountains.

SEC 4

GEOGRAPHY

The region west of Rangeley features a number of large lakes, including Rangeley Lake, Cupsuptic Lake, Mooselookmeguntic Lake, Upper and Lower Richardson lakes, Umbagog Lake, and Aziscohos Lake. Much of this area is drained by the Ellis, Swift, and Sandy rivers, all of which empty into the Androscoggin River. To the northeast are Flagstaff Lake and its feeder, the Dead River. The Carrabassett River and Sandy Stream drain this area and flow south into the Kennebec River.

A nearly continuous chain of mountains extends from the East B Hill Rd. at the eastern margin of the Mahoosucs northeast to Long Falls Dam Rd. east of Flagstaff Lake. The AT traverses this stretch for 88 mi., and along here are ten of Maine's fourteen 4,000-ft. peaks. Many of the trails are on large swaths of public land, including Grafton Notch State Park, Mahoosuc Public Lands, Tumbledown Public Lands, Mt. Blue State Park, and Bigelow Preserve. Maine Huts & Trails has four backcountry lodges on 80 mi. of multiuse trails in and around Bigelow Preserve. Outside of these areas, the trails are mostly on private property and are open for public use through the generosity of the various landowners.

Rumford Whitecap (2,214 ft.) is a local favorite that rises above the Androscoggin River valley in the area east of Bethel and west of Rumford. A new trail now connects neighboring Black Mtn. (2,350 ft.), which is home to a ski area. The ledges on Glassface Mtn. (1,910 ft.) overlook the wide and winding Androscoggin. To the east along the river is the craggy bump of Sugarloaf (1,590 ft.) in Dixfield. North of Black Brook Notch is Old Blue Mtn. (3,600 ft.) and the five summits on the long ridge of Bemis Mtn. (the highest is 3,592 ft.). Just east, concentrated in a semicircular ring

around the village of Weld, are the high peaks and great cliffs of Tumbledown Mtn. (3,068 ft.), the summits of Little Jackson Mtn. (3,470 ft.),
Jackson Mtn. (3,568 ft.), Blueberry Mtn. (2,952 ft.), and the conical form
of Mt. Blue (3,192 ft.). Nearby Center Hill (1,658 ft.) has a picnic area with
a fine view of Tumbledown. Just southwest, Bald Mtn. (2,370 ft.) is connected to Saddleback Wind (2,590 ft.) by a new ridgeline trail.

West of the Rangeley Lakes are the lightly traveled summits of Aziscohos Mtn. (3,215 ft.) and West Kennebago Mtn. (3,713 ft.), both former
fire tower sites. The popular Bald Mtn. (2,470 ft.) in Oquossoc occupies a
commanding location between Mooselookmeguntic Lake and Rangeley
Lake, with views of both.

In the 30-mi. stretch of the AT between ME 17 and ME 4 north of
Rangeley and south of Stratton is a string of 4,000-ft. summits: Saddleback Mtn. (4,210 ft.), The Horn (4,041 ft.), Spaulding Mtn. (4,010 ft.),
Mt. Abraham (4,049 ft.), Sugarloaf (4,250 ft.), North Crocker Mtn.
(4,228 ft.), and South Crocker Mtn. (4,050 ft.). Neighboring Mt. Redington (4,010 ft.) is a formerly trailless summit that can now be reached by a
rough herd path. Third in line on the alpine Saddleback ridgeline is Saddleback Jr. (3,655 ft.). The open summit of Burnt Hill (3,609 ft.), next
door to Sugarloaf, is now part of the Sugarloaf ski area's backcountry trail
system. North of ME 27 is the Bigelow Range and the craggy 4,000-ft.
summits of Avery Peak (4,088 ft.) and West Peak (4,145 ft.), along with
the shapely subsidiary peaks of North Horn (3,792 ft.), South Horn
(3,805 ft.), Cranberry Peak (3,194 ft.), and Little Bigelow Mtn. (3,070 ft.),
all overlooking Flagstaff Lake and Carrabassett Valley.

ROAD ACCESS

US 2 ranges across the region's southern margin from Gilead on the New
Hampshire border east to Farmington. ME 16 slices across the northern
tier of lakes and mountains from west to east between Lincoln Plantation
and Kingfield. A number of major south–north roads and highways cut
across the high mountains traversed by the AT. From west to east, these
are: ME 5 and South Arm Rd. between Rumford and South Arm on
Lower Richardson Lake; ME 17 between Mexico and Oquossoc; ME 4
between Farmington and Rangeley; and ME 27 from Kingfield to Stratton. Long Falls Dam Rd. bookends the section east of Flagstaff Lake. ME
142 connects Kingfield to Phillips to Dixfield in a more or less north to
south direction. ME 156 from Wilton connects to ME 142 in Weld near
Tumbledown and Mt. Blue.

CAMPING & LODGING

Nineteen lean-tos and campsites along the AT provide for trailside camping. There are public campgrounds at Mt. Blue State Park in Weld (136 campsites) and at Rangeley Lake State Park in Rangeley Plantation (50 campsites). At least eight privately operated campgrounds are found throughout this region. Four backcountry huts operated by Maine Huts & Trails (MHT) around the south and east margins of the Bigelow Range offer lodging and meals.

Maine Huts & Trails

Maine Huts & Trails operates year-round backcountry lodges along more than 80 mi. of people-powered trails through the foothills, rivers, and valleys of the western mountains, between ME 27/16 in Carrabassett Valley and US 201 in West Forks. Four huts—Stratton Brook, Poplar, Flagstaff, and Grand Falls—are located respectively amid the spectacular terrain of the Bigelow Preserve, Poplar Stream Falls, Flagstaff Lake, and Grand Falls on the Dead River. Inspired by European huts, the off-grid facilities each feature a great room, a reading area, a screened-in porch, hearty meals served family-style, bagged trail lunches, hot showers, composting toilets, heated bunkrooms (shared or private), gear drying rooms, and a small store with trail necessities during two full-service seasons (summer through fall, and winter). Day visitors are welcome; overnight guests must make a reservation. MHT strives to minimize environmental impact, operating the huts sustainably with solar power, hydropower, wood gasification stoves, advanced composting systems, recycling, gardens, and locally sourced food.

The extensive trails built and maintained by MHT accommodate non-motorized use, from hiking, paddling, and mountain biking in summer to groomed cross-country skiing, fat biking, and snowshoeing in winter. Guests can visit an individual hut or travel between them on a hut-to-hut adventure. Trail access is free.

Stratton Brook Hut

Stratton Brook Hut features panoramic views of the Bigelow Range, Carrabassett Valley, and Sugarloaf Mtn. To reach Stratton Brook Trailhead from the jct. of ME 27 and ME 16 in Kingfield, drive north on ME 27/16 for 14.8 mi. to the MHT-signed trailhead parking lot on the right (less than 0.1 mi. beyond Sugarloaf Access Rd.). From the trailhead, follow Narrow Gauge Pathway and Maine Hut Trail, and take either Oak Knoll Trail or Newton's Revenge to reach the hut.

SEC 4

Poplar Hut

The very first hut of the MHT system is located southeast of Little Bigelow Mtn., just a stone's throw from pretty Poplar Falls. Poplar Hut can be reached from Airport Trailhead on ME 27/16 in Carrabassett Valley by way of Maine Hut Trail, Larry's Trail, or Warren's Trail. From the jct. of ME 27 and ME 16 in Kingfield, drive north on ME 27/16 for 8.9 mi. to the signed trailhead parking lot on the right.

Flagstaff Hut

Flagstaff Hut is the most approachable hut in the MH&T system due to its gentle lakeside terrain. The hut is on the sandy eastern shore of Flagstaff Lake and features wonderful views across the lake to the north side of the Bigelow Range. Flagstaff Hut can be reached from Long Falls Dam/Flagstaff Trailhead on Long Falls Dam Rd. in Carrying Place Township. From the jct. of ME 27 and ME 16 in Kingfield, travel east on ME 16 for 7.5 mi. to New Portland. Turn left (north) on Long Falls Dam Rd. and drive 22.8 mi. to the signed trailhead parking lot on the left.

Grand Falls Hut

The most remote and secluded of the four huts, and the northernmost, Grand Falls Hut is in Lower Enchanted Township on a wooded bluff high above the Dead River a short distance east of thundering Grand Falls and Spencer Stream.

Grand Falls Hut can be reached from the west at Lower Enchanted Trailhead (summer only) or from the south at Big Eddy/Grand Falls Trailhead.

Directions to Lower Enchanted Trailhead: From the jct. of US 201 and US 201A/ME 8 in Solon, drive north on US 201 for 34.2 mi. (through the towns of Bingham, Moscow, Caratunk, and The Forks) to Lower Enchanted Rd. on the left; turn left. Reset odometer. At 4.2 mi. from US 201, keep right on the most heavily used road. At 4.7 mi., turn left to remain on Lower Enchanted Rd. At 7.0 mi., at a four-way intersection, stay straight on Lower Enchanted Rd. At 8.9 mi., turn left, and at 9.6 mi., stay right on the better-used road. At 13.3 mi., pass through a grove of tall Norway pines, and at 13.7 mi., at a white sign for Grand Falls hut access, turn left on Hut Rd. The signed trailhead parking lot is just ahead on the right.

Directions to Big Eddy/Grand Falls Trailhead: From the jct. of ME 27 and ME 16 in Kingfield, travel east on ME 16 for 7.5 mi. to New Portland. Here, turn left (north) on Long Falls Dam Rd. and drive 35.0 mi. to the signed trailhead parking lot on the left in the township of T3 R4 BKP WKR.

MT. BLUE STATE PARK

Mt. Blue State Park is Maine's largest state park, encompassing about 8,000 acres, the bulk of it in the town of Weld, with small portions in Temple and Avon. The largest section of the park lies east of Webb Lake and includes the iconic peak of Mt. Blue and a picnic area on Center Hill. A 136-site campground, beach, picnic area, and nature center are on the southwest shore of Webb Lake. Adjoining the park are the mountainous 22,000 acres of Tumbledown Public Lands, making this area one of Maine's premier outdoor recreation destinations.

TUMBLEDOWN PUBLIC LANDS

This large swath of public land encompasses the Tumbledown Mtn. Range in Township 6 North of Weld. The Maine Bureau of Parks and Lands owns 10,000 acres and holds easements on an additional 12,000 acres in the vicinity, bringing the total of this extraordinary conservation property to 22,000 acres. Tumbledown Public Lands include Tumbledown Mtn., Tumbledown Pond, Little Jackson Mtn., Jackson Mtn., Jackson Pond, and the top of Blueberry Mtn.

Seven trails provide miles of hiking opportunities in this scenic and rugged mountain region. Byron Rd. two primary trailhead parking areas. Loop Trail trailhead is the start of Loop Trail only. Brook Trail trailhead is the start for Brook Trail and Little Jackson Connector, both of which connect to other trails.

BIGELOW PRESERVE

The Bigelow Preserve was established by public referendum in 1976, the first time in Maine a statewide vote was held to create a public parkland. Since then, a series of land donations and purchases have brought the preserve to its present size of 36,000 acres. The Maine Bureau of Parks and Lands manages Bigelow Preserve.

The scenic Bigelow Range sprawls 12 mi. from west to east, encompassing a vast swath of forestland, six high peaks, more than 30 mi. of hiking trails, and miles of pristine lakefront. An 18-mi. section of the AT crosses the preserve, while the Maine Hut Trail cuts across the southwest corner.

The predominant natural features are the alpine summits of Avery Peak and West Peak, both exceeding 4,000 ft. in elevation, and the symmetrical twin peaks of North Horn and South Horn, which rise just shy of the 4,000-ft. mark. From these high peaks, there are spectacular vistas over the rugged forested wilderness of hills and mountains, lakes, ponds, rivers, and streams ranging north to Katahdin and the jumble of mountains in the

SEC 4

southern part of BSP and south to Sugarloaf, the Crockers, the summits of Mt. Abraham, and far beyond. Horns Pond is tucked into the ridge crest at the base of The Horns. The craggy upper reaches of Cranberry Peak bookend the range to the west, and pretty Cranberry Pond is at its base. East of Avery Peak, and separated by the deep defile of Safford Notch, is the long ridge of Little Bigelow Mtn. Artificially constructed Flagstaff Lake, Maine's fourth-largest body of water, lies just north of the Bigelow Range. Like the range, the lake stretches east to west, from one end of the Bigelows to the other.

Three trails approach the range from the south. Fire Warden's Trail is the most direct, albeit steep, route to the main peaks of the Bigelow Range, while Horns Pond Trail provides quick access to Horns Pond, where the trail joins the AT to follow the ridge between The Horns, over South Horn (and past the side trail to North Horn) and West Peak, and on to Avery Peak. A third approach is via the AT, which extends from ME 27 to the ridge west of Horns Pond. A fourth and longer approach is by way of Bigelow Range Trail, which leads east from Stratton to join the AT near Cranberry Pond. From East Flagstaff Rd. at Flagstaff Lake, gain access to the high peaks via Safford Brook Trail and the AT.

SUGGESTED HIKES

■ Easy
BALD MTN. (IN OQUOSSOC)

	🔁	↗	⏱
RT via Bald Mtn. Trail	2.6 mi.	960 ft.	1:50

Enjoy grand lake and mountain views of the Rangeley Lakes region from an observation tower atop Bald Mtn. See Bald Mtn. Trail, p. 207.

CENTER HILL

	🔁	↗	⏱
LP via Center Hill Nature Trail	0.5 mi.	75 ft.	0:20

A self-guided nature trail loop offers outstanding views of Tumbledown and the Jacksons from ledges en route. See Center Hill Nature Trail, p. 211.

BALD MTN. (IN WASHINGTON TOWNSHIP)

	↕	↗	○
RT via Bald Mtn. Trail	2.2 mi.	1,320 ft.	1:50

Hike a long and beautiful ridge to fine views from the open ledges on the summit of Bald Mtn. See Bald Mtn. Trail, p. 217.

GLASSFACE LEDGES

	↕	↗	○
RT via Glassface Ledges Trail	1.6 mi.	670 ft.	1:15

Enjoy fabulous views over the bucolic Androscoggin River valley from the craggy outlook at trail's end. See Glassface Ledges Trail, p. 223.

SEC 4

■ Moderate

BURNT HILL

	↕	↗	○
RT via Burnt Hill Trail	5.6 mi.	1,670 ft.	3:50

Hike to the alpine terrain on Burnt Hill for great views of the Sugarloaf ski slopes, the Crockers, and the Bigelows. See Burnt Hill Trail, p. 186.

STRATTON BROOK HUT

	↕	↗	○
RT via Narrow Gauge Pathway, Maine Hut Trail, and Oak Knoll Trail	8.2 mi.	630 ft.	4:30

Grab a quick lunch or stay overnight at this Maine Huts & Trails back-country lodge. Either way, enjoy great views of the Bigelow Range and Sugarloaf. To begin, see Narrow Gauge Pathway, p. 187.

SADDLEBACK MTN.

	↕	↗	○
RT via Berry Picker's Trail and AT Southbound	8.4 mi.	2,240 ft.	5:20

Hike a historical route used by local residents to harvest berries then continue on to bag the alpine summit of Saddleback Mtn. via the AT. To begin, See Berry Picker's Trail, p. 203.

AZISCOHOS MTN.

	⇅	↗	○
RT via Aziscohos Mtn. Trail	3.4 mi.	1,460 ft.	2:25

This craggy mountaintop well west of Rangeley offers a 360-degree panorama that is one of the finest in Maine: from Katahdin to Saddleback to Mt. Washington, plus a handful of large lakes. See Aziscohos Mtn. Trail, p. 209.

MT. BLUE

	⇅	↗	○
RT via Mt. Blue Trail	3.2 mi.	1,738 ft.	2:30

The summit of this conical peak is home to an observation tower with spectacular views in all directions. See Mt. Blue Trail, p. 210.

TUMBLEDOWN MTN.

	⇅	↗	○
LP via Loop Trail, Tumbledown Mtn. Trail, and Parker Ridge Trail	5.4 mi.	1,750 ft.	3:35

Combine these trails for an excellent tour of the high terrain on Tumbledown, including beautiful Tumbledown Pond. To begin, see Loop Trail, p. 213.

RUMFORD WHITECAP

	⇅	↗	○
LP via Red/Orange Trail and Starr Trail	4.9 mi.	1,600 ft.	3:20

Take Red/Orange Trail to the long, bald summit ridge of Rumford Whitecap (then take ledgy Starr Trail on the descent) for panoramic views and plenty of blueberries in season. To begin, see Red/Orange Trail, p. 220.

■ Strenuous
BIGELOW HIGH PEAKS

	⇅	↗	○
LP via Firewarden's Trail, AT Northbound, and Horns Pond Trail	14.5 mi.	3,750 ft.	9:10

Bag Avery Peak and West Peak (both 4,000-footers) and South Horn and North Horn (both a little less than 4,000 ft.) on this grand circuit hike in the Bigelow Range. The pretty Horns Pond is a bonus en route. To begin, see Firewarden's Trail, p. 179.

CRANBERRY PEAK

⬛ ❄ 🔺 🎾 🎿

RT via AT Northbound and Bigelow Range Trail	10.4 mi.	1,850 ft.	6:10

Climb past secluded Cranberry Pond to craggy Cranberry Peak, the western-most summit in the Bigelow Range. To begin, see AT Northbound, p. 182.

THE CROCKERS AND MT. REDINGTON

⬛ 🏃 🔺 🎾 🎿

RT via AT Northbound and herd path	9.8 mi.	4,000 ft.	6:55

Bag the two Crockers, both 4,000-footers, via the AT then go for a third, Mt. Redington, via a herd path. To begin, see AT Northbound, p. 193.

MT. ABRAHAM

⬛ ❄ 🏃 🔺 🎾 🎿

RT via Fire Warden's Trail	9.0 mi.	3,050 ft.	6:05

The summit of Mt. Abraham features panoramic views and the second-largest alpine zone in Maine. See Fire Warden's Trail, p. 198.

TRAIL DESCRIPTIONS

BIGELOW PRESERVE AND VICINITY

■ AVERY PEAK (4,088 FT.) AND WEST PEAK (4,145 FT.)

FIRE WARDEN'S TRAIL (MATC; MAP 3: B2–B3)

Cumulative from Stratton Brook Pond Rd. (1,250 ft.) to:	⇅	↗	↻
Horns Pond Trail (1,750 ft.)	2.1 mi.	500 ft.	1:20
Moose Falls Campsite (2,500 ft.)	3.5 mi.	1,250 ft.	2:25
Bigelow Col, Myron Avery Campsite, AT (3,800 ft.)	4.7 mi.	2,550 ft.	3:40
From Stratton Brook Pond Rd. (1,250 ft.) to:			
Avery Peak summit (4,088 ft.) via AT Northbound	5.1 mi.	2,840 ft.	4:00
From Stratton Brook Pond Rd. (1,250 ft.) to:			
West Peak summit (4,145 ft.) via AT Southbound	5.0 mi.	2,895 ft.	4:00

This trail provides direct and steep access to Avery Peak and West Peak from the south.

From ME 27/16, at a point 3.2 mi. north of the blinking light at its jct. with Sugarloaf Access Rd., and 18.5 mi. north of the jct. of ME 27 and ME 16 in Kingfield, turn right (north) onto Stratton Brook Pond Rd. (small sign for Bigelow Preserve). Ahead on this dirt road, cross the AT at 0.9 mi. (limited parking). At 1.6 mi. from ME 27, arrive at the trailhead parking area for Fire Warden's Trail and Horns Pond Trail (kiosk).

From the parking area, follow the rough road up and then down to Stratton Brook. Cross Stratton Brook on a footbridge. There are campsites before and after the bridge. The trail continues along the shore of the pond on the old woods road. Beyond the pond, the trail reaches a fork near a campsite. Bear left and soon reach the posted start of Fire Warden's Trail in a clearing. The trail ascends gradually, then narrows and steepens to climb rocky slopes and rock slabs. After a level stretch, the trail crosses a section of bog bridge and then a small stream to meet the jct. of Horns Pond Trail on the left at 2.1 mi. Beyond, make a rising traverse, climb the occasional rock steps, and cross a rocky brook. After a steep rock staircase, reach the spur to Moose Falls Campsite on the left at 3.5 mi. Over the next 1.2 mi. to Bigelow Col, Fire Warden's Trail gains more than 1,300 ft. A long series of rock staircases lead directly up the increasingly steep mountainside. Eventually, the angle eases and the trail soon passes through Myron H. Avery Campsite to end at the jct. with the AT at 4.7 mi.

From this jct. in Bigelow Col, the AT goes right (north) to Avery Peak or left (south) to West Peak. For Avery Peak, go right on the AT and follow a rocky trail up and out of the trees and onto the peak's alpine summit at 0.4 mi. Just beyond the summit along the open ridge is the old fire tower base and a plaque honoring Myron Avery. The view is magnificent in every direction: north over Flagstaff Lake all the way to White Cap Mtn. and beyond to Katahdin, northwest over a rugged landscape to Canada, and southward to the ski slopes of shapely Sugarloaf, the Crockers, Spaulding Mtn., Mt. Abraham, and more. For West Peak, go left from Bigelow Col and climb through the trees before breaking out onto the craggy summit at 0.3 mi. The spectacular view takes in the Bigelow Range east to Avery Peak and the long ridge of Little Bigelow; to the west, the pyramidal peaks of South Horn and North Horn; and in every direction, for many miles, a panorama of mountains and lakes.

■ SOUTH HORN (3,805 FT.) AND NORTH HORN (3,792 FT.)

HORNS POND TRAIL AND AT (MATC; MAP 3: B2–B3)

Cumulative from Stratton Brook Pond Rd. (1,250 ft.) to:	↕	↗	↺
Start of trail (1,750 ft.) via Fire Warden's Trail	2.1 mi.	500 ft.	1:20
AT (3,150 ft.)	4.6 mi.	1,960 ft.	3:20
Horns Pond Lean-tos (3,150 ft.) via AT	4.8 mi.	1,960 ft.	3:25
North Horn side trail (3,685 ft.)	5.2 mi.	2,435 ft.	3:50
North Horn summit (3,792 ft.) via side trail	5.4 mi.	2,550 ft.	4:00
From Stratton Brook Pond Rd. (1,250 ft.) to:			
South Horn summit (3,805 ft.) via AT	5.3 mi.	2,555 ft.	3:55

SEC 4

Horns Pond Trail provides the most direct access to Horns Pond, a scenic tarn high on the ridgeline of the Bigelow Range at the western base of The Horns. From Horns Pond, the AT leads north to South Horn and North Horn (via short spur).

The route starts from Fire Warden's Trail, diverging left at a point 2.1 mi. from the parking area west of Stratton Brook Pond. Horns Pond Trail heads northwest, climbing gradually, sometimes on rocky terrain, and paralleling a brook for a stretch. On a shelf above, the trail skirts the southern edge of a grassy meadow (an old bog) with a good view of South Horn. Beyond, the trail continues to rise gradually and then gets increasingly steeper, climbing through boulders and up rock staircases. At 4.6 mi., the trail intersects the AT. Bear right on the AT for 0.2 mi. to reach Horns Pond and The Horns Pond Lean-tos at the old AT lean-to turned day-use shelter. From this jct., the pond is to the left and the two shelters and tentsites are to the right.

Continue north on the AT, passing by the caretaker's tent platform and then a spring. Beyond, climb steadily up the west side of South Horn to a jct., where a 0.2-mi. side trail leads to the summit of North Horn (the lightly visited wooded summit has outlooks and is well worth the effort). Continue the steep climb to reach the ledges atop South Horn at 5.3 mi.

AT NORTHBOUND (MATC; MAP 3: B2–B3)

Cumulative from ME 27 (1,390 ft.) to:	⇅	↗	◷
Stratton Brook Pond Rd. (1,270 ft.)	0.8 mi.	-120 ft.	0:25
Cranberry Stream Campsite (1,300 ft.)	1.9 mi.	60 ft.	1:00
Bigelow Range Trail (2,400 ft.)	3.4 mi.	1,050 ft.	2:10
Horns Pond Trail (3,150 ft.)	5.2 mi.	2,050 ft.	3:40
Horns Pond Lean-tos (3,150 ft.)	5.4 mi.	2,050 ft.	3:45
North Horn side trail (3,685 ft.)	5.8 mi.	2,600 ft.	4:10
South Horn summit (3,805 ft.)	5.9 mi.	2,700 ft.	4:20
West Peak summit (4,145 ft.)	8.2 mi.	3,500 ft.	5:50
Bigelow Col, Fire Warden's Trail, Myron Avery Campsite (3,800 ft.)	8.5 mi.	3,500 ft.	6:00
Avery Peak (4,088 ft.)	8.9 mi.	3,900 ft.	6:25
Safford Brook Trail jct. (2,250 ft.)	11.1 mi.	3,900 ft.	7:30

SEC 4

The AT crosses ME 27/16 in Wyman Township at a point 2.6 mi. north of the blinking light at the jct. of Sugarloaf Access Rd. and 17.8 mi. north of the jct. of ME 27 and ME 16 in Kingfield. Ample AT trailhead parking is available on the left (south) side of ME 27.

The trail descends gradually, crosses a brook, and reaches Stratton Brook Rd. at 0.9 mi. Shortly after, it crosses Jones Pond Rd. and then descends to cross Stratton Brook on a footbridge. Beyond, the trail joins an old tote road, turns left, and soon crosses a stream. At 1.9 mi., turn right off the road and soon reach Cranberry Stream Campsite. Cross a tote road at 2.5 mi., pass an old beaver pond, and then climb gradually but steadily into the basin of Cranberry Pond. Pass a spring (last reliable water before Horns Pond). At 3.2 mi., the trail reaches a jct. Here, the AT turns sharply right (north). Bigelow Range Trail (sign) continues straight ahead (west) to reach the east end of pretty Cranberry Pond in 0.2 mi., the summit of Cranberry Peak in 1.8 mi., and the trailhead at the end of Currie St. in Stratton at 5.0 mi.

Ahead on the AT, the trail climbs steeply on a rough route through rocks and boulders, and at 4.0 mi., reaches the crest of the ridge. It turns right (east) and follows the ridge crest, crossing a minor summit. Where the trail takes a sharp left, there is a lookout a few yards to the right over Horns Pond to The Horns. The trail descends steeply, and at 5.2 mi., Horns Pond Trail enters from the right. The AT continues through the woods, paralleling the south shore of Horns Pond, passing a side trail to The Horns Pond Lean-tos at 5.4 mi.

From Horns Pond, the AT continues east, climbing South Horn. At 5.8 mi., the blue-blazed North Horn Trail leads 0.2 mi. left to North Horn. Ahead, the AT crosses the peak of South Horn (5.9 mi.) and continues along the undulating crest of the range, reaching West Peak at 8.2 mi. The trail then descends to the Bigelow Col and Myron H. Avery Campsite at 8.5 mi. Here, Fire Warden's Trail enters from the right. The AT continues east, climbing to the summit of Avery Peak at 8.9 mi. From Avery Peak, the AT descends east 2.2 mi. to its jct. with Safford Brook Trail in rugged Safford Notch.

SEC 4

■ CRANBERRY PEAK (3,194 FT.)

This craggy summit is the westernmost of the six Bigelow Range peaks. Cranberry Pond is a scenic tarn high on the Bigelow Range crest at the eastern base of the peak. The Bigelow Range Trail traverses Cranberry Peak from the village of Stratton to the AT, which offers access from the south at ME 27/16.

BIGELOW RANGE TRAIL (MATC; MAP 3: B1–B2)

Cumulative from Currie St. (1,180 ft.) to:	↕	↗	○
Cranberry Peak (3,194 ft.)	3.2 mi.	2,000 ft.	2:40
AT (2,400 ft.)	5.0 mi.	2,000 ft.	3:30

This blue-blazed trail starts from the village of Stratton at the western end of the Bigelow Range, climbs to Cranberry Peak, and continues east to meet the AT just beyond Cranberry Pond.

From the center of Stratton, drive 0.8 mi. south on ME 27/16 to Currie St. (opposite the town ball fields). Take Currie St. for 0.7 mi. to its end, where there is trailhead parking.

Bigelow Range Trail proceeds easily through the woods, then climbs gradually on an old woods road. The trail crosses a brook at 1.0 mi., then climbs steeply to reach Arnold's Well (a deep cleft in the rocks named for Benedict Arnold; no drinking water) at about 1.5 mi. Beyond, the trail reaches open ledges and good views. Ahead, pass a short side trail leading 200 ft. to a huge overhanging slab of rock known as "the Cave."

Beyond, the trail continues its steep ascent, much of it over open ledges, to reach the summit of Cranberry Peak at 3.2 mi. Enjoy excellent views of Flagstaff Lake and the major summits along the Bigelow Range from this vantage point. Beyond the peak, the trail descends steeply and then more gradually into a narrow valley, where it reaches the north shore of Cranberry Pond. The trail follows a scenic route along the pond before ending at a jct. with the AT at 5.0 mi.

■ LITTLE BIGELOW MTN. (3,070 FT.)

Little Bigelow Mtn. is the easternmost peak of the Bigelow Range, separated from Avery Peak by a deep, rugged notch known as Safford Notch. The mountain's ridgeline is long and narrow, with steep cliffs along its southern side. The northern slope descends steadily to the south shore of Flagstaff Lake. Access to the Little Bigelow summit is via the AT Southbound from East Flagstaff Rd. or via Safford Brook Trail and the AT Northbound.

AT SOUTHBOUND (MATC; MAP 3: B3–B4)

Cumulative from East Flagstaff Rd. (1,170 ft.) via AT to:	↕	↗	↺
Little Bigelow Lean-to (1,800 ft.)	1.4 mi.	630 ft.	1:00
Little Bigelow Mtn. summit (3,070 ft.)	3.5 mi.	1,900 ft.	2:40
Safford Brook Trail (2,250 ft.)	6.7 mi.	1,900 ft.	4:15

The AT traverses the long and craggy ridgeline of Little Bigelow Mtn., connecting East Flagstaff Rd. with Safford Notch Trail in Safford Notch.

From the jct. of ME 16 and Long Falls Dam Rd. in New Portland, drive 17.3 mi. north on Long Falls Dam Rd. to Bog Brook Rd., on the left. Bear left on the gravel-surfaced Bog Brook Rd. and drive 0.8 mi., then bear left onto East Flagstaff Rd. Reach the AT crossing in another 0.2 mi. Parking is on the right in an old gravel pit.

The AT continues north along the road from the parking area for a short distance, then bears left into the woods and climbs through hardwoods alongside a brook. At 1.4 mi., a blue-blazed side trail leads right 0.1 mi. across the brook to Little Bigelow Lean-to. Beyond, the trail continues through the woods, leaves the brook, and climbs a series of open ledges. At 3.0 mi., the trail reaches a viewpoint at the southeastern end of the summit ridge. The true summit is about 0.5 mi. farther along the trail. Multiple outlooks offer fine views down the Bigelow Range and south to the ski slopes of Sugarloaf. The AT continues to a jct. with Safford Brook Trail in rugged Safford Notch at 6.7 mi. Safford Notch Campsite is 0.3 mi. to the left (south).

SAFFORD BROOK TRAIL (MATC; MAP 3: A4 AND B3–B4)

Cumulative from East Flagstaff Rd. (1,230 ft.) to:	⇅	↗	○
AT (2,250 ft.) via Safford Brook Trail	2.3 mi.	1,000 ft.	1:40
Little Bigelow Mtn. summit (3,070 ft.) via AT Northbound	5.5 mi.	1,850 ft.	3:40
From East Flagstaff Rd. (1,230 ft.) to:			
Avery Peak (4,088 ft.) via AT Southbound	4.5 mi.	2,850 ft.	3:40

This trail affords access to Little Bigelow Mtn. and Avery Peak from the north at Flagstaff Lake.

To reach the start of Safford Notch Trail, follow the driving directions for the AT to Little Bigelow Mtn. as described on p. 184. From the AT crossing, continue to drive northwest on East Flagstaff Rd. In 4.1 mi., the road crosses Safford Brook and, just ahead, reaches the trailhead parking area on the right (kiosk). (*Note:* Safford Notch Trail officially starts 0.25 mi. north at Round Barn Campsite on the shore of Flagstaff Lake, but most hikers headed for Bigelow skip this short stretch and start from the parking lot on East Flagstaff Rd.)

From the road, Safford Brook Trail ascends gradually along Safford Brook, then crosses the brook at 0.7 mi. Beyond, it climbs steeply to a side trail on the left leading to Safford Overlook. Continuing on, the main trail maintains a steep ascent into the wild and rugged environs of Safford Notch, with its jumble of house-sized boulders. Here at 2.3 mi. is the jct. with the AT, which leads north to Little Bigelow Mtn. and south to Avery Peak.

About 50 yd. east (left) on the AT is a blue-blazed trail that leads south (right) 0.3 mi. to Safford Notch Campsite. Continuing in this direction, the AT reaches the highest peak of Little Bigelow Mtn. at 5.5 mi.

To the right, heading southbound on the AT, the trail rises steeply west toward Avery Peak, with several excellent vistas en route. At 3.2 mi., the AT reaches the crest of the ridge. Here, a side trail leads left 0.1 mi. to the top of Old Man's Head, a huge cliff on the south side of the mountain. From this jct., the AT continues to climb steeply, reaching the timberline and, shortly thereafter, the alpine summit of Avery Peak and the concrete and stone base of an old fire tower. Outstanding views are possible in all directions.

SEC 4

■ BURNT HILL (3,609 FT.)

This lightly visited peak in Carrabassett Valley, also known as Burnt Mtn., lies just east of Sugarloaf Mtn. A forest fire in the early 1900s burned 5,500 acres on the mountain (hence its name) as well as a portion of neighboring Sugarloaf. The mountain offers extensive views from its open alpine summit, including Sugarloaf and its ski slopes, Spaulding Mtn., the long alpine ridge of Mt. Abraham, the Crockers, and the Bigelow Range.

From the jct. of ME 16 and ME 27 in Kingfield, drive north on ME 27/16 for 15.2 mi. Turn left (south) onto the access road to the Sugarloaf ski resort. Continue about 2.0 mi. to the base area. Parking is available at several large lots near the Sugarloaf base lodge and the Sugarloaf Mtn. Hotel.

Walk through the breezeway of the hotel into the courtyard beyond. With the hotel on your left and the base lodge to your right, follow the paved walk (aka Main St.) east. Pass behind the base lodge, follow the driveway past Gondola Village, and then walk along Adams Mtn. Rd. Continue past the condominium complex, cross Mountainside Rd., and then continue on Bigelow Mtn. Rd. to its end, where there is a sign for Burnt Mtn. Trail.

BURNT HILL TRAIL (SMSR; USGS SUGARLOAF MTN. QUAD, GAZETTEER MAP 29, MTF BURNT HILL HIKING TRAIL MAP)

From Bigelow Mtn. Rd (1,940 ft.) to:	⇅	↗	↻
Burnt Mtn. summit (3,609 ft.)	2.8 mi.	1,670 ft.	2:25

A wide ski trail leads into the woods a short distance to Burnt Hill Trail, which starts on the right just after a small bridge over the West Branch of Brackett Brook. Follow the blue-blazed trail along the brook, crossing it several times. The trail veers away from the brook and begins to climb steadily, reaching the col between Burnt Mtn. and Sugarloaf. The remainder of the hike is above treeline, marked by cairns and blue blazes. The summit is at 2.8 mi.

Since 2010, Sugarloaf has been expanding its ski trail system to the east into the upper basin of Brackett Brook as far as the summit of Burnt Mtn., which has opened up 650 acres of backcountry glade skiing. Burnt Mtn. Trail threads a route through these trails and glades. While the treadway is well defined, hikers should still look carefully for trail markers (blazes, cairns) whenever crossing any areas cleared for skiing. Sugarloaf is committed to minimizing impact to the hiking trail.

MAINE HUTS AND TRAILS
■ STRATTON BROOK HUT

NARROW GAUGE PATHWAY, MAINE HUT TRAIL, AND OAK KNOLL TRAIL (CV, MHT; GAZETTEER MAP 29, MHT TRAIL MAP)

Cumulative from Stratton Brook Trailhead (1,294 ft.) to:	↥↧	↗	⟳
Maine Hut Trail (1,250 ft.)	0.9 mi.	-50 ft.	0:25
Oak Knoll Trail (1,280 ft.)	1.3 mi.	30 ft.	0:40
Newton's Revenge (1,830 ft.)	3.8 mi.	580 ft.	2:15
Stratton Brook Hut (1,880 ft.)	4.1 mi.	630 ft.	2:25

SEC 4

From the parking lot kiosk, follow Trailhead spur trail 0.1 mi. to connect with Narrow Gauge Pathway. Turn left, cross a bridge over the Carrabassett River, and at 0.3 mi., turn right to stay on Narrow Gauge Pathway. Continue down the old graveled rail corridor, gently losing elevation. At 0.9 mi., turn left on Maine Hut Trail (also signed for Newton's Revenge). At 1.3 mi., reach the blue-blazed Oak Knoll Trail on the left (sign), a single-track trail with well-crafted stone switchbacks that climb the south side of the hill. Near Stratton Brook Hut, Oak Knoll Trail crosses the hut service road twice. Beyond the first service road crossing, at a T jct. with Newton's Revenge, turn right, and in 80 yd., cross the service road for the second time (the hut is 100 yd. up the service road to the left). Ahead, the single-track winds through the woods to a great view of the Bigelow Range before reaching Stratton Brook Hut at 4.1 mi.

NARROW GAUGE PATHWAY, MAINE HUT TRAIL, AND NEWTON'S REVENGE (CV, MHT; GAZETTEER MAP 29, MHT TRAIL MAP)

Cumulative from Stratton Brook Trailhead (1,294 ft.) to:	↥↧	↗	⟳
Maine Hut Trail (1,250 ft.)	0.9 mi.	-50 ft.	0:25
Oak Knoll Trail (1,280 ft.)	1.3 mi.	30 ft.	0:40
Newton's Revenge (1,540 ft.)	2.5 mi.	290 ft.	1:25
Stratton Brook Hut (1,880 ft.) via Newton's Revenge	3.2 mi.	630 ft.	1:55

From the parking lot kiosk, follow Trailhead spur trail 0.1 mi. to connect with Narrow Gauge Pathway. Turn left, cross a bridge over the Carrabassett River, and at 0.3 mi., turn right to stay on Narrow Gauge Pathway. Continue down the old narrow-gauge rail corridor, gently losing elevation.

At 0.9 mi., turn left on Maine Hut Trail (also signed for Newton's Revenge). At 1.3 mi., reach the blue-blazed Oak Knoll Trail on the left (sign). Continue ahead on Maine Hut Trail, which winds up the south slope of the knoll to a jct. at 2.5 mi. with Newton's Revenge, Maine Hut Trail to Poplar Hut, and a single-track bike trail. Here, Maine Hut Trail either turns right and downhill toward Poplar Hut or continues straight and uphill as Newton's Revenge to Stratton Brook Hut. The single-track trail on the left at this intersection braids on and off Newton's Revenge, ending at Oak Knoll Trail. Stay straight on Newton's Revenge, climbing the east ridge to the jct. with Oak Knoll Trail at 3.0 mi. In another 80 yd., Newton's Revenge comes to a T intersection with the hut service road; take a left to follow the road, arriving at Stratton Brook Hut at 3.2 mi.

NEWTON'S REVENGE, APPROACH TRAIL, ESKER TRAIL, FIRE WARDEN'S TRAIL, DEAD MOOSE TRAIL, AND MOUNTAIN TRAIL (CV, MHT; GAZETTEER MAP 29, MHT TRAIL MAP)

Cumulative from Stratton Brook Hut (1,880 ft.) to:	⇅	↗	○
Newton's Revenge (1,850 ft.)	100 yd.	-30 ft.	0:02
Oak Knoll Trail (1,820 ft.)	180 yd.	-50 ft.	0:04
Approach Trail (1,685 ft.)	0.4 mi.	-195 ft.	0:25
Esker Trail (1,270 ft.)	2.1 mi.	-610 ft.	1:05
Fire Warden's Trailhead, Dead Moose Trail (1,250 ft.)	4.0 mi.	20 ft.	2:00
Mountain Trail (1,370 ft.)	4.7 mi.	140 ft.	2:25
Stratton Brook Hut service road (1,600 ft.)	5.7 mi.	370 ft.	3:00
Stratton Brook Hut (1,880 ft.)	6.3 mi.	650 ft.	3:30

From Stratton Brook Hut follow the hut service road to its intersection with Newton's Revenge, and turn right at 100 yd. Stay straight past Oak Knoll Trail, which turns downhill to the left in about 80 yd. (sign). Continue the steep descent along Newton's Revenge, blazed with MHT white diamond trail markers. At 0.4 mi., at a large hairpin right-hand corner, Approach Trail takes a left from Newton's Revenge. This sustainable hiking, snowshoeing, and backcountry-skiing trail follows the knoll's north-facing contours downhill, eventually crossing the (motorized) Mountain Trail, a power-line corridor, and a footbridge over Stratton Brook to a T intersection with Esker Trail.

To loop around Stratton Brook Pond back to Stratton Brook Hut, turn left on Esker Trail from Approach Trail and go 1.2 mi. Stay straight past the Fire Warden's Trail intersection on the right and continue for another 0.7 mi. to Fire Warden's Trailhead. At 3.9 mi., turn left at Fire Warden's Trailhead onto the double-tracked, locally named Dead Moose Trail (when facing the trailhead kiosk, the trail is to the right and makes a Y with Fire Warden's Trail and Stratton Brook Pond Rd.). Dead Moose Trail, marked with MHT blue diamond blazes, leads back to Mountain Trail (ATVs and snowmobiles have right-of-way) at 4.7 mi. Follow MHT cedar and blue diamond trail signs on Mountain Trail, braiding along a power-line corridor. At 5.7 mi., turn right at a directional cedar-diamond trail sign with a blue blaze, and travel 0.3 mi. to the Stratton Brook Hut service road at 6.0 mi. (going straight leads back to the Mountain Trail crossing of the Approach Trail, 0.4 mi. farther up Mountain Trail). At the wide landing area, turn left onto the Stratton Brook service road, climb steeply uphill, pass the Oak Knoll Trail crossings, and arrive at Stratton Brook Hut at 6.3 mi.

SEC 4

■ POPLAR HUT

MAINE HUT TRAIL (MHT; GAZETTEER MAP 29, MHT TRAIL MAP)

Cumulative from Airport Trailhead (883 ft.) to:

	⇅	↗	↻
Carriage Rd. X-ing 1, Warren's Trail (900 ft.)	1.3 mi.	20 ft.	0:40
Larry's Trail (1,050 ft.)	1.8 mi.	170 ft.	1:00
Poplar Hut (1,314 ft.)	3.3 mi.	430 ft.	1:50

From the parking lot kiosk, follow the multiuse trail north to a bridge over the Carrabassett River at 0.2 mi. Cross the bridge to reach a large five-way intersection. Turn right on Huston Brook Rd. and immediately branch left to follow Maine Hut Trail uphill. The trail parallels the Carrabassett River and Huston Brook Rd. before trending away and around the base of a ridge to meet Carriage Rd. at Carriage Rd. X-ing 1 at 1.3 mi. Here a bridge crosses Poplar Stream. Warren's Trail departs north to follow the west side of Poplar Stream toward Poplar Hut. To continue on Maine Hut Trail, take the bridge over Poplar Stream and keep left. The trail starts out flat, then rises to the jct. with Larry's Trail on the left at 1.8 mi. Beyond Larry's Trail, Maine Hut Trail climbs moderately through the valley of Poplar Stream before leveling off for the final stretch to a bridge over Poplar Hut's modest hydro reservoir at 3.2 mi. Cross the bridge and follow the reservoir before turning right at a signed intersection to reach Poplar Hut at 3.3 mi.

LARRY'S TRAIL (MHT; GAZETTEER MAP 29, MHT TRAIL MAP)

Cumulative from Airport Trailhead (883 ft.) to:	↥↧	↗	↺
Warren's Trail (900 ft.)	1.3 mi.	20 ft.	0:40
Larry's Trail (1,050 ft.)	1.8 mi.	170 ft.	1:00
Poplar Hut (1,314 ft.)	3.1 mi.	430 ft.	2:00

Larry's Trail departs left from Maine Hut Trail 1.8 mi. from Airport Trailhead. The trail follows the east side of Poplar Stream, winding through the forest over rolling terrain. Cross the South Branch of Poplar Stream at 2.6 mi. on a native timber footbridge. The cascades of Poplar Falls are on the right, while Larry's Trail climbs a steep stone staircase straight ahead. At the top of the staircase, Warren's Trail intersects on the left, creating a loop back toward Airport Trailhead. Continue straight for 0.1 mi. and turn right at the T intersection with Maine Hut Trail. Climb uphill beside South Brook (which feeds Poplar Falls and Poplar Hut's hydropower) for 0.3 mi. before reaching a left-hand jct. that leads to Poplar Hut at 3.1 mi.

WARREN'S TRAIL (MHT; GAZETTEER MAP 29, MHT TRAIL MAP)

Cumulative from Airport Trailhead (883 ft.) to:	↥↧	↗	↺
Warren's Trail (900 ft.)	1.3 mi.	20 ft.	0:40
Poplar Hut service road (1,150 ft.)	2.8 mi.	250 ft.	1:50
Larry's Trail (1,170 ft.)	3.0 mi.	270 ft.	1:55
Maine Hut Trail (1,190 ft.)	3.1 mi.	290 ft.	2:00
Poplar Hut (1,314 ft.)	3.5 mi.	430 ft.	2:15

Warren's Trail departs left from the Maine Hut Trail at 1.3 mi. from Airport Trailhead. After crossing Carriage Rd. at Carriage Rd. X-ing 1, but before crossing the bridge over Poplar Stream, turn left onto Warren's Trail. This primitive trail along the west side of Poplar Stream passes through mature tree growth and makes for a great hike to see waterfalls and wildlife. At 2.8 mi., Warren's Trail reaches the Poplar Hut service road. Turn right on the service road and cross Poplar Stream Bridge. Immediately after the bridge at an MHT cedar trail sign, head back into the forest to continue on the trail, following the boulder-strewn path for 0.1 mi. to the jct. with Larry's Trail. To continue to Poplar Hut, take a left on Larry's Trail. The trail from here is a gradual ascent to Maine Hut Trail at 3.1 mi. Turn right on Maine Hut Trail. Climb uphill beside South Brook (which feeds Poplar Falls and Poplar Hut's hydropower) for 0.3 mi. before reaching a left-hand jct. that leads to Poplar Hut at 3.5 mi.

■ FLAGSTAFF HUT

MAINE HUT TRAIL (MHT; GAZETTEER MAP 29, MHT TRAIL MAP)

From Long Falls Dam/Flagstaff Trailhead (1,202 ft.) to:	⇅	↗	↻
Flagstaff Hut (1,164 ft.)	2.1 mi.	50 ft.	1:10

Hike south on the trailhead spur of Maine Hut Trail (white diamond trail markers) for 0.2 mi. to a four-way jct. with Maine Hut Trail (goes left and right, south and north) and Shore Trail, which goes straight to reach Flagstaff Lake. Take a right on Maine Hut Trail, which meanders northwest over rolling terrain through cedar, fir, and broadleaf forest. At 1.6 mi., a spur leads to Shore Trail. Take a hard right to stay on Maine Hut Trail. Continue for 0.3 mi., and bear left on the hut service road. In another 0.1 mi., continue straight along the service road past the intersection of the Grand Falls–bound Maine Hut Trail for an additional 0.2 mi. to reach Flagstaff Hut.

SEC 4

SHORE TRAIL (MHT; GAZETTEER MAP 29, MHT TRAIL MAP)

Cumulative from Long Falls Dam/ Flagstaff Trailhead (1,202 ft.) to:	⇅	↗	↻
Shore Trail (1,180 ft.)	0.2 mi.	-20 ft.	0:05
Flagstaff Hut (1,164 ft.)	2.1 mi.	50 ft.	1:05

Hike south on the trailhead spur of Maine Hut Trail (white diamond trail markers) for 0.2 mi. to a four-way jct. with the Maine Hut Trail (goes left and right, south and north) and Shore Trail, which goes straight to reach Flagstaff Lake. Continue ahead on Shore Trail. At Flagstaff Lake, Shore Trail turns northwest to follow the shoreline for more than 1 mi. At 1.6 mi., a spur turns right to Maine Hut Trail; bear left to continue on Shore Trail. At 1.9 mi., Beaver Trail leads right to a dam and beaver hut viewpoint. A spur on the left at 2.0 mi. leads to a fantastic vista of Flagstaff Lake. Bear right to arrive at Flagstaff Hut at 2.1 mi.

■ GRAND FALLS HUT

MAINE HUT TRAIL (MHT; GAZETTEER MAP 29, MHT TRAIL MAP)

Cumulative from Big Eddy/ Grand Falls Trailhead (1,058 ft.) to:	⇅	↗	↻
Tom & Kate Chappell Bridge over the Dead River (1,030 ft.)	6.5 mi.	50 ft.	3:15
Grand Falls (1,030 ft.) via Falls Trail	6.7 mi.	50 ft.	3:20
Lower Enchanted Trailhead Spur (1,020 ft.)	7.1 mi.	70 ft.	3:35
Grand Falls Hut (1,049 ft.)	7.8 mi.	100 ft.	3:55

From the MHT parking area at Big Eddy, walk back along Long Falls Dam Rd for 0.3 mi. Turn left on Dead River Rd. (a private camp road), continue 0.1 mi. and cross a bridge, then turn left on Maine Hut Trail at 0.6 mi. Maine Hut Trail rejoins Dead River Rd. for a short time at 1.1 mi., then splits off again, left, beyond a boat put-in. At a gate across the dirt camp road, keep left and follow the trail 5.5 mi. through forests and fields while hugging the eastern shore of the quiet Dead River. Cross seven large bridges along the way.

At 6.6 mi., reach the Tom & Kate Chappell Footbridge that impressively spans the river above Grand Falls. After the bridge is a jct. with Falls Trail. Continue straight along Maine Hut Trail for 0.6 mi. (passing multiple ATV/snowmobile crossings and merging with ITS 89 before Spencer Stream), or turn right onto the narrower Falls Trail for 0.3 mi. to view the Grand Falls vista. Where Maine Hut Trail and Falls Trail converge ahead, continue on for another 0.2 mi. to a gated bridge that crosses Spencer Stream. Cross this bridge and continue uphill to the right to a road intersection (follow MHT cedar and white diamond trail markers). Downhill to the right is the popular Dead River boat put-in and parking area; turn left and immediately right back onto Maine Hut Trail. From here, the trail climbs to Grand Falls Hut at 7.8 mi. from the Big Eddy parking area.

APPALACHIAN TRAIL CORRIDOR

■ NORTH CROCKER MTN. (4,228 FT.) AND SOUTH CROCKER MTN. (4,050 FT.)

North Crocker Mtn. and South Crocker Mtn. are just west of Sugarloaf Mtn. in Carrabassett Valley. They are separated from Sugarloaf by Caribou Valley and the South Branch of the Carrabassett River. The two peaks and a portion of nearby Mt. Redington are part of the 12,000-acre Crocker Mtn. property, a new addition to Maine's public lands system, thanks to the Forest Legacy Program, Land for Maine's Future Program, in cooperation with private foundations and individual donors. The AT extends across the Crockers for 8.0 mi. North Crocker Mtn., despite its height, is heavily wooded to the top and has few views. South Crocker Mtn., although also wooded, offers fine views on the ascent from Caribou Valley as well as from a ledge outcrop on its summit. Hikers can approach North Crocker Mtn. from the north via the AT from ME 27, and South Crocker Mtn. from the east at Caribou Valley Rd.

AT SOUTHBOUND (MATC; USGS SUGARLOAF MTN. AND BLACK NUBBLE QUADS, GAZETTEER MAP 29, MATC MAP 6, MTF AT–CROCKER CIRQUE MAP)

Cumulative from ME 27 (1,390 ft.) to:	↧↥	↗	↻
North Crocker Mtn. (4,228 ft.)	5.2 mi.	2,800 ft.	4:00
South Crocker Mtn. (4,050 ft.)	6.2 mi.	3,160 ft.	4:40
Side trail to Crocker Cirque Campsite (2,700 ft.)	7.3 mi.	3,160 ft.	5:15
Caribou Valley Rd. (2,220 ft.)	8.3 mi.	3,160 ft.	5:45
Parking area and yellow gate (2,130 ft.)	8.8 mi.	3,160 ft.	6:00

In Carrabassett Valley, from the jct. of ME 27 and the blinking light at the jct. of Sugarloaf Access Rd., drive north on ME 27 for 2.6 mi. to the AT crossing, where there is a trailhead parking lot on the left (south) side of the highway.

Follow the AT Southbound, climbing steadily through woods for 1.4 mi. to reach a knoll on the north ridge of Crocker Mtn. Beyond, pass through a long section of coniferous forest. Ahead, the trail angles up the western side of the ridge through hardwood forest. It continues up the ridge, reenters softwoods at about 3.5 mi., and crosses a small stream at 4.2 mi. (usually reliable; last water until Crocker Cirque Campsite). Then the trail rises more steeply to the crest and reaches the north peak of Crocker Mtn. at 5.2 mi. The descent into the col begins immediately. The trail leads to the low point of the col and soon begins to climb toward the rocky South Crocker Mtn. At 6.2 mi., at a signed jct. on top of South Crocker Mtn., where the AT makes a sharp left turn for the descent to Caribou Valley Rd., bear right and up 50 yd. to the true summit, where an open ledge offers fine views to Sugarloaf, Spaulding Mtn., and Mt. Abraham. The herd path to Mt. Redington leaves right just before the ledge opening.

AT NORTHBOUND (MATC; USGS SUGARLOAF MTN. AND BLACK NUBBLE QUADS, GAZETTEER MAP 29, MATC MAP 6, MTF AT–CROCKER CIRQUE MAP)

Cumulative from Caribou Valley Rd. parking area and yellow gate (2,130 ft.) to:	↧↥	↗	↻
AT crossing (2,220 ft.)	0.5 mi.	90 ft.	0:15
Side trail to Crocker Cirque Campsite (2,700 ft.)	1.5 mi.	570 ft.	1:00
South Crocker Mtn. (4,050 ft.)	2.6 mi.	1,920 ft.	2:15
North Crocker Mtn. (4,228 ft.)	3.6 mi.	2,500 ft.	3:00
ME 27 (1,390 ft.)	8.8 mi.	2,500 ft.	5:40

SEC 4

From the jct. of ME 27 and Caribou Valley Rd. (no sign), at a point 1.0 mi. north of the blinking light at the jct. of the Sugarloaf Access Rd., turn left (south) on Caribou Valley Rd. and drive 3.8 mi. to the end of the maintained road (blocked by a yellow gate) and a parking area.

To reach the AT, go around the yellow gate and walk north on Caribou Valley Rd. for 0.5 mi., passing over three bridges en route (the first is metal, the second and third are wooden). A small cairn on the right marks where the AT enters the woods on the right (west) side of the old road. The AT climbs steadily to a jct. and brook on the right at 1.0 mi., where a 0.2-mi. side trail leads to Crocker Cirque Campsite. Beyond the jct., the AT climbs steeply via switchbacks, then crosses a talus field with views ahead to North Crocker and behind to Sugarloaf. Continuing up the west ridge of the mountain, there are nice views of Crocker Cirque below and the Bigelow Range to the north. The moderate climb along the ridge ends at a signed jct. atop South Crocker. Here, the AT bears right and down, while a side trail bears left and up 50 yd. to the true summit and a nice ledge viewpoint. Just before the view opening, the herd path to Mt. Redington leaves to the right.

■ MT. REDINGTON (4,010 FT.)

Mt. Redington straddles the town lines of Redington Township and Carrabassett Valley in the wild region of high peaks southwest of South Crocker Mtn. and North Crocker Mtn. and east of Sugarloaf Mtn. and Spaulding Mtn. The eastern half of the mountain, nearly to the summit, is on conservation land owned by the state of Maine, while everything west of that line is privately owned.

The mountain is the only "trailless" 4,000-footer in Maine and the only bushwhack described in this guide. A good herd path, not officially marked or maintained, connects the summit of South Crocker Mtn. with the top of Mt. Redington. Once a fierce bushwhack, this path has become increasingly popular with peak baggers and, as such, is beaten down and pretty obvious the entire way, with bits of colored surveyor's tape marking the route. (*Note:* Even with the presence of a herd path, an attempt on Mt. Redington should not be underestimated and must be treated as a bushwhack. Hikers should be prepared for travel into remote terrain with proper gear and the requisite navigational skills.)

Prior to the development of the herd path, logging on the eastern slopes of the mountain enticed hikers to avoid the difficult bushwhack by ascending via a series of logging roads and skidder trails from Caribou Pond. Then, to many hikers' dismay, a work road was constructed to the summit to service an experimental wind gauge tower, making the ascent that much easier. The wind project proposal was withdrawn and the tower removed. The summit is now being reclaimed by forest, but good views remain. A register canister is attached to a tree in the thick fir growth adjacent to the summit clearing; it still bears the old (pre-1989 USGS survey) elevation of 3,984 ft.

MT. REDINGTON HERD PATH (NFTM; USGS BLACK NUBBLE QUAD, GAZETTEER MAP 29, MATC MAP 6)

Cumulative from South Crocker Mtn. summit (4,050 ft.) to:	⥮	↗	○
Low point between peaks (3,440 ft.)	0.6 mi.	-610 ft.	0:20
Mt. Redington summit (4,010 ft.)	1.3 mi.	570 ft.	1:00

To reach the start of the Mt. Redington herd path, follow the driving directions and trail description for South Crocker Mtn. (the AT Northbound from Caribou Valley Rd.). At the signed jct. atop South Crocker, the AT Northbound bears right and down, while a side trail bears left and up 50 yd. to the true summit and a nice ledge viewpoint. Just before the view opening, the herd path to Mt. Redington leaves to the right. A small tentsite is visible to the right of the trail at the herd path start.

Follow the flagged path along the ridge and over a low knoll. Drop down to a yellow-blazed boundary line at 0.1 mi. Turn west along the boundary, follow it around a corner, and then reach a jct. at 0.15 mi., with a low cairn on the left and a low brush pile blocking the boundary corridor ahead. Leave the boundary line here by turning left onto a narrow trail. Descend southwest through thick woods, and as the trail descends, views of Mt. Redington ahead are possible through the trees. At 0.4 mi., there's an awkward step off a boulder. The descent is mostly moderate with a few steep sections. At 0.55 mi., the trail bears south along a contour. Reach a small clearing, the low point between South Crocker and Mt. Redington, where there is a view to the northwest. Just ahead, in a semi-open stretch of fir, the dome of Mt. Redington is in view, while behind is a good look to North Crocker and the shoulder of South Crocker. Climb, then follow a contour, then climb again to reach an old skidder road at 0.7 mi. (cairn on left, small log barrier across road to right). Turn left up the road, and in another 0.1 mi., reach the saddle between South Crocker Mtn. and Mt. Redington. Here, turn right off the skidder road and follow the trail southwest up the ridge. At a well-flagged jct. at 1.1 mi., the old bushwhack "path" from Caribou Pond enters from the left. Ahead, climb easily, and soon cross a faint yellow-blazed boundary line at 1.3 mi. Just beyond, an old trail, likely the former work road built to service the former wind gauge on top, enters from the left. Bear right here into the summit clearing, and in 75 ft., reach the summit. A bench is to the left, and a small summit sign is tucked into the woods on the right. Ahead, through one row of firs, there is a nice view north to North

SEC 4

Crocker, South Crocker, and the Bigelow Range. From the summit sign, follow flagging around to the right to the register canister.

■ SUGARLOAF MTN. (4,250 FT.)

AT AND SUGARLOAF MTN. TRAIL
(MATC; USGS SUGARLOAF MTN. QUAD, GAZETTEER MAP 29,
MATC MAP 6, MTF AT–SUGARLOAF MTN. MAP)

Cumulative from Caribou Valley Rd. parking area and yellow gate (2,130 ft.) to:	⇅	↗	○
AT crossing (2,220 ft.)	0.5 mi.	90 ft.	0:15
Sugarloaf Mtn. Trail (3,640 ft.)	2.8 mi.	1,500 ft.	2:10
Sugarloaf Mtn. summit (4,250 ft.) via Sugarloaf Mtn. Trail	3.4 mi.	2,100 ft.	2:45

Sugarloaf Mtn. in Carrabassett Valley is the second-highest mountain in Maine. It is best known and most frequented for the ski resort on its northern slopes. For hikers, the view from the symmetrical, bare summit cone is well worth the climb. The number of peaks visible may be unequaled in the state, except perhaps from Katahdin. Spaulding Mtn. is south of Sugarloaf and is connected to it by a high ridge, while the two peaks of Crocker Mtn. are to the west, across a branch of the Carrabassett River in Caribou Valley.

The approach to Sugarloaf is via the AT Southbound. From the jct. of ME 27 and Caribou Valley Rd. (no sign), at a point 1.0 mi. north of the blinking light at the jct. of Sugarloaf Access Rd., turn left (south) on Caribou Valley Rd. and drive 3.8 mi. to the end of the maintained road (blocked by a yellow gate) and a parking area.

To reach the AT, go around the yellow gate and walk north on Caribou Valley Rd. for 0.5 mi., passing over three bridges en route (the first is metal, the second and third are wooden). A small cairn on the right marks where the AT enters the woods on the right (west) side of the old road. Just ahead, look left into the thick brush to find the AT going southbound; this is the route.

The AT soon crosses the South Branch of the Carrabassett River (no bridge; can be difficult, if not impossible, in high water). Sugarloaf Mtn. Trail follows the river for a time and then begins to climb, at first gently and then more steeply (very rough and steep in some sections). Ahead, the trail crosses open ledges and skirts the top of a huge cirque on the western side of Sugarloaf. The last water is a stream at 1.8 mi. At a jct. at 2.3 mi., the AT turns right toward Spaulding Mtn. and Sugarloaf. Sugarloaf Mtn. Trail leaves left, climbing steadily up the southwest flank of Sugarloaf for 0.6 mi., and emerges into the open near the top. One last rocky scramble is required to reach the summit and a cluster of towers. The Octagon, the old building that once housed the Sugarloaf gondola, is below to the left, and just beyond that, the top of the Timberline Chairlift.

■ SPAULDING MTN. (4,010 FT.)

AT SOUTHBOUND FROM SUGARLOAF MTN. TRAIL (MATC; USGS SUGARLOAF MTN. QUAD, GAZETTEER MAP 29, MATC MAP 6)

Cumulative from Caribou Valley Rd. parking area and yellow gate (2,130 ft.) to:	⬇⬆	↗	◯
AT crossing (2,220 ft.)	0.5 mi.	90 ft.	0:15
Sugarloaf Mtn. Trail (3,640 ft.)	2.8 mi.	1,500 ft.	2:10
Bronze AT plaque (3,500 ft.)	4.2 mi.	1,650 ft.	3:00
Spaulding side trail (3,900 ft.)	4.9 mi.	2,350 ft.	3:40
Spaulding Mtn. summit (4,010 ft.) via side trail	5.0 mi.	2,450 ft.	3:45
Spaulding Mtn. Lean-to (3,100 ft.)	5.7 mi.	2,450 ft.	4:00
Mt. Abraham Trail (3,350 ft.)	6.8 mi.	2,450 ft.	4:35

Spaulding Mtn. in Mt. Abram Township rises high above the long, undulating ridgeline extending southwest from Sugarloaf Mtn. toward the north ridge of Mt. Abraham. The final 2 mi. of the AT were cut and blazed along this stretch in 1937.

From its jct. with Sugarloaf Mtn. Trail, at a point 2.3 mi. from Caribou Valley Rd., the AT continues southbound, traversing the crest of the rugged ridge between Sugarloaf Mtn. and Spaulding Mtn., with views and steep cliffs on the left. En route, a large bronze plaque on the north side of the trail honors the members of the Maine Civilian Conservation Corps, who completed the AT near this spot in 1937. Beyond, the AT descends steeply to a deep notch in the ridge, and the ascent of Spaulding Mtn. begins, steeply at first, then more gradually. At 4.9 mi., a side trail leads left 0.1 mi. to the wooded summit. There are limited views at the summit sign, but a cleared narrow corridor leads north 200 ft. to fine views of Sugarloaf and the Bigelows. Continuing south, the AT descends to Spaulding Mtn. Lean-to (via a 150-ft. side trail) at 5.7 mi. Following an easy route along the wide, mostly level ridge, reach the jct. of Mt. Abraham Trail at 6.8 mi. (this spur leads 1.7 mi. south to the open 4,043-ft. summit of Mt. Abraham). For a description of the AT south of this point, refer to the *The Official Appalachian Trail Guide to Maine* (MATC).

■ MT. ABRAHAM (4,049 FT.)

Mt. Abraham (or "Abram") in Mt. Abram Township and Salem Township lies to the south of Sugarloaf Mtn. and Spaulding Mtn. in the 6,200-acre

Mt. Abraham Public Lands unit, most of which is an ecological reserve. Mt. Abraham has an impressive ridgeline that extends for about 4.5 mi. in a northwest-southeast direction and consists of eight peaks ranging from 3,400 ft. to more than 4,000 ft. Mt. Abraham is home to the second-largest alpine zone in Maine (behind Katahdin), some 350 acres in size. Two trails ascend to the summit: Fire Warden's Trail climbs the mountain from the Kingfield side in the east, and Mt. Abraham Trail approaches from the north via the AT just south of Spaulding Mtn.

FIRE WARDEN'S TRAIL (MATC; USGS MT. ABRAHAM QUAD, GAZETTEER MAP 29, MATC MAP 6, MTF MT. ABRAHAM–FIRE WARDEN TRAIL MAP)

Cumulative from grassy pullout before the Rapid Stream bridges (990 ft.) to:	⇅	↗	↻
Trailhead at T jct. (1,163 ft.)	0.6 mi.	175 ft.	0:20
Campsite at former fire warden's cabin site (2,100 ft.)	3.2 mi.	1,100 ft.	2:00
Mt. Abraham summit (4,049 ft.)	4.5 mi.	3,050 ft.	3:50

From the jct. of ME 27 and ME 16 in Kingfield, drive north on ME 27 for 0.5 mi., crossing a bridge over the Carrabassett River en route. Turn left (west) onto West Kingfield Rd. At 3.3 mi. from ME 27, the road becomes gravel. At a crossroads at 3.5 mi., proceed straight ahead on Rapid Stream Rd. At 6.0 mi., reach a major fork. Take the left fork, and in about 100 yd., cross the first of two bridges over Rapid Stream. Cross the second bridge; the road forks again immediately after the bridge. Follow the right fork for 0.5 mi. to a T intersection. The trail starts here (sign). Parking is on the side of the road to the left or right. (*Note:* A high-clearance vehicle is recommended for the final stretch of road beyond the bridges, which is quite tough. If in doubt, park at the grassy pullout before Rapid Stream and walk the remaining 0.6 mi. to the trailhead.)

The trail passes through deciduous forest to cross a logging road at 1.3 mi. Beyond, the trail eventually crosses a stream and reaches a campsite at 2.6 mi., with two earthen tent pads and a moldering privy. Soon after the campsite, the trail begins a steady and steep ascent. At 3.4 mi., it emerges into the open at treeline and is completely exposed to the weather for the final 0.5 mi. to the summit. Marked by cairns, the trail rises steadily up and across a huge talus field to the summit and the site of a former fire tower (the metal framework of the old tower lies on its side near the summit). Here, Mt. Abraham Trail leads 1.7 mi. north to connect with the AT at a point 1.8 mi. south of Spaulding Mtn. Lean-to. The 360-degree panorama from the Mt. Abraham summit is extraordinary.

MT. ABRAHAM TRAIL (MATC; USGS MT. ABRAHAM QUAD, GAZETTEER MAP 29, MATC MAP 6)

Cumulative from parking area and yellow gate on Caribou Valley Rd. (2,130 ft.) to:	⮃	↗	◷
AT crossing (2,220 ft.)	0.5 mi.	90 ft.	0:15
Sugarloaf Mtn. Trail (3,640 ft.)	2.8 mi.	1,500 ft.	2:10
Bronze AT plaque (3,500 ft.)	4.2 mi.	1,650 ft.	3:00
Spaulding side trail (3,900 ft.)	4.9 mi.	2,350 ft.	3:40
Spaulding Mtn. summit (4,010 ft.) via side trail	5.0 mi.	2,450 ft.	3:45
Spaulding Mtn. Lean-to (3,100 ft.)	5.7 mi.	2,450 ft.	4:00
Mt. Abraham Trail (3,350 ft.)	6.8 mi.	2,450 ft.	4:35
Mt. Abraham summit (4,049 ft.)	8.5 mi.	3,150 ft.	5:50

This trail leaves from the AT south of Spaulding Mtn. at a point 6.8 mi. south of the Caribou Valley Rd. parking area and yellow gate. Refer to the trail description for Spaulding Mtn. to reach the start of the trail.

From the AT, Mt. Abraham Trail leads southeast along the route of a very old tote road, climbing gradually and then steeply up the densely forested northern ridge of Mt. Abraham. The trail emerges from the trees and crosses a talus field at 1.1 mi., then reaches treeline at 1.3 mi. The alpine summit and site of the former fire tower is at 1.7 mi.

■ SADDLEBACK MTN. (4,120 FT.), THE HORN (4,041 FT.), AND SADDLEBACK JUNIOR (3,655 FT.)

Saddleback Mtn. sprawls across Sandy River Plantation, Madrid Township, and Redington Township southeast of Rangeley. The long ridge's undulating crest extends in a northeast-southwest direction for more than 3 mi., with pronounced saddles separating its high peaks. Two of the summits, Saddleback and The Horn, exceed 4,000 ft. Saddleback Junior is only slightly lower at 3,655 ft. The Saddleback Mtn. ski area is on the northwestern slope of the mountain.

The bare summits of these peaks have extensive areas above treeline and thereby offer expansive views in all directions. Because of this exposure, however, hikers should proceed with caution during periods of high winds and low visibility. Further, due to the fragile ecology of the alpine terrain on Saddleback, hikers must exercise care to stay on the trail and avoid stepping on plants or disturbing shallow soils. Pets should be leashed.

The AT traverses the four high peaks of Saddleback, while Berry Picker's Trail climbs to the high col between Saddleback Mtn. and The Horn. Fly

Rod Crosby Trail connects the village of Madrid with the base of the Saddleback ski area on a route over the west shoulder of the mountain.

AT NORTHBOUND (MATC; USGS SADDLEBACK MTN. AND REDINGTON QUADS, GAZETTEER MAPS 19 AND 29, MATC MAP 6, MTF AT–SADDLEBACK MTN. MAP)

Cumulative from ME 4 (1,750 ft.) to:	↑↓	↗	○
Piazza Rock Lean-to (2,000 ft.)	1.8 mi.	250 ft.	1:00
Fly Rod Crosby Trail (2,650 ft.)	3.9 mi.	900 ft.	2:35
Saddleback Mtn. summit (4,120 ft.)	5.7 mi.	2,370 ft.	4:00
Berry Picker's Trail (3,600 ft.)	6.5 mi.	2,370 ft.	4:25
The Horn summit (4,041 ft.)	7.3 mi.	2,800 ft.	5:00
Saddleback Junior (3,655 ft.)	9.3 mi.	3,375 ft.	6:20
Poplar Ridge (3,120 ft.)	10.9 mi.	3,475 ft.	7:10
Orbeton Stream (1,550 ft.)	13.4 mi.	3,475 ft.	8:30
Mt. Abraham Trail (3,350 ft.)	17.6 mi.	5,325 ft.	11:30

To approach Saddleback Mtn. from the south, follow ME 4 for 32.0 mi. north from the jct. of ME 4 and US 2 in Farmington. From the north, at the jct. of ME 4 and ME 16 in Rangeley, the trailhead is 9.9 mi. south on ME 4. The AT crosses ME 4 at a steep, winding section of the road. A large trailhead parking lot is on the west side of the highway.

From ME 4, the AT descends and crosses the Sandy River via a bridge at 0.1 mi. The trail climbs out of the valley, crossing a gravel logging road at 1.1 mi. At 1.8 mi., the trail passes Piazza Rock Lean-to. A side trail leads left 200 yd. to the top of Piazza Rock, a large granite slab protruding from the cliff. Just ahead along the side trail are the Caves, a series of boulder caves with narrow passages.

The AT then climbs steeply, skirting the west shore of Ethel Pond. Turning sharply left at the end of the pond, the trail climbs to pass Mud Pond, then descends slightly to reach Eddy Pond (last reliable water). Watch for a point near the east shore of Eddy Pond about 3.7 mi. from ME 4 where the trail, after turning left onto a gravel road for a few feet, turns sharply right off the road and continues (this gravel road is the Fly Rod Crosby Trail). Beyond, the AT rises steeply through conifers, emerging on a scrub-covered slope.

The exposed open crest of Saddleback, which extends for the next 3.0 mi., is a particularly scenic hike on a good day, but can be difficult in bad weather. Use care to follow the rock cairns and white blazes marking the route. After a long stretch over rocky slopes and heath, the trail descends slightly into a sag, then climbs ahead to reach the summit of Saddleback at 5.7 mi.

The AT continues ahead over the open alpine slopes, descending steeply into the col between Saddleback and The Horn. At 6.5 mi., Berry Picker's Trail enters from the south. Ahead, the AT crosses the wide col, then climbs slabs and ledges to reach the summit of The Horn at 7.3 mi. Continuing north, the AT descends steeply off the peak, reaches treeline, and arrives at a side trail to Redington Stream Campsite on the left at 8.0 mi. The descent continues, reaching a low point on the west side of Saddleback Junior at 8.8 mi. A steep climb ahead leads to the open summit of Saddleback Junior at 9.3 mi., which has 360-degree views. Poplar Ridge, the valley of Orbeton Stream, Lone Mtn., Mt. Abraham, Mt. Redington, Black Nubble, Spaulding Mtn., and more fill the scene.

The AT carries on northward, descending steeply off Saddleback Junior to reach a brook, then continuing along Poplar Ridge Lean-to at 10.7 mi. Beyond the shelter, the AT climbs to the ledges on Poplar Ridge, then drops steeply down into the deep canyon that holds Orbeton Stream, climbs up and out to Lone Mtn., and reaches the jct. of Mt. Abraham Trail at 17.6 mi. Refer to the trail descriptions for Spaulding Mtn. and Mt. Abraham Trail for details beyond this point.

FLY ROD CROSBY TRAIL (HPA; USGS SADDLEBACK MTN. AND REDINGTON QUADS, GAZETTEER MAPS 29 AND 19, MTF FLY ROD CROSBY TRAIL MAP)

Cumulative from Reeds Mill Rd. trailhead (950 ft.) to:	↥↧	↗	○
Berry Picker's Trail, lower jct. (2,100 ft.)	7.2 mi.	1,150 ft.	4:10
Berry Picker's Trail, upper jct. (2,250 ft.)	7.8 mi.	1,300 ft.	4:35
AT crossing near Eddy Pond (2,650 ft.)	10.2 mi.	1,800 ft.	6:00
Saddleback ski area base lodge and parking (2,450 ft.)	12.3 mi.	1,800 ft.	7:05

The Fly Rod Crosby Trail is a proposed 45-mi. heritage hiking trail that when completed will extend from Strong to Oquossoc along the Sandy River, Orbeton Stream, and Hardy Stream, across the AT, and on to Rangeley Lake and the Outdoor Sporting Heritage Museum in Oquossoc. Cornelia "Fly Rod" Crosby (1854–1946), a journalist, fly-fisher extraordinaire, hunter, early conservationist, and outdoor enthusiast, was Maine's first registered guide. Crosby grew up in Phillips, guided in Rangeley, worked for the Maine Central Railroad and Sandy River & Rangeley Lakes Railroad, and is buried in Strong. The trail named for Crosby is closely linked to the landscape of her life. The blue and white trail signs sport the drawing of a fishing fly.

Fly Rod Crosby Trail links existing motorized trails, woods roads, and streets and creates some new ones for nonmotorized recreation only. The motorized trails open to foot traffic are referred to as "multiuse" trails. Most of Fly Rod Crosby Trail is on privately owned land; please respect these lands and practice Leave No Trace. The trail is under the care of High Peaks Alliance in partnership with local recreational trail groups.

Currently there are two sections open, which total 19 mi. of continuous trail. A lower elevation 7-mi. section of the trail begins in Phillips, crosses the Sandy River, and follows abandoned railroad beds and an existing multiuse trail along the river to Orbeton Stream in Madrid. The 12-mi. section immediately to the north extends through moderate to strenuous mountain terrain between Madrid and Saddleback Mtn.; this section is described here.

Trailhead parking for the Madrid to Saddleback section is at Star Barn Yoga on Reeds Mill Rd. From the jct. of ME 4 and ME 142 in Phillips, drive 4.9 mi. north on ME 4. Turn right on Toothaker Pond Rd., and continue 2.25 mi. Turn left on Fish Hatchery Rd. (dirt) and continue for another 2.0 mi. to the kiosk and parking lot at the top of the hill on the right, immediately after crossing Orbeton Stream. Check in at the trailhead kiosk to pick up a map and to find out current trail conditions.

From the kiosk, follow the blue-blazed footpath into the woods. This section of the trail exists on private land actively managed as a working forest. The trail route, while well marked, can vary according to timber-harvesting activities. For about 3 mi., the trail goes north through a mixed forest and runs parallel to Orbeton Stream on the western bank. The next 4.0 mi. of trail closely follow Hardy Stream (along the southern and then western bank), with great views to the north of some of the neighboring high peaks, including Saddleback, Mt. Abraham, and Spaulding Mtn. The footpath passes the "Horse Hobble," remains of an old horse logging camp, before joining up with a 3.5-mi. stretch of multiuse trail that passes Moose Pond and Deer Pond and meets the AT on the western shoulder of Saddleback Mtn. near Eddy Pond. At the start of this multiuse stretch, Berry Picker's Trail enters from the left. At a point 0.6 mi. ahead, Berry Picker's Trail, which leads to the AT high on the ridgeline of Saddleback Mtn., departs to the right, just before a stream crossing. About 1 mi. beyond the AT crossing near Eddy Pond, the trail joins with Rock Pond Trail, a 2-mi. section that passes Midway Pond and Rock Pond before ending at an emergency vehicle turnaround a short distance from the Saddleback ski area base lodge. To reach this trailhead: From ME 4 just south of Rangeley, turn east on Dallas Hill Rd. and drive 2.5 mi., then bear right on Saddleback Mtn.

Rd. In another 4.5 mi., the road enters the Saddleback ski area, with the base lodge on the left and three large parking lots to the right. Park in any of these and walk up the main road (first left) as it turns away from the lodge and winds up the mountain through condos. There are signs for the Rock Pond and Fly Rod Crosby trails at the end of the road.

BERRY PICKER'S TRAIL (MATC; USGS MADRID AND REDINGTON QUADS, GAZETTEER MAPS 19 AND 29, MTF BERRY PICKER'S TRAIL TO SADDLEBACK OR THE HORN [VIA THE AT] MAP)

Cumulative from ATV gate (1,800 ft.) to:	⇅	↗	○
Fly Rod Crosby Trail (2,100 ft.)	0.9 mi.	300 ft.	0:35
Start of Berry Picker's Trail (2,250 ft.)	1.5 mi.	450 ft.	1:00
Col between Saddleback and The Horn (3,600 ft.)	3.0 mi.	1,600 ft.	2:20
Saddleback Mtn. summit (4,120 ft.) via AT	3.8 mi.	2,320 ft.	3:05
The Horn summit (4,041 ft.) via AT	4.2 mi.	2,240 ft.	3:15

The Berry Picker's Trail is a side trail between the multiuse Fly Rod Crosby Trail and the AT. It follows, in part, a route used by local residents for more than 150 years to harvest blueberries and cranberries on Saddleback Mtn. This was also the route originally planned for the AT in 1933. The trail crosses the Orbeton Stream conservation easement, land owned by ATC, and land owned by the Maine Appalachian Trail Land Trust before finally entering the AT corridor, owned by the National Park Service. Except for occasional double blazes that indicate sharp or unexpected turns, the trail is marked by single rectangular blue blazes and rock cairns. The route follows open ledges with outstanding views.

To reach the trailhead, turn off ME 4 in the center of the village of Madrid and cross the Sandy River over the one-lane bridge onto the blacktop Reeds Mill Rd. At 3.0 mi., immediately after crossing a bridge in front of a white house (on the right), turn left onto a gravel road. Follow this private road (a very good gravel road that has deteriorated some) for 3.1 mi. Do not turn right on the older, but still high-quality, gravel road. This gravel "cross road" has two connections, creating a pie-shaped island in the middle, and is signed for snowmobile use. Follow the good gravel road, which bears left at this point, and, shortly after crossing a stream (watch out for holes in the bridge), you will arrive at an ATV gate. Park here, but do not block the gate.

From the ATV gate, walk 0.9 mi. up the ATV trail and turn left onto the multiuse Fly Rod Crosby Trail at a group of signs on two wooden posts. At 1.45 mi., you will reach the Berry Picker's Trail trailhead proper, which is on the right side just before a bridge over Winship Stream. From the trailhead at Winship Stream, Berry Picker's Trail ascends through mixed hardwood and softwood forest along the stream, which has beautiful cascades. The trail becomes steeper, turns away from the stream, and at 1.95 mi., turns up the ridges to Saddleback to the left (northwest). On the right, the former route of the historic Berry Picker's Trail is visible on the slope. The trail transitions to open ledges dominated by dwarf spruce, alpine blueberry, and mountain cranberry. At 2.1 mi., it reaches Boundary Ledge, which is marked with yellow blazes to denote the boundary line between the landowners. At 2.65 mi., Berry Picker's Trail reaches the Erratic (a large boulder), and then the AT at 3.0 mi. at the top of the ridge. From here, it is 0.8 mi. south to the summit of Saddleback and 1.2 mi. north to the summit of The Horn.

SEC 4

■ BEMIS MTN., WEST PEAK (3,592 FT.), EAST PEAK (3,532 FT.), THIRD PEAK (3,115 FT.), SECOND PEAK (2,915 FT.), AND FIRST PEAK (2,604 FT.)

Bemis Mtn. in Township D rises south of Mooselookmeguntic Lake, and its long ridge crest extends in a northeast-southwest direction. The AT traverses the range and offers outstanding views from the five peaks en route. West Peak is the highest. Bemis Stream Trail is an alternate route for ascent or descent and, combined with the AT, makes a loop hike over the range possible, with an overnight option at Bemis Lean-to. Views from the Bemis summits are excellent in all directions.

AT SOUTHBOUND (MATC; USGS HOUGHTON AND METALLAK MTN. QUADS, GAZETTEER MAP 18, MATC MAP 7, MTF AT—BEMIS MTN. AND BEMIS STREAM LOOP MAP)

Cumulative from ME 17 (2,200 ft.) via AT to:	⇅	↗	○
Bemis Mtn., First Peak (2,604 ft.)	2.2 mi.	1,050 ft.	1:40
Bemis Mtn., Second Peak (2,915 ft.)	3.1 mi.	1,500 ft.	2:20
Bemis Mtn. Lean-to (2,800 ft.)	4.6 mi.	1,600 ft.	3:05
Bemis Mtn., Third Peak (3,115 ft.)	5.0 mi.	1,900 ft.	3:35
Bemis Mtn., West Peak (3,592 ft.)	6.3 mi.	2,500 ft.	4:25
Bemis Stream Trail (3,300 ft.)	7.3 mi.	2,500 ft.	4:55
Complete loop (via AT, Bemis Stream Trail, and ME 17)	13.6 mi.	2,850 ft.	8:15

Access to the AT is on ME 17 from a spot known as Height of Land, 11.0 mi. south of Oquossoc and 26.0 mi. north of Rumford. Parking is available 0.5 mi. south on ME 17, opposite the trailhead for Bemis Stream Trail. (*Note:* The Height of Land parking lot is not meant for hiker parking.)

The trail descends 0.8 mi. to Bemis Stream. Ford the stream at a point where it divides around an island (may be difficult to cross in high water). At 1.0 mi., cross the gravel Bemis Rd., a former railroad grade. Just ahead, pass a small spring, the last water source southbound for 3.5 mi. Ahead, climb steeply through woods to emerge on open ledges at 1.5 mi., then cross a series of rocky knobs, the first at 1.7 mi. Beyond, the trail is marked by cairns and white blazes and follows the ridge crest to reach First Peak at 2.2 mi. and Second Peak at 3.1 mi.

Bemis Mtn. Lean-to is reached at 4.6 mi.; Third Peak is at 5.0 mi. Cross East Peak at 6.2 mi. and West Peak at 6.3 mi. Arrive at the jct. with Bemis Stream Trail at 7.3 mi. Ahead on the AT, it is 3.2 mi. to the summit of Old Blue Mtn. and 6.0 mi. to South Arm Rd. By way of Bemis Stream Trail, it is 6.3 mi. back to ME 17.

SEC 4

BEMIS STREAM TRAIL (MATC; USGS HOUGHTON AND METALLAK MTN. QUADS, GAZETTEER MAP 18, MATC MAP 7, MTF AT—BEMIS MTN. AND BEMIS STREAM LOOP)

Cumulative from ME 17 (2,050 ft.) to:	↕	↗	↺
Bemis Rd. (1,700 ft.)	1.0 mi.	-350 ft.	0:30
AT (3,300 ft.)	6.3 mi.	1,600 ft.	4:00
Bemis Mtn., West Peak (3,592 ft.)	7.3 mi.	1,900 ft.	4:40

This trail, formerly part of the AT, provides an alternate route to the Bemis Mtn. peaks and, using the AT, makes a loop hike possible. Bemis Stream Trail starts from ME 17 at a point 0.5 mi. south of the AT crossing, 11.5 mi. south of Oquossoc, and 25.5 mi. north of Rumford. The trailhead parking lot is directly across the road from the start of the trail.

Following blue blazes, cross three small side streams at 0.1 mi., then descend gradually on a wide trail. At 0.8 mi., the forest opens up, affording views of Bemis Mtn. to the west and Brimstone Mtn. to the east. Descend steeply, and at 1.0 mi., cross the gravel-surfaced Bemis Rd., a former railroad grade. Follow a wide trail past a pool in Bemis Stream at 1.3 mi., then climb to finally cross Bemis Stream (may be difficult in high water) at 2.2 mi. Continue to climb, with the stream on the left, and cross several side streams. At 4.2 mi., reach a gravel logging road. Turn left to cross a bridge, then reenter the woods on the right immediately after. Follow Bemis Stream and cross it again at 5.2 mi. Ascend steadily through a mature spruce forest, and pass several glacial erratics. Reach the jct. with the AT at 6.3 mi. To the north, it is 1.0 mi. to the summit of West Peak of Bemis Mtn., 2.7 mi. to Bemis Mtn. Lean-to, and 7.3 mi. to ME 17 via the AT. To the south, it is 3.2 mi. to the summit of Old Blue Mtn. and 6.0 mi. to South Arm Rd.

■ OLD BLUE MTN. (3,600 FT.)

This mountain in Township D rises steeply above Black Brook, south of Elephant Mtn. and west of Lower Richardson Lake. Gain access from the south or north via the AT. To reach the AT from ME 5 in Andover, go 0.6 mi. east on ME 120 to South Arm Rd. Turn left onto South Arm Rd., and drive north for 7.7 mi. to the AT crossing at Black Brook Notch. Limited parking is available on the right side of the road.

AT NORTHBOUND (MATC; USGS EAST ANDOVER QUAD, GAZETTEER MAP 18, MATC MAP 7)

From South Arm Rd. (1,430 ft.) to:	↓↑	↗	↻
Old Blue Mtn. summit (3,600 ft.)	2.8 mi.	2,170 ft.	2:25

Leaving South Arm Rd., the AT climbs very steeply up the north wall of Black Brook Notch, gaining 900 ft. in 0.6 mi. The climb includes a bare section of rock that must be ascended with the aid of iron rungs and handrails. At the top of the climb is an overlook with good views south to Black Brook Notch and the peaks beyond. Ahead, the trail climbs gradually to the base of the upper south slope of Old Blue Mtn., reaching it at 2.3 mi. Beyond, the trail makes the final ascent to the summit at 2.8 mi. There are outstanding views all around over the tops of the stunted spruce and fir growth.

From the summit, the AT descends north into the high valley between Old Blue Mtn. and Elephant Mtn. At 4.3 mi., it reaches a col and an impressive stand of old-growth spruce. Bemis Stream Trail enters from the right at 6.0 mi. It is 6.1 mi. to ME 17 via this trail. Ahead on the AT, it is 7.3 mi. to ME 17.

RANGELEY LAKES AREA

■ BALD MTN. (IN OQUOSSOC; 2,470 FT.)

This mountain in Oquossoc, a village of Rangeley, occupies a scenic location between Mooselookmeguntic Lake and Rangeley Lake, and is the central natural feature of the 1,923-acre Bald Mtn. Public Lands. The mountain was the site of the short-lived Bald Mountain Skiway, which operated from 1960 into the early 1970s. Views from the summit observation tower range from the surrounding lakes of Mooselookmeguntic,

Rangeley, and Cupsuptic to the peaks of Saddleback Mtn., the Bemis Range, Elephant Mtn., and on to Mt. Washington and the Presidential Range. Two trails ascend the peak, from west and from the north.

BALD MTN. TRAIL (MBPL; USGS OQUOSSOC QUAD, GAZETTEER MAP 28, MTF BALD MTN. TRAIL–OQUOSSOC MAP)

Cumulative from Bald Mtn. Rd. (1,510 ft.) to:	⬇⬆	↗	⟳
Bald Mtn. Link (1,640 ft.)	0.3 mi.	130 ft.	0:10
Bald Mtn. summit (2,470 ft.)	1.3 mi.	960 ft.	1:10

From the jct. of ME 4 and ME 17 in Oquossoc, drive west on ME 4 (also called Dam Rd.) for 1.2 mi. toward its terminus at Haines Landing. Before the landing, turn left (south) onto Bald Mtn. Rd. and follow this road for 0.8 mi. to the trailhead parking area for Bald Mtn. on the left (sign).

The trail leaves the lot left of the kiosk and climbs gradually east on a wide gravel path marked with blue blazes. After crossing a footbridge, reach a jct., where Bald Mtn. Link enters from the left. Continue straight ahead on Bald Mtn. Trail, a wide, well-used footway of rocks and roots. At 1.5 mi., the angle increases as the ascent becomes moderate to steep on eroded trail. Climb sections of bedrock and ledges. The angle finally eases, and the trail crosses a wet section on bog bridges. Climb a slab beyond, dip down, and then continue to the observation tower on top of the summit ledges. There is a picnic area in the small clearing below the tower, but views are limited at ground level. Climb the 30-foot tower for a 360-degree panorama that takes in Mooselookmeguntic Lake, Cupsuptic Lake, Rangeley Lake, and a long chain of mountains, from Katahdin to Bigelow to Saddleback and all the way to Mt. Washington.

BALD MTN. LINK (MBPL; USGS OQUOSSOC QUAD, GAZETTEER MAP 28, MTF BALD MTN. TRAIL–OQUOSSOC MAP)

Cumulative from boat launch parking lot on ME 4 (aka Dam Rd.; 1,490 ft.) to:	⬇⬆	↗	⟳
Bald Mtn. Trail (1,640 ft.)	1.0 mi.	150 ft.	0:30
Bald Mtn. summit (2,470 ft.)	2.0 mi.	980 ft.	1:30

This longer alternative route on Bald Mtn. leaves from the boat launch parking lot on ME 4, just east of Haines Landing. From the jct. of ME 4 and ME 17 in Oquossoc, drive west on ME 4 (also called Dam Rd.) for 1.0 mi. to the large boat launch parking lot on the left. The trail (not signed as Bald Mtn. Link) leaves the far end (south) of the lot at the kiosk. The well-trodden route reaches a jct. at 0.2 mi. Turn left, and at the grassy meadow ahead, turn sharply right. The old tote road crosses a wet area on

SEC 4

bog bridges, then begins a gentle ascent. Ahead, the trail proceeds on a contour and then crosses a footbridge, an old skidder road, and a second footbridge. Immediately after, reach the jct. with Bald Mtn. Trail at 1.0 mi. Turn left to continue toward the summit, which is another 1.0 mi. ahead.

■ WEST KENNEBAGO MTN. (3,713 FT.)

This isolated peak in Upper Cupsuptic Township, north of Cupsuptic Lake and west of Kennebago Lake, is the highest of the several summits of the north-south ridge that forms the mountain. Local volunteers from the Trails for Rangeley Area Coalition maintain West Kennebago Mtn. Trail.

To reach the start of the trail, turn right (north) from ME 16 onto Morton Cutoff Rd., 4.8 mi. west of the ME 4 and ME 16 jct. in Oquossoc and 0.3 mi. west of the Maine Forest Service buildings at Cupsuptic Lake. Drive 3.2 mi. from ME 16 to a jct. with Lincoln Pond Rd. Turn right (east), and in 5.5 mi., the road reaches a parking area on the left. The trail begins at the right end of the parking area.

WEST KENNEBAGO MTN. TRAIL
(TRAC; USGS KENNEBAGO QUAD, GAZETTEER MAP 28,
MTF WEST KENNEBAGO MTN. TRAIL MAP)

Cumulative from Lincoln Pond Rd. (2,007 ft.) to:	↿⇂	↗	↻
Site of old fire warden's camp (3,050 ft.)	1.2 mi.	1,050 ft.	1:10
West Kennebago Mtn. summit (3,713 ft.)	1.9 mi.	1,700 ft.	1:50

The red-blazed trail starts as an old woods road. It soon narrows to a footpath and climbs rather steeply. At 0.9 mi., the trail levels out among conifers and bears left. Then it begins to climb again, crosses a small stream, and turns sharply right. Beyond, the trail becomes heavily eroded. At 1.2 mi., it reaches a small clearing, the site of the old fire warden's camp. A spring is 100 yd. into the woods to the left of the clearing via a faint path.

The trail leaves the site of the old camp from the upper right (northwest) corner of the clearing. At 1.5 mi., it reaches the ridge, where it turns left (south) and follows the ridge nearly to the summit. The old fire tower was removed in 2012 to make way for a communications tower, which is fenced off, and trespassing is prohibited. Just before reaching the tower, there is a clearing and a wooden platform (used as a helipad) that offers a good place to rest and nice views of Kennebago Lake to the east, Cupsuptic Lake and Mooselookmeguntic Lake to the south, and the skyline of summits on Saddleback Mtn. (*Note:* West Kennebago Mtn. Trail is on private land and is open to the public through the generosity of the landowner. Please respect the trail and the land to ensure future access.)

■ AZISCOHOS MTN. (3,215 FT.)

This mountain in Lincoln Plantation, shown as Low Aziscohos Mtn. on some USGS maps, is just south of Aziscohos Lake and offers excellent views over the Rangeley Lakes region and far beyond. The abandoned fire tower on the summit was removed in 2004. Local volunteers from the Trails for Rangeley Area Coalition maintain Aziscohos Mtn. Trail.

From the jct. of ME 4 and ME 16 in Oquossoc, drive west for 17.8 mi. The trail starts on the south side of ME 16, 100 ft. east of a gravel road leading left (south) into an old wood yard. Park along the shoulder on the south side of the road. There is no sign, and the entrance into the woods is obscure. (As a check, the trailhead is 1.2 mi. east of the bridge over Magalloway River at Aziscohos Lake Dam.)

**SEC
4**

AZISCOHOS MTN. TRAIL (TRAC; USGS RICHARDSON POND AND WILSONS MILLS QUADS, GAZETTEER MAPS 27, 28, AND 18, MTF AZISCOHOS MTN. MAP)

From ME 16 (1,730 ft.) to:	⇅	↗	↺
Aziscohos Mtn. summit (3,190 ft.)	1.7 mi.	1,460 ft.	1:35

Once into the woods, the trail follows red paint blazes. In 100 yd., pass a trail sign for "Aziscohos." The trail leads gradually uphill on an old tote road (can be quite wet at times) through open hardwood and mixed forest. Ahead, the trail turns sharply left and soon passes through several old cutover areas. Through here are occasional views north to the hamlet of Wilsons Mills. Beyond, the trail enters conifers, then crosses a small brook. It then continues more steeply, becoming quite rough as it leads over boulders and exposed roots. The angle finally eases, and the trail reaches the abandoned Tower Man's Trail, entering from the right (northwest) at 1.6 mi. Turn left here and climb on bedrock trail through low spruce growth to the open summit ledges and the concrete footings of the old fire tower.

The mountaintop offers a 360-degree panorama that is one of the finest in Maine and includes Katahdin, Big Moose, Big Spencer, Saddleback, Bald Mtn., Tumbledown, Mt. Blue, Bemis, Elephant, Old Blue, the Baldpates, Old Speck, the Carter–Moriah Range, the Presidential Range, and the many lakes around the Rangeley area, including Rangeley, Mooselookmeguntic, Cupsuptic, and Richardson. (*Note:* Aziscohos Mtn. Trail is on private land and is open to the public through the generosity of the landowner. Please respect the trail and the land to ensure future access.)

MT. BLUE STATE PARK

■ MT. BLUE (3,192 FT.)

Rising steeply east of Webb Lake in Weld, Mt. Blue is known for its conical profile, which is unmistakable when viewed from surrounding summits. The former fire tower on the summit has been replaced with an observation tower and offers outstanding panoramic views. Mt. Blue Trail ascends from the west.

From the jct. of ME 156 and ME 142 in the village of Weld, drive east on Center Hill Rd. Pass the driveway to Center Hill picnic area, which is on the right at 2.6 mi. (this winding 0.5-mi. drive leads to the start of Center Hill Nature Trail). At 3.5 mi., where Center Hill Rd. bears left, continue straight ahead on Mt. Blue Rd. Follow it for another 2.5 mi. to the trailhead parking lot (sign and kiosk) at the end of the road. The trail leaves from the north end of the lot.

MT. BLUE TRAIL (MBPL; USGS WELD QUAD, GAZETTEER MAP 19, MBPL MT. BLUE STATE PARK AND TUMBLEDOWN PUBLIC LANDS MAP)

From Mt. Blue Rd. (1,409 ft.) to:	↕	↗	↻
Mt. Blue summit (3,192 ft.)	1.6 mi.	1,783 ft.	1:40

The well-worn Mt. Blue Trail ascends steadily up the fall line of the mountain at moderate to steep grades, passing through thick woods en route. About 1 mi. into the hike, a side trail leads to the old fire warden's cabin with a small stream behind it. Back on the main trail, continue the ascent. Reach an outlook with views just below the summit and then quickly top out at the small grassy field on the summit, where there are two buildings, a safety communications tower, and a solar array. Stairs lead to an observation platform halfway up the tower, which was erected in 2011 and designed to look like an old fire tower. The views are spectacular in all directions and include Saddleback Mtn., The Horn, Mt. Abraham, Spaulding Mtn., Sugarloaf Mtn., the Presidential Range, the Carter–Moriah Range, peaks of the Mahoosuc Range, and nearby Bald Mtn.

■ CENTER HILL (1,658 FT.)

A short circuit around this hill on the way to Mt. Blue yields maximum views for minimal effort. Follow the driving directions for the Mt. Blue trailhead; the side road to Center Hill is passed en route. Parking is in the large lot at the end of the drive.

CENTER HILL NATURE TRAIL (MBPL; USGS WELD QUAD, GAZETTEER MAP 19, MBPL MT. BLUE STATE PARK AND TUMBLEDOWN PUBLIC LANDS MAP)

From Center Hill picnic area (1,570 ft.) to:	⇅	↗	↺
Complete loop	0.5 mi.	75 ft.	0:20

This interesting and scenic self-guided nature loop hike leaves the parking lot and leads around Center Hill at a consistent contour, passing eleven interpretive stations that describe the natural history and ecology of the area. Outstanding views of Tumbledown, Blueberry Mtn., Little Jackson Mtn., and Jackson Mtn. are possible from open ledges along the trail.

SEC 4

TUMBLEDOWN PUBLIC LANDS AND VICINITY

Directions to the Loop Trail trailhead: From the west, leave ME 17 in Byron at a point 22 mi. south of Oquossoc and 13.0 mi. north of Mexico. Travel east on Dingle Hill Rd. to cross over Coos Canyon and the Swift River. Stay on this road for 4.5 mi. to trailhead parking on the left, noting that the road name changes from Weld to Byron en route. From the east, begin at the jct. of ME 156 and ME 142 in Weld. Go north on ME 142 for 2.3 mi. Turn left onto West Side Rd. At 2.7 mi., where the paved West Side Rd. bears left, continue straight on the gravel-surfaced Byron Rd. Pass the Brook Trail trailhead on the right at 6.4 mi. Reach the Loop Trail trailhead at 7.7 mi.

Directions to the Brook Trail trailhead: From the west, leave ME 17 in Byron at a point 22.0 mi. south of Oquossoc and 13.0 mi. north of Mexico. Travel east on Dingle Hill Rd. to cross over Coos Canyon and the Swift River. Stay on this road for 5.8 mi. to trailhead parking on the right, noting that the road name changes from Weld to Byron en route. From the east, begin at the jct. of ME 156 and ME 142 in Weld. Go north on ME 142 for 2.3 mi. Turn left on West Side Rd. At 2.7 mi., where the paved West Side Rd. bears left, continue straight on the gravel-surfaced Byron Rd. Reach the Brook Trail Trailhead on the left at 6.4 mi.

■ TUMBLEDOWN MTN., WEST PEAK (3,068 FT.)

Tumbledown Mtn. features an extensive alpine area on its high ridges and an impressive 700-ft. cliff on its south face, which has attracted rock climbers for years. Another natural feature is Tumbledown Pond, a pretty tarn tucked into a bowl beneath the peaks of Tumbledown and Little Jackson Mtn. The views from the open summit ridges are exceptional. Loop Trail, Brook Trail, Parker Ridge Trail, and Pond Link Trail reach the high

SEC
4

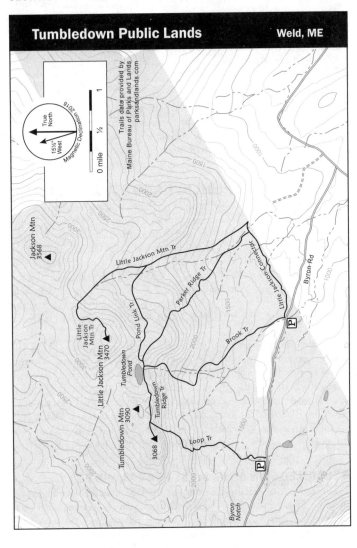

Tumbledown Public Lands

Weld, ME

True North

15½° West

Magnetic Declination 2018

0 mile   ½   1

Trails data provided by
Maine Bureau of Parks and Lands
parksandlands.com

Jackson Mtn
3568

Little Jackson Mtn Tr

Little
Jackson
Mtn Tr

Little Jackson Mtn
3470

Parker Ridge Tr

Pond Link Tr

Little Jackson Connector

Byron Rd

Brook Tr

Tumbledown
Pond

Tumbledown Mtn
3090

Tumbledown Ridge Tr

3068

Loop Tr

Byron
Notch

terrain on Tumbledown, while Tumbledown Mtn. Trail connects Tumbledown Pond with the west peak of the mountain.

LOOP TRAIL (MBPL; TUMBLEDOWN PUBLIC LANDS, P. 212)

Cumulative from Loop Trail trailhead on Byron Rd. (1,330 ft.) to:	⇅	↗	⟳
Tumbledown Mtn. Trail (2,900 ft.)	1.5 mi.	1,570 ft.	1:35
Tumbledown Mtn., west peak (3,068 ft.), via Tumbledown Mtn. Trail	1.7 mi.	1,750 ft.	1:45

Loop Trail is a direct route to the west peak of Tumbledown. Ascent of this interesting trail requires considerable rock scrambling at its upper end before reaching Tumbledown Mtn. Trail high on the mountain, just west of the summit. While nontechnical, the extensive steep rock scrambling makes this trail unsuitable for novices, dogs, and less agile hikers.

The blue-blazed trail rises gradually to the north, crossing a brook twice, and soon passes the huge Tumbledown Boulder. From here, the trail rises steeply to emerge in the open at the Great Ledges, where there are splendid views of the impressive 700-ft. cliffs. On the ledges, Loop Trail turns right at a large cairn. Ahead, it crosses a brook and then climbs steeply up a gully. Near the top of the gully, a side trail leads to a narrow chimney-like fissure known as Fat Man's Misery. Above this is an opening in the boulders with iron rungs to aid in the ascent. The scramble from the Great Ledges cairn leads to the saddle between the craggy high peaks, and a spring (unreliable in dry weather). From this jct. at 1.5 mi., Tumbledown Mtn. Trail leads left (west) to the main summit in 0.2 mi., and right (east) to Tumbledown Pond and the jct. with Brook Trail in 0.6 mi.

BROOK TRAIL (MBPL; TUMBLEDOWN PUBLIC LANDS, P. 212)

From Brook Trail trailhead on Byron Rd. (1,150 ft.) to:	⇅	↗	⟳
Tumbledown Pond (2,670 ft.)	1.8 mi.	1,500 ft.	1:40

This trail along Tumbledown Brook is a direct route to scenic Tumbledown Pond, tucked high into the mountain's upper reaches, where the trail connects with Tumbledown Mtn. Trail and Parker Ridge Trail.

Brook Trail follows an old woods road for the first half of its route. After crossing Tumbledown Brook, the trail turns right and parallels the brook as it climbs. Ahead, cross the brook another time before arriving at a jct. with Parker Brook Trail, which enters from the right. Just ahead, Brook Trail reaches Tumbledown Pond and a jct. Here, Tumbledown Mtn. Trail leads left 0.6 mi. to Loop Trail and 0.8 mi. to the west peak of Tumbledown Mtn.

SEC 4

LITTLE JACKSON CONNECTOR (MBPL; TUMBLEDOWN PUBLIC LANDS, P. 212)

From Brook Trail trailhead on Byron Rd. (1,150 ft.) to:	Distance	Elevation gain	Time
Parker Ridge Trail and Little Jackson Trail (1,200 ft.)	1.1 mi.	150 ft.	0:35

This trail connects Brook Trail trailhead with Little Jackson Trail and Parker Ridge Trail. From Brook Trail trailhead, Little Jackson Connector heads easily northeast across the lower slopes of Tumbledown and ends at 1.1 mi. in a large clearing (a former trailhead and parking area that is permanently closed to vehicles and camping) at the jct. with Parker Ridge Trail and Little Jackson Trail.

PARKER RIDGE TRAIL (MBPL; TUMBLEDOWN PUBLIC LANDS, P. 212)

Cumulative from Brook Trail trailhead on Byron Rd. (1,150 ft.) to:	Distance	Elevation gain	Time
Start of Parker Ridge Trail (1,200 ft.) via Little Jackson Connector	1.1 mi.	150 ft.	0:35
Tumbledown Pond (2,670 ft.)	2.9 mi.	1,500 ft.	2:15

This trail, one of the oldest on the mountain, ascends to Tumbledown Pond from the southeast via Parker Ridge. Access to the start is by Little Jackson Connector, which leads 1.1 mi. to a large clearing. Here, Little Jackson Trail bears to the right, while Parker Ridge Trail bears left (west) into the woods and crosses a brook. The trail then turns northwest to join an old woods road. For the next mile, it rises gently through second-growth forest, then steeply for a short distance over three ledges. Beyond, the trail continues to climb steadily and then crosses the open ledges of Parker Ridge with views of the peaks of Tumbledown ahead. Beyond, the trail descends west, passing a jct. with Pond Link Trail on the right. Tumbledown Pond and the jct. with Brook Trail and Tumbledown Mtn. Trail are just ahead at 2.9 mi.

TUMBLEDOWN MTN. TRAIL (MBPL; TUMBLEDOWN PUBLIC LANDS, P. 212)

Cumulative from Tumbledown Pond outlet (2,670 ft.) to:	Distance	Elevation gain	Time
Loop Trail (2,900 ft.)	0.6 mi.	230 ft.	0:25
Tumbledown Mtn., west peak (3,068 ft.)	0.8 mi.	400 ft.	0:35

Tumbledown Mtn. Trail connects Tumbledown Pond with the west peak of Tumbledown Mtn. From the outlet of Tumbledown Pond and the jct. with Brook Trail and Parker Ridge Trail, Tumbledown Mtn. Trail ascends west over mostly open ledges with wonderful views all around. Loop Trail is in 0.6 mi. Beyond, Tumbledown Ridge Trail climbs to the west peak of Tumbledown, where there are great views of the Swift River valley and the summits of Old Blue Mtn. and Elephant Mtn., among many others.

POND LINK TRAIL (MBPL; TUMBLEDOWN PUBLIC LANDS, P. 212)

Cumulative from Tumbledown Pond (2,670 ft.) to:	↥↧	↗	↺
Start of Pond Link Trail (2,670 ft.) via Parker Ridge Trail	88 yd.	0 ft.	0:02
Little Jackson Trail (2,350 ft.)	1.1 mi.	180 ft.	0:40

This trail links Tumbledown Pond with Little Jackson Trail. From Parker Ridge Trail at a point just east of Tumbledown Pond, Pond Link Trail leaves to the left (north) and skirts the east end of the pond for about 100 yd. The trail then turns east to ascend to a height-of-land between Parker Ridge and Little Jackson Mtn. at 0.3 mi. from the pond. The trail continues generally east and down to the jct. with Little Jackson Trail.

SEC 4

■ LITTLE JACKSON MTN. (3,470 FT.)

This mountain in the heart of the Tumbledown Public Lands features an extensive alpine area and fine views east to Jackson Mtn. and Mt. Blue, west overlooking Tumbledown Pond and the rugged peaks of Tumbledown Mtn., and southeast to Webb Lake.

LITTLE JACKSON TRAIL
(MBPL; TUMBLEDOWN PUBLIC LANDS, P. 212)

Cumulative from Brook Trail trailhead on Byron Rd. (1,150 ft.) to:	↥↧	↗	↺
Start of Little Jackson Trail (1,200 ft.) via Little Jackson Connector	1.1 mi.	150 ft.	0:35
Pond Link Trail (2,350 ft.)	2.3 mi.	1,300 ft.	1:50
Col between Jackson Mtn. and Little Jackson Mtn. (3,050 ft.)	3.1 mi.	2,000 ft.	2:35
Little Jackson Mtn. summit (3,470 ft.)	3.7 mi.	2,400 ft.	3:05

From the Brook Trail trailhead on Byron Rd., follow Little Jackson Connector 1.1 mi. northeast to its end in a large clearing. Here, Parker Ridge Trail bears left, while Little Jackson Trail (blue sign) bears right. The trail soon crosses a stream and, just beyond, takes a sharp right (sign) onto an old woods road, which climbs steadily at a moderate grade. Ahead, the old road becomes steeper and more eroded before reaching the jct. with Pond Link Trail at 2.3 mi. (leads 1.1 mi. to Tumbledown Pond via Parker Ridge

Trail). Here, where Pond Link Trail continues straight ahead, Little Jackson Trail turns sharply right and continues to climb, getting progressively steeper with a rough footway. Soon after crossing a brook, the trail reaches the open ledges of the col between Jackson Mtn. and Little Jackson Mtn. Here is the jct. with Jackson Mtn. Trail, which leads right (north) 0.7 mi. to the summit of Jackson Mtn. Just ahead, Little Jackson Trail turns left and ascends over ledges with many fine outlooks to the alpine summit of Little Jackson Mtn. and 360-degree views.

■ JACKSON MTN. (3,568 FT.)

Jackson Mtn. is a rambling, heavily forested mountain with a large clearcut, helicopter landing pad, and radio structure on its summit. There are very limited views to the west from the summit, but excellent views looking south, east, and west are possible from open ledges about halfway up. The unofficial, unmaintained, and lightly used trail is narrow. Exercise caution in following it.

JACKSON MTN. TRAIL
(MBPL; USGS JACKSON MTN. QUAD, GAZETTEER MAP 19)

From Little Jackson Trail in col (3,050 ft.) to:	⇅	↗	⏱
Jackson Mtn. summit (3,568 ft.)	0.7 mi.	525 ft.	0:40

Jackson Mtn. Trail diverges right (north) from Little Jackson Trail in the col between Little Jackson Mtn. and Jackson Mtn., about 120 ft. beyond the first open ledges on Little Jackson Trail. From the jct., continue over open ledges for about 300 ft., where the route turns sharply left (west) and descends gradually into the woods on a snowmobile trail. In another 180 ft., the route leaves the snowmobile trail to the right (sign) and heads northeast. The snowmobile trail descends to Jackson Pond below.

From the snowmobile trail, the foot trail begins to climb toward Jackson Mtn. It is clearly defined and marked by a few cairns, but there are no blazes. Reach an open ledge with views southeast to Little Jackson. Beyond, the path is less defined, and there are numerous small blowdowns. Reach the mostly wooded summit of Jackson Mtn. at 0.7 mi.

■ BLUEBERRY MTN. (2,962 FT.)

This mountain is in Township 6 North of Weld, east of Jackson Mtn., Little Jackson Mtn., and Tumbledown Mtn. and north of Webb Lake. Blueberry Mtn. is part of the 22,000-acre Tumbledown Public Lands. The bare summit features interesting geologic formations and excellent views in all directions.

From the jct. of ME 142 and ME 156 in Weld, drive north on ME 142. Pass West Side Rd. on the left at Weld Corner at 2.2 mi. At 3.5 mi., turn left onto the gravel-surfaced Blueberry Mtn. Rd. at a sign for Blueberry Mtn. Bible Camp and Conference Center. At 1.6 mi. from ME 142, look for a small hand-lettered sign next to the road that reads "Hiker Parking." Park in the clearing on the left.

BLUEBERRY MTN. TRAIL (MBPL; USGS MADRID QUAD, GAZETTEER MAP 19, MBPL MT. BLUE STATE PARK AND TUMBLEDOWN PUBLIC LANDS MAP)

From parking area (1,500 ft.) to:	⇅	↗	↻
Blueberry Mtn. summit (2,962 ft.)	2.2 mi.	1,450 ft.	1:50

SEC 4

A sign at the end of the clearing shows the start of the trail. Follow blue markers into the woods along a grassy skidder road, which can be wet and mucky. This new access bypasses the bible camp complex and joins the old road of the former trail start just past the end of the athletic fields. Continue on the old woods road, which rises steeply and crosses a logged area. Beyond, the trail forks right from the old road and climbs steeply. After a series of ledges, the grade moderates and the trail passes through a section of large boulders. Arrive at the open summit at 2.2 mi., where views range from the nearby peaks of Tumbledown and the Jacksons to the high peaks along the AT from Saddleback and Sugarloaf to the Bigelow Range.

■ BALD MTN. (IN WASHINGTON TOWNSHIP; 2,370 FT.)

Bald Mtn. straddles the town lines of Washington Township and Perkins Township a few miles south of Mt. Blue. Featuring a long and narrow northeast-southwest ridgeline, the peak has been a local favorite for many years. The state of Maine owns a portion of the mountaintop in Perkins Township. The craggy summit of Bald Mtn. yields fine views in every direction. Neighboring Saddleback Wind was tantalizing but trailless until recently, when a new path was blazed from the summit of Bald Mtn.

The trailhead for Bald Mtn. is on the west side of ME 156 about 9 mi. northwest of the jct. of ME 4 and ME 156 in Wilton and 5.3 mi. southeast of the jct. of ME 142 and ME 156 in Weld. Parking is on the broad shoulder on the south side of the road.

BALD MTN. TRAIL (NFTM; USGS MT. BLUE QUAD, GAZETTEER MAP 19)

From ME 156 (1,050 ft.) to:	⇅	↗	↻
Bald Mtn. summit (2,370 ft.)	1.1 mi.	1,320 ft.	1:15

Immediately cross Wilson Stream (last sure water) on stepping stones and enter the woods. The well-defined trail climbs steeply through the young woods that were logged a few years back. Ahead, the trail reaches open ledges and climbs these bare slabs to the summit. Blue blazes and cairns mark the route. Atop the open summit, there are fine views in all directions. (*Note:* This trail is on private property and open to the public through the generosity of Carrier Timberlands, the landowner. Please respect the land, stay on the trail, and follow all posted rules.)

■ SADDLEBACK MTN. (AKA SADDLEBACK WIND; 2,590 FT.)

This mountain, also known as Saddleback Wind, is in Carthage just south of Bald Mtn. The two mountains are connected by a trail. The southwestern ridge of Saddleback Mtn. is the site of the 12-turbine, 34-megawatt Saddleback Ridge Wind Project.

SADDLEBACK WIND TRAIL (NFTM; USGS MT. BLUE QUAD, GAZETTEER MAP 19, MTF BALD MTN. AND SADDLEBACK WIND TRAIL MAP)

From Bald Mtn. summit (2,370 ft.) to:	⇅	↗	⟳
Saddleback Mtn. summit (2,590 ft.)	1.8 mi.	750 ft.	1:20

From the summit of Bald Mtn., the trail continues west following blue blazes. In 200 ft., a sign reads "Saddleback Wind 1.4 mi." Continue down over open ledges with excellent views and then through wooded areas to the col separating the peaks at 0.9 mi. From here, the trail rises steadily through the woods, then breaks out into the open. On the summit, wind turbines are nearby, and the views in all directions are outstanding. (*Note:* This trail passes through private property, Town of Carthage property, and Maine Public Lands; please be a considerate user to ensure continued public access.)

RUMFORD

■ RUMFORD WHITECAP MTN. (2,214 FT.)

The 752-acre Rumford Whitecap Mtn. Preserve in Rumford is the signature conservation property of the Mahoosuc Land Trust. The preserve includes the bald summit ridge and south slopes of Rumford Whitecap Mtn., which offers panoramic views and plenty of blueberries in season. Two maintained trails ascend the mountain from the southwest.

From the jct. of US 2 and ME 5, 0.5 mi. west of Rumford Point, go north on ME 5 toward Andover. At 2.8 mi., turn right (east) and cross the Ellis River. At 3.2 mi., turn left onto East Andover Rd. and, in another 0.2 mi., reach the trailhead parking area on the left. Red/Orange Trail

Rumford Whitecap Mtn. Rumford, ME

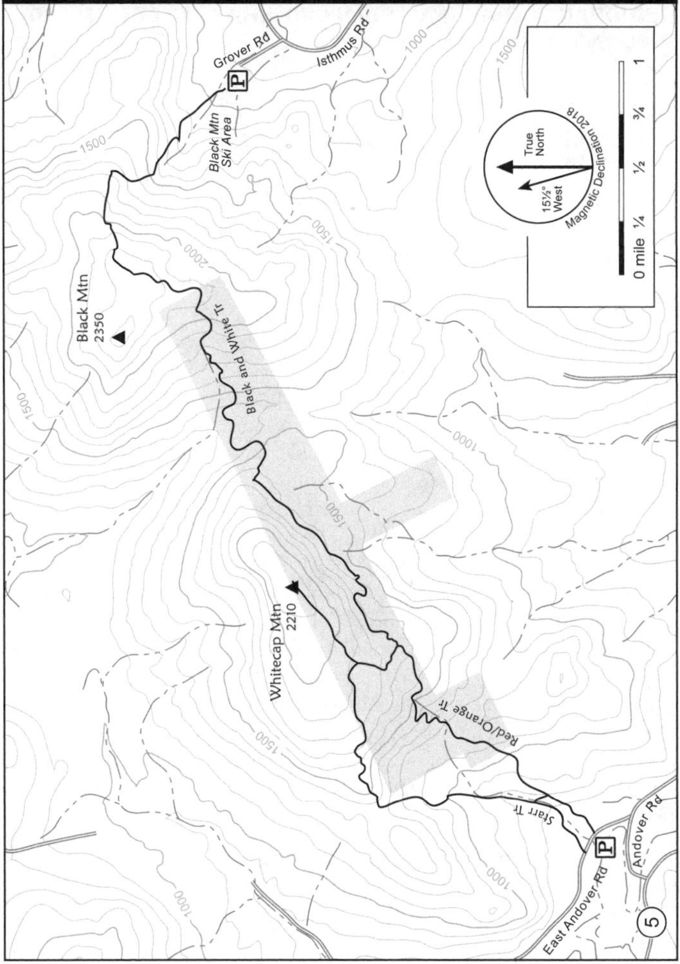

SEC 4

Grover Rd
Isthmus Rd
1000
1500

True North
151½° West
Magnetic Declination 2018

0 mile   ¼   ½   ¾   1

P
Black Mtn Ski Area
1500

Black Mtn
2350
▲

2000

Black and White Tr

1500

1000

Whitecap Mtn
2210

1500

Red/Orange Tr

Start Tr

1500

Andover Rd

P

East Andover Rd

1000

1000

5

begins at a red gate directly across the road. Starr Trail begins about 100 yd. north on East Andover Rd. at a gray gate.

RED/ORANGE TRAIL (MLT; RUMFORD WHITECAP MTN., P. 219)

Cumulative from red gate on East Andover Rd. (630 ft.) to:	⇅	↗	⟳
Black and White Trail (1,750 ft.)	1.5 mi.	1,100 ft.	1:20
Starr Trail (1,880 ft.)	1.8 mi.	1,280 ft.	1:40
Rumford Whitecap Mtn. summit (2,214 ft.)	2.3 mi.	1,600 ft.	2:00

From the gate (red/orange markers), follow the woods road and soon reach a register box on the right. Pass through a log yard and bear left. Climb gradually to reach a trail jct. on the left at 0.3 mi. This trail (green markers) leads northwest about 0.1 mi. to cross a stream on a bridge before joining Starr Trail.

Beyond the jct., Red/Orange Trail continues to follow the woods road, climbing moderately. Ahead, the road narrows in a level area and bears left (sign: to foot trail). Climb steeply on switchbacks and rock steps, contour to the east for a short distance, and then resume climbing. Cross a semi-open area, then cross a wide track (the old trail route to the summit, more direct but steep and eroded). Ahead, follow cairns over ledges to finally merge with the old trail route. Turn right on the wide, eroded trail and climb easily to the jct. with Black and White Trail on the right at 1.5 mi. (leads 4.8 mi. to the summit of Black Mtn. and then to the base lodge of the Black Mtn. ski area), and with Starr Trail (yellow markers) on the left at 1.8 mi. Continuing ahead on Red/Orange Trail, climb gradually up the ridgeline through semi-open terrain to reach the ledges of the open summit at 2.5 mi. The 360-degree view is spectacular and includes Black Mtn. to the east, the high peaks of the Mahoosuc Range to the west, the White Mountains of New Hampshire farther west, and to the south, Mt. Zircon and many other summits of the Oxford Hills. (*Note:* A portion of the Rumford Whitecap summit is privately owned. Please stay on the trail and practice Leave No Trace.)

STARR TRAIL (MLT; RUMFORD WHITECAP MTN., P. 219)

Cumulative from gray gate on East Andover Rd. (630 ft.) to:	⇅	↗	⟳
Red/Orange Trail jct. (1,880 ft.)	2.1 mi.	1,280 ft.	1:40
Rumford Whitecap Mtn. summit (2,214 ft.)	2.6 mi.	1,600 ft.	2:10

Pass beyond the gray gate and follow the grassy tote road to a clearing. A signpost directs hikers out of the old log yard to the right. At 0.25 mi., pass a trail register on the right next to a stream. Climbing alongside the stream, at 0.35 mi., a short connector trail on the right (green markers) crosses a bridge over the stream to join Red/Orange Trail in about 0.1 mi. Starr Trail continues straight ahead on the old road and proceeds up a long hill. At 0.8 mi., the trail leaves the old road to the left and proceeds on a foot trail marked with yellow blazes and yellow flagging. The trail enters a large bowl at 1.0 mi. and climbs at a steady, moderate grade. The route crosses a small brook and an old woods road at 1.2 mi., then climbs through the woods beside the old road, with ledges to the right.

At 1.25 mi., reach a saddle. Signs point left to E. Andover Rd. and right to the summit. From here, climb steeply to the right through the ledges. After crossing a dip, continue to climb steeply through ledges. At 1.35 mi., bear right and up over open ledges with sweeping views that range from Mt. Abram's ski slopes and Puzzle Mtn. in the west to the Mahoosucs in the north. Ahead, follow cairns into the woods and proceed easily over the shoulder of the mountain. Beyond, climb ledges and slabs through the trees, then angle up and right over steep slabs. The summit of Old Speck is revealed between the peaks of Puzzle Mtn. and Long Mtn. Cross a steep slope in the open, with views to US 2 and Mt. Abraham. Continue to follow cairns over slabs, mostly in the open. When the angle eases, traverse right, reenter the woods, and drop slightly to the jct. with Red/Orange Trail at 2.1 mi. The summit of Rumford Whitecap is 0.5 mi. northeast (left) via this trail.

■ BLACK MTN. (2,350 FT.)

Black Mtn. in Rumford, best known for the ski resort on its eastern slopes, Black Mountain of Maine, rises just east of Rumford Whitecap. The mountain's two summits both have communications towers. The Black and White Trail is a new connector trail linking Rumford Whitecap with Black Mtn. This strenuous route gains a little more than 1,000 ft. of elevation en route, but loses 1,700 ft. from its high point to the ski area base. The hike is best done from Rumford Whitecap to Black Mtn. (west to east), as the start of this trail on Rumford Whitecap is easy to find, whereas negotiating the ski runs and cleared areas on Black Mtn. can be challenging on the ascent. A car spot is probably a good idea for the hike from Rumford Whitecap. Mountain Valley Cab in Rumford does shuttles (207-364-9900).

BLACK AND WHITE TRAIL
(MLT; RUMFORD WHITECAP MTN., P. 219)

Cumulative from Red/Orange Trail on Rumford Whitecap (1,750 ft.) to:	↥↧	↗	↻
High point on Black Mtn. at cell tower (2,295 ft.)	3.3 mi.	1,050 ft.	2:10
Black Mountain of Maine ski resort base lodge (960 ft.)	4.75 mi.	1,050 ft.	3:00

From the jct. of Red/Orange Trail at a point 1.5 mi. from East Andover Rd. and 0.8 mi. from the summit of Rumford Whitecap, Black and White Trail diverges to the right and heads northeast toward Black Mtn. The trail follows a contour below the summit dome of Rumford Whitecap, then descends via several tight switchbacks. At 0.6 mi., pass a large split glacial erratic. Beyond, cross multiple drainages. The treadway is not well defined (as of 2017), so follow the markers (white blazes and orange ribbons). After climbing a short, steep pitch, arrive at several rocks and trees splotched with red paint at 1.4 mi. Ignore the red-blazed trail (and one white blaze) going straight and then left uphill. Instead, turn right and proceed downhill to a small clearing, join an old woods road, and continue to descend. At 1.8 mi., reach the bottom of the valley between Rumford Whitecap and Black Mtn.

Ahead, descend rock steps to cross a stream. Reach a meadow (an emergency helicopter landing zone) at 2.0 mi. Bear right to a woods road, then bear left into the woods (signs with hiker symbol at these points). Cross a brook, then meet the brook and go right and up. Cross the brook again, then go right and up next to the drainage. Crest the ridge at 2.8 mi. Bear left and up to cross an old boundary line (orange and yellow blazes, old ax blazes). Level off, then climb higher still. Level off again and reach a cell tower and an old building on the east peak of Black Mtn. at 3.3 mi. Pass left around the cell tower complex, then continue along a gravel road. On the road, with another tower in view, bear right into the woods at the sign "Black Mtn. Lodge." Follow a well-defined trail through thick softwoods. Drop down to a sag, then climb out to a knob. Reach a viewpoint on the left at 3.4 mi., which offers a good look at the Tumbledown peaks, Mt. Blue, and the ridgeline of Bald Mtn. and Saddleback Wind.

Descend off the ridge toward the Mt. Blue view (to the northeast), passing through a logged area. Reach a cairn on a ski trail at 3.5 mi. Bear left for 100 ft., then bear right to the next cairn. Head down the skidder trail with a big view to Black Mtn. base area far below. At a cairn and viewpoint, bear left into the woods and descend steeply along the edge of a ravine. Ahead at a cairn next to a ski trail, bear right downhill, following the right margin of the ski trail (occasional cairns). At 3.75 mi., turn right into the woods and descend steeply over ledges. Reach the next ski trail and descend along its right edge, then quickly reenter the woods. Descend the steep slope at an angle, cross another ski trail (cairns at both sides of opening; base lodge visible on left), and reenter the woods again. Soon cross a brook and then descend a moderate to steep slope above the brook. Ahead, a set of rock steps leads to an old woods road; here, bear left downhill. At 4.2 mi., turn right off the old road and descend the slope below. At 4.4 mi., reach a ski trail, where signs point to Black Mtn. and Whitecap. Go left to the top of the blue lift, in sight 100 yd. beyond. Bear right at the blue lift and follow it to the Black Mtn. base lodge at 4.75 mi.

SEC 4

■ GLASSFACE MTN. (1,910 FT.)

This mountain rises above the north bank of the Androscoggin River in Rumford Center. On the southwestern slopes, Mahoosuc Land Trust owns the 32-acre Glassface Mtn. Conservation Area, where Glassface Ledges Trail climbs to a viewpoint overlooking the river valley.

From the jct. of US 2 and ME 232 in Rumford Point, drive east on US 2 for 3.3 mi. to the Rumford Boat Launch parking area (and trailhead parking), which is on the right immediately across from Rumford Center Meeting House and Rumford Center Cemetery.

GLASSFACE LEDGES TRAIL (MLT; USGS RUMFORD QUAD, GAZETTEER MAP 18, MTF GLASSFACE LEDGES TRAIL MAP)

From US 2 (610 ft.) to:	⇅	↗	⟳
Glassface Ledges (1,280 ft.)	0.8 mi.	670 ft.	0:45

Cross US 2 to the cemetery and follow the old road (path) through the center of the grounds. Beyond the cemetery, at 0.15 mi., enter the woods near a white rail fence. Immediately after, bear right to meet a small brook and begin climbing. Ascend via switchbacks through the semi-open logged area. The way gets steeper above, weaving a route via more switchbacks to enter a ravine with a small brook. At 0.65 mi., cross the brook and then climb rock steps through boulders along the other side. Soon turn away from the brook and reach the end of the trail at the ledges. The view takes in Mt. Zircon, Mt. Abram, the bucolic Androscoggin River valley, and the village of Rumford Center.

■ SUGARLOAF (IN DIXFIELD; 1,590 FT.)

Sugarloaf in Dixfield is conspicuous because of its two prominent and shapely summits. The mountain offers fine vistas from its open northern summit. En route to Sugarloaf, a side trail leads to Bull Rock and good views of the woods and fields of the Dixfield area.

From the jct. of US 2 and ME 142 in Dixfield, drive north on ME 142 for 1.2 mi. Turn right (east) on Holt Hill Rd. and continue 0.5 mi. to Moxie Heights Rd. Turn left and park in a wide spot in the dip (the former parking area ahead on Red Ledge Rd. is now posted "private, no parking").

SUGARLOAF TRAIL
(NFTM; USGS DIXFIELD QUAD, GAZETTEER MAP 19)

Cumulative from parking (750 ft.) to:	⇅	↗	○
Side trail to Bull Rock (1,000 ft.)	0.5 mi.	250 ft.	0:20
Sugarloaf summit (1,590 ft.)	1.2 mi.	840 ft.	1:00

To begin the hike, turn right and walk uphill on Red Ledge Rd., staying straight where a private driveway goes left. The road soon turns left at a sharp, steep curve. At 0.3 mi., where the road bears slightly right (gray house visible on left), the trail to Sugarloaf, an old woods road/snowmobile trail, continues straight ahead at a lower level. At about 0.5 mi., an ATV track leaves left. (A sign reads "recreational trail." This is the side trail to the ledges of Bull Rock, which is in about 0.5 mi. and offers nice views. Partway along this side trail is a four-way intersection; take a sharp right to reach Bull Rock.)

Continuing ahead on the trail to Sugarloaf, cross a large log yard at 0.6 mi. Follow red blazes out of the log yard, beyond the first, lower peak. At 0.9 mi., leave the old road and bear sharply right uphill on a footpath (maroon blazes). Climb steadily up the steep slope to a col at 1.1 mi. (*Note:* The trail may be hard to follow through this area because of logging.) Proceed straight across the col to a large rock with a maroon blaze on the left by a large vernal pool. Climb steeply from this point (*Caution:* poor footing) to the summit ledges of Sugarloaf at 1.2 mi., where there are fine views of the White Mountains.

SECTION 5

MAHOOSUC RANGE
AND GRAFTON NOTCH

Pull-Out Map
Map 6: Mahoosuc Range–Evans Notch

INTRODUCTION

The Mahoosuc Range extends roughly 25 mi. in a northeast–southwest direction from the Androscoggin River, east of Berlin and north of Gorham and across the Maine state line to Shelburne, New Hampshire; to Old Speck Mtn. and the peaks of Baldpate Mtn. and the jumble of rugged mountains around Grafton Notch in Grafton Township, Andover West Surplus Township, and Newry. The Mahoosucs end at the West Branch of the Ellis River in Andover. This rugged range, part of the White Mountains but not part of the WMNF, is bounded by NH 16 to the west, by US 2 to the south, and by East B Hill Rd. to the northeast.

This section covers the trails in the Maine portion of the Mahoosuc Range extending from the Maine–New Hampshire border to its northern end. Map 6: Mahoosuc Range–Evans Notch graphically portrays nearly the entire range and all the trails on both sides of the state line. In all, this section, on Mahoosuc Range and Grafton Notch, describes 17 trails on 15 mountains. AMC maintains trails along the AT corridor between the Maine state line and Grafton Notch, as well as the west side of Grafton Loop Trail; the Maine Bureau of Parks and Lands maintains trails in Grafton Notch State Park; the Maine Appalachian Trail Club maintains the AT between ME 26 and East B Hill Rd., as well as the east side of Grafton Loop Trail.

GEOGRAPHY

Close to 35,000 acres of the Mahoosuc Range in Maine are protected in Mahoosuc Public Lands (31,800 acres) and Grafton Notch State Park (3,200 acres). The state of Maine owns and manages the land. The abutting Stowe Mountain easement places conservation protection on an additional 3,400 acres. Outside of these properties, a number of trails start or end on private property with permission of the various landowners.

Among the more than two dozen jumbled mountains that compose the Mahoosuc Range are sixteen summits that exceed 3,000 ft. In New Hampshire, this includes Bald Cap (3,065 ft.) and Mt. Success (3,565 ft.). In Maine, the high peaks include Mt. Carlo (3,565 ft.), Goose Eye Mtn. (3,870 ft.) and its three summits, Fulling Mill Mtn. (3,450 ft.) and its lower south peak, Mahoosuc Arm (3,765 ft.), and Old Speck Mtn. (4,170 ft.) along the main Mahoosuc crest. West of Grafton Notch along Grafton Loop Trail are Slide Mtn. (3,250 ft.) and Sunday River Whitecap (3,335 ft.). East of Grafton Notch along Grafton Loop Trail are Puzzle Mtn. (3,133 ft.)

and the west and east peaks of Baldpate Mtn. (3,662 ft. and 3,780 ft. respectively). Old Speck Mtn. (4,170 ft.) is the highest in the Mahoosuc Range and the fifth-highest summit in Maine. The highest body of water in Maine is Speck Pond, which lies tucked in between Old Speck Mtn. and Mahoosuc Arm at an elevation of 3,400 ft. South of Grafton Notch is Mt. Will (1,736 ft.), which rises above the Androscoggin River in Newry. The AT traverses the entire Mahoosuc Range, a meandering distance of 41 mi.

ROAD ACCESS

Primary access to trails in the Grafton Notch area is by ME 26. This includes the AT and Grafton Loop Trail. For ease of travel, refer to this table for trailheads and points of interest east and west of ME 26:

Cumulative from jct. of ME 26 and US 2 in Newry via ME 26 north to:
Grafton Loop Trail (southern trailhead),
    Stewart Family Preserve (east) — 4.6 mi.
Step Falls Preserve (east) — 7.8 mi.
Screw Auger Falls (west) — 9.4 mi.
Mother Walker Falls (east) — 10.6 mi.
Moose Cave (east) — 11.3 mi.
Grafton Notch, trailhead parking and AT crossing (west) — 12.1 mi.
Spruce Meadow Picnic Area (west) — 13.1 mi.
North Rd. (access to Success Pond Rd. trailheads) — 16.9 mi.

SEC 5

Access to the peaks of Mahoosuc Range from the west is possible via Success Pond Rd., which extends the length of the lower western slopes of the range. From the trailhead parking area on ME 26 in Grafton Notch at the AT crossing, drive north for 4.9 mi. Turn left on North Rd., and follow it for 4.0 mi. to a jct. with Success Pond Rd. and York Pond Rd. (*Note:* The former access from ME 26 was via York Pond Rd. In 2011, this road washed out and was closed.) Bear right on Success Pond Rd., and continue south to reach the Speck Pond, Notch, Carlo Col and Goose Eye, and Success trailheads. Refer to the following summary table for detailed mileage between points.

From ME 26 via North Rd. and Success Pond Rd. to:
Speck Pond Trail trailhead — 9.4 mi.
Notch Trail spur road to trailhead — 10.7 mi.
Carlo Col and Goose Eye trailhead — 13.5 mi.
Success Trail trailhead — 16.2 mi.
Hutchins St., Berlin, NH — 21.6 mi.

Reach the AT on the north side of Baldpate Mtn. by East B Hill Rd. from the village of Andover, which in turn is reached via ME 5 from US 2 in Rumford Point.

CAMPING

There is no camping in Grafton Notch State Park. In Mahoosuc Public Lands, which includes the AT corridor, there is backcountry camping at five shelter sites: Carlo Col, Full Goose, Speck Pond, Baldface, and Frye Notch. Carlo Col, Full Goose, and Speck Pond are AMC sites. Groups of six or more persons planning to camp at AMC backcountry sites are asked to use the group notification system. Find more info at outdoors.org/lodging-camping/campsites. A caretaker fee is charged at Speck Pond. Camping is prohibited above treeline. Below treeline, dispersed camping is allowed, but fires are not. Along the west side of Grafton Loop Trail, backpackers may tent at Bald Mtn., Sargent Brook, Slide Mtn., and Bull Run. On the east side of Grafton Loop Trail, tentsites include Stewart, Town Corner, and Lane. Along Wright Trail, there is a tentsite on Goose Eye Brook. Fires are not permitted at Stewart and Sargent Brook campsites, which are on private land. There are three privately operated drive-in campgrounds on the outskirts of the Mahoosuc Range and Grafton Notch section, two in Bethel and one in Newry.

GRAFTON NOTCH STATE PARK

Grafton Notch State Park comprises 3,191 acres of mountainous terrain on the east and west sides of ME 26, from the Newry–Grafton Township town line to about 1.5 mi. north of the height-of-land in Grafton Notch at the AT crossing. The park includes the summit and northeastern slopes of Old Speck Mtn. and the lowest western and southwestern slopes of Baldpate Mtn., including Table Rock.

In addition to the AT, there are trails to the Eyebrow, an impressive cliff forming the great western wall of Grafton Notch, and to Table Rock high on the east side. Along ME 26 are a number of short graded trails and paths leading to interesting natural features, including Step Falls, Screw Auger Falls, Mother Walker Falls, and Moose Cave.

A large trailhead parking area with toilet, trail register, and information kiosk is on the west side of ME 26 at the head of Grafton Notch, 12.1 mi. north of the jct. of ME 26 and US 2 in Newry. The AT routes to Old Speck Mtn. and Baldpate Mtn. and to Eyebrow and Table Rock trails leave from this point. No camping is allowed in the park.

SEC 5

MAHOOSUC PUBLIC LANDS

The Mahoosuc PL unit comprises 31,764 acres of the Mahoosuc Range in Maine and essentially surrounds Grafton Notch State Park. North of the park, Mahoosuc PL encompasses the entirety of Baldpate Mtn. South of the park, the unit extends to the Maine–New Hampshire border and the summits of Old Speck, Mahoosuc Arm, Fulling Mill, and Goose Eye mountains and Mt. Carlo. The AT crosses most of the major summits of the Mahoosuc Range. Half of the eastern section and most of the western section of Grafton Loop Trail runs through Mahoosuc PL. Backcountry camping is available at a dozen sites within the unit.

Nearly 10,000 acres of Mahoosuc PL are designated by the state of Maine as an ecological reserve to protect the sensitive ecosystems within. Close to 8,500 acres of the reserve are classified as subalpine forest, while 269 acres are classified as alpine ridge. The subalpine tarn, Speck Pond, is at the highest elevation of any water body in Maine.

SEC 5

SUGGESTED HIKES

■ Easy

Given the rugged terrain of the Mahoosuc Range, there are very few easy hikes, and none can be safely recommended.

■ Moderate

EYEBROW CLIFF

	⥀	⤤	◔
LP via Eyebrow Trail and Old Speck Trail (AT)	2.4 mi.	1,050 ft.	1:45

This loop hike features some steep climbing using iron rungs and ladders to reach spectacular views of Grafton Notch from atop the 800-ft. Eyebrow Cliff. To begin, see Eyebrow Trail, p. 231.

TABLE ROCK

	⥀	⤤	◔
LP via Table Rock Trail and AT Northbound	2.4 mi.	900 ft.	2:00

A moderately steep but spectacular climb leads to a prominent rock ledge overlooking Grafton Notch and an extensive slab cave system. Return via the AT for a nice loop hike. To begin, see Table Rock Trail, p. 232.

MT. WILL

	⇅	↗	⟳
LP via Mt. Will Trail	3.0 mi.	750 ft.	2:30

Hike the loop over Mt. Will to the North Ledges and South Cliffs for good views of the Androscoggin River valley. To begin, see Mt. Will Trail, p. 252.

■ Strenuous

GRAFTON LOOP, EASTERN SECTION

	⇅	↗	⟳
OW via Grafton Loop Trail (Eastern Section)	21.1 mi.	5,300 ft.	2–3 days

Enjoy great views from the alpine summits of Puzzle Mtn. and Baldpate Mtn.'s West Peak on this fine backpacking route, with three primitive campsites en route. See Grafton Loop Trail, p. 232.

OLD SPECK MTN.

	⇅	↗	⟳
RT via Old Speck Trail and Mahoosuc Trail	7.6 mi.	3,000 ft.	5:20

This moderately steep route leads to panoramic views from the observation tower atop Old Speck, Maine's fifth-highest peak. To begin, see Old Speck Trail, p. 233.

BALDPATE MTN.

	⇅	↗	⟳
RT via AT Northbound	8.0 mi.	2,600 ft.	6:20

Climb to the extensive alpine area atop Baldpate Mtn.'s East Peak for outstanding views of the Mahoosuc Range. Bag the more wooded West Peak en route. See AT Northbound, p. 234.

SPECK POND

	⇅	↗	⟳
RT via Speck Pond Trail	7.2 mi.	4,000 ft.	5:40

Hike to this pretty mountain tarn, the highest body of water in Maine. Grab the nearby summit of Mahoosuc Arm en route. See Speck Pond Trail, p. 236.

SEC
5

MAHOOSUC NOTCH

	⇅	↗	⟳
RT via Notch Trail	3.8 mi.	800 ft.	2:40

Hike at easy grades to the southeast end of Mahoosuc Notch, one of the wildest spots in the Maine mountains. If you've still got steam, explore some of the rugged notch before making the return trip. See Notch Trail, p. 236.

GOOSE EYE MTN. AND MT. CARLO

	⇅	↗	⟳
LP via Goose Eye Trail, Mahoosuc Trail, Carlo Col Trail	7.6 mi.	2,750 ft.	5:10
RT via Wright and Mahoosuc trails	9.6 mi.	3,050 ft.	6:20

Hike a rewarding loop over two open peaks with some very steep spots. Or go for Goose Eye only via the very scenic Wright and Mahoosuc trails. To begin the loop, see Goose Eye Trail, p. 237. To begin the round trip, see Wright Trail, p. 238.

SEC
5

GRAFTON LOOP, WESTERN SECTION

	⇅	↗	⟳
OW via Grafton Loop Trail (Western Section)	17.1 mi.	5,500 ft.	2–3 days

Enjoy excellent vistas from the bare summit of Sunday River Whitecap and the observation tower on Speck Mtn. Fine hiking leads to four primitive campsites along the way. See Grafton Loop Trail, p. 249.

TRAIL DESCRIPTIONS

GRAFTON NOTCH STATE PARK

EYEBROW TRAIL (MBPL; MAP 6: B13)

From Old Speck Trail, lower jct. (1,550 ft.) to:	⇅	↗	⟳
Old Speck Trail, upper jct. (2,480 ft.)	1.2 mi.	930 ft.	1:10

This trail provides a steep and rough alternative route to the lower part of Old Speck Trail, passing along the edge of the sweeping cliff called the Eyebrow that overlooks Grafton Notch. Eyebrow Trail is better suited for ascent than descent.

The orange-blazed Eyebrow Trail leaves Old Speck Trail on the right, 0.1 mi. from the parking area on ME 26 in Grafton Notch. Eyebrow Trail climbs moderately northwest and north for 0.4 mi., then swings left and ascends more steeply with the aid of cable handrails. The trail turns right at the base of a rock face, crosses a rock slab where iron rungs and a small ladder have been placed to assist hikers (potentially dangerous if icy), then turns sharply left and ascends steeply, bearing right where a side path leaves straight ahead for an outlook. Soon the trail runs at a moderate grade along the top of the cliff (with good views at several lookouts), then descends to an outlook and runs mostly level until it ends at Old Speck Trail.

TABLE ROCK TRAIL (MBPL; MAP 6: B13)

Cumulative from trailhead parking area on ME 26 (1,450 ft.) to:	⇅	↗	⏱
Start of Table Rock Trail (1,500 ft.) via AT	0.1 mi.	50 ft.	0:05
Table Rock and jct. with upper part of loop trail (2,350 ft.)	1.0 mi.	900 ft.	1:00
Complete loop, including AT	2.4 mi.	900 ft.	2:00

Table Rock Trail offers a short but steep climb to the prominent rock ledge of Table Rock on Baldpate Mtn. on the east side of Grafton Notch and spectacular views of Old Speck Mtn. across the notch. From the ledge, the trail continues on to rejoin the AT. Table Rock Trail also features an extensive slab cave system, possibly the largest in the state.

Table Rock Trail leaves the AT to the right (south), 0.1 mi. north of the trailhead on ME 26 in Grafton Notch. From this jct., Table Rock Trail rises gently for 0.3 mi. along the side of a hill above a marsh until reaching a dropoff. From here, the trail climbs to reach a rocky, caribou-moss-covered area at 0.6 mi. After several switchbacks along ledges, the trail enters a deep ravine between two rock faces. At the top of the ravine, bear right. The trail climbs less steeply to a prominent outlook at 0.8 mi. At 0.9 mi., it reaches the base of the ledges that form Table Rock, where the slab caves begin. (*Caution:* Be careful if you explore the caves. Some are quite deep, and a fall could mean serious injury.)

On the trail, continue around the bottom of Table Rock. (Note the weather-formed rock that looks like a shark's fin on the ledges above.) At 1.0 mi., after swinging behind Table Rock, reach a side trail leading left 20 yd. to Table Rock. To the right, the upper part of Table Rock Trail continues with little change in elevation, reaching the AT in 0.5 mi. Turn right (east) to head for the peaks of Baldpate Mtn.; go left (west) to return to the trailhead on ME 26.

MAHOOSUC PUBLIC LANDS

■ OLD SPECK MTN. (4,170 FT.)

Old Speck Mtn., named for its speckled appearance caused by large areas of exposed rock and tree cover (and to distinguish it from the Speckled Mountains in Stoneham and Peru), dominates the western side of Grafton Notch. Old Speck is Maine's fifth-highest mountain, after Katahdin, Hamlin, Sugarloaf, and North Crocker Mtn. The open observation tower on the wooded summit offers outstanding views of Grafton Notch and of West Peak and East Peak on Baldpate Mtn. to the north, the jumbled peaks of the Mahoosuc Range to the south, and beyond to the Presidential Range.

OLD SPECK TRAIL (AMC; MAP 6: B13–C13)

Cumulative from ME 26 (1,450 ft.) to:	⇅	⬈	⟳
Eyebrow Trail, upper jct. (2,480 ft.)	1.1 mi.	1,030 ft.	1:05
Mahoosuc Trail (4,030 ft.)	3.5 mi.	2,580 ft.	3:05
Old Speck Mtn. summit (4,170 ft.) via Mahoosuc Trail	3.8 mi.	2,720 ft.	3:20

SEC 5

This trail, part of the AT, ascends Old Speck Mtn. from a well-signed parking area (small fee) on ME 26 at the height-of-land in Grafton Notch. From a kiosk on the north side of the parking lot, follow the trail leading to the left (the right-hand trail goes to Baldpate Mtn. via the AT). In 0.1 mi., Eyebrow Trail leaves right. (It circles around the top of the impressive 800-ft. cliff of the Eyebrow [named for its shape] and rejoins Old Speck Trail ahead at 1.1 mi.). Old Speck Trail crosses a brook and soon begins to climb, following a series of switchbacks with many rock steps to approach the falls on Cascade Brook. Above the falls, the trail, now heading more north, crosses the brook for the final time (last water), turns left at a ledge with a view up to Old Speck Mtn., and, at 1.1 mi., passes the upper terminus of Eyebrow Trail on the right.

Here, Old Speck Trail bears left and ascends gradually to the north ridge, where the trail swings more to the left and follows the ridge, with frequent bedrock footing and numerous short descents interspersed through the ascent. High up, the trail turns southeast toward the summit, and at 3.0 mi. there is an outlook east from the top of a ledgy hump. The trail descends again briefly then ascends steadily to the south, passing the abandoned and closed Link Trail on the left. Old Speck Trail climbs a fairly steep and rough pitch, passing an excellent north outlook just before its jct. with Mahoosuc Trail, where Old Speck Trail ends. The flat, wooded summit of Old Speck is 0.3 mi. left (east). There is an observation tower in the cleared summit area that affords fine views. Speck Pond Campsite is 1.1 mi. to the right (west).

■ BALDPATE MTN., EAST PEAK (3,780 FT.) AND WEST PEAK (3,662 FT.)

Baldpate Mtn. rises to the east of Grafton Notch. The two prominent peaks of the mountain include the alpine summit of East Peak and the more wooded West Peak. Access to Baldpate is via the AT, which makes a complete traverse of the mountain. Table Rock is an interesting side hike to spectacular ledges high above Grafton Notch.

BALDPATE MTN. VIA AT NORTHBOUND (MATC; MAP 6: B13–B14)

Cumulative from Grafton Notch trailhead parking on ME 26 (1,450 ft.) to:	⇅	↗	↻
Table Rock Trail, lower jct. (1,500 ft.)	0.1 mi.	50 ft.	0:05
Table Rock Trail, upper jct. (2,100 ft.)	0.8 mi.	650 ft.	0:45
Side trail to Baldpate Lean-to (2,600 ft.)	2.3 mi.	1,150 ft.	1:45
Baldpate Mtn., West Peak (3,662 ft.)	3.1 mi.	2,212 ft.	2:40
Baldpate Mtn., East Peak (3,780 ft.) and Grafton Loop Trail	4.0 mi.	2,600 ft.	3:10
East B Hill Rd. (1,450 ft.)	10.3 mi.	3,100 ft.	6:40

The AT leaves from the kiosk on the north side of the parking area on ME 26 in Grafton Notch. At a fork, the AT heads to the right. The trail soon crosses ME 26 and then runs briefly through woods and beside a marsh until, at 0.1 mi., it crosses a brook on a log footbridge. Just ahead, the AT passes Table Rock Trail, which leaves to the right. The AT rises gradually on an old woods road. At 0.8 mi., it passes the upper end of Table Rock Trail. Ahead, the AT climbs steadily and then more steeply to the western knob of Baldpate Mtn., where there are good views to the northwest. The AT then angles up the north side of the knob to a ridge extending toward West Peak, soon descending to a brook where, at 2.3 mi., a side trail leads south to Baldpate Lean-to.

Beyond, the trail climbs steeply to West Peak and good views at 3.1 mi. It continues north to dip several hundred feet before climbing to East Peak at 4.0 mi., marked by a large cairn. The alpine summit offers extensive views of the western Maine mountain and lake country. Also at the summit, Grafton Loop Trail enters from the right (south). From here, the AT continues north for 6.3 mi. to East B Hill Rd.

BALDPATE MTN. VIA AT SOUTHBOUND FROM EAST B HILL RD. (NFTM; USGS B POND AND OLD SPECK QUADS, GAZETTEER MAP 18, MATC MAP 7)

Cumulative from East B Hill Rd. (1,400 ft.) to:	⬇⬆	↗	↻
Dunn Notch, West Branch of Ellis River (1,300 ft.)	0.8 mi.	-100 ft.	0:55
Frye Notch Lean-to (2,250 ft.)	4.5 mi.	1,550 ft.	3:00
Baldpate Mtn., East Peak (3,780 ft.)	6.3 mi.	2,900 ft.	4:30
Baldpate Mtn., West Peak (3,662 ft.)	7.2 mi.	3,200 ft.	5:10
Trailhead parking area on ME 26 (1,450 ft.)	10.3 mi.	3,200 ft.	7:00

The trail leaves the left (south) side of East B Hill Rd. about 8.0 mi. west of the village of Andover. It descends from the road, crosses a small brook, and then turns south along the edge of a progressively deeper gorge cut by this brook, which the AT follows for 0.5 mi. before turning west into the mouth of Dunn Notch. At 0.8 mi., the trail crosses the West Branch of the Ellis River (a large stream at this point) at the top of a double waterfall plunging 60 ft. into Dunn Notch. (You can reach the bottom of the falls via an old logging road across the stream. Upstream, you will find a small, rocky gorge and the beautiful upper falls.)

The AT crosses the old road and climbs steeply up the eastern rim of the notch, then climbs moderately to the south. At 1.3 mi., the trail turns left and climbs gradually through open hardwoods along the edge of the northern arm of Surplus Mtn. At 3.0 mi., it angles right (southwest) around the nose of Surplus, climbs gently along a broad ridge, and passes near the summit. Beyond, the trail descends steeply over rough ground to reach Frye Notch Lean-to, near the head of Frye Brook, at 4.5 mi. From the lean-to, the trail climbs gradually, then more steeply, gaining more than 1,300 ft. in less than 1.0 mi., to the open summit of East Peak on Baldpate Mtn. at 6.3 mi. The trail descends to a sag between the peaks, then climbs to West Peak at 7.2 mi. Beyond, the AT descends into Grafton Notch via the trail from the south, passing the upper jct. and lower jct. of Table Rock Trail and then the Baldpate Lean-to en route.

■ MAHOOSUC ARM (3,765 FT.)

This mountain is located along the AT, between Mahoosuc Notch and Speck Pond.

SEC 5

SPECK POND TRAIL (AMC; MAP 6: C12–C13)

From Success Pond Rd. (1,730 ft.) to:	⇅	↗	↻
Mahoosuc Trail and Speck Pond Campsite (3,400 ft.)	3.6 mi.	2,000 ft.	2:50

This trail ascends to Speck Pond and Mahoosuc Trail, passing May Cutoff to the summit of Mahoosuc Arm en route. The trail begins on the west side of the Mahoosuc Range at Success Pond Rd., from a point 9.4 mi. southwest of ME 26 via North and Success Pond roads. Parking is on the left before the trailhead, opposite the entrance to Speck Pond Rd.

Speck Pond Trail departs Success Pond Rd., enters the woods, and in 100 yd. makes a crossing of Sucker Brook that can sometimes be difficult. In another 75 yd., the trail recrosses the brook. (*Note:* In high-water conditions, it may be best to walk 200 yd. up Speck Pond Rd. and then bushwhack south to the trail, which runs a short distance away on the near side of the brook, parallel to the road and the brook.) The trail follows the north side of the brook at easy then moderate grades for 1.4 mi., passing through brushy logged areas (follow with care). It then turns left, away from the brook, and traverses northward across another area of recent logging, crossing several skid roads and the top of an open brushy area. Follow markings carefully here, especially where the trail bears right at a cairn as it leaves the open area. The trail swings right (east) and climbs moderately, crossing a relatively level section. It then bears left and climbs rather steeply and roughly, with one wooden ladder up a wet ledge, to the jct. at 3.1 mi. with May Cutoff, which diverges right. Speck Pond Trail continues over a height-of-land, passes an outlook over the pond and up to Old Speck Mtn., and descends steeply to the pond. It skirts the west shore of the pond, swings right at Speck Pond Campsite, passes left of the shelter (where a closed former section of trail is on the left), and continues 80 yd. to a new jct. with Mahoosuc Trail (p. 241), which goes ahead (southbound) and left (northbound, on a short relocation).

May Cutoff (AMC; Map 6: C13). This short trail extends from Speck Pond Trail to Mahoosuc Trail—0.3 mi., 50 ft. ascent, 10 min.—with only minor ups and downs, ascending across a scrubby hump along the way that is probably the true summit of Mahoosuc Arm.

NOTCH TRAIL (AMC; MAP 6: C12–C13)

From parking area on Shelter Brook Rd. (1,650 ft.) to:	⇅	↗	↻
Mahoosuc Trail (2,460 ft.)	1.9 mi.	800 ft.	1:20

Notch Trail ascends at easy grades to the southwest end of Mahoosuc Notch, providing the easiest access to that wild and beautiful place. At the west end of Mahoosuc Notch, Notch Trail meets Mahoosuc Trail, which heads north through the notch to Mahoosuc Arm and Speck Pond, and south to Fulling Mill Mtn. and Goose Eye Mtn.

The trail begins on Shelter Brook Rd. (sign for Notch Trail), a spur that leaves Success Pond Rd. 10.7 mi. southwest of ME 26 via North and Success Pond roads and runs 0.3 mi. to a jct., where there is limited parking on the left. Shelter Brook Rd. turns right here (the road ahead is blocked off) and crosses two bridges. At 0.6 mi. from Success Pond Rd., a parking area is on the right, and 50 yd. farther, the trail leaves the road on the left (sign).

The trail ascends easily, following old logging roads along Shelter Brook, crossing to the brook's north side at 0.9 mi. then back to the south side at 1.1 mi. Here, the trail swings left (northeast), soon crosses the brook again, skirts to the left of an area of beaver activity, and continues with many bog bridges up to the height-of-land, where Notch Trail meets Mahoosuc Trail (p. 241); turn left to traverse the notch. A short distance along Mahoosuc Trail, the valley, which has been an ordinary one, changes sharply to a chamber formation, and the high cliffs of the notch, which have not been visible at all on Notch Trail, come into sight.

SEC 5

■ GOOSE EYE MTN. (3,870 FT.) AND GOOSE EYE MTN., EAST PEAK (3,974 FT.)

This striking mountain in Riley Township offers excellent panoramic views from its high, rocky summit, including the Presidential Range and the surrounding peaks in the heart of the Mahoosuc Range. Goose Eye Mtn. (West Peak) and its subsidiary East Peak can be reached from the east via Wright and Mahoosuc trails, from the north via Notch and Mahoosuc trails, from the west via Goose Eye Trail, and from the south via Carlo Col and Mahoosuc trails.

GOOSE EYE TRAIL (AMC; MAP 6: C12–C13)

Cumulative from Carlo Col Trail (1,660 ft.) to:	⇅	↗	↻
Goose Eye Mtn. summit (3,870 ft.)	2.9 mi.	2,200 ft.	2:35
Mahoosuc Trail (3,800 ft.)	3.0 mi.	2,200 ft. (rev. 50 ft.)	2:40

Goose Eye Trail ascends Goose Eye Mtn. from Carlo Col Trail, 0.2 mi. from Success Pond Rd., and ends at Mahoosuc Trail 0.1 mi. beyond the summit. The trail has easy to moderate grades for most of its length and then climbs very steeply, with some ledge scrambling, to the scenic summit. Follow the lower part of the trail with care through logged areas.

From the gravel logging road that Carlo Col Trail follows, Goose Eye Trail diverges left at a sign, drops down an embankment, follows a newer section of trail for 90 yd., and turns right onto the original route, an old logging road. Goose Eye quickly crosses a brook, runs through a brushy, overgrown area, crosses another brook, and bears left onto a gravel road at 0.3 mi. from Carlo Col Trail (descending, bear right into the woods here at a sign). Goose Eye follows this road for 0.1 mi., then diverges right (watch carefully for sign) and passes through a clear-cut area where the footway may be very obscure through tall grass. The trail swings to the right (southeast) across a wet spot at 0.6 mi. and climbs gradually through woods between logged areas, crossing an overgrown skid road at an angle.

At 1.2 mi., the trail reaches the Maine–New Hampshire state line and enters a fine hardwood forest. The trail swings right at 1.7 mi. and angles up the south side of a ridge at a moderate grade, climbs more steeply uphill, and then becomes eases at the crest of the ridge in dense conifers; at 2.4 mi., there is a glimpse of Goose Eye Mtn. ahead. The trail ascends moderately along the north side of the ridge, then climbs steeply, swinging left to bypass a very difficult ledge, then scrambling up a somewhat less difficult ledge. It soon comes out on the open ledges below the summit, which requires a steep scramble to attain. From the summit, which is at 2.9 mi. and has magnificent views in all directions, the trail descends gradually over ledges 0.1 mi. to Mahoosuc Trail (p. 241), which turns right (southbound) and runs straight ahead at the jct. (northbound).

WRIGHT TRAIL (MBPL; MAP 6: C13)

Cumulative from parking area on Bull Branch Rd. (1,240 ft.) to:	⇅	↗	↺
MBPL tentsite and former loop jct. (2,300 ft.)	2.5 mi.	1,150 ft.	1:50
Mahoosuc Trail (3,630 ft.)	4.4 mi.	2,600 ft.	3:30
West Peak of Goose Eye Mtn. (3,870 ft.) via Mahoosuc and Goose Eye trails	4.8 mi.	2,850 ft.	3:50
East Peak of Goose Eye Mtn. (3,790 ft.) via Mahoosuc Trail	4.5 mi.	2,750 ft.	3:35

This trail, steep and rough in places, provides access to Goose Eye Mtn. and the Mahoosuc Range via a scenic route from the east that begins in a place known as Ketchum, located on a branch of the Sunday River. The upper part of the trail formerly had two separate branches, but the north branch, which ascended through a small glacial cirque, has been closed because of erosion and safety concerns. The south branch, which follows a craggy ridge, is now the sole route up to the main ridge crest.

To reach the trailhead, leave US 2, 2.8 mi. north of Bethel, and follow Sunday River Rd. to the left (northwest). At a fork at 2.2 mi., bear right (signs for Jordan Bowl and covered bridge), and at 3.3 mi., bear right again (sign for covered bridge) and continue past Artist Covered Bridge (left) at 3.8 mi. from US 2. At 6.5 mi., the road becomes gravel. At 7.8 mi., turn left across two new bridges and immediately take the first right, which is Bull Branch Rd. (Both of these turns may have signs: "Frenchmans" and "Goose Eye." Frenchman's Hole is a popular swimming area on Bull Branch Rd.) At 9.3 mi., cross Goose Eye Brook; the trailhead is on the left at 9.5 mi. from US 2. Parking is available here or a short distance up the road. The trail starts at a signboard with a small trail sign.

Leaving Bull Branch Rd., the blue-blazed trail immediately splits into two branches, which rejoin in 0.5 mi. The left and more scenic branch descends toward Goose Eye Brook, then follows its north side upstream past several cascades and pools and a 30-ft. gorge. It then turns left on an old woods road, which the right branch has followed from the trailhead. The single trail now follows this woods road for 0.2 mi. and then makes a right turn onto an older road. At 0.9 mi., the trail bears left off the road and descends gradually 100 yd. to Goose Eye Brook at its confluence with a tributary. Here the trail bears right and follows the tributary for 0.1 mi., then turns sharply left and crosses it. From this point, the trail roughly follows the north side of Goose Eye Brook, with minor ups and downs, crossing two small tributaries, until it reaches the former loop jct. at 2.5 mi. A designated MBPL tentsite is on the right just before the jct.

From the former loop jct., where the north branch (now closed) continued ahead across a tributary brook, the south branch of the trail immediately crosses Goose Eye Brook to the left and starts to climb, gradually at first and then moderately by switchbacks, with rough sections and wooden steps, to the ridge crest at 3.1 mi. At 3.4 mi., after a rough ascent, the trail reaches an open spot, then descends slightly back into the woods. It then resumes a steep, rough ascent on ledges to an open knob with beautiful views at 3.6 mi. The trail continues along the ridge with several open areas and occasional minor descents to cross small sags, then finally climbs moderately to Mahoosuc Trail (p. 241) in the small gap between East Peak and West Peak (main summit) of Goose Eye Mtn. at 4.4 mi. Reach the main summit in 0.4 mi. by following Mahoosuc Trail to the left (southbound) and then Goose Eye Trail. Reach craggy East Peak by climbing steeply for 0.1 mi. on Mahoosuc Trail to the right (northbound).

SEC 5

■ MT. CARLO (3,565 FT.)

Mt. Carlo in Riley Township is just east of the Maine–New Hampshire border, roughly in the middle of the Mahoosuc Range. Mt. Carlo can be climbed from the west via Carlo Col Trail and from the north via either Goose Eye and Mahoosuc trails or Wright and Mahoosuc trails.

CARLO COL TRAIL (AMC; MAP 6: C12 AND D12–D13)

Cumulative from Success Pond Rd. (1,630 ft.) to:	⇅	↗	↻
Goose Eye Trail (1,660 ft.)	0.2 mi.	50 ft.	0:10
Spur to Carlo Col Campsite (2,960 ft.)	2.5 mi.	1,350 ft.	1:55
Mahoosuc Trail (3,170 ft.)	2.7 mi.	1,550 ft.	2:10

Carlo Col Trail ascends to Mahoosuc Trail at the small box ravine called Carlo Col and, in combination with Goose Eye Trail, makes possible a scenic loop over Mt. Carlo and Goose Eye Mtn. Carlo Col Trail departs Success Pond Rd. on a gravel logging road (AMC trail sign and road sign for Carlo Col trailhead) that begins 16.2 mi. southwest of ME 26 via North and Success Pond roads. Parking for several cars is available a few yards up the road on the left.

From the parking area, the trail follows the road southeast, and in 0.2 mi. Goose Eye Trail (sign) diverges left down an embankment. Carlo Col Trail continues straight ahead on the road, climbing easily through a logged area. At 0.7 mi., the trail takes the left-hand road at a fork, descends on the road for 0.1 mi., then turns left (sign) onto a footpath into the woods and immediately crosses the brook that flows from Carlo Col (may be difficult to cross at high water). The trail ascends easily, and at 1.0 mi. it turns right onto a relocated section where the older route climbed left into a brushy clearcut area. The trail runs through woods between the brook and the clearcut, swings right to cross the brook at 1.3 mi., and crosses it again in another 100 yd. The trail then skirts the edge of the clearcut, crosses the brook again, and climbs moderately, turning right onto the original route at 1.8 mi. At 2.2 mi., the trail bears right onto a newer relocation, climbs steadily via switchbacks with many log steps, and swings left to a jct. at 2.5 mi. (Here, a spur trail, the former route of Carlo Col Trail, descends left to cross a small, mossy brook—the last water, perhaps for several miles—and then ascends to Carlo Col Campsite, about 60 yd. from the jct.) The main trail turns right at the jct. and climbs moderately to Mahoosuc Trail (p. 241) at Carlo Col. Mt. Carlo is 0.4 mi. to the left on this trail; to the right, there's a fine outlook ledge in a short distance via a fairly difficult scramble.

MAHOOSUC TRAIL

Crossing the Mahoosuc Public Land, Mahoosuc Trail extends across the length of the Mahoosuc Range from Gorham, New Hampshire, to the summit of Old Speck Mtn. in Maine. Beyond its jct. with Centennial Trail, Mahoosuc Trail is a link in the AT. Water may be scarce, particularly in dry weather. This spectacular route is among the most rugged and strenuous of its kind in the Maine and New Hampshire mountains, with numerous minor humps and deep cols, and many ledges, some of them quite steep and likely to be slippery when wet. Parts of the trail may require significantly more time than that provided by the guidebook formula, particularly for backpackers with a full pack.

Mahoosuc Notch, in particular, may require several hours to traverse. The notch is regarded by experienced hikers to be one of the most difficult sections of the entire AT. It can be hazardous in wet or icy conditions and can remain impassable due to snow through the end of May and perhaps longer. Some alpine sections, especially the section traversing the peaks of Goose Eye Mtn., have significant weather exposure.

SEC 5

The entirety of Mahoosuc Trail is described in detail in AMC's *White Mountain Guide* (30th Edition, 2017). The trail is also shown from end to end on Maine Mountains Trail Map 6: Mahoosuc Range–Evans Notch, included with this guide.

MAHOOSUC TRAIL IN NEW HAMPSHIRE (AMC; MAP 6: E10–E11 AND D11–D12)

Cumulative from Hogan Rd. parking area north of Androscoggin River in Gorham, NH (820 ft.), north to:	⤊	↗	○
Mt. Hayes summit (2,555 ft.)	2.5 mi.	1,750 ft.	2:10
Centennial Trail (2,550 ft.)	2.7 mi.	1,750 ft.	2:15
Cascade Mtn. summit (2,631 ft.)	4.5 mi.	2,450 ft.	3:30
Trident Col (2,030 ft.)	5.7 mi.	2,550 ft.	4:05
Page Pond (2,220 ft.)	6.7 mi.	2,950 ft.	4:20
Wocket Ledge viewpoint (2,700 ft.)	7.3 mi.	3,450 ft.	5:20
Dream Lake, inlet brook crossing (2,620 ft.)	8.4 mi.	3,750 ft.	6:05
Austin Brook Trail (2,155 ft.)	10.5 mi.	3,950 ft.	7:15
Mt. Success summit (3,565 ft.)	13.3 mi.	5,850 ft.	9:35
Success Trail (3,170 ft.)	13.9 mi.	5,850 ft.	9:55
Carlo Col Trail at Carlo Col (3,170 ft.)	15.7 mi.	6,450 ft.	11:05

MAHOOSUC TRAIL IN MAINE (AMC; MAP 6: D13, C13, AND B13)

Cumulative from Carlo Col (3,170 ft.) north to:	⇅	↗	⟳
Mt. Carlo summit (3,565 ft.)	0.4 mi.	400 ft.	0:25
Goose Eye Trail jct. (3,800 ft.)	1.8 mi.	1,100 ft.	1:25
Wright Trail jct. (3,630 ft.)	2.1 mi.	1,100 ft.	1:35
Goose Eye Mtn., East Peak (3,794 ft.)	2.2 mi.	1,300 ft.	1:45
Goose Eye Mtn., North Peak (3,675 ft.)	3.4 mi.	1,600 ft.	2:30
Full Goose Campsite (2,950 ft.)	4.4 mi.	1,600 ft.	3:00
Notch Trail (2,460 ft.)	5.9 mi.	2,050 ft.	4:00
Foot of Mahoosuc Notch (2,150 ft.)	7.0 mi.	2,050 ft.	4:45
Mahoosuc Arm and May Cutoff (3,750 ft.)	8.6 mi.	3,750 ft.	6:15
Speck Pond Campsite (3,400 ft.)	9.5 mi.	3,750 ft.	6:40
Old Speck Trail jct. (4,030 ft.)	10.6 mi.	4,700 ft.	7:35
Old Speck Mtn. summit (4,170 ft.)	10.9 mi.	4,850 ft.	7:50

MAHOOSUC TRAIL IN MAINE, IN REVERSE (AMC; MAP 6: B13, C13, AND D13)

Cumulative from Old Speck Mtn. summit (4,170 ft.) south to:	⇅	↗	⟳
Old Speck Trail jct. (4,030 ft.)	0.3 mi.	0 ft.	0:10
Speck Pond Campsite (3,400 ft.)	1.4 mi.	200 ft.	0:50
Mahoosuc Arm summit (3,770 ft.)	2.3 mi.	600 ft.	1:25
Foot of Mahoosuc Notch (2,150 ft.)	3.9 mi.	700 ft.	2:15
Notch Trail (2,460 ft.)	5.0 mi.	1,000 ft.	3:00
Full Goose Campsite (2,950 ft.)	6.5 mi.	1,950 ft.	4:15
Goose Eye Mtn., North Peak (3,675 ft.)	7.5 mi.	2,650 ft.	5:05
Goose Eye Mtn., East Peak (3,794 ft.)	8.7 mi.	3,050 ft.	5:55
Wright Trail (3,630 ft.)	8.8 mi.	3,050 ft.	5:55
Goose Eye Trail (3,800 ft.)	9.1 mi.	3,200 ft.	6:10
Mt. Carlo (3,565 ft.)	10.5 mi.	3,700 ft.	7:05
Carlo Col Trail at Carlo Col (3,170 ft.)	10.9 mi.	3,700 ft.	7:20

From Carlo Col, 0.3 mi. east of Carlo Col Shelter and 2.6 mi. from Success Pond Rd., the trail climbs steadily to the bare southwest summit of Mt. Carlo at 0.4 mi., where there are views over the trees. The trail descends briefly and then climbs a lower knob to the northeast, crosses a mountain meadow that has a fine view of Goose Eye Mtn. ahead, then descends steeply over many slippery ledge slabs and reaches a col at 1.0 mi. From the col, the trail swings left and climbs moderately by switchbacks to a southern shoulder of Goose Eye Mtn., crosses an open meadow with excellent views, then climbs a short, steep pitch to an open craggy knoll below the summit. The trail then passes through a sag and climbs a very steep pitch (with two sets of iron rungs and a large wooden ladder on the steepest ledges) to the narrow ridge of the main peak of Goose Eye Mtn. at 1.8 mi. (Use care on this section.) Here, at the ridge top, Goose Eye Trail branches sharply left, reaching the open summit and its spectacular views in 0.1 mi., and continues to Success Pond Rd. in 3.2 mi. Mahoosuc Trail turns sharply right (east) here and follows the ridge crest through mixed ledge and scrub to a col at 2.1 mi., where the trail meets Wright Trail (leads 1.9 mi. to a campsite and 4.4. mi. to Bull Branch Rd. in Ketchum). Beyond, Mahoosuc Trail climbs steeply for 0.1 mi. through woods and open ledges to the bare summit of East Peak of Goose Eye Mtn. at 2.2 mi.

SEC 5

■ GOOSE EYE MTN., NORTH PEAK (3,675 FT.), AND FULLING MILL MTN., SOUTH PEAK (3,395 FT.)

From East Peak of Goose Eye Mtn., Mahoosuc Trail turns north and descends steeply, with one tricky ledge scramble, then makes a long switchback out to the east, heading downhill through scrub over plank walkways, passing the former jct. with the now-closed north branch of Wright Trail. Mahoosuc Trail descends steeply again over ladders and ledges to a minor col, then rises slightly and emerges in open subalpine meadows on the broad ridge. Ahead, the trail swings left on a relocation, passes a view over a valley from the western edge of the ridge, and swings right back to the original route in 0.1 mi. In another 0.1 mi., it drops to the bottom of a box ravine (possible but unreliable water), the true col between East and North peaks. The trail climbs steeply out of the ravine and continues mostly in the open at easy grades for another 0.4 mi., nearly to the foot of the North Peak. The trail climbs moderately through woods and emerges in the open on the broad summit of the North Peak at 3.4 mi.

Here, the trail swings right (east) on a relocation that bypasses the high point, turning right back onto the original route in 70 yd. It then swings northeast down a steep slope with fine views, winding through several patches of scrub and dropping over several steep ledges. At the foot of the steep slope, the trail enters the woods, contours along the west side of a hump, then angles steeply down the west face of the ridge, with two sets of iron rungs, to a col at 4.4 mi. The trail ascends a ladder to Full Goose Campsite, located on a ledge shelf near the col; there's a spring 80 yd. downhill to the right (east of the campsite). In front of the shelter, the trail turns sharply left, descends a ladder, ascends steeply then moderately, and comes into the open 0.1 mi. below the bare summit of South Peak of Fulling Mill Mtn., which is at 4.9 mi. At the broad summit ledge, the trail turns sharply left and runs through a meadow. It descends northwest through woods, first gradually then steeply, with two more sets of iron rungs and many rock steps, to the head of Mahoosuc Notch at 5.9 mi. Here, Notch Trail diverges sharply left (southwest) and leads 2.2 mi. to Success Pond Rd.

From the head of Mahoosuc Notch, Mahoosuc Trail turns sharply right (northeast) and descends the length of the narrow notch along a rough footway with numerous rock scrambles, some of which are fairly difficult, and passes through a number of boulder caverns, some with narrow openings where progress will be slow and where ice remains into summer. The trail is blazed on the rocks with white paint. (*Caution:* Exercise great care in the notch because of the numerous slippery rocks and dangerous holes. Large packs will be a particular hindrance. The traverse of the notch is not recommended for dogs. The notch may be impassable through early June because of snow, even with snowshoes. Heavy backpacks will impede progress considerably.)

At the lower end of the notch, at 7.0 mi., the trail skirts to the left of a small beaver pond, bears left soon after, and ascends moderately but roughly at times under the east end of Mahoosuc Mtn. along the valley that leads to Notch 2. Then it crosses to the north side of a brook and winds upward among rocks and ledges on the very steep wooded slope of Mahoosuc Arm with a rough footway and many slabs that may be slippery when wet. A little more than halfway up, the trail passes the head of a little flume, in which there is sometimes water. Near the top of the climb, an open ledge a few yards to the right of the trail affords an excellent view of Mahoosuc Notch and the Mahoosuc Range. At 8.6 mi., a few yards past the top of the flat ledges near the summit of Mahoosuc Arm, May Cutoff diverges left and leads 0.3 mi. over the true summit to join Speck Pond Trail.

Mahoosuc Trail swings right (southeast) and wanders across the semi-open summit plateau, turns left twice and climbs slightly, then drops steeply to Speck Pond (3,430 ft.), the highest pond in Maine, bordered by thick woods. The trail crosses the outlet brook and continues around the east side of the pond to a jct. a short distance east of Speck Pond Campsite at 9.5 mi. (in summer, there is a caretaker and a fee for overnight camping). Here, Speck Pond Trail leads ahead 80 yd. to the shelter and continues to Success Pond Rd. in another 3.1 mi. At this jct., Mahoosuc Trail turns right (north) on a relocation and in 100 yd. turns right again to rejoin the original route.

Mahoosuc Trail turns right a third time and climbs to the southeast end of the next hump on the ridge, passes over it, and runs across the east face of a second small hump. In the gully beyond, a few yards east of the trail, is an unreliable spring. The trail climbs steeply up the west shoulder of Old Speck, reaching an open ledges area with excellent views, where the footway is well defined on the crest. Near the top of the shoulder, the trail bears right, reenters the woods, descends slightly, then ascends along the wooded crest. Shortly after entering Grafton Notch State Park, Old Speck Trail, which continues the AT north, diverges left to Grafton Notch at 10.6 mi. Mahoosuc Trail leads straight ahead, ascending moderately southeast to the cleared summit of Old Speck Mtn. and its observation tower at 10.9 mi. Grafton Loop Trail leaves from this point and heads southeast toward Sunday River Whitecap.

SEC 5

GRAFTON LOOP TRAIL

Grafton Loop Trail offers extensive hiking along a route that connects a series of scenic peaks and other natural features in the vicinity of Grafton Notch. This major trail project was a cooperative effort among private landowners, the state of Maine, and nonprofit organizations, such as AMC and the Maine Appalachian Trail Club. The goal of the project was to develop multiday hiking opportunities as alternatives to heavily used sections of the AT. For AMC, this was the first major trail constructed since the Centennial Trail in the Mahoosucs in 1976. About 32 mi. of new trail were built on either side of Grafton Notch, which, along with a 7-mi. section of the AT between Old Speck Mtn. and Baldpate Mtn., created an impressive 39-mi. loop.

Parking for the southern trailhead (used for both eastern and western sections) is on the east side of ME 26, 4.9 mi. north of its jct. with US 2 in Newry and just north of Eddy Rd. To reach the western section trailhead (no parking), walk 0.6 mi. south on the shoulder of ME 26 to a sign for Grafton Loop Trail. The northern trailhead is located on ME 26 in the Grafton Notch parking area, where the AT crosses ME 26, 12.1 mi. north of US 2.

■ PUZZLE MTN. (3,133 FT.) AND LONG MTN. (3,062 FT.)

These two summits are found lie astride the Newry–Andover town line, east of ME 26 and Grafton Notch along the lower half of the eastern section of Grafton Loop Trail.

GRAFTON LOOP TRAIL, EASTERN SECTION
(MATC; MAP 6: B13–B15 AND C15)
Cumulative from southern trailhead on ME 26 (730 ft.) to:

	⇅	↗	◯
Woodsum Spur Trail, lower jct. (2,900 ft.)	3.2 mi.	2,150 ft.	2:45
Puzzle Mtn. (3,133 ft.)	3.6 mi.	2,380 ft.	3:00
Stewart Campsite spur trail (2,500 ft.)	4.9 mi.	2,380 ft.	4:00
Long Mtn. spur trail (2,950 ft.)	9.4 mi.	3,100 ft.	6:30
Town Corner Campsite spur trail (2,400 ft.)	10.4 mi.	3,100 ft.	7:00
Lane Campsite spur trail (1,950 ft.)	13.2 mi.	3,400 ft.	8:30
Baldpate Mtn., East Peak (3,780 ft.)	17.1 mi.	5,200 ft.	11:30
Grafton Notch parking area on ME 26 (1,450 ft.) via AT	21.1 mi.	5,600 ft.	13:40

The eastern section of Grafton Loop Trail was completed and opened to the public in 2003. It consists of a 17.1-mi. route that leaves ME 26 in Newry and returns to ME 26 in Grafton Notch State Park via a 4.0-mi. section of the AT. The trail traverses four peaks and includes three primitive campsites and an AT shelter. About half of the trail crosses private lands, with the remainder crossing public lands managed by the MBPL as part of the Mahoosuc PL and Grafton Notch State Park.

At the parking lot on ME 26, Grafton Loop Trail begins at a post with a blue blaze. The trail heads through a young forest and crosses a small brook and an overgrown logging road. It switchbacks several times on a gradual incline along parts of another old logging road, passing through a section of young spruce and white birch and then through an area thick with downed balsam fir. The trail continues gradually uphill, using sections of a logging road and switchbacks. It is clearly marked with blue blazes and cairns. Avoid turning left onto smaller unmarked paths. At about 2 mi., turn left and begin a steep climb. At about 2.4 mi., the trail crosses several exposed granite boulders and ledges, offering views of the Sunday River ski area, Grafton Notch, and the distant Presidential Range. The trail cuts back into the woods before climbing a steep boulder staircase with some mild rock scrambling. (*Caution:* The exposed granite areas are very slippery in wet weather.)

Reach the south summit of Puzzle Mtn., marked by a large rock cairn, at 3.2 mi. Excellent views appear in all directions. The lower end of Woodsum Spur Trail enters from the right (not recommended from this direction). Ahead, at 3.6 mi., the trail reaches the rocky ledges on top of Puzzle Mtn. Here, the upper end of Woodsum Spur Trail diverges to the right.

Descend the mountain to the north, following cairns. Grafton Loop Trail traverses rolling terrain with a few boulder scrambles and an iron ladder. Beyond, the trail descends gradually on stone steps. At 4.9 mi., it reaches the jct. with the spur trail leading 300 ft. to Stewart Campsite.

SEC 5

After the jct., Grafton Loop Trail makes a winding descent on switchbacks. The trail crosses an overgrown road before leveling out as it approaches Chase Hill Brook. Take care to follow only the blue blazes in this area. At 6.3 mi., cross Chase Hill Brook (crossing may be difficult during times of high water). At the base of the mountain (6.7 mi.), the trail intersects an old road. Turn right, walk 0.25 mi., and reenter the woods at the cairn on the left side of the road. The trail winds up Long Mtn., crossing, following, and leaving the woods road several times. It eventually leaves the woods road for good and continues through mature forest. The trail contours up a ridge on long, gradual switchbacks with occasional steep sections. As the trail gains altitude, gaps in the trees afford views of the Sunday River ski area and the summit of Mt. Washington. The trail becomes steeper and uses a stone staircase and wooden staircase/ladder to assist with the ascent.

At 9.4 mi., a short spur trail near the summit of Long Mtn. leads north to a viewpoint. Grafton Loop Trail reaches a high point on Long Mtn. at 9.5 mi. Beyond, the trail winds easily downhill, crossing several small streams. At 10.4 mi., it reaches the 440-ft. spur to Town Corner Campsite. At 11.1 mi., the route crosses a snowmobile trail and a log bridge. Grafton Loop Trail then descends along a brook to a jct. at 11.9 mi. Ahead, the trail follows Wight Brook through a level area, crossing the brook several times (may be difficult to cross in high water).

At 13.2 mi., reach the jct. with a spur trail leading 450 ft. to Lane Campsite on Wight Brook. The spur continues beyond the campsite to a lovely waterfall and pool. Beyond the spur, the main trail climbs steeply to reach a short spur to Lightning Ledge at 14.2 mi., where there are good views of Puzzle Mtn. and the Bear River valley. At 14.5 mi., the trail reaches the knob of Lightning Ledge (2,644 ft.), where there are good views of Baldpate Mtn.

The trail heads back into the woods and descends through the forest with rugged rock faces to the left. A short, moderate descent brings it back to Wight Brook, which it crosses at 14.9 mi. After a short ascent, the trail passes a huge glacial erratic at 16.4 mi. At 17.1 mi., it reaches the open summit of East Peak of Baldpate and spectacular views of mountains and lakes in all directions. (Take care to stay on the trail to avoid disturbing the fragile alpine vegetation.) Grafton Loop Trail joins the AT on the summit for the 4.0 mi. descent to ME 26 and the Grafton Notch parking area.

WOODSUM SPUR TRAIL (MLT; MAP 6: C15)

Cumulative from Grafton Loop Trail, upper jct. (3,100 ft.) to:	⇅	↗	↻
Low point on loop (2,600 ft.)	1.0 mi.	-500 ft.	0:50
Grafton Loop Trail, lower jct. (2,900 ft.)	1.4 mi.	300 ft.	1:15

This loop trail on the south side of Puzzle Mtn. is part of the Stewart Family Preserve, a 485-acre parcel of land protected by a conservation easement held by Mahoosuc Land Trust. The trail is fairly rugged with significant elevation gains and losses for its relatively short length. MLT recommends hiking the trail in a clockwise direction from the upper jct.

The upper end of the spur leaves Grafton Loop Trail and heads east below the true summit of Puzzle Mtn. Woodsum Spur Trail passes through a wet area, then descends to a col on the southeastern ridge. A short, steep pitch climbs to the southeast peak with limited views. The trail then drops off the peak to the south and west, descending through shrub and forest with occasional open ledges. It passes through a wet area before crossing a stream. Gradually ascending as it traverses westward, the trail turns sharply to the northeast and climbs steeply to a boulder field. It intersects Grafton Loop Trail on an open ledge at 1.4 mi.

■ BALD MTN. (2,085 FT.), STOWE MTN. (2,730 FT.), AND SUNDAY RIVER WHITECAP (3,335 FT.)

These three summits are found west of ME 26 and Grafton Notch in Newry, along the western section of Grafton Loop Trail.

GRAFTON LOOP TRAIL, WESTERN SECTION
(AMC; MAP 6: B13–C15)

Cumulative from Grafton Loop Trail, eastern section, trailhead parking area on ME 26 (730 ft.) to:	↥↧	↗	↺
Start of western section via ME 26 (730 ft.)	0.6 mi.	0 ft.	0:20
Bald Mtn. Tentsite spur (1,370 ft.)	2.2 mi.	650 ft.	1:25
High point on Bald Mtn. (2,070 ft.)	3.2 mi.	1,350 ft.	2:15
Stowe Mtn. summit (2,730 ft.)	4.5 mi.	2,250 ft. (rev. 250 ft.)	3:25
Sargent Brook Tentsite spur (2,650 ft.)	6.0 mi.	2,500 ft.	4:15
Sunday River Whitecap summit (3,335 ft.)	7.1 mi.	3,250 ft.	5:10
Miles Notch (2,350 ft.)	8.3 mi.	3,250 ft.	5:45
Slide Mtn. Tentsite spur (2,550 ft.)	10.4 mi.	3,850 ft.	7:10
Bull Run Tentsite spur (2,700 ft.)	11.4 mi.	4,050 ft.	7:45
Old Speck Mtn. summit (4,170 ft.)	13.3 mi.	5,500 ft.	9:25
Grafton Notch (1,450 ft.) via Mahoosuc Trail and AT	17.1 mi.	5,500 ft.	11:45

SEC 5

The western section of Grafton Loop Trail opened in 2007 and provides access to spectacular views from Sunday River Whitecap (views from the rest of this section are somewhat limited). Grades are mostly easy to moderate, with a few short, steep pitches. The first 7.0 mi. of this section pass through private land (some of which is under conservation easement), where landowners have generously granted public access. Camping is allowed only at the four designated campsites, and fires are not permitted.

By agreement with the landowner, parking is prohibited at the western section trailhead. Parking at the south end of the western section of the trail is allowed only at the trailhead for the eastern section. This parking area is on the east side of ME 26, 4.9 mi. north of its jct. with US 2 at Newry and almost opposite Eddy Rd. To reach the western section trailhead, walk 0.6 mi. south on the shoulder of ME 26 to a sign for Grafton Loop Trail on the west side of the road. Mileages are given from the eastern section trailhead parking area and include the 0.6-mi. walk to the western trailhead.

From ME 26, the trail follows a farm road along the left edge of a field for 90 yd., then bears left off the road (sign) and, in another 125 yd., turns right to cross Bear River on a snowmobile bridge. Marked with snowmobile trail arrows, the route crosses two fields and enters the woods, following an old road south. At 1.2 mi., the road swings left, and in another 50 yd., the trail turns right (west) off the road (sign) onto a footpath. In

20 yd., the blue-blazed trail crosses a small brook and swings right to follow it, climbing at mostly easy grades and crossing the brook three more times in the next 0.4 mi.; between the second and third crossings, the trail passes a small flume.

The trail continues following the brook at moderate grades up the northeast slope of Bald Mtn., occasionally making use of old woods roads. It crosses the brook twice more, and at 2.2 mi., just beyond the second of these crossings, a spur trail leads 60 yd. left across the brook to Bald Mtn. Tentsite. At 2.4 mi., the main trail turns left, crosses the brook (or its dry bed) for the last time, and climbs steadily by switchbacks to the broad crest of Bald Mtn. It continues at easy grades across the plateau, crosses a small sag, and reaches its high point on Bald Mtn. at 3.2 mi. The trail then descends moderately to a flat saddle, where it runs nearly level to the right of a brushy logged area.

The trail soon begins the ascent of Stowe Mtn., first at easy grades, then steeply, with many rock steps, as it enters spruce woods. At 4.3 mi., the trail ascends a series of wooden ladders. The grade eases as the trail crosses the flat, wooded crest of Stowe Mtn. at 4.5 mi. It then descends to a minor col at 4.8 mi., where it crosses a small brook, and ascends briefly to the semi-open ledges on the west knob of Stowe Mtn., where there are limited views. Marked by cairns, the trail runs across the ledges for 0.1 mi., then reenters the woods. It follows a winding course through dense growth, then swings north and descends at mostly easy grades. The trail now traverses the southwestern slope of Sunday River Whitecap through open woods, with minor ups and downs, crossing several small, unreliable brooks.

At 6.0 mi., a spur trail diverges left and descends 0.2 mi. to Sargent Brook Tentsite, crossing a small brook (reliable) in 50 yd. The main trail traverses to the west, then turns right (north) at 6.2 mi. and ascends moderately along the west slope of Sunday River Whitecap, gaining the ridge crest in a small col at 6.7 mi. The trail follows the ridge over a hump, descends to another col, then climbs again, emerging on open ledges at 7.0 mi., where AMC trail crews have used innovative construction techniques—scree walls and raised wooden walkways—to protect the fragile alpine vegetation. Hikers are urged to stay on the defined trail and outlook areas. At 7.1 mi., just before the summit, a side path descends 25 yd. right to a designated viewing area looking east. In another 20 yd., a similar path leads 20 yd. left to a western outlook with a fine view of the northern Mahoosucs and the distant Presidential Range.

The main trail crosses the summit and descends steeply north over open ledges, then swings more to the northeast, winding down over ledges and through patches of scrub, with excellent views of the peaks around Grafton

Notch. The trail descends into a belt of woods, then in 125 yd. swings left (west) and emerges on an open shoulder. At 7.6 mi., it enters the woods for good and descends steadily west, then southwest, through an area where some yellow blazes remain from a former unofficial trail. The grade eases in open woods, and at 8.3 mi., the trail swings left (south) on the broad floor of Miles Notch, runs nearly level for 0.1 mi., and then bears right (west) and ascends through partly logged areas onto the lower slope of Slide Mtn. The trail turns left (south) again and contours along the slope, with occasional rough footing, then descends through an area of boulders to a low point at 9.1 mi.

The trail soon swings west and ascends briefly, then runs northwest at easy grades, with minor ups and downs, passing to the left of a large boulder at 9.5 mi. It runs at easy grades through fine hardwood forest for some distance along the base of Slide Mtn., then rises gradually into mixed woods. At 10.4 mi., a spur on the right ascends 110 yd. to Slide Mtn. Tentsite. About 35 yd. past this jct., the main trail crosses a small brook (the water source for the campsite), runs west, then soon swings right and ascends through a hardwood glade. It then bears left and winds gradually up the east side of a valley.

At 11.4 mi., a spur trail leads 0.1 mi. left to Bull Run Tentsite, crossing a brook that is the water source. The main trail enters conifers and climbs more steadily across the slope, gaining the crest of a southeastern spur of Old Speck Mtn. at 11.9 mi. Here, the trail swings left and ascends the ridge crest, then bears left again and climbs by easy switchbacks with good footing. At 12.2 mi., the trail climbs through a blowdown patch with restricted views south. The grade increases at 12.7 mi., and the footway becomes rough with rocks, roots, and holes as the trail angles the south slope of Old Speck. At 13.0 mi., there is an outlook southeast toward Sunday River Whitecap and the Bear River valley. The trail soon swings right, and the footing improves. After a steadier climb, the trail levels, passes a trail sign, and 10 yd. farther emerges in the clearing at the summit of Old Speck Mtn. Here are fine views northeast, and visitors can get a full panorama by ascending the metal ladder on the observation tower. From the summit, Mahoosuc Trail leads 0.3 mi. northwest to Old Speck Trail.

BETHEL

■ MT. WILL (1,726 FT.)

Mt. Will straddles the town lines of Bethel and Newry. A nice blue-blazed loop trail, maintained by Bethel Conservation Commission, ascends to two viewpoints high on the mountain. Several interpretive signs are along

SEC 5

the lower portion of the trail. The section of trail to North Ledge goes through Bethel Town Forest, but the rest of the trail is on private land. The marked trailhead parking area is opposite the Bethel recycling center, on the west side of US 2 at a point 1.9 mi. north of the Riverside Rest Area.

MT. WILL TRAIL (BCC; MAP 6: D15)
Cumulative from ME 26 (730 ft.) to:

	⇅	⤴	↻
North Ledges (1,500 ft.)	0.9 mi.	770 ft.	0:50
Mt. Will north summit (1,704 ft.)	1.5 mi.	1,000 ft.	1:15
South Cliffs (1,620 ft.)	2.1 mi.	1,000 ft.	1:30
Complete loop	3.1 mi.	1,000 ft.	2:30

The trail enters the woods at a kiosk and splits in 150 ft. Go right, the recommended direction to hike the route. Ahead, cross a brook and bear left. Soon, the trail bears away from the brook and begins to contour across the mountain's lower east face. It turns steeply uphill toward mossy cliffs, makes a sharp switchback left, then contours west. After a series of steep switchbacks past mossy cliffs, crest the ridge and reach a jct. To the right, it is 150 ft. to a lookout atop North Ledges, where there are views over the farms and fields in the Androscoggin River valley.

From the jct., continue left on the ridge, then make a slight descent to a ledge and a narrow view window. Beyond, climb the rocky ridge and, in thick spruce and fir, pass over the north summit of Mt. Will, marked by a large cairn. Descend to a sag between the north and south summits. Pass a tote road on the right with signs for Gray Memorial, which leads a short distance off-trail uphill to a memorial for Leroy and Brenda Gray, who died in a plane crash on the mountain in 1992.

Beyond, the trail contours south beneath the steep face of the south summit, on a rough path of rocks and roots. The descent moderates to reach the viewpoint at South Cliffs, which provides a good look to the Androscoggin River, the Sunday River ski area, the village of Bethel, Mt. Abram, and the White Mountains. Ahead, weave down across the mountain into a huge bowl on the east side, following switchbacks. Reach a brook and stone steps, and then walk through an area of extensive logging. Cross a brook, then bear right on the wide track along it. Close the loop at the original trail jct., and turn right to reach the trailhead.

SECTION 6

WHITE MOUNTAIN NATIONAL FOREST AND EVANS NOTCH

Pull-Out Map
Map 6: Mahoosuc Range–Evans Notch

INTRODUCTION

This section includes the entire Maine portion of the White Mountain National Forest in the region around Evans Notch, and the valleys of Evans Brook and Cold River that lead up to Evans Notch from the north and south, respectively. The area is bounded on the west by the New Hampshire state line from the Androscoggin River south roughly to the village of Stow, a few miles south of AMC's Cold River Camp. US 2 and the Androscoggin River form the northern boundary, from Gilead east roughly to Bethel. ME 5/35 outlines the eastern boundary from Bethel south to North Waterford. The south is bounded by ME 5 between North Waterford and Lovell, and by Kezar Lake and local roads west to Stow.

This section describes 33 trails on 18 mountains. The WMNF maintains most of these trails; the remainder are cared for by AMC and the Chatham Trails Association (CTA). Map 6: Mahoosuc Range–Evans Notch covers the entire area, which straddles the Maine–New Hampshire state line. All of the Maine trails are described in this guide, while some, but not all, of the trails entering New Hampshire to the west are mentioned but not described. Hikers heading for the Baldfaces, Mt. Meader, the Wild River valley, and beyond will want to refer to AMC's *White Mountain Guide* (30th Edition, 2017). CTA publishes a detailed map of its trail system in the Cold River valley.

A central feature of the WMNF in Maine is the 11,236-acre Caribou–Speckled Mtn. Wilderness. In accordance with USFS Wilderness policy, the trails in the Wilderness are generally maintained to a lower standard than are non-Wilderness trails. Considerable care may be required to follow them.

GEOGRAPHY

The WMNF in Maine encompasses a jumbled mass of mountains and ridges with numerous ledges; although the peaks are not high, they offer a variety of fine walks. With the exception of a few trails off ME/NH 113, this section probably receives less hiking traffic than any comparable portion of the WMNF, allowing visitors to enjoy relative solitude on trails in an area that is quite rugged and scenic.

The highest summit in the section is East Royce Mtn. (3,114 ft.). Its eastern escarpment forms the western walls of Evans Notch. On the east side of Evans Notch is the bulk of Speckled Mtn. (2,906 ft.). The second-tallest peak in the section, Speckled is one of at least three mountains in Maine that are known by this name; its open summit ledges have excellent views in nearly all directions. The wooded west ridge of Speckled Mtn., which descends toward ME/NH 113, includes Ames Mtn. (2,686 ft.) and Spruce Hill (2,510 ft.). Blueberry Ridge, ending in Blueberry Mtn.

SEC
6

(1,781 ft.), is a long, flat spur running south from Speckled Mtn. The top of Blueberry is mostly one big open ledge, where mature trees are slowly reclaiming what was once a burned-over summit with only sparse and stunted trees. Numerous open spaces afford excellent views, especially from the southwest ledges on Blueberry Mtn. In the valley between Blueberry Mtn. and the southwest ridge of Speckled Mtn., Bickford Brook passes the Bickford Slides, a series of beautiful flumes and waterfalls. The southeast ridge of Speckled Mtn. also bears many open ledges with fine views. A long ridge extends east from Speckled Mtn. to Miles Notch, running over Durgin Mtn. (2,404 ft.), Butters Mtn. (2,246 ft.), Red Rock Mtn. (2,141 ft.), and Miles Knob (2,090 ft.). Durgin Mtn. and Red Rock Mtn. offer interesting views from ledges near their summits, and the south cliff of Red Rock Mtn. is one of the most impressive features of the region.

To the north of Speckled Mtn. is Caribou Mtn. (2,850 ft.), the third-highest peak in the area; its bare, ledgy summit affords excellent views. South of Caribou Mtn. is Haystack Notch, with the cliffs of trailless Haystack Mtn. (2,205 ft.) rising on its north side. Peabody Mtn. (2,462 ft.) is a wooded mountain that rises north of Caribou Mtn. Northeast of Caribou Mtn. is The Roost (1,374 ft.), a low mountain near Hastings, with open ledges that afford fine views of the Wild River valley, the Evans Brook valley, and surrounding mountains. Located on the eastern edge of the WMNF, Albany Mtn. (1,930 ft.) has open ledges near its summit with excellent views in several directions.

Deer Hill (1,367 ft.), often called Big Deer Hill, is south of Speckled Mtn. and east of Cold River. The views from the east and south ledges are excellent. Little Deer Hill (1,090 ft.), a lower hill west of Deer Hill that rises only about 600 ft. above the valley, gives fine views of the valley and the Baldfaces from its summit ledges. Pine Hill (1,250 ft.) and Lord Hill (1,257 ft.) rise southeast of Deer Hill, with scattered open ledges that afford interesting views. Several short paths in the vicinity of AMC's Cold River Camp are not covered in this guide because they are not open to the public, although some are mentioned where they intersect other more important trails.

ROAD ACCESS

The primary access to the western side of the WMNF and Evans Notch area is by ME/NH 113, also known as the Evans Notch Rd. This scenic auto road extends from US 2 in Gilead south to US 302 in Fryeburg. It generally follows an undulating route along the Maine–New Hampshire state line, bisecting the Evans Notch region. Three WMNF campgrounds (Basin, Cold River, and Hastings) are accessible from this road. Many

SEC 6

trailheads are along the route, to the east and west of the road. To assist in locating these points, this mileage summary is provided:

Cumulative along ME/NH 113 southbound from US 2 in Gilead to:

The Roost, north trailhead (east)	2.9 mi.
Wild River Rd. to Wild River Campground (west)	3.1 mi.
Hastings CG (east)	3.3 mi.
The Roost, south trailhead (east)	3.6 mi.
Forest Route 8/Little Lary Brook Rd. to Wheeler Brook Trail (east)	3.7 mi.
Caribou/Mud Brook trailhead (east)	4.7 mi.
Haystack Notch trailhead (east)	6.1 mi.
East Royce (west) and Spruce Hill (east) trailheads	7.5 mi.
Laughing Lion trailhead (west)	8.4 mi.
Brickett Place (east) and Royce Trail (west)	10.4 mi.
Cold River CG and access road to Basin CG (west)	10.7 mi.
Mt. Meader Trail (west)	12.2 mi.
Baldfaces trailhead (east)	12.8 mi.
AMC's Cold River Camp (east)	13.0 mi.
Stow Corner	18.5 mi.
US 302 in Fryeburg	29.8 mi.

In winter, ME/NH 113 is not plowed between Cold River CG and the access road to Basin Pond and a gate 1.7 mi. south of US 2. Stone House Rd. (private) leads 1.1 mi. east from ME/NH 113 (1.3 mi. north of AMC's Cold River Camp) to a gate and parking area; the road is not plowed in winter. Deer Hill Rd. (FR 9) runs between ME/NH 113 in North Chatham, New Hampshire (0.7 mi. south of AMC's Cold River Camp), and Adams Rd. in Stoneham; Deer Hill Rd. is not plowed in winter. Trails emanating from the Androscoggin River valley are accessed from US 2. Trails along the southern and eastern sides of the section are accessed from ME 5 and ME 5/35.

CAMPING

There are no shelters or established trailside campsites in this section; any backcountry camping must be dispersed. The WMNF operates five campgrounds in this region: at Crocker Pond just west of ME 5 in Albany Township, and at Hastings, Wild River, Cold River (in NH), and Basin along ME/NH 113 in Evans Notch. There is no camping, and no wood or charcoal fires are allowed within 0.25 mi. of any trailhead, picnic and day-use site, or Wild River Rd. Six privately operated campgrounds with a variety of amenities are found on the outer perimeter of the section.

WHITE MOUNTAIN NATIONAL FOREST

The White Mountain National Forest encompasses a diverse landscape of mountains, forests, lakes, ponds, rivers, and streams totaling 769,000 acres: 722,000 acres across central northern New Hampshire and 47,000 acres in western Maine. The Weeks Act of 1911, also known as the Organic Act, authorized the federal government to purchase private forestland for the protection of rivers and watersheds in the eastern United States. This important conservation legislation led to the establishment of the WMNF in 1918.

The WMNF is not a national park but, rather, a national forest. Whereas parks are established primarily for preservation and recreation, national forests are managed for multiple use: recreation, timber production, watershed protection, and wildlife habitat. About 45 percent of the WMNF is open to timber harvesting on a carefully controlled basis. The boundaries of the WMNF are usually marked wherever they cross roads or trails, typically by red-painted corner posts and blazes. Hunting and fishing are permitted in the WMNF under state laws; state licenses are required. Organized groups, including those sponsored by nonprofit organizations, must apply for an outfitter-guide permit if they conduct trips on WMNF land for which they charge a fee. Pets are allowed on WMNF trails; however, be sure to control your pet so it won't be a nuisance to other hikers, and clean up after your pet along the trail.

SEC 6

WMNF Trailhead Parking Fees

Certain established WMNF trailhead parking sites have a posted fee sign indicating that hikers must display an annual or weekly WMNF Recreation Pass on their windshield or dashboard or should be prepared to purchase a daily parking pass at the trailhead. Almost all the proceeds from these passes are used for improvements in the WMNF. Annual and weekly parking passes are available at WMNF ranger offices, information centers, and other locations.

A WMNF Recreation Pass is required to park in Evans Notch at the Brickett Place Day Use Site, where a convenient self-serve day-pass station is available. Valid passes include the daily pass, WMNF weekly and annual passes, and Interagency Passes and Golden Age and Access passes. Any one of these passes displayed on the parked vehicle authorizes the holder to use the site.

For more information on the WMNF, Forest Protection Areas, backcountry camping rules, parking fees, and related items, visit fs.usda.gov/whitemountain.

CARIBOU–SPECKLED MTN. WILDERNESS

This 11,236-acre Wilderness Area east of Evans Notch, established in 1990 and managed by the USFS, encompasses the peaks of Caribou, Red Rock, Butters, Durgin, Speckled, Ames, and Blueberry mountains and Spruce Hill. Twelve trails lead into the Wilderness and provide extensive opportunities to explore this unique mountain environment.

In accordance with USFS Wilderness policy, the trails in Caribou–Speckled Mtn. Wilderness are generally maintained to a lower standard than are non-Wilderness trails. The trails here may be rough, overgrown, or essentially unmarked with minimal signage, and considerable care may be required to follow them. Use of the Wilderness is governed by USFS Wilderness policy. Hiking groups may not exceed ten people, and no more than ten people may occupy a campsite. Motorized equipment or mechanical transport is not allowed, and there is no storing of equipment, personal property, or supplies, including geocaching and letterboxing.

SEC 6

SUGGESTED HIKES

■ Easy

THE ROOST

	↻	↗	○
RT via Roost Trail	1.2 mi.	700 ft.	0:55

A short climb leads to ledges with views of Evans Notch and the Wild River valley. See Roost Trail, p. 274.

ROUND POND

	↻	↗	○
RT via Albany Brook Trail	2.0 mi.	250 ft.	1:10

Take an easy ramble to this pretty pond on a pleasant round-trip hike. See Albany Brook Trail, p. 280.

DEER HILLS

	↻	↗	○
RT via Deer Hills Connector, Deer Hills Trail, and Deer Hills Bypass to Little Deer Hill	2.6 mi.	700 ft.	1:40
LP to Little and Big Deer hills via Deer Hills Connector, Deer Hills Trail, and Deer Hills Bypass	4.3 mi.	1,250 ft.	2:45

For good views of the Cold River valley and the Baldfaces, take the shorter out-and-back trip to Little Deer Hill, or make a longer loop over Little and Big Deer hills. To begin, see Deer Hills Connector, p. 283.

■ Moderate
CARIBOU MTN.

	�763	↗	○
LP via Caribou Trail and Mud Brook Trail	6.9 mi.	1,950 ft.	4:25

Enjoy a loop hike with panoramic views from the extensive open ledges on the Caribou Mtn. summit. To begin, see Caribou Trail, p. 261.

BLUEBERRY MTN.

	�763	↗	○
LP via Shell Pond Trail, White Cairn Trail, Overlook Loop, and Stone House Trail	4.3 mi.	1,200 ft.	2:45

There are many ledges with views on this loop, but you'll still want to add the short side trip to beautiful Rattlesnake Pool. To begin, see Shell Pond Trail, p. 269.

SEC
6

EAST ROYCE MTN.

	�763	↗	○
RT via East Royce Trail	2.6 mi.	1,650 ft.	2:10

A steep and rugged ascent leads to fine views of the Evans Notch area. See East Royce Trail, p. 277.

ALBANY MTN.

	�763	↗	○
RT via Albany Mtn. Trail and Albany Mtn. Spur	4.4 mi.	1,200 ft.	2:25

The small mountain offers good views of western Maine. To begin, see Albany Mtn. Trail, p. 278.

■ Strenuous
SPECKLED MTN.

▓ 🏂 🏂 🏕 🐕 🦆 ⛷	⇅	↗	⟳
LP via Blueberry Ridge Trail and Bickford Brook Trail	8.6 mi.	2,500 ft.	5:35

This scenic circuit includes the open summits of Blueberry and Speckled mountains. To begin, see Blueberry Ridge Trail, p. 267.

RED ROCK MTN.

▓ 🏕 🐾 🦆 ⛷	⇅	↗	⟳
LP via Miles Notch Trail, Red Rock Trail, and Great Brook Trail	10.3 mi.	2,900 ft.	6:35

This interesting valley and ridge loop for experienced hikers covers a wild, less-visited area, with fine views from Red Rock Mtn. The trails require care to follow in places. To begin, see Miles Notch Trail, p. 271.

SEC 6

TRAIL DESCRIPTIONS

CARIBOU–SPECKLED MTN. WILDERNESS
■ CARIBOU MTN. (2,850 FT.)

The extensive open summit ledges on this mountain, located in the townships of Batchelders Grant and Mason, afford excellent views. Caribou Mtn. and much of the surrounding area are part of the Caribou–Speckled Mountain Wilderness. Combine Caribou Trail and Mud Brook Trail for a pleasant loop hike.

The western trailhead for Caribou Mtn., which is the start of both Caribou and Mud Brook trails, is at a parking area on the east side of ME 113, 6.0 mi. north of the WMNF Cold River CG and 4.8 mi. south of US 2. The eastern trailhead is on Bog Rd. (FR 6), which leaves the south side of US 2 4.9 mi. west of the jct. of US 2 and ME 26 in Bethel, and 5.0 mi. east of the jct. of US 2 and ME 113 in Gilead. From US 2, Bog Rd. (sign for Pooh Corner Farm) leads 2.8 mi. to a gate and parking at the end of public travel on the road.

CARIBOU TRAIL (WMNF; MAP 6: E13–E14)

Cumulative from ME 113 (935 ft.) to:	⇅	↗	⟳
Mud Brook Trail (2,420 ft.)	3.0 mi.	1,550 ft.	2:15
Caribou Mtn. summit (2,850 ft.) via Mud Brook Trail	3.6 mi.	1,950 ft.	2:45
Bog Rd. (860 ft.)	5.5 mi.	1,550 ft. (rev. 400 ft.)	3:30

From the parking area on ME 113, Caribou Trail runs north, ascending slightly and then descending. The trail crosses Morrison Brook at 0.4 mi. (no bridge) and turns east to follow the brook, crossing it five more times and entering the Wilderness. The third crossing, at 2.0 mi., is at the head of Kees Falls, a 25-ft. waterfall; a side path descends steeply on the north side of the brook to a good view of the falls. Ahead, the trail climbs steadily, then levels off at the height-of-land as the trail crosses the col between Gammon and Caribou mountains at 2.9 mi. Soon, Mud Brook Trail leaves right to reach the summit of Caribou in 0.6 mi. and ME 113 in 3.9 mi.

Caribou Trail continues ahead at the jct., descending steadily into a ravine and swinging left to cross a small brook. The trail leaves the Wilderness at 3.4 mi., continues down the valley of Bog Brook, and turns northeast, crossing Bog Brook at 4.3 mi. and a tributary in another 0.2 mi. The trail continues at easy grades, bears right across a brook, and at 5.2 mi., just after crossing another brook, the trail turns left onto a logging road (FR 6). At 5.4 mi., the trail turns right at a jct. with another logging road and continues to the gate on Bog Rd. (Ascending, turn left at 0.1 mi. and bear right off the logging road at 0.3 mi.)

SEC 6

MUD BROOK TRAIL (WMNF; MAP 6: E13–F13)

Cumulative from ME 113 (935 ft.) to:	⇅	↗	⟳
Caribou Mtn. summit (2,850 ft.)	3.4 mi.	1,915 ft.	2:40
Caribou Trail (2,420 ft.)	3.9 mi.	1,915 ft.	2:55

This trail begins on ME 113 at the same trailhead as Caribou Trail (refer to driving directions above). The trail passes over the summit of Caribou Mtn. and ends at Caribou Trail in the col between Caribou Mtn. and Gammon Mtn. Despite its name, the footing on Mud Brook Trail is generally dry and good. The eastern section of this trail is in the Caribou–Speckled Mtn. Wilderness.

From ME 113, the trail runs generally south, then turns east along the north side of Mud Brook, rising gradually. The trail crosses the brook at 1.5 mi., then crosses it again at 1.9 mi. and swings left (north) uphill, climbing more steeply. The trail crosses several smaller brooks and, at 3.0 mi., comes out on a small bare knob with excellent views east. It turns left into the woods and makes a short descent into a small ravine, then emerges in the open, passing a short side path on the right leading to ledges with excellent views east.

The trail scrambles up to open ledges on the south summit knob, with views south and west. (*Note:* Hikers should walk only on bare rock in the summit area to preserve fragile vegetation.) The trail, which is poorly marked and requires care to follow, runs northeast across the broad summit ledges, descending slightly and generally keeping to the right (southeast) side of the crest. At 3.4 mi., the trail turns left up a short scramble, then turns right (sign), with the open ledges of the north summit knob a few steps to the left. Ahead, the trail enters the woods and descends north, passes Caribou Spring (unreliable) on the left at 3.6 mi., and meets Caribou Trail in the col.

HAYSTACK NOTCH TRAIL (WMNF; MAP 6: E14 AND F13–F14)

Cumulative from ME 113 (1,070 ft.) to:	⇅	↗	⟳
Haystack Notch (1,810 ft.)	2.1 mi.	750 ft.	1:25
WMNF gate (900 ft.)	5.5 mi.	750 ft.	3:05

This trail, with mostly easy grades but some potentially difficult brook crossings, runs through Haystack Notch, the pass between Haystack Mtn. and the Speckled Mtn. Range. The trail is lightly used and in places requires care to follow. The middle section is in the Caribou–Speckled Mtn. Wilderness.

The west trailhead is on the east side of ME 113, 6.1 mi. south of the jct. of US 2 and ME 113 in Gilead, and 4.7 mi. north of WMNF Cold River CG. Roadside parking is available a short distance to the north or south.

Haystack Notch Trail shares its east trailhead with the north trailhead for Miles Notch Trail. To reach this trailhead, follow Flat Rd. south from US 2 opposite the West Bethel Post Office, and at 3.2 mi., turn right (west) on Grover Hill Rd. Stay straight at 0.5 mi. from Flat Rd. on Tyler Rd. (FR 5). Paving ends at 1.0 mi., and the surface changes to a narrow but sound gravel road that was passable for most vehicles in 2016, with a rough spot at the very end that might prevent low-clearance vehicles from driving all the way to the trailhead. At 2.4 mi. the road rises steeply, bears right at a fork, descends to cross Miles Brook on a bridge, then rises again over a rough spot to a grassy clearing at 2.5 mi. with a signboard and arrow, where the road continues to the left (southwest) past a WMNF gate. (Alternative parking is available on the right side of Tyler Rd. at 2.0 mi. and 2.4 mi.) Park here and continue on foot up the road past the gate for 0.1 mi., where the road emerges in a large brushy clearing with signs for Haystack Notch Trail and Miles Notch Trail on the right.

From the west trailhead on ME 113, the trail runs generally east along the East Branch of Evans Brook, crossing the branch and its south fork, then following its north fork, with three more crossings. The first crossing in particular may be difficult at high water. The trail enters the Wilderness at 1.3 mi. and climbs under the cliffs of Haystack Mtn. to the broad height-of-land in Haystack Notch at 2.1 mi. It then descends moderately through fine hardwood forest into the valley of the Pleasant River's West Branch, where the grade becomes easy. The trail leaves the Wilderness at 3.4 mi. and, at 4.4 mi., after crossing a tributary brook, makes the first of three crossings of the West Branch in the next 0.4 mi., which may be difficult at high water.

Beyond the crossings, the trail rises slightly to an open brushy area at 5.2 mi. Here it makes a diagonal crossing of a small gravel road at a point where the road curves sharply. The trail is very obscure in the brush on the far side of the road; do not follow the road descending to the left. About 50 yd. beyond, the trail turns left onto a grassy old logging road and follows it east and then northeast along the north edge of the large clearing, with views south to Miles Notch. At 5.4 mi. Haystack Notch Trail meets the northern end of Miles Notch Trail at the trail signs, 0.1 mi. southwest of the WMNF gate at the east trailhead. To reach the gate and trailhead, follow the logging road left (northeast). In the reverse direction, from the trail signs in the brushy clearing, Haystack Notch Trail begins as a faint track leading to the right (west) along the north side of the clearing, to the right of the signs. Bear left at a fork 80 yd. west of the trail signs, then bear right and downhill (small cairn, blaze) off the grassy logging road, 0.2 mi. from the trail signs. Cross the gravel road in 50 yd. and continue down into the woods.

SEC
6

■ SPECKLED MTN. (2,906 FT.), SPRUCE HILL (2,510 FT.), AND AMES MTN. (2,686 FT.)

This mountain lies east of Evans Notch, in Batchelders Grant and Stoneham. Speckled Mtn. is one of at least three mountains in Maine that are known by this name. The open summit ledges have excellent views in all directions. A spring is 0.1 mi. northeast of the summit, just off Red Rock Trail. Subsidiary peaks include Spruce Hill, Ames Mtn., and Blueberry Mtn.

SPRUCE HILL TRAIL (WMNF, CTA; MAP 6: F13)

Cumulative from ME 113 (1,425 ft.) to:	⇅	↗	⏱
Bickford Brook Trail (2,400 ft.)	1.9 mi.	1,150 ft.	1:30
Speckled Mtn. summit (2,906 ft.) via Bickford Brook Trail	3.1 mi.	1,650 ft.	2:25

This trail begins on the east side of ME 113, 7.5 mi. south of US 2 and 2.9 mi. north of Brickett Place, opposite the start of East Royce Trail. Spruce Hill Trail combined with Bickford Brook Trail forms the shortest route to the summit of Speckled Mtn. Most of this trail is in the Caribou–Speckled Mtn. Wilderness.

Spruce Hill Trail ascends moderately through woods, passing the Wilderness boundary sign at 0.6 mi., to reach the summit of Spruce Hill at 1.5 mi. The trail then descends into a sag and climbs to meet Bickford Brook Trail on the ridge crest west of Ames Mtn.

BICKFORD BROOK TRAIL (CTA; MAP 6: F12–F13)

Cumulative from ME 113 (600 ft.) to:	⇅	↗	⏱
Blueberry Ridge Trail, lower jct. (970 ft.)	0.7 mi.	350 ft.	0:30
Spruce Hill Trail (2,400 ft.)	3.1 mi.	1,800 ft.	2:25
Blueberry Ridge Trail, upper jct. (2,585 ft.)	3.8 mi.	2,000 ft.	2:55
Speckled Mtn. summit (2,906 ft.)	4.3 mi.	2,300 ft.	3:20

This trail ascends Speckled Mtn. from Brickett Place, a historical brick building (built by John Brickett in the early 1800s as part of his farmstead) that serves as a WMNF visitor center during summer. Brickett Place is on ME 113, 10.4 mi. south of US 2 and 8.1 mi. north of Stow Corner. Most of Bickford Brook Trail is in the Caribou–Speckled Mtn. Wilderness. The trail enters the woods near the garage adjacent to Brickett Place and climbs moderately. At 0.3 mi., it turns to the right onto an old WMNF service road built for access to the former fire tower on Speckled Mtn. (The trail follows this old road for the next 2.5 mi.) The trail soon enters the Wilderness, and at 0.7 mi., Blueberry Ridge Trail leaves on the right (east) for the lower end of Bickford Slides and Blueberry Mtn.; it rejoins Bickford Brook Trail 0.5 mi. below the summit of Speckled Mtn., affording the opportunity for a loop hike.

At 1.1 mi., the upper end of Bickford Slides Loop enters on the right. Bickford Brook Trail crosses a tributary at 1.5 mi., swings away from the main brook, and winds up a southwest spur to the crest of the main west ridge of the Speckled Mtn. Range, where Spruce Hill Trail enters from the left at 3.1 mi. Bickford Brook Trail then passes west and north of the summit of Ames Mtn. into the col between Ames Mtn. and Speckled Mtn., where Blueberry Ridge Trail rejoins from the right at 3.8 mi. Bickford Brook Trail then climbs steadily to the open summit of Speckled Mtn. The trail continues 30 yd. beyond the summit to a signed jct. with Red Rock Trail (straight ahead, northeast) and Cold Brook Trail (on the right, southeast).

COLD BROOK TRAIL (WMNF; MAP 6: F13–F14)

Cumulative from Adams Rd. (485 ft.) to:	↧↥	↗	↺
Evergreen Link Trail (1,175 ft.)	2.7 mi.	800 ft.	1:45
Speckled Mtn. summit (2,906 ft.)	4.9 mi.	2,500 ft.	3:40

This trail ascends Speckled Mtn. from the southeast and affords fine views from numerous open ledges in its upper part, which is in the Caribou–Speckled Mtn. Wilderness. Below the jct. with Evergreen Link Trail, Cold Brook Trail mostly follows logging roads on private land and is poorly marked. There has been extensive recent logging on parts of this section. The trailhead is reached from ME 5 in North Lovell, 2.0 mi. south of Keewaydin Lake, by following West Stoneham Rd. for 1.9 mi. and turning right onto Adams Rd. (Evergreen Valley Inn sign), just after the bridge over Great Brook. Continue to gravel-surfaced Enid Melrose Rd. on the right, 2.2 mi. from ME 5. The WMNF sign is on paved Adams Rd., where parking is very limited. It may be possible to drive 0.5 mi. on the rough Enid Melrose Rd. to a small parking spot on the right. The upper part of Cold Brook Trail can also be approached via Evergreen Link Trail, a shorter and much more attractive alternative to the lower section of Cold Brook Trail.

Beyond the parking area, from which hikers should proceed on foot, the road becomes rougher, and at 0.7 mi. from Adams Rd., Cold Brook Trail bears left past a gate. The next 1.0 mi. is on a road, muddy in places, that climbs and then circles at a nearly level grade to a cabin (the Duncan McIntosh House). Continuing ahead on the road, take the left fork, then the right. The trail descends to Cold Brook and crosses it at 1.9 mi., then crosses a logging yard, bearing right on the far side. The trail, which soon enters an area that has been extensively logged, may be difficult to follow due to diverging logging roads. It climbs moderately, crosses a branch brook, and passes west of Sugarloaf Mtn. The trail then climbs easily past

SEC 6

the WMNF boundary at 2.5 mi. to a jct. on the left at 2.7 mi. with Evergreen Link Trail (sign) from Evergreen Valley.

Cold Brook Trail ascends moderately, then swings left and climbs rather steeply up the southeast side of the south ridge of Speckled Mtn. The grade eases as the trail swings more to the north and emerges on semi-open ledges at 3.5 mi.; follow cairns and blazes carefully as the trail winds over ledges and through patches of scrub. The trail crosses an open ledgy area with excellent views south. It dips and passes a small pond on the left, then climbs to another open ledgy area. Above this fine viewpoint, the trail swings left across a ledgy shoulder and reenters the woods at 4.4 mi. It descends slightly, then ascends through dense conifers. At 4.9 mi., the trail emerges on semi-open ledges again and soon reaches a signed jct. with Red Rock Trail on the right and Bickford Brook Trail on the left; the summit of Speckled Mtn. is 30 yd. left (southwest) on Bickford Brook Trail.

EVERGREEN LINK TRAIL (WMNF; MAP 6: F13)

Cumulative from upper end of gravel parking lot (550 ft.) to:	⇅	↗	↻
Cold Brook Trail (1,175 ft.)	1.4 mi.	650 ft.	1:00
Speckled Mtn. summit (2,906 ft.) via Cold Brook Trail	3.6 mi.	2,350 ft.	3:00

This trail provides the easiest access to Speckled Mtn. via the scenic ledges on the upper Cold Brook Trail. Evergreen Link Trail is lightly used but easily followed by experienced hikers. To reach the trailhead, leave ME 5 in North Lovell, 2.0 mi. south of Keewaydin Lake, and follow West Stoneham Rd. northwest for 1.9 mi. Just beyond the bridge over Great Brook, turn right onto Adams Rd. (sign for Evergreen Valley) and follow it for 1.5 mi., passing the trailhead for Cold Brook Trail. Then turn right onto Mountain Rd. (sign for Evergreen Valley Inn); the trail begins as a gravel road diverging right 0.5 mi. from Adams Rd. Trailhead parking is available in a gravel parking area located a short distance along a side road to the left off Mountain Rd., 0.3 mi. from Adams Rd., or it may be possible to park at the inn (ask for permission) at 0.4 mi.

From either parking area (distances are given from the upper end of the gravel parking lot), follow paved Mountain Rd. uphill on foot; where it bears left at 0.1 mi., take the gravel road (soon blocked by a cable) straight ahead and climb steeply. At 0.5 mi., turn left onto a grassy logging road (arrow and yellow blaze), then right onto yellow-blazed Evergreen Link Trail proper at 0.8 mi. (sign: Speckled Mtn. via Cold Brook Trail). The trail crosses a woods road at 1.1 mi. and reaches Cold Brook Trail at 1.4 mi. (sign for Evergreen Link only); turn left for the ledges and Speckled Mtn.

■ BLUEBERRY MTN. (1,781 FT.)

This mountain, a long outlying spur extending southwest from Speckled Mtn. and Ames Mtn., has extensive open ledges offering fine views in all directions.

BLUEBERRY RIDGE TRAIL (CTA; MAP 6: F13)

Cumulative from Bickford Brook Trail, lower jct. (970 ft.), to:	↿⇂	↗	↻
Stone House Trail (1,780 ft.)	0.9 mi.	900 ft.	0:55
Bickford Brook Trail, upper jct. (2,585 ft.)	3.1 mi.	1,850 ft.	2:30

This route begins and ends on Bickford Brook Trail, leaving it at a sign 0.7 mi. from its trailhead at Brickett Place on ME 113 and rejoining it 0.5 mi. below the summit of Speckled Mtn. (The upper part of Blueberry Ridge Trail may also be reached from Stone House Rd. via Stone House or White Cairn trails.) Blueberry Ridge Trail is in the Caribou–Speckled Mtn. Wilderness.

Leaving Bickford Brook Trail, Blueberry Ridge Trail descends toward Bickford Brook, and at 0.1 mi., a graded spur descends 50 yd. to the right to a view of the Lower Slide from a high bank. In a short distance, the lower end of Bickford Slides Loop diverges left from Blueberry Ridge Trail, just before the latter crosses Bickford Brook. Take care to avoid several unofficial side paths in this area.

Bickford Slides Loop (CTA). This side path, 0.5 mi. long, leaves Blueberry Ridge Trail on the left just before Blueberry Ridge Trail crosses Bickford Brook, 0.1 mi. from its lower jct. with Bickford Brook Trail. About 20 yd. from its beginning, Bickford Slides Loop crosses Bickford Brook (may be difficult at high water) and climbs northeast alongside it for 0.2 mi., with three minor stream crossings. The loop climbs steeply over a low rise and descends to a jct. at 0.3 mi., where a short side path descends steeply left to a pool at the base of the Middle Slide. (The former continuation of this branching path up the steep west wall of the ravine has been abandoned.)

Bickford Slides Loop then climbs on a narrow, rough footway past the Middle and Upper Slides and drops sharply to cross the brook above the Upper Slide. Here, the loop turns sharply left and climbs easily to Bickford Brook Trail, 0.4 mi. above that trail's lower jct. with Blueberry Ridge Trail (ascent 400 ft., 25 min.). From the jct. with the spur to the Lower Slide and Bickford Slides Loop, Blueberry Ridge Trail crosses Bickford Brook (may be difficult at high water) and ascends steeply southeast past a good western outlook to an open area just over the crest of Blueberry Ridge, where White Cairn Trail enters from the right at 0.7 mi.

SEC 6

Overlook Loop (CTA). This side path, 0.4 mi. long, with excellent views to the south, leaves Blueberry Ridge Trail on the right after that trail's jct. with Stone House Trail. Overlook Loop runs nearly level out to the south cliffs of Blueberry Mtn., then loops back to the north and rejoins Blueberry Ridge Trail just before the latter drops over a ledge to the jct. with Stone House Trail on the right, at 0.9 mi.

From the jct. with Stone House Trail, marked by signs and a large cairn, Blueberry Ridge Trail bears left and descends gradually to a col. Here it bears right and ascends northeast and then north up the long ridge at easy to moderate grades, alternating through patches of spruce woods and across ledges with fine views, where the trail is marked by cairns. The best viewpoints are at 1.5 mi., 1.8 mi., and 2.5 mi. After crossing one more ledgy area at 2.8 mi., the trail swings right into spruce woods, climbs slightly, then turns right and descends to meet Bickford Brook Trail in the shallow pass at the head of the Rattlesnake Brook ravine, 0.5 mi. below the summit of Speckled Mtn.

STONE HOUSE TRAIL (CTA; MAP 6: F13)

From Stone House Rd./Shell Pond Trail (615 ft.) to:	⇅	↗	⟳
Blueberry Ridge Trail (1,780 ft.)	1.5 mi.	1,150 ft.	1:20

This trail ascends to the scenic ledges of Blueberry Mtn. from Stone House Rd. (formerly Shell Pond Rd.). The upper part of this trail is in the Caribou–Speckled Mtn. Wilderness. To reach the trailhead, leave NH 113 on the east side 1.3 mi. north of AMC's Cold River Camp and follow Stone House Rd. 1.1 mi. to a padlocked steel gate, where a parking area is on the right. The lower part of this route, including Rattlesnake Flume and Rattlesnake Pool, is on private land, and hikers are requested to stay on the marked trails.

The trail leaves the road (which here is also Shell Pond Trail) on the left (north), 0.5 mi. beyond the gate, east of an open shed. Stone House Trail follows a logging road and approaches Rattlesnake Brook. At 0.2 mi. from Stone House Rd., the trail merges with a private road (descending, bear right at arrow) and immediately reaches the jct. with a spur path that leads right 30 yd. to a bridge overlooking Rattlesnake Flume, a small, attractive gorge.

The main trail soon swings right (arrow), and at 0.5 mi., just after crossing a bridge over a small brook, another spur leads right 0.1 mi. to the exquisite Rattlesnake Pool, which lies at the foot of a small cascade. The main trail soon enters the WMNF, and at 1.2 mi., it swings left and begins to climb rather steeply straight up the slope, running generally northwest to the top of the ridge, where Stone House Trail ends at Blueberry Ridge Trail, only a few steps from the top of Blueberry Mtn. The eastern jct. with Overlook Loop is 30 yd. to the left up a ledge. For Speckled Mtn., turn right onto Blueberry Ridge Trail.

WHITE CAIRN TRAIL (CTA; MAP 6: F13)

From Stone House Rd./Shell Pond Trail (600 ft.) to:	⬆⬇	↗	↻
Blueberry Ridge Trail (1,750 ft.)	1.4 mi.	1,150 ft.	1:15

This trail, steep in places, provides access to the open ledges on Blueberry Mtn. and, with Stone House Trail, makes a rewarding half-day circuit. The upper part of this trail is in the Caribou–Speckled Mtn. Wilderness. The trail begins on Stone House Rd. (formerly Shell Pond Rd.), which leaves NH 113 on the east side 1.3 mi. north of AMC's Cold River Camp and runs 1.1 mi. to a padlocked steel gate, where parking is available on the right.

White Cairn Trail leaves Stone House Rd. (which is also Shell Pond Trail here) at a small clearing 0.3 mi. beyond the gate. The trail follows an old logging road north across a flat area then ascends moderately, entering the WMNF at 0.3 mi. from Stone House Rd. At 0.8 mi., the trail climbs steeply up a well-constructed rock staircase then turns sharply left and begins to climb on ledges along the edge of the cliffs that are visible from the road. The grade moderates as the trail runs northwest along the crest of the cliffs, with excellent views to the south.

At 1.2 mi., the trail passes a spring then swings right (north) at easy grades; follow cairns carefully as the trail winds through areas of ledge. The trail passes another spring just before ending at the jct. with Blueberry Ridge Trail, 0.2 mi. west of the upper terminus of Stone House Trail. Overlook Loop, which leaves Blueberry Ridge Trail just east of its jct. with White Cairn Trail, provides a scenic alternate route, 0.4 mi. long, to Stone House Trail.

SHELL POND TRAIL (CTA; MAP 6: G13)

From gate on Stone House Rd. (600 ft.) to:	⬆⬇	↗	↻
Deer Hill Rd. (755 ft.)	1.8 mi.	150 ft.	1:00

This trail runs between Stone House Rd. (formerly Shell Pond Rd.), at the locked gate 1.1 mi. from NH 113, and Deer Hill Rd. (FR 9), 3.5 mi. from NH 113 (limited roadside parking nearby). Stone House Rd. leaves NH 113 on the east side 1.3 mi. north of AMC's Cold River Camp. Much of

SEC 6

this trail is on private property, and hikers are requested to stay on the marked trails, especially in the vicinity of the Stone House. The trail itself does not come within sight of the pond, but Shell Pond Loop provides access to a viewpoint on the shore.

From the gate on Stone House Rd., continue east on the road on foot. Shell Pond Loop leaves right at 0.2 mi., and in another 80 yd., White Cairn Trail leaves left. At 0.4 mi., the road emerges at the side of a large field and soon turns right onto a grassy airplane landing strip. Here, at 0.5 mi., Stone House Trail diverges left, and the road ahead (not open to hikers) leads to a private house.

Shell Pond Trail soon swings left and heads east across the field, with good views of the surrounding mountains, passing to the right of the Stone House at 0.6 mi. The trail leaves the landing strip at 0.8 mi., entering a patch of woods to the left, and follows a grassy old road through an orchard. (The trail is not clearly marked in this area; in the reverse direction, bear left at a fork to reach the landing strip.) The trail crosses Rattlesnake Brook on a bridge at 1.1 mi., passes through a wet area, and turns left off the road at 1.2 mi., where Shell Pond Loop bears right. From here, Shell Pond Trail ascends gradually to Deer Hill Rd.

SHELL POND LOOP (CTA; MAP 6: F13–G13)

From western jct. with Shell Pond Trail (600 ft.) to:	↧↥	↗	○
Eastern jct. with Shell Pond Trail (610 ft.)	1.9 mi.	200 ft.	1:05

This trail skirts the south side of Shell Pond, making possible a pleasant loop hike in combination with Shell Pond Trail. Shell Pond Loop is almost entirely on private property and also serves as an ATV trail; hikers are requested to stay on the marked route, which leaves the south side of Shell Pond Trail 0.2 mi. east of the gate on Stone House Rd. (formerly Shell Pond Rd.) and leads through woods near the edge of a field, making several turns marked by yellow blazes.

At 0.2 mi., the trail turns right onto a grassy road, crosses a bridge over Shell Pond Brook, and soon swings left (east) on a well-worn woods road. It traverses the slope well above the south shore of Shell Pond, with several minor ups and downs. At 1.3 mi., the trail turns left off the road and descends, then meanders through the woods behind the east shore of the pond, crossing several small brooks. At 1.7 mi., a spur path leads 25 yd. left to a clearing and a bench with a fine view across the pond to the Baldfaces and Mt. Meader. Shell Pond Loop bears right here and continues at easy grades to Shell Pond Trail, 0.6 mi. west of the latter's eastern trailhead on Deer Hill Rd. and 1.2 mi. from the gate on Stone House Rd.

■ DURGIN MTN. (2,440 FT.), BUTTERS MTN. (2,246 FT.), RED ROCK MTN. (2,141 FT.), AND MILES KNOB (2,090 FT.)

This group of lightly visited mountains forms the long ridge extending east from Speckled Mtn. into the heart of the Caribou–Speckled Mtn. Wilderness as far as Miles Notch.

MILES NOTCH TRAIL (WMNF; MAP 6: E14–F14)

Cumulative from southern terminus (490 ft.) to:	↥↧	↗	⟳
Red Rock Trail (1,740 ft.)	3.2 mi.	1,800 ft.	2:30
WMNF gate (900 ft.)	5.5 mi.	1,800 ft.	3:40

This yellow-blazed trail runs through Miles Notch, giving access to the east end of the long ridge that culminates in Speckled Mtn. The trail is lightly used and sparsely marked, and in places requires care to follow. Future logging activity is planned on the southern 1.5 mi. To reach the trail's southern trailhead, leave ME 5 in North Lovell 2.0 mi. south of Keewaydin Lake, on West Stoneham Rd., and follow that road northwest for 1.8 mi. Then turn right onto Hut Rd. just before the bridge over Great Brook. Continue 1.5 mi. to the trailhead (sign), where parking is available on the left. To reach the northern trailhead for Miles Notch Trail, refer to the directions for the eastern trailhead of Haystack Notch Trail.

From the southern trailhead, the trail climbs north on an old logging road, soon bearing left (sign: no ATVs) as a snowmobile trail bears right and downhill. At 0.3 mi., the trail bears left off the old road (arrow), then climbs over a small ridge and descends steadily northeast into the valley of Beaver Brook. At 1.2 mi., at the bottom of the descent, the trail turns left onto another old logging road and follows it for 0.2 mi., then bears right off the road and soon crosses a branch of Beaver Brook. The trail climbs steadily, crosses Beaver Brook at 2.3 mi., and continues to ascend the east side of the valley through an ice-damaged area where undergrowth may obscure the footway.

The trail runs along the gully of a small brook, then turns left away from the brook and reaches Miles Notch at 2.9 mi.; while ascending to the notch, the cliffs of Miles Knob up to the left are in view. Just north of the notch, the trail enters the Caribou–Speckled Mtn. Wilderness. The trail now descends gradually along the east side of a ravine, and at 3.2 mi., Red Rock Trail leaves on the left for the summit of Speckled Mtn. Miles Notch Trail soon leaves the Wilderness and descends moderately, making six crossings of the various branches of Miles Brook. The trail bears left onto a grassy logging road at 4.6 mi. (in the reverse direction, bear right off the road at an arrow) and swings left down through a clearing to cross Miles Brook at 5.0 mi. It ascends slightly across a drainage dip and past a road forking to the right, then continues on the main road into the large brushy clearing (with a view of Caribou Mtn.), where the trail meets the eastern end of Haystack Notch Trail at the trail signs. Follow the logging road northeast for 0.1 mi. to reach the WMNF gate at the northern trailhead. In the reverse direction, from the trail signs in the brushy clearing 0.1 mi. southwest of the WMNF gate, Miles Notch Trail begins as a grassy, two-track road leading ahead (south) across the clearing.

RED ROCK TRAIL (WMNF; MAP 6: F13–F14)

Cumulative from Miles Notch Trail (1,740 ft.) to:	�??↑	↗	○
Red Rock Mtn. summit (2,141 ft.)	1.2 mi.	550 ft.	0:55
Butters Mtn. summit (2,246 ft.)	2.5 mi.	850 ft.	1:40
Great Brook Trail (2,000 ft.)	3.4 mi.	850 ft.	2:15
Durgin Mtn. summit (2,404 ft.)	4.4 mi.	1,250 ft.	2:50
Speckled Mtn. summit (2,906 ft.)	5.6 mi.	1,900 ft.	3:45

This trail ascends to Speckled Mtn. from Miles Notch Trail 0.3 mi. north of Miles Notch, 3.2 mi. from its southern trailhead, and 2.2 mi. from its northern trailhead. Red Rock Trail traverses the long eastern ridge of the Speckled Mtn. Range, affording fine views of the surrounding mountains. The trail is lightly used, sparsely marked, and in places requires great care to follow. This entire trail is in the Caribou–Speckled Mtn. Wilderness.

Red Rock Trail leaves Miles Notch Trail, descends to cross Miles Brook in its deep ravine, then angles up the north slope of Miles Knob and gains the ridge crest northwest of that summit. The trail descends to a col, then ascends to the east knob of Red Rock Mtn., where it passes an obscure side path that leads left 50 yd. downhill to a spectacular ledge viewpoint (potentially dangerous if wet or icy) at the top of the sheer south cliffs of Red Rock Mtn.; the side path leaves the trail 10 yd. east of a more obvious path that leads to a ledge with a limited view. Red Rock Trail continues to the ledgy true summit of Red Rock Mtn. at 1.2 mi., which provides a view to the north.

A short distance beyond the summit, at a ledge with a view southwest, the trail swings right and descends over more ledges to the Red Rock–Butters col. The trail crosses the col (avoid a beaten path leading to the right through the col) then ascends to the east knob of Butters Mtn. The trail follows the ridge, with several ups and downs, passing near the summit of Butters Mtn. at 2.5 mi. and then continuing on to the next sag to the west. Here, at 3.4 mi., Great Brook Trail diverges left (east) and descends southeast to its trailhead, which is very close to the southern trailhead of Miles Notch Trail.

Beyond, Red Rock Trail swings southwest and climbs to the summit of Durgin Mtn. and ledges with some outlooks (the best is located on an obscure side path just before the high point) at 4.4 mi. The trail descends easily to a notch, climbs sharply, then ascends generally southwest to the signed jct. with Cold Brook Trail (on the left) and Bickford Brook Trail (straight ahead); the latter trail leads 30 yd. southwest to the summit of Speckled Mtn. There's a spring near the trail, about 0.1 mi. east of the summit.

GREAT BROOK TRAIL (WMNF; MAP 6: F13–F14)

Cumulative from trailhead on Hut Rd. (500 ft.) to:	⇅	↗	⏱
Red Rock Trail (2,000 ft.)	3.7 mi.	1,500 ft.	2:35
Speckled Mtn. summit (2,906 ft.) via Red Rock Trail	5.9 mi.	2,600 ft.	4:15

SEC 6

This trail ascends to Red Rock Trail east of Speckled Mtn. The upper part of Great Brook Trail is in the Caribou–Speckled Mtn. Wilderness; this section is sparsely marked, requires care to follow, and has poor footing in places. To reach the trailhead, leave ME 5 in North Lovell, 2.0 mi. south of Keewaydin Lake, on West Stoneham Rd. and follow that road northwest for 1.8 mi. Turn right just before the bridge over Great Brook onto Hut Rd. (FR 4; paved, then gravel) and continue 1.5 mi. to the trailhead, which is just before a gate, about 100 yd. past the southern trailhead for Miles Notch Trail. (*Note:* The WMNF plans to relocate this trailhead in the near future to the next gate on FR 4, 0.8 mi. north of the present trailhead.)

Great Brook Trail follows the gravel road north past the gate, and at 0.8 mi. it passes a second gate (the location of the future trailhead, with parking available near a small cascade) and crosses Great Brook on a bridge. At times in the past, the first gate has been open, making it possible to drive to the second gate. About 80 yd. past the bridge, the trail turns right onto FR 823, an extension of FR 4. (Avoid an older road that diverges right just after the bridge and another road that continues ahead where the trail turns right.) At 1.6 mi., the older road rejoins from the right (bear right here on the descent).

At a fork at 1.9 mi., the trail turns left onto a grassy older road and follows Great Brook, passing a stone wall, cellar hole, and gravesite marking the mid-1800s homestead of the Butters family on the left at 2.1 mi., just before crossing a tributary brook. The trail narrows to a footpath and, at 2.5 mi., crosses Great Brook, with some interesting cascades below and above the crossing. In another 0.1 mi. the trail enters the Wilderness, then bears left (arrow) and climbs, steeply at times, keeping well above the brook. At the head of the valley, the trail crosses the brook twice and soon reaches the ridge crest, where Great Brook Trail meets Red Rock Trail in the col between Butters Mtn. and Durgin Mtn.

REST OF WMNF AND EVANS NOTCH

■ THE ROOST (1,364 FT.)

This small hill in Batchelders Grant Township offers fine views of the Wild River and Evans Brook valleys.

ROOST TRAIL (WMNF; MAP 6: E13)

Cumulative from ME 113, north trailhead (820 ft.) to:	⇅	↗	○
The Roost (1,374 ft.)	0.5 mi.	550 ft.	0:30
ME 113, south trailhead (850 ft.)	1.2 mi.	550 ft.	0:55

This trail starts from two trailheads 0.7 mi. apart on the east side of ME 113. The north trailhead (sign, parking on shoulder) is 2.9 mi. south of US 2. The south trailhead is 0.2 mi. south of Hastings CG and 0.1 mi. north of Forest Route 8/Little Lary Brook Rd.

Leaving the north trailhead, the trail ascends a steep bank for 90 yd., then bears right (east) and ascends gradually along a wooded ridge, rejoining an older route of the trail at 0.1 mi. Roost Trail crosses a small brook at 0.3 mi., then rises somewhat steeply, swings right, and emerges on a ledge at the Roost summit (no views) at 0.5 mi. Here, a spur trail descends steeply for 0.1 mi. and then 150 ft. right (southwest) through woods to spacious open ledges, where the views are excellent. The main trail descends generally southeast from the summit at a moderate grade and crosses a small brook, then turns right (southwest) on an old road (no sign) and follows it past a cellar hole and a brushy area back to ME 113.

WHEELER BROOK TRAIL (WMNF; MAP 6: E13)

From US 2 (680 ft.) to:	⇅	↗	○
Gate on Little Lary Brook Rd./FR 8 (1,240 ft.)	3.5 mi.	1,350 ft.	2:25

There are two trailheads for this wooded, viewless trail. Find the northern trailhead on US 2, 7.7 mi. west of the jct. of ME 26 and US 2 in Bethel, and 2.2 mi. east of the jct. of US 2 and ME 113 in Gilead. Parking along the south shoulder of US 2 is limited. For the southern trailhead, from US 2 in Gilead, drive south on ME 113 for 3.7 mi. to FR 8 (Little Lary Brook Rd.) on the left. Proceed east on this road for 1.8 mi. to its end at a gate and parking. The trail is lightly used and requires care to follow.

From US 2, the trail follows a gated, grassy logging road (FR 711) south, soon crossing an old woods road and then passing junctions with another woods road on the right and a snowmobile trail on the left. Wheeler Brook Trail enters the WMNF at 0.3 mi., bears left on a grassy road, and joins and follows Wheeler Brook, crossing it four times.

The trail turns left (arrow) at a logging road fork at 1.0 mi., just before the third crossing of the brook. It rises steadily to its highest point, a little more than 2,000 ft., at the crest of the northwest ridge of Peabody Mtn. (2,462 ft.) at 2.1 mi. (There is no route to the wooded summit of Peabody Mtn.) The trail then descends generally southwest, merges onto an old logging road (FR 8) that comes down from the left, and reaches Little Lary Brook Rd. Turn left onto Little Lary Brook Rd. and continue about 100 yd. to a locked gate beyond the bridge over Little Lary Brook, 1.6 mi. from ME 113.

To hike the trail in the reverse (west to east) direction: From the locked gate at the end of Little Lary Brook Rd., walk west on the old road, cross a bridge and hike uphill. About 100 yd. from the gate and parking, reach an unsigned jct. Here, where FR 185 goes straight, turn sharply right uphill on FR 8. Wheeler Brook Trail (arrow) leaves the left side of the old road in another 0.3 mi.

■ EAST ROYCE MTN. (3,114 FT.) AND WEST ROYCE MTN. (3,210 FT.)

The Royces rise to the west of Evans Notch and Cold River. East Royce Mtn. is in Batchelders Grant Township, and West Royce Mtn. is in Bean's Purchase, New Hampshire.

ROYCE TRAIL (AMC; MAP 6: F12)

Cumulative from ME 113 (600 ft.) to:

	⇅	↗	⟳
Mad River Falls (900 ft.)	1.6 mi.	300 ft.	0:55
Laughing Lion Trail (2,200 ft.)	2.7 mi.	1,600 ft.	2:10
Royce Connector Trail (2,650 ft.)	2.9 mi.	2,050 ft.	2:30
Burnt Mill Brook Trail (2,610 ft.)	3.6 mi.	2,150 ft.	2:55
West Royce Mtn. summit (3,210 ft.)	4.3 mi.	2,750 ft.	3:30

This trail runs to the summit of West Royce Mtn. from its start on the west side of ME 113, opposite Brickett Place (a USFS information center), 10.4 mi. south of US 2 and 2.6 mi. north of AMC's Cold River Camp.

The first two crossings of the Cold River are difficult in high water. Leaving ME 113, the trail follows a narrow road for about 0.3 mi., bears right where another road joins from the left, then crosses the Cold River and bears off the road to the right onto a yellow-blazed footpath. The trail recrosses the river at 0.7 mi., crosses a tributary at 1.1 mi., and crosses the river again at 1.3 mi.

Then, after crossing the West Branch of the Mad River, the trail rises more steeply and soon passes Mad River Falls, where a side path leads left 25 yd. to a viewpoint. The trail climbs moderately up the valley, passing several cascades as it comes back near the Mad River. Then it becomes rather rough and rises steeply under the imposing ledges for which East Royce Mtn. is famous. At 2.7 mi., Laughing Lion Trail enters from the right, and at a height-of-land at 2.9 mi., after a very steep and rough ascent, Royce Connector Trail branches right, leading to East Royce Trail for East Royce Mtn.

Royce Connector Trail (AMC). This short trail, 0.2 mi. long (50 ft. ascent, 10 min.), links Royce Trail and East Royce Trail, permitting the ascent of either summit of Royce from either trail, crossing some ledges with restricted views.

Royce Trail bears left at this jct. and descends somewhat, crossing a small brook, then climbs to the height-of-land between the Royces at 3.6 mi., where Burnt Mill Brook Trail to Wild River Rd. diverges right. Here, Royce Trail turns abruptly left (west) and zigzags up the steep wall of the pass, turns sharply left (southeast), then swings more to the southwest. The trail climbs moderately up the ridge over ledges and through stunted spruce, crossing a ledge with a view east at 4.1 mi. It passes side paths to two more outlooks on the left shortly before reaching the summit area of West Royce Mtn., where the trail meets Basin Rim Trail.

LAUGHING LION TRAIL (CTA; MAP 6: F12–F13)

From ME 113 (1,370 ft.) to:	⇵	↗	↻
Royce Trail (2,200 ft.)	1.1 mi.	1,000 ft.	1:05

This trail, which begins on the west side of ME 113, 2.0 mi. north of Brickett Place, extends to Royce Trail. Parking is available at a small parking area on the west side of the road.

Laughing Lion Trail (sign) starts from the north end of the parking area, passes an old gate, and follows the left side of the guardrail. The trail descends to and then crosses Cold River (here, a rather small brook) before ascending west to a ridge crest, which it follows north. With alternating moderate and steep sections, the trail passes two outlooks on the left looking down the valley. It then swings west and levels off just before ending at Royce Trail.

EAST ROYCE TRAIL (AMC; MAP 6: F12–F13)

Cumulative from ME 113 (1,420 ft.) to:	⤵⤴	↗	○
Royce Connector Trail (2,610 ft.)	1.0 mi.	1,200 ft.	1:05
Ledge at end of East Royce Trail (3,070 ft.)	1.3 mi.	1,650 ft.	1:30

This trail climbs steeply to East Royce Mtn. from a parking area on the west side of ME 113, just north of the height-of-land in Evans Notch and 2.9 mi. north of Brickett Place.

Leaving the parking area, the trail immediately crosses Evans Brook and ascends, soon swinging left to cross a brook on ledges at the top of a fine cascade. The trail continues up, steeply at times, crossing several other brooks in the first 0.5 mi. At the final brook crossing at 1.0 mi., Royce Connector Trail leaves on the left, leading in 0.2 mi. to Royce Trail for West Royce Mtn.

After ascending a steep and rough section with several scrambles, East Royce Trail emerges on open ledges at 1.1 mi. with a view east to Speckled Mtn. The trail soon reaches a subsidiary summit with views to the south, then turns right and climbs to a broad open ledge at 1.3 mi. with wide-ranging views, where the plainly marked trail ends. An unmaintained path continues north 0.2 mi. along the summit ridge, dropping off a ledge, crossing several ledgy knobs (including the true summit), and ending at a ledge with a USFS radio repeater and wide views west and north.

■ ALBANY MTN. (1,930 FT.)

On the eastern edge of the WMNF is a cluster of low hills, with Albany Mtn. being the highest and the only one with trails. Views from its open summit ledges are excellent in all directions.

SEC 6

ALBANY MTN. TRAIL (WMNF; MAP 6: F14–F15)

Cumulative from FR 18 (820 ft.) to:	⇅	↗	◔
Spur trail to summit of Albany Mtn. (1,740 ft.)	1.5 mi.	900 ft.	1:10
Albany Notch (1,500 ft.)	1.9 mi.	900 ft.	1:25
Trailhead on Birch Ave. (750 ft.)	4.4 mi.	950 ft.	2:40
Cumulative from north trailhead (820 ft.) to:			
Albany Mtn., northeast outlook, via Albany Mtn. Trail and Spur (1,925 ft.)	1.9 mi.	1,100 ft.	1:30
Cumulative from south trailhead (750 ft.) to:			
Albany Mtn., northeast outlook, via Albany Mtn. Trail and Spur (1,925 ft.)	3.3 mi.	1,200 ft.	2:15

This yellow-blazed trail provides access to ledges and views on Albany Mtn. from trailheads to the north and the south. Due to extensive beaver flooding north of Albany Notch, a 1.1-mi. section of Albany Notch Trail has been abandoned, and the remainder of that trail—0.6 mi. on the north end, 2.5 mi. on the south end, and a 0.4-mi. connecting path—has been combined with Albany Mtn. Trail into a single through route under the name of Albany Mtn. Trail, with Albany Mtn. Spur leading to the summit of Albany Mtn. (Trail signs for Albany Notch Trail may still be present until new signage is in place.)

The southern section, which is located partly on old, rather overgrown logging roads, is poorly marked, wet in places, and requires care to follow. Logging activity is planned for the near future south of Albany Notch. Most use of this trail is on the northern end, which is well maintained, with many recent volunteer-built improvements, and provides the easiest access to Albany Mtn.

To reach the north trailhead, follow Flat Rd., which leads south from US 2 opposite the West Bethel Post Office and becomes FR 7 (gravel, not plowed in winter) when it enters the WMNF at 4.5 mi. At 5.8 mi., turn right on FR 18, following signs for WMNF Crocker Pond CG. The trailhead parking lot and kiosk are on the right in another 0.6 mi.

The north trailhead can also be reached from ME 5, just south of Songo Pond, by turning west onto Patte Brook Rd., which becomes FR 7. At 2.8 mi., turn left onto FR 18 and follow it 0.6 mi. to the trailhead on the right. The south trailhead is reached by leaving ME 5 at the west end of Keewaydin Lake, 2.4 mi. west of the East Stoneham Post Office and 0.7 mi. east of the Lovell–Stoneham town line, and following Birch Ave. north. Bear right on Birch Ave. at 0.4 mi. from ME 5; the trail begins at a sign at 1.0 mi., where pavement ends and the road ahead becomes gravel, narrow, and rough. The trail begins in a residential area, but parking is available in a dirt lot on the right, by the end of pavement; parking is extremely limited beyond this point.

Leaving the parking lot for the north trailhead on FR 18, Albany Mtn. Trail follows an old logging road, with one relocation up to the left. At 0.4 mi. it turns left on another relocation, then in 75 yd. turns right, crosses an old beaver dam, and reenters the woods. It swings left at 0.5 mi. and bears left again at 0.6 mi. toward Albany Mtn., where the abandoned section of Albany Notch Trail continues ahead. Albany Mtn. Trail now ascends moderately southwest, crosses a brook at 1.0 mi., swings left, and climbs through several turns to a signed jct. at 1.5 mi.

Here, Albany Mtn. Spur diverges left, soon crossing a ledge with a view of the Moriahs and Mt. Washington over the treetops. It winds upward at easy grades across ledges and through stands of red pine and reaches an open ledge with restricted northeast views near the summit of Albany Mtn. at 0.4 mi. from the main trail, where blazing ends. The best view here is found by descending 50 yd. east to the ledges at the edge of the ridge-crest. The best views on the mountain are from the southwest ledges, reached by a well-defined path marked by cairns, easy to follow for experienced hikers. From the ledge where the blazed trail ends, this path leads south 100 yd. across ledges to the true summit, marked by a larger cairn. Here the path turns right (west) and descends, then swings back to the south and slabs along the west side of the ridge with minor ups and downs, crossing several ledges with views west. It ends at an open ledge with wide views south and west, 0.3 mi. from the end of the blazed trail.

At the jct. with Albany Mtn. Spur, Albany Mtn. Trail turns sharply right (west), rises slightly, then descends moderately for 0.4 mi. to the height-of-land in Albany Notch; partway down, the trail crosses a ledge with a view west. In the notch, the trail turns sharply left (south); in the reverse direction, be sure to make this right turn where the abandoned section of Albany Notch Trail continues ahead. Albany Mtn. Trail now descends moderately, with a steeper pitch just below the pass, and crosses two small brooks; this section may be overgrown. The trail then runs at easy grades until it reaches a logging road used as a snowmobile trail at 2.6 mi., and turns left on this road. (If ascending from the south, turn sharply right off the road onto a narrow footpath leading into the woods, just before the road dips to cross a small brook; the arrow marking this turn is easily missed.)

This road is fairly easy to follow, but is very wet in places and overgrown with tall grasses and other vegetation that permit little evidence of a footway. At 3.0 mi., the trail bears right off the logging road onto an older road (arrow), which is also wet and overgrown. At 3.3 mi., the newer road rejoins from the left. The trail soon passes a WMNF gate and then merges with a gravel road that joins from the left. The trail passes a branch road on the right (in the reverse direction, bear right at this fork) and a camp on the left, crosses Meadow Brook at 3.8 mi., and climbs gradually past several private homes and camps to the trailhead on Birch Ave.

ALBANY BROOK TRAIL (WMNF; MAP 6: F15)

From WMNF Crocker Pond CG (830 ft.) to:	⇅	↗	⟳
Round Pond (790 ft.)	1.0 mi.	100 ft.	0:35

This short, easy trail follows the shore of Crocker Pond and then leads to attractive, secluded Round Pond. In 2016 the WMNF began upgrading the first 0.2 mi. for universal accessibility. Logging activity is planned for the near future along parts of this trail. Albany Brook Trail begins at the turnaround at the end of FR 18, the main road at Crocker Pond CG (do not enter the actual camping area), 0.9 mi. south of the north trailhead for Albany Mtn. Trail; see that trail description for driving directions.

Leaving the west side of the turnaround, the trail descends around to the left and follows the west shore of Crocker Pond for 0.2 mi., makes a short and moderate ascent, then runs along the lower east slope of Albany Mtn. with minor ups and downs. It then descends, crosses an old logging road at 0.9 mi. with a clearing visible on the right, and soon reaches the north end of Round Pond.

■ HARNDON HILL (1,395 FT.), LORD HILL (1,257 FT.), AND PINE HILL (1,250 FT.)

This compact group of hills just west of Horseshoe Pond in Stoneham, Stow, and Lovell can be climbed via an intricate network of three trails.

CONANT TRAIL (CTA; MAP 6: G13)

From trailhead off Deer Hill Rd. (550 ft.) to:	⇅	↗	⟳
Complete loop over Pine Hill and Lord Hill via Conant Trail	5.2 mi.	1,050 ft.	3:10
From trailhead off Deer Hill Rd. (550 ft.) to:			
Loop over Lord Hill via north branch of Conant Trail and Mine Loop	4.3 mi.	850 ft.	2:35

This loop trail to Pine Hill and Lord Hill is an interesting and fairly easy walk with several good outlooks. Much of Conant Trail, especially the south loop, is on private land. The trail is frequently referred to (and may be signed as) Pine-Lord-Harndon Trail, though it does not go particularly close to the summit of Harndon Hill. Do not confuse this trail with Conant Path, a short trail (not open to the public) near AMC's Cold River Camp. Conant Trail is reached by following Deer Hill Rd. (FR 9) from NH 113, 0.7 mi. south of AMC's Cold River Camp, and making a right turn onto FR 9A, 1.5 mi. from NH 113. The best parking is at a four-way jct. about 100 yd. from Deer Hill Rd., where there is a sign for North Barbour Rd. There may be a trail sign here.

Continue on foot along the road that leads east (left at the four-way jct.), soon descending to the dike across swampy Colton Brook. Beyond the dike, the yellow-blazed trail continues on a gravel road to the loop jct. at 0.4 mi., where the path divides. From here, the trail is described in a counterclockwise direction. The south branch, also a snowmobile route, turns right and follows a logging road (Hemp Hill Rd.). At 0.7 mi., the trail reaches a road section that leads through an area of beaver activity that had been flooded but in 2016 was once again dry and passable. Beyond, the road climbs to a level spot at 1.0 mi. near the old Johnson cellar hole. Here the trail turns left on a logging road, then left again in a few steps.

Conant Trail swings right and then left again at 1.2 mi. and ascends Pine Hill, rather steeply at times, passing a ledge with a fine view west at 1.4 mi. Here the trail turns right and climbs to the west end of the summit ridge and continues to the most easterly knob, which has a good view north, at 2.0 mi. The trail swings left off the ledges and zigzags steeply down through hemlock forest. It crosses Bradley Brook at 2.3 mi. and then quickly crosses a logging road that can be followed 0.2 mi. left to Mine Loop Trail, 0.4 mi. below the mine on Lord Hill. Conant Trail then climbs moderately to an outlook over Horseshoe Pond. Here, the trail turns left and climbs ledges to a jct. near the summit of Lord Hill at 3.0 mi., where Mine Loop leaves on the left.

Mine Loop. This path is 1.0 mi. long, 0.1 mi. shorter than the section of Conant Trail it bypasses. Except for the one critical turn mentioned later, Mine Loop is fairly easy to follow. From the jct. with Conant Trail near the summit of Lord Hill, Mine Loop climbs briefly to the ledge at the top of the old mica mine, swings left then quickly right onto a woods road, descends 40 yd., and turns left at 0.1 mi., where a spur path leads right 30 yd. to the mine. The trail soon swings right, and at 0.3 mi., turns sharply left on a clear logging road. At 0.5 mi., the trail reaches a fork and turns sharply right back onto a less-used branch road (sign), a turn that is easily missed. (The main road, continuing straight at this fork, crosses Conant

Trail between Pine Hill and Lord Hill in 0.2 mi. and continues south toward Kezar Lake.) Mine Loop descends to a flat area and climbs easily over a shoulder. At a clearing, the trail leaves the road on the right and descends 50 yd. to rejoin Conant Trail 1.1 mi. from its trailhead (ascent 100 ft., rev. 250 ft., 35 min.).

From Lord Hill, Conant Trail descends, with one tricky drop over a ledge, to the jct. with Horseshoe Pond Trail on the right at 3.2 mi. Here, the trail bears left then left again through a gap in a stone wall and runs at a fairly level grade, with minor ups and downs, along the south side of Harndon Hill. The trail passes a cellar hole, and Mine Loop rejoins on the left at 4.1 mi. At 4.5 mi., the road passes a gate, becomes wider (in the reverse direction, avoid logging roads branching to the right), passes a cemetery on the right, reaches the loop jct., and continues straight ahead across the dike to the trailhead.

HORSESHOE POND TRAIL (CTA; MAP 6: G13)

From Deer Hill Rd. (700 ft.) to:	⇅	↗	○
Conant Trail (1,115 ft.)	1.1 mi.	500 ft.	0:50

This yellow-blazed trail starts from Deer Hill Rd. (FR 9), 4.7 mi. from NH 113 at a small pull-off at a curve in the road. It ends on Conant Trail, 0.2 mi. north of the ledges near the summit of Lord Hill. The former Horseshoe Pond Loop is now closed to public use, so there is no public trail access to the shore of this pond.

From Deer Hill Rd., the trail descends moderately for 0.1 mi. past the Styles grave, which is on the right of the trail and is enclosed by a stone wall. Then it turns right onto a gravel logging road. The trail follows this road, keeping straight at a jct. in 100 yd. At 0.3 mi., the trail turns right onto a grassy road that leads up into a brushy area and ascends through a regenerating area. The trail continues ascending moderately to the southwest through woods to Conant Trail.

■ LITTLE DEER HILL (1,090 FT.) AND BIG DEER HILL (1,367 FT.)

Rising southwest of Shell Pond, these low hills are crisscrossed by six interconnected trails that provide several miles of pleasant hiking in close proximity to AMC's Cold River Camp.

DEER HILLS TRAIL (CTA; MAP 6: G12–G13)

Cumulative from ME 113 at Baldface Circle Trail parking area (500 ft.) via Deer Hills Connector to:	⇅	↗	↺
Little Deer Hill summit (1,090 ft.)	1.3 mi.	650 ft.	1:00
Big Deer Hill summit (1,367 ft.)	2.0 mi.	1,100 ft.	1:35
Deer Hills Bypass, eastern jct. (1,025 ft.)	2.5 mi.	1,100 ft.	1:50
Deer Hill Rd. (530 ft.)	3.3 mi.	1,100 ft.	2:10

This trail ascends Little Deer Hill and Big Deer Hill, providing a relatively easy trip that offers interesting views. The trail runs from a jct. by the Cold River, near AMC's Cold River Camp, to Deer Hill Rd. (FR 9), 1.4 mi. from NH 113. Roadside parking is limited.

Deer Hills Connector. Access to the north end of the trail is from Baldface Circle Trail (refer to AMC's *White Mountain Guide*) trailhead parking area on the east side of NH 113 (0.2 mi. north of the entrance to AMC's Cold River Camp) via a yellow-blazed path called Deer Hills Connector. Deer Hills Connector (yellow blazes, no sign in 2016) leaves the east side of the lot, runs level for 150 yd., then turns left down a short pitch and descends gradually on the south side of Charles Brook, in an area where the trail was eroded by Tropical Storm Irene in 2011. Deer Hills Connector passes an unmarked private path on the right at 0.3 mi. and reaches a dam on the Cold River at 0.4 mi. Here, a trail from AMC's camp enters on the right (this trail is not open to the public). At this jct., Deer Hills Trail begins; distances given here include those traveled on Deer Hills Connector.

Deer Hills Trail crosses Cold River on the dam abutments (may be difficult in high water). In the reverse direction, after crossing the dam, turn right onto Deer Hills Connector (at the sign: Baldface Parking Lot). The trail soon passes the jct. on the left with Leach Link Trail, crosses the state line into Maine, and quickly passes the jct. on the right with Deer Hills Bypass. Deer Hills Trail continues straight ahead and climbs moderately past an outlook west, then bears left onto ledges and reaches the open summit of Little Deer Hill at 1.3 mi., where there is a fine view of the Baldfaces. Here, Frost Trail enters on the right, having ascended from Deer Hills Bypass.

Deer Hills Trail descends into a sag, then climbs to a point near the summit of Big Deer Hill at 2.0 mi. Here, the trail turns right, descends 40 yd., and turns right again where there is a fine eastern outlook 20 yd. to the left. The trail then descends the south ridge, passing another outlook, and

SEC 6

turns left at 2.5 mi., where Deer Hills Bypass leaves on the right. Soon Deer Hills Trail turns left again, then turns right onto an old logging road at 2.7 mi. Here, a spur path (sign) follows the logging road left for 20 yd., then turns right and descends in 0.2 mi. and 150 ft. to Deer Hill Spring, a shallow pool with air bubbles rising through a small area of light-colored sand. The main trail descends south from the jct. to Deer Hill Rd.

DEER HILLS BYPASS (CTA; MAP 6: G12–G13)

From western jct. with Deer Hills Trail (460 ft.) to:	↧↥	↗	↻
Eastern jct. with Deer Hills Trail (1,025 ft.)	1.4 mi.	650 ft.	1:00

This trail skirts the south slopes of the Deer hills, making possible various loop hikes over the summits. Deer Hills Bypass leaves Deer Hills Trail on the right (southeast), just east of the Cold River Dam, and follows a level grassy road along the river. At 0.4 mi., Deer Hills Bypass turns left off the road and soon ascends a steep ledge with a view west. The trail swings left, and at 0.6 mi., Ledges Trail leaves left, and Deer Hills Bypass climbs steadily alongside a stone wall. At 0.8 mi., Frost Trail leaves left, climbing 0.15 mi. and 150 ft. to the summit of Little Deer Hill, passing a jct. left with Ledges Trail 70 yd. before the summit. Deer Hills Bypass descends into a shallow ravine, crosses two small brooks, and ascends again. The trail soon turns left onto a woods road, follows it for 0.1 mi., then turns left off it (both turns are marked with signs and arrows). The trail then ascends easily to rejoin Deer Hills Trail on the south ridge of Big Deer Hill, 0.5 mi. below the summit.

LEDGES TRAIL (CTA; MAP 6: G12)

From Deer Hills Bypass (730 ft.) to:	↧↥	↗	↻
Little Deer Hill summit (1,090 ft.)	0.3 mi.	350 ft.	0:20

This trail passes interesting ledges and a cave but is very steep and rough, dangerous in wet or icy conditions, lightly used, and not recommended for descent. The trail diverges left from Deer Hills Bypass, 0.6 mi. from the Cold River Dam, and climbs steeply with several outlooks. At 0.2 mi., Ledges Trail divides: the left branch (sign: Ledges Direct) ascends through a small cave, while the slightly longer right branch (sign: By-Pass) loops out through the woods, then swings left across an excellent outlook ledge and rejoins the left branch in 140 yd. About 40 yd. above the point where these branches rejoin, Ledges Trail meets Frost Trail, a connecting path from Deer Hills Bypass. The summit of Little Deer Hill is 70 yd. left on Frost Trail.

LEACH LINK TRAIL (CTA; MAP 6: F12–G12)

From Stone House Rd. (540 ft.) to:	⇕	↗	↻
Deer Hills Trail (450 ft.)	1.2 mi.	0 ft.	0:35

This trail gives access to Little Deer Hill and Big Deer Hill from Stone House Rd. (formerly Shell Pond Rd.), which leaves NH 113 on the east side 1.3 mi. north of AMC's Cold River Camp. The trail starts at a gated road on the right side of Stone House Rd. 0.3 mi. from NH 113; roadside parking is available. The northern part of the route uses the former Shell Pond Brook Trail.

Beyond the gate, Leach Link Trail follows a grassy road across a snow-mobile bridge over Shell Pond Brook. At 0.2 mi., the trail turns right off the road (sign), then in another 50 yd. bears left and runs through hemlock woods along a bank high above the brook. The trail then descends, and at 0.5 mi., it turns left where the former route of the trail came across the brook from the right. The trail continues south along the Cold River at easy grades and ends at Deer Hills Trail a few steps east of Cold River Dam. To ascend the Deer hills, turn left onto Deer Hills Trail.

SEC 6

SECTION 7
OXFORD HILLS

Pull-Out Map
Map 6: Mahoosuc Range–Evans Notch

INTRODUCTION

This section, on the Oxford Hills, includes much of central and southern Oxford County and the part of Androscoggin County west of the Androscoggin River. To the north, the region is bounded by US 2 and the Androscoggin River as far west as Bethel. The Androscoggin River also constitutes the eastern boundary as the river turns south at Jay on its run through the urban environs of Auburn and Lewiston to eventually merge with the Kennebec River at Merrymeeting Bay in Topsham. The Cumberland County line and the Fryeburg town line form the southern boundary. To the west, the region is bounded by the New Hampshire border and the western boundary of the Maine portion of the White Mountain National Forest, which is roughly outlined by ME 5 and Kezar Lake, and then ME 5/35 between Lovell and Bethel.

This section describes 28 trails on 17 mountains in the Oxford Hills. Most of the trails in this section are on private property and are open for public use through the generosity of various landowners. Notable exceptions include a portion of the trail on Bald Mtn. and the loop trail on Sabattus Mtn., which are on state land managed by the Maine Bureau of Parks and Lands.

GEOGRAPHY

SEC 7

The Oxford Hills extend west from the Androscoggin River to the WMNF boundary. Among the scattered lakes, ponds, streams, and rivers are a series of mountains generally ranging in elevation from around 1,000 ft. to a little more than 2,200 ft. Sabattus Mtn. (1,253 ft.) is east of Kezar Lake in Center Lovell. The sweeping granite cliffs of its south face afford big views to Pleasant Mtn., the Baldfaces, and the White Mountains. A few miles north, east of the Upper Bay of Kezar Lake in North Lovell, is Heald and Bradley Ponds Reserve, a pleasant 802-acre preserve owned and managed by Greater Lovell Land Trust. The reserve is home to three small mountains: Amos Mtn. (995 ft.), Whiting Hill (801 ft.), and Flat Hill (891 ft.). West of pretty Keoka Lake in Waterford is Mt. Tire'm (1,104 ft.); on its summit are fine examples of old stone walls. In the shadow of Mt. Abram and its ski slopes, rising above the tranquil shores of South Pond in Greenwood, is Maggie's Nature Park, 86 town-owned acres where a lovely network of color-coded trails crisscross the slopes of Ring Hill (1,095 ft.) and Peaked Mtn. (1,250 ft.). Nearby, adjacent to North Pond, are the impressive cliff faces of Buck's Ledge (1,200 ft.) and Lapham Ledge (1,100 ft.).

Just south of Rumford and the Androscoggin River, straddling the town lines of Milton Township and Peru, is Mt. Zircon (2,240 ft.), the highest peak in the Oxford Hills, which affords wonderful panoramic views from its summit ledges. Straddling the town lines of Woodstock and Peru, rising steeply above Little Concord Pond and Shagg Pond, is Bald Mtn. (1,692 ft.), with its precipitous cliffs, and the craggy mountaintop of Speckled Mtn. (2,183 ft.). To the east, straddling the Sumner and Peru town lines, is Black Mtn. (2,133 ft.), a broad, flat mass with five distinct summits running roughly east to west. Directly south in Paris is Crocker Hill (1,374 ft.), which hikers climb via an old carriage road. Also in Paris, the open ledges high on the south side of Singepole Mtn. (1,420 ft.) offer fine views. Just east in Hebron is Streaked Mtn. (1,770 ft.), well known for its distinctive west face of steep granite slabs. Bear Mtn. (1,208 ft.) in Hartford, the easternmost of the Oxford Hills with a trail, looks out over Bear Pond.

ROAD ACCESS

SEC 7

Trailheads are scattered far and wide across the Oxford Hills. Connecting Bethel and Lovell, ME 5 is the major road at the western edge of the region and is useful for access to Sabattus Mtn. and the hills of the Heald and Bradley Ponds Reserve. Just east, ME 35 and ME 37 provide access to Mt. Tire'm in Waterford. ME 26 is a busy highway that slices across the Oxford Hills from the southeast at Oxford northwest to Bethel. From ME 26, hikers can access the trails at Maggie's Nature Park and Buck's Ledge in Greenwood. From ME 26 in South Paris, use ME 177 to get to Crocker Hill, Singepole Mtn., and Streaked Mtn. Use US 2 or ME 219 to get to trailheads for Mt. Zircon, Black Mtn., Bald Mtn., and Speckled Mtn. in the Milton and Peru area. Bear Mtn. is best accessed from ME 4 in Livermore.

CAMPING

There are about a dozen privately-operated campgrounds in the Oxford Hills region.

HEALD AND BRADLEY PONDS RESERVE

This 802-acre conservation land in Lovell, a property of Greater Lovell Land Trust, includes more than 1 mi. of shoreline on Heald Pond and more than 0.5 mi. on Bradley Pond. A 9-mi. network of trails extends through the reserve and reaches the summits of three hills: Amos Mtn., Whiting Hill, and Flat Hill.

SUGGESTED HIKES

■ Easy

WHITING HILL

	↻↑	↗	○
LP via Whiting Hill Trails, Westways Spur, Red and Blue Trail, Blue Trail, Red Trail, and Otter Rocks Spur	2.3 mi.	350 ft.	1:20

Enjoy views of Kezar Lake and Mt. Kearsarge then visit Otter Rock on Heald Pond. To begin, see Whiting Hill Trails, p. 292.

SABATTUS MTN.

	↻↑	↗	○
LP via Sabattus Mtn. Trail	1.6 mi.	550 ft.	2:10

This fine loop hike to the sweeping cliffs atop Sabattus Mtn. offers views from Pleasant Mtn. to the Presidential Range. See Sabattus Mtn. Trail, p. 294.

RING HILL

	↻↑	↗	○
LP via Ring Hill Loop Trail	1.1 mi.	300 ft.	0:40

This woodland loop hike through Maggie's Nature Park features ledges and views of Mt. Abram. See Ring Hill Loop Trail, p. 295.

SEC 7

BUCK'S LEDGE

	↻↑	↗	○
LP via Buck's Ledge Trail	2.8 mi.	650 ft.	1:30

Enjoy impressive cliff-top views from open ledges overlooking scenic North Pond. See Buck's Ledge Trail, p. 297.

MT. TIRE'M

	↻↑	↗	○
RT via Daniel Brown Trail	1.4 mi.	600 ft.	1:20

Hike to a beautiful vista overlooking Keoka Lake. See Daniel Brown Trail, p. 300.

CROCKER HILL

		🔃	↗	⟳
RT via Crocker Hill Trail		1.8 mi.	475 ft.	1:20

Follow Old Crocker Hill carriage road then a footpath to fine views over the central Oxford Hills. To begin, see Crocker Hill Trail, p. 301.

STREAKED MTN.

		🔃	↗	⟳
RT via Streaked Mtn. Trail		1.2 mi.	740 ft.	1:20

Hike distinctive granite slabs to panoramic views from Streaked Mtn.'s extensive summit ledges. See Streaked Mtn. Trail, p. 302.

■ Moderate

BALD MTN. AND SPECKLED MTN.

		🔃	↗	⟳
RT via Bald Mtn. Trail and Speckled Mtn. Trail		4.6 mi.	1,350 ft.	4:20

Hike past Little Concord Pond to Bald Mtn.'s cliffs then on to craggy Speckled Mtn.'s open ledges with extensive views. To begin, see Bald Mtn. Trail, p. 298.

MT. ZIRCON

		🔃	↗	⟳
RT via Mt. Zircon Trail		5.6 mi.	1,630 ft.	4:30

Hike past the springhouse of the old Zircon Water Bottling Company en route to a downed fire tower on the open summit of Mt. Zircon, with exceptional views south and east. See Mt. Zircon Trail, p. 304.

■ Strenuous

The Oxford Hills area does not have any strenuous hikes.

TRAIL DESCRIPTIONS

HEALD AND BRADLEY PONDS RESERVE AND VICINITY

■ AMOS MTN. (995 FT.)

Rising west of Bradley Pond and north of Heald Pond, this mountain is the highest and most northerly in the reserve. Follow driving directions for Whiting Hill. From the parking area opposite Westways Rd., continue north on ME 5 for 1.3 mi. to trailhead parking in the woods on the right. This parking lot is locally known as the "Cemetery Parking Lot."

AMOS MTN. TRAILS (GLLT; USGS CENTER LOVELL AND NORTH WATERFORD QUADS, GAZETTEER MAP 10, GLLT HEALD AND BRADLEY PONDS RESERVE MAP)

Cumulative from ME 5 trailhead (500 ft.) to:	⇅	↗	○
Amos Mtn. summit (955 ft.)	1.0 mi.	455 ft.	0:45
Complete loop	1.9 mi.	455 ft.	1:10

This loop over Amos Mtn. combines Blue Trail, Orange Trail, Green Trail, and Opi's Trail. An unnamed trail leaves the end of the parking lot on the left and follows white markers with red dots. The trail soon crosses a low stone wall and, 100 ft. beyond, reaches a jct. Take a sharp right turn (easy to miss, as a wide trail continues straight ahead) onto Blue Trail. At 0.2 mi., the trail crosses a brook on a footbridge then climbs gradually beyond it. The trail reaches a jct. at 0.35 mi., with Blue Trail continuing straight ahead and Orange Trail going to the right. Go right on Orange Trail. Ahead, at the base of low cliffs, Orange Trail bears right and then sharply left, steeply uphill beside the cliff face. Partway up, Orange Trail goes left again, up a mossy crevice in the rocks. This is the Devil's Staircase; just above it, the cliff-bypass route goes right and down. Continue up and left, weaving through rocks to reach a T jct., where Green and Orange trails head right. Go left to stay on Orange Trail and make a rising traverse to another T jct. at 0.7 mi. Turn right here on Blue Trail (sign: Amos Mtn. summit). Ahead at 0.8 mi., where a purple-blazed connector trail goes straight (to El Pulpito, a large boulder), continue right and up on Blue Trail. Blue Trail climbs a ledge step to a small rocky meadow and the jct. with Green Trail, which enters from the right at 0.9 mi. Turn left on the merged Blue Trail and Green Trail to quickly reach the wooded summit of Amos Mtn., which features a cairn and bench.

SEC 7

Start down the west side of Amos Mtn. on the obvious grassy forest road; there are no trail markers for a while. At 1.1 mi., reach a jct. with a foot trail on the left: Opi's Trail. Leave the woods road here and hike the path (marked with purple dots) to a jct. at several boulders, large and small ("El Pulpito"). From here, go right and descend on tight switchbacks. Reach a T jct. with Blue Trail at 1.3 mi.; go right and downhill from here. In another 0.1 mi., pass an old wooden corner post set in rocks. At 1.5 mi., close the loop at the jct. with Orange Trail. Follow Orange Trail straight ahead, then Blue Trail, to return to the trailhead.

■ WHITING HILL (801 FT.)

Rising directly west of Heald Pond, this hill is the most southerly and lowest of the three in the Heald and Bradley Ponds Reserve. From the jct. of ME 93 and ME 5 in Lovell, drive north on ME 5 for 6.7 mi. to the trailhead parking area on the right, immediately opposite Westways Rd. (En route, you'll pass Slab City Rd. on the right at 6.3 mi.; this is the turnoff leading to the Flat Hill trailhead.)

WHITING HILL TRAILS (GLLT; USGS CENTER LOVELL AND NORTH WATERFORD QUADS, GAZETTEER MAP 10, GLLT HEALD AND BRADLEY PONDS RESERVE MAP)

Cumulative from ME 5 (510 ft.) to:	⇅	↗	↻
Whiting Hill summit (801 ft.) via short spur	0.7 mi.	290 ft.	0:30
Heald Pond (471 ft.) via Red Trail and Otter Rocks Spur	1.2 mi.	290 ft.	0:45
Complete loop	2.3 mi.	350 ft.	1:20

This loop over Whiting Hill to Heald Pond combines Westways Spur, Red and Blue Trail, Blue Trail, Red Trail, and Otter Rocks Spur.

Westways Spur (green markers) leaves the parking area just left of the kiosk. Follow the old forest road, which soon peters out into a trail of mossy rocks. In 0.2 mi., reach an unsigned jct., where an unmarked trail enters sharply from the right. Continue straight/slightly left, and at 0.3 mi., arrive at a T jct. (The loop hike returns to this jct.) Turn left to continue to Whitten Hill. A short distance ahead, make a sharp right turn on an old forest road and hike uphill, now following red and blue paint blazes and dots. Ahead, climb to the left of jumbled ledges and boulders. Reach a jct. at 0.6 mi. A spur path leads 200 ft. to the wooded summit, from which Whiting Overlook is another 50 ft. to the right, marked by a cairn and a bench. The view is westerly and takes in Kezar Lake and Mt. Kearsarge.

Return to the main trail and continue to the right, descending to the northeast. At 0.7 mi., Red Trail departs to the left. Continue straight on Blue Trail, which heads downhill to join an old forest road then slabs down the mountainside. Reach a grassy woods road and jct. at 0.95 mi. To get a look (and maybe a swim) at Heald Pond, head left on Red Trail for 0.1 mi. then turn right onto Otter Rock Spur. In another 500 ft., reach the west shore of Heald Pond at the obvious Otter Rock.

From Otter Rock, retrace your steps back to the jct. of Red and Blue Trail and Red Trail. Follow the woods road south and, at 1.8 mi., reach a jct. and kiosk. Straight ahead, the road leads to a boat launch and parking at the south end of Heald Pond. Instead, turn sharply right and head gradually uphill. The path levels off then uses a footbridge to cross a wet area. Close the loop at 2.0 mi. then turn left to return to the trailhead on ME 5.

■ FLAT HILL (891 FT.)

This hill east of Bradley Pond and Heald Pond is the most easterly of the three peaks in the reserve. Refer to the driving directions for Whiting Hill. From the jct. of ME 5 and Slab City Rd., at a point 6.3 mi. north of the jct. of ME 5 and ME 93 in Lovell, turn east on Slab City Rd. Pass the southern end of Heald Pond and, at a fork in 1.2 mi., bear left on the dirt-surface Heald Pond Rd. and follow it 2.0 mi. to trailhead parking at the end of the road.

FLAT HILL TRAIL
(GLLT; USGS NORTH WATERFORD QUADS, GAZETTEER MAP 10,
GLLT HEALD AND BRADLEY PONDS RESERVE MAP)

Parking at end of Heald Pond Rd. (530 ft.) to:	↥↧	↗	⟳
Flat Hill summit (891 ft.)	0.7 mi.	360 ft.	0:30

Flat Hill Trail starts across the road from the kiosk. Following purple dots, it soon crosses a small creek on a footbridge then follows an old forest road. At a fork in 0.1 mi., go right toward Flat Hill (Perky's Path is to the left) and begin a gradual ascent. In a tiny clearing with a cairn and arrow posted on a tree at 0.4 mi., Flat Hill Trail bears right. After a moderate stretch where the angle eases, bear left at the trail arrows and continue at an easier grade onto the ridge. The path ends at a small rocky outcrop with a view to the west, toward the White Mountains.

■ SABATTUS MTN. (1,253 FT.)

From the top of the immense cliffs on the southwest face of Sabattus Mtn. in Lovell, hikers will enjoy extensive views ranging from Pleasant Mtn. to the Baldfaces on the eastern edge of the White Mountains. The trail and protection of the mountain is a joint partnership between the MBPL and Greater Lovell Land Trust.

SABATTUS MTN. TRAIL (MBPL; USGS NORTH WATERFORD QUAD, GAZETTEER MAP 10, MTF SABATTUS MTN. MAP)

Cumulative from Sabattus Trail Rd. (700 ft.) to:	⇅	◸	↻
Sabattus Mtn. summit (1,253 ft.)	0.9 mi.	500 ft.	0:40
Complete loop	1.6 mi.	550 ft.	1:05

From the jct. of ME 5 and ME 93 in Lovell, drive north on ME 5 for 4.5 mi., through the village of Center Lovell, to Sabattus Rd. Reset odometer. Turn right on Sabattus Rd. and continue to a fork at 1.5 mi. Bear right onto Sabattus Trail Rd. and drive 0.7 mi. on this dirt road to the trailhead parking lot (sign) on the right.

The loop trail splits 200 ft. into the woods. Take the left fork and climb steadily, gradually at first and then moderately, with occasional switchbacks. Reach the summit ridge, and in a small opening with a large outcrop, bear sharply right at an easy grade to reach an outlook and a large outcrop of white quartzite. Pass another viewpoint to reach the site of the old fire tower on the summit. (Attached to one of the concrete stanchions is a memorial to Steven Hickey, a local young man who died while trying to save his brother after a boating accident.) Just below, in the opening at the top of the cliff, is a park bench, an unusual find on a mountaintop. The views take in numerous ponds and Pleasant Mtn. to the south and extend as far as Mt. Washington and the Presidential Range to the west. A second park bench is just below.

To descend, return to the tower site and bear left. Sabbatus Mtn. Trail descends easily at first and then moderately to the base of the mountain before closing the loop and returning to the parking area.

GREENWOOD–WOODSTOCK–PERU

■ RING HILL (1,095 FT.) AND PEAKED MTN. (1,250 FT.)

Mahoosuc Land Trust maintains an interconnected system of color-coded trails on Ring Hill and adjacent Peaked Mtn. in Greenwood. Ring Hill is part of Maggie's Nature Park, an 86-acre woodland preserve donated to the town by Maggie Ring, a lifelong resident.

From the post office in Bryant Pond, at the jct. of Railroad St. and North Main St. (ME 26), drive north on ME 26 for 3.4 mi. to the jct. with Howe Hill Rd. (sign for the Mt. Abram ski area). Turn left onto Howe Hill Rd., cross the railroad tracks, and turn left onto Greenwood Rd. Follow it for 1.4 mi. to trailhead parking on the right (sign).

RING HILL LOOP TRAIL (MLT; USGS BRYANT POND QUAD, GAZETTEER MAP 10, MTF MAGGIE'S NATURE PARK MAP)

Cumulative from Greenwood Rd. (750 ft.) to:	⬍	↗	↺
Ledges (1,050 ft.)	0.7 mi.	300 ft.	0:25
Complete loop	1.1 mi.	300 ft.	0:40

This trail circumnavigates Ring Hill, which rises west of South Pond. Starting to the right of the kiosk at the back of the parking lot, follow orange blazes 50 ft. to a jct. Bear right to hike Ring Hill Loop Trail (also referred to as Harriet's Path) counterclockwise. Pass Maggie's Path on the left; ahead at 0.2 mi., Abner's Path (blue blazes) leaves right. Just beyond, pass Mae's Path (green blazes) on the right. Cross the upper end of Abner's Path and head gradually uphill, switchbacking several times. At 0.6 mi., the trail levels off and soon reaches an open ledge with good views of Mt. Abram. Cross the ledge and descend to the left. After several switchbacks, cross Abner's Path again at 0.8 mi. Abner's Path continues to the right, leading to Peaked Mtn. Trail and on to the summit of Peaked Mtn. in about 0.6 mi. Continue downhill on Ring Hill Loop Trail. At 1.0 mi., Maggie's Path (purple blazes) leaves left. Beyond, close the loop and reach the parking area at 1.1 mi.

ABNER'S PATH (MLT; USGS BRYANT POND QUAD, GAZETTEER MAP 10, MTF MAGGIE'S NATURE PARK MAP)

Cumulative from Greenwood Rd. (730 ft.) to:	⬍	↗	↺
Start of trail via Ring Hill Loop Trail (800 ft.)	0.2 mi.	70 ft.	0:10
High point on east slope of Ring Hill (1,000 ft.)	0.5 mi.	270 ft.	0:25
Peaked Mtn. Trail (970 ft.)	0.8 mi.	300 ft.	0:35

Abner's Path, also referred to as Alternate Loop Trail, starts from Ring Hill Loop Trail at a point 0.2 mi. north of the trailhead. From this jct., blue-blazed Abner's Path makes a rising traverse around the north slope of Ring Hill, passing Mae's Path on the left before reaching the jct. with Ring Hill Loop Trail at 0.4 mi. Beyond, Abner's Path takes a mildly undulating route across the east slope of Ring Hill to a saddle between Ring Hill and

SEC 7

Peaked Mtn. at 0.7 mi., where it crosses Ring Hill Loop Trail again. Continuing on, Abner's Path ends at its jct. with Peaked Mtn. Trail at 0.8 mi.

PEAKED MTN. TRAIL (MLT; USGS BRYANT POND QUAD, GAZETTEER MAP 10, MTF MAGGIE'S NATURE PARK MAP)

Cumulative from Greenwood Rd.
(730 ft.) to:

	⇅	↗	↻
Peaked Mtn. summit (1,250 ft.) and ledges	0.9 mi.	520 ft.	0:45
Complete loop and return to trailhead	1.8 mi.	520 ft.	1:10

This trail climbs to the summit ledges of Peaked Mtn., just south of Ring Hill. Leave the far end of the parking lot, away from the kiosk, following yellow blazes. In 100 yd., turn right off the woods road and head uphill into the woods on a foot trail. Climb gradually via switchbacks to the lower jct. with Ledge Trail (red blazes) on the left at 0.3 mi. Pass Abner's Path (blue blazes) on the right at 0.4 mi., and the upper jct. of Ledge Trail on the left at 0.5 mi.

Arrive at a blue-painted stake at 0.5 mi. that marks the boundary of Maggie's Nature Park. Beyond, the ridge levels off, and a jct. with the summit loop is reached at 0.6 mi. Continue straight ahead on the old woods road, trending easily up along the ridgeline. At 0.9 mi., make a sharp left (unmarked trail to right). The summit of Peaked Mtn. and a series of ledges with nice views of Mt. Abram are just ahead. Beyond, leave the ledges and descend briefly, then remain on a contour before closing the loop at the jct. at 1.2 mi. Turn right and retrace your steps to the parking area, which is at 1.8 mi.

LEDGE TRAIL (MLT; USGS BRYANT POND QUAD, GAZETTEER MAP 10, MTF MAGGIE'S NATURE PARK MAP)

This short 0.2-mi. path makes a nice loop to ledges offering good views east over North Pond and South Pond and to Buck's Ledge and Lapham Ledge. The trail is best hiked from its upper jct. with Peaked Mtn. Trail, which is 0.4 mi. from the trailhead on Greenwood Rd. Following red blazes, descend 0.1 mi. to a spur leading 100 ft. right to the ledges. From the spur jct., continue left on a contour, then switchback down to rejoin Peaked Mtn. Trail 0.3 mi. from the trailhead.

■ BUCK'S LEDGE (1,200 FT.) AND LAPHAM LEDGE (1,100 FT.)

On the southwest ridge of Moody Mtn. in Woodstock, Buck's Ledge offers good views west over North Pond and South Pond to the ski trails on Mt. Abram, and on the peaks of Evans Notch and the White Mountains beyond.

From the post office in Bryant Pond, at the jct. of Railroad St. and North Main St. (ME 26), drive north on ME 26 for 1.4 mi. to a gravel woods road (the trail) on the right just before a small house. Park along the side of ME 26 south of the house and the woods road, taking care not to block the woods road.

BUCK'S LEDGE TRAIL AND LAPHAM LEDGE TRAIL (WCC; USGS BRYANT POND QUAD, GAZETTEER MAP 10, MTF BUCK'S AND LAPHAM LEDGES MAP)

Cumulative from ME 26 (750 ft.) to:	⥮	↗	↻
Side trail to Lapham Ledge (900 ft.)	0.5 mi.	150 ft.	0:15
Lapham Ledge (1,100 ft.) via side trail	1.0 mi.	350 ft.	0:40
Buck's Ledge (1,200 ft.)	1.2 mi.	450 ft.	0:50
Complete loop via Mann Rd. and ME 26	2.8 mi.	650 ft.	1:45

Immediately pass a small sign and register box. Beyond, pass through an old gate and follow the woods road north uphill. At 0.5 mi., reach a jct. with a foot trail on the right (sign and orange flagging) that leads an easy 0.5 mi. to Lapham Ledge and good views south to Bryant Pond and the surrounding hills.

Continuing ahead on the woods road, pass through a clearing (old log yard) and bear left off the road at a sign for Buck's Ledge at 0.6 mi. At 0.7 mi., bear sharply right onto the wide trail and soon begin to climb moderately. Then, after a short, steep climb, reach the top of the ledges at 1.2 mi. Continue along the ledges, passing several viewpoints, before descending steeply to a jct. with Mann Rd. at 1.5 mi., just above the shore of North Pond. Turn left and follow the road south. Reach a jct. with Rocky Rd. and ME 26 just ahead at 2.5 mi. Walk the shoulder of ME 26 to return to the trailhead at 2.8 mi.

■ BALD MTN. (1,692 FT.)

This mountain is in the northeastern corner of Woodstock, near Shagg Pond. Together with neighboring Speckled Mtn. to the east, Bald Mtn. offers interesting hiking with good cliff-top and summit views.

From the jct. of ME 26 and ME 219 in West Paris, go east on ME 219 for 4.8 mi. to Tuell Hill Rd. and turn left. Take this road to where it dead-ends and turn left onto Redding Rd. Follow Redding Rd. for 3.4 mi. to

Shagg Pond. Continue along the road for 0.5 mi. to two parking areas on the left at the top of the hill.

BALD MTN. TRAIL (MBPL; USGS MT. ZIRCON QUAD, GAZETTEER MAP 11, MTF LITTLE CONCORD POND STATE PARK MAP)

Cumulative from Redding Rd. (970 ft.) to:	⇅	↗	⟳
Little Concord Pond jct. (1,110 ft.)	0.4 mi.	140 ft.	0:15
Bald Mtn. summit and ledges (1,692 ft.) via Bald Mtn. Loop	1.0 mi.	725 ft.	0:50

Bald Mtn. Trail begins across the road from the parking area and follows an old road into the woods gradually uphill for 0.4 mi. As Little Concord Pond comes into view, the trail reaches a jct. Straight ahead, a short side trail leads to the pond. Bald Mtn. Trail (blue-blazed) turns sharply right onto a foot trail and, just ahead, makes another sharp right (here, an unmaintained trail bears left along the edge of the pond), climbing up over the rocks.

The trail levels off near the ridge crest and soon reaches a jct. with Bald Mtn. Loop Trail. The loop trail (0.2 mi., yellow-blazed) heads right, follows the summit ledges, and reenters the woods before returning to this jct. with Bald Mtn. Trail. (Speckled Mtn. Trail departs left from this jct.) The loop offers excellent views over Shagg Pond to the White Mountains.

■ SPECKLED MTN. (2,183 FT.)

Speckled Mtn. lies to the east of Bald Mtn. in Peru. The route to Speckled Mtn. from the summit of Bald Mtn. drops steeply into a col and then follows the ridge to the Speckled Mtn. summit, with extensive views in all directions. Speckled Mtn. can also be climbed from the north via Speckled Mtn. Pasture Trail.

SPECKLED MTN. TRAIL (MBPL; USGS MT. ZIRCON QUAD, GAZETTEER MAP 11)

From Bald Mtn. ledges (1,692 ft.) to:	⇅	↗	⟳
Speckled Mtn. summit (2,183 ft.)	1.3 mi.	650 ft.	1:00

From the jct. with Bald Mtn. Loop Trail, Speckled Mtn. Trail descends steeply to a col and a small stream. In 0.3 mi., it joins a blazed survey line for about 50 ft., passing a survey rock en route. The trail bears right off the survey line into the woods and soon crosses a flat ledge. At 0.8 mi., in a level area, it bears right toward a yellow survey blaze (ignore the old blue blaze straight ahead) and ascends steeply over the ledges of Speckled Mtn.

with views to the west. The trail makes a final steep climb to the summit ridge and reaches the metal pole on top of Speckled Mtn. at 1.3 mi.

SPECKLED MTN. PASTURE TRAIL
(NFTM; USGS MT. ZIRCON QUAD, GAZETTEER MAP 11)

Cumulative from Dickvale Rd. (800 ft.) to:	↥↧	↗	↻
Logging haul road (1,200 ft.)	1.7 mi.	400 ft.	1:05
Base of east ridge (1,600 ft.)	2.2 mi.	800 ft.	1:35
Speckled Mtn. summit (2,183 ft.)	3.2 mi.	1,400 ft.	2:25

Speckled Mtn. Pasture Trail offers a direct approach to the mountain instead of the route from Bald Mtn. From ME 108 in West Peru, turn right onto Main St. Go through West Peru, staying on Main St., which becomes Dickvale Rd. in 4.3 mi. Continue on Dickvale Rd. until the pavement ends at 4.8 mi. Park on the side of the road. The trail starts to the left behind a gate. (*Note:* This trail is quite overgrown in places and hard to follow.)

The trail begins as a gated, grassy road (sign: Dearles Orchard) and soon reaches a structure resembling a dog house on the right. Another road joins from the left at 0.5 mi. (This road leads to an old log yard, now a grown-in clearing. When descending, it is easy to mistake this converging road for the actual route. Take care.) At a four-way jct. at 0.9 mi., bear right onto the roadbed (sign: No ATVs) and emerge into a cutover area. Beyond the four-way jct., where the more-obvious road bears right and ascend to a private camp, Speckled Mtn. Trail continues straight, making a quick transition to a very grassy and overgrown road with no footbed (in places, evergreen boughs extend into the trail, making the way rather obscure). In a short distance, the trail reaches a line of boulders and is briefly overtaken by young hardwoods and thorny growth. Pushing through through the thick brush, reemerge on the grassy track. The ground is swampy and the footing poor, as tall grass obscures ruts and uneven terrain, although there is a nice view of the ridge. At 1.6 mi., the trail reaches a stone wall and bears left to join a new skid road. (On the return trip, it is easy to miss this right turn right.) Following this road a short distance reaches a section of significant flooding that requires care to pass. Just beyond the flooding, the route reaches a T intersection and joins a wide haul road at 1.7 mi. Speckled Mtn. Pasture Trail goes right and passes several red posts hidden by hard-wood growth then takes a quick left onto a yellow-blazed path. (This turn is easy to miss due to low boughs but quite obvious once you leave the haul road.) The path is heavily eroded and marked with yellow boundary blazes and occasional orange flagging. The trail reaches ledges with nice views

SEC 7

and then reenters the woods (sign: Caution). After crossing ledges, the trail passes a fire pit with a grill and becomes a very narrow footbed, tight and obscure at times, following cairns and occasional flagging. Once the trail passes to the side of a false summit, the cairns and flagging lead briefly downhill on a discreet footbed. Soon the path levels out then ascends on open rock, following cairns to the summit at 3.2 mi.

WATERFORD–NORWAY–PARIS–BUCKFIELD

■ MT. TIRE'M (1,104 FT.)

Mt. Tire'm in Waterford offers an easy hike that yields good views of the Long Lake region.

DANIEL BROWN TRAIL
(NFTM; USGS WATERFORD FLAT QUAD, GAZETTEER MAP 10)

From Plummer Hill Rd. (510 ft.) to:	↧↥	↗	↻
Mt. Tire'm summit (1,104 ft.)	0.7 mi.	600 ft.	0:40

From the jct. of ME 35 and ME 37 in the center of Waterford, drive south on the combined ME 35/37 for just 100 yd. Turn right (northwest) onto Plummer Hill Rd. and follow it uphill for 500 ft. On the left, a stone wall and a plaque set into a rock (hard to see) mark the start of the Daniel Brown Trail (also often referred to as Old Squire Brown Trail). Parking is along the left side of the road on the wide dirt shoulder.

Take the wide trail uphill into the woods, following the line of the stone wall on the left. The path is not blazed but is well defined and easy to follow. The trail contours up the east side of the hill through the forest, with occasional glimpses of Keoka Lake. Soon after, it reaches a viewpoint overlooking Bear Pond, Bear Mtn., and Long Lake. Just ahead on the summit ledges are views to Pleasant Mtn. and the ski trails on Shawnee Peak. Explore around the summit area to find a number of old stone walls in remarkable condition.

■ CROCKER HILL (1,374 FT.)

Crocker Hill in Paris is the site of the 1868 panorama of the White Mountains painted by George L. Vose, a Bowdoin College professor of civil engineering, and offers fine views of the surrounding countryside and other mountains. Leave from Paris Hill Rd. in Paris, just north of Paris Hill Country Club, and turn right (east) onto Lincoln St. (which soon becomes Mt. Mica Rd.). At 1.1 mi., turn left onto Thayer Rd., and proceed 0.7 mi. to where the road turns left. Limited parking is along the shoulder.

CROCKER HILL TRAIL
(NFTM; USGS WEST SUMNER QUAD, GAZETTEER MAP 11)

From Thayer Rd. (900 ft.) to:	↧↥	↗	↻
Crocker Hill summit (1,374 ft.)	0.9 mi.	475 ft.	0:40

The Old Crocker Hill carriage road leaves from beyond the gate (sign: Crocker Hill Tree Farm). At 0.2 mi., the road makes a sweeping left turn where a snowmobile trail continues straight ahead. Stay left to follow the carriage road. Crocker Hill Trail ascends gradually and then veers sharply right on a switchback. A few yards after the switchback is an old mine shaft. Soon, the trail switchbacks to the left once more. The view to the left is partially obscured by trees, and a short walk toward the overlook affords limited views, as well. Leave the carriage road at 0.6 mi. by turning right onto a foot trail marked by a small cairn and a red-orange blaze. Climb steadily for 0.2 mi. to the western viewpoint. Red-orange blazes mark the trail. To reach the eastern viewpoint, follow the trail 0.1 mi. past a cairn on left. A bench sculpted out of a fallen tree adorns the outlook.

■ SINGEPOLE MTN. (1,420 FT.)

Across the valley southwest of Streaked Mtn. is Singepole Mtn. in Paris. Although the trail does not reach the actual summit, open ledges on the south side of the mountain offer broad views to the south and west. From the jct. of ME 117 and ME 119 just east of downtown South Paris, drive east on ME 117 for 2.5 mi. to Brett Hill Rd. on the right. Turn right on Brett Hill Rd. and proceed to a jct. in another 0.4 mi. Here, Brett Hill Rd. turns right, and Durrell Hill Rd. continues straight ahead. Park here alongside the road.

SEC 7

SINGEPOLE MTN. TRAIL
(NFTM; USGS OXFORD QUAD, GAZETTEER MAP 11)

From jct. of Brett Hill Rd. and Durrell Hill Rd. (900 ft.) to:	↧↥	↗	↻
Singepole Mtn. ledges and overlook (1,300 ft.)	1.2 mi.	400 ft.	0:50

From its jct. with Brett Hill Rd., follow the dirt Durrell Hill Rd. uphill on foot. In 0.4 mi., bear left off the road onto a driveway, and reach a residence and a garage in another 350 ft. Beyond the garage, the trail—an ATV trail—heads into the woods. A handwritten sign and a wooden sign that both read "Cornell" mark the way. The numerous side roads/trails can be confusing; follow the main track, marked by ATV trail markers and orange flagging tape.

At 1.1 mi., reach an obscured fork, which can easily be missed. To the right is a steep shortcut leading to the top of the ridge. The left fork—the main trail—winds up past an old quarry. (Both routes converge on the ridge above.) Just past the quarry, the trail emerges on an open ledge with tailings from a mine. Turn right and descend briefly into the woods, then follow a track to open ledges. Cairns lead to the cliff edge overlooking Hall Pond.

■ STREAKED MTN. (1,770 FT.)

The distinctive west face of Streaked Mtn. in Hebron can be seen for miles in the Norway–South Paris area. The mountain offers a short but steep half-mile hike to the open ledges on its top. Hebron Academy maintains the trail. From the jct. of ME 117 and ME 119 just east of downtown South Paris, proceed east on ME 117 for 4.5 mi. to Streaked Mtn. Rd. Turn right (south) on this road and drive another 0.5 mi., where there is parking along either side of the road. The trail (sign) starts on the left (north) side of the road, next to a brook.

STREAKED MTN. TRAIL
(HA; USGS OXFORD QUAD, GAZETTEER MAP 11)

From Streaked Mtn. Rd. (1,030 ft.) to:	⇅	↗	⟳
Streaked Mtn. summit (1,770 ft.)	0.6 mi.	740 ft.	0:40

Start by following a brook and an old telephone line along the edge of a field. The trail quickly becomes steep, rocky, and eroded. It passes through a section of dense forest before emerging onto smooth rock slabs. Soon the grade moderates and the trail crosses under the phone line. Beyond, it climbs to reach the broad summit and a complex of communications towers and buildings. ATV trails crisscross the mountaintop. Follow these tracks right (east) to more viewpoints and ledges. Descending, leave the phone line at the second pole to drop down to the ledges to the left.

SUMNER–HARTFORD

■ BLACK MTN. (2,133 FT.)

This mountain in Sumner and Peru, just east of Speckled Mtn., is a broad, flat mass with multiple summits extending roughly east to west. A trail ascends to the easternmost summit from the Sumner side. From the jct. of ME 26 and ME 219 in West Paris, go 7.9 mi. east on ME 219 to Greenwood Rd. Turn left and follow Greenwood Rd. 1.3 mi. to Black Mtn. Rd. Follow Black Mtn. Rd. for 2.3 mi. to an apparent T intersection. Here, a driveway leaves right; turn left and park ahead on the left.

BLACK MTN. TRAIL
(NFTM; USGS WORTHLEY POND QUAD, GAZETTEER MAP 11)
From Black Mtn. Rd.
(950 ft.) to:

	⇅	↗	↻
Black Mtn., eastern summit (2,133 ft.)	1.6 mi.	1,200 ft.	1:30

Hike up the road 0.2 mi. and diverge right from the road onto an old woods road. Three white triangles mark important turns in the first 0.5 mi. of the hike. Bear left in a small open space and cross a brook on a stone culvert. Ahead, in a logged area, past what appears to be an old cellar hole on the left, follow occasional cairns and orange flagging. At 0.3 mi., pass a large pile of stones in the trees to the left. Continue uphill on the woods road. At 0.45 mi., the woods road turns right and, shortly after, levels out on a skidder trail. At 0.7 mi., where the skidder trail turns left steeply uphill, Black Mtn. Trail leaves right at a whitish boulder and orange arrow (important turn, but easy to miss). The trail continues, rocky and heavily eroded, for another 100 yd.

At 0.75 mi., bear right across a large skidder trail (orange flagging), follow a smaller skidder trail a short distance, then bear right into the woods on a foot trail (marked by white triangle and orange flagging). Reach a major skidder trail at 0.95 mi. (double orange flag) and follow it right, going steeply uphill (flagging, cairns). At 1.15 mi., bear right off the skidder trail onto an older logging road, which ends at 1.25 mi. Here, Black Mtn. Trail continues into the woods and climbs steeply along a brook, crosses it at 1.35 mi., and then levels out before reaching the east summit of Black Mtn. at 1.6 mi., where there are fine views to the southeast. Bear left and walk along the plateau, noting the old carvings (dating to 1889) in the rock on the left, just steps from the trail. The summit ridge is criss-crossed with paths; several lead to outcroppings with views.

SEC 7

■ BEAR MTN. (1,208 FT.)

This mountain in Hartford offers fine views overlooking Bear Pond and the surrounding countryside of the upper valley of the Androscoggin River. From ME 4 at North Turner, turn west onto ME 219 (Bear Pond Rd.). Follow it for 4.0 mi. to Pratt Hill Rd. Turn right and drive 0.9 to the jct. of Berry Rd. (right) and Mahoney Rd. (left). Proceed straight ahead through this intersection to trailhead parking (sign) in a grassy field immediately on the right.

BEAR MTN. TRAIL
(NFTM; USGS BUCKFIELD QUAD, GAZETTEER MAP 11)

Cumulative from parking area (400 ft.) to:	⥮	↗	↻
Side trail to western summit (1,100 ft.)	0.9 mi.	700 ft.	0:45
Bear Mtn. main summit (1,208 ft.)	1.9 mi.	800 ft.	1:20

The trail follows a dirt road past several houses, crossing a brook along the way. Ascend gradually as the wide road deteriorates to a woods road. At a fork, bear right and continue up the rocky, eroded route.

Partway up the hill, a narrow trail leaves the dirt road to the right and heads for the western summit. Turn right onto this trail, which contours easily along the ridgeline. The path makes a sharp right at a metal culvert and, a short distance beyond, breaks out onto open ledges. Just ahead is an outlook at a large boulder and good views to the southeast. Return to the dirt road to continue.

To reach the main summit, where the narrow trail leaves the dirt road to the right, continue straight ahead on the dirt road toward the height-of-land. At 1.1 mi., a road from the north comes in on the left, and the trail (also a road) swings around to the right (south). Ahead are good views to the west, south, and southeast from the summit.

ANDROSCOGGIN RIVER VALLEY

■ MT. ZIRCON (2,240 FT.)

This mountain, straddling the town lines of Milton Township and Peru, rewards hikers with exceptional views to the south and east from its craggy alpine summit.

MT. ZIRCON TRAIL (RWD; USGS MT. ZIRCON AND RUMFORD QUADS, GAZETTEER MAPS 10, 11, 18, AND 19, MTF MT. ZIRCON TRAIL MAP)

Cumulative from South Rumford Rd. (610 ft.) to:	⥮	↗	↻
Mt. Zircon spring house (1,210 ft.)	1.5 mi.	600 ft.	1:05
Start of trail via old Zircon Rd. (1,350 ft.)	2.1 mi.	740 ft.	1:25
Mt. Zircon summit (2,240 ft.)	2.9 mi.	1,630 ft.	2:15

To reach Mt. Zircon from the south, from the jct. of ME 26 and ME 232 in Woodstock, go north on ME 232 for 6.8 mi. to Abbotts Mill. Turn right onto South Rumford Rd. and drive 6.4 mi. to a gated gravel road on the right, by a Rumford Water District tree farm sign. Park in the grassy area along South Rumford Rd. (Do not block the gravel road.) From the east, from the jct. of US 2 and ME 108 in Rumford, drive west on US 2 for 0.5 mi. Turn left and cross the Androscoggin River, then follow South Rumford Rd. west for 3.2 mi. to the trailhead.

Begin by walking south on the gravel road (old Zircon Rd.) past the locked red gate, then uphill on an easy but steady grade. At 0.9 mi., just past an old logging area on the left, a snowmobile trail goes to the right. Bear left here, and follow the gravel road to a gated spring house at 1.5 mi. This remnant of the old Zircon Water Bottling Company is fenced in, but across the road, cold, clear water gushes from a spring pipe. Nearing the height-of-land, look for a white Mt. Zircon Trail sign on the left at 2.1 mi. Turn off the road here and follow the footpath, on a moderate grade at first, then more steep, with rough footing. Finish by climbing over slabs to the top. A large cairn and a downed, rusting old fire tower (cut down in 1976) mark the summit.

SECTION 8

SOUTHWESTERN MAINE

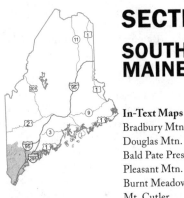

SEC
8

INTRODUCTION

This section, on Southwestern Maine, includes all of York County and Cumberland County, as well as the southern part of Oxford County. The area is bordered by Casco Bay, Saco Bay, and miles of sandy beaches to the south; the Piscataqua River, Salmon Falls River, and the state of New Hampshire to the west; an abundance of natural lakes to the north; and low hills to the east. The Saco River slices through the region, entering Maine at Fryeburg and emptying into the Gulf of Maine at Camp Ellis just south of Old Orchard Beach. The predominant natural feature in this part of the state is Sebago Lake; at 46 sq. mi., it is the second-largest body of water in Maine after Moosehead Lake.

The hills and mountains in this region are relatively low, rising to less than 1,000 ft. near the coast and ranging from 1,000 to 2,000 ft. farther inland. Pleasant Mtn. is the highest peak at 2,006 ft. Many of the hills and mountains are wooded all the way to the top, but others have semi-open and open summits that provide fine views of the surrounding countryside, as well as northwest to the White Mountains and east and southeast to the coast.

This section describes 85 trails on 25 mountains. This is Maine's most populous region, and many of the trails are well traveled, although others, in contrast, see little use. One-third of the trails listed are on private property, and the rest are on lands protected by land trusts and public and private conservation agencies, including the state of Maine.

SEC 8

GEOGRAPHY

The hills of Pownal and New Gloucester are a few miles northwest of Freeport on Casco Bay. Bradbury Mtn. State Park is one of Maine's five original state parks, protecting 800 acres around Bradbury Mtn. (484 ft.). Popular with hikers of all ages and abilities, Bradbury is perhaps Maine's most climbed mountain. Tryon Mtn. (395 ft.), the site of historical feldspar quarries, is connected to Bradbury by an ambitious multiagency conservation corridor that ranges west to Pineland Public Lands. Nearby, Pisgah Hill (385 ft.) rises above the farmlands along the Pownal–New Gloucester town line; it's a property of Royal River Conservation Trust. The town of Freeport owns Hedgehog Mtn. (308 ft.), an oasis of woods and trails close to the hustle and bustle of downtown. Just west of the din of the Maine Turnpike/I-95 corridor in Gray, the extensive network of trails on Libby Hill (477 ft.) offer miles of peace and quiet. The ridgeline of Rattlesnake

Mtn. (1,035 ft.) in Casco offers fine views of Crescent Lake, Panther Pond, and on to the big blue waters of Sebago Lake. Pismire Mtn. (833 ft.) in Raymond, just east of Crescent Lake, is the natural focal point of the Raymond Community Forest.

Douglas Mtn. (1,382 ft.) in Sebago is the highest of the four peaks of the Saddleback Hills, which rise immediately west of Sebago Lake. An old stone tower on top of Douglas rewards hikers with wonderful views. Just north of Peabody Pond in South Bridgton, a preserve owned by Loon Echo Land Trust encompasses Bald Pate Mtn. (1,150 ft.), with its pitch pine woods, pretty meadows, and granite ledges. Pleasant Mtn. (2,006 ft.), its distinctive ridgeline extending for 4 mi. across the Denmark–Bridgton town line, rises abruptly from the comparatively flat surrounding countryside around Moose Pond just south of US 302. Six popular hiking trails are on the slopes of Pleasant Mtn., which offers fine vistas of the White Mountains. The summit ledges on Mt. Tom (1,073 ft.) in Fryeburg, partially owned by The Nature Conservancy, make for excellent lookout points over the lovely valley of the wide and winding Saco River.

Just east of the New Hampshire state line, Jockey Cap (610 ft.) is a massive granite dome on the outskirts of Fryeburg that rises nearly 200 ft. above surrounding woods and fields, offering outstanding views for a small amount of time and effort. West of ME 113/5, the open ledges of Peary Mtn. (958 ft.) in Brownfield afford good views of the White Mountains and the mountains of western Maine. A little farther south in Brownfield, the mass of Burnt Meadow Mtn. (1,510 ft.) consists of three main summits and two lesser summits, all of nearly equal height. Deep cols separate Stone Mtn. (1,624 ft.) from the north and south peaks of Burnt Meadow Mtn. Continuing south on ME 113/5, in the village of Hiram, the extensive open ledges of Mt. Cutler (1,232 ft.) reward hikers with fine views of nearby hills and farmlands, the Saco River valley to the south, and the White Mountains to the north. Preservation efforts are under way to permanently protect Mt. Cutler and its system of trails. The precipitous cliffs on Bald Ledge (1,187 ft.) in Porter yield a fabulous vista eastward over Colcord Pond to the pretty hills and woods of north-central York County.

In Limerick and Limington, Sawyer Mtn. (1,213 ft.), the dominant natural feature of the Sawyer Mtn. Highlands, is part of the largest unfragmented block of undeveloped forestland in York and Cumberland counties. Knox Mtn. (830 ft.), in Newfield, and Abbott Mtn. (1,078 ft.), in Shapleigh, are amid the expansive Vernon S. Walker Wildlife Management Area, which spans more than 5,600 acres across the towns of Newfield,

SEC 8

Limerick, and Shapleigh. Bauneg Beg Mtn. (860 ft.), part of an 89-acre conservation property in North Berwick owned by Great Works Regional Land Trust, is the only major mountaintop in southern York County without a communications tower. The Mt. Agamenticus Conservation Region, a cooperative of seven landowners, encompasses more than 10,000 acres of coastal woods and hills in York and South Berwick in southern York County. The central feature of these lands is Mt. Agamenticus (the southernmost mountain in this guide), which rises distinctively above the coastal plain. Just northeast of Mt. Agamenticus is Second Hill, and to the east of that, Third Hill. The mountain's geographic location makes it a unique mixing ground for a number of southern and northern plant and animal species at the limits of their ranges.

ROAD ACCESS

Trailheads are scattered far and wide across the three counties of southwestern Maine: Cumberland, York, and Oxford. The main travel corridor between Portland and Brunswick is I-295.

From this major highway, local and state roads lead to the trails in Freeport, Pownal, and New Gloucester. The Maine Turnpike/I-95 route gets close to the trails in Gray and those in the area of Mt. Agamenticus in York. ME 11 slices across the region from Raymond and Sebago Lake to Lebanon on the New Hampshire border; many trails can be accessed from this major artery. US 302 and ME 113/5 are major transportation routes that connect the urban environs of Portland to Fryeburg; these two roads will get visitors within striking distance of nearly half the mountains in the area. ME 4 is an important north-south highway through central York County.

CAMPING

In addition to at least 72 privately operated campgrounds, camping is available in this region at two state parks: Bradbury Mtn. State Park in Pownal has 35 campsites, and Sebago Lake State Park in Casco has 129 sites. Both parks provide hot showers, restrooms, and other amenities. No backcountry camping is available.

BRADBURY MTN. STATE PARK

The federal government acquired Bradbury Mtn. in 1939, and soon after, it became one of Maine's five original state parks, along with Sebago Lake, Aroostook, Mt. Blue, and Lake St. George. The west side of the 800-acre park features a 5-mi. network of hiking trails on Bradbury Mtn., while the east side of the park is home to 14 mi. of mountain bike trails. A 35-site campground, complete with showers and restrooms, sits just north of the park entrance on the east side of ME 9.

MT. AGAMENTICUS CONSERVATION REGION

The Mt. Agamenticus Conservation Region encompasses more than 10,000 acres of coastal woods and hills in southern York County. The region is a cooperative of seven public, quasi-public, and nonprofit land-owners working together for conservation, watershed protection, and rec-reation: the towns of York and South Berwick, York Water District, DIFW, GWRLT, York Land Trust, and TNC.

The central feature is Mt. Agamenticus, which rises distinctively above the coastal plain of southern York County. The main mountain is also known as First Hill; just northeast of Mt. Agamenticus is Second Hill, and to the east of that, Third Hill. Because of its location, the mountain's envi-ronment is a unique mixing ground for a number of southern and northern plant and animal species at the limits of their ranges. More than 40 mi. of trails are available for public use, from hiking and mountain biking to horseback riding and ATVs.

SUGGESTED HIKES

■ Easy
BRADBURY MTN.

RT via Summit Trail	0.5 mi.	220 ft.	0:30

This is the shortest and most direct route to the open ledge atop Bradbury Mtn. See Summit Trail, p. 317.

TRYON MTN.

RT via Bradbury to Pineland Corridor Trail	0.6 mi.	200 ft.	0:40

Take a nice trek to see the remains of a feldspar mining operation on top of Tryon Mtn. See Bradbury to Pineland Corridor Trail, p. 322.

SEC 8

PISGAH HILL

🚶 🐕 �snowshoe

	🔁	↗	⏱
LP via Pisgah Hill Loop	1.3 mi.	300 ft.	0:45

Enjoy a variety of wildlife habitats, mixed forests, and old quarries on this loop. See Pisgah Hill Loop, p. 323.

PISMIRE MTN.

🚶 🐕 � ❄

	🔁	↗	⏱
RT via Pismire Bluff Trail	1.6 mi.	360 ft.	1:10

Climb the west side of Pismire Mtn. for a pleasant view of Crescent Lake and Rattlesnake Mtn. from the ledges at Pismire Bluff. See Pismire Bluff Trail, p. 328.

BALD PATE MTN.

🚶 🐕 � 🎿 ❄

	🔁	↗	⏱
LP via Bob Chase Scenic Loop and South Face Loop Trail	1.4 mi.	300 ft.	1:00

Hike through pitch pine woods to granite ledges atop Bald Pate Mtn., where there are good views of Peabody Pond and Sebago Lake. See Bob Chase Scenic Loop, p. 331.

SEC 8

JOCKEY CAP

🚶 🐕 � ❄

	🔁	↗	⏱
LP via Jockey Cap Trail	0.5 mi.	185 ft.	0:25

Scamper to the top of this amazing granite dome for outstanding views. Use the monument to the polar explorer Robert Peary, a bronze profile of the surrounding mountains, to identify all the peaks in a 360-degree arc. See Jockey Cap Trail, p. 339.

BALD LEDGE

🚶 🐕 � ❄

	🔁	↗	⏱
RT via Bald Ledge Trail	1.4 mi.	320 ft.	1:00

This trip rewards hikers with a fabulous vista eastward over Colcord Pond to the pretty hills and woods of north-central York County. See Bald Ledge Trail, p. 349.

KNOX MTN.

RT via Knox Mtn. Trail	1.5 mi.	330 ft.	1:00

Meander through a 5,600-acre wildlife management area for mountaintop views over the Little Ossipee River valley. See Knox Mtn. Trail, p. 352.

BAUNEG BEG MTN.

LP via Bauneg Beg Trail and North Peak Loop	1.5 mi.	340 ft.	0:55

Climb to the top of the only major summit in southern York County without a communications tower. Bonus: good views and rocky Devil's Den. See Bauneg Beg Trail and North Peak Loop, p. 354.

MT. AGAMENTICUS

LP via Ring Trail and Blueberry Bluff Trail	2.7 mi.	360 ft.	1:40

Circle all the way around Mt. Agamenticus then make a jaunt to the grassy summit. On top, enjoy the observation deck and Learning Lodge. To begin, see Ring Trail, p. 355.

■ Moderate

LIBBY HILL

LP via Libby Hill Loop	3.6 mi.	400 ft.	2:00

Take a good look around the woodland of the old Libby homestead on Lynx Trail, Harold Libbey Trail, Outback Trail, and Moose Odyssey Trail. To begin, see Libby Hill Loop, p. 324.

RATTLESNAKE MTN.

RT via Bri-Mar Trail	2.0 mi.	600 ft.	1:30

Revel in views of Crescent Pond, Panther Pond, and Sebago Lake from high on the ridgeline of Rattlesnake Mtn. See Bri-Mar Trail, p. 325.

SEC 8

DOUGLAS MTN.

🧍🐕🐾🏂🧎   ⤵   ↗   ⟳

LP via Eagle Scout Trail, Nature Loop, Ledges Trail, Douglas Mtn. Rd., and Ledges Rd.	2.4 mi.	380 ft.	1:35

Hike up to the old stone observation tower (1925) atop Douglas Mtn. for fantastic views ranging from Sebago Lake to the White Mountains. To begin, see Eagle Scout Trail, p. 327.

MT. TOM

💧🐾🏂   ⤵   ↗   ⟳

RT via West Ridge Trail	3.4 mi.	710 ft.	2:30

Hike across The Nature Conservancy land to the summit ledges of Mt. Tom and a nice lookout over the Saco River to Pleasant Mtn. See West Ridge Trail, p. 338.

BURNT MEADOW MTN.

🐕🐾🏂   ⤵   ↗   ⟳

LP via Burnt Meadow Trail and Twin Brook Trail	3.8 mi.	1,200 ft.	3:00

Make a big loop over this scenic mountaintop for fine views of the Saco River valley and the surrounding hills and mountains. To begin, see Burnt Meadow Trail, p. 342.

MT. CUTLER

🏂🐕🐾🏂   ⤵   ↗   ⟳

LP via Barnes Trail and Saco Ridge Trail	2.6 mi.	950 ft.	1:45

This excellent loop on Mt. Cutler rewards hikers with a series of far-reaching ledge views along the way. To begin, see Barnes Trail, p. 344.

SAWYER MTN.

💧🧍🐕🐾🏂   ⤵   ↗   ⟳

RT via Smith Trail	3.0 mi.	600 ft.	2:00

Get a good look at the largest unfragmented block of undeveloped forestland in York and Cumberland counties. See Smith Trail, p. 350.

■ Strenuous
PLEASANT MTN.

🐕 🎿 🏃 🏕

	↕	↗	○
RT via Southwest Ridge Trail	5.8 mi.	1,700 ft.	4:40

Pass an interesting wooden tepee on this long and scenic route to fine views of Moose Pond. From the main summit and fire tower, views to the west include Fryeburg, the Saco River valley, and numerous ponds. See Southwest Ridge Trail, p. 334.

MT. AGAMENTICUS, SECOND HILL, THIRD HILL

◐ 🐕 🎿 🏃 🏕

	↕	↗	○
LP via Ring Trail, Sweet Fern Trail, Second Hill Loop, Great Marsh Trail, Wheel Trail, Third Hill Trail, Bobcat Trail, and Ledge Trail	7.6 mi.	1,340 ft.	4:40

Make a grand loop over Mt. Agamenticus to the backcountry beyond, including Second Hill and Third Hill. To begin, see Ring Trail, p. 355.

SEC 8

TRAIL DESCRIPTIONS

BRADBURY MTN. STATE PARK

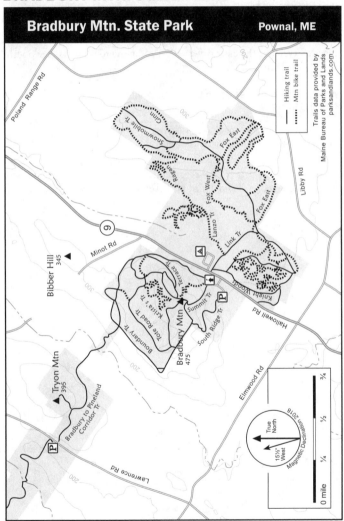

Bradbury Mtn. State Park   Pownal, ME

Hiking trail
Mtn bike trail

Trails data provided by Maine Bureau of Parks and Lands parksandlands.com

Poland Range Rd

Snowmobile Tr

Fox East

Fox West

Ragan Tr

Fox East

Lanzo Tr

Link Tr

Minot Rd

Bibber Hill
345

Terrace Tr

Krista's Tr

Tote Road Tr

Boundary Tr

Bradbury Mtn
475

Summit Tr

South Ridge Tr

Knight Woods Tr

Hallowell Rd

Libby Rd

Tryon Mtn
395

Bradbury to Pineland Corridor Tr

Lawrence Rd

Elmwood Rd

True North

15½° West

Magnetic Declination 2018

0 mile   ¼   ½   ¾

■ BRADBURY MTN. (484 FT.)

A network of pleasant foot trails and multiuse trails wends through the wooded Bradbury Mtn. State Park, many of which lead to the extensive open ledges on the summit of Bradbury Mtn., where there are good views of Casco Bay and the Portland skyline. Bradbury Mtn. trails are color coded. Fifteen numbered map posts at key intersections help you locate your position in the woods.

To reach Bradbury Mtn. State Park, take I-95 to Exit 22 in Freeport. Drive west on ME 136/125 and immediately turn left onto Pownal Rd. Drive 4.0 mi. to Pownal Center and the jct. with ME 9 (Pownal Rd. becomes Elmwood Rd. en route). Turn right on ME 9 and go 0.8 mi. to the main entrance of Bradbury Mtn. State Park on the left. Past the entrance station (fee), the park road bends to the right and leads to the main trailhead parking lot, a picnic area, and pit toilets.

SUMMIT TRAIL (MBPL; BRADBURY MTN. STATE PARK, P. 316)

From main trailhead parking lot (265 ft.) to:	⮁	↗	⏱
Bradbury Mtn. summit (484 ft.)	0.3 mi.	220 ft.	0:15

Summit Trail offers the shortest and most direct route to the top of Bradbury Mtn. This trail leaves the main trailhead parking lot and follows a rock-lined route through the pines of the picnic area. The white-blazed trail climbs easily through mostly hemlock woods, then ascends rock steps past a large, horizontally fractured ledge outcrop on the right. A final set of rock steps winds up and right to the large and open summit ledge, where there are broad views to the south and southeast.

NORTHERN LOOP TRAIL (MBPL; BRADBURY MTN. STATE PARK, P. 316)

From main trailhead parking lot (265 ft.) to:	⮁	↗	⏱
Bradbury Mtn. summit (484 ft.)	1.1 mi.	220 ft.	0:40

Northern Loop Trail follows the eastern base of Bradbury Mtn. before swinging around to ascend its northeast slope. This blue-blazed trail leaves from the east end of the main trailhead parking lot, going between the two pit toilets. Just past the information kiosk, cross a wide footbridge, then bear left on a spacious path. In 350 ft., Switchback Trail departs left. Continuing on Northern Loop Trail, view remnants of an old feldspar quarry to the left. At 0.15 mi., the stone walls of an old cattle pound are on the right. Continue easily along the base of the mountain to meet Terrace Trail on the left at 0.45 mi. (map post 1). Just 20 ft. beyond this jct., Ski Trail departs left. Bear right here to continue on Northern Loop Trail. At 0.5 mi., Boundary Trail leaves to the right (map post 2); continue straight ahead on Northern Loop Trail. Reach a four-way jct. and a bench at 0.7 mi. (map post 3). Here, Tote Road Trail leaves right, and a short connector to Ski Trail leaves left. In another 100 ft., Ski Trail departs to the left (map post 4). Continuing ahead, Northern Loop Trail reaches the lower jct. of Bluff Trail on the left at 0.8 mi. (map post 5). A nice viewpoint is 100 ft. along Bluff Trail. Northern Loop Trail turns to the right, climbing easily to the upper jct. of Bluff Trail on the left at 1.0 mi. (map post 6). Soon, Switchback Trail enters from the left (map post 7), and 10 ft. after that, Tote Road Trail enters from the right. The summit ledges atop Bradbury Mtn. are immediately beyond at 1.1 mi.

TOTE ROAD TRAIL (MBPL; BRADBURY MTN. STATE PARK, P. 316)

Cumulative from main trailhead parking lot (265 ft.) to:	⇅	↗	↻
Start of Tote Road Trail (365 ft.) via Northern Loop Trail	0.7 mi.	100 ft.	0:20
Bradbury Mtn. summit (484 ft.)	1.8 mi.	220 ft.	1:00

Tote Road Trail (white blazes) diverges from Northern Loop Trail (map post 3) at a point 0.7 mi. from the main trailhead parking lot. From there, head west on a contour and quickly pass the first and second entrances to Krista's Loop, a mountain bike trail. Crest a ridge, then descend gently to a connector trail on the right at 0.2 mi. (map post 17); this short path leads north to Boundary Trail. Ahead on Tote Road Trail, cross a dip, then climb easily southwest around the back side of Bradbury Mtn. The mostly level trail leads to a bench at 0.6 mi. Trend southeast up to a connector trail at 0.7 mi. (map post 15); this connector goes straight up a rooty pitch to join with Boundary Trail. Tote Road Trail turns sharply left at this jct. Ahead, cross a wide boardwalk, then follow gently rolling trail to a log bench. Beyond, reach the jct. with Northern Loop Trail at 1.1 mi. The summit ledges are 200 ft. to the right.

SKI TRAIL (MBPL; BRADBURY MTN. STATE PARK, P. 316)

This short, wide route, an old downhill ski trail that sported a rope tow for a time in the 1940s, cuts off a short section of Northern Loop Trail. Ski Trail is 0.15 mi. long and gains 90 ft. in elevation. Ski Trail begins at map post 1 and runs to map posts 3 and 4.

TERRACE TRAIL (MBPL; BRADBURY MTN. STATE PARK, P. 316)

Cumulative from main trailhead parking lot (265 ft.) to:	⇅	↗	⟳
Start of Terrace Trail (285 ft.) via Northern Loop Trail	0.5 mi.	20 ft.	0:15
Bradbury Mtn. summit (484 ft.) via Bluff Trail and Northern Loop Trail	1.0 mi.	220 ft.	0:35

Terrace Trail (gray blazes) leaves left from Northern Loop Trail (map post 1) at a point 0.45 mi. from the main trailhead parking lot. In 250 ft., go through a gap in an old stone wall. Slab across the east face of Bradbury Mtn. on a wide trail that passes the remains of rock-walled terraces used to cultivate grapes back in the 1800s. Ahead, the trail climbs moderately to its end at the jct. of Bluff Trail (map post 8). To continue to the top of Bradbury Mtn., bear left on Bluff Trail. Follow it to Northern Loop Trail and the summit ledges.

BLUFF TRAIL (MBPL; BRADBURY MTN. STATE PARK, P. 316)

Cumulative from main trailhead parking lot (265 ft.) to:	⇅	↗	⟳
Start of Bluff Trail (425 ft.) via Northern Loop Trail	0.8 mi.	160 ft.	0:30
Bradbury Mtn. summit (484 ft.) via Northern Loop Trail	1.0 mi.	220 ft.	0:35

From Northern Loop Trail (map post 5), the red-blazed Bluff Trail climbs 100 ft. to a ledge viewpoint on the left, reached by a 30-ft. spur. Beyond, after a quick, short drop, Terrace Trail enters from the right (map post 8). Bear left through a gap in a stone wall, then continue to the end of Bluff Trail at its jct. with Northern Loop Trail (map post 6). Turn left to reach the summit ledges on atop Bradbury Mtn. in another 0.1 mi.

SEC 8

BOUNDARY TRAIL (MBPL; BRADBURY MTN. STATE PARK, P. 316)

Cumulative from main trailhead parking lot (265 ft.) to:	⇅	↗	⟳
Start of Boundary Trail (290 ft.) via Northern Loop Trail	0.5 mi.	35 ft.	0:15
Bradbury Mtn. summit (484 ft.)	2.2 mi.	250 ft.	1:15

Follow Northern Loop Trail to the start of Boundary Trail on the right at 0.5 mi. (map post 2). Boundary Trail (orange blazes) soon reaches a stone wall and bears left along it. Ahead, the trail bears left away from the wall, crosses a wide boardwalk, and then reaches a connector trail, which enters from the left (map post 9). Turn right here and soon reach a green-blazed connector trail and map post 16. Continue straight ahead to stay on Boundary Trail. After a wet area on the left, pass map post 10, then return to the stone boundary wall. Pass a gate in the wall, with a meadow just below. Beyond, where an unnamed trail continues straight, bear sharply right around a corner in the stone wall. Cross an intermittent stream on a footbridge.

At 1.2 mi. from the main trailhead parking lot, reach a jct. Here, the Bradbury to Pineland Corridor Trail (sign) enters from the right, and another connector trail leaves left. Continue straight through the jct., climbing a moderate pitch up along the stone wall. At 1.3 mi., pass a split log bench on the right. At 1.6 mi., a connector trail leaves left (map post 11). Just ahead, make a sharp left at the corner of two boundary walls. Pass another connector trail on the left (map post 12), and continue along the park's southern boundary. Climb a short, moderate pitch, then cross three sections of boardwalk (two long, one short). Soon after another connector trail (map post 13) enters from the left, South Ridge Trail joins from the right (map post 14). Bear left to stay on Boundary Trail, and follow it easily to the top of Bradbury Mtn., 2.2 mi. from the main trailhead parking lot.

SOUTH RIDGE TRAIL
(MBPL; BRADBURY MTN. STATE PARK, P. 316)

From group campsite parking lot (210 ft.) to:	⇅	↗	↻
Bradbury Mtn. summit (484 ft.) via Boundary Trail	0.7 mi.	275 ft.	0:30

South Ridge Trail starts from the far (west) end of the group campsite parking lot, 0.1 mi. from the park entrance station. In 750 ft., climb a wooden staircase with a handrail. Beyond, the ascent is moderate over sections of bedrock trail. At 0.2 mi., bear left and climb another wooden staircase. Make a rising traverse to the next staircase. At 0.3 mi., reach a jct. Here, a shortcut to the summit leaves right; continue straight ahead to the South Ridge Overlook. At a signpost, an impressive 30-ft. cliff face is in the woods to the right; to the left, a side trail leads 150 ft. to the overlook and view. From the signpost, climb rock steps up and left around the cliff face. On top, the summit shortcut trail enters from the right. South Ridge Trail continues to its end at Boundary Trail, marked by a stone wall and a map post (14). Turn right here to continue 0.2 mi. to the top of Bradbury Mtn. via Boundary Trail.

FREEPORT–POWNAL–NEW GLOUCESTER–GRAY

■ HEDGEHOG MTN. (308 FT.)

This mountain is part of a 195-acre property owned by the town of Freeport. A 5-mi. network of trails, maintained by the town with volunteer help, is on the slopes of the mountain, the highest point in town. From I-95, Exit 22 in Freeport, proceed west briefly on ME 136/125 to Pownal Rd. (sign for Bradbury Mtn. State Park). Turn left here and go 1.5 mi. Turn left on Hedgehog Rd. (signs for Freeport Transfer and Recycling, and Hedgehog Mtn., Town of Freeport) and proceed 0.3 mi. to trailhead parking on the left, immediately before the transfer station gate (sign, kiosk).

HEDGEHOG TRAIL (TOF; USGS YARMOUTH AND FREEPORT QUADS, GAZETTEER MAP 6, TOWN OF FREEPORT–HEDGEHOG MTN. TRAILS MAP)

Cumulative from Hedgehog Rd. trailhead (160 ft.) to:	⇅	↗	↺
Hedgehog Mtn. Summit Overlook (300 ft.)	0.5 mi.	140 ft.	0:15
Complete loop via Hedgehog Trail, Summit Trail, and Stonewall Trail	1.2 mi.	140 ft.	0:40

Follow Hedgehog Trail toward the Hedgehog Mtn. Summit Overlook. Watching for blue blazes, cross a bridge over a creek. Ahead on the wide trail, cross a second bridge. Pass along the base of the mountain to a jct. at 0.2 mi. Turn left here for the Summit Overlook, Stonewall Trail, and Wentworth Trail. Thirty ft. ahead, an unmarked trail goes straight; go left. At 0.25 mi., make a sharp left turn and proceed uphill through rocks. Just ahead, reach a jct. Here, Stonewall Trail and Wentworth Trail are to the right; turn sharply left uphill on Summit Trail and climb a wooded ridge. Above, pass an old log bench on the left. Crest the ridge then descend briefly. At 0.45 mi., the trail reaches a ledge outcrop, the Hedgehog Mtn. Summit Overlook, and a bench. The view window is to Bradbury Mtn. and, on very clear days, Mt. Washington. Beyond, drop down off the ledge and continue through the woods. At 0.7 mi., turn right on Stonewall Trail and ascend along a stone wall. At 0.9 mi., close the loop. Continue right and out to the trailhead.

SEC
8

■ TRYON MTN. (395 FT.)

This low, wooded mountain in Pownal is named for the Tryon family, whose roots in the area date back to 1800. The remains of an old feldspar mining operation are on top. The mountain is reached by way of the Bradbury to Pineland Corridor Trail. This route connects a series of conservation lands between Bradbury Mtn. State Park and Pineland Public Lands, which spans the towns of Pownal, New Gloucester, Gray, and North Yarmouth. The ambitious project is the work of the Maine Bureau of Parks and Lands, Royal River Conservation Trust, Casco Bay Estuary Project, and New England Mountain Bike Association.

From I-95, Exit 22 in Freeport, drive west briefly on ME 136/125 to Pownal Rd. Turn left on Pownal Rd. and follow it for 2.4 mi. to its jct. with Verrill Rd. Here, Pownal Rd. becomes Elmwood Rd. Continue on Elmwood Rd. for 2.0 mi. to its jct. with ME 9 (convenience store on left, sign for Bradbury Mtn. State Park on right). Continue straight through the intersection (still on Elmwood Rd.) and drive an additional 2.3 mi. Turn right onto Lawrence Rd. and follow it for 0.9 mi. to trailhead parking on the left (sign, kiosk).

BRADBURY TO PINELAND CORRIDOR TRAIL (MBPL; BRADBURY MTN. STATE PARK, P. 316)

Cumulative from Lawrence Rd. trailhead (200 ft.) to:	↰↑	↗	◷
Tryon Mtn. side trail (300 ft.)	0.3 mi.	100 ft.	0:10
Tyron Mtn. summit, old feldspar quarries (395 ft.)	0.5 mi.	200 ft.	0:20
Bradbury Mtn. SP western boundary, jct. with Boundary Trail (250 ft.)	1.4 mi.	330 ft.	1:00

The trail begins on the opposite side of Lawrence Rd. about 100 ft. south of the parking area. Follow an old woods road gently uphill to a signed jct. Bear left here, cross a dip, then pass right of a wet area to reach another old woods road and, just ahead, a side trail to the top of Tryon Mtn. The green-blazed side trail follows an old road 0.15 mi. to the old feldspar quarries atop the mountain.

Back at the main trail, turn left (east) and soon descend to cross a stone wall. Ahead at a fork, a faint trail goes right; continue left to follow the wide main track. Descend a moderate slope of crushed rock. Beyond, where the valley narrows, turn sharply right across a low, often wet area. Turn up the other side of the valley and then, ahead at a woods road, turn left to cross Thoit's Brook on a nice footbridge. Soon after the bridge, bear left, then right onto a footpath. Wind upslope to a stone wall marking the northwestern boundary of Bradbury Mtn. State Park. If desired, turn right here to continue on Boundary Trail to reach the summit of Bradbury Mtn. in another 1.0 mi.

■ PISGAH HILL (385 FT.)

This wooded ridge in New Gloucester is part of Pisgah Hill Preserve, a nearly 300-acre public landscape that protects a wide variety of wildlife habitats, mixed forests, and old quarries. A loop hike offers a good look around the conservation property, which is owned by Royal River Conservation Trust.

From the jct. of Elmwood Rd. and ME 9 in Pownal, travel west on Elmwood Rd. for 2.4 mi. Turn left on Allen Rd. and follow it for 0.5 mi. Turn right on Chadsey Rd. In 0.5 mi., at the Pownal–New Gloucester town line, the dirt Chadsey Rd. becomes the paved Dougherty Rd. The trailhead parking lot is on the right (sign, kiosk) in another 0.4 mi.

PISGAH HILL LOOP (RRCT; USGS NORTH POWNAL QUAD, GAZETTEER MAP 5, RRCT PISGAH HILL PRESERVE MAP)

From Dougherty Rd. trailhead (95 ft.) to:	⮃	↗	⏱
Pisgah Hill summit (385 ft.)	1.3 mi.	300 ft.	0:45

Pass a wooden fence, then hike up along the edge of the field next to the fence. Enter the woods beyond. Descend to cross Quarry Brook on a metal bridge. At 0.2 mi., reach the loop jct. Go right to hike the loop counterclockwise. Climb through mixed forest. At 0.3 mi., make a sharp left in a semi-open area of ledges and boulders. Beyond, climb bedrock trail through pines, oak, and juniper. Cross a large open area of ledge, then drop off its back side. Proceed easily on the level for a distance, then climb higher on bedrock trail, a short, moderate pitch. Reach the wooded high point on Pisgah Hill at 0.6 mi., marked by a cairn with a rebar stake in it. Descend next to a property boundary, passing through pleasant groves of mature hemlock and pine. At 1.0 mi., a side trail leads to private land; please continue to follow RRCT trail markers. Close the loop at 1.1 mi. Turn right to return to the trailhead.

■ LIBBY HILL (477 FT.)

Libby Hill Forest Trails in Gray is home to wooded Libby Hill and a pleasant network of color-coded recreation trails on about 200 acres. Founded in 1999, the trail system was created on land donated by descendants of the Libby family. School Administrative District 15, the town of Gray, and Gray Community Endowment own the forest properties; Friends of Libby Hill maintains the trails.

The trailhead for Libby Hill Forest is adjacent to Gray-New Gloucester Middle School on Libby Hill Rd. From the Maine Turnpike, Exit 63 in

Gray, drive north on ME 26A for 1.5 mi. Turn left on Libby Hill Rd. and drive 0.25 mi. to trailhead parking on the right (kiosk).

LIBBY HILL LOOP (LHFT; USGS GRAY QUAD, GAZETTEER MAP 5, LHFT LIBBY HILL FOREST TRAILS MAP)

From Libby Hill Rd.
(325 ft.) to:

	⇅	↗	↻
Complete loop via Lynx, Moose Odyssey, Harold Libbey, and Outback trails	3.6 mi.	400 ft.	2:00

For a good look around Libby Hill Forest, this hike combines the Lynx, Harold Libbey, Outback, and Moose Odyssey trails. From the small parking area, cross to the Gray-New Gloucester school, then bear right to the start of Lynx Trail. The trail soon merges right with Moose Odyssey Trail, which crosses a snowmobile/ATV trail and in 400 ft. turns left to cross over to where Lynx Trail breaks off from Moose Odyssey Trail and climbs Libby Hill. Beyond the hill crest, Lynx Trail descends to a jct. Here, turn left onto Harold Libbey Trail, which leads down the back side of Libby Hill, passing glacial boulders and little canyons en route. At the next jct., Outback Trail leaves to the left. Outback Trail leads through the most remote portion of Libby Hill Forest. The trail soon reaches Thayer Brook, which drains the back side of Libby Hill and eventually empties into the Pleasant River/ Presumpscot River water system. Cross the brook on stepping stones and quickly arrive at the loop jct.; bear left to hike it clockwise.

Outback Trail next climbs a ridge, then descends to a beaver bog. Leaving the bog, the trail regains the ridge and returns to the Outback loop jct. and Harold Libbey Trail. Bear left on Harold Libbey Trail and climb a "horseback," or esker, to pass a large boulder known as Whale Rock. Continue on to meet Lynx Trail, which enters from the right. Ahead, the trail passes by Ghost Trail (enters on the left) and soon meets Moose Odyssey Trail. Turn right on Moose Odyssey Trail, and at the next intersection, bear left toward the summit of Libby Hill. At a long rock wall, bear right to pass through the wall. (To the left, it's a short walk to Secret Garden of the Woods, a perennial garden created out of the old homestead foundation of James Libby). Continue on Moose Odyssey Trail, then bear left on Lynx Trail to return to the trailhead.

SEBAGO LAKE

■ RATTLESNAKE MTN. (1,035 FT.)

This mountain, in Raymond and Casco, offers fine ridge walking with views of Sebago Lake to the south and the White Mountains to the north. The mountain is privately owned by the Huntress family, which has maintained the Bri-Mar Trail to the top of the mountain since 1965. The trail is named in memory of Huntress family members Brian and Marlene, who enjoyed this hike. The trailhead in Raymond is on ME 85, 0.9 mi. south of its jct. with ME 11 in the hamlet of Webb's Mills in Raymond, or 7.1 mi. north of its jct. with US 302 in Raymond. Parking is in a small fenced-in area at the edge of a field. Please observe the rules posted on the green and white sign at the start of the trail. (*Note:* No dogs are allowed, and the trail is closed from April 1 to May 1 each spring.)

BRI-MAR TRAIL (HUNTRESS FAMILY; USGS RAYMOND QUAD, GAZETTEER MAP 5)

From ME 85 trailhead (440 ft.) to:	↧↥	↗	○
Rattlesnake Mtn. main summit (1,035 ft.)	1.0 mi.	600 ft.	0:45

Bri-Mar Trail crosses a field and enters the forest, following a woods road for a short distance. The road forks, but both forks rejoin ahead. Shortly, bear right onto a foot trail and, following red markers, climb steadily up the hillside. The path levels off atop the ridge and reaches several lookouts with views south to Crescent Lake and Panther Pond. Ahead, a faint side trail marked by red dots leads right (north) 100 yd. to a small clearing with limited views through the trees to Mt. Washington and the Presidential Range. Beyond, climb over a rock knob to reach the wooded summit and the end of Bri-Mar Trail. (*Note:* A trail continues west to ledges with views to Sebago Lake, then descends the southwest side of the mountain, following blue and orange flagging; but it is obscure in places, is steep and rough, and is not recommended.)

■ DOUGLAS MTN. (1,382 FT.)

Douglas Mtn. in Sebago is the highest of the four peaks of the Saddleback Hills, which rise immediately west of Sebago Lake. The town of Sebago owns 169 acres on the mountain, where four trails offer a little more than 3 mi. of tramping. Local stewards and volunteers maintain the preserve and its trails and charge a small fee to help support these activities. The summit features a stone observation tower built in 1925 and a large boulder with the Latin inscription *non sibi sed omnibus*, which translates to "not for

SEC
8

one but for all." The top of Douglas affords panoramic views of the surrounding countryside, as well as the Presidential Range, Pleasant Mtn., and the Atlantic Ocean.

From the jct. of ME 113 and ME 11/107 in East Baldwin, turn north on ME 11/107. In 1.8 mi., ME 11 bears right. Continue on ME 107, and at 6.4 mi., reach Dyke Mtn. Rd. Turn left here (a small sign reads "Douglas Mtn.—1 mile"). In 1.0 mi., turn left onto Douglas Mtn. Rd., drive 0.2 mi., and turn left onto Ledges Rd. Just ahead is the parking lot for all trails (sign, kiosk).

Four trails lead to the top of Douglas Mtn. Eagle Scout Trail leaves from the parking lot and joins Nature Loop not far from the summit. Access Ledges Trail and Woods Trail by walking 0.2 mi. on Ledges Rd. to Douglas Mtn. Rd. and then following it uphill for 0.2 mi. to the upper trailhead. Vehicles may also drive to this point to drop off hikers, but no parking is allowed.

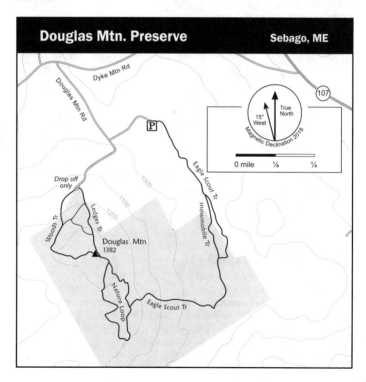

Douglas Mtn. Preserve   Sebago, ME

EAGLE SCOUT TRAIL (TOS; DOUGLAS MTN. PRESERVE, P. 326)

Cumulative from Ledges Rd. parking lot (1,000 ft.) to:	⇅	↗	○
Nature Loop (1,250 ft.)	1.3 mi.	250 ft.	0:45
Douglas Mtn. summit (1,382 ft.) via Nature Loop	1.5 mi.	380 ft.	0:55

This trail, delineated with orange markers, enters the woods and alternately follows a snowmobile trail/woods road and footpath, crossing several small brooks and wet areas. At a sign reading "To Nature Loop," the trail leaves the woods road and climbs steeply to a jct. with Nature Loop. To the right, Nature Loop leads 0.25 mi. to the summit of Douglas Mtn. and the stone tower. Nature Loop is delineated with pink markers.

NATURE LOOP (TOS; DOUGLAS MTN. PRESERVE, P. 326)

Cumulative from Douglas Mtn. summit (1,382 ft.) to:	⇅	↗	○
Eagle Scout Trail (1,250 ft.)	0.5 mi.	45 ft.	0:15
Complete loop	0.8 mi.	175 ft.	0:25

From the summit tower on Douglas Mtn., head east into the woods, then turn south to reach the loop jct. of Nature Loop in 200 ft. Turn right to follow Nature Loop counterclockwise. The pink-blazed trail descends through a hemlock grove, then levels off. Just beyond a wet area, bear sharply left, make a short climb, then level off. Ahead, limited views are possible from a ledge on the right. Descend through hemlocks, then swing north to meet Eagle Scout Trail, which enters from the right at 0.5 mi. Beyond, drop easily into a shallow ravine, then climb a short, moderate to steep pitch to the Nature Loop jct. Continue on to the Douglas summit and tower, which is at 0.75 mi.

SEC 8

LEDGES TRAIL (TOS; DOUGLAS MTN. PRESERVE, P. 326)

Cumulative from Ledges Rd. parking lot (1,000 ft.) to:	⇅	↗	○
Upper trailhead and drop-off point (1,150 ft.)	0.4 mi.	200 ft.	0:15
Douglas Mtn. summit (1,382 ft.)	0.9 mi.	430 ft.	0:40

This wide and eroded trail is the shortest and most popular route to the summit. From the upper trailhead and drop-off point 0.4 mi. from the Ledges Rd. parking lot, proceed past two stone pillars, and follow slabs and ledges 0.5 mi. to the top of Douglas Mtn. Pass two white-blazed connector trails leading west to Woods Trail en route. Ledges Trail is delineated with yellow markers.

WOODS TRAIL (TOS; DOUGLAS MTN. PRESERVE, P. 326)

Cumulative from Ledges Rd. parking lot (1,000 ft.) to:	↕	↗	↺
Upper trailhead and drop-off point (1,150 ft.)	0.4 mi.	200 ft.	0:15
Douglas Mtn. summit (1,382 ft.)	1.2 mi.	430 ft.	0:45

This trail leaves the left end of the upper trailhead and drop-off point, 0.4 mi. from the Ledges Rd. parking lot. Woods Trail follows an old woods road for 300 ft. before turning left uphill. Soon, pass an old concrete tank on the left. Beyond, pass a white-blazed connector leading east to Ledges Trail. Above, bear sharply left to avoid private property. The final part of the climb trends easily up the west ridge of the mountain. Woods Trail is delineated with green markers.

LOON ECHO LAND TRUST

■ PISMIRE MTN. (833 FT.)

A portion of this mountain in Raymond is in the Raymond Community Forest, 356 acres of mixed woods and unique natural communities owned and managed by Loon Echo Land Trust. Outlooks high on the mountain offer stunning views west over Crescent Lake to Rattlesnake Mtn. and beyond, to Sebago Lake. Pismire Bluff Trail and Highlands Loop are hiking-only trails that wend over the southern slopes of Pismire Mtn. A short section of Spiller Homestead Loop, a mountain-biking and hiking trail, provides access to these trails.

From the jct. of US 302 and ME 11 in Naples, drive north on ME 11 for 7.0 mi. to Edwards Rd. Turn right on Edwards Rd. and proceed 0.9 mi. to where it merges with Conesca Rd. Continue on Conesca Rd. for 0.7 mi. to trailhead parking on the right (sign, kiosk).

PISMIRE BLUFF TRAIL (LELT; USGS RAYMOND QUAD, GAZETTEER MAP 5, LELT RAYMOND COMMUNITY FOREST TRAILS MAP)

From Conesca Rd. trailhead (415 ft.) to:	↕	↗	↺
Start of trail (460 ft.) via Spiller Homestead Loop	0.1 mi.	45 ft.	0:05
Highlands Loop (775 ft.)	0.7 mi.	360 ft.	0:30
Pismire Bluff scenic overlook (760 ft.)	0.8 mi.	360 ft.	0:35

From the trailhead kiosk, head northwest on Spiller Homestead Trail (pink markers) to a jct. at 0.1 mi. Here, turn right on Pismire Bluff Trail (blue markers) and soon cross Conesca Rd. The trail heads northeast, then turns sharply southeast on a rising traverse along the base of a talus slope to reach a large set of stone steps. It climbs moderately via short switchbacks for a distance, then rises more gradually to the south ridge of Pismire Mtn. At a jct. at 0.7 mi., a spur of Pismire Bluff Trail leads left 0.1 mi. to Pismire Bluff, a scenic overlook with good westerly views. Also at the jct. is the start and finish of Highlands Loop, which makes an 0.7-mi. circuit on the upper south slopes of Pismire Mtn.

HIGHLANDS LOOP (LELT; USGS RAYMOND QUAD, GAZETTEER MAP 5, LELT RAYMOND COMMUNITY FOREST TRAILS MAP)

From Pismire Bluff Trail (775 ft.) to:	⇅	↗	○
Complete loop	0.8 mi.	150 ft.	0:30

From the jct. of the Pismire Bluff Trail spur to the scenic overlook, head north on Highlands Loop toward the top of Pismire Mtn., trending easily along the ridge. Reach a property boundary at the base of the summit cone of Pismire (through the trees, a house is visible on the hilltop); bear right here, away from the upper face of the mountain. The trail descends easily down the back side, then heads south to join an old woods road. Bear right, and ahead, bear right again off the woods road to climb a narrow old track to the loop jct. Turn left here to return to the Conesca Rd. trailhead via Pismire Bluff Trail and Spiller Homestead Loop.

■ BALD PATE MTN. (1,150 FT.)

SEC 8

Loon Echo Land Trust established the 486-acre Bald Pate Mtn. Preserve of forests, meadows, and granite ledges in South Bridgton in 1997 to protect the land from development. The 7 mi. of hiking on the preserve's seven trails offer plenty of opportunity for exploration, highlighted by a mountaintop pitch pine forest and numerous outlooks with views of Peabody Pond and Sebago Lake.

From the jct. of US 302 and ME 107/117, 1.5 mi. south of Bridgton, turn left (west) onto ME 117. At 0.8 mi., ME 117 proceeds straight. Turn left (south) here onto ME 107. At 4.3 mi., pass Five Fields Farm on the left. Just ahead, at the top of the hill at 4.6 mi., reach a dirt drive (sign) on the left leading to the main trailhead parking (kiosk).

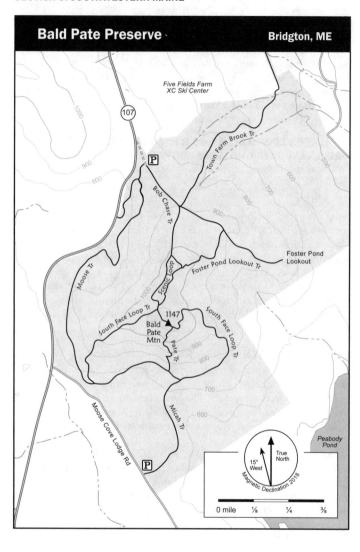

SEC
8

BOB CHASE SCENIC LOOP (LELT; BALD PATE PRESERVE, P. 330)

Cumulative from main trailhead on ME 107 (850 ft.) to:	↕	↗	○
South Face Loop Trail (1,100 ft.)	0.6 mi.	250 ft.	0:25
Bald Pate Mtn. summit (1,150 ft.) via South Face Loop Trail	0.7 mi.	300 ft.	0:30

Follow the wide, grassy track of Bob Chase Scenic Loop (blue markers) to a jct. at 0.2 mi. Here, Town Farm Brook Trail comes in from the left (leads 2.0 mi. north to Holt Pond Trail and on to Holt Pond), and Foster Pond Lookout Trail proceeds straight (leads 0.2 to a jct., where a spur leads 0.3 mi. east to a viewpoint over Foster Pond; to the right [south], the trail ascends easily to merge with Bob Chase Scenic Loop at 0.4 mi.).

Continuing on Bob Chase Scenic Loop, turn right (south) and climb gradually, crossing a wide track (ski trail in winter) to reach a jct. at 0.4 mi. where the trail splits. Both paths climb moderately past viewpoints to merge again at 0.6 mi. and a jct. with South Face Loop Trail. Follow this to reach the summit at 0.7 mi., with views through the trees. A bronze plaque on the summit honors conservation supporters of Bald Pate Mtn. Several loop possibilities from this point are possible using South Face Loop Trail and Pate Trail.

FOSTER POND LOOKOUT TRAIL
(LELT; BALD PATE PRESERVE, P. 330)

Cumulative from main trailhead on ME 107 (850 ft.) to:	↕	↗	○
Foster Pond Lookout (890 ft.) via Bob Chase Scenic Loop	0.7 mi.	60 ft.	0:20
Bald Pate Mtn. summit (1,150 ft.) via Bob Chase Scenic Loop and South Face Loop Trail	1.5 mi.	320 ft.	0:55

Follow the wide, grassy track of Bob Chase Scenic Loop (blue markers) to a jct. at 0.2 mi. Here, Town Farm Brook Trail comes in from the left (leads 2.0 mi. north to Holt Pond Trail and on to Holt Pond), and Foster Pond Lookout Trail proceeds straight ahead, while Bob Chase Scenic Loop turns right.

Go straight on Foster Pond Lookout Trail to the next jct. Here, a spur of Foster Pond Lookout Trail leads 0.3 mi. to Foster Pond Lookout and a view of Foster Pond. Return to the spur jct. and turn left to climb to a jct. with the upper east loop of Bob Chase Scenic Loop at a viewpoint to Peabody Pond. From here, Bob Chase Scenic Loop ascends to join South Face Loop Trail, which leads to the top of Bald Pate Mtn.

MICAH TRAIL AND PATE TRAIL
(LELT; BALD PATE PRESERVE, P. 330)

From the south trailhead on Moose Cove Lodge Rd. (650 ft.) to:	⇅	↗	↺
Bald Pate Mtn. summit (1,150 ft.) via Micah Trail, South Face Loop Trail, and Pate Trail	0.8 mi.	500 ft.	0:40

From the main trailhead, drive south on ME 107 for 0.9 mi. Turn left onto the dirt Moose Cove Lodge Rd. (sign for Camp Micah), and go 0.5 mi. to a small parking lot on the left.

Follow Micah Trail (white markers) to a bridge over a creek and then gradually up to the jct. with South Face Loop Trail (orange markers). Turn left on South Face Loop Trail; at 0.1 mi. along this trail, Pate Trail (green markers) diverges right (north) and climbs 0.2 mi. at a moderate to steep grade past cliffs to the Bald Pate Mtn. summit. South Face Loop Trail may be used to form a loop hike east or west from the summit back to the south trailhead.

MICAH TRAIL AND SOUTH FACE LOOP TRAIL
(LELT; BALD PATE PRESERVE, P. 330)

Cumulative from the south trailhead on Moose Cove Lodge Rd. (650 ft.) to:	⇅	↗	↺
Bald Pate Mtn. summit (1,150 ft.) via right side of South Face Loop Trail	1.1 mi.	500 ft.	0:50
Complete loop via South Face Loop Trail and Micah Trail	2.5 mi.	600 ft.	1:30

From the south trailhead on Moose Cove Lodge Rd. (see above), follow Micah Trail (white markers) to a bridge over a creek and then gradually up to a jct. with South Face Loop Trail (orange markers). To hike the loop counterclockwise, turn right on South Face Loop Trail, which leads 0.6 mi. to the top of Bald Pate Mtn., climbing the right side of the south face, past a viewpoint.

From the summit, descend the mountain's west ridge on South Face Loop Trail, passing a viewpoint en route. At the base of the mountain, Moose Trail diverges right. (*Note:* Moose Trail is prone to ticks due to high grass and is therefore recommended as a winter trail only.) Continue easily east, pass the bottom of Pate Trail, and reach the jct. with Micah Trail. Turn right on Micah Trail to return to the south trailhead.

■ PLEASANT MTN. (2,006 FT.)

This isolated mountain mass on the Denmark–Bridgton town line rises abruptly from the comparatively flat surrounding countryside around Moose Pond, its ridgeline extending 4 mi. in a generally north-south line.

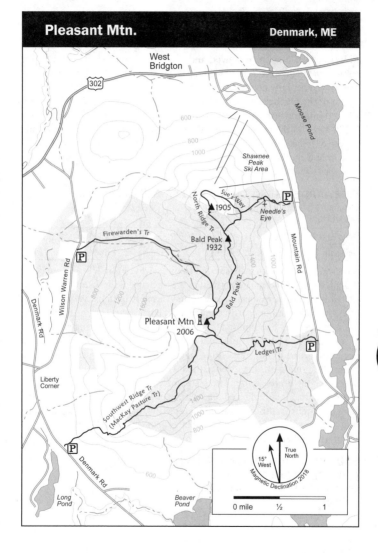

Pleasant Mtn.   **Denmark, ME**

West
Bridgton

302

600
800
1000

Moose Pond

Shawnee
Peak
Ski Area

Sue's Way

1905

Needle's
Eye

North Ridge Tr

Firewarden's Tr

Bald Peak
1932

Mountain Rd

1400

1000

Bald Peak Tr

Wilson Warren Rd

800
1200
1600

Pleasant Mtn
2006

Denmark Rd

Ledges Tr

SEC
8

Liberty
Corner

Southwest Ridge Tr
(MacKay Pasture Tr)

1400

1000

800

Denmark Rd

600

Long
Pond

Beaver
Pond

15°
West
True
North

Magnetic Declination 2018

0 mile   ½   1

The 10 mi. of hiking trails converge at the main summit, where an old fire tower has stood since 1920. The summit was once known as House Peak because of the hotel that stood there from 1873 to 1907. Around 1860, Pleasant Mtn. was burned over, and the forests and ledges remain open enough today for outstanding views. Mt. Washington, 29 mi. to the northwest, is particularly noticeable. The Shawnee Peak ski area operates on the slopes of the northern peak. LELT owns a little more than 2,000 acres on the mountain's eastern slopes, while The Nature Conservancy protects 1,400 acres on the western slopes through conservation easements. Maine Forest Service owns 20 acres on the main summit. Portions of the trail system and mountain are privately owned and can be used thanks to the generosity of the landowners.

FIREWARDEN'S TRAIL (LELT; PLEASANT MTN., P. 333)

Cumulative from Wilton Warren Rd. trailhead (450 ft.) to:	↕	↗	○
Bald Peak Trail (1,900 ft.)	2.3 mi.	1,450 ft.	1:50
Pleasant Mtn. main summit (2,006 ft.)	2.5 mi.	1,560 ft.	2:00

This trail climbs to the main summit from the west. From US 302, at a point 2.3 mi. west of Mountain Rd. (road to the Shawnee Peak ski area) and 7 mi. east of Fryeburg, turn south onto Wilton Warren Rd. At 1.2 mi. south of US 302, a yellow farmhouse is on the left and a large barn is on the right. Parking is on the left. The trail starts at the right end of the parking area (sign).

The first half of the trail is old woods road with few views. In recent years, this road has been used for logging and is deeply rutted in places. Several logging roads cross the path and can be confusing. Follow the red blazes to stay on the route. The trail crosses a brook several times before narrowing to a rough old jeep road with exposed bedrock much of the way. It swings right (southeast) and climbs steadily to the summit ridge. In the final 0.2 mi., Bald Peak Trail (blue blazes) comes in on the left (sign). An old storm shelter is just off the trail to the right.

SOUTHWEST RIDGE (MACKAY PASTURE) TRAIL (LELT; PLEASANT MTN., P. 333)

Cumulative from Denmark Rd. trailhead (450 ft.) to:	↕	↗	○
Pleasant Mtn. southwest summit (1,900 ft.)	1.7 mi.	1,450 ft.	1:35
Ledges Trail (1,800 ft.)	2.7 mi.	1,450 ft.	2:05
Pleasant Mtn. main summit (2,006 ft.) via Ledges Trail	2.9 mi.	1,700 ft.	2:20

From the jct. of ME 117 and ME 160 in Denmark, take ME 160 for 0.3 mi. to the Moose Pond Dam. Turn right onto Denmark Rd. and drive 3.5 mi. to the parking area on the right, opposite the sign for Spiked Ridge Rd. (Forest Route 78). Visitors may also approach the parking area from US 302 in East Fryeburg by following Denmark Rd. for 3.4 mi.

The trail, marked by cairns and yellow blazes, begins on private property (sign) and follows an old woods road gradually northeast, then becomes steeper. At approximately 0.4 mi., the trail turns sharply right (southeast), angles across the slope, turns left, and reaches open ledges at 0.6 mi. Beyond, the trail ascends northeasterly along the mostly open ridge to an old wooden tepee at the southwestern summit (1,900 ft.) at 1.7 mi., with good views over Moose Pond and Beaver Pond. The trail keeps to the ridge, then descends to a short saddle and angles across and down the hillside to a deep gully. Beyond, the trail ascends back to the ridge, becoming more gradual until it reaches Ledges Trail (blue blazes) at 2.7 mi., which is 0.2 mi. from the summit.

LEDGES TRAIL (LELT/AMC; PLEASANT MTN., P. 333)

Cumulative from Mountain Rd. (450 ft.) to:	↕	↗	○
Overlook (1,300 ft.)	1.1 mi.	850 ft.	1:00
Southwest Ridge Trail (1,800 ft.)	1.6 mi.	1,350 ft.	1:30
Pleasant Mtn. main summit (2,006 ft.)	1.8 mi.	1,560 ft.	1:40

This trail leaves the west side of Mountain Rd. at a point 3.3 mi. south of US 302, 1.5 mi. south of Bald Peak Trail, and 0.6 mi. north of Walker's Bridge (which separates the two sections of Moose Pond). A small parking area is on the east side of the road next to FR 54.

SEC 8

The blue-blazed trail (sign) begins by climbing a stone stairway to an information kiosk and then gradually ascending along an old woods road. At 0.5 mi., it crosses two often dry streambeds. Continue to climb moderately for 0.6 mi., noting changes in direction as the trail traverses to the open ledges with views south and southeast. The trail follows the ledges, with the southwestern summit and a cell tower visible ahead on the left. At 1.6 mi., Southwest Ridge Trail comes in on the left (sign). Ahead, Ledges Trail climbs through an area of ledges and scrub to the main summit and fire tower. Views to the west include Fryeburg, the Saco River valley, and numerous ponds.

BALD PEAK TRAIL (LELT; PLEASANT MTN., P. 333)

Cumulative from Mountain Rd. (450 ft.) to:	⮑⮑	↗	⟳
Brook crossing and Sue's Way (1,300 ft.)	0.7 mi.	850 ft.	0:45
North Ridge Trail (1,800 ft.)	1.0 mi.	1,350 ft.	1:10
Firewarden's Trail (1,900 ft.)	2.2 mi.	1,600 ft.	1:55
Pleasant Mtn. main summit (2,006 ft.) via Firewarden's Trail	2.4 mi.	1,700 ft.	2:05

This trail climbs the eastern side of Pleasant Mtn. to Big Bald Peak and then runs south along the ridge to join Firewarden's Trail just below the main summit. When combined with Ledges Trail and a 1.5-mi. walk on Mountain Rd., Bald Peak Trail forms an enjoyable circuit. Both trails follow blue blazes. There is no sure water on this trail during dry periods.

To reach Bald Peak Trail, follow Mountain Rd. along the western shore of Moose Pond to a point 1.8 mi. south of the road's jct. with US 302, and 1.2 mi. beyond the entrance to the Shawnee Peak ski area. The trailhead is on the right between utility poles 49 and 50 (sign). Limited roadside parking is available.

The trail starts westward, crosses a brook, and climbs steeply. At 0.2 mi., turn left and follow the north side of the brook. At 0.4 mi., a short but rough spur trail (sign) leads left to the Needle's Eye, a brook cascading through a cleft in a ledge. At 0.7 mi., just before the second of two small brooks, turn left (Sue's Way turns right; see sign). Climb a steep 0.3 mi. over exposed bedrock, emerging onto ledges (cairn). Turn left and quickly reach Big Bald Peak (1,932 ft.) and excellent views at 1.1 mi. From Big Bald Peak, the trail follows the crest of the ridge, first south and then southwest over two humps, toward the main summit. At 2.2 mi., it joins Firewarden's Trail, which leads left (south) past the storm shelter to the top of Pleasant Mtn. and the fire tower.

SUE'S WAY (LELT; PLEASANT MTN., P. 333)

From Bald Peak Trail (1,300 ft.) to:	⮑⮑	↗	⟳
North Ridge Trail (1,750 ft.)	0.5 mi.	450 ft.	0:30

This orange-blazed trail starts 0.7 mi. up Bald Peak Trail and leads 0.5 mi. to a jct. with North Ridge Trail (sign). At the jct., turn right and leave the woods. Go past the Shawnee Peak ski area summit warming hut and uphill a short distance to the top of the ski area for views to the north. Combined, Sue's Way and North Ridge Trail allow for an interesting loop hike.

SEC
8

There's a spring one-third of the way up Sue's Way, and the trail is often wet in season.

NORTH RIDGE TRAIL (LELT; PLEASANT MTN., P. 333)

From Sue's Way (1,750 ft.) to:	↧↥	↗	⟳
Bald Peak Trail (1,800 ft.)	0.8 mi.	200 ft.	0:30

This white-blazed trail begins at the jct. with Sue's Way, 100 yd. downhill (southeast) from the top of the Shawnee Peak ski area. North Ridge Trail heads due west on the level before turning left to pass through a granite slab. The trail then circles around the northwest side of the mountain's north peakbefore reaching the top. Beyond, it bears right to cross an open ledge, where there are views of Big Bald Peak and the main summit of Pleasant Mtn. The trail then drops steeply into a col before ascending Big Bald Peak. Just below the top, Bald Peak Trail comes in from the left.

FRYEBURG

■ MT. TOM (1,073 FT.)

Mt. Tom in Fryeburg offers hikers a pleasant walk through the woods, capped by summit ledges with rewarding views of the Saco River valley and Pleasant Mtn. Two trails access the top. Much of the land on the north side of Mt. Tom is owned by the Carter family of Fryeburg, who maintain Mt. Tom Trail. The 995-acre Mt. Tom Preserve, owned by The Nature Conservancy, protects a sizeable chunk of the west, south, and east slopes of the mountain between Menotomy Rd. and the Saco River, as well as 3,500 feet of frontage on that river. TNC maintains West Ridge Trail.

SEC 8

MT. TOM TRAIL (CARTER FAMILY; USGS FRYEBURG QUAD, GAZETTEER MAP 4)

Cumulative from Menotomy Rd. (490 ft.) to:	↧↥	↗	⟳
West Ridge Trail (1,060 ft.)	1.1 mi.	570 ft.	0:50
Mt. Tom summit (1,073 ft.) via West Ridge Trail	1.2 mi.	585 ft.	0:55

This old trail climbs Mt. Tom from the northwest. From the intersection of US 302 and ME 113 in Fryeburg, drive south on US 302 for 2.3 mi. Turn left (north) onto Menotomy Rd. and proceed 2.3 mi. to a small parking area (sign) on the right next to a large barn and field.

Mt. Tom Trail follows the Old Mountain Rd. south through the field to a dirt road and the Mt. Tom Cabin (1883), which is owned by the Carter family. A short distance beyond the cabin, pass a house on the right. This vantage point offers lovely views to the west, including Mt. Kearsarge and other peaks of the White Mountains. The road soon turns to grass and ascends gradually to a firewood log yard. Ahead at a fork, bear left and continue easily upward through a mix of forest types, including a stand of mature hemlock. Just shy of the summit, the trail merges with West Ridge Trail, which enters from the right. The south-facing ledges and summit sign are just 0.1 mi. ahead.

WEST RIDGE TRAIL (TNC; USGS FRYEBURG QUAD, GAZETTEER MAP 4, TNC MT. TOM PRESERVE MAP)

Cumulative from Menotomy Rd. (350 ft.) to:	⇅	↗	⟳
Mt. Tom Trail (1,060 ft.)	1.6 mi.	700 ft.	1:10
Mt. Tom summit ledges (1,073 ft.)	1.7 mi.	710 ft.	1:15

This trail climbs Mt. Tom from the southwest. Refer to driving directions for Mt. Tom Trail above. From the jct. of US 302 and Menotomy Rd., turn north on Menotomy Rd. and drive 1.1 mi. to Fire Rd. 31B on the right (sign for TNC trailhead). Park as far to the right on this road as possible; do not block the road.

Walk 150 ft. down the fire road to the start of West Ridge Trail on the left (sign). Just into the woods are several old foundations. Pass between these, following the white blazes of the trail. Ahead, cross a small stream, and soon bear right on an old woods road (sign: trail). In another 100 ft., where the woods road crosses a stream on a bridge, bear left off the road (sign: trail). Begin a steady ascent. At 0.9 mi., the ascent becomes steep. Follow along a lichen-covered rock wall, then climb up to the left through a break in the wall. Reach the northeast ridge of Mt. Tom at 1.0 mi. A brief descent leads to an old woods road (sign). Bear left onto the old road, and a short distance ahead, bear right off the road (sign). Beyond, climb at a steady moderate grade with several steep pitches. Ahead, a rising contour leads to an outcrop and a view to the southwest. Ascend steadily along the steep, forested west face of Mt. Tom. At 1.45 mi., climb over two rock slabs, then go up and around to gain a narrow ridge. The angle soon eases as the trail contours to reach a cairn with a painted rock at 1.6 mi. Just beyond is the jct. with Mt. Tom Trail. Bear right here to reach the top of Mt. Tom and its impressive south-facing ledges in 0.1 mi.

■ JOCKEY CAP (610 FT.)

This impressive ledge on the outskirts of Fryeburg rises nearly 200 ft. above the surrounding countryside and offers outstanding views for a small amount of time and effort. Jockey Cap was the site of the first rope ski tow in Maine, installed in 1936. At the top, a bronze profile of the nearby peaks is a monument to polar explorer Robert E. Peary, who lived in Fryeburg from 1878 to 1879. The monument affords a great way to identify neighboring mountains, including Mt. Washington.

The trailhead is on the north side of US 302 at the Jockey Cap Country Store, 1.6 mi. east of the jct. of US 302 and ME 113 (traffic light) in the center of Fryeburg. To the left side of the store, there are two signed parking spaces for hikers.

JOCKEY CAP TRAIL
(NFTM; USGS FRYEBURG QUAD, GAZETTEER MAP 4)

Cumulative from US 302 at Jockey Cap Country Store (425 ft.) to:	⇅	↗	⏱
Jockey Cap summit (610 ft.)	0.2 mi.	185 ft.	0:15
Complete loop	0.5 mi.	185 ft.	0:25

The trail begins through the gateway to the left of the store (sign). It quickly bears left, then right, and soon reaches Molly Lockett's Cave. The last of the Pequawkets, she is said to have used the cave for a shelter. Follow the trail to the left around the large rocks and circle up the west side of the cliff, which is visible through the trees. Climbing to the back side of the dome, emerge from the woods and scramble across the open summit ledges to the Peary monument and commanding views that range from Pleasant Mtn. and the Presidential Range and Carter–Moriah Range to the peaks in the Evans Notch area. To make a loop, return to the back side and take the path to the right, which descends along the east side of Jockey Cap out to a path that parallels US 302 through the woods. Follow the path west, passing behind Dollar General and the Jockey Cap Country Store to return to the trailhead parking.

SEC 8

ME 113 CORRIDOR

■ PEARY MTN. (958 FT.)

The open ledges of this mountain in Brownfield afford good views of the White Mountains and the mountains of western Maine, including Mt. Chocorua, the Moats, Kearsarge, the Presidential Range, Carter–Moriah Range, and the peaks around Evans Notch.

From the jct. of ME 160 and ME 113 in East Brownfield, proceed north on ME 113 for 2.2 mi. to Farnsworth Rd. Turn left (west) onto Farnsworth Rd. and drive 1.3 mi. to a bridge over Little Saco River. A small parking area is located on the right before the bridge. There is a snowmobile trail signpost and a kiosk with maps of the snowmobile trails.

PEARY MTN. TRAIL
(NFTM; USGS BROWNFIELD QUAD, GAZETTEER MAP 4)

Cumulative from Farnsworth Rd. (400 ft.) to:	⇅	↗	○
Saddle (800 ft.)	0.8 mi.	400 ft.	0:35
Peary Mtn. south summit (910 ft.)	1.0 mi.	510 ft.	0:45
Peary Mtn. main summit (958 ft.)	1.4 mi.	560 ft.	1:00

The trail starts on the opposite side of Farnsworth Rd. from the parking area. Follow the old woods road (snowmobile trail) past a gate on the east side of the river. Just ahead, in a small clearing (old log yard), bear right. The trail heads south on the level and then climbs at a gradual grade to a saddle at 0.8 mi., in a small clearing with an old foundation and stone wall. Turn left (southeast) off the woods road, and immediately left again onto another woods road. In 100 ft., turn right (cairn) onto a footpath and ascend through open woods and over ledges (following cairns) for 0.2 mi. to the south summit. Here is a granite bench and outstanding views to the north and west. To reach the main summit, follow the trail 0.4 mi. northeast across open ledges and through scrub. At trail's end are views to the east and north, including Pleasant Mtn. and Pleasant Pond.

■ BURNT MEADOW MTN., NORTH PEAK (1,575 FT.)

Located in Brownfield, this mountain mass consists of three main summits and two lesser summits, all of nearly equal height. Deep cols separate Stone Mtn. from the north and south peaks of Burnt Meadow Mtn. Fine views may be had of the Saco River valley, the western Maine mountains, and the White Mountains. A ski area operated on the north slope of the mountain from 1971 into the early 1980s.

From the jct. of ME 113/5 and ME 160 in East Brownfield, drive west on ME 160 through Brownfield. In 0.9 mi., bear sharply left (south) past the Brownfield Community Church. Continue past Burnt Meadow Pond to trailhead parking (kiosk) on the right at 3.1 mi.

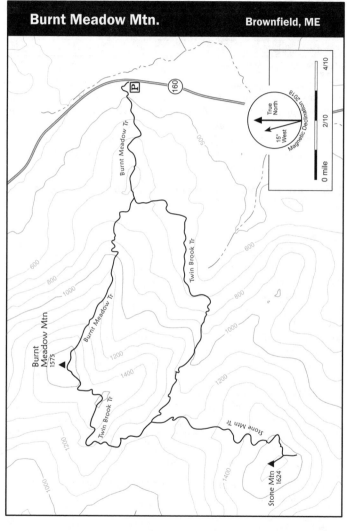

Burnt Meadow Mtn.

Brownfield, ME

BURNT MEADOW TRAIL (FOBMM; BURNT MEADOW MTN., P. 341)

Cumulative from ME 160 (430 ft.) to:	⇅	↗	⟳
Twin Brook Trail (770 ft.)	0.5 mi.	340 ft.	0:25
Burnt Meadow Mtn., north peak (1,575 ft.)	1.3 mi.	1,200 ft.	1:15

The trail (blue blazes) climbs westerly up the slope, staying on the southern edge of the east ridge. At 0.4 mi., it passes over a small hump and drops slightly into a shallow col and the jct. with Twin Brook Trail at 0.5 mi. Beyond the col, Burnt Meadow Trail continues up the crest of the spur, which becomes steeper and more open, with a sharp dropoff on the left. Cairns as well as blazes mark the upper part of the route, which climbs via a series of ledges and a short scramble to reach the open summit at 1.3 mi.

TWIN BROOK TRAIL (FOBMM; BURNT MEADOW MTN., P. 341)

Cumulative from Burnt Meadow Trail (770 ft.) to:	⇅	↗	⟳
Stone Mtn. Trail (1,160 ft.)	1.2 mi.	390 ft.	0:50
Burnt Meadow Mtn., north peak (1,575 ft.)	2.0 mi.	865 ft.	1:25

This trail forms a loop over the summit of Burnt Meadow Mtn. when combined with Burnt Meadow Trail. Twin Brook Trail (yellow blazes) leaves Burnt Meadow Trail at a point 0.5 mi. from the trailhead on ME 160. It follows a brook up the ravine between Stone Mtn. and North Peak of Burnt Meadow Mtn. At 1.2 mi., the trail reaches a col and the jct. with Stone Mtn. Trail (leads left [south] 0.7 mi. to the 1,624-ft. summit of Stone Mtn.). Beyond, the trail climbs ledges on the southern flank of North Peak, reaching the summit at 2.0 mi. and the jct. with Burnt Meadow Trail.

■ STONE MTN. (1,624 FT.)

This mountain is the highest of the three summits of the Burnt Meadow Mtn. mass in Brownfield. Stone Mtn. Trail to the peak was constructed by AMC and Friends of Burnt Meadow Mountains volunteers. It opened in 2010. See the descriptions for Burnt Meadow Trail and Twin Brook Trail for directions to the start of Stone Mtn. Trail.

STONE MTN. TRAIL (FOBMM; BURNT MEADOW MTN., P. 341)

From Twin Brook Trail (1,160 ft.) to:	⇅	↗	⟳
Stone Mtn. summit (1,624 ft.)	0.7 mi.	460 ft.	0:35

This trail heads south from near the height-of-land between Stone Mtn. and Burnt Meadow Mtn. (North Peak) at a point 1.2 mi. from ME 160 via Burnt Meadow Trail and Twin Brook Trail. Stone Mtn. Trail ascends the

SEC 8

north shoulder of Stone Mtn., crosses a dry brook, and then switchbacks to reach the ledges on the south flank of the mountain before continuing west to the summit at 0.7 mi.

■ MT. CUTLER (1,232 FT.)

The extensive open ledges of this mountain in the village of Hiram reward hikers with fine views of nearby hills and farmlands, the Saco River valley to the south, and the White Mountains to the north. The 4 mi. of trails on Mt. Cutler are almost entirely on privately owned lands, the bulk of which have been owned since 2007 by conservation-minded Dan Hester of Hiram, who formed the Mt. Cutler Preservation Trust. Visitors enjoy access to these trails by permission of the various landowners.

As of 2017, efforts were under way to permanently preserve Mt. Cutler. With the assistance of a Land and Water Conservation Fund grant, Hiram is now working to purchase 173 acres on the mountain to create the

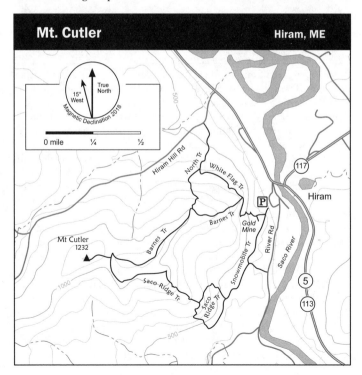

SEC
8

Mt. Cutler Park and Conservation Area, which will be open for multiple public uses. Francis Small Heritage Trust has contributed effort and resources for this project and may take care of trail maintenance. The Nature Conservancy has also provided a grant in support of this park development. A new large trailhead parking area is planned for Hiram Hill Rd. at the start of North Trail, along with new signage and trail maps. Existing trails will continue to be maintained, both on the park property and on adjacent lands, and about 1 mi. of new trails are planned, increasing the opportunities for loop hikes on Mt. Cutler.

BARNES TRAIL (AMC; MT. CUTLER, P. 343)

Cumulative from old Maine Central Railroad Depot trailhead (375 ft.) to:	⇵	↗	⟳
Front Ledges (625 ft.)	0.4 mi.	250 ft.	0:20
White Flag Trail (625 ft.)	0.5 mi.	250 ft.	0:25
South View Ledge (970 ft.)	0.7 mi.	600 ft.	0:40
North Trail (1,030 ft.)	0.9 mi.	650 ft.	0:50
Notch/ATV trail (1,090 ft.)	1.2 mi.	850 ft.	1:00
Mt. Cutler main summit (1,232 ft.)	1.3 mi.	1,000 ft.	1:10

Barnes Trail starts from the site of the old Maine Central Railroad Depot in Hiram. From the jct. of ME 113/5 and ME 117 in Hiram, cross the Saco River Bridge, turn left (south) on River Rd., then immediately turn right on Mountain View Ave. Where the ave. turns nearest to the mountain, cross the first set of railroad tracks and park in the area between the tracks. There is a kiosk, and a trail sign is across the tracks, south of the parking area. This is the trailhead for Barnes Trail and Snowmobile Trail. Barnes Trail, established by Dr. Lowell "Bud" Barnes in the 1950s, is the original trail to the front ledges on Mt. Cutler. Sections of this trail are very steep. The trail is marked by red blazes on trees and rocks and, on ledge areas, by rock cairns.

After crossing the tracks to the trail sign, Barnes Trail and Snowmobile Trail stay together up a steady grade. At about 100 yd., the trails divide. Snowmobile Trail continues straight, while Barnes Trail forks to the right and enters Merrill Botanical Park, a grove of large pines (severely damaged in 2010). Before Barnes Trail leaves the park, a short path branches to the south, through an opening in a stone wall, leading to the "Gold Mine," described in books of local lore written by Raymond Cotton. Barnes Trail makes a slight dip as it leaves the southwest corner of the park and crosses the (usually dry) outlet of a large vernal pool. Historical dug wells are found in this small valley. The trail ascends quickly to enter the ravine between Mt. Cutler and the south shoulder of the mountain. Stay on the south side of the seasonal stream, and follow the steep ascent up the ravine over rough rocks. After going west and up for about 100 yd., Barnes Trail turns sharply right and crosses a very rough boulder area. The trail passes under an overhanging ledge and makes a very steep ascent of the ledges. At the top of the ledges, the trail turns sharply right and runs north along the top of the Front Ledges, which offer excellent views overlooking Hiram.

Northwest of the Front Ledges, the trail makes a sharp left turn, passes the jct. with White Flag Trail, enters a hardwood forest, and steadily ascends toward the west. Some short sections are steep. Before entering a hemlock grove, there are good views to the northeast to Pleasant Mtn. Above, the trail continues a steady, moderate ascent before emerging from a small evergreen thicket into the open at South View Ledge, where there are spectacular panoramic views to the southeast, sometimes as far as the Maine coast. This vista point is not actually a summit, although it appears to be so when viewed from the village. These ledges are the easternmost end of a long ridge, with the westward end at a notch just below the true summit of Mt. Cutler.

Barnes Trail continues, gradually ascending the long east-west ridge of Mt. Cutler. Along this ridge are alternating outlooks with excellent views to the northwest (the Presidential Range) and to the south (Saco Bay and Casco Bay). Cairns and some red blazes mark the trail, although it is usually discernible without markers. At 0.9 mi., North Trail enters from the north. Just beyond this jct. are good views north to Burnt Meadow Mtn. and Mt. Washington. Ahead, Barnes Trail crosses a mostly wooded secondary summit (1,080 ft.) then descends quickly to a notch traversed by a sometimes-used ATV trail at 1.2 mi. The true summit of Mt. Cutler is a short scramble west of this notch.

SEC 8

SNOWMOBILE TRAIL (AMC; MT. CUTLER, P. 343)

Cumulative from old Maine Central Railroad Depot trailhead (375 ft.) to:	⇅	↗	⏲
Saco Ridge Trail (430 ft.)	0.5 mi.	55 ft.	0:15
Old Saco Ridge Trail (430 ft.)	0.7 mi.	55 ft.	0:20

Snowmobile Trail starts at the same trailhead as Barnes Trail. After the initial 100 yd. uphill, where Barnes Trail forks to the right, Snowmobile Trail continues straight. It remains nearly level, passing two houses that are on the left (below the elevation of the trail). Ahead, the trail descends slightly before it enters open fields. Turning toward the mountain, away from the fields, the trail reenters woods, turns left, and crosses a small stream. Just beyond this stream crossing, Saco Ridge Trail leaves to the right at a small cairn at 0.5 mi. Continuing mostly on the level, Snowmobile Trail passes close to a steep shoulder of the mountain, where the original Saco Ridge Trail (now called Old Saco Ridge Trail) begins at 0.7 mi.

SACO RIDGE TRAIL (AMC; MT. CUTLER, P. 343)

Cumulative from Notch/ATV trail and Barnes Trail upper end (1,090 ft.) to:	⇅	↗	○
Old Saco Ridge Trail (790 ft.)	0.5 mi.	25 ft.	0:15
Snowmobile Trail (430 ft.)	0.7 mi.	25 ft.	0:20
Old Maine Central Railroad Depot trailhead (375 ft.)	1.2 mi.	25 ft.	0:35

Saco Ridge Trail is often used as a descent route and is therefore described in that direction. With Barnes Trail, Saco Ridge Trail forms a nice loop hike. Saco Ridge Trail (also known as South Ridge Trail) runs from the notch/ATV trail high on Mt. Cutler, at the upper end of Barnes Trail, down the most prominent southern ridge, joining Snowmobile Trail at the eastern base of the mountain. Leaving the notch, descend a short distance to the south, watching for cairns and red blaze marks. The trail bears left and slabs along the south side of Mt. Cutler, gradually descending until it reaches a small notch between the bulk of the mountain and the upper part of this ridge. The trail makes a short ascent to an open area with views to the east. Near the easternmost edge of this clearing, it turns sharply right (at a cairn), enters hardwoods, and descends the ridge. There are several good viewpoints looking down to the Saco River and the neighboring farmland. Before the lowest overlook on Saco Ridge, reach a jct. with Old Saco Ridge Trail; steep and sometimes slippery, it is not recommended (but for a nice view, walk 100 ft. on Old Saco Ridge Trail). The relocated Saco Ridge Trail turns north in a small clearing spotted with pines. The descent continues northward, eventually making a right turn to descend eastward on an old logging road to reach Snowmobile Trail. Turn left to return to the trailhead in Hiram.

NORTH TRAIL (AMC; MT. CUTLER, P. 343)

Cumulative from Hiram Hill Rd. (450 ft.) to:	⇅	↗	○
Moraine Trail (500 ft.)	0.2 mi.	50 ft.	0:10
White Flag Trail (620 ft.)	0.3 mi.	170 ft.	0:15
Barnes Trail (1,030 ft.)	0.5 mi.	580 ft.	0:35
Notch/ATV trail (1,100 ft.) via Barnes Trail	1.0 mi.	780 ft.	0:55
Mt. Cutler main summit (1,232 ft.)	1.1 mi.	920 ft.	1:00

This trail (blue blazes) ascends from the north to meet Barnes Trail high on the long east ridge of Mt. Cutler. In Hiram, from the jct. of ME 113/5 and River Rd. on the west side of the bridge over the Saco River, drive north 0.6 mi. to Hiram Hill Rd. (on the left just before the concrete bridge over Red Mill Brook). Turn left on Hiram Hill Rd. and park along the road before the railroad tracks (plans for a new parking area are being developed). Walk up Hiram Hill Rd., cross the railroad tracks, and look up the road; you should see two large pine trees straight ahead, where the road curves uphill to the right. North Trail starts on the south side of the road, 0.1 mi. past the railroad crossing, under the obvious "twin pines." Look for blue blazes marking the trail, a well house in the woods near the road and trail, and a small trail sign.

As the trail leaves the road, it passes a well house uphill from the trail (this is an active water supply; do not approach or tamper with the well house or water source). In 100 yd., North Trail crosses a small stream next to a property corner marker (please do not disturb iron pins and flagging tape used to mark the trail and property lines). The trail continues at moderate uphill grade through hardwood forest in a southerly direction toward the mountain. At 0.1, at the crest of a small ridge, Moraine Trail forks to the left. North Trail follows the west side of a small valley with a brook, then ascends a steep ridge notched by this brook. The trail parallels the brook for 150 yd., passing several gullies visible to the south. At 0.25 mi., the trail turns left, crosses the brook in a grove of large hemlocks, and ascends southwest away from the water. At 0.3 mi. above the crossing, White Flag Trail diverges to the left. In another 150 yd., North Trail reaches the foot of a steep, rocky slope, turns left, and works its way uphill into dense hemlock woods. Short switchbacks ascend steeper sections below the hemlock thickets. Climbing higher, through narrow passages in thick hemlocks, the trail emerges on sloping, open ledges with excellent views to the north and northeast. In wet weather, the moss and lichens covering the ledges can be slippery. Passing through hemlocks, the trail reemerges to continue up sloping ledges to join Barnes Trail at a cairn marker at 0.5 mi. Turn right to continue up Mt. Cutler via Barnes Trail.

SEC 8

WHITE FLAG TRAIL (AMC; MT. CUTLER, P. 343)

Cumulative from Hiram Hill Rd. (450 ft.) to:	⇅	↗	⟳
Start of White Flag Trail (620 ft.) via North Trail	0.3 mi.	170 ft.	0:15
Barnes Trail (625 ft.)	0.5 mi.	210 ft.	0:25

White Flag Trail forks left off North Trail at 0.25 mi., a short distance above the highest brook crossing. After crossing a small ridge, it ascends gradually to the southeast through overgrown pastures and gentle ledges. Passing large boulders, stone walls, and remains of pasture fences, the trail joins the Barnes Trail near the Front Ledges.

MORAINE TRAIL (AMC; MT. CUTLER, P. 343)

Cumulative from Hiram Hill Rd.
(380 ft.) to:

	⇅	↗	⟳
Start of Moraine Trail via railroad tracks (380 ft.)	0.2 mi.	0 ft.	0:05
North Trail (500 ft.)	0.4 mi.	120 ft.	0:15

From the railroad crossing on Hiram Hill Rd., walk 0.2 mi. south on the abandoned Mountain Division railroad tracks. On the right, a trail sign indicates the start of this trail, which is marked with white paint blazes. Ascending through hardwoods via two switchbacks, Moraine Trail climbs to the east end of an interesting ridge (a glacial moraine), crosses a stone wall, then follows this ridge to the jct. with North Trail. (*Note:* The Mountain Division rail line has not been used for rail transport since the 1980s; however, this line is state-owned property and may be considered for return to active use in the near future. In Fryeburg and near Sebago Lake, sections of the rail line have been developed, with multiuse paths to allow continued pedestrian use even if rail transport resumes, and similar development may be considered in the Hiram area. For Mt. Cutler, the railroad line should be considered part of the trail system. Walking the RR tracks connects Hiram Hill Rd. to Moraine Trail and the Hiram Depot trailhead. Using the RR tracks along with the mountain trails provides for several different loop hikes.)

SEC 8

FRANCES SMALL HERITAGE TRUST

■ BALD LEDGE (1,187 FT.)

From the precipitous cliffs atop this crag in Porter, not far from the New Hampshire border, hikers are rewarded with a fabulous vista eastward over Colcord Pond to the pretty hills and woods of north-central York County. Francis Small Heritage Trust owns 25 acres of land next to the ledges, while the Giovanella family of the nearby Bickford Pond area owns 200 acres, which includes most of Bald Ledge and its summit overlook. FSHT maintains a trail to the top from the west side.

From the jct. of Old County Rd. and ME 25/160 in Porter, drive north on Old County Rd. for 1.5 mi. Bear left on Colcord Pond Rd. and continue 2.8 mi. to a fork. Here, Colcord Pond Rd. goes right; bear left and proceed on Dana Weeks Rd. a very short distance then bear right again to continue on Kennard Hill Rd. Drive 1.5 mi. up several steep hills to Danforth Lane. Turn right on Danforth Lane then, at a split in the road ahead, bear right on Varney Rd. There is a water bar on this old road, so be careful. Parking is a short way down Varney Rd. at a grassy open space on the right.

BALD LEDGE TRAIL
(FSHT; USGS KEZAR FALLS QUAD, GAZETTEER MAP 4)

From parking on Kennard Hill Rd. (870 ft.) to:	⇅	↗	◔
Bald Ledge summit overlooks (1,187 ft.)	0.7 mi.	320 ft.	0:30

Start by walking north on Varney Rd. Follow this wide old road easily uphill, passing a shed on the left. Soon after, at 0.3 mi., look for a red block of wood on the right with the carved outline of a turtle painted yellow; this marks the start of the foot trail to Bald Ledge. Cross the stone wall bordering the road, then follow along another stone wall. Ahead, go right at a stone wall. Pass a huge bull pine on the left, then bear sharply left to cross a low, mossy stone wall. Pass through woods of red and white pine. Follow to the right of a large stone wall, then cross another low, mossy wall. Wend upslope through hemlocks to reach a jct. Here, an old trail from the Colcord Pond side enters from the left. Turn right and climb through a hemlock grove to a big ledge outlook on the left (best views of Colcord Pond and the hills and woods beyond). Continue easily along the ridge to trail's end at the top of Bald Ledge and another outlook.

■ SAWYER MTN. (1,213 FT.)

SEC 8

Sawyer Mtn. is the central natural feature of the Sawyer Mtn. Highlands, a parcel of 1,472 contiguous acres spanning the town lines of Limerick and Limington. Owned and managed by FSHT, the property is part of the largest unfragmented block of undeveloped forestland in York and Cumberland counties, just 22 mi. from the major urban center of Portland. Sawyer Mtn. may be reached from Limerick on the west side or from Limington on the east.

More than 5 mi. of trails thread through the hilly terrain, which is home to stands of old-growth red oak, hemlock, sugar maple, and beech, miles of stone walls, and the remains of the historical Sawyer homestead. Trails are marked with small blocks of wood that have the outline of a turtle carved into them and painted yellow; this is the mark of Captain Sandy, also known as Chief Wesumbe, of the Newichewannock Abenaki, the native people of the area.

SMITH TRAIL (FSHT; USGS LIMERICK QUAD, GAZETTEER MAP 4, MTF SAWYER MTN. HIGHLANDS MAP)

Cumulative from Sawyer Mtn. Rd.
(650 ft.) to:

	⇅	↗	○
Old Sawyer Mtn. Rd. (950 ft.)	0.8 mi.	330 ft.	0:35
Summit side trail (1,100 ft.)	1.2 mi.	480 ft.	0:50
Sawyer Mtn. summit (1,213 ft.)	1.5 mi.	600 ft.	1:00

This trail climbs Sawyer Mtn. from the Limerick side. From the post office at the jct. of ME 5 and ME 11 in the village of Limerick, drive northeast on ME 11 for 0.9 mi. Just after the boat launch and outlet dam on Sokokis Lake, turn left on Emery Corner Rd. Follow it for 0.8 mi. to a four-way intersection, where Quarry Rd. goes left and Pickerel Pond Rd. goes right. Proceed straight through the intersection to continue on Emery Corner Rd. In another 1.2 mi., Coffin Hill Rd. diverges right; here, bear sharply left onto Sawyer Mtn. Rd. to reach Emery Corner in another 0.5 mi. Continue straight on the dirt-surfaced Sawyer Mtn. Rd., while the paved Lombard Hill Rd. goes left and the dirt Shaving Hill Rd. goes right. In another 0.6 mi., Nason Corner Rd. diverges left; continue straight ahead on Sawyer Mtn. Rd. to reach the gravel trailhead parking lot on the right in another 0.3 mi. If you reach a town turnaround in sight of a red barn on a hill up to the right, you've gone just a little too far. (*Note:* During spring mud season, the parking lot is closed, requiring hikers to park along the roadside.)

Smith Trail leaves from the right-hand corner of the lot and proceeds uphill on a wide track. Ahead, bear left up a ridge, which climbs next to a stream in a rocky ravine. The trail soon levels off and crosses the stream. Proceeding on a contour, the path follows a jeep trail, but soon bears left onto a footpath (arrow) and climbs up and left below a ridge of mossy boulders. The angle soon eases, and the path continues through parklike woods. Beyond, swing up and right to pass a huge ancient oak 25 ft. to the right of the trail. Just beyond, the trail veers gently left and easily ascends the slope beyond. The trail then bears sharply left (arrow) and passes through a gap in a stone wall. Along a wide, level stretch, it passes through two more stone walls, then trends gently downhill, passes through a fourth stone wall, and soon reaches the jct. with the old Sawyer Mtn. Rd. The stone foundations, cellar holes, and well of the old Sawyer family homestead (settled in 1794) are directly ahead in the woods across from the jct. Turn right on old Sawyer Mtn. Rd. and follow this wide, eroded, and often wet old road north to the height-of-land on the northwest shoulder of the mountain. Here, a side trail leaves right to follow the ridge crest for 0.3 mi. to the summit of Sawyer Mtn.

Visible from the ocean, the summit of Sawyer was once the site of a whale oil light that helped guide ships into Portland Harbor in the eighteenth

SEC 8

century. In 1884, the U.S. Geological Survey erected a 15-ft. stone monument on the site, which was destroyed by lightning in 1913. Scattered stones from the tower still remain. From the summit sign, the trail continues to a fine flat rock in a grassy clearing, where it ends. Beyond the trees, views to the south and west stretch over the lowland of York County. On the northeast side, views range to Sebago Lake, the second-largest and deepest lake in Maine.

SAWYER MTN. ROAD TRAIL (FSHT; USGS STEEP FALLS, CORNISH, AND LIMERICK QUADS, GAZETTEER MAP 4, MTF SAWYER MTN. HIGHLANDS MAP)

Cumulative from ME 117 (500 ft.) to:	⮃	↗	◷
Summit side trail (1,100 ft.)	1.5 mi.	600 ft.	1:05
Sawyer Mtn. summit (1,213 ft.)	1.8 mi.	725 ft.	1:15

From the jct. of ME 25 and ME 117 in Limington, drive south on ME 117 for 2.5 mi. to a parking area (sign) on the right. The trailhead can also be reached by driving north on ME 117 for 2.4 mi. from the jct. of ME 117 and ME 11 in Limington.

The trail leaves the parking area and follows the right-hand branch road, the Old Sawyer Mtn. Rd. This road is rough, rocky, and severely eroded in places. Pass several camps on the right, and be sure to observe private property signs. Continue straight through several intersections (signed) and pass the Estes Cemetery on the right. At 1.5 mi. on the north shoulder of the mountain, reach a jct. Here, the summit side trail on the left leads 0.3 mi. to the top of Sawyer Mtn. and a large grassy clearing with a number of nice viewpoints.

SHERWOOD LIBBY TRAIL (FSHT; USGS STEEP FALLS, CORNISH, AND LIMERICK QUADS, GAZETTEER MAP 4, MTF SAWYER MTN. HIGHLANDS MAP)

Cumulative from ME 117 (500 ft.) to:	⮃	↗	◷
High pasture of Ebenezer Walker (960 ft.)	1.2 mi.	460 ft.	0:50
New Skidway Rd. (840 ft.)	1.8 mi.	460 ft.	1:10
Summit side trail (1,180 ft.)	2.2 mi.	800 ft.	1:30
Sawyer Mtn. summit (1,213 ft.)	2.3 mi.	830 ft.	1:35

This trail leaves from the same trailhead parking area as Sawyer Mtn. Road Trail, described above.

Take the left-hand branch road from the parking area to follow old Littlefield Pond Rd. Sherwood Libby Trail is marked by orange wooden signs featuring yellow turtles. (At the start of the trail is an optional 0.7-mi.

Nature Trail, marked with blue turtles, that loops back to the parking area.) Littlefield Pond Rd. goes slightly uphill, and at 0.4 mi., Sherwood Libby Trail leaves on the right (sign). Sherwood Libby Trail continues uphill through a beech forest, crosses a small stream, and skirts a grassy area at the base of John Douglass Mtn., which is named for one of the first settlers in the area. The trail continues to the right below towering, rocky cliffs and ascends via rock stairs to the high pasture of Ebenezer Walker, who cleared the land here in 1815. Beyond, the trail descends slightly through old fields bounded by stone walls then ascends again and crosses the New Skidway Rd. The trail continues to ascend the mountain, joining the summit side trail 0.1 mi. northwest of the summit of Sawyer Mtn.

VERNON S. WALKER WILDLIFE MANAGEMENT AREA

■ KNOX MTN. (830 FT.)

This mountain in Newfield is in the northern part of the expansive Vernon S. Walker Wildlife Management Area, which spans 5,617 acres across the towns of Newfield, Limerick, and Shapleigh. The Maine Dept. of Inland Fisheries and Wildlife manages the area. An unmarked trail climbs Knox Mtn. from the north.

From the jct. of ME 110 and ME 11 in Newfield, drive east on ME 11 for 2.0 mi. to an unsigned turnout on the right, directly across from the eastern end of Symmes Pond.

KNOX MTN. TRAIL
(NFTM; USGS LIMERICK QUAD, GAZETTEER MAP 2)

From ME 11 turnout (500 ft.) to:	↥↧	↗	↻
Knox Mtn. summit (830 ft.)	0.8 mi.	330 ft.	0:30

From the turnout, take the foot trail into the woods. (*Note:* The start is at an old paint-blazed boundary line; look closely, the entrance may be obscure.) Climb along a stone wall to a knoll. Descend through a cutover area, pass through a stone wall, and then cross a low wet area. Beyond, at a stone wall, bear right and up, following the line of the wall. At 0.5 mi., pass around the upper end of the stone wall to join an ATV track. Continue uphill at a moderate grade, following the wide ATV track along the north ridge. As the ridge narrows, hike over bedrock trail. At 0.7 mi., pass an obvious square-angled cut in a low ledge to the right of the trail. The tree canopy thins beyond this point. Reach the summit ledges just ahead, and enjoy fine views of the surrounding Little Ossipee River valley countryside from this vantage point.

■ ABBOTT MTN. (1,078 FT.)

This mountain in Shapleigh is in the southeast corner of the Vernon S. Walker Wildlife Management Area. Managed by DIFW, the area encompasses 5,617 acres in the towns of Shapleigh, Newfield, and Limerick. An unmarked trail ascends the mountain from the south.

In the center of Shapleigh, at the intersection of ME 11 and Owl's Nest Rd., and opposite a large white church, turn north on Owl's Nest Rd. and drive 3.3 mi. to the jct. of Owl's Nest Rd. and Pitts Rd. (pavement ends 0.3 mi. before this jct.). Park here on the right side of Owl's Nest Rd.

ABBOTT MTN. TRAIL
(NFTM; USGS MOUSAM LAKE QUAD, GAZETTEER MAP 2)

From parking at jct. of Owl's Nest Rd. and Pitts Rd. (580 ft.) to:	⇅	↗	↺
Abbott Mtn. summit (1,078 ft.)	1.3 mi.	500 ft.	0:55

Start by walking up Pitts Rd. While this private road is drivable, the landowner requests that users access Abbott Mtn. by "foot and hoof" only; please respect these wishes. At 0.2 mi., Pitts Rd. ends (No Parking signs). A driveway (number 43) is to the right. Walk straight ahead on the obvious old woods road, Abbott Mtn. Rd. At a jct. at 0.4 mi., turn left to follow the wide, rocky, eroded old jeep trail. Ahead, pass an old camper trailer in the woods on the right and then a small pond on the left. At 0.85 mi., where the jeep road continues straight, the "trail" (an ATV trail) to Abbott Mtn. turns left and climbs steeply up the ledges in view. Climb a series of ledge steps on the eroded bedrock trail, which is crisscrossed by ATV tracks. Stick to the most obvious route uphill. At 1.0 mi., enter a clearing of bedrock and grass with a lone pine in its center. Go left past the pine and continue upward. A multitrunked pine is in the center of the next clearing. Behind you now are good views south and west. Ahead, climb a moderate to steep stretch over open ledges. Reach the summit rock at 1.3 mi. at an ATV roundabout. Good views of the surrounding woodland extend west to the White Mountains. Another viewpoint ledge is 100 yd. north.

SEC 8

BAUNEG BEG MTN. CONSERVATION AREA

■ BAUNEG BEG MTN., MIDDLE PEAK (860 FT.) AND NORTH PEAK (830 FT.)

The middle peak of this mountain in North Berwick is part of the 89-acre Bauneg Beg Mtn. Conservation Area, which is owned and managed by

Great Works Regional Land Trust. The mountain's north peak is on land owned by the town of North Berwick. Bauneg Beg Mtn. (pronounced like "Bonny Beg") is the only major mountaintop in southern York County without a communications tower. Summit views range from the White Mountains and western Maine to the Atlantic Ocean.

From North Berwick, drive north on US 4 for 2.1 mi. Turn left onto Boyle Rd. and continue straight as it turns into Ford Quint Rd., about 5.5 mi. from US 4. Turn left onto Fox Farm Rd., and proceed 0.3 mi. to the trailhead parking area on the left (sign).

BAUNEG BEG TRAIL AND NORTH PEAK LOOP
(GWRLT; USGS SANFORD QUAD, GAZETTEER MAP 2, GWRLT BAUNEG BEG MTN. CONSERVATION AREA MAP)

Cumulative from Fox Farm Hill Rd. (600 ft.) to:

	↥↧	↗	◐
Bauneg Beg Mtn., Middle Peak (860 ft.), via Ginny's Way	0.6 mi.	260 ft.	0:25
Bauneg Beg Mtn., North Peak (830 ft.), via Linny's Way and North Peak Loop	1.0 mi.	340 ft.	0:40
Complete loop	1.5 mi.	340 ft.	0:55

Bauneg Beg Trail and North Peak Loop form a fine loop hike, climbing the mountain from the east. The white-blazed Bauneg Beg Trail leaves from the kiosk at the back of the parking lot. After a series of bog bridges, the path climbs gradually to the jct. of North Peak Loop, which enters from the right. Continue straight to the next jct., where Linny's Way departs right, climbing the mountain via Devil's Den. Bear left to continue the hike on Ginny's Way, which swings around the south and west sides of the mountain. After a short rise, the trail bears sharply right and ascends the southeast ridge to the jct. of Tom's Way, which departs left, down and out to Bauneg Beg Hill Rd. At 150 ft. beyond this jct., reach the north-facing summit ledges atop Middle Peak of Bauneg Beg Mtn. The view includes North Peak, part of Sanford, the towers on Mt. Hope, and, on a good day, even Mt. Washington.

From the summit, the trail bears left and down to a second area of open ledges. Follow the edge of the ridge, then bear sharply right onto Linny's Way to descend into the rocks of Devil's Den. Scamper down a narrow passage in the rocks beneath the overhangs of the summit ledges. Reach the base of the descent and a jct. where a sign points right to Ginny's Way. Continue straight on North Peak Loop, which crosses a shallow valley between the peaks. Climb easily out the other side to a jct. Here, a spur leads right 75 ft. to an open ledge and a nice look back at Middle Peak and the rocks of Devil's Den. Ahead, pass through a stone wall to reach the semi-open summit area on North Peak. Turn sharply right to walk over the low summit, which is marked by a large cairn. Beyond, cross another stone wall and reenter the woods. Beyond one more stone wall, the going is easy to the jct. of Bauneg Beg Trail. Turn left to return to the Fox Farm Rd. trailhead.

MT. AGAMENTICUS CONSERVATION REGION

From Maine Turnpike/I-95, Exit 7 in York, follow Chases Pond Rd. west and north for 3.5 mi. Turn left onto Mountain Rd., and in 2.5 mi., reach the base of the mountain and the main trailhead parking lot on the right. The paved Mt. Agamenticus Rd. begins from this point, climbing 0.7 mi. to the top of the mountain and the summit parking lot. On the open, grassy summit of Mt. Agamenticus are two observation decks, an old fire tower (1941; no public access), several communications towers, a workshop, and the old lodge of the long-defunct Big A ski area (now the Learning Lodge, an environmental education center).

Mt. Agamenticus trails are open year-round, as is Mt. Agamenticus Rd. (weather permitting; gate closes at sunset). The Learning Lodge is open weekends from 11 A.M. to 3 P.M. from Memorial Day through Columbus Day. (*Note:* Many cairns on Mt. Agamenticus, Second Hill, and Third Hill are scheduled to be replaced with paint blazes.)

■ MT. AGAMENTICUS (691 FT.)

RING TRAIL (MACR; MT. AGAMENTICUS, P. 356)

Cumulative from main trailhead parking on Mountain Rd. (347 ft.) to:	⇅	↗	⏱
Ring Trail loop jct. (400 ft.)	0.1 mi.	50 ft.	0:05
Blueberry Bluff Trail (480 ft.)	0.3 mi.	130 ft.	0:15
Wintergreen Trail (500 ft.)	0.6 mi.	150 ft.	0:25
Fisher Trail (540 ft.)	0.7 mi.	190 ft.	0:30
Vultures View Trail (500 ft.)	0.9 mi.	210 ft.	0:35
Sweet Fern Trail (510 ft.)	1.0 mi.	240 ft.	0:40
Goosefoot Trail, Chestnut Oak Trail (490 ft.)	1.0 mi.	240 ft.	0:40
Witch Hazel Trail (570 ft.)	1.2 mi.	320 ft.	0:45
Rocky Road Trail, Hairpin Trail (550 ft.)	1.3 mi.	340 ft.	0:50
Complete loop	1.9 mi.	360 ft.	1:10

SEC 8

This loop makes a circuit around Mt. Agamenticus, connecting to many of the mountain's summit trails. From the main trailhead parking lot on Mountain Rd., Ring Trail enters the woods from the right side (near the

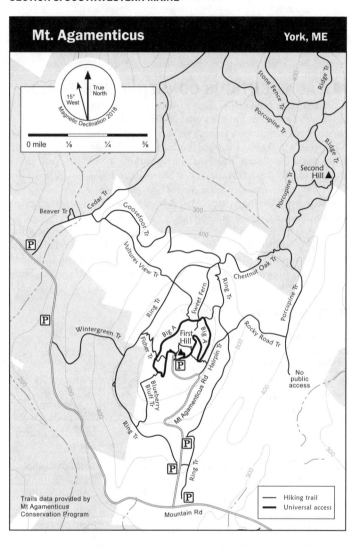

Mt. Agamenticus   York, ME

True North
15° West
Magnetic Declination 2018

0 mile   ⅛   ¼   ⅜

Stone Fence Tr
Ridge Tr
Porcupine Tr
Ridge Tr
Second Hill ▲
Porcupine Tr
Cedar Tr
Beaver Tr
Goosefoot Tr
Vultures View Tr
Chestnut Oak Tr
Ring Tr
Sweet Fern
Ring Tr
Porcupine Tr
Wintergreen Tr
Big A
First Hill
Big A
Rocky Road Tr
Fisher Tr
Hairpin Tr
No public access
Blueberry Bluff Tr
Mt Agamenticus Rd
Ring Tr
Ring Tr
Mountain Rd

Trails data provided by
Mt Agamenticus
Conservation Program

— Hiking trail
— Universal access

SEC 8

toilet), passes an information kiosk and fee station (an iron ranger, a slotted metal box for accepting the day-use fee), and proceeds easily north to the loop jct. at 0.1 mi. Turn left to follow Ring Trail in a clockwise direction. Just ahead, cross Mt. Agamenticus Rd. (parking) and continue following white blazes on the wide, well-used trail. At 0.3 mi., Blueberry Bluff Trail departs on the right. Ahead, crest the west shoulder of the mountain and soon reach a spur to a viewpoint on the left. At 0.6 mi., Wintergreen Trail enters from the left. Climb a short, moderate pitch to reach Fisher Trail on the right at 0.7 mi. After a gentle descent, arrive at a clearing, an old ski lift line, and then ahead, several semi-open old ski runs. At 0.9 mi., cross Vultures View Trail.

Swinging around the north side of the mountain, reach the jct. with Sweet Fern Trail, also an old ski run, at 1.0 mi. on the right. Just ahead on the left is the base of an old T-bar lift. At the fork just beyond, Goosefoot Trail leaves at an angle to the left, while Chestnut Oak Trail departs at an angle to the right. Ring Trail continues to the immediate right and climbs the north shoulder via a series of switchbacks to the jct. with Witch Hazel Trail on the right at 1.2 mi. Crest the shoulder, then descend to the east side of the mountain. Arrive at a jct. at 1.3 mi. Here, Rocky Road Trail enters from the left, while Hairpin Trail leaves to the right. Continue to descend on a narrow footpath, climb briefly, follow an undulating route, descend on a wide trail, and then bear right onto a narrow path in a regrowth area. At 1.7 mi., a spur on the right leads 25 ft. to the auto road; bear sharply left here. Close the Ring Trail loop at the jct. at 1.8 mi. Proceed straight ahead to the trailhead parking lot on Mountain Rd., which is in 0.1 mi.

**SEC
8**

BLUEBERRY BLUFF TRAIL
(MACR; MT. AGAMENTICUS, P. 356)

Cumulative from main trailhead parking on Mountain Rd. (347 ft.) to:	⮕⬆	↗	⟳
Start of Blueberry Bluff Trail (480 ft.)	0.3 mi.	130 ft.	0:15
Big A Trail (660 ft.)	0.5 mi.	180 ft.	0:10
Mt. Agamenticus summit (691 ft.) via Big A Trail	0.7 mi.	210 ft.	0:15

Blueberry Bluff Trail is one of three "hiking only" trails on Mt. Agamenticus (the others are Wintergreen Trail and Vultures View Trail). The route begins from Ring Trail, at a point 0.3 mi. from Mountain Rd. Blueberry Bluff Trail starts up the south ridge via several switchbacks, then climbs ledges, steps, and slabs. Following bedrock trail out of the trees, the trail reaches an overlook and a bench on the left. From this point, continue on Big A Trail, turning right just ahead to follow the loop counterclockwise up to the summit observation deck.

FISHER TRAIL (MACR; MT. AGAMENTICUS, P. 356)

Cumulative from main trailhead parking on Mountain Rd. (347 ft.) to:	⇅	↗	⭘
Start of Fisher Trail (540 ft.)	0.7 mi.	190 ft.	0:30
Big A Trail, second crossing (670 ft.)	0.9 mi.	320 ft.	0:40
Mt. Agamenticus summit (691 ft.) via Big A Trail	1.0 mi.	340 ft.	0:45

Fisher Trail starts from Ring Trail at a point 0.7 mi. from Mountain Rd. The trail ascends easily via switchbacks, and as it breaks out into the open, the summit fire tower and communications tower come into view. Cross Big A Trail and pass around the left side of a workshop. Head straight for the rail fence and stone steps just ahead. At a gate on the old fire tower service road, look right to see the summit parking lot. A large information kiosk, the summit observation deck, and the old Big A ski lodge (now the Learning Lodge) are straight ahead. Seasonal portable toilets are immediately to the left; the fire tower (no access) is a short distance beyond the toilets. Follow Big A Trail left over the grassy field to the observation deck.

BIG A TRAIL (MACR; MT. AGAMENTICUS, P. 356)

From large information kiosk near summit parking lot (691 ft.) to:	⇅	↗	⭘
Complete Big A Trail circuit	1.0 mi.	50 ft.	0:30

Completed in 2017, this universally accessible trail makes a circuit around the summit area of Mt. Agamenticus through shrubs and meadows, offering many fine viewpoints en route. There are several slight variants to the start and finish of Big A Trail. The most straightforward start is to walk east from the large information kiosk, make the quick side trip over to the summit observation deck, and then continue around the southeast side of the summit lodge. Pass Summit Staircase, which joins from the right, then pass the signs and rock pile representing the folklore of St. Aspinquid, a Micmac chief who died in 1906, and cultural practices of native people. With good views ahead to Second Hill and Third Hill, go around the old lift tower and snow roller (Sweet Fern Trail begins here) then continue right around the hairpin. At 0.2 mi., Summit Staircase crosses the trail.

Proceeding north along a contour, at 0.35 mi., Witch Hazel Trail departs right. At 150 ft. beyond, Sweet Fern Trail crosses Big A Trail at the remains of the old T-bar lift line. Immediately ahead is a footbridge. Pass a ledge outcrop to reach the jct. with Vultures View Trail, which enters from the right at 0.4 mi. Then pass the concrete base of an old lift line tower. To the left here, a side trail leads to an observation deck. At the jct. and atop the deck are expansive views northwest. Continuing on, with the old fire tower and communications tower on the left, enter woods. At 0.6 mi., with a workshop up to the left, cross Fisher Trail. Just beyond, a spur on the right leads to an overlook and bench and to Blueberry Bluff Trail. Big A Trail winds ahead to cross a footbridge over a gully, then goes past the other side of the workshop. Cross Fisher Trail again. A spur on the left just ahead goes to an overlook. The fire tower and interpretive signs at its base are to the left; toilets are to the right. At the T intersection here, go right to the large information kiosk and parking lot, or continue left to walk around the north side of the lodge.

SWEET FERN TRAIL (MACR; MT. AGAMENTICUS, P. 356)

Cumulative from Mt. Agamenticus summit lodge (691 ft.) to:	↧↥	↗	○
Big A Trail, upper jct. (670 ft.)	0.1 mi.	-20 ft.	0:05
Ring Trail (510 ft.)	0.3 mi.	-160 ft.	0:10

This trail, which connects the Mt. Agamenticus summit to Ring Trail, is described on the descent. From the front of the summit lodge, hike around the east side of the building on Big A Trail. At the first hairpin turn near the old ski lift tower and snow roller, leave Big A Trail and start down the wide path ahead, Sweet Fern Trail. Pass another old lift tower. At the next jct. with Big A Trail below, with a lift tower immediately to the right and a bridge to the left, go straight ahead on Sweet Fern Trail. Just below, enter the woods. The trail follows an old ski run down over slabs and eroded trail, passing another old lift tower en route. Sweet Fern Trail ends at Ring Trail at 0.2 mi.

WITCH HAZEL TRAIL (MACR; MT. AGAMENTICUS, P. 356)

This short 0.1-mi. connector trail, which links Big A Trail to Ring Trail, is described on the descent, a loss of 70 ft. in elevation. Witch Hazel Trail departs from Big A Trail on the right at 0.35 mi. from the summit lodge. The trail passes an ancient hemlock tree along its route.

HAIRPIN TRAIL (MACR; MT. AGAMENTICUS, P. 356)

This short, wide trail extends from the jct. of Ring Trail and Rocky Road Trail to Mt. Agamenticus Rd. about 0.2 mi. before the summit parking area, passing Summit Staircase along the way. Hairpin Trail gains 60 ft. of elevation over 0.15 mi.

SUMMIT STAIRCASE (MACR; MT. AGAMENTICUS, P. 356)

This trail is a short, direct route from Hairpin Trail to the summit lodge, crossing Big A Trail on the way. As its name implies, this moderate to steep trail is composed of hand-set granite rocks that form a staircase to the summit and gains 80 ft. of elevation in 375 ft.

ROCKY ROAD TRAIL (MACR; MT. AGAMENTICUS, P. 356)

This short path extends from Porcupine Trail to the jct. of Ring Trail and Hairpin Trail, climbing partway up the mountain from the east. Rocky Road Trail gains 140 ft. of elevation over 0.25 mi.

WINTERGREEN TRAIL (MACR; MT. AGAMENTICUS, P. 356)

From Mountain Rd. (270 ft.) to:	⤿⤴	↗	⏱
Ring Trail (500 ft.)	0.4 mi.	230 ft.	0:20

This hiker-only trail climbs the west side of Mt. Agamenticus to Ring Trail. From the main trailhead parking lot at the jct. of Mountain Rd. and Mt. Agamenticus Rd., continue west on Mountain Rd., which quickly turns to dirt. In 0.8 mi., Wintergreen Trail starts on the right. Parking for the trail is just downhill on the left side of Mountain Rd.

The wide, red-blazed trail trends south for 0.1 mi. before swinging back to the north to follow a contour. At 0.2 mi., it ascends east and soon enters a ravine of hemlocks, then climbs moderately on some rock steps. Wintergreen Trail ends at Ring Trail a short distance south of Fisher Trail.

VULTURES VIEW TRAIL (MACR; MT. AGAMENTICUS, P. 356)

Cumulative from Mountain Rd. (180 ft.) to:	⤿⤴	↗	⏱
Start of Vultures View Trail via Cedar Trail and Goosefoot Trail (200 ft.)	0.3 mi.	20 ft.	0:10
Ring Trail (500 ft.)	0.6 mi.	320 ft.	0:30
Big A Trail (640 ft.)	0.8 mi.	460 ft.	0:40
Mt. Agamenticus summit (691 ft.) via Sweet Fern Trail and Big A Trail	0.9 mi.	510 ft.	0:45

This trail, the longest "hiking only" trail on Mt. Agamenticus, climbs the mountain from the northwest. From the main trailhead parking lot at the junction of Mountain Rd. and Mt. Agamenticus Rd., drive west on

Mountain Rd., which quickly turns to dirt. In 1.1 mi., reach a large parking lot on the right, where there is a red gate and a sign for Mt. Agamenticus Wildlife Management Area.

Walk by the left side of the red gate on Cedar Trail, a wide multiuse road. After a first and then second jct. with Beaver Trail on the left, cross a beaver pond outlet on a culvert. At 0.25 mi., turn right on Goosefoot Trail. This is the base of an old ski lift line for the long-defunct Big A ski area. Pass the concrete stanchions of an old lift. In 250 ft., reach a fork. Here, Goosefoot Trail bears left. Bear right to continue on red-blazed Vultures View Trail, and climb the rocky footway of the wide path. At 0.4 mi., pass through a clearing, part of a former ski run. Just beyond, climb a rock staircase, then head up a series of smooth slabs. Continue to climb the wide and eroded trail. At 0.6 mi., reach the jct. of Ring Trail. Continue straight ahead up slabs on more eroded trail. Pass double metal pipes, part of an old snowmaking system. At 0.75 mi., emerge into the semi-open summit area. Climb rock steps to reach Big A Trail. Go left or right to reach the summit observation deck and summit lodge.

GOOSEFOOT TRAIL
(MACR; MT. AGAMENTICUS, P. 356)

Ring Trail and Chestnut Oak Trail jct. (490 ft.) to:	⇅	↗	○
Cedar Trail (190 ft.)	0.7 mi.	-300 ft.	0:20
Mountain Rd. (180 ft.)	1.0 mi.	-310 ft.	0:30

This trail can be combined with Vultures View Trail and any of several other short trails for a nice loop hike. Goosefoot Trail is described on the descent. From the jct. of Ring Trail and Chestnut Oak Trail, follow the wide, white-blazed Goosefoot Trail on a contour along the west slope of the mountain. At 0.15 mi., veer left onto a narrow footpath and descend moderately via switchbacks. Ahead, regain the wide, rocky, eroded trail. For the better part of the next 0.4 mi., the trail alternates between footpath and the old road. At 0.6 mi., Vultures View Trail enters from the left. Goosefoot Trail continues to the right to reach Cedar Trail at 0.7 mi. Turn left to reach Mountain Rd. in another 0.3 mi.

SEC 8

■ SECOND HILL (555 FT.)

Located in the backcountry northeast of Mt. Agamenticus, Second Hill has a long north-south ridge of ledges and pleasant woods. The South Berwick town line is to the west, and the valley of Chicks Brook is to the east. Second Hill is reached by trail from the summit of Mt. Agamenticus.

SECOND HILL LOOP
(MACR; MT. AGAMENTICUS, P. 356)

Cumulative from Mt. Agamenticus summit
(691 ft.) to:

	⇅	↗	↻
Ring Trail, Goosefoot Trail, and Chestnut Oak Trail jct. (490 ft.)	0.2 mi.	-200 ft.	0:05
Porcupine Trail (380 ft.)	0.5 mi.	-310 ft.	0:15
Second Hill (555 ft.) via Porcupine Trail and Second Hill Trail	0.9 mi.	175 ft.	0:30
Complete loop via Ridge, Notch, Stone Fence, Porcupine, Chestnut Oak, Ring, Sweet Fern or Witch Hazel, and Big A trails	3.7 mi.	650 ft.	2:10

Combine some or all of the following trails for a nice loop hike over Second
Hill: Chestnut Oak, Porcupine, Second Hill, Ridge, Notch, and Stone
Fence. Several variations are possible.

From the summit of Mt. Agamenticus, follow any of several short trail
segments (Big A Trail, Sweet Fern Trail, and Ring Trail or Big A Trail, Witch
Hazel Trail, and Ring Trail—both combinations are about 0.2 mi. long) north
to the jct. of Ring Trail, Goosefoot Trail, and Chestnut Oak Trail.

From this jct., bear right on the wide Chestnut Oak Trail and descend
at a moderate grade via switchbacks, contour easily east, then wind down
to the jct. with Porcupine Trail at 0.5 mi. Go left on Porcupine Trail, cross
a brook on a footbridge, then reach an unmarked trail that leaves right. Go
straight at this jct. to remain on Porcupine Trail. Ascend gradually along
the western base of Second Hill to a small clearing with a cairn. Turn right
here on Second Hill Trail and climb easily by switchbacks on wide trail at
first, then ascend a short, moderate pitch through ledge outcrops to the
ridge. An unmarked trail enters from the right; turn left here, and in 75 ft.,
look left to see the summit sign for Second Hill nailed to a tree (the sign
faces away from the trail).

From the top of Second Hill, continue north on Ridge Trail. Walk easily
along the north ridge on a rolling path. At 1.1 mi., an unmarked trail leaves
left. Just ahead, Incline Trail enters from the right. Stay straight on Ridge
Trail. Hidden Trail departs left at 1.2 mi. Ridge Trail winds over a knoll
through parklike woods then switchbacks down at an easy to moderate
grade. Walk along the base of a boulder slope and, at 1.9 mi., reach the jct.
of Notch Trail. (Hikers headed for Third Hill should turn right here.)

From the Notch Trail jct., turn left (west) on the wide Notch Trail. At
2.2 mi., turn left onto Stone Fence Trail and head south. Over the next
0.5 mi., Stone Fence Trail passes through gaps in several stone walls and
parallels several more impressive old walls. A short distance beyond the jct.

with Hidden Trail, Stone Fence Trail ends at Porcupine Trail at 2.7 mi. Go left on Porcupine Trail, pass Second Hill, and soon meet Chestnut Oak Trail on the right at 3.2 mi.

Return to the summit of Mt. Agamenticus via Chestnut Oak Trail and either Ring Trail, Sweet Fern Trail, and Big A Trail or Ring Trail, Witch Hazel Trail, and Big A Trail—about 0.5 mi. either way.

■ THIRD HILL (526 FT.)

This wooded peak is east of Second Hill in the backcountry northeast of Mt. Agamenticus. Chick Brook is at the western base of the hill, and the Ogunquit River is to the north. Third Hill can be reached by combining several trails from the summit of Second Hill.

SECOND HILL TO THIRD HILL TRAILS
(MACR; USGS YORK HARBOR QUAD, GAZETTEER MAP 1,
MACR MT. AGAMENTICUS TRAILS MAP)

From Second Hill summit (555 ft.) to:	⮃	↗	⟳
Base of Third Hill (230 ft.) via Ridge, Notch, Wheel, and Great Marsh trails	1.4 mi.	-325 ft.	0:45

From the top of Second Hill, continue north on Ridge Trail. Walk easily along the north ridge on a mildly undulating path. At 0.2 mi., an unmarked trail leaves left. Just ahead, Incline Trail enters from the right. Stay straight on Ridge Trail. Hidden Trail departs left at 0.3 mi. Beyond, wind over a knoll through the parklike woods, then switchback down at easy to moderate trail. In a large, wooded amphitheater, walk along the base of a boulder slope. At 1.0 mi., reach the jct. of Notch Trail. Turn right on wide Notch Trail and reach Wheel Trail on the left at 1.2 mi. Cross a low wet area to the T intersection. at Great Marsh Trail. Go left on Great Marsh Trail, and in 1.3 mi. reach the jct. of Third Hill Trail on the right.

THIRD HILL TRAIL (MACR; USGS YORK HARBOR QUAD,
GAZETTEER MAP 1, MACR MT. AGAMENTICUS TRAILS MAP)

Cumulative from north jct. of Great Marsh Trail and Third Hill Trail (230 ft.) to:	⮃	↗	⟳
Ledge Trail, lower jct. (280 ft.)	88 yd.	50 ft.	0:02
Third Hill summit (526 ft.)	0.9 mi.	250 ft.	0:35
Bobcat Trail (330 ft.)	1.4 mi.	250 ft.	0:50
Great Marsh Trail, south jct. (280 ft.)	1.5 mi.	250 ft.	0:55

This trail makes a north-south traverse of Third Hill. From the jct. of Great Marsh Trail, hike east on Third Hill Trail. In 350 ft., Ledge Trail

SEC 8

leaves to the right. Stay straight on Third Hill Trail, climb the slope ahead, then contour easily north to a ledge outcrop in a small clearing. At 0.45 mi., reach an unsigned jct. with a knee-high cairn. Turn right to stay on Third Hill Trail. Pass another cairn, then wind easily to moderately up the north ridge. Hike over bedrock trail edged with moss to reach a cairn in a semi-open area at 0.8 mi. Here is the jct. of Ledge Trail, which enters from the right. Climb ahead, level off, and easily cross the upper ridge to reach the top of Third Hill and a 5-ft. cairn at 0.9 mi.

Beyond the summit, trend gently down to a large open ledge and, below that, a semi-open ridgeline. Descend on wide trail at first, then on eroded trail over ledges to reach Bobcat Trail on the right at 1.4 mi. Third Hill Trail continues ahead to reach Great Marsh Trail in another 0.1 mi., at a point 0.5 mi. south of the base of Third Hill at the start of Third Hill Trail.

BOBCAT TRAIL (MACR; USGS YORK HARBOR QUAD, GAZETTEER MAP 1, MACR MT. AGAMENTICUS TRAILS MAP)

Cumulative from south side of Third Hill Trail (330 ft.) to:	⇅	↗	○
Ledge Trail (370 ft.)	0.4 mi.	40 ft.	0:10
Third Hill Trail (280 ft.) via Ledge Trail	0.6 mi.	40 ft.	0:20

To make a loop on Third Hill, from the jct. of Third Hill Trail and Bobcat Trail, follow the narrow Bobcat Trail north on a contour over the lower western slope of the hill, passing by ledges, outcrops, and small cliff faces, to reach Ledge Trail at 0.4 mi. Go left down Ledge Trail, an eroded, moderate pitch at the start, then a long series of switchbacks. Join Third Hill Trail at 0.6 mi.

LEDGE TRAIL (MACR; USGS YORK HARBOR QUAD, GAZETTEER MAP 1, MACR MT. AGAMENTICUS TRAILS MAP)

Cumulative from Third Hill Trail, lower jct. (280 ft.), to:	⇅	↗	○
Third Hill Trail, upper jct. (490 ft.)	0.5 mi.	210 ft.	0:20
Third Hill summit (526 ft.)	0.6 mi.	250 ft.	0:25

This trail offers a direct route up the west side of Third Hill. From the jct. of Third Hill Trail, climb through an area of ledges via a long series of switchbacks to Bobcat Trail at 0.2 mi. Continue the climb on Ledge Trail through ledges on switchbacks. At 0.35 mi., make an arc north over an open slab. Cross the slabs and then bear right and up toward the obvious cairns. Ascend one final ledge step to the cairn and sign at the jct. of Third Hill Trail. The top of Third Hill is 0.1 mi. right (south).

THIRD HILL TO SECOND HILL TRAILS (MACR; USGS YORK HARBOR QUAD, GAZETTEER MAP 1, MACR MT. AGAMENTICUS TRAILS MAP)

From north jct. of Third Hill Trail and Great Marsh Trail (230 ft.) to:	⮃	↗	⏱
Second Hill summit (555 ft.) via Great Marsh, Darter, Notch, Incline, and Ridge trails	1.4 mi.	365 ft.	0:55

From the jct. of Third Hill Trail and Great Marsh Trail at the base of Third Hill, hikers can choose to retrace their steps to Second Hill via Great Marsh Trail, Wheel Trail, Notch Trail, and Ridge Trail, and then out to Mt. Agamenticus from that point.

Another option is to hike south on Great Marsh Trail for 0.6 mi. to the jct. of Darter Trail on the right. Turn onto Darter Trail and follow it northwest over a low rise (ledges up to right). Beyond, cross a wet area on stepping-stones then climb switchbacks to a long rock ledge. Bear right to reach Notch Trail at 1.0 mi. Follow Notch Trail, a wide old woods road, north for 0.2 mi. to Incline Trail. Go left on Incline Trail, pass through a mature stand of beech, hemlock, and birch, then make a short, moderate to steep ascent to join Ridge Trail on Second Hill at 1.4 mi. Turn left (south) on Ridge Trail to return to the top of Second Hill. From there, follow Second Hill Trail, Porcupine Trail, and Chestnut Oak Trail back toward Mt. Agamenticus.

Another option is to connect directly to Darter Trail via Great Marsh Trail from the south end of Third Hill Trail.

SECTION 9
MIDCOAST

In-Text Maps
Ragged Mtn.

387

Pull-Out Map
Map 4: Camden Hills

SEC
9

INTRODUCTION

The Midcoast region includes the entirety of Waldo County, Knox County, Lincoln County, and Sagadahoc County. It is bounded by the counties of Cumberland, Androscoggin, Kennebec, Somerset, and Penobscot to the west and north. The Penobscot River and Penobscot Bay form the eastern boundary: the river from Winterport to Stockton Springs, and the bay from there to Spruce Head and the Muscle Ridge Islands. The sinuous coastline along the Gulf of Maine composes the southern boundary, with a series of long, fingerlike peninsulas, craggy headlands, bays and sounds, and many islands, ranging from Casco Bay to Penobscot Bay. The Androscoggin River and Kennebec River merge at Merrymeeting Bay and flow into the Atlantic east of Popham Beach, and numerous other rivers, including the Damariscotta, Sheepscot, and Georges, slice across the landscape before emptying into the ocean. Rolling hills, farmland, and lakes characterize much of the interior of the region. A mountainous belt extends from the Unity area southeast to Penobscot Bay at Camden and Rockport, near which the greatest concentration of high mountains (to just above 1,300 ft.) is found. This section describes 41 trails on 18 mountains.

GEOGRAPHY

The Camden Hills are a compact and attractive complex of mountains rising above the western shore of Penobscot Bay in the towns of Lincolnville, Camden, and Rockport. These coastal summits share many characteristics with the mountains of Acadia on Mt. Desert Island a few miles to the east, including fragrant forests of spruce and fir; bold cliffs and ledges; and broad vistas of oceans, lakes, and mountains. Camden Hills State Park encompasses 6,200 acres of the scenic Camden Hills. At 1,385 ft., Mt. Megunticook is the highest peak in the Camden Hills and, with the exception of Cadillac Mtn., the highest point on the Atlantic seaboard of the United States. The great cliffs at Ocean Lookout on the southeastern ridge of Megunticook are some of the finest viewpoints anywhere along the Midcoast.

North of Megunticook are the extensive open blueberry fields atop Cameron Mtn. (811 ft.). A series of mountains continues northeast of Megunticook for several miles and includes Bald Rock Mtn. (1,100 ft.) and its summit ledges overlooking Penobscot Bay, and, farther along, the wooded ridges of Derry Mtn. (777 ft.) and Frohock Mtn. (454 ft.). Mt. Battie (790 ft.) rises steeply just south of Megunticook. A popular auto road climbs to the Mt. Battie summit, which is adorned by a stone observation tower. Just outside the state park, near the end of the northwestern ridge of Megunticook, trails lead to Maiden Cliff, which overlooks Megunticook Lake. More than 30 mi. of well-maintained, blue-blazed trails crisscross the park.

Megunticook Lake and Megunticook River separate the main peaks of the Camden Hills from the mountains extending to the southwest, which include Bald Mtn. (1,280 ft.) in Camden and Ragged Mtn. (1,280 ft.) astride the Camden–Rockport line. The northeastern slope of Ragged Mtn. is home to the downhill ski area known as Camden Snow Bowl. Ragged Mtn. and Bald Mtn. are both the focus of conservation and trail-building efforts by Coastal Mountains Land Trust and Georges River Land Trust. Just west of Rockport Harbor, Beech Hill has open blueberry fields and a historical stone hut on its summit.

Another area of hills with elevations in and around the 1,000-ft. level is about 15 mi. northeast of the Camden Hills, mostly in the town of Montville. Frye Mtn. (1,139 ft.) is the high point in the 5,240-acre Gene Letourneau Wildlife Management Area. Neighboring Hogback Mtn. (1,115 ft.) has a fine summit overlook. Just west is Whitten Hill (865 ft.), which is part of the Sheepscot Headwaters Preserve, a property of Midcoast Conservancy. North of that is the rolling Goose Ridge (930 ft.), with its high fields and lovely views. To the south, in Liberty, Haystack Mtn. (850 ft.) affords nice views of Lake St. George, the headwater of the Sheepscot River.

A few miles east of Verona Island and the mouth of the Penobscot River, the summit ledges of Mt. Waldo (1,064 ft.) loom large over Frankfort. And far to the southwest, on the crest of Georgetown Island, between the Kennebec River and Sheepscot Bay, is Higgins Mtn. (259 ft.).

SEC 9

ROAD ACCESS

The bulk of the trails in this section are in Waldo County, from its northwestern corner to the coast at Penobscot Bay between Lincolnville and Rockport. Most of the remaining trails are near the coast in the northeastern corner of Knox County. The major highway routes leading to local roads and trailheads are ME 3 and ME 17 from east to west, and ME 220 and US 1 from south to north. Important connectors are ME 52 out of Camden and ME 90 out of Rockport. ME 127 from US 1 in Woolwich is the route to Georgetown Island.

CAMPING

Camping is available in the Midcoast region at Camden Hills State Park in Camden, with 106 campsites, and at Lake St. George State Park in Liberty, with 38 campsites. Both locations have showers, restrooms, and other amenities. Approximately twenty privately operated campgrounds are also available. There is backcountry camping only in Camden Hills State Park, at two primitive shelters on Bald Rock Mtn., and at the Megunticook Ski Shelter in the valley between Bald Rock Mtn. and Mt. Megunticook.

HILLS TO SEA TRAIL

The Hills to Sea Trail stretches 47 mi. through the hills and mountains of eastern Waldo County from Unity to Belfast through Montville, Knox, and Waldo. Opened to the public in 2016, the trail was designed and built over five years by WCTC. The project included volunteers from nine non-profit entities in the county. More than 60 landowners have generously allowed trail access across their lands. The trail also traverses more than 7,000 acres of state and private conservation land.

The trail is for foot travel only. There are eight kiosks along the route, multiple points of entry where the trail crosses roads, and seven year-round parking areas (the village of Unity, Unity College, Freedom General Store, Whitten Hill trailhead and ME 220/Walker Ridge Rd. trailhead in Montville, the ME 7 crossing in Waldo, and City Point Train Station in Belfast), each with a kiosk and maps. The entire trail is rated easy to moderate in terms of difficulty. The route was planned to use some existing trails, including GHP. It is identified in most places with blue blazes and, where helpful, small yellow and black "Hills to Sea" signs. There is no camping along the trail.

Portions of Hills to Sea Trail on Goose Ridge, Whitten Hill, Hogback Mtn., and Frye Mtn. are described in detail under those headings elsewhere in this section.

CAMDEN HILLS STATE PARK

This state park encompasses 6,200 acres of mountainous terrain on the west shore of Penobscot Bay in the towns of Camden and Lincolnville. The beautiful Camden Hills share many characteristics with the mountains of Acadia on Mt. Desert Island 30 mi. to the east, including fragrant softwood forests, bold cliffs and ledges, and far-reaching vistas of ocean, lakes, and mountains. At 1,385 ft., Mt. Megunticook is not only the highest summit in the park but also the highest mainland mountain on the Atlantic coast of the United States. The park offers more than 30 mi. of hiking on 21 trails, which cover—in addition to Megunticook—Mt. Battie, Bald Rock Mtn., Cameron Mtn., and several other wooded summits. The park features a campground with 106 sites and many amenities.

SUGGESTED HIKES

■ Easy

JENNIFER HILL AND LUNCH ROCK

OW via Hills to Sea Trail	2.5 mi.	100 ft.	1:15

Hike this pretty segment of the 47-mi. Hills to Sea Trail between ME 7 and Belfast, taking in Jennifer Hill and Lunch Rock en route to Belfast Harbor. See Hills to Sea Trail, p. 374.

MT. BATTIE

RT via Mt. Battie Trail	1.0 mi.	580 ft.	1:00

This short but steep hike to Mt. Battie's stone observation tower provides superb views of Penobscot Bay and its many islands. See Mt. Battie Trail, p. 378.

MAIDEN CLIFF

RT via Maiden Cliff Trail, Scenic Trail, and Ridge Trail	1.4 mi.	550 ft.	1:00

This fine hike makes a loop over Maiden Cliff, where there is a large memorial cross and an excellent view of Megunticook Lake. To begin, see Maiden Cliff Trail, p. 382.

SEC 9

BALD MTN.

RT via Bald Mtn. Trail	2.6 mi.	680 ft.	1:40

Revel in the good views of Penobscot Bay, Ragged Mtn., and the surrounding Camden Hills from these craggy heights. See Bald Mtn. Trail, p. 395.

BEECH HILL

	⇅	↗	◌
RT via Summit Trail	1.7 mi.	121 ft.	0:55

A short, scenic walk leads through blueberry fields to the open summit of Beech Hill, the historical Beech Nut stone hut, and sweeping coastal views. See Summit Trail, p. 395.

HIGGINS MTN.

	⇅	↗	◌
LP via Higgins Mtn. Trail	0.6 mi.	130 ft.	0:20

Visit one of the high points on Georgetown Island on this fun circuit. See Higgins Mtn. Trail, p. 403.

■ Moderate
MT. MEGUNTICOOK

	⇅	↗	◌
LP via Megunticook Trail, Ridge Trail, Slope Trail, and Ski Shelter/Multi-use Trail	4.5 mi.	935 ft.	2:45

From the state park campground, make a pleasant circuit over Mt. Megunticook, with the spectacular view from Ocean Lookout as your highpoint. To begin, see Megunticook Trail, p. 380.

MT. MEGUNTICOOK–MAIDEN CLIFF TO MT. BATTIE

	⇅	↗	◌
OW via Maiden Cliff Trail, Scenic Trail, Ridge Trail, Tablelands Trail, and Mt. Battie Trail	5.5 mi.	1,550 ft.	3:35

This combination of trails—equally good in either direction—makes for the finest long hike in the Camden Hills, offering excellent views and plenty of great ridge walking. To begin, see Maiden Cliff Trail, p. 382.

BALD ROCK MTN.

	⇅	↗	◌
LP via Ski Shelter/Multi-use Trail, Bald Rock Trail, and Frohock Mtn. Trail	3.3 mi.	840 ft.	2:05

Enjoy views of Penobscot Bay from the summit ledges of Bald Rock Mtn. To begin, see Ski Shelter/Multi-use Trail, p. 383.

RAGGED MTN.

		⮏⮙	↗	○
OW via Georges Highland Path		4.9 mi.	950 ft.	3:00

Tackle this pretty section of Georges Highland Path, which features extensive open ledges with outstanding coastal views from the long ridge-line of Ragged Mtn. See Georges Highland Path, p. 388.

WHITTEN HILL

		⮏⮙	↗	○
LP via Northern Headwaters Trail		3.8 mi.	500 ft.	2:10

Stroll past old stone walls and along the headwater of the Sheepscot River on this pleasant walk over Whitten Hill. See Northern Headwaters Trail, p. 400.

GOOSE RIDGE

		⮏⮙	↗	○
OW via Goose Ridge Trail		3.6 mi.	600 ft.	2:00

Trundle over Goose Ridge for a nice stretch of ridge hiking that leads to several high fields and bucolic views of the hilly, rural landscape. See Goose Ridge Trail, p. 401.

■ Strenuous
FRYE MTN.

		⮏⮙	↗	○
LP via Frye Mtn. Trail		10.9 mi.	1,100 ft.	6:00

A good autumn foliage hike, this route travels through the scenic woods of the Gene Letourneau (aka Frye Mtn.) Wildlife Management Area and over the wooded summit of Frye Mtn. See Frye Mtn. Trail, p. 397.

SEC 9

TRAIL DESCRIPTIONS

WEST AND NORTH OF BELFAST

HILLS TO SEA TRAIL
(WCTC; USGS UNITY, LIBERTY, MORRILL, AND BELFAST QUADS, GAZETTEER MAPS 22 AND 14, WCTC HILLS TO SEA TRAIL MAP)

Cumulative from Unity (200 ft.) to:	⇅	↗	↺
Quaker Hill Rd.	3.0 mi.	350 ft.	1:40
Maine Organic Farmers and Gardeners Association Common Ground Education Center	5.7 mi.	450 ft.	3:05
Hunter Rd.	7.5 mi.	650 ft.	4:05
Clark Rd.	11.8 mi.	850 ft.	6:20
Stevens Rd.	13.7 mi.	1,100 ft.	7:25
ME 137, Freedom	15.8 mi.	1,150 ft.	8:30
Freedom Pond Rd.	17.1 mi.	1,300 ft.	9:15
Penney Rd., Montville	20.8 mi.	1,700 ft.	11:15
Halldale Rd.	25.6 mi.	2,100 ft.	13:50
ME 220	29.5 mi.	2,600 ft.	16:00
Jeep road east of Frye Mtn.	35.0 mi.	3,200 ft.	19:00
Mixer Pond Rd. at ME 137	37.2 mi.	3,200 ft.	20:00
Savage Rd., Waldo	39.5 mi.	3,400 ft.	21:30
ME 137, Waldo	42.7 mi.	3,600 ft.	23:00
ME 7 at Waldo County Tech Center	44.3 mi.	3,650 ft.	24:00
City Point Train Station, Belfast	46.8 mi.	3,750 ft.	25:30

Hills to Sea Trail begins in Unity, just south of the jct. of ME 139 and US 202/ME 9. Parking is across the road at Unity Barn Raisers. The trail crosses Sandy Stream on a footbridge, then heads south to the Unity College campus, crossing Quaker Hill Rd. en route. It follows a pedestrian path through campus, crosses Loop Rd., then follows the west margin of the soccer fields. Beyond, the trail climbs Quaker Hill, where there are expansive views from the fields, then descends to reach Quaker Hill Rd. and parking at 3.0 mi.

The trail heads east and descends to cross Mussey Brook, passes Mussey Rd., loops north around a hilltop, then drops down to Sandy Stream. The stream has steep banks and may require shallow wading. (If the stream is impassable due to high water, use Mussey Rd. as a cutoff route to avoid the crossing.) Beyond the crossing, the trail follows the stream south through Maine Organic Farmers and Gardeners Association's Maine Heritage Orchard, then arrives at the association's Common Ground Education Center and parking on Crosby Brook Rd. at 5.7 mi.

Walk south on Crosby Brook Rd. for 0.5 mi. to Berry Rd. Go right on Berry Rd. and follow it over Sandy Stream to meet Mussey Rd. Go left on Mussey Rd. to Hunter Rd. The trail leaves Mussey Rd. and enters the woods at a point 0.3 mi. beyond the intersection of Town Farm Rd. and Mussey Rd. at 7.5 mi.

Between Hunter Rd. and Clark Rd., Hills to Sea Trail negotiates rolling terrain with minor elevation changes. From Hunter Rd., the trail heads east to reach Sandy Stream, then follows its west bank southward before trending west again to cross Fly Brook (normally a stepping stone crossing, it may be impassable in high water). Clark Rd. is south up the hill. Parking is just east on Clark Rd. at 11.8 mi.

From Clark Rd., the trail winds through mature forest and across undulating terrain before recrossing Clark Rd. Ahead, it winds through a cedar swamp on bog bridges to reach Stevens Rd. at 13.7 mi. For the next 0.9 mi., the trail follows Stevens Rd. north and then Weed Rd. west to parking. From here, the trail reenters the woods and follows Sand Stream south for about 1.0 mi. before reaching ME 137. It heads west on ME 137 toward the village of Freedom for 150 yd., where it leaves the road and continues south. This point is 15.8 mi. from the start of the trail in Unity.

From ME 137, it is 0.3 mi. to a spur jct. The spur leads west 0.4 mi. to Freedom and Freedom General Store, where there is parking. Beyond the spur, the trail reaches Freedom Pond Rd. at 17.1 mi.

From Freedom Pond Rd., Hills to Sea Trail follows the route of Goose Ridge Trail, which is maintained by MCC. Goose Ridge Trail is described in detail on p. 401. It meanders south through the mixed forest, climbing over several miles to Goose Ridge, with captivating views of farms and fields to the northeast. Beyond the high point, the trail descends steeply along a pipeline corridor before reentering the woods and intersecting Penney Rd. in Montville at 20.8 mi.

Ahead, the route follows more MCC trails through a portion of 1,100 acres of conserved land that protect the Sheepscot River headwater. From Penney Rd., Goose Ridge Trail continues, descending to cross several branches of the Sheepscot River before joining Northern Headwaters Trail. From this point to Hemlock Hollow Trail beyond the summit of Whitten Hill, the route of Hills to Sea Trail is described as part of Northern Headwaters Trail on p. 400. The trail follows the Sheepscot River south before climbing away toward Whitten Hill and the Whitten Hill

SEC 9

Trail at 24.3 mi. From this jct., the Whitten Hill trailhead parking lot on Halldale Rd. is just 0.1 mi. east. Northern Headwaters Trail continues north along the wooded ridgeline of Whitten Hill, following alongside numerous fine old stone walls. Ahead, Hills to Sea Trail veers right onto Hemlock Hollow Trail and soon reaches Halldale Rd. at 25.6 mi.

The next 9.4 mi. of Hills to Sea Trail are described in detail on pp. 397–399 as part of the trails on Frye Mtn. and Hogback Mtn.

From Halldale Rd., Hills to Sea Trail continues on Hemlock Hollow Trail to join Hogback Connector Trail, which links the trails of MCC and GRLT's GHP. Hills to Sea Trail climbs to the summit of Hogback Mtn. and several nice viewpoints before descending to the north and east to reach ME 220 at 29.5 mi. Parking is just south on Walker Ridge Rd. at the DIFW maintenance building (which can be reached by walking 0.25 mi. on an ATV/snowmobile trail that proceeds straight immediately after crossing the highway). Beyond ME 220, Hills to Sea Trail, now part of GHP, passes through the GLWMA (fires and camping prohibited). For the next 2 mi., the trail undulates with minor elevation gain, crossing Bartlett Stream and two gravel roads. Beyond the second gravel road, the trail ascends quickly to a jct. on the southwestern end of the Frye Mtn. ridgeline. Here, it turns left to follow the ridge, while GHP splits to form a loop over the mountain. Hills to Sea Trail continues on to the wooded summit of Frye Mtn., then descends gradually over a series of ridges to the northeast, breaks away to the left from the GHP loop, and reaches an old jeep road at 35.0 mi., where it exits state land. There is seasonal parking here.

Turn left on the jeep road and follow it north for 0.5 mi., then turn right on a smaller dirt road, where there is seasonal parking. After 0.6 mi., leave the road, and in another 0.6 mi., reach ME 137 in Knox. Turn right, and in 0.2 mi., reach the Mixer Pond Rd. kiosk at 37.2 mi. Beyond, the trail follows ME 137 for 0.7 mi., then enters the woods on the south side of the highway. A short distance into the woods, it climbs a steep 100-ft. escarpment, and in another 1.3 mi., it intersects ME 131. Now in Waldo, from this point the trail follows Savage Rd. south for 1.0 mi. to a kiosk on the left at 39.5 mi.

The trail leaves Savage Rd. to the left just past the kiosk. It follows the Central Maine Power power line, crosses Pendleton Stream on a bridge, and continues uphill through woods onto a dirt road, going back into the woods before coming out onto the gravel-surfaced Gurney Hill Rd. Follow this to ME 137, turn right and follow the highway south for 0.5 mi., then turn right onto Bonne Terre Rd. for 0.5 mi. Ahead, leave the road on the left and enter the woods. In another 1.25 mi., reach ME 137 at 42.7 mi. Here, next to Waldo County Technical Center, is a kiosk.

Crossing ME 137, Hills to Sea Trail goes past a beaver pond and on through the hilly woods, turns left on a woods road for a short distance, then goes back into the woods. It passes through a recent logging cut before emerging into a field—where there is a kiosk, portable toilets, and parking—for the last short stretch to ME 7 at 44.3 mi. From ME 7, the trail follows a dirt road for 0.5 mi., then turns right into a remote, wooded stretch that for the next 2 mi. features hilly terrain, mossy boulders, and a bridge across Marsh Fork. Reaching the CMP substation, the trail crosses Waldo Rd. and proceeds through the woods to Oak Hill Rd. at City Point Train Station at 46.8 mi., where there is a kiosk and parking. This is the eastern terminus of Hills to Sea Trail. The Belfast Rail Trail continues from this point for 2.6 mi. to the public wharf on Belfast Bay at the base of Main St.

■ MT. WALDO (1,064 FT.)

This attractive mountain in Frankfort is best known for the granite quarries on its eastern side. Its many open ledges offer excellent views that include Penobscot Bay and the islands of Islesboro, North Haven and Vinalhaven; the mountains of Acadia on Mt. Desert Island; Blue Hill; and Tunk Mtn. and Schoodic Mtn.

From the jct. of US 1A and Loggin Rd. in Frankfort (just west of the bridge over the North Branch of the Marsh River), head south on US 1A for 0.3 mi. Turn right onto Old Belfast Rd., go beneath a railroad overpass, and at 0.5 mi., turn right onto Tyler Ln. At 0.7 mi., the road forks. Here, where Old Stage Rd. bears right, continue straight on Tyler Ln. Beyond, the dirt road gets rough. At 2.2 mi., pass another dirt road and a power line on the left. Park here on the side of Tyler Ln.

NORTH TRAIL
(NFTM; USGS MT. WALDO QUAD, GAZETTEER MAP 23)

From Tyler Ln. (470 ft.) to:	⇅	↗	↻
Mt. Waldo summit (1,064 ft.)	1.0 mi.	600 ft.	0:50

From Tyler Ln., follow the dirt road (gated after 100 ft.) and power line south toward the mountain and its summit communications towers to reach a large commercial blueberry field on the right. Ahead, the dirt road bends sharply right at the upper corner of the field (power line continues straight up the mountain; this was the former trail route, but is now posted "no trespassing"). Follow the road as it traverses along the top of the blueberry barrens for about 150 yd. Then bear left and up on the road, which climbs mostly exposed granite ledge to the summit of the mountain.

SEC 9

CAMDEN HILLS STATE PARK

■ MT. BATTIE (790 FT.)

Located just south of Mt. Megunticook, this mountain features one of the most popular hikes in the Camden Hills, due to both its open ledges that offer outstanding views of the coast and its proximity to the village of Camden. In 1897, a carriage road was built to the summit, and a hotel named the Summit House was built. The hotel was torn down in 1920. A 26-ft. stone observation tower—a World War I memorial—was erected in its place the following year. The paved auto road from the east side was constructed by the Maine State Park Commission in 1965; the road leaves from the state park entrance on US 1 and climbs gradually to the top in 1.6 mi.

MT. BATTIE TRAIL (MBPL; MAP 4: C1)

From Megunticook St. parking (210 ft.) to:	�it	↗	○
Mt. Battie summit (790 ft.)	0.5 mi.	580 ft.	0:35

This trail rises steeply over the rocky nose of Mt. Battie from the south. Follow ME 52 (Mountain St.) from its jct. with US 1 in Camden. Take the fourth turn on the right, and then the first left onto Megunticook St. Continue steeply uphill to a small parking area.

The trail climbs steadily and then more steeply north to emerge on open ledges before reaching the stone tower on top. The expansive view of Camden Harbor and the islands in Penobscot Bay is a Maine coast classic.

CARRIAGE ROAD TRAIL (MBPL; MAP 4: C1)

Cumulative from ME 52 (250 ft.) to:	↕	↗	○
Carriage Trail (270 ft.)	0.3 mi.	20 ft.	0:10
Tablelands Trail (600 ft.)	1.0 mi.	350 ft.	0:40
Mt. Battie summit (790 ft.)	1.2 mi.	540 ft.	0:50

This trail climbs along the gradual western slopes of Mt. Battie via the route of an old carriage road. It leaves the right (northeast) side of ME 52 1.3 mi. from the jct. of US 1 and ME 52 in Camden. Look for a small wooden sign: Old Carriage Road—Mt. Battie Rd. 1 mile. Parking is along the road.

Carriage Road Trail runs north 0.3 mi. to a jct. Here, Carriage Road Trail forks right, and Carriage Trail continues ahead to meet Tablelands Trail. Carriage Road Trail rises gently on or near the old carriage road to join Mt. Battie Auto Rd. just north of the summit parking area. Cross the road to merge with Tablelands Trail at 1.0 mi., turning right onto this trail to reach the summit of Mt. Battie in another 0.2 mi.

CARRIAGE TRAIL (MBPL; MAP 4: C1–C2)

Cumulative from ME 52 (250 ft.) to:	⥮	↗	⟳
Carriage Road Trail (270 ft.)	0.3 mi.	20 ft.	0:10
Tablelands Trail (700 ft.)	1.0 mi.	450 ft.	0:45
Mt. Battie summit (790 ft.) via Tablelands Trail	1.8 mi.	540 ft.	1:10
Ocean Lookout (1,250 ft.) via Tablelands Trail	1.7 mi.	1,000 ft.	1:20

This trail leaves Carriage Road Trail at a point 0.3 mi. from ME 52 and climbs gradually to reach Tablelands Trail just north of the saddle between Mt. Battie and Mt. Megunticook at 1.0 mi. To the right, it is 0.8 mi. to the summit of Mt. Battie via Tablelands Trail. To the left, it is 0.7 mi. to Ocean Lookout via Tablelands Trail.

TABLELANDS TRAIL (MBPL; MAP 4: B2, C1–C2)

From Mt. Battie summit (790 ft.) to:	⥮	↗	⟳
Ocean Lookout (1,250 ft.)	1.4 mi.	680 ft.	1:00

This trail starts from the summit of Mt. Battie near the stone tower, crosses the parking area, and descends gradually to the north. The trail meets Carriage Road Trail coming in from the left (west) at 0.2 mi., and crosses Mt. Battie Auto Rd. at 0.5 mi. At 0.7 mi., it passes Nature Trail on the right, and at 0.8 mi., Carriage Trail on the left. Beyond, Tablelands Trail ascends and passes Adam's Lookout Trail on the right at 1.2 mi. The route keeps to the right (east) of two lines of cliffs and, again swinging to the northwest, climbs steeply to Ocean Lookout at 1.4 mi. From the expansive lookout cliffs, the views of Mt. Battie and Camden Harbor are extraordinary. The true summit of Mt. Megunticook is 0.4 mi. ahead via Ridge Trail.

SEC 9

NATURE TRAIL (MBPL; MAP 4: C2)

From Mt. Battie Auto Rd. hiker parking lot (250 ft.) to:	⥮	↗	⟳
Megunticook Trail (450 ft.) via right turn on Nature Trail	0.3 mi.	200 ft.	0:15
From Mt. Battie Auto Rd. hiker parking lot (250 ft.) to:			
Tablelands Trail (650 ft.) via left turn on Nature Trail	0.8 mi.	400 ft.	0:30

Nature Trail links the lower part of Megunticook Trail with Tablelands Trail and provides access to both Mt. Battie (via Tablelands Trail) and

Mt. Megunticook (via either Megunticook or Tablelands Trail and Ridge Trail). Nature Trail starts from the Mt. Battie hikers parking lot, on the right 0.25 mi. up Mt. Battie Auto Rd. from the park entrance and US 1. Nature Trail proceeds to a jct. at 0.1 mi. Turn left (west) here to reach Tablelands Trail in a col between Mt. Battie and Mt. Megunticook at 0.7 mi. Turn right (north) here to reach Megunticook Trail in 0.2 mi.

■ MT. MEGUNTICOOK (1,385 FT.)

Mt. Megunticook, a 6-mi.-long mountain ridge extending in a northwest–southeast direction between Youngtown Rd. and US 1, is the highest peak in the Camden Hills. The true summit is forested and has no view, but just to the southeast, Ocean Lookout takes in the expanse of Penobscot Bay and the nearby coastal hills. Several outlooks along Ridge Trail also offer views over Megunticook Lake. Maiden Cliff is a prominent escarpment near the northwest end of the ridge.

MEGUNTICOOK TRAIL (MBPL; MAP 4: B1–C2)

Cumulative from campground upper loop (350 ft.) to:	⇅	↗	⟳
Nature Trail (450 ft.)	0.1 mi.	100 ft.	0:05
Ocean Lookout, Tablelands Trail (1,250 ft.)	1.1 mi.	800 ft.	1:00
Mt. Megunticook summit (1,385 ft.) via Ridge Trail	1.5 mi.	935 ft.	1:15

Find the start of Megunticook Trail on the outer edge of the upper campground loop, a 0.5-mi. walk from the day-use parking lot across from the park entrance station. Megunticook Trail and Ski Shelter/Multi-use Trail coincide for a short stretch before Ski Shelter/Multi-use Trail breaks off to the right. Shortly after crossing a bridge, Nature Trail departs to the left. At 0.7 mi., pass Adam's Lookout Trail on the left (leads 0.3 mi. to Tablelands Trail). At 1.1 mi., Megunticook Trail reaches Ocean Lookout, where Tablelands Trail from Mt. Battie comes up from the left (south). From Ocean Lookout, follow Ridge Trail 0.4 mi. to the Mt. Megunticook summit.

ADAM'S LOOKOUT TRAIL (MBPL; MAP 4: B2)

From Megunticook Trail (850 ft.) to:	⇅	↗	⟳
Tablelands Trail (1,100 ft.)	0.3 mi.	250 ft.	0:15

This short trail connects Megunticook Trail and Tablelands Trail while providing an excellent lookout over Penobscot Bay to the east.

SKI SHELTER/MULTI-USE TRAIL NORTHBOUND
(MBPL; MAP 4: C2, B2, AND A2)

Cumulative from campground upper loop (350 ft.) to:	�??↓↑	↗	⟳
Summer Bypass Trail (550 ft.)	1.0 mi.	200 ft.	0:35
Slope Trail (550 ft.) and Megunticook Ski Shelter	2.0 mi.	200 ft.	1:05
Youngtown Rd. trailhead (250 ft.)	4.8 mi.	350 ft.	2:35

Ski Shelter/Multi-use Trail diverges right from Megunticook Trail a short distance from the latter's start at the upper campground loop. Ski Shelter/Multi-use Trail heads north to a fork at 1.0 mi. Here, Summer Bypass Trail leaves to the left, while Ski Shelter/Multi-use Trail continues to the right. Both trails contour easily to the west and merge 0.8 mi. ahead at 1.8 mi. Cross Spring Brook to reach the jct. with Slope Trail at 2.0 mi. To the left, Slope Trail ascends 1.0 mi. to the summit of Mt. Megunticook. Here also is the Megunticook Ski Shelter, a small cabin that can be reserved for overnight use. Continuing ahead, Ski Shelter/Multi-use Trail traverses the interior of the park, passing the northern base of Bald Rock Mtn. before reaching the Youngtown Rd. trailhead, 2.3 mi. from the jct. of ME 173 and US 1 in Lincolnville.

SLOPE TRAIL (MBPL; MAP 4: B1–B2)

From Ski Shelter/Multi-use Trail (550 ft.) to:	↓↑	↗	⟳
Mt. Megunticook summit (1,385 ft.)	1.0 mi.	835 ft.	0:55

Slope Trail leaves Ski Shelter/Multi-use Trail at a point 2.0 mi. north of the latter's start at the upper campground loop, opposite Megunticook Ski Shelter. Slope Trail crosses over Spring Brook and climbs steeply up the northeast slope of the mountain to reach Ridge Trail at 1.0 mi. The true summit of Mt. Megunticook is 100 ft. right up Ridge Trail from this jct. in a small viewless clearing.

JACK WILLIAMS TRAIL (MBPL; MAP 4: B1–B2)

From Tablelands Trail (1,100 ft.) to:	↓↑	↗	⟳
Ridge Trail (900 ft.)	1.6 mi.	200 ft.	1:15

This mostly wooded trail leaves Tablelands Trail just below its jct. with Ridge Trail and contours across the southwest face of Mt. Megunticook, passing through some impressive stands of hardwoods. Near its end, the trail rises to meet Ridge Trail at a point 1.2 mi. west of the Mt. Megunticook summit and 1.0 mi. east of Maiden Cliff. Jack Williams Trail is named in honor of a local trail volunteer.

SEC 9

MAIDEN CLIFF TRAIL (MBPL; MAP 4: B1)

Cumulative from ME 52 parking (189 ft.) to:	↧↥	↗	↻
Ridge Trail (500 ft.)	0.4 mi.	300 ft.	0:20
Scenic Trail (750 ft.) and Maiden Cliff	0.8 mi.	550 ft.	0:40

Maiden Cliff rises abruptly above the eastern shore of Megunticook Lake. A steel cross on top stands near the spot where 12-year-old Elenora French fell to her death in 1864 in an attempt to catch her windblown hat. The trail starts from the northeast side of ME 52 at a signed parking area, 2.8 mi. north of the jct. of ME 52 and US 1 in Camden, where the road passes above Barrett's Cove on Megunticook Lake and just beyond the impressive walls of Barrett's Cove Cliff.

The trail climbs north and west, at first following an eroded woods road along a small brook. Cross the brook on a footbridge and follow the rocky trail beyond. At 0.4 mi., Ridge Trail continues ahead (north). Maiden Cliff Trail branches left (west) and climbs more steeply via switchbacks before making a mostly level run northwest to the jct. with Scenic Trail. Follow a short spur left to the top of Maiden Cliff then scramble down a few feet for an outstanding view over Megunticook Lake to Ragged Mtn. and the ski slopes of Camden Snow Bowl, as well as Bald Mtn.

SCENIC TRAIL (MBPL; MAP 4: B1)

From Maiden Cliff (750 ft.) to:	↧↥	↗	↻
Ridge Trail (850 ft.)	0.4 mi.	150 ft.	0:20

This trail bears right (east) from Maiden Cliff Trail just above Maiden Cliff. Scenic Trail follows over several knobs with extensive open ledges. Occasional cairns mark the route. Views are excellent over Megunticook Lake. The trail then descends slightly to the jct. with Ridge Trail, at a point 0.6 mi. from ME 52 via Maiden Cliff Trail and Ridge Trail.

RIDGE TRAIL (MBPL; MAP 4: B1–B2)

Cumulative from Maiden Cliff Trail (500 ft.) to:	↧↥	↗	↻
Scenic Trail (850 ft.)	0.2 mi.	350 ft.	0:20
Jack Williams Trail (900 ft.)	0.8 mi.	400 ft.	0:35
Zeke's Trail (1,150 ft.)	1.1 mi.	650 ft.	0:55
Mt. Megunticook summit and Slope Trail (1,385 ft.)	2.0 mi.	885 ft.	1:30
Ocean Lookout (1,250 ft.) and Tablelands Trail	2.4 mi.	885 ft.	1:45

Ridge Trail leaves Maiden Cliff Trail 0.4 mi. from ME 52 at a signed jct. and runs southeast along the main ridge of Mt. Megunticook, over the wooded summit (1,385 ft.), and on to Ocean Lookout, with its fine views of Penobscot Bay.

From Maiden Cliff Trail, climb steeply via switchbacks to the ridgeline and the jct. of Scenic Trail, which leaves left at 0.2 mi. Ridge Trail now proceeds east, makes a brief descent to cross a couple of small brooks, then trends gradually upward past several outlooks. On a sometimes rough trail of rocks and roots, pass Jack Williams Trail on the right. Soon, after detouring up a shallow ravine, pass Zeke's Trail entering from the left. On a level stretch ahead is a window view to Mt. Battie and its auto road and to the Megunticook River valley. After crossing a subsidiary summit (1,290 ft.), Ridge Trail descends slightly and then climbs gradually to the true summit of Mt. Megunticook, which is wooded and marked by a large rock pile. Just beyond, Slope Trail diverges left (north). In another 0.4 mi., Ridge Trail descends to meet Tablelands Trail at Ocean Lookout.

■ BALD ROCK MTN. (1,100 FT.), DERRY MTN. (777 FT.), AND FROHOCK MTN. (454 FT.)

Bald Rock Mtn., which rises several miles northeast of Mt. Megunticook, is the second-highest peak in the state park. The mountain's open summit ledges provide excellent views east over Penobscot Bay. Extending northeast of Bald Rock Mtn. are the wooded ridgelines and the viewless summits of Derry Mtn. and Frohock Mtn.

SKI SHELTER/MULTI-USE TRAIL SOUTHBOUND
(MBPL; MAP 4: A2, B2, AND C2)

Cumulative from Youngtown Rd. (260 ft.) to:	↧↥	↗	○
Frohock Mtn. Trail (400 ft.)	0.5 mi.	140 ft.	0:20
Bald Rock Mtn. Trail and Cameron Mtn. Trail jct. (600 ft.)	1.2 mi.	340 ft.	0:45
Sky Blue Trail (650 ft.)	1.5 mi.	390 ft.	1:00
Zeke's Trail (650 ft.)	2.4 mi.	400 ft.	1:25
Slope Trail (550 ft.) and Megunticook Ski Shelter	2.8 mi.	400 ft.	1:35
Megunticook Trail (350 ft.) and upper campground loop	4.8 mi.	400 ft.	2:35

This trail, a wide, gravel-surfaced service road, serves as the approach to the mountains in the northern part of Camden Hills State Park, including Bald Rock Mtn., Cameron Mtn., Derry Mtn., and Frohock Mtn. The trail may also be used to reach several trails that climb the north side of Mt. Megunticook. From the jct. of US 1 and ME 173 in Lincolnville, drive west on ME 173. At 2.3 mi., bear left onto Youngtown Rd., and in 200 ft. turn left into a small parking area (iron ranger, day-use fee).

In 0.5 mi. from the trailhead, reach the jct. with Frohock Mtn. Trail, which leads left (south) to meet Bald Rock Mtn. Trail in 0.3 mi. and continues northeast over Derry Mtn. The trail ends atop the wooded Frohock Mtn. in 2.1 mi. Continuing on Ski Shelter/Multi-use Trail, reach the jct. of two trails at 1.2 mi. Here, Bald Rock Mtn. Trail heads left (south) 0.8 mi. to the summit of Bald Rock Mtn., while Cameron Mtn. Trail leaves right and climbs 2.0 mi. to a spur that leads another 0.1 mi. to Cameron Mtn.

Ahead on Ski Shelter/Multi-use Trail, Sky Blue Trail leaves right at 1.5 mi. At 2.4 mi. from Youngtown Rd., Ski Shelter/Multi-use Trail passes Zeke's Trail on the right (leads 1.4 mi. to Ridge Trail), and at 2.8 mi., Ski Shelter/Multi-use Trail reaches a jct. with Slope Trail (leads 1.0 mi. to the true summit of Mt. Megunticook) and the Megunticook Ski Shelter (overnight shelter by reservation only). Ski Shelter/Multi-use Trail continues to swing low around the northeast side of Mt. Megunticook to reach its end at Megunticook Trail, just a short distance from the outer ring of the upper campground loop.

FROHOCK MTN. TRAIL (MBPL; MAP 4: A2–A3)

Cumulative from Ski Shelter/Multi-use Trail (400 ft.) to:	⇅	↗	⟳
Bald Rock Mtn. Trail (650 ft.)	0.3 mi.	250 ft.	0:15
Frohock Mtn. (454 ft.)	2.1 mi.	230 ft.	1:10

The trail leaves from Ski Shelter/Multi-use Trail at a point 0.5 mi. from the Youngtown Rd. trailhead. From the jct. with Ski Shelter/Multi-use Trail, turn left onto Frohock Mtn. Trail and climb southeast. In 0.3 mi., reach a jct. with Bald Rock Mtn. Trail (leads 0.5 mi. to the summit of Bald Rock Mtn.). Frohock Mtn. Trail turns hard left (northeast) and climbs easily to the wooded summit of Derry Mtn. Beyond, the trail descends gradually to a sag before a brief climb to its end atop Frohock Mtn.

BALD ROCK MTN. TRAIL (MBPL; MAP 4: A2 AND B2)

Cumulative from jct. with Ski Shelter/Multi-use Trail (600 ft.) to:	⇅	↗	⟳
Bald Rock Mtn. summit (1,100 ft.) and shelters	0.8 mi.	500 ft.	0:40
Frohock Mtn. Trail (650 ft.)	1.3 mi.	500 ft.	0:55

Bald Rock Mtn. Trail diverges to the left (southeast) from Ski Shelter/ Multi-use Trail at a point 1.2 mi. from Youngtown Rd. Bald Rock Mtn. Trail climbs easily at first, then more steeply to the open summit slabs, where there are fabulous views over Penobscot Bay to the island beyond. Just before the summit, a short side trail leads left to a campsite and shelter (available on a first-come, first-served basis). Coming off the top of the mountain, the trail quickly reaches a second shelter on the right. Beyond, the trail drops steeply, then eases and slowly curves left to reach Frohock Mtn. Trail.

■ CAMERON MTN. (811 FT.)

In 2007, The Nature Conservancy acquired a 45-acre parcel that includes the open summit of Cameron Mtn. The following year the land was transferred to the state of Maine and is now part of Camden Hills State Park. Commercial blueberry fields are located on the summit, and hikers are asked to stay on the trail.

CAMERON MTN. TRAIL (MBPL; MAP 4: A1–A2 AND B1–B2)

Cumulative from jct. with Ski Shelter/Multi-use Trail (600 ft.) to:	⇅	↗	○
Cameron Mtn. summit (811 ft.) via side trail	1.1 mi.	210 ft.	0:35
Jct. of Sky Blue Trail and Zeke's Trail (950 ft.)	2.0 mi.	510 ft.	1:15

This trail diverges right (west) from Ski Shelter/Multi-use Trail at its jct. with Bald Rock Mtn. Trail, 1.2 mi. from the Youngtown Rd. trailhead. Shortly after the trails split, Cameron Mtn. Trail turns left (avoid the first left), following an old road. The trail crosses Black Brook and rises gradually past abandoned farmland, old cellar holes, and apple trees to a point just below the summit of Cameron Mtn., where a short side trail leads right (north) 0.1 mi. to the mountaintop. Beyond the jct., the main trail descends for a short distance before turning left (south) and starting to climb. Soon, Sky Blue Trail enters from the left, and at 2.0 mi., Cameron Mtn. Trail merges with Zeke's Trail.

SEC 9

SKY BLUE TRAIL (MBPL; MAP 4: B1–B2)

From Ski Shelter/Multi-use Trail (650 ft.) to:	⇅	↗	○
Jct. of Cameron Mtn. Trail and Zeke's Trail (950 ft.)	1.5 mi.	300 ft.	0:55

Sky Blue Trail leaves Ski Shelter/Multi-use Trail at a point 0.3 mi. beyond the start of Cameron Mtn. Trail and follows a course roughly parallel to that trail. At 1.5 mi., Sky Blue Trail merges with the upper end of Cameron Mtn. Trail and, just beyond, reaches the jct. with Zeke's Trail.

ZEKE'S TRAIL (MBPL; MAP 4: B1–B2)

Cumulative from Ski Shelter/Multi-use Trail (650 ft.) to:	⭥	↗	↺
Cameron Mtn. Trail (950 ft.)	0.6 mi.	300 ft.	0:30
Zeke's Lookout spur trail (1,100 ft.)	0.9 mi.	450 ft.	0:40
Ridge Trail (1,150 ft.)	1.4 mi.	500 ft.	1:00

This trail diverges right (west) from Ski Shelter/Multi-use Trail at a point 2.4 mi. from the Youngtown Rd. trailhead and ascends gradually. At 0.6 mi., Sky Blue Trail enters from the right. At 0.9 mi., a spur leads right 100 yd. to Zeke's Lookout (1,150 ft.), which offers limited but very nice views of Bald Rock Mtn. and Penobscot Bay. Zeke's Trail ends at its jct. with Ridge Trail at 1.4 mi., 0.9 mi. northwest of the summit of Mt. Megunticook.

GEORGES HIGHLAND PATH AND CAMDEN SNOW BOWL

The Georges River Land Trust was established in 1987. Soon after, its founders conceived the Georges Highland Path as a long-distance walking trail connecting the headwater of the St. George River in Montville to the Gulf of Maine at Port Clyde. Today, the GHP network has more than 50 mi. of hiking trails in five distinct sections scattered from north to south throughout the watershed.

Hikers can enjoy sections of GHP on Ragged Mtn. in Camden and Rockport, Spruce Mtn., and Mt. Pleasant in Rockport, the top of a prominent ridgeline west of the St. George River in Appleton, and on Hogback Mtn. and Frye Mtn. at the north end of the watershed in Montville and Knox. The Hogback-Frye portion of GHP connects to the trails of Midcoast Conservancy in the northern reaches of the adjoining Sheepscot River watershed. The MCC and GRLT trails in this area are part of the 47-mi. Hills to Sea Trail that connects Unity to Belfast, a monumental project completed by Waldo Countyrails Coalition in 2017.

■ RAGGED MTN. (1,303 FT.)

Ragged Mtn. straddles the town lines of Camden and Rockport. The northeast slope is home to the Camden Snow Bowl ski area. Ragged Mtn., the focus of ambitious conservation efforts by Coastal Mountains Land Trust and a number of private landowners, features extensive ledges and outlooks, wild blueberries, and considerable subalpine terrain.

Three trail sections of GHP are on the mountain. Access to the sections is from Thorndike Brook on Hope St., from ME 17 west of Mirror Lake, and from Barnestown Rd. Two trails ascend the mountain from the Camden Snow Bowl base area.

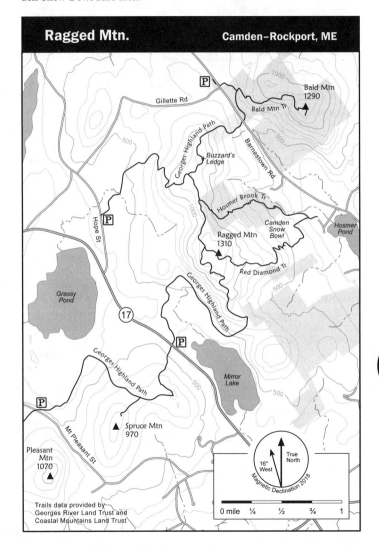

GHP FROM HOPE ST. (GRLT; USGS WEST ROCKPORT QUAD, GAZETTEER MAP 14, RAGGED MTN., P. 387)

Cumulative from Hope St. trailhead (450 ft.) to:	↕	↗	↻
Barnestown Rd. via Buzzard's Ledge (1,200 ft.)	1.5 mi.	750 ft.	1:10
Hosmer Brook Trail (1,150 ft.)	1.8 mi.	750 ft.	1:20
Sundown Ledge (1,260 ft.) and Red Diamond Trail	2.2 mi.	900 ft.	1:40
Ragged Mtn. summit (1,303 ft.) via Red Diamond Trail	2.4 mi.	950 ft.	1:50
ME 17 trailhead (420 ft.)	4.9 mi.	1,100 ft.	3:00

GHP climbs the southwest ridge of Ragged Mtn., offering a series of good viewpoints en route. Traversing the entire ridge from north to south (or vice versa) and walking back to the start along ME 17 makes for a fine loop hike of about 5 mi. From the jct. of US 1 and ME 90 in Rockport, travel west on ME 90 for 2.7 mi. Turn right (northeast) on ME 17 and drive 2.7 mi. to Hope St. Turn right and reach the trailhead (sign and kiosk) on the right in 0.5 mi.

The initial going is easy through old fields and young woods, across Thorndike Brook, past stone walls, and on and off old woods roads. Beyond, climb moderately to an overlook above Grassy Pond. Ahead, the trail switchbacks and then angles across the mountainside to a jct. with GHP from Barnestown Rd. via Buzzard's Ledge. Descend gradually to a sag on the ridge, then climb easily to a jct. at 1.75 mi., where Hosmer Brook Trail from Camden Snow Bowl enters from the left. Proceed along the ridgeline, reach another sag, climb again, then follow along on a contour. Ahead, bear left to avoid the obvious outcrops, and then climb a short, steep pitch to the semi-open ledges above. Just beyond, reach a large open outcrop known as Sundown Ledge, where there are views all the way to the White Mountains. Red Diamond Trail enters the woods atop Sundown Ledge; this jct. is unsigned and easily missed. (In 2017, a small square of plywood signboard tacked to a gnarled white birch marked the entrance of this trail in the woods.) Red Diamond Trail leads easily to the true summit of Ragged Mtn. in 0.15 mi.

Continuing on GHP, descend Sundown Ledge. The trail remains out in the open for a fair distance, crossing several ledges and knobs with good views. Climb to a cairn out on the open ledges of the west face of the mountain, where there are big views to the ocean and to Spruce Mtn. and Mt. Pleasant. Descend the cliff face with the Ragged Mtn. summit towers off to the left. Turn a corner to get a wonderful view of Mirror Lake.

Continue in the open toward the towers. Bear left and up the rocks, then zigzag down a short, steep pitch into a wooded ravine.

Cross a small stream, then climb out of the ravine onto big, open slabs of rock. Follow cairns and blazes up the open slope of rocks and ledges toward the towers. Just below the towers at 2.7 mi., veer to the right and enter a grove of scrub oaks. The trail continues down the south ridge, in and out of the trees, with several more good viewpoints. At 3.2 mi., it joins an old carriage road and then descends steadily toward Mirror Lake (the trail avoids the lake, a public water supply). Leveling off below, the trail traverses north along the base of the mountain, bears left to cross a brook, and soon reaches the trailhead at 4.9 mi. at ME 17.

GHP FROM ME 17 (GRLT; USGS WEST ROCKPORT QUAD, GAZETTEER MAP 14, RAGGED MTN., P. 387)

Cumulative from ME 17 trailhead (420 ft.) to:	⇅	↗	↻
Sundown Ledge (1,260 ft.) and Red Diamond Trail	2.7 mi.	1,000 ft.	1:50
Ragged Mtn. summit (1,303 ft.) via Red Diamond Trail	2.9 mi.	1,050 ft.	2:00
Hope St. trailhead (450 ft.)	4.9 mi.	1,050 ft.	3:00
Barnestown Rd. trailhead (650 ft.)	5.1 mi.	1,050 ft.	3:05

This trail ascends the southwest face of Ragged Mtn. and affords good views of Camden and the ocean, as well as the nearby peaks of Mt. Pleasant and Spruce Mtn. From the jct. of US 1 and ME 90 in Rockport, travel west on ME 90 for 2.7 mi. Turn right (northeast) on ME 17. Follow this for 1.8 mi. to trailhead parking (sign and kiosk) on the right, a short distance past Mirror Lake.

GHP enters the woods, and in about 0.5 mi., crosses a small brook. Turning right, it contours along the base of the mountain before ascending steadily with views through the trees to Mirror Lake. Reach an old carriage road and follow this easily north along the upper face of the mountain. Continue up the ridge on a foot trail, emerging on open ledges with views to the south. The trail ducks into scrub growth for a short distance before breaking into the open on ledges high on Ragged Mtn. just beneath the summit towers. From here, it continues around the west face and to Sundown Ledge and the jct. with Red Diamond Trail at 2.7 mi. Ahead on the north ridge, GHP reaches Hosmer Brook Trail at 3.1 mi., then proceeds to the next GHP jct. at 3.4 mi. Here, to the left, it is 1.5 mi. via GHP to Hope St. (Thorndike Brook Access); to the right, it is 1.1 mi. via GHP to Barnestown Rd. and another 0.6 mi. to the trailhead parking area.

GHP FROM BARNESTOWN RD. (GRLT; USGS WEST ROCKPORT QUAD, GAZETTEER MAP 14, RAGGED MTN., P. 387)

Cumulative from Barnestown Rd. trailhead (650 ft.) to:	↥↧	↗	○
Hope St. (1,200 ft.)	1.7 mi.	650 ft.	1:10
Sundown Ledge and Red Diamond Trail (1,260 ft.)	2.4 mi.	800 ft.	1:35
Ragged Mtn. summit (1,303 ft.) via Red Diamond Trail	2.6 mi.	850 ft.	1:45

This trail ascends Ragged Mtn. from the northeast, offering good views from Buzzard's Ledge, along the north ridge, and from the high point just below the summit. From US 1 at a point 0.8 mi. from the center of Camden, turn northwest on John St. At 0.8 from US 1, John St. becomes Hosmer Pond Rd. Follow this past the entrance to Camden Snow Bowl on the left. Beyond this point, the road is known as Barnestown Rd. Continue past the intersection with Gillette Rd. on the left to the height-of-land and a trailhead parking lot on the left at 4.3 mi.

The trail begins in a small field and then crosses the road to a larger hay field. Ahead at 0.3 mi., bearing right at the jct. with Bald Mtn. Trail, GHP descends slightly, paralleling a brook. Below, cross the brook and begin to ascend Ragged Mtn. At 0.6 mi., cross Barnestown Rd. Ascend a short, steep pitch to a wide trail that winds up the hill at a moderate grade. Bear right at the lip of a ravine and soon reach Buzzard's Ledge at 1.5 mi. with views northeast to Bald Mtn. Continue up the ridge over a series of open ledges. Reach a knob, then descend slightly to a jct. at 1.7 mi., where GHP from Hope St. comes in from the right and merges. From here, it is 0.3 mi. to Hosmer Brook Trail, 0.7 mi. to Sundown Ledge and Red Diamond Trail, 0.9 mi. to the summit of Ragged Mtn. via Red Diamond Trail, and 3.4 mi. via GHP to ME 17. To continue from this point, follow the directions for GHP from Hope St.

SEC 9

HOSMER BROOK TRAIL (CMLT; USGS CAMDEN QUAD, GAZETTEER MAP 14, RAGGED MTN., P. 387)

Cumulative from Camden Snow Bowl parking lot (240 ft.) to:	↥↧	↗	○
GHP (1,150 ft.)	1.4 mi.	910 ft.	1:10
Sundown Ledge and Red Diamond Trail (1,260 ft.)	2.1 mi.	950 ft.	1:30
Ragged Mtn. summit (1,303 ft.) via Red Diamond Trail	2.3 mi.	1,000 ft.	1:40
Camden Snow Bowl base area (240 ft.) via Red Diamond Trail	3.9 mi.	1,000 ft.	2:30

Hosmer Brook Trail climbs from the Camden Snow Bowl base area to the north ridge of Ragged Mtn. where it connects with the GHP. From downtown Camden, travel north on US 1 for 0.8 mi. to John St. Turn right and drive 0.8 mi. then bear left onto Mechanic St., which beomes Hosmer Pond Rd. then Barnestown Road. In 2.1 mi., the entrance road for Camden Snow Bowl is on the left, just after Hosmer Pond. Park near the Camden Snow Bowl base lodge, the obvious A-frame building.

From the right side of the A-frame, walk straight up the grassy slope for about 400 ft. Two mountain bike tracks cross the slope; at the second, turn right and follow it under the triple-chair lift line then cross a gravel access road. Cross a ski trail and at a trail sign (Hosmer Brook Trail) ahead, bear left up another ski trail, the farthest right on the mountain. The trail zigzags up the slopes, trending in and out of the woods to either side of the wide ski trail, but you can simply follow the obvious path straight up the slope. At 0.25 mi. from the base lodge, leave the ski trail to the right and enter the woods (sign). About 400 ft. ahead, reach an unsigned fork. A mountain bike trail continues to the left; continue on Hosmer Brook Trail to the right.

At 0.5 mi., the trail reaches the lower loop jct. The right fork is shorter (0.2 mi.) and more popular; the left fork is 0.4 mi. Both sections rejoin a short distance ahead. Take the right fork by going straight ahead and soon cross over a stone wall. Beyond, at a rocky stream bed, turn left and up a ravine, following switchbacks to the upper loop jct., which enters from the left. Continue straight, climbing gradually up the mountainside on switchbacks. Hosmer Brook Trail passes to the left of a large, sloping, mossy outcrop. Climb a single rock step then bear right around several huge, mossy outcrops. Reach the jct. with the GHP at 1.4 mi., on the north ridge in a semi-open area of oak and spruce. Follow GHP to the left to reach Sundown Ledge and Red Diamond Trail, which leads to the top of Ragged Mtn.

SEC 9

RED DIAMOND TRAIL (CMLT; USGS CAMDEN QUAD, GAZETTEER MAP 14, RAGGED MTN., P. 387)

Cumulative from Sundown Ledge (1,260 ft.) and GHP to:	⇅	↗	○
Ragged Mtn. summit (1,303 ft.)	0.2 mi.	50 ft.	0:10
Camden Snow Bowl base area (240 ft.)	1.8 mi.	50 ft.	1:00

Red Diamond Trail connects Sundown Ledge on GHP to the true summit of Ragged Mtn. and then continues on through the woods and over ski slopes of the Camden Snow Bowl to its base area. The numerous outlooks en route include Bald Mtn., Mt. Megunticook, Mt. Battie, and Camden Harbor. This trail is not open during ski season. Red Diamond Trail is often combined with Hosmer Brook Trail and a portion of GHP to form a loop on Ragged Mtn. and is therefore described on the descent.

Standing on Sundown Ledge with your back to the view, look for a gnarled white birch with a small square of plywood (but no sign) nailed to a branch. This marks the trail's entrance into the woods. In 750 ft., reach a T jct. A side trail to the left leads 75 ft. to the summit ledges atop Ragged Mtn. and fine views to the east. Back on the main trail, drop down to a sag between the two wooded peaks of Ragged Mtn. then bear left and down past a large ledge outcrop. Descend a wide eroded path then bear sharply left and contour to the top of Downeast Glade. Cross the open area above the top of the triple-chair lift station. Enter the woods beyond and continue the descent. At 0.5 mi., pass the South Overlook tent platform. Continue down through the woods just south of the ski trail.

At 0.65 mi., an open-front shelter is 150 ft. to the left. Continue to follow the red diamond trail markers. Cross an open ledge with a cairn then proceed through the oak forest. Below, join with a narrow ski trail then cross a wider ski trail. Pass through Mainsail Glade. At 1.0 mi., at the next wide ski trail, make a sharp switchback right, back into the woods. Red Diamond Trail continues to switchback down through the woods on the shared mountain bike and hiking trail. (Please do not cut switchbacks.) Cross a narrow ski trail then reach a wide ski trail and turn left down it. Follow the right edge of the ski trail to reach a gravel access road just to the left of the upper station of the double-chair lift. Follow this track across the main ski slopes. At the triple chair lift, turn right and follow the gravel access road to the base area. Cross the grassy ski slope to reach the A-frame base lodge and the end of the trail.

SEC 9

■ SPRUCE MTN. (955 FT.)

This mountain lies just southwest of Ragged Mtn. in Rockport. East and west summits offer good views of the Camden Hills, Penobscot Bay, and beyond. The section of GHP described here heads west from Ragged Mtn. Spruce Mtn. may also be hiked from the west starting at Mt. Pleasant St. in Rockport. The Spruce Mtn. trailhead is the same as for GHP to Ragged Mtn. from ME 17.

SPRUCE MTN. TRAIL/GHP (GRLT; USGS WEST ROCKPORT QUAD, GAZETTEER MAP 14, RAGGED MTN., P. 387)

Cumulative from ME 17 trailhead (420 ft.) to:	↿⇂	↗	○
Spruce Mtn. high point (935 ft.)	1.3 mi.	650 ft.	1:00
Mt. Pleasant St. trailhead (550 ft.)	3.0 mi.	750 ft.	1:55

The trail begins directly across ME 17 from the Ragged Mtn. trailhead parking lot and ascends steadily through mixed hardwoods and past old stone walls. At 0.4 mi., atop a steep rock outcrop, there are blueberry fields and views of Grassy Pond to the northwest, Ragged Mtn. to the north, and Penobscot Bay to the east. Descend briefly, reenter the woods, and continue ascending. At 0.6, emerge on the east summit of Spruce Mtn. From here, there are excellent views of Mirror Lake and Ragged Mtn. across ME 17, the islands of Penobscot Bay to the east, and Mt. Desert Island beyond.

After reentering the woods, the undulating trail trends down, crosses an old woods road, and reaches a large rock outcrop at the jct. with the spur trail to the west summit outlook. The spur climbs steeply before emerging on rock ledges among spruce trees below the summit at 1.3 mi. The trail does not ascend to the wooded summit. The best observation point is from a rock outcrop below where the spur emerges. From there, enjoy excellent views of Hatchett Mtn. to the west, with Moody Mtn. peeking over its ridgeline, and of the North Haven, Vinalhaven, and Mt. Desert islands to the east.

Return to the main trail. At the jct., turn left and begin a gradual descent off the north flank of the west summit to the valley between Spruce Mtn. and Mt. Pleasant. The trail travels through a young hardwood forest and gradually flattens out in the valley as the forest becomes more mature. In the lower section, there may be wet spots that are easily crossed, and there are two bridges over streams. Shortly after crossing the second bridge, the trail begins to climb toward Mt. Pleasant. Ascend gradually at first, then more steeply, crossing power lines and reaching Mt. Pleasant St. in Rockport at 3.0 mi. There is a parking area on the side of the road. GHP continues on toward Mt. Pleasant across the road. There are small GHP signs and blue blazes at the crossing.

SEC 9

■ MT. PLEASANT (1,070 FT.)

This mountain straddles the Rockport–Warren town line just southwest of Spruce Mtn. From the jct. of US 1 and ME 90 in Rockport, travel west on ME 90 for 2.7 mi. Turn right (northeast) on ME 17, drive 0.4 mi., and turn left on Mt. Pleasant St. Follow Mt. Pleasant St., passing blueberry fields and the height-of-land between Mt. Pleasant and Spruce Mtn. before reaching the trailhead at 2.4 mi. at a wide spot in the road. There are small GHP signs and blue blazes (no kiosk) marking the spot.

MT. PLEASANT TRAIL/GHP (GRLT; USGS WEST ROCKPORT QUAD, GAZETTEER MAP 14, RAGGED MTN., P. 387)

Cumulative from Mt. Pleasant St. trailhead (550 ft.) to:	⤴	↗	◷
Overlook at highest point (800 ft.)	0.8 mi.	250 ft.	0:30
Mt. Pleasant viewpoint (750 ft.)	0.9 mi.	250 ft.	0:35

This trail is a continuation of the Ragged Mtn. and Spruce Mtn. section of GHP. The segment leads to an outlook with long views on the west flank of Mt. Pleasant. Although the trail formerly extended to a trailhead on Mt. Pleasant Rd. in Union, that portion has been discontinued. The trail now ends at the viewpoint.

The trail enters the woods on the west side of Mt. Pleasant St., across the street from the Ragged Mtn. section of GHP. It begins as an abandoned logging road and ascends gradually through a regenerating hardwood stand. At 0.3 mi., the trail turns sharply left and enters land protected by TNC, commemorated by a plaque embedded in a rock on the right side of the trail. Here, the trail begins ascending through a mature mixed forest to reach an overlook at the highest point on the trail at 0.75 mi. Descend gradually, briefly merge with a jeep trail, and quickly emerge at the upper edge of an old blueberry field, where there are good views to the west. (*Note:* The trail ends here. Please respect landowners' wishes and retrace your steps to the start.)

COASTAL MOUNTAINS LAND TRUST

■ BALD MTN. (1,280 FT.)

This mountain in Camden is part of the 537-acre Bald Mtn. Preserve, which is owned and managed by CMLT. Good views from the summit ledges of Bald Mtn. include Penobscot Bay, Ragged Mtn., and the surrounding Camden Hills. The rocky heath on top is home to rare subalpine natural communities.

From US 1 at a point 0.8 mi. from the center of Camden, turn northwest on John St. At 0.8 from US 1, John St. becomes Hosmer Pond Rd. Follow this past the entrance to Camden Snow Bowl on the left. Beyond this point, the road is known as Barnestown Rd. Continue past the intersection with Gillette Rd. on the left to the height-of-land and a trailhead parking lot on the left at 4.3 mi.

BALD MTN. TRAIL (CMLT; USGS CAMDEN QUAD, GAZETTEER MAP 14, RAGGED MTN., P. 387)

From Barnestown Rd. (650 ft.) to:	⇅	↗	○
Bald Mtn. summit (1,280 ft.)	1.3 mi.	680 ft.	1:00

The trail starts in a small field and crosses the road to a larger hay field. It then enters the woods and arrives at a jct at 0.3 mi. Here, GHP continues ahead toward Ragged Mtn., while Bald Mtn. Trail turns left. Climb steadily on switchbacks and rock steps. Leveling off, the trail reaches a viewpoint. Beyond, scramble up a short, steep pitch to an open ledge and views of Ragged Mtn. and Buzzard's Ledge across the notch.

After an easy traverse, Bald Mtn. Trail swings back toward the mountain and ascends steeply on rocks and ledges. At the top of the climb, hike along the cliffs with good views of the ocean and the peak of Bald Mtn. Bear left away from the cliffs and up to a knob. Cross a shallow col, then pass beneath the summit cliffs. Reach the base of a rock staircase and ascend steeply. Above, angle upward through woods and then climb switchbacks to the huge cairn and interpretive sign on the summit at 1.3 mi.

■ BEECH HILL (533 FT.)

The 295-acre Beech Hill Preserve in Camden is owned by CMLT and managed for bird habitat and blueberries. The preserve protects the area's only bald hilltop, which offers panoramic views of Penobscot Bay and the Camden Hills. Atop the summit is Beech Nut, a sod-roofed stone hut built in 1914.

SUMMIT TRAIL (CMLT; USGS CAMDEN QUAD, GAZETTEER MAP 14, CMLT BEECH HILL MAP)

From Beech Hill Rd. (412 ft.) to:	⇅	↗	○
Beech Hill summit (533 ft.)	0.85 mi.	121 ft.	0:30

SEC
9

This trail climbs Beech Hill from the west through blueberry fields and grasslands. From the jct. of US 1 and ME 90, travel south 0.3 mi. to Beech Hill Rd on right. Follow this 1.6 mi. to trailhead parking on the left.

Follow a footpath through young woods and then through a field along the edge of the road. At a stone gate, turn right uphill on the farm road. Please observe signs asking hikers to remain on the trail. The road angles across the hillside in the open with fine views of the surrounding landscape, the Camden Hills, and the islands of Penobscot Bay. Beech Nut, a stone hut, sits atop Beech Hill.

WOODS LOOP (CMLT; USGS CAMDEN QUAD, GAZETTEER MAP 14, CMLT BEECH HILL MAP)

From Rockville St. (240 ft.) to:	⇅	↗	⟳
Beech Hill summit (533 ft.) via right fork	1.1 mi.	290 ft.	0:40
From Rockville St. (240 ft.) to:			
Beech Hill summit (533 ft.) via left fork	0.9 mi.	290 ft.	0:35

This trail ascends Beech Hill from the south through the forest. The trail forms a loop, providing hikers with alternative routes of about equal length for ascent and descent. From the jct. of US 1 and ME 90, travel south on US 1 for 1.7 mi. Turn right onto Rockville St. and follow it 0.7 mi. to trailhead parking on the right.

Hike through a sugar maple grove then bear left and soon reach the loop jct. The right fork makes an arc around the east side of the hill before reaching the summit. The left fork winds back and forth up the slope through young forest. The two trails meet 0.25 mi. below the summit. At that point, the stone hut and the summit spruce trees are visible up ahead to the west. Reach them at 1.05 mi. (right fork) or 0.85 mi. (left fork).

MONTVILLE AND KNOX

■ FRYE MTN. (1,139 FT.)

Frye Mtn. in Montville and Knox is in the 5,240-acre Gene Letourneau (Frye Mtn.) Wildlife Management Area. The area is managed by the Maine Dept. of Inland Fisheries & Wildlife. The wooded summit, formerly the site of a Maine Forest Service fire tower, is reached via a loop trail that is part of GHP and maintained by GRLT. Part of the Frye Mtn. Trail coincides with the 47-mi. Hills to Sea Trail from Unity to Belfast, an ambitious project of WCTC.

From the jct. of ME 3 and ME 220 in Liberty, travel north on ME 220. Bear sharply right at Whites Corner at 3.2 mi. and reach Walker Ridge Rd. and the entrance to GLWMA on the right at 6.6 mi. Parking is available behind the DIFW maintenance building on the left.

FRYE MTN. TRAIL/GHP (GRLT; USGS LIBERTY AND MORRILL QUADS, GAZETTEER MAP 14, GRLT FRYE MTN. TRAIL MAP)

Cumulative from DIFW maintenance building parking area (550 ft.) to:	↰↱	↗	↻
Frye Mtn. Trail/Hogback Mtn. Trail jct. near ME 220 (550 ft.)	0.3 mi.	0 ft.	0:05
Frye Mtn. summit (1,139 ft.)	4.1 mi.	700 ft.	2:25
Complete loop	10.9 mi.	1,100 ft.	6:00

To reach the start of the trail, walk behind the maintenance building and enter the woods on a snowmobile/ATV trail. Follow the well-established trail for 0.25 mi. through the woods as it curves back toward ME 220. (*Note:* The start of the trail to Hogback Mtn. is reached via this same route.)

The snowmobile trail joins GHP 50 ft. before ME 220. Immediately, the Frye Mtn. Trail turns right and begins to climb a ridge. (If you were headed for Hogback Mtn., you would turn left here and cross the road.) Traversing east, the trail passes through open woods and an old field before reaching Walker Ridge Rd. at 1.0 mi. (*Note:* This is 0.4 mi. east of the DIFW maintenance building parking area, and when the road is not closed to traffic beyond the parking area, hikers may drive to this point to start the hike.) Cross the road, reenter the woods, and quickly reach a kiosk. Ahead, cross a brook, continue on the trail, and cross Bartlett Stream. (*Note:* A high-water-crossing path is available on the left a short distance before the stream.) The trail follows Bartlett Stream and then gradually bears away and heads south. Cross a number of stone walls and an old road before climbing to cross a third brook. Continue up a rocky ravine, and beyond, cross a gravel road. (*Note:* Depending on road conditions, when the management area road system is not closed to traffic, hikers may also park here.) Climb to a jct. at 3.2 mi. and the start of a loop over Frye Mtn. From the jct., climb up to and across a series of ledges, passing many impressive stone walls and stone piles to reach the summit at 4.1 mi.

Just beyond the summit, the trail bears right and descends quickly off the large ledge (look for a small cairn and a blue blaze). Continue easily along to the east, then descend gradually. Just before reaching the eastern-most point on the loop, pass a massive oak tree. Shortly, the Hills to Sea Trail departs to the right toward ME 137 in Morrill. Here, Frye Mtn. Trail continues straight ahead, swings back to the south, and contours along the southeast face of the mountain, passing through many different types and ages of forest stands and past numerous stone walls and foundations. Cross a brook and begin to climb under a rock outcrop. Reach a ledge where there

SEC 9

are views to the south. Continue to climb, eventually reaching a ledge above the jct. where the loop began. From here, there are views to the northwest. Descend briefly, reaching the loop trail jct. at 7.8 mi. Bear left and follow the trail 3.2 mi. back to ME 220, which is at 10.9 mi.

■ HOGBACK MTN. (1,115 FT.)

This mountain in Montville, which lies just west of Frye Mtn. and consists of several rocky summits, is mostly wooded but provides an excellent view of Lake St. George and the St. George River watershed to the south. GRLT maintains Hogback Mtn. Trail, which is part of GHP. It connects to MCC's Northern Headwaters Trail in the Sheepscot River watershed to the west. The entire trail and the Hogback Connector beyond are part of the 47-mi. Hills to Sea Trail from Unity to Belfast.

Directions to the trailhead and parking are the same as for Frye Mtn.

HOGBACK MTN. TRAIL/GHP (GRLT; USGS LIBERTY QUAD, GAZETTEER MAP 14, GRLT HOGBACK MTN. TRAIL MAP)

Cumulative from DIFW maintenance building parking area (550 ft.) to:	⇅	↗	⟳
ME 220 crossing (550 ft.)	0.3 mi.	0 ft.	0:05
Hogback Overlook (1,050 ft.)	2.1 mi.	500 ft.	1:20
Hogback Connector (900 ft.)	2.8 mi.	600 ft.	1:45

Follow the start of Frye Mtn. Trail. At 0.25 mi., where Frye Mtn. Trail diverges right from the snowmobile trail, Hogback Mtn. Trail continues straight ahead, reaching ME 220 in 50 ft., and crosses directly to the other side (the trail diverges from the snowmobile trail, which crosses the road diagonally to the right). On the west side of ME 220, Hogback Mtn. Trail immediately crosses a wet area on bog bridges and ascends a short, steep pitch. Beyond, follow a skidder trail for 50 ft., then bear left uphill through a stand of mature hemlock. After another steep pitch, the grade moderates. Contour along the hillside with minor ups and downs, passing several rock outcrops, glacial erratics, and a 50-ft. cliff that has tiny waterfalls in the wet season. After about 1.0 mi., the trail bears distinctly left. A rough gravel road paralleling the trail along the edge of an open area is visible through the trees.

In a short distance, the trail bears left, away from the road, and reenters a more wooded area. Continue to the left and climb on a well-worn tread-way, passing occasional cairns. Cross the rocky spine of the ridge in the semi-open with views to the east and west. From the ridge, cross several woods roads and jeep tracks, descend slightly, then ascend easily to reach the steep south face of the mountain, where there are limited views through the trees. Ahead, reach Hogback Overlook, a large cleared area with a picnic table and good views to the southeast at 2.1 mi. These are the last views along this part of the trail, and the part of the trail ahead that formerly looped back to connect with the trail below the first ridge has been closed at the request of the landowner, so most hikers may choose to turn around and return to the parking lot from here.

For those continuing on from the overlook, the trail bears away from the south face, reenters the woods, and passes over several high points, including the wooded summit of Hogback Mtn. Beyond, descend easily to reach a woods road, Howard Rd. This is the end of Hogback Mtn. Trail and is the northern terminus of GHP. Hogback Connector Trail begins immediately across the road.

WHITTEN HILL TRAIL, BOG BROOK TRAIL, AND HOGBACK CONNECTOR TRAIL (MCC; USGS LIBERTY QUAD, GAZETTEER MAP 14, MCC SHEEPSCOT HEADWATERS TRAIL NETWORK MAP)

Cumulative from Halldale Rd. (785 ft.) to:	⇅	↗	↺
Bog Brook Trail (650 ft.)	0.3 mi.	-135 ft.	0:10
Jct. with Hogback Connector Trail (660 ft.)	0.7 mi.	10 ft.	0:20
Hogback Mtn. Trail (900 ft.)	2.0 mi.	250 ft.	1:10
Hogback Overlook (1,050 ft.)	2.7 mi.	500 ft.	1:35

This route, which includes part of Whitten Hill Trail and Bog Brook Trail and all of Hogback Connector Trail, connects with Hogback Mtn. Trail, which climbs Hogback Mtn. to reach scenic views. From the jct. of ME 3 and ME 220 in Liberty, travel north on ME 220 to Whites Corner at 3.2 mi. Turn left onto Burnham Hill Rd. At 3.8 mi., bear right on Halldale Rd., which turns to dirt at 4.7 mi. Trailhead parking is on the left at 4.8 mi.

From the parking area and kiosk, cross Halldale Rd. to find the sign for Whitten Hill Trail to Bog Brook Trail. Follow the blue blazes through a regenerating field then quickly enter a forested area with a stone wall running along the trail. Pass Eric Bruun Trail on the left and continue on Whitten Hill Trail through a dense hemlock forest until the Bog Brook Trail jct. at 0.3 mi. Turn left to follow Bog Brook Trail through a forest of hemlock, striped maple, and fir. At 0.6 mi. the trail crosses Bog Brook several times before briefly joining a woods road. At 0.7 mi. the trail intersects with Hogback Connector Trail. Follow Hogback Connector Trail to the left and begin a gentle climb that soon levels out. At 1.4 mi. Hogback

SEC 9

Connector Trail joins with Hills to Sea Trail, which enters from the west. Turning right, the climb up Hogback Mtn. begins in earnest. At 2.0 mi. the trail reaches the dirt Howard Rd. Here, Hogback Mtn. Trail continues across the road, climbing to reach Hogback Overlook in another 0.6 mi. Return to Halldale Rd. via the same route, or continue on Hogback Mtn. Trail (GHP) toward ME 220.

MIDCOAST CONSERVANCY TRAILS

■ WHITTEN HILL (865 FT.)

The 410-acre Whitten Hill property in Montville is part of 1,500 acres of conservation lands in the towns of Freedom, Liberty, Montville, and Palermo. MCC owns Whitten Hill and maintains the trails there as part of the 20-mi. Sheepscot Headwaters Trail Network. The Northern Headwaters Trail climbs easily over Whitten Hill and follows a section of the headwater of the Sheepscot River, making for a pleasant and interesting woods walk. A portion of the trail coincides with the 47-mi. Hills to Sea Trail from Unity to Belfast.

From the jct. of ME 3 and ME 220 in Liberty, travel north on ME 220 to Whites Corner at 3.2 mi. Turn left onto Burnham Hill Rd. At 3.8 mi., bear right on Halldale Rd., which turns to dirt at 4.7 mi. Trailhead parking is on the left at 4.8 mi.

NORTHERN HEADWATERS TRAIL
(MCC; USGS LIBERTY QUAD, GAZETTEER MAP 14, MCC
SHEEPSCOT HEADWATERS TRAIL NETWORK MAP)

Cumulative from Halldale Rd. (785 ft.) to:	↧↥	↗	↻
Whitten Hill summit (865 ft.)	0.5 mi.	80 ft.	0:15
Sheepscot River (450 ft.)	1.6 mi.	80 ft.	0:50
Complete loop	3.8 mi.	500 ft.	2:10

SEC 9

From the kiosk, follow the trail 100 ft. to the Whitten Hill Trail jct. To the left, Whitten Hill Trail connects to Bog Brook Trail and a series of trails south of Halldale Rd. Turn right on Whitten Hill Trail to reach the jct. of Northern Headwaters Trail in 0.1 mi. Turn right and follow blue blazes easily along the ridge top, passing a series of stone walls on the left. Cross the unmarked and wooded summit of Whitten Hill at 0.5 mi. Hemlock Hollow Trail joins from the right at 0.8 mi. Beyond, descend easily to the west, passing a spur leading right (north) to the Northern Headwaters trailhead on Whitten Hill Rd.

Ahead, pass Goose Ridge Trail on the right at 1.2 mi., and soon after, pass Mink Run Trail, also on the right. Continue downhill to reach the east bank of the Sheepscot River at 1.6 mi. Continue south along the north side of Whitten Hill, following the course of the river with minor ups and downs. At 2.2 mi., turn away from the river and ascend gradually to reach an old woods road. Leave the road and emerge into a large field with views to the south and west. At 2.9 mi., Whitten Fields Trail goes right, across the fields. Beyond the jct., reenter the woods and trend easily uphill to gain the ridge. Close the loop at the original jct. at 3.7 mi., and turn right (east) to reach the trailhead in another 0.1 mi.

■ GOOSE RIDGE (930 FT.)

This scenic hill in Montville is just north of Whitten Hill and features good ridge walking and several open fields with nice views of the rural countryside. Goose Ridge is part of the MCC trail system, and the trail over the ridge coincides with the 47-mi. Hills to Sea Trail from Unity to Belfast.

From the jct. of ME 3 and ME 220 in Liberty, travel north on ME 220; bear sharply right at Whites Corner at 3.2 mi. Pass Walker Ridge Rd. and the entrance to GLWMA on the right at 6.6 mi. At a jct. at 9.4 mi., where ME 220 bears right and Halldale Rd. goes left, continue straight ahead on Freedom Pond Rd. Reach the trailhead on the left 10.5 mi. Parking is along the road.

GOOSE RIDGE TRAIL (MCC; USGS LIBERTY QUAD, GAZETTEER MAP 14, MCC SHEEPSCOT HEADWATERS TRAIL NETWORK MAP)

Cumulative from Freedom Pond Rd. (510 ft.) to:	Distance	Elevation gain	Time
Goose Ridge (930 ft.)	2.1 mi.	560 ft.	1:15
Penney Rd. (450 ft.)	3.6 mi.	600 ft.	2:00

Follow the red-blazed trail into the woods, climbing easily. Begin a descent at 0.6 mi., pass an unsigned trail on the left, and then climb steadily. After a sharp right, reach a level area. Pass a sign for Spirited Horse Ranch (please stay on the trail). Bear left onto a two-wheel track, and at 1.2 mi. reach an open field with good views. Climb to the top of the field and reenter the woods at 1.3 mi. Hike easily along the ridge, and at a second field, bear right over a stone wall at 1.5 mi. Cross the field with views to the Camden Hills. Reenter the woods at 1.6 mi. Immediately take a right onto a woods road and proceed on level ground. Pass through a stand of young birch and maple trees, then cross a swampy area. Pass through a stone wall at 1.8 mi., then ascend to the ridge top. At 2.1 mi., reach the high point on Goose Ridge.

Beyond, continue along the level ridge, then begin a gentle descent next to a stone wall on the left. In a semi-open area, merge with a wide track coming in from the right. Reach a signpost at 2.7 mi., bear left, and follow a grassy road. At the next signpost, bear right into the woods and climb slightly over a knob. Reach a pipeline corridor at 2.9 mi. For the next 0.4 mi., the trail alternates between the woods and the pipeline. At 3.3 mi., bear left into the woods and soon cross a wet and overgrown area with difficult footing. Emerge into a field and follow along the woods line. Bear left at a corner of the field, then right out to Penney Rd. at 3.6 mi.

■ HAYSTACK MTN. (850 FT.)

This mountain in Liberty overlooks the village and Lake St. George and Little Pond. Haystack Mtn. Trail, a local favorite, climbs from behind the Walker Memorial School athletic fields to a beautiful overlook to the south. From ME 3 between South China and Belfast, take ME 220 south for 0.8 mi. Turn left at the sign for the Vena M. Roberts Memorial Ball Field. Park in the lot behind Walker Health Center. The trailhead is at the far corner, past the ball field.

HAYSTACK MTN. TRAIL (MCC; USGS LIBERTY QUAD, GAZETTEER MAP 14, MTF HAYSTACK MTN. TRAIL [LIBERTY] MAP)

Cumulative from Walker Memorial School parking (530 ft.) to:	↥↧	↗	○
Scenic overlook (790 ft.)	0.6 mi.	260 ft.	0:25
Complete loop	1.1 mi.	260 ft.	0:40

From the trailhead, take an immediate left to begin the loop hike, following blue blazes. The trail weaves through sections of oak, pine, and birch forest. Some sections are steep. At 0.5 mi., please note that the short spur trail to the summit of Haystack Mtn. has been closed to the public. Instead, enjoy the pocket overlook at 0.6 mi., which affords a nice southerly view to Lake St. George.

GEORGETOWN

■ HIGGINS MTN. (259 FT.)

This small mountain in Georgetown is one of the highest points on George-town Island. The summit, burned over in the Great Georgetown Fire of 1908 and subsequent blazes is home to pitch pines, blueberries, and the rare broom crowberry. It offers excellent views east to Robinhood Cove and south to Sheepscot Bay and the Gulf of Maine. Billie Todd donated the mountain to the Kennebec Estuary Land Trust in 2000, after the death of her husband, Warren Todd. A plaque atop the summit honors both.

From the jct. of US 1 and ME 127 in Woolwich, drive south on ME 127 for 7.6 mi. to trailhead parking on the right.

HIGGINS MTN. TRAIL (KELT; USGS PHIPPSBURG QUAD, GAZETTEER MAP 6, KELT HIGGINS MTN. MAP)

From ME 127 (130 ft.) to:	⇅	↗	↻
Complete loop (130 ft.)	0.6 mi.	130 ft.	0:20

Begin the loop by going left, uphill. Scamper up ledges, following cairns. In the semi-open above, the trail turns sharply right and traverses the ridge to the memorial plaque in a trailside rock. It continues across the ridge, crosses two footbridges, then descends over ledges into the woods below. Hike south along the base of the mountain to complete the loop.

SEC
9

SECTION 10
ACADIA NATIONAL PARK

SEC
10

INTRODUCTION

Much, but by no means all, of Acadia National Park is on the 80,000-acre Mt. Desert Island, situated east of Penobscot Bay about two-thirds of the way up Maine's coast between New Hampshire and New Brunswick, Canada. About 10 mi. south of the city of Ellsworth, Mt. Desert Island is connected to the mainland by a short bridge and causeways. Portions of Schoodic Peninsula and Isle au Haut are also preserved as part of ANP, which in its entirety encompasses 50,200 acres. The park owns 30,700 acres on Mt. Desert Island (about 38 percent of the island), 3,400 acres on Schoodic Peninsula, 2,900 acres on Isle au Haut, 700 acres on a number of scattered islands, and has 12,500 acres in conservation easements.

ANP was established as Sieur de Monts National Monument in 1916. The monument became the first national park east of the Mississippi River in 1919 and was named Lafayette National Park in honor of the Marquis de Lafayette, a key French supporter of the American Revolution. The park was renamed ANP in 1929.

Acadia is the eleventh-smallest national park but is consistently one of the top ten most visited. It features more than 150 mi. of hiking trails and 45 mi. of carriage roads for human-powered recreation. A range of 26 granite mountain peaks extend across Mt. Desert Island from east to west, and eight of these summits exceed 1,000 ft. in elevation. Cadillac Mtn. rises to 1,528 ft., the highest point on the entire eastern seaboard of the United States. Scoured by the powerful action of glaciers eons ago, the U-shaped valleys between the mountain ridges hold forests of coniferous and deciduous trees and a multitude of streams, meadows, and peat lands that support more than 1,200 plant species and 26 pristine lakes and ponds have thriving fish populations (28 species). The island's 41 mi. of coastal shoreline feature cliffs and tidepools; beaches of sand, pebbles, and cobbles; mud flats and tidal marshes; and many other islands large and small. Rich with wildlife, ANP is home to 37 species of mammals, 11 species of amphibians, 7 species of reptiles, and more than 300 species of birds (resident and migratory). Twelve species of marine mammals are found in the ocean waters around the island, including whales, seals, dolphins, and porpoises.

The 27-mi. Park Loop Rd. and the 3.5-mi. Cadillac Mtn. Rd. visit the major scenic highlights of the park on Mt. Desert Island. Acadia receives more than 3 million visitors each year, most of those from July through September.

The ANP section describes 105 trails on 32 mountains.

For more on outdoor recreation in ANP, see the 2017 National Outdoor Book Award-winning *Outdoor Adventures Acadia National Park: Your Guide to the Best Hiking, Biking, and Paddling*, by Jerry and Marcy Monkman, and AMC's *Acadia National Park Map* (both AMC Books, 2017).

ACADIA NATIONAL PARK ON MT. DESERT ISLAND

Geography

Mt. Desert Island is roughly 15 mi. across from east to west and 13 mi. long from north to south. Shaped much like a lobster claw, the island is divided into distinct east and west sides by Somes Sound, a natural fjord. Frenchman Bay is to the east of the island, Blue Hill Bay to the west. ANP encompasses a little more than one-third of Mt. Desert Island. Many of Acadia's mountain summits, especially on the east side of the island, are relatively treeless and open and provide far-reaching ocean and mountain views.

On Mt. Desert Island's east side, just south of Bar Harbor, runs the long ridgeline of Champlain Mtn. (1,058 ft.), which trends south to encompass the Bowl, a beautiful mountain tarn (glacial pool). The east face, or Precipice Wall, of Champlain Mtn. rises more than 900 ft. from the woods and meadows near Schooner Head. Great Head (145 ft.) is the easternmost point on the island, and Sand Beach is tucked into Newport Cove at its base. The steep pink cliffs of the Beehive (520 ft.) make it a distinctive landmark in this part of the park. Flanking Ocean Drive is the long, low ridge of Gorham Mtn. (522 ft.), which peters out near Monument Cove a short distance north of Otter Cliff.

Between ME 3 and Eagle Lake is the mass of Dorr Mtn. and Cadillac Mtn. The east face of Dorr Mtn. (1,265 ft.) rises dramatically above the Tarn (a lovely but aging pond that is slowly reverting to a meadow). Kebo Mtn. (407 ft.) is a subsidiary peak on the north ridge of Dorr Mtn. A branch of Otter Creek has its start on the south slopes of Dorr Mtn. A significant gorge separates Dorr Mtn. from its lofty neighbor Cadillac Mtn. (1,528 ft.). The long and mostly barren south and north ridges on Cadillac combine for a wonderful 6-mi. traverse, the longest on the island. A road winds to the top of the popular mountain, where there is a large parking lot; a gift shop; restrooms; and a short accessible, interpretive loop trail. For several weeks each year, around the spring and fall equinoxes, the summit of Cadillac is the first spot in the United States to see the sunrise.

The bare summit of Pemetic Mtn. (1,247 ft.) is south of Eagle Lake, west of Cadillac Mtn., and east of Jordan Pond. From the extensive lawn at Jordan Pond House, visitors can enjoy the famous view of the shapely Bubbles (North Bubble [872 ft.] and South Bubble [766 ft.] across Jordan Pond, one of the clearest in Maine. From Jordan Pond west to ME 3/198

SEC 10

near Upper Hadlock Pond is a compact jumble of rugged peaks, including Sargent Mtn. (1,379 ft.). Its extensive barren upper flanks form the second-highest summit on the island. Sargent Mtn. Pond is a lovely and secretive spot just north of the long, open ridgeline of Penobscot Mtn. (1,196 ft.). Jordan Cliffs form the steep walls of the mountain's east face above Jordan Pond. Subsidiary but very hike-worthy summits with fine views west of Sargent and Penobscot include Gilmore Peak (1,030 ft.), Bald Peak (971 ft.), Parkman Mtn. (950 ft.), and Cedar Swamp Mtn. (950 ft.). The long, wooded ridge of Norumbega Mtn. (852 ft.) forms the eastern escarpment of Somes Sound.

On the west side of Mt. Desert Island, between Somes Sound and ME 102, is the flat-topped Acadia Mtn. (681 ft.). Just south, St. Sauveur Mtn. rises spectacularly over Valley Cove, its 500-ft. cliffs the highest on the island. Flying Mtn. (284 ft.) looms over the Narrows at the entrance to Somes Sound. Rising precipitously above Echo Lake are Beech Cliff and Canada Cliff. Beech Mtn. (841 ft.) and its summit fire tower lie just west. Long Pond is the largest water body on Mt. Desert Island, and immediately west rises the bulk of Western Mtn., which comprises two wooded peaks, Mansell Mtn. (938 ft.) and Bernard Mtn. (1,010 ft.). Great Notch and Little Notch are high and rugged defiles between these summits. The broad west ridge of Bernard Mtn. leads down to Seal Cove Pond, which is within striking distance of Blue Hill Bay.

Road Access

Mt. Desert Island is reached via ME 3 from Trenton. ME 3 is the major highway around the east side of the island, connecting the towns of Bar Harbor and Northeast Harbor before ending at its jct. with ME 102/198 in Somesville near the head of Somes Sound. ME 233 is a major east–west connector between Bar Harbor and Somesville. ME 102 is the primary north–south route from the head of Mt. Desert Island through Southwest Harbor and on to Bass Harbor.

The 27-mi. Park Loop Rd. and the 3.5-mi. Cadillac Mtn. Rd. are open from April 15 through November 30 (weather dependent). Park roads can be very congested during the busy summer months, so visitors are encouraged to take advantage of the free Island Explorer shuttle service that operates from late June through Columbus Day.

Island Explorer buses run on eight routes that serve Acadia, local towns and villages, and the regional airport in Trenton. These regularly scheduled buses stop at points throughout the park, including campgrounds, carriage road entrances, and many trailheads. Hikers can also flag down buses along their routes. The bus is an easy and efficient way to get around and see the park while helping to ease traffic congestion, alleviate parking problems, and reduce air pollution on the island.

Hikers may also consider leaving their cars parked in Bar Harbor and hiking the village connector trails that link the town to park trails. These easy routes include Schooner Head Path, Great Meadow Loop, and Jesup Path. The ball field on Main St. in Bar Harbor has ample parking and is near these trails.

FEES AND SEASONS

ANP is open year-round. A park entrance pass is required from May 1 through October 31, regardless of how or where visitors enter. The passes can be purchased at Hulls Cove Visitor Center, Sand Beach Entrance Station, Thompson Island Information Center, Bar Harbor Village Green, Blackwoods CG, Seawall CG, and Schoodic Woods CG, Cadillac Mountain Gift Shop, Jordan Pond Gift Shop, Mount Desert Town Office (Northeast Harbor), Bar Harbor Chamber of Commerce, Southwest Harbor/Tremont Chamber of Commerce (Southwest Harbor), and Schoodic Institute (Rockefeller Hall Welcome Center). All visitors must display a valid pass on their vehicles at all park facilities. Park passes can be purchased online in advance.

Thompson Island Information Center on ME 3 at the northern tip of the island is open from mid-May to mid-October. Hulls Cove Visitor Center at the start of Park Loop Rd. is open from April 15 through October 31. Outside of that period, information is available at the park's headquarters on ME 233 west of Bar Harbor. Operating hours of these facilities vary by season.

Pets are allowed on leashes shorter than 6 ft. Visitor amenities are limited in winter months, when most park buildings are closed. Park Loop Rd. and Cadillac Mtn. Rd. are closed from December 1 through April 14 and at other times when conditions warrant.

CAMPING

SEC 10

The National Park Service operates two campgrounds on Mt. Desert Island, one on Schoodic Peninsula, and one on Isle au Haut. No backcountry camping is allowed in any unit of ANP.

Blackwoods CG

This campground is on ME 3, about 5 mi. south of Bar Harbor. The campground is open all year and features 306 campsites that accommodate tents, campers, and RVs (up to 35 ft.). No hookups are available. Amenities include restrooms with cold running water, a dump station, picnic tables, fire rings, and water faucets. Showers and a small store are available during the summer season a short distance from the campground. A fee is charged from May 1 through October 31, and reservations are recommended during this period. Campground facilities are limited in winter, and the entrance road is not plowed. Winter campers should check with park officials in advance of arrival.

Seawall CG

This campground is on ME 102A about 4 mi. south of Southwest Harbor, is open from late May through September 30, and features 214 campsites. Reservations are recommended. Amenities are similar to those at Blackwoods. A privately operated shower facility is available a short distance from the campground.

A good selection of accommodations are available elsewhere on Mt. Desert Island, from about a dozen campgrounds to many bed-and-breakfasts, motels, and hotels. Bar Harbor and numerous other island villages offer a wide range of other visitor amenities, including restaurants and grocery stores.

Schoodic Woods CG

Located on Schoodic Peninsula, described in subsection.

Duck Harbor CG

Located on Isle au Haut, described in subsection.

AMC's Echo Lake Camp

Located in Southwest Harbor just outside ANP, the waterfront camp (established in 1925) is an exceptional vacation spot amid the spectacular scenery of Acadia. Facilities consist of platform tents with canvas sides equipped with cots, blankets, mattresses and pillows, full-service dining hall providing three meals a day, recreation hall and library. Flush toilets and running hot and cold water are located in two areas of the camp. Hot showers and a bathhouse are available at the bathhouse in the center of camp, which is handicapped accessible. Other amenities include a volleyball court, basketball net, swimming floats and boating dock with canoes, kayaks, rowboats, three sunfish and a windsurfer.

TRAILS AND NPS TRAIL RATINGS

Many of Acadia's mountain summits are relatively treeless, open. Rock cairns mark the routes along these open stretches, and hikers should take care to locate the next cairn before moving ahead. Although the trails in

Acadia are mostly within a short distance of roads and villages, the terrain is often sharp and precipitous, and hikers who stray off the marked paths may encounter rough going and dead ends at cliff edges and ravines. Hikers should be prepared for the changeable weather of the Maine coast, which can, for example, turn quickly from bright sun to thick fog and rain.

The described trails in this section are, for the most part, well-marked, officially recognized, maintained paths that provide access to all of the preferred summits on Mt. Desert Island, Schoodic Peninsula, and Isle au Haut. Most of the individual summits can be reached in comfortable half-day walks.

To simplify reference and to conform to ANP nomenclature, the hikes on Mt. Desert Island have been divided into two districts: east of Somes Sound, and west of Somes Sound. NPS maintains all of the trails described, with the exception of those trails within Land & Garden Preserve. Trail markings include blue paint blazes, signs, and rock cairns (many of which are the traditional Bates cairns: two base stones, a mantle rock, and a pointer rock).

NPS rates trails based on these criteria:

Easy = fairly level ground

Moderate = uneven ground with some steep grades and/or gradual climbing, and footing may be difficult in places

Strenuous = steep and/or long grades, steady climbing or descending, sometimes difficult footing, difficult maneuvering

Ladder = iron rungs, ladders, handrails, and walkways placed on steep grades or difficult terrain (these trails are considered very difficult)

A 57-mi. system of fine-gravel carriage paths (45 mi. within ANP, 15 mi. outside the park, and all closed to vehicular traffic) offers additional opportunities for pleasant walking, bicycling, horseback riding, and, in winter, cross-country skiing and snowshoeing. The trail descriptions in this section are limited primarily to mountain trails and, as such, don't cover some of the easier walks or the carriage paths. These paths are, however, delineated on Map 5.

For ease of traveling to ANP trailheads on the east side of Mt. Desert Island, the following mileages are provided, to be used in conjunction with Map 5.

SEC 10

From Hulls Cove Visitor Center via Park Loop Rd. (two-way traffic) south to:

jct., ramp to ME 233	2.6 mi.
start of one-way section of Park Loop Rd.	3.1 mi.

Start of one-way Park Loop Rd. to:

Cadillac North Ridge Trail (no parking during summer/early fall)	0.3 mi.
Gorge Path	0.9 mi.
Kebo Mtn. Trail (no parking, park at Stratheden)	1.5 mi.
Stratheden Path	1.7 mi.
Sieur de Monts Spring access road	2.7 mi.
Champlain North Ridge Trail	3.5 mi.
Orange & Black Trail crossing	4.1 mi.
Precipice Trail	4.6 mi.
Park Entrance Station	5.4 mi.
Sand Beach	6.0 mi.
Gorham Mtn.	7.1 mi.
Otter Cliff Rd.	7.2 mi.
Hunter Brook Trail	11.6 mi.
Triad-Day Mtn. Bridge	12.6 mi.
Stanley Brook Rd., end of one-way traffic	13.4 mi.

From Hulls Cove Visitor Center via Park Loop Rd. (two-way section) south to:

jct., ramp to ME 233	2.5 mi.
start of Kebo Brook Trail at Island Explorer bus stop	2.7 mi.
jct., start of one-way section of Park Loop Rd.	3.1 mi.
jct., Cadillac Mtn. Rd.	3.6 mi.
Bubble Pond	5.1 mi.
Bubble Rock	6.2 mi.
Jordan Pond trailhead parking area	7.7 mi.
Jordan Pond House	7.8 mi.
Stanley Brook Rd.	8.6 mi.
Seal Harbor and jct., ME 3	10.1 mi.

SEC 10

LAND & GARDEN PRESERVE

This lovely 1,165-acre preserve is separate from but adjacent to ANP, in Seal Harbor and Northeast Harbor on Mt. Desert Island's east side. The preserve, on land owned by the Rockefeller family for generations, includes the historic Thuya Garden, Thuya Lodge, and Asticou Azalea Garden, as well as Asticou Terraces and Asticou Landing. In 2015, David Rockefeller donated 1,022 acres around and including scenic Little Long Pond, bringing the preserve to its present size. Ten trails offer more than 8 mi. of hiking, much of it on Eliot Mtn. Miles of carriage roads also wend through the property.

ACADIA NATIONAL PARK
ON SCHOODIC PENINSULA

The only mainland unit of ANP is on Schoodic Peninsula, south of the town of Winter Harbor, which is east of Mt. Desert Island and the bulk of the park. Flanked by Frenchman Bay to the west and the Gulf of Maine to the east, the peninsula features bold oceanfront granite cliffs and ledges, fragrant spruce and fir woods, and a craggy high point with wonderful panorama views on Schoodic Head (440 ft.). Buck Cove Mtn. (225 ft.) is just to the north of Schoodic Head.

Much of Schoodic Peninsula was once owned by John G. Moore, a Maine native and Wall Street financier. Moore's heirs donated the land to the Hancock County Trustees of Reservations in the 1920s, and in 1929, the spectacular 2,050-acre parcel became part of ANP. From 1935 to 2002, the U.S. Navy operated a radio communications station on Schoodic Point. This facility is now the Schoodic Education and Research Center, where the nonprofit Schoodic Institute is working to advance ecosystem science and learning for all ages through a unique partnership with ANP.

In 2015, the National Park Foundation donated 1,400 acres of land abutting the park on Schoodic Peninsula to NPS, bringing the total size of ANP at Schoodic to 3,450 acres. Prior to acquisition, new infrastructure was privately built and donated to the park, including 4.7 mi. of hiking trails and 8.3 mi. of biking paths, and at the 94-site Schoodic Woods CG, a hybrid ranger station/information center and a 100-space day-use parking area. There are now more than 9 mi. of trails for hiking enjoyment.

From the jct. of US 1 and ME 186 in West Gouldsboro, drive south on ME 186 for 6.5 mi. to Winter Harbor. In the town, at the intersection of ME 186 and Main St., turn left on ME 186 and travel east another 0.5 mi. to Schoodic Loop Rd. Turn right on Schoodic Loop Rd. at a sign for ANP and drive 0.9 mi. south to Schoodic Woods Campground and Information Center. The campground, information center, parking, and toilets are 0.1 mi. left on this access road. Schoodic Woods CG, open late May through Columbus Day, has primitive sites, car camping sites, RV sites with water and electric, potable water, and toilets (no showers).

Schoodic Peninsula may also be reached by passenger ferry from Bar Harbor (the Bar Harbor Inn pier or the College of the Atlantic pier). Debarking at Winter Harbor, visitors can then ride the Island Explorer bus (in season).

Schoodic Loop Rd. guides visitors around the peninsula, touching most of the major scenic attractions. From ME 186 east of Winter Harbor past the Schoodic Woods complex to the picnic area at Frazer Point, Schoodic

SEC 10

Loop Rd. allows two-way traffic. From Frazer Point to the east side of the peninsula at the head of Schoodic Harbor, the road is one-way only. Partway along, at 3.5 mi. from Frazer Point, the two-way Arey Cove Rd. leads past Schoodic Education and Research Center to a magnificent viewpoint at the tip of Schoodic Point, perhaps the most visited spot in this unit of ANP.

ACADIA NATIONAL PARK ON ISLE AU HAUT

Isle au Haut is located 5 mi. out to sea from the southern tip of Deer Isle and the town of Stonington, and 16 mi. southwest of Mt. Desert Island. Isel au Haut features a range of low mountains extending from north to south along the length of the 6-mi. island, including Mt. Champlain (545 ft.), Rocky Mtn. (511 ft.), Sawyer Mtn. (495 ft.), Jerusalem Mtn. (455 ft.), Bowditch Mtn. (425 ft.), Wentworth Mtn. (299 ft.), and Duck Harbor Mtn. (309 ft.). The ANP unit on Isle au Haut encompasses most of the southern half of the island, some 2,700 incredibly scenic and remote acres. These lands were donated to the federal government in 1943. Isle au Haut ("High Island") was named by the French explorer Samuel de Champlain in 1604. The highest island in Penobscot Bay, it boasts a bumpy ridgeline that runs its length. Mt. Champlain, at an elevation of 540 feet, is the apex among the seven named mountains. The island has a year-round population of 65, which grows to several hundred in summer. (*Note:* ANP limits the number of visitors to the island, and on rare occasions, visitors may be denied access. See Appendix A, p. 564 for contact information.) Outside of tourism, fishing is the economic mainstay. Amenities are few: a small general store, an ice cream stand, Maine's smallest post office, and an inn.

Isle au Haut is reached by a passenger ferry from Stonington on the southern tip of Deer Isle. The trip takes about 45 min. one-way. The ferry, operated on a first-come, first-served basis, runs year-round to a landing in the town of Isle au Haut. From mid-June to late September, the ferry also continues on to Isle au Haut's Duck Harbor. (Contact Isle au Haut Boat Services at 207-367-5193 or visit isleauhaut.com for schedule and rate information.) An ANP ranger station is 0.25 mi. south of the landing. During the summer season, a park ranger may board the ferry at the landing to answer visitors' questions en route to Duck Harbor.

There are no private campgrounds on Isle au Haut, but there are very limited ANP facilities: Five lean-tos offer primitive camping at Duck Harbor CG from May 15 to October 14. Advance reservations are required (no walk-ins) for these highly coveted spots and must be made through recreation.gov (starting on April 1 at 10 A.M. each spring). Camping is limited to one stay per year, with a three-night maximum for up to six persons. Each lean-to is equipped with a fire ring, a picnic table, and a storage locker for food and toiletries. A hand pump for water is nearby, as are several composting toilets. No trash containers are available, and campers must carry out all trash.

Twelve surprisingly rugged trails offer 18 mi. of hiking along the island's rocky shoreline and pebbly beaches, up to craggy peaks and ridgelines, through dense spruce forests, and along marshes and bogs. A partially paved 12-mi. road circumnavigates the bulk of the island, offering additional walking options.

SUGGESTED HIKES

■ Easy
KEBO MTN.

	↥↧	↗	◷
LP via Kebo Mtn. Trail, Hemlock Trail, and Stratheden Path	1.8 mi.	275 ft.	1:05

Combine these trails for a fine walk through the piney woods on the ridge of Kebo Mtn. To begin, see Kebo Mtn. Trail, p. 433.

BUBBLE ROCK

	↥↧	↗	◷
RT via Pemetic Northwest Trail	1.4 mi.	350 ft.	0:35

Climb South Bubble to check out the spectacular Bubble Rock, a 110-ton glacial erratic perched on the cliff edge, and take in excellent views of Jordan Pond, Pemetic Mtn., and Penobscot Mtn. See Pemetic Northwest Trail, p. 437.

SEC 10

DAY MTN.

	↥↧	↗	◷
RT via Day Mtn. Trail	2.6 mi.	330 ft.	1:30

Visit the Champlain Monument and cross several pretty carriage roads on this lightly visited peak, which offers ocean and mountain vistas. See Day Mtn. Trail, p. 440.

JORDAN POND

	⤵	↗	○
LP via Jordan Pond Path	3.4 mi.	0 ft.	1:40

Follow the mostly graded pathway all the way around the deepest body of water on Mt. Desert Island, also one of the cleanest, clearest ponds in Maine. Bonus: excellent views of Jordan Cliff and the Bubbles. See Jordan Pond Path, p. 442.

FLYING MTN.

	⤵	↗	○
LP via Flying Mtn. Trail and Valley Cove fire road	1.4 mi.	230 ft.	0:45

A short climb leads to a fine panoramic view of Somes Sound, Southwest Harbor, and the islands beyond. To begin, see Flying Mtn. Trail, p. 461.

BEECH CLIFF

	⤵	↗	○
LP via Beech Cliff Loop Trail	0.6 mi.	50 ft.	0:20

Meander out to the lip of the dramatic escarpment of Beech Cliff overlooking Echo Lake, where the views are far-reaching and breathtaking. See Beech Cliff Loop Trail, p. 464.

BEECH MTN.

	⤵	↗	○
LP via Beech Mtn. Loop	1.0 mi.	340 ft.	0:45

Visit the old fire tower atop Beech Mtn. (usually open on summer weekends) then drink in the views of Long Pond and Western Mtn. from the ledges on the west side of Beech Mtn. See Beech Mtn. Loop Trail, p. 464.

■ Moderate
CHAMPLAIN MTN.

	⤵	↗	○
OW via Champlain North Ridge Trail, Champlain South Ridge Trail, and Bowl Trail	3.3 mi.	1,000 ft.	2:40

Enjoy ocean and mountain views for most of the route over Champlain Mtn. To begin, see Champlain North Ridge Trail, p. 422.

BEEHIVE–BOWL

			�??↺	↗	↺
LP via Beehive Trail and Bowl Trail			1.4 mi.	500 ft.	1:05

Tackle the steep cliffs of the Beehive via iron rungs, ladders, and walkways then visit the Bowl before looping back to Sand Beach. To begin, see Beehive Trail, p. 425.

GREAT HEAD

					↗	↺
LP via Great Head Trail			2.0 mi.	150 ft.	1:05

Explore Sand Beach and the cliffs atop Great Head, including the ruins of an old teahouse, on this circuit wth great views of the Beehive, Ocean Drive, and Otter Cliff. See Great Head Trail, p. 425.

CADILLAC NORTH RIDGE–GORGE PATH

			↗	↺
LP via Gorge Path		4.0 mi.	1,275 ft.	2:40

Explore the scenic gorge between Cadillac Mtn. and Dorr Mtn. then summit Cadillac Mtn., the highest peak in ANP. Finish via the lovely north ridge. See Gorge Path, p. 434.

PEMETIC MTN. SOUTH RIDGE

			↗	↺
RT via Bubbles & Jordan Ponds Path and Pemetic South Ridge Trail		2.6 mi.	800 ft.	1:50

Go east then up the beautiful south ridge of Pemetic Mtn. for views to Cadillac Mtn. and Jordan Pond. To begin, see Bubbles & Jordan Ponds Path, p. 437.

PENOBSCOT MTN. SOUTH RIDGE

			↗	↺
RT via Asticou & Jordan Pond Path and Penobscot Mtn. Trail		5.4 mi.	1,050 ft.	3:25

Emerge from a wooded hike onto the mostly open south ridge of Penobscot Mtn. for great views over Jordan Pond. To begin, see Asticou & Jordan Pond Path, p. 443.

SEC 10

SARGENT MTN. SOUTH RIDGE

	⇅	↗	○
RT via Hadlock Brook Trail and South Ridge Trail	4.2 mi.	1,075 ft.	2:40

Climb to the expansive summit of the second highest peak on Mt. Desert Island. To begin, see Hadlock Brook Trail, p. 449.

BALD PEAK AND PARKMAN MTN.

	⇅	↗	○
LP via Hadlock Brook Trail, Bald Peak Trail, and Parkman Mtn. Trail	2.8 mi.	700 ft.	1:50

Bag these two rocky knobs for great views of Upper Hadlock Pond, Norumbega Mtn., and Sargent Mtn. To begin, see Hadlock Brook Trail, p. 449.

NORUMBEGA MTN.

	⇅	↗	○
RT via Goat Trail	1.2 mi.	550 ft.	1:00

Hike to a series of lookouts amid the trees on the summit ridgeline of Norumbega Mtn., which rises immediately east of Somes Sound. See Goat Trail, p. 453.

ACADIA MTN.

	⇅	↗	○
LP via Acadia Mtn. Trail and Man O' War Brook fire road	2.4 mi.	530 ft.	1:25

Enjoy dramatic views of Somes Sound and the Cranberry Isles on this pleasant loop. To begin, see Acadia Mtn. Trail, p. 457.

MANSELL MTN.

	⇅	↗	○
LP via Perpendicular Trail, Mansell Mtn. Trail, and Cold Brook Trail	2.6 mi.	890 ft.	2:55

Climb Mansell Mtn. via the more than 1,000 rock steps of Perpendicular Trail (you'll follow the other two trails on your return) for views over Long Pond, toward Beech Mtn. To begin, see Perpendicular Trail, p. 468.

SEC 10

BERNARD MTN.

		⤵	↗	⏱
LP via Bernard Mtn. Trail		2.6 mi.	860 ft.	1:45

Enjoy viewpoints en route to the mountaintop then return to Mill Field. See Bernard Mtn. Trail, p. 470.

SCHOODIC HEAD

		⤵	↗	⏱
LP via Anvil Trail, Schoodic Head Trail, and Alder Trail		2.5 mi.	480 ft.	1:25

Climb to the top of Schoodic Head for great views of MDI's mountain skyline then circle back to Blueberry Hill. To begin, see Anvil Trail, p. 474.

WESTERN HEAD

		⤵	↗	⏱
LP via Western Head Trail, Cliff Trail, and Western Head Rd.		3.6 mi.	325 ft.	2:00

This outstanding shoreline route follows the southern edge of Isle au Haut. To begin, see Western Head Trail, p. 479.

■ Strenuous

CHAMPLAIN MTN.–PRECIPICE

		⤵	↗	⏱
LP via Precipice Trail, Champlain North Ridge Trail, Orange & Black Path, and Precipice Trail		3.0 mi.	900 ft.	2:00

Tackle the steep, exposed, and exhilarating east wall of Champlain Mtn. via iron rungs, ladders, handrails, and walkways. To begin, see Precipice Trail, p. 421.

SAND BEACH–JORDAN POND

SEC 10

		⤵	↗	⏱
OW via Bowl Trail, Beehive Trail, Champlain South Ridge Trail, Beachcroft Path, Kane Path, Canon Brook Trail, Cadillac South Ridge Trail, Bubble & Jordan Ponds Path, and Asticou & Jordan Pond Path		10.1 mi.	2,700 ft.	6:30

This lengthy traverse of the east side of Mt. Desert Island takes in some of the best known natural features and quietest trails in ANP on its route from Sand Beach to Jordan Pond via the south ridge of Cadillac Mtn. The summits of Champlain and Cadillac are included; add side trips to Dorr and Pemetic for more miles and more fun. Spot a second car at the finish or ride the Island Explorer bus in season. To begin, see Bowl Trail, p. 424.

CADILLAC MTN. SOUTH RIDGE

		↻	↗	○
RT via Cadillac South Ridge Trail		6.54 mi.	1,375 ft.	4:00

From ME 3, hike to Eagle Crag and the Featherbed then revel in the views from the long and wide-open upper south ridge to the top of Cadillac Mtn. See Cadillac South Ridge Trail, p. 435.

SIX PEAKS

		↻	↗	○
LP via Hadlock Brook Trail, Bald Peak Trail, Grandgent Trail, Sargent South Ridge Trail, Penobscot Mtn. Trail, and Amphitheater Trail		6.8 mi.	2,110 ft.	5:00

Tackle six summits and enjoy extraordinary ocean, island, and mountain views on this rugged loop over the jumble of high peaks between Jordan Pond and Somes Sound, including Bald Peak, Parkman Mtn., Gilmore Peak, Sargent Mtn., Penobscot Mtn., and Cedar Swamp Mtn. Don't miss the scenic bonus of tiny Sargent Mtn. Pond en route. Start and finish at Norumbega Mtn. trailhead on ME 3/198; see Hadlock Brook Trail, p. 449.

SEC 10

TRAIL DESCRIPTIONS

EASTERN MT. DESERT ISLAND

■ CHAMPLAIN MTN. (1,058 FT.)

Champlain Mtn., the easternmost major ridge on Mt. Desert Island, consists of the main peak of Champlain Mtn. and the subsidiary peak of Huguenot Head, just west. The Beehive and Gorham Mtn. are immediately south of Champlain Mtn. All of these summits provide excellent views. Champlain and the Beehive are very popular because of their exciting ladder trails that climb steep cliff faces overlooking Frenchman Bay. Easier trails that are better suited for children or those with a fear of heights provide access to both peaks.

PRECIPICE TRAIL (NPS; MAP 5: D8 AND E8)

NPS rating: ladder; cumulative from Park Loop Rd. (150 ft.) to:	⇅	↗	↻
Orange & Black Path (400 ft.)	0.6 mi.	250 ft.	0:25
Champlain Mtn. summit (1,058 ft.)	1.3 mi.	900 ft.	1:05

Precipice Trail climbs the east wall of Champlain Mtn. in spectacular fashion, using a series of iron rungs, ladders, handrails, and walkways to guide hikers over the many exposed ledges. This route starts from the Precipice Trail parking area at the eastern base of Champlain Mtn., located on Park Loop Rd., 1.9 mi. beyond Sieur de Monts Spring entrance and 0.8 mi. before the park entrance station.

(*Caution:* According to the NPS, Precipice Trail is maintained as a nontechnical climbing route, not a hiking trail. Hikers should attempt this route only if they are in good physical condition, are wearing proper footwear, and have experience climbing near exposed cliffs and heights. Avoid this route in inclement weather or darkness. Please stay on the trail, and do not throw or dislodge rocks onto hikers below. Precipice Trail may be closed for an undetermined amount of time each spring and summer, usually until early to mid-August, to protect nesting peregrine falcons, a Maine endangered species, from inadvertent disturbance or harassment. Violators of the closure are subject to a $10,000 fine. When Precipice Trail is closed, visitors may experience alternative ladder hikes on the Beehive, Ladder [Dorr Mtn.], Beech Cliff, or Perpendicular trails.)

From the parking lot, Precipice Trail climbs steps to pass a gate and kiosk, then climbs slabs to a warning sign. Steps beyond lead to the base of the Precipice Wall. The trail climbs a short wall via a strenuous iron rung, then negotiates a rugged talus field of large boulders beyond, climbing

SEC 10

northwest. After passing two cave formations, the trail makes a traverse using a long handrail. Ahead, the undulating route across the exposed face uses a series of walkways and handrails. At 0.6 mi., reach the jct. with Orange & Black Path (leads right to Champlain North Ridge Trail in 0.5 mi., and to Park Loop Rd. in 0.7 mi.).

From this jct., Precipice Trail climbs southwest, rising steeply to a point directly west of the parking area. Iron rungs, strenuous pull-ups, a rock slot, sloping ledges with a handrail, and more iron rungs up a short wall lead to a traverse left along a narrow ledge with handrails. More rungs and ladders lead ever higher over vertical ledges on the very exposed face. After the final ladders and rungs, the angle eases and the trail climbs to the summit over gentle slopes and ledges, reaching the top of Champlain Mtn. at 1.3 mi.

ORANGE & BLACK PATH (NPS; MAP 5: D8–E8)

NPS rating: ladder; cumulative from Schooner Head Rd. (50 ft.) to:	⥮	↗	○
Park Loop Rd. (200 ft.)	0.2 mi.	150 ft.	0:10
Champlain North Ridge Trail (550 ft.)	0.4 mi.	500 ft.	0:30
Precipice Trail (400 ft.)	0.9 mi.	500 ft.	0:45
Champlain Mtn. summit (1,058 ft.) via Precipice Trail	1.6 mi.	1,000 ft.	1:20

Orange & Black Path begins from Schooner Head Rd. at a point 1.3 mi. south of the jct. with ME 3 in Bar Harbor. Parking is along the road.

Start out on Schooner Head Trail. In 50 ft., Orange & Black Path diverges right. Follow this easily uphill to Park Loop Rd. at 0.2 mi. Cross the road and proceed into the woods. Ahead, scramble over rocks and climb via stone steps to a jct. The trail to the right leads 0.1 mi. to a jct. with Champlain North Ridge Trail.

Continuing left from the jct. on Orange & Black Path, traverse the face of the mountain with minor ups and downs and numerous viewpoints en route. Descend a crevice in the rocks on stone steps, then continue to the south. Cross a steep section of the slope using wooden steps and an iron ladder to reach a jct. with Precipice Trail at 0.9 mi. To the right, it is 0.7 mi. to the summit of Champlain Mtn. To the left, it is 0.6 mi. to Park Loop Rd. and the Precipice Trail parking area.

CHAMPLAIN NORTH RIDGE TRAIL (NPS; MAP 5: D8)

NPS rating: moderate; cumulative from Park Loop Rd. (200 ft.) to:	⥮	↗	○
Orange & Black Path (550 ft.)	0.5 mi.	350 ft.	0:25
Champlain Mtn. summit (1,058 ft.)	1.1 mi.	860 ft.	1:00

Beginning on Park Loop Rd., 0.2 mi. east of the entrance to Bear Brook picnic area, this trail ends at the summit of Champlain Mtn., where Champlain South Ridge Trail continues on to meet Bowl Trail at the south end of the Bowl, a pretty mountain tarn.

The trail climbs gradually from Park Loop Rd. through a mixed forest of birch, pine, and spruce on the north slope of Champlain Mtn. to a jct. at 0.5 mi. To the left, a connector trail leads 0.1 mi. to Orange & Black Path. Continuing ahead on Champlain North Ridge Trail, the path climbs steadily to emerge from the forest canopy, giving outstanding views of Frenchman Bay and Schoodic Peninsula on the mainland to the east. Atop the summit ridge, Beachcroft Trail enters from the right (west), and just ahead at 1.1 mi., the trail reaches the open, rocky summit of Champlain Mtn. At the large summit cairn is the jct. with Precipice Trail and Champlain South Ridge Trail.

CHAMPLAIN SOUTH RIDGE TRAIL (NPS; MAP 5: D8 AND E8)

NPS rating: moderate; cumulative from Park Loop Rd. (50 ft.) near Sand Beach to:	⇅	↗	○
Start of Champlain South Ridge Trail (450 ft.) via Bowl Trail	0.8 mi.	400 ft.	0:35
Champlain Mtn. summit (1,058 ft.)	2.2 mi.	1,000 ft.	1:40

This trail provides a route from Sand Beach and the Bowl to the summit of Champlain Mtn. The trail begins at a jct. with Bowl Trail, 0.7 mi. from Park Loop Rd. near the Sand Beach parking area.

Champlain South Ridge Trail skirts the south shore of the Bowl, a small glacial tarn west of the Beehive, before ascending to the south ridge of the mountain. Ahead, the trail climbs moderately before entering a semi-open forest of pitch pines. Climbing over pink granite, the trail reaches open views and the summit of Champlain Mtn. at 2.3 mi., the jct. with Champlain North Ridge and Precipice trails.

BEACHCROFT PATH (NPS; MAP 5: D7–D8)

SEC 10

NPS rating: moderate; cumulative from north end of the Tarn (50 ft.) to:	⇅	↗	○
ME 3 parking area (100 ft.)	0.1 mi.	50 ft.	0:02
Champlain Mtn. summit (1,058 ft.)	1.4 mi.	1,000 ft.	1:10

This path offers a convenient route from the Sieur de Monts Spring area to the summit of Champlain Mtn. via Huguenot Head. The trail officially starts at the jct. of Jesup Path, Kurt Diederich's Climb, and Kane Path, 0.1 mi. west of ME 3 and the parking area at the north end of the Tarn. Most hikers, however, will simply start from ME 3. From the village green in Bar Harbor (jct. Mt. Desert St. and Main St.), drive south on ME 3 for 1.6 mi. to the Tarn parking lot on the right, immediately beyond the Sieur de Monts Spring entrance to ANP.

After crossing ME 3, Beachcroft Path starts up a flight of granite steps and then heads southeast, often on carefully placed stonework. Following switchbacks and stone steps, the trail rises across the west slope of Huguenot Head. It passes just below the summit of Huguenot Head at about 0.7 mi. A brief, gradual descent into the notch between Huguenot Head and Champlain Mtn. is followed by a sharp, difficult ascent over rocks up the northwest slope of the mountain to the summit at 1.4 mi.

■ THE BEEHIVE (520 FT.)

Rising dramatically above Sand Beach and Park Loop Rd., the Beehive is one of the most popular mountains in ANP. The Beehive Trail is challenging and not for hikers who may be uneasy on precipitous heights. Atop the summit cliffs, the views of Frenchman Bay, Sand Beach, and Otter Cliff are spectacular. Bowl Trail and Beehive Trail combine for a fine loop over the Beehive.

BOWL TRAIL (NPS; MAP 5: E8)

NPS rating: moderate; cumulative from Sand Beach parking area (50 ft.) to:	↧↥	↗	○
Beehive Trail (150 ft.)	0.2 mi.	100 ft.	0:10
Gorham Mtn. Trail, lower jct. (250 ft.)	0.5 mi.	200 ft.	0:20
Gorham Mtn. Trail, upper jct. (350 ft.)	0.6 mi.	300 ft.	0:25
The Bowl, Beehive Trail, Champlain South Ridge Trail (450 ft.)	0.7 mi.	400 ft.	0:30

This trail leaves from Park Loop Rd. just opposite the entrance to the Sand Beach parking area, 0.6 mi. south of the Sand Beach entrance station. Bowl Trail is a gently sloping path that connects Sand Beach to the Bowl, a pretty mountain tarn in a wild setting. On the ascent to the Bowl, the route passes trails to the Beehive and Gorham Mtn. At the Bowl, Beehive Trail bears right and climbs over the Beehive, while Champlain South Ridge Trail bears left around the pond to Champlain Mtn.

BEEHIVE TRAIL (NPS; MAP 5: E8)

NPS rating: ladder; cumulative from Sand Beach parking area (50 ft.) to:	⇅	↗	○
Start of Beehive Trail (150 ft.) via Bowl Trail	0.2 mi.	100 ft.	0:10
The Beehive summit (520 ft.)	0.4 mi.	470 ft.	0:25
The Bowl summit at jct. of Bowl Trail and Champlain South Ridge Trail (450 ft.)	0.7 mi.	500 ft.	0:35

This route begins from Bowl Trail, 0.2 mi. west of Park Loop Rd., opposite the entrance to the Sand Beach parking area. At the jct., take a sharp right at the sign marked "Beehive." For 0.3 mi., the trail rises abruptly via switchbacks, climbing via iron ladders, rungs, and walkways over steep ledges to the summit of the Beehive. It continues down the northwest slope, passing a connector trail leading left (south) to Bowl Trail. Ahead, Beehive Trail climbs briefly, then drops steeply to the Bowl, bearing left around the tarn to reach the jct. with Bowl Trail and Champlain South Ridge Trail.

■ GREAT HEAD (150 FT.)

The easternmost high point on Mt. Desert Island, Great Head offers stunning vistas west over Sand Beach and Newport Cove to Champlain Mtn., the Beehive, Gorham Mtn., and Otter Point, and east across Frenchman Bay to Egg Rock Light and Schoodic Peninsula.

GREAT HEAD TRAIL (NPS; MAP 5: E8)

NPS rating: moderate; from Sand Beach parking area (sea level) to:	⇅	↗	○
Complete loop	2.0 mi.	150 ft.	1:05

This scenic, short walk passes largely along cliffs directly above the sea. From the Sand Beach parking area on Park Loop Rd., cross Sand Beach to its east end. Near the seaward end of the interior lagoon, look for a series of granite steps with a handrail ascending a high bank, which lead quickly to a huge millstone and the loop jct. To hike Great Head counterclockwise (recommended), turn sharply right (south) here. Weave upward over ledges and slabs to a jct. on top, where a connector path leads left to join with the return loop of the trail.

SEC
10

Great Head Trail traces the perimeter of the peninsula, at first high above Newport Cove and then along the southern cliffs before turning northeast, high above Frenchman Bay. Cross several open ledges to reach the high point, where there are ruins of a stone teahouse. The route descends northwest on a wide trail to a jct. with a shortcut trail on the left leading back to Sand Beach. Continuing on, Great Head Trail leads easily north on good terrain and soon reaches the old Satterlee Rd., named for the family whose estate once occupied this property. At this jct., it is 250 ft. right to parking on Schooner Head Rd. Turn left here to follow the old road through the former Satterlee estate. Ahead at a fork, take either path; both lead to the close of the loop at the millstone. Turn right to return to Sand Beach and the parking area.

■ GORHAM MTN. (522 FT.)

Located south of Champlain Mtn. and the Beehive, the long, low ridge of Gorham Mtn. offers fine walking and outstanding views east over Ocean Drive to Frenchman Bay and Schoodic Peninsula, and west to Cadillac Mtn. and Dorr Mtn.

GORHAM MTN. TRAIL (NPS; MAP 5: E8)

NPS rating: moderate; cumulative from Gorham Mtn. parking area (50 ft.) to:	⇅	↗	↺
Gorham Mtn. summit (522 ft.)	1.1 mi.	470 ft.	0:45
Bowl Trail (250 ft.)	1.6 mi.	470 ft.	1:05
Park Loop Rd. at Sand Beach	2.0 mi.	470 ft.	1:15

This trail starts at the Gorham Mtn. parking area (also known as Monument Cove parking area) on Park Loop Rd., 1.1 mi. south of Sand Beach.

Gorham Mtn. Trail quickly reaches the jct. with Otter Cove Trail, which leads left (west) 0.4 mi. to Park Loop Rd. at the Otter Cove Causeway, crossing Otter Creek Rd. en route. Beyond, Gorham Mtn. Trail rises gently over open ledges to a jct. with a side trail on the right to Cadillac Cliffs (NPS rating: strenuous) at 0.3 mi. This short loop rejoins Gorham Mtn. Trail in 0.3 mi., after first passing ancient sea cliffs and an ancient sea cave.

Beyond the jct., Gorham Mtn. Trail continues easily over open granite ledges to where the Cadillac Cliffs loop rejoins it. Then the trail climbs north to the bare summit of Gorham Mtn. at 1.1 mi. and some of the finest panoramas in ANP. Descending the north ridge, it reaches a connector trail that leaves left, offering a direct route to the Bowl, reaching the tarn in 0.3 mi. Ahead, Gorham Mtn. Trail reaches a jct. with Bowl Trail. From here, it is 0.3 mi. left to the Bowl. To the right, it is 0.2 mi. to Beehive Trail and 0.4 mi. to Park Loop Rd. near Sand Beach.

■ DORR MTN. (1,265 FT.)

This mountain, named for the founding father of ANP, George B. Dorr, lies immediately west of Sieur de Monts Spring and the Tarn. Two routes up the mountain originate from Sieur de Monts Spring, while two more trails begin from the Tarn on ME 3. Trails also ascend from the north and south over long ridges, and another trail rises from the gorge east of Cadillac Mtn. The east slope of Dorr Mtn. is particularly steep, and views from the high ridgeline on Dorr are superb. Ten trails form an extensive network for exploring this mountain from all sides.

EMERY PATH (NPS; MAP 5: D7)

NPS rating: strenuous; cumulative from Sieur de Monts Spring (50 ft.) to:	⇅	↗	⟳
Homans Path (400 ft.)	0.3 mi.	350 ft.	0:20
Jct. of Kurt Diederich's Climb and Schiff Path (550 ft.)	0.5 mi.	500 ft.	0:30
Dorr Mtn. summit (1,265 ft.) via Schiff Path	1.7 mi.	1,215 ft.	1:30

Emery Path originates from Sieur de Monts Spring and climbs the east face of Dorr Mtn. to join Schiff Path and Homans Path. From the village green in Bar Harbor (jct. of Mt. Desert St. and Main St.), drive south on ME 3 for 1.5 mi. to the Sieur de Monts entrance to ANP. Turn right here, and then left, to reach the large Sieur de Monts Spring parking area (toilets). Wild Gardens of Acadia is on the right, and the Nature Center is just ahead.

To reach the start of Emery Path, from the patio at the Nature Center, take the gravel path to the right of the kiosk. In just a few feet, at the entrance to Wild Gardens of Acadia, turn left and cross a footbridge. At a fork just beyond, walk left for 150 ft. to a large rock inscribed "Sweet Waters of Acadia." The spring house is ahead. From here, Emery Path follows a series of switchbacks up the northeast shoulder of Dorr Mtn. The first half of the climb features many stone steps. At 0.3 mi., Homans Path enters from the right. At 0.5 mi., Emery Path ends at its jct. with Kurt Diederich's Climb (descends left [east] 0.6 mi. to the north end of the Tarn) and Schiff Path, which continues on a rising traverse to meet Ladder Trail before ascending to the summit ridge of Dorr Mtn. in another 1.2 mi. Near the top, turn left to finish the hike via Dorr North Ridge Trail, which reaches the peak of Dorr Mtn. in 100 yd.

SEC 10

HOMANS PATH (NPS; MAP 5: D7)

NPS rating: strenuous; cumulative from Hemlock Rd. (50 ft.) near Sieur de Monts Spring to:	⇅	↗	⟳
Emery Path (400 ft.)	0.4 mi.	350 ft.	0:20
Dorr Mtn. summit (1,265 ft.) via Emery Path, Schiff Path, and Dorr North Ridge Trail	1.8 mi.	1,215 ft.	1:30

Homans Path features some of the most amazing stonework of any trail in ANP. To reach the start of Emery Path, from the patio at the ANP

Nature Center, take the gravel path to the right of the kiosk. In just a few feet, at the entrance to Wild Gardens of Acadia, turn left and cross a footbridge. At a fork just beyond, walk right along the garden fence to intersect Jesup Path. Continue straight (right) on Jesup Path, and in 0.1 mi., turn left on Hemlock Rd. and follow it for 40 ft., where Homans Path begins on the left.

Soon after the start, Homans Path climbs rock steps. Ahead, the route gets steeper as the trail negotiates a stretch of boulders. Climb through a natural archway, then follow a sidewalk-like trail across an open slope of boulders. Here are views east over Great Meadow to Schoodic Mtn. Climb steps on tight switchbacks, and just above, climb through a narrow crevice topped by a small block of granite. The trail is almost entirely rock steps from this point on. In the woods above, it levels off and contours south to meet Emery Trail at 0.4 mi. From this point, it is another 1.4 mi. to the summit of Dorr Mtn. via Emery Path and Schiff Path.

SCHIFF PATH (NPS; MAP 5: D7)

NPS rating: strenuous; cumulative from jct. of Emery Path and Kurt Diederich's Climb (550 ft.) to:	↰↱	↗	⟳
Ladder Trail (800 ft.)	0.6 mi.	250 ft.	0:25
Dorr Mtn. summit (1,265 ft.) · via Dorr North Ridge Trail	1.2 mi.	715 ft.	1:00

This trail begins partway up the east slope of Dorr Mtn. at the jct. of Emery Path and Kurt Diederich's Climb, 0.5 mi. above Sieur de Monts Spring and 0.6 mi. above the north end of the Tarn. Schiff Path traverses above the steep east face of the mountain, ascending moderately, to reach a jct. with Ladder Trail. Here, Schiff Path makes a sharp right and climbs steeply, then more moderately, to meet Dorr North Ridge Trail at 1.2 mi. Follow Dorr North Ridge Trail south for 0.1 mi. to the summit of Dorr Mtn.

KURT DIEDERICH'S CLIMB (NPS; MAP 5: D7)

NPS rating: strenuous; cumulative from the Tarn parking area on ME 3 (100 ft.) to:	↰↱	↗	⟳
Start of trail (50 ft.) via Beachcroft Trail	0.1 mi.	-50 ft.	0:05
Jct. of Emery Path and Schiff Path (550 ft.)	0.7 mi.	500 ft.	0:40

This trail takes a direct route from the north end of the Tarn to the jct. of Schiff Path and Emery Path partway up the east side of Dorr Mtn. Start at the Tarn parking area on ME 3, and proceed west via Beachcroft Trail for 0.1 mi. to the jct. with Kane and Jesup paths. Look for an inscription in the stone steps that reads "Kurt Diederich's Climb." The trail climbs steeply up the steps to good views and a jct. with Emery and Schiff paths at 0.6 mi.

KANE PATH (NPS; MAP 5: D7 AND E7)

NPS rating: moderate; cumulative from north end of the Tarn (50 ft.) to:	⇅	↗	○
Ladder Trail (150 ft.)	0.5 mi.	100 ft.	0:15
Canon Brook Trail (150 ft.)	0.8 mi.	100 ft.	0:25

This trail starts at the north end of the Tarn, 0.1 mi. west of the parking area on ME 3 via Beachcroft Path. Kane Path leads south to Canon Brook Trail and links the Sieur de Monts Spring area to the southern trails of Dorr Mtn. and Cadillac Mtn. At its start, Kane Path runs south over a talus slope directly along the west side of the Tarn. After reaching the south end of the pond, the path continues past Ladder Trail at 0.5 mi. to end at Canon Brook Trail at 0.8 mi. Follow Canon Brook Trail south and then west to reach Dorr South Ridge Trail and A. Murray Young Path.

LADDER TRAIL (NPS; MAP 5: D7)

NPS rating: ladder; cumulative from ME 3 (150 ft.) to:	⇅	↗	○
Schiff Path (800 ft.)	0.6 mi.	650 ft.	0:40
Dorr Mtn. summit (1,265 ft.) via Schiff Path and Dorr North Ridge Trail	1.2 mi.	1,215 ft.	1:15

This trail leaves from ME 3 just south of the Tarn and 0.5 mi. south of the Tarn trailhead parking lot. Parking for Ladder Trail is along the west (Dorr Mtn.) side of ME 3. From ME 3, the trail soon crosses Kane Path, then makes a steady ascent to reach Schiff Path at 0.6 mi. The trail is steep, climbing some 1,200 stone steps and over several sets of iron ladders. At the end of Schiff Path on the summit ridge, turn left (south) to reach the top of Dorr Mtn. in 100 yd.

CANON BROOK TRAIL (NPS; MAP 5: D7 AND E7)

NPS rating: strenuous; cumulative from ME 3 (150 ft.) to:	⇅	↗	○
Kane Path (150 ft.)	0.2 mi.	0 ft.	0:10
Dorr South Ridge Trail (250 ft.)	0.9 mi.	100 ft.	0:25
A. Murray Young Path (250 ft.)	1.1 mi.	100 ft.	0:30
Cadillac South Ridge Trail jct. (950 ft.) at the Featherbed	2.0 mi.	800 ft.	1:25
Bubble & Jordan Ponds Path (300 ft.)	2.7 mi.	800 ft.	1:45

SEC 10

This trail begins on ME 3, 0.8 mi. south of the Tarn trailhead parking area. There is parking in a paved lot on the east side of ME 3 and in a gravel area along the west side of ME 3. Canon Brook Trail leaves from the south end of the gravel lot. It descends west to cross a beaver flowage, then intersects Kane Path at 0.2 mi. Turn left (south) at the jct. and follow the beaver flowage down through the valley. After a brief, sharp rise, the trail reaches a jct. with Dorr South Ridge Trail, which diverges right at 0.9 mi. Canon Brook Trail then descends to a jct. with A. Murray Young Path, which goes right at 1.1 mi. Here, Canon Brook Trail crosses a branch of Otter Creek and climbs gently along the north side of Canon Brook before crossing the brook and then climbing steeply past the cascades on the upper part.

The trail then swings away from the brook, passes a beaver pond, and ascends to a small wetlands area known as the Featherbed. Here, it intersects Cadillac South Ridge Trail, which leads 2.0 mi. south to ME 3 near Blackwoods CG, and 1.2 mi. north to the summit of Cadillac Mtn. Ahead, Canon Brook Trail skirts the north side of the wetlands to reach a large ledge and view to Pemetic Mtn. and the Cranberry Isles. The trail then descends steeply via stone steps, a rough and rocky treadway, then more steps. Below, the trail continues its steep descent; two iron rungs and four iron railings are aids in the strenuous section, which includes a narrow rock cleft. After a footbridge across a seep, then a bridge over a small stream, the angle eases. Follow the course of the stream, cross the outlet of a beaver pond on bog bridges, then make a short jaunt to a jct. Canon Brook Trail ends here, while Bubble & Jordan Ponds Path begins. Via this path, it is 0.4 mi. west to a carriage road and 1.1 mi. farther to Park Loop Rd. near Jordan Pond.

DORR SOUTH RIDGE TRAIL (NPS; MAP 5: D7 AND E7)

NPS rating: moderate; cumulative from ME 3 (150 ft.) to:	⇅	↗	○
Start of Dorr South Ridge Trail (250 ft.) via Canon Brook Trail	0.9 mi.	100 ft.	0:25
Dorr Mtn. summit (1,265 ft.)	2.4 mi.	1,115 ft.	1:45

This trail diverges right (north) from Canon Brook Trail 0.9 mi. from ME 3 at the southern end of Dorr Mtn. Dorr South Ridge Trail rises at a moderate grade over rocky ledges and through semi-open softwood forest. Views of Champlain Mtn. and Cadillac Mtn. and the ocean are frequent during the ascent of the long ridge. At the summit, the trail ends at the jct. with Dorr North Ridge Trail.

A. MURRAY YOUNG PATH (NPS; MAP 5: D7 AND E7)

NPS rating: moderate; from Canon Brook Trail (250 ft.) to:	⇅	↗	⟳
Jct. of Gorge Path and Cadillac–Dorr Connector (1,050 ft.)	1.3 mi.	800 ft.	1:05

Ascending the narrow valley between Dorr Mtn. and Cadillac Mtn. from the south, this path leaves Canon Brook Trail at a point 1.1 mi. west of ME 3. A. Murray Young Path climbs gradually in close proximity to a branch of Otter Creek, crossing the creek several times on stepping stones. Beyond, the trail makes a short, steep climb into a narrow, rocky defile sandwiched between the walls of the two high peaks. North along the floor of this dramatic gorge, the path ends at a jct. Here, Gorge Path arrives from the north, and the Cadillac–Dorr Connector enters from the east (leads 0.25 mi. to the summit of Dorr Mtn.). Gorge Path continues to the left (west) to climb steeply to the top of Cadillac Mtn. in another 0.4 mi.

Cadillac–Dorr Connector. This short trail (only 0.2 mi.) starts just north of the summit of Dorr Mtn. and runs east to west, connecting Dorr North Ridge Trail with Gorge Path at its jct. with A. Murray Young Path in the high, narrow valley between Cadillac Mtn. and Dorr Mtn.

DORR NORTH RIDGE TRAIL (NPS; MAP 5: D7)

NPS rating: moderate; cumulative from jct. of Kebo Mtn. Trail and Hemlock Trail (250 ft.) to:	⇅	↗	⟳
Jct. of Schiff Path and Cadillac–Dorr Connector (1,250 ft.)	1.0 mi.	1,000 ft.	1:00
Dorr Mtn. summit (1,265 ft.) and Dorr South Ridge Trail	1.1 mi.	1,105 ft.	1:05

Dorr North Ridge Trail offers a more gradual alternative to the summit of Dorr Mtn. than do the trails from the steeper east side. The trail begins as an extension of Kebo Mtn. Trail at 1.0 mi. from Park Loop Rd. and Kebo Brook Trail. Dorr North Ridge Trail climbs the north ridge at a moderate grade, reaching a jct. with Schiff Path and Cadillac–Dorr Connector at 1.0 mi. The summit is just 100 yd. farther ahead (south), at the jct. of Dorr South Ridge Trail. Views high on the north ridge are excellent.

SEC 10

■ KEBO MTN. (407 FT.)

The northernmost mountain in the park and the nearest to Bar Harbor, this low, twin-summited peak lies just off Park Loop Rd. at the end of the long north ridge of Dorr Mtn. Climb Kebo Mtn. on its own or combined with adjacent Dorr Mtn.

KEBO BROOK TRAIL (NPS; MAP 5: D6–D7)

NPS rating: easy; cumulative from Park Loop Rd.

(360 ft.) at Island Explorer bus stop (North Ridge) to:	↕	↗	↻
Cadillac North Ridge Trail (360 ft.)	0.1 mi.	0 ft.	0:05
Gorge Path (220 ft.)	0.5 mi.	-140 ft.	0:15
Kebo Mtn. Trail (180 ft.)	0.8 mi.	-180 ft.	0:25
Stratheden Path (150 ft.)	0.9 mi.	-210 ft.	0:30
Great Meadow Loop at Kebo St. (100 ft.)	1.1 mi.	-260 ft.	0:35

This trail provides an important link between the Island Explorer bus stop (North Ridge) on Park Loop Rd. and Great Meadow. Kebo Brook Trail links trailheads on the north side of Cadillac Mtn. and Kebo Mtn. and provides access to Cadillac North Ridge Trail, Gorge Path, Kebo Mtn. Trail, and Stratheden Path. During the busy summer and early fall months, parking is not allowed at the Cadillac North Ridge trailhead on Park Loop Rd., and there is no parking on Park Loop Rd. at the start of Kebo Mtn. Trail. Parking is roadside and limited at both Gorge Path and Stratheden Path. Therefore, hikers are urged to take advantage of the Island Explorer bus (route 4 or 5) when planning to hike these trails.

From the bus stop, look for a trail sign just right of the power line. Follow the wide gravel path into the woods. In 0.1 mi. reach the jct. with Cadillac North Ridge Trail, which leads 50 ft. up a stone staircase to Park Loop Rd. and to the summit of Cadillac Mtn. in another 2.2 mi. Kebo Brook Trail continues, trending downhill but still parallel to Park Loop Rd. At 0.5 mi., Gorge Path leaves to the right (leads 0.35 mi. to Park Loop Rd., where the path passes through the arch of a stone bridge, crosses a stream, and continues right up steps along the bridge and south into the woods. From here, it is 1.8 mi. to the top of Cadillac Mtn.). Ahead on Kebo Brook Trail, cross a brook on stepping stones, with Kebo Valley Golf Course below to the left. At 0.8 mi., Kebo Mtn. Trail departs to the right, leading 25 ft. up steps to Park Loop Rd. From there, it is 0.3 mi. to the top of Kebo Mtn. At 0.9 mi. on Kebo Brook Trail, Stratheden Path leaves to the right to reach Park Loop Rd. in 100 ft. (from there, the trail goes on to join Hemlock Trail in another 0.7 mi.). Kebo Brook Trail ends ahead at 1.05 mi. at its jct. with Great Meadow Loop at Kebo St.

SEC 10

KEBO MTN. TRAIL (NPS; MAP 5: D7)

NPS rating: easy; cumulative from Park Loop Rd. (180 ft.) to:	⇅	↗	⟳
Kebo Mtn. summit (407 ft.)	0.3 mi.	227 ft.	0:15
Jct. of Hemlock and Dorr North Ridge trails (250 ft.)	0.9 mi.	275 ft.	0:35
Dorr Mtn. summit (1,265 ft.) via Dorr North Ridge Trail	1.9 mi.	1,085 ft.	1:40

This trail leaves the south side of Park Loop Rd. 1.5 mi. after the road becomes one-way. (*Note:* No parking is available at the start of Kebo Mtn. Trail on Park Loop Rd. Parking is available 0.2 mi. east at the gravel pull-out for Stratheden Path. Hikers can then walk Kebo Brook Trail 0.1 mi. west to the start.) Kebo Mtn. Trail climbs south to the summit of Kebo Mtn. at 0.3 mi., traverses a minor summit, and reaches its end at a jct. with Hemlock and Dorr North Ridge trails 0.9 mi. from Park Loop Rd.

STRATHEDEN PATH (NPS; MAP 5: D7)

NPS rating: easy; from Park Loop Rd. (150 ft.) to:	⇅	↗	⟳
Hemlock Trail (50 ft.)	0.7 mi.	-100 ft.	0:20

Extending from Park Loop Rd. to Hemlock Trail, this easy walk wends along the eastern base of Kebo Mtn. Stratheden Path begins on Park Loop Rd., 0.2 mi. east of Kebo Mtn. Trail. The path takes a fairly level route through hemlocks on its way to Hemlock Trail, which it reaches at 0.7 mi. Turn right on Hemlock Trail to access Kebo Mtn. Trail and Dorr North Ridge Trail in 0.2 mi.

HEMLOCK TRAIL (NPS; MAP 5: D7)

NPS rating: easy; cumulative from Gorge Path (250 ft.) to:	⇅	↗	⟳
Jct. of Dorr North Ridge Trail and Kebo Mtn. Trail (250 ft.)	0.2 mi.	50 ft.	0:10
Stratheden Path and Hemlock Rd. (50 ft.)	0.4 mi.	50 ft.	0:20

SEC 10

This trail on the lower end of the north ridge of Dorr Mtn. connects Gorge Path to Dorr North Ridge and Kebo Mtn. trails and on to Stratheden Path and Hemlock Rd. Hemlock Trail begins on Gorge Path, 1.0 mi. north of the Cadillac–Dorr notch and 0.4 mi. south of Park Loop Rd. It heads east, rising slightly to the jct. of Dorr North Ridge Trail and Kebo Mtn. Trail in 0.2 mi. Hemlock Trail then descends moderately to end at a jct. with Stratheden Path and Hemlock Rd. (closed to vehicles) at 0.4 mi. From this jct., Sieur de Monts Spring is 0.5 mi. south via Hemlock Rd.

■ CADILLAC MTN. (1,528 FT.)

The highest point on Mt. Desert Island, this mountain is also the highest on the eastern seaboard of the Atlantic Ocean between Newfoundland and Brazil. An automobile road, the Cadillac Mtn. Rd., leads 3.5 mi. to the summit, where there is a parking area, a paved 0.4-mi. walking trail with interpretive signs, a small gift shop, and restrooms. The open expanse offers commanding views in all directions. Accessibility by car makes this rocky summit the busiest in ANP. Six trails traverse the mountain's slopes.

CADILLAC NORTH RIDGE TRAIL (NPS; MAP 5: D7)

NPS rating: moderate; from Park Loop Rd. (400 ft.) to:	↕	↗	↺
Cadillac Mtn. summit (1,528 ft.)	2.2 mi.	1,125 ft.	1:40

The trailhead is on Park Loop Rd., 0.3 mi. east of where it becomes one-way. A pullout on the north side of the road provides very limited parking. (*Note:* During the busy summer and early fall months, hikers may *not* park at this trailhead but must access the start of this route from Kebo Brook Trail, which they can reach by riding the Island Explorer. See Kebo Brook Trail for details.)

The trail starts on the south side of Park Loop Rd. and climbs the north ridge of Cadillac Mtn., rising steadily through stunted softwoods onto open ledges. The trail always keeps to the east of Cadillac Mtn. Rd., although it closely approaches road switchbacks on two occasions. For much of the way, both sides of the ridge are visible. The views of Bar Harbor, Eagle Lake, Egg Rock, and Dorr Mtn. are excellent as the trail wends over open slabs and ledges to its end on top of Cadillac Mtn., emerging onto the pavement of the summit parking lot a short distance west of the gift shop and restrooms.

GORGE PATH (NPS; MAP 5: D7)

NPS rating: moderate; cumulative from Park Loop Rd. (250 ft.) to:	↕	↗	↺
Dorr–Cadillac notch (1,050 ft.) at jct. of Cadillac–Dorr Connector and A. Murray Young Path	1.4 mi.	800 ft.	1:10
Cadillac Mtn. summit (1,528 ft.)	1.8 mi.	1,275 ft.	1:35

This trail ascends the scenic gorge between Cadillac Mtn. and Dorr Mtn. and provides good access to both peaks. The trailhead is on Park Loop Rd., 0.9 mi. east of where it becomes one-way. The trail rises moderately up the gorge, passing Hemlock Trail at 0.4 mi. Ascending a narrow valley next to a brook much of the time, Gorge Path finally reaches a jct. with

Cadillac–Dorr Connector and A. Murray Young Path at 1.4 mi. in the deep notch between the two mountains. At this point, Gorge Path turns right (west) and climbs steeply to the summit of Cadillac Mtn., reaching it at 1.8 mi.

CADILLAC SOUTH RIDGE TRAIL (NPS; MAP 5: D7, E7, AND F7)

NPS rating: moderate; cumulative from ME 3 (150 ft.) to:	⇅	↗	↻
Eagles Crag loop, south jct. (600 ft.)	0.9 mi.	450 ft.	0:40
Canon Brook Trail (950 ft.) at the Featherbed	2.0 mi.	800 ft.	1:25
Cadillac Mtn. summit (1,528 ft.)	3.2 mi.	1,375 ft.	2:20

A relatively long hike for ANP, this trail starts on the north side of ME 3 about 50 yd. west of the entrance to Blackwoods CG. (A level 0.7-mi. connector trail also links the campground to the road and trailhead.) Parking is along the north shoulder of ME 3. The trail climbs generally north. At 0.9 mi., a short loop trail on the right leads to Eagles Crag, with good views to the southeast and Otter Creek and Otter Cove. The loop trail rejoins the main trail in 0.3 mi.

Ahead, Cadillac South Ridge Trail wends through a semi-open forest of pitch pines and jack pines. After leaving the woods, the trail rises gently over open ledges before dropping down to meet Canon Brook Trail at the Featherbed at 2.0 mi. Continuing a long climb of the broad south ridge, mostly in the open, Cadillac South Ridge Trail reaches a jct. with Cadillac West Face Trail on the left at 2.7 mi. Ahead, the trail passes close to a switchback in the Cadillac Mtn. Rd. near Blue Hill Overlook and then ends at the Cadillac Mtn. summit parking area, adjacent to the gift shop and restrooms. The true summit of Cadillac, often overlooked, is 100 yd. before this—a large flat rock with a USGS marker on its surface 30 ft. west of the trail.

CADILLAC WEST FACE TRAIL (NPS; MAP 5: E6–E7)

NPS rating: strenuous; cumulative from Bubble Pond parking lot (350 ft.) to:	⇅	↗	↻
Cadillac South Ridge Trail (1,350 ft.)	1.1 mi.	1,000 ft.	1:05
Cadillac Mtn. summit (1,528 ft.) via Cadillac South Ridge Trail	1.6 mi.	1,175 ft.	1:30

SEC 10

This steep trail, the shortest route to the summit of Cadillac Mtn., is difficult anytime, but especially in wet weather, when the rock slabs can be extremely slippery. The trailhead is at Bubble Pond parking lot on Park Loop Rd., 5.1 mi. south of Hulls Cove Visitor Center and 2.7 mi. north of Jordan Pond House. (*Note:* This is a very small lot, so visitors often find it full. Plan to arrive early or ride the Island Explorer bus.)

From the parking lot, cross a carriage road and proceed south for 100 ft. to Bubble Pond. Here, Pemetic North Ridge Trail departs right (west), while Cadillac West Face Trail leaves to the left (east). Follow Cadillac West Face Trail along the pond shore, past a picnic table, to cross the pond's outlet. Just after, leave the wide path and turn sharply right on a footpath. The trail quickly ascends on rocky treadway. Ahead, scramble over ledges and across steep slabs, then climb steeply. Views of Bubble Pond and Pemetic Mtn. emerge, and then above, the vista widens to include Penobscot Mtn., Sargent Mtn., and Eagle Lake.

After more steeply sloping ledges, North Bubble and Connors Nubble enter the view. A rising traverse leads to more steep, sloping slabs and now ocean views to the Cranberry Isles. After the final slabs, the trail wends easily to join Cadillac South Ridge Trail at 1.1 mi. Turn left to follow Cadillac South Ridge Trail, which passes close to a switchback in the Cadillac Mtn. Rd. near Blue Hill Overlook, climbs some rocky terrain through the woods, and ends at the Cadillac Mtn. summit parking area adjacent to the gift shop and restrooms at 1.6 mi.

■ PEMETIC MTN. (1,247 FT.)

This mountain, the fourth-highest in ANP, is located roughly in the center of the eastern half of Mt. Desert Island. Its long ridgeline offers some of the best panoramic views in ANP. Trails up the west side are short and relatively steep, whereas routes from the north and south are more gradual and wooded.

For the trails from the south, park at the Jordan Pond trailhead parking area; from the north, park at Bubble Pond; and from the west, park at Bubble Rock. Gain access to all parking areas via Park Loop Rd. Summer crowds tend to fill these lots quickly, so plan to arrive early or ride the Island Explorer bus.

PEMETIC NORTH RIDGE TRAIL (NPS; MAP 5: E6)

NPS rating: strenuous; cumulative from Bubble Pond parking area (350 ft.) to:	⇅	↗	↺
Pemetic Northwest Trail (1,150 ft.)	1.1 mi.	800 ft.	1:00
Pemetic Mtn. summit (1,247 ft.)	1.2 mi.	900 ft.	1:05

This trail ascends the mountain from the north and offers outstanding views of Jordan Pond, the Bubbles, Sargent Mtn., and Eagle Lake. It leaves from the small Bubble Pond parking area at the north end of Bubble Pond on Park Loop Rd., 5.1 mi. south of Hulls Cove Visitor Center and 2.6 mi. north of the Jordan Pond trailhead parking area.

From the parking lot, cross a carriage road and proceed south for 100 ft. to Bubble Pond. Here, Pemetic North Ridge Trail departs right (west), while Cadillac West Face Trail leaves to the left (east). Pemetic North Ridge Trail parallels the pond for a distance, then crosses a carriage road. From there, the trail climbs steadily through the forest to a jct. with Pemetic Northwest Trail high on the mountain at 1.1 mi. Pemetic North Ridge Trail reaches the summit of Pemetic Mtn. and the jct. with Pemetic South Ridge Trail at 1.2 mi. The summit offers excellent views of the Triad, Cadillac Mtn., Jordan Pond, Penobscot Mtn., and Sargent Mtn.

PEMETIC NORTHWEST TRAIL (NPS; MAP 5: E6)

NPS rating: strenuous; cumulative from Bubble Rock parking area (450 ft.) to:	⇅	↗	○
Pemetic North Ridge Trail (1,150 ft.)	0.6 mi.	700 ft.	0:40
Pemetic Mtn. summit (1,247 ft.) via Pemetic North Ridge Trail	0.7 mi.	800 ft.	0:45

This trail begins at the Bubble Rock parking area on the west side of Park Loop Rd., 6.2 mi. south of Hulls Cove Visitor Center. It enters the woods east of the road and climbs through thick forest cover. Sometimes following a rocky streambed, the trail ends at a jct. with Pemetic North Ridge Trail 0.1 mi. north of the summit.

BUBBLE & JORDAN PONDS PATH (NPS; MAP 5: E6–E7)

NPS rating: moderate; cumulative from Jordan Pond (275 ft.) to:	⇅	↗	○
Pemetic South Ridge Trail (450 ft.)	0.5 mi.	175 ft.	0:20
Carriage road (350 ft.)	1.1 mi.	175 ft.	0:40
Canon Brook Trail (400 ft.)	1.5 mi.	225 ft.	0:55

This path extends from the southeast shore of Jordan Pond to the valley south of Bubble Pond, where the path meets the west end of Canon Brook Trail. Parking is at the Jordan Pond parking area. From there, follow Jordan Pond Path east for 0.4 mi. to cross an outlet and reach the jct. with Bubble & Jordan Ponds Path.

Bubble & Jordan Ponds Path leaves the pond and climbs east to cross Park Loop Rd. (there is limited roadside parking here). Continuing through heavy woods and by easy grades, the path ascends the valley between the Triad and Pemetic Mtn. It passes Pemetic South Ridge Trail on the left at 0.5 mi. and, ahead, turns left at a jct. with Triad Pass. Bubble & Jordan Ponds Path continues northeast to a jct. with Pemetic East Cliff Trail (goes left) and Triad Trail (goes right) at 0.8 mi. Beyond, Bubble &

SEC 10

Jordan Ponds Path gently descends to join a carriage road at 1.1 mi., bearing left (north). After a short distance, the trail leaves the road (but parallels it through the woods to the east) and continues 0.4 mi. to merge with Canon Brook Trail (climbs steeply to the south ridge of Cadillac Mtn. at the Featherbed, 1.2 mi. south of the summit) in a low area of beaver activity.

PEMETIC SOUTH RIDGE TRAIL (NPS; MAP 5: E6)

NPS rating: strenuous; cumulative from Bubble & Jordan Ponds Path (450 ft.) to:	⇅	↗	○
Pemetic East Cliff Trail (950 ft.)	0.6 mi.	500 ft.	0:35
Pemetic Mtn. summit (1,247 ft.)	1.3 mi.	800 ft.	1:10

This trail climbs to the summit of Pemetic Mtn. via the south ridge. The trail begins at Bubble & Jordan Ponds Path, 0.4 mi. east of its jct. with Jordan Pond Path and 0.8 mi. east of the Jordan Pond trailhead parking area. Pemetic South Ridge Trail climbs steadily to a jct. at 0.6 mi. with Pemetic East Cliff Trail, which enters from the right. Continuing straight ahead, it climbs over open ledges with spectacular views to reach the summit and the jct. with Pemetic North Ridge Trail at 1.3 mi.

PEMETIC EAST CLIFF TRAIL (NPS; MAP 5: E6)

This short but steep trail—NPS rating: strenuous—climbs from the intersection of Bubble & Jordan Ponds Path and Triad Trail to Pemetic South Ridge Trail in 0.3 mi., gaining 400 ft. and requiring about 10 min.

■ THE TRIAD (698 FT.)

The Triad is a compact group of three peaks nestled between Pemetic Mtn. and Day Mtn., just east of Jordan Pond. Hunters Brook Trail and Triad Trail crisscross its slopes.

TRIAD TRAIL (NPS; MAP 5: E6 AND F6)

NPS rating: moderate; cumulative from Bubble & Jordan Ponds Path (550 ft.) to:	⇅	↗	○
Hunters Brook Trail (650 ft.)	0.4 mi.	100 ft.	0:15
The Triad summit (698 ft.)	0.5 mi.	150 ft.	0:20
Day Mtn. Trail (250 ft.)	1.0 mi.	150 ft.	0:35

This trail provides a route from Pemetic Mtn. to Day Mtn. via the Triad. The start of Triad Trail is best reached from the Jordan Pond trailhead parking area via a 1.1-mi. hike on Jordan Pond Path and Bubbles & Jordan

Ponds Path. From the jct. of Bubbles & Jordan Ponds Path and Pemetic East Cliff Trail, Triad Trail rises moderately for 0.4 mi. to cross Hunters Brook Trail before reaching the top of the Triad. From there, the trail descends for 0.6 mi. to end at a carriage road jct. and the Triad-Day Mtn. Bridge over Park Loop Rd. The northern end of Day Mtn. Trail is here also.

TRIAD PASS (NPS; MAP 5: E6)

This short link—NPS rating: easy—provides trail access from Jordan Pond to the Triad and Day Mtn. The pass begins on Bubble & Jordan Ponds Path, 0.4 mi. east of Jordan Pond and 0.8 mi. from the Jordan Pond trailhead parking area. Triad Pass heads southeast for 0.2 mi. to connect with Hunters Brook Trail.

HUNTERS BROOK TRAIL (NPS; MAP 5: F6–F7 AND E6–E7)

NPS rating: moderate; cumulative from Park Loop Rd. (50 ft.) to:	⇅	↗	⟳
Carriage path (350 ft.)	1.4 mi.	300 ft.	0:45
Triad Trail (650 ft.)	1.9 mi.	600 ft.	1:00
Triad Pass (550 ft.)	2.2 mi.	600 ft.	1:25
Carriage road (350 ft.)	2.7 mi.	600 ft.	1:40

This trail begins on Park Loop Rd., 0.1 mi. north of the ME 3 bridge over Park Loop Rd. The bridge is 0.4 mi. southwest of the entrance to Blackwoods CG via ME 3. Park on the side of ME 3 after the bridge and scramble down the embankment to Park Loop Rd.

The trail follows the course of pretty Hunters Brook through beautiful spruce forest. At 1.25 mi., at the remnants of an old road and bridge, the trail bears west away from the brook and climbs to a carriage road at 1.4 mi. Beyond, the trail climbs to a jct. with Triad Trail at 1.9 mi., just north of the true summit of the Triad.

From here, Triad Trail leads south over the Triad to Park Loop Rd. in 0.6 mi. to meet Day Mtn. Trail. Turning right (north), Hunters Brook Trail and Triad Trail coincide for 20 ft. Then Triad Trail continues straight ahead to the summit of Pemetic Mtn. in 1.4 mi., while Hunters Brook Trail continues left and down to cross a deep ravine, then descends rock steps and log stairs to reach Triad Pass. (Triad Pass is a short connector leading 0.2 mi. to Bubble & Jordan Ponds Path.) Hunters Brook Trail takes a left and heads south (views to Wildwood Stables on the descent), ending at a carriage road at 2.7 mi., 0.3 mi. west of signpost 17 at the Triad-Day Mtn. Bridge over Park Loop Rd. Follow Park Loop Rd. back to the original trailhead.

SEC 10

■ DAY MTN. (583 FT.)

This little mountain at the southern edge of the eastern side of ANP offers sweeping views from many points on its upper slopes. Reach the top via Day Mtn. Trail and a pretty carriage road that winds its way to the summit.

DAY MTN. TRAIL (NPS; MAP 5: F6–F7)

NPS rating: moderate; cumulative from ME 3 (250 ft.) to:	↥↧	↗	⏱
Day Mtn. summit (583 ft.)	0.8 mi.	330 ft.	0:40
Jct. of carriage road (300 ft.) and Triad Trail	1.3 mi.	330 ft.	0:50

This trail starts on the north side of ME 3, 1.3 mi. south of the entrance to Blackwoods CG. A parking area is on the south side of the road. A few feet into the woods, a side trail leads right 150 ft. to the Champlain Monument, a tribute to Samuel de Champlain, the French navigator and explorer who visited Mt. Desert Island in 1604 and named it.

The trail climbs moderately through the forest for its entire length. Periodically crossing carriage roads (six different times), it offers good views of Hunters Beach and Seal Harbor from ledges at 0.7 mi. The trail reaches the summit at 0.9 mi. Beyond, it descends into the forest and ends at a carriage road and the Triad-Day Mtn. Bridge over ME 3 at 1.4 mi. Here, Triad Trail continues north toward the Triad and Pemetic Mtn. For a nice loop, go either left or right on the carriage road to return to ME 3.

■ NORTH BUBBLE (872 FT.), SOUTH BUBBLE (766 FT.), AND CONNERS NUBBLE (510 FT.)

The finely shaped, almost symmetrical North Bubble and South Bubble rise above the north end of Jordan Pond. Formerly covered with heavy tree growth, they were swept by fire in 1947, leaving many open views. The 110-ton glacial erratic precariously perched atop the east face of South Bubble is Bubble Rock, one of the park's most recognized natural features. The best access is from the Bubble Rock parking area on the west side of Park Loop Rd., 1.1 mi. south of Bubble Pond and 6.2 mi. south of Hulls Cove Visitor Center.

BUBBLES DIVIDE TRAIL (NPS; MAP 5: E6)

NPS rating: moderate; cumulative from Bubble Rock parking area (450 ft.) to:	↥↧	↗	⏱
Jordan Pond Carry	0.1 mi.	-50 ft.	0:05
Bubbles Trail, lower jct. (600 ft.)	0.3 mi.	200 ft.	0:15
Bubbles Trail, upper jct. (650 ft.)	0.4 mi.	250 ft.	0:20
Jordan Pond Path (250 ft.)	0.7 mi.	250 ft.	0:30

SEC 10

Bubbles Divide Trail bisects South and North Bubble on its route west to Jordan Pond. The trail offers the shortest route to the summit of either mountain. From its start, the trail drops a short distance to cross Jordan Pond Carry, which connects Jordan Pond with Eagle Lake. Beyond, the wide and well-used trail climbs toward the small notch between the Bubbles. Here, the northern section of Bubbles Trail leaves to the right (leads 0.3 mi. to North Bubble). Follow the southern section of Bubbles Trail in the notch proper; from this point, it climbs 0.3 mi. to the top of South Bubble and a short spur leading out to Bubble Rock.

Continuing west, Bubbles Divide Trail descends, on steep, rocky trail at times, to the north shore of Jordan Pond, ending at the jct. with Jordan Pond Path. To the left, it is 0.9 mi. back to the Bubble Rock parking area via Jordan Pond Path and Jordan Pond Carry.

BUBBLES TRAIL (NPS; MAP 5: D6 AND E6)

NPS rating: strenuous; cumulative from Jordan Pond Path (275 ft.) to:	⇅	↗	⟳
South Bubble summit (766 ft.)	0.4 mi.	490 ft.	0:30
Bubbles Divide Trail (650 ft.)	0.7 mi.	490 ft.	0:40
North Bubble summit (872 ft.)	1.0 mi.	715 ft.	0:55
Conners Nubble (550 ft.)	1.8 mi.	765 ft.	1:20
Eagle Lake Trail (250 ft.)	2.3 mi.	765 ft.	1:35

This trail connects the north shore of Jordan Pond with Eagle Lake, taking the high route and climbing over the Bubbles and Conners Nubble en route. It leaves from Jordan Pond Path at a point 0.5 mi. from Bubble Rock parking area on Park Loop Rd. via Bubbles Divide Trail and Jordan Pond Carry.

Bubbles Trail rises very steeply almost immediately, climbing via tight switchbacks over boulders and ledges. It levels off just before reaching the summit of South Bubble at 0.4 mi. Here, the views of Jordan Pond and beyond from the wide, open ledges below the summit are spectacular. At the summit, a short spur trail leads right to Bubble Rock, the large and unmistakable glacial erratic perched on the edge of the cliff face.

From the summit of South Bubble, the trail descends moderately over ledges to a notch, then turns right, traveling with Bubbles Divide Trail for a short distance before turning left and making a steep climb to the summit of North Bubble. Bubbles Trail then continues north past the summit, descending at an easy pace over open ridgeline for a distance.

Beyond, the trail crosses a carriage road before making a short climb to the open ledges on the summit of Conners Nubble, where there are excellent views of Eagle Lake and Cadillac Mtn. The trail continues north over

SEC 10

the summit, descends into the woods, and reaches Eagle Lake Trail near the shore of Eagle Lake. From here, it is 1.8 mi. back to the Bubble Rock parking area via Eagle Lake Trail and Jordan Pond Carry.

JORDAN POND

The Jordan Pond area is a central starting point for many good hiking trails, ranging from Pemetic Mtn. to the east, around Jordan Pond to the Bubbles in the north, and to Penobscot Mtn. and Sargent Mtn. to the west. Jordan Pond, its deep, sparkling waters considered some of the cleanest in Maine, is also home to the namesake and highly popular Jordan Pond House. Known for its fine dining and scenic view of the Bubbles and Penobscot Mtn., Jordan Pond House has been serving ANP visitors since 1871. Hiker parking is discouraged here due to congestion during the busy summer months. A large trailhead parking lot with a toilet is on Park Loop Rd. just 0.1 mi. north of Jordan Pond House or 7.7 mi. south of Hulls Cove Visitor Center. The Island Explorer bus is another good option for reaching trails in this busy area of the park.

JORDAN POND PATH (NPS; MAP 5: E6)

NPS rating: easy; cumulative (counterclockwise) from Jordan Pond parking area (250 ft.) to:

	⇅	↗	↻
Bubble & Jordan Ponds Path (250 ft.)	0.4 mi.	0 ft.	0:10
Jct. of Jordan Pond Carry and Bubbles Trail (250 ft.)	1.3 mi.	0 ft.	0:40
Bubbles Divide Trail (250 ft.)	1.7 mi.	0 ft.	0:50
Deer Brook Trail (250 ft.)	1.9 mi.	0 ft.	0:55
Complete circuit	3.4 mi.	0 ft.	1:40

This circuit around beautiful Jordan Pond connects with six trails to the mountain summits beyond. The description provided here is for travel in a counterclockwise direction, hiking the eastern shore of Jordan Pond first. The trail is fairly level, with negligible elevation gain and loss.

From the Jordan Pond trailhead parking area, follow the gravel boat-launch road to the south shore of the pond, which frames the classic view north to North and South Bubble. At the pond, turn right to start the circuit, which is also part of the Jordan Pond Nature Trail for a short distance. Follow the south shore, and just after crossing an inlet on a stone causeway, reach a jct. at 0.4 mi. with Bubble & Jordan Ponds Path, which departs to the right (leads to trails on Pemetic Mtn. and the Triad).

Continue left on Jordan Pond Path, a graded, fine-gravel trail that meanders easily along the east shore of the pond, offering excellent views of Penobscot Mtn. and Jordan Cliffs en route. At 1.3 mi., Jordan Pond

Carry and Bubbles Trail diverge to the right. Winding along the northeast shore at the base of South Bubble, reach the jct. with Bubbles Divide Trail at 1.7 mi. This trail climbs to Bubbles Gap, a high notch between North Bubble and South Bubble. Beyond, Jordan Pond Path crosses a picturesque footbridge over an inlet to reach the jct. with Deer Brook Trail, which leads to trails on Penobscot Mtn. and Sargent Mtn.

Finally, the trail turns south along the west shore of Jordan Pond and runs under the precipitous Jordan Cliffs. At first the trail alternates between graded pathway and a footpath through shoreline boulders. The last mile is a delightful combination of wooden boardwalks and graded gravel pathway. Views east take in the long ridge of Pemetic Mtn. and the Bubbles. Jordan Pond House and its long, sloping lawn come into view ahead. At the south end of the pond, merge with a carriage road and bear left to cross a bridge over Jordan Stream just south of a small dam. Beyond, follow the path along the shore and, with Jordan Pond House up to the right, continue ahead to the boat-launch road. Turn right here to return to the parking area.

ASTICOU & JORDAN POND PATH (NPS; MAP 5: E6 AND F5–F6)

NPS rating: easy; cumulative from Jordan Pond House (250 ft.) to:	⮃	↗	⏱
Spring Trail	0.1 mi.	0 ft.	0:05
Jct. of Penobscot Mtn. and Amphitheater trails (150 ft.)	1.1 mi.	-100 ft.	0:30
Asticou Ridge Trail (350 ft.)	1.5 mi.	200 ft.	0:50
Sargent South Ridge Trail (250 ft.)	1.8 mi.	200 ft.	1:00
Asticou Map House (250 ft.)	2.1 mi.	200 ft.	1:10

Asticou & Jordan Pond Path follows a mostly level course for much of its distance, yet gains some elevation to reach Asticou Ridge Trail. The path provides an important link to Eliot Mtn., as well as to trails on the southern ridges of Penobscot, Cedar Swamp, and Sargent mountains.

Park at the Jordan Pond trailhead parking area and follow any number of short signed paths to Jordan Pond House. From the ramada at the front of the facility, follows signs for the restrooms and water fountain, which are on the left (west side) of the building. On the patio adjacent to the restrooms, look for a sign on the left for Sargent Mtn., Penobscot Mtn., and Asticou trails. Asticou & Jordan Pond Path begins here.

Proceed down the wide steps of logs and gravel. Cross a carriage road at signpost number 15. In 50 ft., where the carriage road crosses a stream, bear right onto a footpath, marked with a sign for Penobscot Mtn. and Sargent Mtn. trails. Ahead, cross Jordan Stream on a footbridge to reach the jct. on the right with Spring Trail, which leads uphill via rock steps to connect with Jordan Cliffs and Penobscot Mtn. trails. Asticou & Jordan Pond Path turns left here.

The wide, graded path contours for a distance with minor variations in elevation. Ahead, cross a carriage road, then trend easily downhill to cross another carriage road. Here, the start of Amphitheater Trail is 0.3 mi. north via this carriage road. At 1.0 mi., reach the jct. with Penobscot Mtn. Trail, which leaves to the right. A short distance ahead, Harbor Brook Trail departs to the left (leads 2.0 mi. south to ME 3). At 1.4 mi., Asticou & Jordan Pond Path winds upward on a long series of stone steps to arrive at the jct. with Asticou Ridge Trail, which leads 0.8 south to Eliot Mtn.

On the gentle descent beyond, Sargent South Ridge Trail departs to the right (leads 1.4 mi. to Cedar Swamp Mtn. and 2.6 mi. to Sargent Mtn.). Asticou & Jordan Pond Path ends at the Map House, a small day shelter with benches and a posted map of ANP. Here also is the jct. with Charles Savage Trail, which leads 0.6 mi. to Eliot Mtn. and beyond to Thuya Gardens. The quiet lane adjacent to the Map House leads downhill to the left for 0.5 mi. to ME 3 at Asticou in Northeast Harbor; to the right, the lane leads to 0.6 mi. to a carriage road and Brown Mtn. Gatehouse on ME 3/198. Parking is discouraged near the Map House. There is a small parking lot on ME 3 at Asticou, signed for visitors of Thuya Gardens.

■ PENOBSCOT MTN. (1,196 FT.)

This mountain, the fifth highest in ANP, rises steeply west of Jordan Pond. The long and high Jordan Ridge atop the sweeping face of Jordan Cliffs offers commanding panoramic views in every direction. Sandwiched between ME 3/198 and Jordan Pond, the two major trailheads, Penobscot Mtn. is part of a compact group of six peaks that are home to an intricate network of trails allowing for many fun and interesting hike combinations.

SEC 10

SPRING TRAIL (NPS; MAP 5: E6)

NPS rating: strenuous; cumulative from Jordan Pond House (250 ft.) to:	↥↧	↗	↻
Jordan Cliffs Trail (350 ft.)	0.3 mi.	100 ft.	0:15
Penobscot Mtn. Trail (650 ft.)	0.5 mi.	400 ft.	0:30

This trail provides the quickest access to Penobscot Mtn. from Jordan Pond House. Short, but very steep in places, it should be avoided for descents, especially in wet conditions. The trail leaves from Asticou & Jordan Pond Path, 0.1 mi. west of Jordan Pond House.

Spring Trail extends easily west to the jct. with Jordan Cliffs Trail at 0.3 mi. Just beyond, Spring Trail crosses a carriage road and then climbs steeply, with the assistance of iron rungs and wooden handrails, boardwalks, and rock staircases, to join Penobscot Mtn. Trail at 0.5 mi., which leads 1.0 mi. along the pleasant and mostly open Jordan Ridge to the summit of Penobscot Mtn.

JORDAN CLIFFS TRAIL (NPS; MAP 5: E6)

NPS rating: ladder; cumulative from Jordan Pond House (250 ft.) to:	⇅	↗	↻
Start of Jordan Cliffs Trail (350 ft.) via Asticou & Jordan Pond Path and Spring Trail	0.3 mi.	100 ft.	0:15
East Trail (900 ft.)	1.3 mi.	650 ft.	1:00
Deer Brook Trail (650 ft.)	1.6 mi.	650 ft.	1:10

Although very rugged, Jordan Cliffs Trail is spectacular, with outstanding views over Jordan Pond to the Bubbles and Pemetic Mtn. The start of this challenging and scenic trail is 0.3 mi. west of Jordan Pond House via Asticou & Jordan Pond Path and Spring Trail.

Jordan Cliffs Trail immediately crosses a carriage road and, beyond, rises up the east shoulder of Penobscot Mtn. in gradual pitches to reach the base of Jordan Cliffs. The trail then traverses along the cliffs, via iron ladders and handrails, to a jct. with East Trail at 1.2 mi. (East Trail leads left [west] 0.3 mi. to the summit of Penobscot Mtn.). To the right, Jordan Cliffs Trail descends to join Deer Brook Trail in another 0.3 mi.

East Trail (NPS; Map 5: E5–E6). This short 0.4-mi. trail—NPS rating: moderate—climbs the upper northeast slope of Penobscot Mtn. to connect Jordan Cliffs Trail with the summit of Penobscot Mtn.

PENOBSCOT MTN. TRAIL (NPS; MAP 5: E5–F6)

NPS rating: strenuous; cumulative from Asticou & Jordan Pond Path (150 ft.) to:	⇅	↗	↻
Spring Trail (650 ft.)	0.9 mi.	500 ft.	1:00
Penobscot Mtn. summit (1,196 ft.) at East Trail	1.8 mi.	1,050 ft.	1:30
Deer Brook Trail (1,050 ft.)	1.9 mi.	1,050 ft.	1:35
Sargent South Ridge Trail (1,150 ft.)	2.1 mi.	1,150 ft.	1:40

SEC 10

The trail leaves from Asticou & Jordan Pond Path 0.9 mi. west of Jordan Pond House. Penobscot Mtn. Trail heads north, climbing at an easy pace and crossing three carriage roads in its first 0.3 mi. The trail then climbs more steeply, occasionally breaking out into the open with excellent views to the south. It attains the south ridge of the mountain, known as Jordan Ridge, and the jct. with Spring Trail. Penobscot Mtn. Trail then climbs gradually over open granite ledges to the summit, where East Trail enters. Beyond, Penobscot Mtn. Trail continues north, descending to a rugged notch and the jct. with Deer Brook Trail. Penobscot Mtn. Trail turns left here and soon reaches pretty Sargent Mtn. Pond. From the pond, the trail makes a short climb to join the Sargent South Ridge Trail (leads 1.2 mi. right [north] to the top of Sargent Mtn.).

DEER BROOK TRAIL (NPS; MAP 5: E5–E6)

NPS rating: strenuous; from Jordan Pond Path (250 ft.) to:	↥↧	↗	↺
Penobscot Mtn. Trail (1,050 ft.)	0.8 mi.	800 ft.	0:50

Deer Brook Trail starts from Jordan Pond Path at the north end of Jordan Pond. The trail can be accessed by hiking either east or west around the pond via Jordan Pond Path from Jordan Pond House, or by climbing over the Bubbles on Bubbles Divide Trail from the Bubble Rock parking area on Park Loop Rd. Deer Brook Trail provides good access to the summits of Penobscot Mtn. and Sargent Mtn.

From Jordan Pond, Deer Brook Trail climbs rock steps along Deer Brook, crossing it several times below the double-arched Deer Brook bridge. Cross the carriage road, then climb wooden staircases and rock steps alongside Deer Brook to reach a trail jct. Here, Jordan Cliffs Trail departs left, and Sargent East Cliffs Trail leaves to the right. Ahead on Deer Brook Trail, ascend the narrow valley, crossing the brook several more times before bearing away from it. Above a set of rock steps, the angle eases, and in a notch ahead, reach the end of the trail at the jct. with Penobscot Mtn. Trail. Sargent Mtn. Pond is just a 5-min. walk ahead; the open summit of Penobscot Mtn. is 0.1 mi. left.

■ CEDAR SWAMP MTN. (950 FT.)

This scenic peak, the southernmost of a jumble of six mountains west of Jordan Pond, is just west of Penobscot Mtn. and features a long south ridge that divides the large and remote ravine known as the Amphitheater from the Upper and Lower Hadlock ponds. The Amphitheater and Sargent South Ridge trails cross near the Cedar Swamp summit.

AMPHITHEATER TRAIL (NPS; MAP 5: E5 AND F5)

NPS rating: moderate; cumulative from Harbor Brook Bridge (150 ft.) to:	⇅	↗	↻
Amphitheater Bridge (350 ft.)	0.7 mi.	200 ft.	0:25
Sargent South Ridge Trail at Birch Spring (850 ft.)	1.3 mi.	700 ft.	1:00
Hadlock Brook Trail (700 ft.)	1.7 mi.	700 ft.	1:15

This trail connects Hadlock Brook Trail to Sargent South Ridge Trail high on Cedar Swamp Mtn. The start of Amphitheater Trail is 1.1 mi. west of Jordan Pond House, via a short walk on a carriage road from Asticou & Jordan Pond Path.

From Asticou & Jordan Pond Path, walk north on the carriage road, which quickly crosses Penobscot Mtn. Trail. Continue on the carriage road, paralleling Harbor Brook. In 0.3 mi., cross Harbor Brook Bridge; Amphitheater Trail begins on the right immediately after the bridge.

Amphitheater Trail traces a route along Harbor Brook, crossing it numerous times before and after passing under Amphitheater Bridge (the largest carriage road bridge in the park) at 0.7 mi. Beyond the bridge, the trail climbs more steeply through an area known as the Amphitheater to Birch Spring and the jct. with Sargent South Ridge Trail at 1.3 mi. To the left, it is 0.1 mi. to the top of Cedar Swamp Mtn.; to the right, it is 1.1 mi. to the summit of Sargent Mtn. Ahead, Amphitheater Trail descends to end at Hadlock Brook Trail at 1.7 mi.

SARGENT SOUTH RIDGE TRAIL (NPS; MAP 5: E5)

NPS rating: moderate; cumulative from Asticou & Jordan Pond Path (350 ft.) to:	⇅	↗	↻
Cedar Swamp Mtn. spur trail (950 ft.)	1.4 mi.	600 ft.	1:00
Amphitheater Trail (850 ft.)	1.5 mi.	600 ft.	1:05
Penobscot Mtn. Trail (1,150 ft.)	2.0 mi.	800 ft.	1:25
Hadlock Brook Trail (1,200 ft.)	2.2 mi.	850 ft.	1:30
Maple Spring Trail (1,250 ft.)	2.4 mi.	900 ft.	1:40
Sargent Mtn. summit (1,379 ft.)	2.7 mi.	1,030 ft.	1:55

SEC 10

This trail makes a long climb along the south ridge of Sargent Mtn., topping the subsidiary peak of Cedar Swamp Mtn. en route. Access the trail from Asticou & Jordan Pond Path by way of a 0.3-mi. hike east from the Map House near Asticou or a 1.8-mi. hike west from Jordan Pond House. The trail can also be reached by way of several carriage roads from Brown Mtn. Gatehouse on ME 3/198, which is located 3.7 mi. south of the jct. with ME 233.

From Asticou & Jordan Pond Path, Sargent South Ridge Trail soon crosses a carriage road. Beyond, the trail rises over a wooded shoulder, breaks out of the trees, and passes just southeast of the summit of Cedar Swamp Mtn. at 1.3 mi. (a short spur leads left to the summit). Just ahead, the trail drops to cross Amphitheater Trail at Birch Spring. Sargent South Ridge Trail then leaves the woods and rises sharply to another jct. at 1.9 mi. Here, Penobscot Mtn. Trail enters from the right. Sargent South Ridge Trail continues north over open ledges, past junctions to the left with Hadlock Brook Trail at 2.1 mi. and the Maple Spring Trail at 2.3 mi. The summit is at 2.6 mi.

■ SARGENT MTN. (1,379 FT.)

Sargent Mtn. is the second-highest peak on Mt. Desert Island, just 149 ft. lower than Cadillac Mtn. Rising high west of Eagle Lake, Jordan Pond, and the Bubbles, the bare granite summit of Sargent Mtn. offers sweeping 360-degree views. A fine network of trails leads hikers over its slopes. A small tarn, Sargent Mtn. Pond, is in the wooded col between Sargent Mtn. and neighboring Penobscot Mtn.

SARGENT EAST CLIFFS TRAIL (NPS; MAP 5: E5–E6)

NPS rating: strenuous; from Deer Brook Trail jct. (650 ft.) to:	⇅	↗	○
Sargent Mtn. summit (1,379 ft.)	0.7 mi.	730 ft.	0:45

This short but steep trail connects Deer Brook Trail to the summit of Sargent Mtn. Sargent East Cliffs Trail is recommended more for ascent than descent, especially in wet weather, when the steep climb down wet rocks and ledges can be hazardous. The trail starts at Deer Brook and the jct. of Jordan Cliffs and Deer Brook trails, 0.3 mi. west of Jordan Pond Path at the north end of Jordan Pond. Sargent East Cliffs Trail climbs quickly up the southeast face of Sargent Mtn. and has excellent views for much of its 0.7-mi. length.

GIANT SLIDE TRAIL (NPS; MAP 5: D4–D5 AND E5)

NPS rating: strenuous; cumulative from ME 3/198 (50 ft.) to:	⇅	↗	○
Carriage road crossing (250 ft.)	0.7 mi.	200 ft.	0:25
Jct. of Parkman Mtn. Trail and Sargent Northwest Trail (550 ft.)	1.2 mi.	500 ft.	0:50
Notch between Parkman Mtn. and Gilmore Peak (750 ft.)	1.9 mi.	700 ft.	1:20
Maple Spring Trail (550 ft.)	2.4 mi.	700 ft.	1:35

This trail leaves the east side of ME 3/198, 1.0 mi. south of ME 233 (limited parking is available on both sides of the road).

The trail, on private land at first, climbs a gradual slope to a carriage road. It turns sharply right (south) and, following Sargent Brook, rises steeply over the tumbled boulders of Giant Slide. Hikers must negotiate several small rock passages. At 1.2 mi., Parkman Mtn. Trail diverges to the right, and Sargent Northwest Trail leaves left. Beyond the jct., the trail passes through a long, narrow cave in the rock and several slot passages. It eventually trends away from the brook and onto easier ground. The trail parallels and then crosses a carriage road, picks up Sargent Brook again, and runs along it on bog bridges. In a notch between Gilmore Peak and Parkman Mtn., the trail intersects Grandgent Trail, which goes right to Parkman Mtn. and left to Sargent Mtn. Giant Slide Trail continues south past this jct. to meet Maple Spring Trail lower down at 2.4 mi.

SARGENT NORTHWEST TRAIL (NPS; MAP 5: E5)

NPS rating: moderate; from Giant Slide Trail (550 ft.) to:	⬆⬇	↗	⟳
Sargent Mtn. summit (1,379 ft.)	1.1 mi.	830 ft.	1:10

Sargent Northwest Trail leaves Giant Slide Trail at a point 1.2 mi. from ME 3/198. From this jct., the trail ascends east and crosses a carriage road at 0.3 mi. Ahead, it rises over slanting pitches for another 0.3 mi. before making a sharp right (south) turn. The final stretch to the summit of Sargent Mtn. is over open ledges offering spectacular views of Somes Sound, Blue Hill, the Camden Hills, and the hills around Bangor. At the top of Sargent Mtn., Sargent Northwest Trail meets Sargent South Ridge Trail and Grandgent Trail.

HADLOCK BROOK TRAIL (NPS; MAP 5: E5)

NPS rating: strenuous; cumulative from ME 3/198 (300 ft.) to:	⬆⬇	↗	⟳
Maple Spring Trail (350 ft.)	0.4 mi.	50 ft.	0:15
Amphitheater Trail (700 ft.)	1.1 mi.	400 ft.	0:45
Sargent South Ridge Trail (1,200 ft.)	1.6 mi.	900 ft.	1:15

SEC 10

This trail provides access to Sargent Mtn. from the southwest and leads to a handful of other trails in the area of Penobscot Mtn., Cedar Swamp Mtn., and Gilmore Peak. Hadlock Brook Trail begins from the Norumbega Mtn. Trail parking area on ME 3/198, 2.7 mi. south of its jct. with ME 233.

From the east side of the road, Hadlock Brook Trail enters the woods and heads east, quickly passing Parkman Mtn. and Bald Peak trails on the left. Beyond a carriage road, Hadlock Ponds Trail enters from the south. Bearing left uphill, reach a fork. Here, Maple Spring Trail diverges left, while Hadlock Brook Trail heads right to follow the East Branch of Hadlock Brook through mature forest. Hadlock Brook Trail crosses a carriage road at the stunning Waterfall Bridge, which frames the beautiful 40-ft. Hadlock Falls. Above, the trail gets steeper, continuing to parallel the brook over rough footing. The jct. with Amphitheater Trail is reached at 1.1 mi. Beyond, Hadlock Brook Trail climbs steeply before reaching the open terrain of the south ridge of Sargent Mtn. and Sargent South Ridge Trail at 1.6 mi. From this jct., via Sargent South Ridge Trail, it is 0.7 mi. north to the top of Sargent Mtn. and 0.2 mi. south to Penobscot Mtn. Trail near Sargent Mtn. Pond.

MAPLE SPRING TRAIL (NPS; MAP 5: E5)

NPS rating: strenuous; cumulative from Hadlock Brook Trail jct. (350 ft.) to:	↕	↗	○
Giant Slide Trail (550 ft.)	0.4 mi.	200 ft.	0:15
Grandgent Trail (750 ft.)	0.9 mi.	400 ft.	0:40
Sargent South Ridge Trail (1,250 ft.)	1.4 mi.	900 ft.	1:10
Sargent Mtn. summit (1,379 ft.) via Sargent South Ridge Trail	1.7 mi.	1,030 ft.	1:20

This trail climbs to the south ridge of Sargent Mtn. from the southwest, following the West Branch of Hadlock Brook for much of its length; it also provides access to Gilmore Peak via Grandgent Trail. Reach the start of the trail by following Hadlock Brook Trail from the Norumbega Mtn. parking area on ME 3/198 for 0.4 mi.

From its jct. with Hadlock Brook Trail, Maple Spring Trail leads left. The trail closely follows Hadlock Brook, crossing it several times. In high water, there are some nice cascades and small waterfalls before and after crossing under beautiful Hemlock Bridge at a point 0.3 mi. above Hadlock Brook Trail. Beyond, Maple Spring Trail climbs through a small gorge before reaching Giant Slide Trail at 0.4 mi. and then Grandgent Trail at 0.9 mi. (Gilmore Peak is 0.1 mi. to the left via Grandgent Trail.) Here, Maple Spring Trail makes a sharp right and climbs steeply, reaching the open south ridge and Sargent South Ridge Trail at 1.4 mi. The summit of Sargent Mtn. is 0.3 mi. to the left (north) via Sargent South Ridge Trail.

■ GILMORE PEAK (1,030 FT.), PARKMAN MTN. (950 FT.), AND BALD PEAK (971 FT.)

These three peaks with extensive rocky knobs as summits are part of six high mountains grouped together between Norumbega Mtn. and the Hadlock ponds to the west and Jordan Pond, Sargent Mtn., and Penobscot Mtn. to the east. Vistas from each of these summits are panoramic, spanning the coastal islands just south of Mt. Desert Island, across ANP to the east and west, and north to the mainland hills nearby. Six trails are on these slopes.

PARKMAN MTN. TRAIL (NPS; MAP 5: E5)

NPS rating: moderate; cumulative from ME 3/198 (300 ft.) to:	⇅	↗	○
Bald Peak Trail (850 ft.)	1.3 mi.	550 ft.	1:00
Parkman Mtn. summit (950 ft.)	1.4 mi.	650 ft.	1:10
Jct. of Giant Slide Trail and Sargent North Ridge Trail (550 ft.)	2.1 mi.	650 ft.	1:25

Parkman Mtn. Trail leads 1.2 mi. through woods and over a series of rocky knobs to the open summit of Parkman Mtn. The trail diverges left (north) from Hadlock Brook Trail just 0.1 mi. east of ME 3/198 and the Norumbega Mtn. parking area.

Parkman Mtn. Trail crosses carriage roads three times during the early part of the ascent, which is moderate at most. Views open up to the south, west, and east high on the south ridge. Bald Peak Trail joins from the right, and the craggy peak of Parkman Mtn. is a short distance ahead. At the Parkman Mtn. summit, Grandgent Trail leaves right (east) toward Gilmore Peak. Parkman Mtn. Trail continues north over open ledges, then through the woods, crossing a carriage road 0.5 mi. beyond the summit. The trail ends 0.3 mi. farther at the jct. of Giant Slide and Sargent Northwest trails. From here, Giant Slide Trail leads left 1.2 mi. to ME 3/198.

BALD PEAK TRAIL (NPS; MAP 5: E5)

NPS rating: moderate; cumulative from ME 3/198 (300 ft.) to:	⇅	↗	○
Start of Bald Peak Trail (300 ft.) via Hadlock Brook Trail	0.2 mi.	0 ft.	0:10
Bald Peak summit (971 ft.)	1.2 mi.	671 ft.	0:55
Parkman Mtn. Trail (850 ft.)	1.4 mi.	700 ft.	1:05

This direct route up Bald Peak, one of several small and rocky open mountaintops and ridges to the west of Sargent Mtn., leads quickly to outstanding views from the summit. Bald Peak Trail diverges left (north) from Hadlock

SEC 10

Brook Trail at a point 0.2 mi. from the Norumbega Mtn. parking area on ME 3/198. Bald Peak Trail climbs gradually at first, crosses a carriage road, and then ascends more steeply above to gain the south ridge proper. Mostly in the open now, the trail finally gains the summit of this fine crag. Beyond, it makes a short but sharp drop and then a short scramble up to the jct. with Parkman Mtn. Trail just 0.1 mi. from that mountain's summit.

GRANDGENT TRAIL (NPS; MAP 5: E5)

NPS rating: strenuous; cumulative from Parkman Mtn. summit (950 ft.) to:	↻↑	↗	↻
Giant Slide Trail (750 ft.)	0.2 mi.	-250 ft.	0:10
Gilmore Peak summit (1,030 ft.)	0.5 mi.	280 ft.	0:25
Maple Spring Trail (950 ft.)	0.6 mi.	280 ft.	0:30
Sargent South Ridge Trail (1,250 ft.)	1.1 mi.	580 ft.	0:50
Sargent Mtn. summit (1,379 ft.)	1.4 mi.	710 ft.	1:05

Grandgent Trail connects the summits of Parkman Mtn., Gilmore Peak, and Sargent Mtn. Beginning on the top of Parkman Mtn., Grandgent Trail bears right along the north ridge, then drops to the right into the woods and, farther, into a deep ravine with a streamlet. Here, it intersects with Giant Slide Trail, which passes through the ravine from north to south. Continuing east, Grandgent Trail climbs steeply out of the ravine to reach the open ledges above and the broad summit of Gilmore Peak.

Grandgent Trail leaves Gilmore Peak and continues east, descending into another ravine. At the base of the ravine, the trail crosses a small stream on a footbridge before reaching the jct. with Maple Spring Trail, which enters from the right. Grandgent Trail turns left here and proceeds north up the shallow valley, crossing and recrossing the stream several times. After a stretch of very rocky terrain, Grandgent Trail breaks out of the trees and follows cairns up the broad and barren upper dome of Sargent Mtn. to the large cairn on top. Here is the jct. of Sargent South Ridge, Sargent Northwest, and Sargent East Cliffs trails.

SEC 10

■ NORUMBEGA MTN. (852 FT.)

Rising steeply from the sea-level waters of Somes Sound, shapely Norumbega Mtn. is the westernmost high mountain on the east side of Mt. Desert Island. The upper slopes may appear heavily forested, but the peak actually has a surprising number of excellent lookouts, at times east to Parkman Mtn., Bald Mtn., and Hadlock ponds, and at other times south and west, to Somes Sound and Northeast Harbor. Three trails ascend Norumbega Mtn., and several more wend along its base.

GOAT TRAIL (NPS; MAP 5: E5)

NPS rating: strenuous; from ME 3/198 (300 ft.) to:	⇅	↗	○
Norumbega Mtn. summit (852 ft.)	0.6 mi.	550 ft.	0:35

Goat Trail leaves the Norumbega Mtn. parking area on the west side of ME 3/198, 2.7 mi. south of its jct. with ME 233 and 0.3 mi. north of Upper Hadlock Pond.

The trail ascends quickly and very steeply for the first 0.3 mi. through woods to granite ledges, then swings south to the summit at 0.6 mi. There are occasional nice views eastward from several ledges before reaching the wooded summit. At the summit, Norumbega Mtn. Trail joins from the south; this trail and Lower Norumbega Trail may be combined for a pleasant loop hike. About 150 yd. beyond the summit, Norumbega Mtn. Trail offers excellent views.

NORUMBEGA MTN. TRAIL (NPS; MAP 5: E5 AND F5)

NPS rating: moderate; cumulative from gate on Hadlock Pond Rd. (189 ft.) to:	⇅	↗	○
Start of Norumbega Mtn. Trail (189 ft.)	0.3 mi.	0 ft.	0:10
Golf Course Trail (550 ft.)	0.8 mi.	360 ft.	0:35
Norumbega Mtn. summit (852 ft.)	1.6 mi.	665 ft.	1:20

Norumbega Mtn. Trail climbs the peak from the south at Lower Hadlock Pond. To reach the start, from the jct. of ME 233 and ME 3/198, drive south for 3.8 mi. Just past Brown Mtn. Gatehouse on the left, arrive at Hadlock Pond Rd. on the right. Turn left here. Park at several turnouts to either side of the road over the first 0.2 mi. from ME 3/198. No parking is allowed beyond the gate.

From the gate, walk along Hadlock Pond Rd., paralleling the pond (public water supply, no swimming). Bear right off the road at a fork, then soon pass a cul-de-sac. At 0.2 mi. from the gate, bear right to a jct. Here, Reservoir Trail leaves to the left, while Hadlock Ponds Trail goes straight ahead. Follow Hadlock Ponds Trail across the dam and spillway and past the pumphouse. There is a nice view here north to Parkman Mtn., Bald Peak, Gilmore Peak, Sargent Mtn., and Cedar Swamp Mtn. At 0.3 mi., reach a jct. on the shore of the pond. Here, Hadlock Ponds Trail leads straight ahead, while Norumbega Mtn. Trail begins to the left.

Norumbega Mtn. Trail climbs moderately through spruce woods, then more steeply on rocks and roots. At 0.8 mi., Golf Course Trail from the Northeast Harbor Golf Club enters from the left. At 1.0 mi., reach the high ridgeline of the mountain amid a fragrant forest of pines. Southwest Harbor and the nearby islands, Western Mtn., Somes Sound, Flying Mtn.,

SEC 10

and St. Sauveur Mtn. fill the view. Continue easily on the ridge for about a half-mile to a point just south of the summit where there are nearly 360-degree views. Meet Goat Trail at 1.6 mi. from the start.

LOWER NORUMBEGA TRAIL (NPS; MAP 5: E5 AND F5)

NPS rating: moderate; cumulative from Goat Trail (300 ft.) to:	⇅	↗	○
Hadlock Ponds Trail (250 ft.)	0.9 mi.	25 ft.	0:30
Norumbega Mtn. Trail at Lower Hadlock Pond (189 ft.)	1.4 mi.	25 ft.	0:40

This trail connects Goat Trail, just west of the Norumbega Mtn. parking area, to Hadlock Ponds Trail near the north shore of Lower Hadlock Pond. From the Goat Trail jct., 25 ft. into the woods from the Norumbega Mtn. parking area on ME 3/198, proceed south on Lower Norumbega Trail. The trail contours across the lower east face of the mountain. Soon after passing an old trail on the left (sign: "village"), begin a rising traverse on rough, rooty trail. Cross several streamlets before meeting Hadlock Ponds Trail at 0.9 mi. To the left, Hadlock Ponds Trail leads 0.3 mi. to ME 3/198 at the south end of Lower Hadlock Pond; to the right, Hadlock Ponds Trail continues around the pretty west side of Lower Hadlock Pond to the jct. with Norumbega Mtn. Trail in another 0.5 mi.

GOLF COURSE TRAIL (NHVIS; MAP 5: F5)

Cumulative from Northeast Harbor Golf Club parking lot (90 ft.) to:	⇅	↗	○
Norumbega Mtn. Trail (570 ft.)	0.7 mi.	480 ft.	0:35
Norumbega Mtn. summit (852 ft.) via Norumbega Mtn. Trail	1.5 mi.	760 ft.	1:10

This trail climbs to the south ridge of Norumbega Mtn. from Northeast Harbor Golf Club. The Northeast Harbor Village Improvement Society maintains the lower half of the trail. From the jct. of ME 3/198 and ME 233 near the head of Somes Sound, drive south on ME 3/198 for 1.2 mi. Turn right on Sargent Dr. and travel another 2.8 mi. to Northeast Harbor Golf Club on the left. Drive past the clubhouse and park in the lot beyond. The trail begins at the far end of the lot (sign: Golf Club Trail, to Tennis Club). In 250 ft., reach a confusing jct. Golf Club Trail continues straight ahead, but to climb Norumbega Mtn., turn left here. Follow easily along to the left of the fairway and green on the second hole. At 0.25 mi., cut across the cart path, then go right and up. Pass an NPS boundary marker. Small cairns have marked the path to this point, but now blue blazes lead the way. A moderate but steady ascent leads to the ledges above. Wind up through the rocks and

ledges to join Norumbega Mtn. Trail on the ridge crest at 0.7 mi. Turn left
to continue to the top of Norumbega Mtn. in another 0.8 mi.

LAND & GARDEN PRESERVE

■ ELIOT MTN. (456 FT.)

This wooded peak is named for Charles W. Eliot; along with George B.
Dorr, he is considered one of the founding fathers of ANP. Eliot Mtn.
Trail, Charles Savage Trail, and Asticou Ridge Trail all reach the wooded
summit. The trails on Eliot Mtn. are some of the oldest on Mt. Desert
Island, so please be aware that trail signage, where it is present, often does
not correspond with maps or guides. (*Note:* As of late 2017, LGP was working to install new, updated trail signs throughout the preserve.)

ELIOT MTN. TRAIL (LGP; MAP 5: F5)
From ME 3 (90 ft.) to:

	⇅	↗	○
Eliot Mtn. summit (456 ft.)	0.9 mi.	370 ft.	0:40

This trail climbs Eliot Mtn. via the south ridge. It begins on the north side
of ME 3 in Northeast Harbor, 1.3 mi. east of the jct. of ME 3 and ME 198.
Parking is along the road shoulder. The rooty trail soon skirts a wetlands,
then makes a gradual ascent, passing through a grove of mature spruce. At
0.6 mi., reach a jct. with the Richard Trail, which leads left (west) 0.2 mi. to
the parking lot for Thuya Garden and Thuya Lodge; to the right, the Richard Trail leads to Charles Savage Trail and Harbor Brook Trail. As Eliot
Mtn. Trail continues straight ahead, the angle steepens. Ledges lead into the
semi-open and a large cairn at the Eliot Monument. The angle eases ahead,
and Eliot Mtn. Trail soon reaches a small opening on the summit at 0.9 mi.
and a jct. of trails. Here, Asticou Ridge Trail departs north, while Charles
Savage Trail enters from the right (east) and continues to the left (west).

HARBOR BROOK TRAIL (LGP; MAP 5: F5)
Cumulative from ME 3
(30 ft.) to:

	⇅	↗	○
Richard Trail (50 ft.)	1.0 mi.	20 ft.	0:30
Asticou & Jordan Pond Path (110 ft.)	2.0 mi.	80 ft.	1:00

This trail follows pretty Little Harbor Brook for most of its length. It
begins from a gravel parking area on the north side of ME 3, 1.5 mi. east
of the jct. of ME 3 and ME 198. Enter the woods in the right rear corner
of the parking area. The trail quickly joins the west bank of Little Harbor
Brook and heads north. In the first 0.25 mi., the trail crosses and then
recrosses the brook on sturdy footbridges, then closely follows the brook to

the intersection with the Richard Trail at 0.95 mi. Beyond, Harbor Brook Trail remains close to the brook. At 1.8 mi., at a bend in the brook to the east, the path leaves the brook and ends at Asticou & Jordan Pond Path at 2.0 mi. To the right, Asticou & Jordan Pond Path leads 1.0 mi. to Jordan Pond House; to the left, the path leads 1.1 mi. to the Asticou Map House.

CHARLES SAVAGE TRAIL (LGP; MAP 5: F5)

Cumulative from the Richard Trail (270 ft.) to:	⇅	↗	○
Eliot Mtn. summit (456 ft.)	0.3 mi.	190 ft.	0:15
Map House Trail (250 ft.)	0.7 mi.	190 ft.	0:35

This trail is named for Charles Savage, who designed both Thuya Garden and Asticou Azalea Garden. The path extends from the Richard Trail over Eliot Mtn. to Map House Trail. From the jct. of the Richard Trail and Harbor Brook Trail, head west upslope on the Richard Trail for 0.2 mi. to a fork. Here, the Richard Trail continues left, while Charles Savage Trail diverges right.

On Charles Savage Trail, climb up past low, mossy ledges. The angle soon eases on the ridge above. At 0.3 mi., reach a jct. in a small clearing on top of Eliot Mtn. Here, Asticou Ridge Trail (sign: to Jordan Pond Trail) enters from the north, while Eliot Mtn. Trail (sign: to Little Harbor Brook) enters from the left (south). Continue straight ahead (west) on Charles Savage Trail (sign: Map House). A short distance ahead, the trail makes a sharp left (sign for Asticou and Map House). Switchback down the west slope of Eliot Mtn., contour for stretch, then angle down to a jct., where a foot trail enters from the right (north). Walk 50 ft. to the left (west) to a gravel path, Map House Trail, at 0.7 mi. The Map House is a short distance right; to the left it is 0.4 mi. to Thuya Garden and Thuya Lodge.

THE RICHARD TRAIL (LGP; MAP 5: F5–F6)

From Thuya Garden and Thuya Lodge parking lot (190 ft.) to:	⇅	↗	○
Trail's end, at carriage road between mileposts 32 and 33 (150 ft.)	1.2 mi.	150 ft.	0:40

This trail is named for Richard Rockefeller, son of David Rockefeller; Richard died in a plane crash in New York in June 2014. The Richard Trail leaves from the visitor parking lot at Thuya Garden. To reach the trailhead, from the jct. of ME 3 and ME 198 in Northeast Harbor, drive east on ME 3 for 0.8 mi. to Thuya Drive on the left. The 0.3-mi. drive ends at a cul-de-sac parking lot at Thuya Garden and Thuya Lodge.

From the parking lot, walk back along the drive 150 ft. to the start of the trail on the left. In 300 ft., a trail leaves left to the gardens; stay straight.

Climb easily over ledges to the next jct., where an unmarked trail enters from the right. At 0.2 mi., the Richard Trail crosses Eliot Mtn. Trail. Continue ahead up a series of steps, over a rise, and then on a contour around the south ridge of Eliot Mtn. Pass blocky, mossy ledge faces en route to the jct. with Charles Savage Trail at 0.5 mi. Here, bear right and down to Harbor Brook Trail at 0.75 mi. Cross Little Harbor Brook on a footbridge, then swing north up the valley. Climb a pretty staircase up along a mossy cliff face, and above, at 1.0 mi., make a sharp right turn, then hike easily east to a carriage road at 1.2 mi. where the trail ends. (*Note:* As of late 2017, plans were in the works to extend the Richard Trail eastward to the David & Neva Trail, near Little Long Pond.) To the right, it is 1.0 mi. to ME 3 via the carriage road; to the left, the carriage road leads about 1 mi. to Asticou & Jordan Pond Path.

ASTICOU RIDGE TRAIL (LGP; MAP 5: F5)

From Eliot Mtn. summit (456 ft.) to:	⇅	↗	⟳
Asticou & Jordan Pond Path (350 ft.)	0.8 mi.	-100 ft.	0:25

Asticou Ridge Trail begins on the summit of Eliot Mtn., at the jct. with Eliot Mtn. Trail and Charles Savage Trail. Head north on the ridge (sign: to Jordan Pond Trail), descend gradually, then follow a rolling stretch to a col. An open ledge on the right has views east. After a level stretch, the trail drops moderately off the north ridge, passes an ANP boundary marker, and soon reaches its end at the jct. of Asticou & Jordan Pond Path. Here, it is 1.5 mi. east to Jordan Pond House or 0.6 mi. west to the Asticou Map House.

WESTERN MT. DESERT ISLAND

■ ACADIA MTN. (681 FT.)

This mountain provides dramatic views of Somes Sound and the Cranberry Isles from its open summit ledges interspersed with pitch pines and scrub oaks. Combine Acadia Mtn. Trail and the Man O' War Brook fire road for a loop hike.

SEC 10

ACADIA MTN. TRAIL (NPS; ST. SAUVEUR MTN., P. 459)

NPS rating: strenuous; cumulative from ME 102 (150 ft.) to:	⇅	↗	⟳
Acadia Mtn. summit (681 ft.)	0.8 mi.	530 ft.	0:40
Man O' War Brook fire road (100 ft.)	1.5 mi.	530 ft.	1:00
ME 102 (100 ft.) via Man O' War Brook fire road and Acadia Mtn. Trail	2.4 mi.	530 ft.	1:25

Parking for this trail is at the Acadia Mtn. parking area (toilet) on the west side of ME 102, 3.5 mi. south of Somesville and 3.0 mi. north of Southwest Harbor.

The trail begins on the opposite side of ME 102. Reach a fork at 0.1 mi. and turn left (the right fork heads to St. Sauveur Mtn.). The trail descends gradually to cross Man O' War Brook Rd., then climbs the west slope of the mountain, soon leaving the woods and reaching open ledges with frequent views. The trail passes over the true summit and reaches the open ledges on the east summit, with views of Somes Sound. It then descends southeast and south very steeply to cross Man O' War Brook. Here, a spur leads left to the shore of the sound. Man O' War Brook Rd. is at a jct. about 50 yd ahead.

To return to ME 102 via the Man O' War Brook fire road, go right (west) at the jct. (To continue toward St. Sauveur Mtn., proceed straight to quickly reach the jct. of Valley Cove Trail and Valley Peak Trail). Follow the fire road west over gradual grades for 0.8 mi. to intersect Acadia Mtn. Trail. Turn left here, and at the next jct., turn right to return to the parking area on ME 102.

■ ST. SAUVEUR MTN. (690 FT.)

This mountain overlooking Valley Cove on Somes Sound can be climbed from ME 102 in the west or from Fernald Cove Rd. in the south. The 500-ft. Eagle Cliff, home to nesting peregrine falcons, forms the precipitous east face of the peak.

ST. SAUVEUR MTN. TRAIL (NPS; ST. SAUVEUR MTN., P. 459)

NPS rating: moderate;

cumulative from ME 102 (150 ft.) to:	⇅	↗	⟳
Start of trail (250 ft.) via Acadia Mtn. Trail	0.1 mi.	100 ft.	0:05
Ledge Trail jct. (650 ft.)	0.9 mi.	500 ft.	0:40
St. Sauveur Mtn. summit (690 ft.)	1.1 mi.	540 ft.	0:50
Spur to Valley Peak Trail (650 ft.)	1.2 mi.	540 ft.	0:55
Valley Peak Trail (500 ft.)	1.5 mi.	540 ft.	1:05
Valley Cove fire road (50 ft.) via Valley Peak Trail	1.9 mi.	540 ft.	1:25
Flying Mtn. trailhead at Fernald Point Rd. (50 ft.)	2.0 mi.	540 ft.	1:30

This trail offers an easy route to the summit of St. Sauveur Mtn. from the northwest. Parking for this trail is the same as for Acadia Mtn. Trail.

Start 0.1 mi. up Acadia Mtn. Trail and go right at the fork. St. Sauveur Mtn. Trail runs south through a softwood forest and over open slopes, rising continually to a jct. at 0.9 mi., where Ledge Trail enters on the right. The summit of St. Sauveur Mtn. is at 1.1 mi. St. Sauveur Mtn. Trail

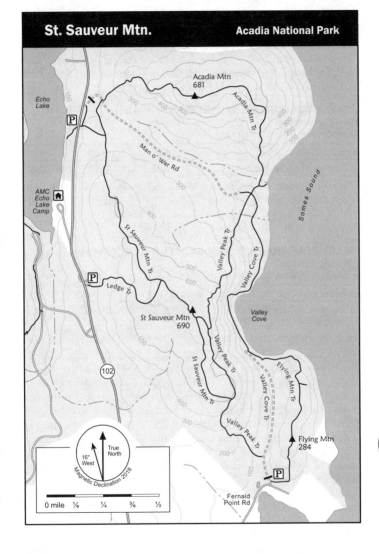

St. Sauveur Mtn.

Acadia National Park

Echo Lake

Acadia Mtn
681

Acadia Mtn Tr

P

Man o' War Rd

Somes Sound

AMC
Echo
Lake
Camp

St Sauveur Mtn Tr

Valley Peak Tr

Valley Cove Tr

P

Ledge Tr

St Sauveur Mtn
690

Valley
Cove

St Sauveur Mtn Tr

Valley Peak Tr

Valley Cove Tr

Flying Mtn Tr

102

Valley Peak Tr

Flying Mtn
284

16°
West

True
North

Magnetic Declination 2018

0 mile   ⅛   ¼   ⅜   ½

Fernald
Point Rd

P

SEC
10

continues past the summit to a jct. Here, a spur to Valley Peak Trail leaves left, while St. Sauveur Mtn. Trail continues right, descending the south ridge of the mountain. At 1.5 mi., the trail ends at its jct. with the lower end of Valley Peak Trail. Ahead, it is 0.4 mi. to the Valley Cove fire road via Valley Peak Trail. At the fire road, turn right to reach the Flying Mtn. trailhead parking lot at Fernald Point Rd.

LEDGE TRAIL (NPS; ST. SAUVEUR MTN., P. 459)

NPS rating: moderate; cumulative from ME 102 (200 ft.) to:	�	↗	↻
St. Sauveur Trail jct. (650 ft.)	0.6 mi.	450 ft.	0:30
St. Sauveur Mtn. summit (690 ft.)	0.8 mi.	490 ft.	0:40

This trail begins at the St. Sauveur Mtn. parking area on ME 102, 0.6 mi. south of the Acadia Mtn. trailhead. Ledge Trail enters the woods and rises quickly over ledges to the jct. with St. Sauveur Trail, 0.3 mi. northwest of the summit of St. Sauveur Mtn.

VALLEY PEAK TRAIL (NPS; ST. SAUVEUR MTN., P. 459)

NPS rating: strenuous; cumulative from Valley Cove fire road (50 ft.) to:	↷↺	↗	↻
St. Sauveur Trail (500 ft.)	0.4 mi.	450 ft.	0:25
St. Sauveur Mtn. summit (690 ft.) via spur trail	0.8 mi.	640 ft.	0:45
Acadia Mtn. Trail and Valley Cove Trail jct. (100 ft.)	1.5 mi.	640 ft.	1:10

This trail leaves the west side of the Valley Cove fire road (no vehicle access) a short distance north of the Flying Mtn. trailhead parking area on Fernald Point Rd. The trail rises steeply northwest through shady woods over Valley Peak (the south shoulder of St. Sauveur Mtn.). At 0.4 mi., St. Sauveur Trail departs left. Stay right on Valley Peak Trail to skirt the top of Eagle Cliff, with outstanding views of Valley Cove below and the mountains east of Somes Sound. At 0.8 mi., a spur path on the left leads to the summit of St. Sauveur Mtn. Valley Peak Trail continues straight, steeply descending the northeast shoulder of the mountain to end at a jct. with Acadia Mtn. Trail and Valley Cove Trail near Man O' War Brook and the east end of the Man O' War fire road at 1.5 mi.

■ FLYING MTN. (284 FT.)

A short climb to the open summit of Flying Mtn. offers a fine panorama of Somes Sound, Southwest Harbor, and the islands to the south, including the Cranberry Isles and Greening, Sutton, Baker, and Bear islands.

FLYING MTN. TRAIL (NPS; ST. SAUVEUR MTN., P. 459)

NPS rating: moderate; cumulative from Fernald Point Rd. parking area (50 ft.) to:	↑↓	↗	↻
Flying Mtn. summit (284 ft.)	0.3 mi.	234 ft.	0:15
Jct. of Valley Cove Trail and fire road (sea level)	0.9 mi.	234 ft.	0:25
Complete loop via Valley Cove fire road	1.4 mi.	234 ft.	0:45

From the jct. of ME 102 and ME 3/198 in Somesville, drive south on ME 102 for 5.4 mi. to Fernald Point Rd. in Southwest Harbor. Turn left (west) on Fernald Point Rd. and drive 0.9 mi. to the trailhead parking lot on the left. This scenic trail leaves the parking area on Fernald Point Rd. in Southwest Harbor. The trail rises quickly through spruce woods, reaching the summit of Flying Mtn. in 0.3 mi. It then follows the long and pleasant ridgeline of the mountain north before descending to the shore of Valley Cove on Somes Sound. The trail follows the cove to the left to end at the jct. of Valley Cove Trail and the Valley Cove fire road at 0.9 mi. For an easy return to the parking area, follow the fire road south for 0.5 mi.

VALLEY COVE TRAIL (NPS; ST. SAUVEUR MTN., P. 459)

NPS rating: strenuous; cumulative from Fernald Point Rd. parking area (50 ft.) to:	↑↓	↗	↻
Start of Valley Cove Trail (sea level) via Valley Cove fire road	0.5 mi.	-50 ft.	0:15
Jct. of Acadia Mtn. Trail and Valley Peak Trail (100 ft.)	1.6 mi.	150 ft.	0:50

Valley Cove Trail starts on the shore of Somes Sound at Valley Cove at the end of the Valley Cove fire road, 0.5 mi. from the Flying Mtn. trailhead parking area on Fernald Point Rd. From the fire road, Valley Cove Trail leads left, while Flying Mtn. Trail goes right. Valley Cove Trail follows the shoreline under the ledge walls of Eagle Cliff high above, traversing a rugged rock slide via a long series of rock staircases. The trail ends at the jct. of Acadia Mtn. Trail and Valley Peak Trail in 1.1 mi., a short distance south of the Man O' War Brook fire road.

SEC 10

■ BEECH MTN. (841 FT.)

This mountain rises steeply between Echo Lake and Long Pond. Its summit, adorned by the only fire tower on Mt. Desert Island, can be reached either from the Beech Mtn. parking area, at the end of Beech Hill Rd. in the notch between Beech Cliff and Beech Mtn., from Echo Lake, or from the pumping station area at the south end of Long Pond. The iron tower

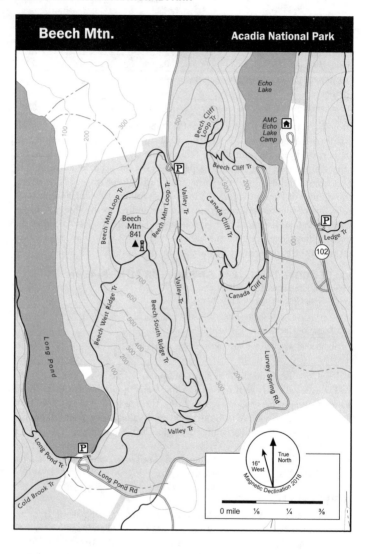

SEC
10

was erected in 1962, replacing the original wooden structure. The tower is often open to visitors on summer weekends.

Beech Cliff and Canada Cliff, on the east side of the mountain overlooking Echo Lake, can be reached by short trails from the Beech Mtn. parking area or from the Echo Lake parking area (follow a short access road from ME 102 north of Southwest Harbor). To reach the pumping station at the south end of Long Pond, follow Seal Cove Rd. west from its jct. with ME 198 in Southwest Harbor. At 0.6 mi., turn right onto Long Pond Rd., and follow the road to its end at the pumping station at 1.8 mi. Parking is limited.

BEECH CLIFF TRAIL (NPS; BEECH MTN., P. 462)

NPS rating: ladder;
from Echo Lake parking area (100 ft.) to:

	⇅	↗	⟳
Jct. of Canada Cliff Trail and Beech Cliff Loop Trail (550 ft.)	0.4 mi.	450 ft.	0:30

This trail offers quick but very steep access to Beech Cliff from the Echo Lake parking area at the south end of Echo Lake. From the jct. of ME 102 and ME 3/198 in Somesville, drive south on ME 102 for 4.4 mi. to the Echo Lake entrance to ANP. A large parking lot is 0.4 mi. ahead at the end of this access road.

The trail begins at the north end of the parking lot and immediately passes an NPS cabin. After about 0.1 mi. of moderate hiking through the woods, the trail climbs very steeply for the rest of the way, via a series of stone staircases and iron ladders. It levels off atop Beech Cliff at 0.4 mi., where Canada Cliff Trail leads left. Beech Cliff Trail continues right for about 100 yd. and ends at Beech Cliff Loop Trail. Views of Echo Lake and the mountains to the east are excellent.

CANADA CLIFF TRAIL (NPS; BEECH MTN., P. 462)

NPS rating: moderate;
from Echo Lake parking area (100 ft.) to:

	⇅	↗	⟳
Fork in trail (400 ft.)	0.6 mi.	300 ft.	0:25
Jct. of Beech Cliff Trail and Beech Cliff Loop Trail (550 ft.)	1.0 mi.	450 ft.	0:45
From Echo Lake parking area (100 ft.) to:			
Beech Cliff parking area (500 ft.) via Canada Cliff spur trail and Valley Trail	1.1 mi.	400 ft.	0:50

SEC 10

This trail starts from the south end of the Echo Lake parking area at a set of wooden stairs (diagonally opposite the Island Explorer bus stop). The trail runs on the level through the woods parallel to the access road for

0.2 mi., then climbs steeply via switchbacks and rock steps to a ravine at 0.4 mi. The trail climbs the left side, then crosses to the right side before reaching a fork at 0.6 mi. The left fork leads 0.4 mi. to the Beech Mtn. parking area via a spur of Canada Cliff Trail and then via Valley Trail.

Continuing right, Canada Cliff Trail contours at first, then makes a rising traverse across the east face of the mountain, with occasional viewpoints. At 0.7 mi., reach open ledges and views to Southwest Harbor. Continue north along the ridge with minor ups and downs. After a short scramble, gain the top of the ridge and break into the open with views to the Beech Mtn. fire tower to the west. Arrive at a large ledge overlooking Echo Lake at 1.0 mi. Here, the views of Somes Sound, Sargent Mtn., Acadia Mtn., and St. Sauveur Mtn. are spectacular. The jct. with Beech Cliff Loop Trail is 100 yd. ahead; at that jct., Beech Cliff Loop Trail leaves right. Turn left (west) to reach the Beech Mtn. parking area in 0.1 mi.

BEECH CLIFF LOOP TRAIL (NPS; BEECH MTN., P. 462)

NPS rating: moderate; cumulative from Beech Hill Rd. parking area (500 ft.) to:	⤵	↗	↻
Loop jct. and Beech Cliff Trail (550 ft.)	0.2 mi.	50 ft.	0:10
Complete loop (500 ft.)	0.6 mi.	50 ft.	0:20

The trail climbs easily to the lip of Beech Cliff from the Beech Mtn. parking area at the end of Beech Hill Rd. To reach this trailhead, follow ME 102 south through Somesville and take Pretty Marsh Rd., the first right after the fire station. Follow Pretty Marsh Rd. west for 0.3 mi. to Beech Hill Rd. Turn left on Beech Hill Rd. and follow it to its end at a large trailhead parking lot (toilet), 3.4 mi. from Pretty Marsh Rd.

Beech Cliff Loop Trail starts to the east, entering the woods where Beech Hill Rd. enters the parking lot. In 0.2 mi., Beech Cliff Loop Trail reaches a jct. Here, Canada Cliff Trail leads right to a jct. with Beech Cliff Trail high above Echo Lake. Beech Cliff Loop Trail leads straight or left, depending on which direction this 0.2-mi. section of the loop is walked. The loop follows the spectacular cliff edge for half of its length, with spectacular views to the east over Echo Lake.

BEECH MTN. LOOP TRAIL (NPS; BEECH MTN., P. 462)

NPS rating: moderate; cumulative from Beech Hill Rd. parking area (500 ft.) to:	⤵	↗	↻
Beech Mtn. summit (841 ft.)	0.4 mi.	340 ft.	0:20
Complete loop	1.0 mi.	340 ft.	0:45

This trail leaves the northwest side of the Beech Mtn. parking area to the left of the toilet. The trail forks in 100 yd. Turn left here to hike the loop clockwise. The trail ascends over ledges through semi-open woods to reach a jct. with Beech Mtn. South Ridge Trail immediately below the summit fire tower. Scramble up 20 ft. to the base of the tower for fine views east. From this jct., hike downhill to the right to the jct. with Beech West Ridge Trail, which enters on the left. Continue right on Beech Mtn. Loop Trail, and quickly reach open ledges and extraordinary views over Long Pond to Mansell Mtn. and Bernard Mtn. Descend over ledges, then enter the woods below. Continue to descend moderately, then swing east on a contour to close the loop near the parking area at the end of Beech Hill Rd.

VALLEY TRAIL (NPS; BEECH MTN., P. 462)

NPS rating: moderate; cumulative from parking area at Long Pond pumping station (50 ft.) to:	↥↧	↗	↻
Beech South Ridge Trail (400 ft.)	0.7 mi.	350 ft.	0:30
Canada Cliff Trail (450 ft.)	1.3 mi.	400 ft.	0:50
Beech Hill Rd. parking area (500 ft.)	1.5 mi.	450 ft.	0:55

This trail makes a convenient link between the pumping station at Long Pond and the Beech Hill Rd. parking area, located in the notch between Beech Cliff and Beech Mtn. It also provides direct access to Beech South Ridge Trail, permitting a circuit or one-way trip over Beech Mtn.

Valley Trail starts from the south side of the parking area (away from the pond) at the south end of Long Pond. The trail enters the woods, heading south and then east to cross a service road at a road jct. Beyond, the trail trends easily over the lower slopes before climbing via a series of switchbacks on the south ridge of Beech Mtn. At 0.7 mi., Beech South Ridge Trail leaves left. Continuing east, Valley Trail soon swings north to make a pleasant rising traverse up the valley separating Beech Mtn. and Canada Cliff. At 1.3 mi., a spur from Canada Cliff Trail enters from the right. Continue directly ahead to reach the parking area at the end of Beech Hill Rd. at 1.5 mi.

SEC 10

BEECH SOUTH RIDGE TRAIL (NPS; BEECH MTN., P. 462)

NPS rating: moderate; cumulative from Long Pond parking area (50 ft.) to:	↥↧	↗	↻
Start of trail (400 ft.) via Valley Trail	0.7 mi.	350 ft.	0:30
Beech Mtn. summit (841 ft.)	1.5 mi.	790 ft.	1:10

This well-marked trail diverges left from Valley Trail at a point 0.7 mi. east of the pumping station parking area at the south end of Long Pond. Beech

South Ridge Trail steadily ascends the south ridge to the summit over a series of semi-open ledges that offer views to the south. The trail ends adjacent to the Beech Mtn. fire tower at the jct. with Beech Mtn. Loop Trail.

BEECH WEST RIDGE TRAIL (NPS; BEECH MTN., P. 462)

NPS rating: moderate; cumulative from Long Pond parking area (50 ft.) to:	↰↱	↗	↻
Beech Mtn. Loop Trail jct. (750 ft.)	0.9 mi.	700 ft.	0:50
Beech Mtn. summit (841 ft.) via Beech Mtn. Loop Trail	1.0 mi.	790 ft.	0:55

Beech West Ridge Trail starts from the east side of parking area (away from the pumping station) at the south end of Long Pond. The trail enters the woods to follow the shore of Long Pond and soon crosses a service road. In 0.3 mi., the trail leaves the pond and climbs by easy grades for a short distance, then climbs steeply up the west ridge. Ledges en route offer good views over Long Pond to Mansell Mtn. At 0.9 mi., the trail reaches Beech Mtn. Loop Trail, which leads right 0.1 mi. to the summit of Beech Mtn. and its fire tower.

■ WESTERN MTN.—BERNARD MTN. (1,010 FT.) AND MANSELL MTN. (938 FT.)

Western Mtn. comprises two main peaks: Bernard Mtn. to the west and Mansell Mtn. to the east. Both summits are mostly wooded, but there are occasional view windows. Trails in this area start from three primary trailheads: at the pumping station at the south end of Long Pond, at Mill Field, and at Gilley Field.

To reach the pumping station, follow Seal Cove Rd. west from ME 102 in Southwest Harbor. At 0.6 mi., take the first right (toward the landfill) onto Long Pond Rd. and follow it until it ends at the pumping station at 1.8 mi. *To reach Mill Field and Gilley Field,* follow Seal Cove Rd. west from ME 102 in Southwest Harbor. The pavement ends at the ANP boundary at 3.9 mi. Take a right off Seal Cove Rd at 4.6 mi. (no sign). Reset odometer. On the dirt access road, reach the jct. with Western Mtn. Rd. at 0.4 mi. (To the left, it is 1.2 mi. to the West Ledge Trail trailhead.) Turn right on Western Mtn. Rd. and follow it to the next jct. at 1.2 mi. To reach Mill Field, turn left here and drive 0.2 mi. to the end of the road and the trailhead parking area for Sluiceway Trail and Bernard Mtn. Trail. To reach Gilley Field, turn right here and drive 0.1 mi. to the end of the road and the trailhead parking area for Gilley Trail, Mansell Mtn. Trail, and Cold Brook Trail.

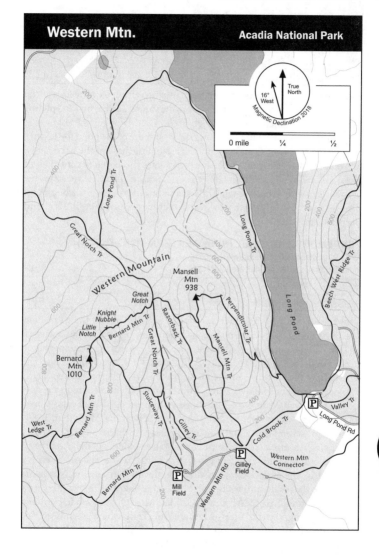

Western Mtn.   Acadia National Park

True North

16° West

Magnetic Declination 2018

0 mile   ¼   ½

Long Pond Tr

Great Notch Tr

Western Mountain

Great Notch

Knight Nubble

Little Notch

Bernard Mtn Tr

Great Notch Tr

Razorback Tr

Mansell Mtn 938

Perpendicular Tr

Long Pond Tr

Long Pond

Beech West Ridge Tr

Bernard Mtn 1010

Mansell Mtn Tr

West Ledge Tr

Bernard Mtn Tr

Sluiceway Tr

Gilley Tr

Cold Brook Tr

Valley Tr

Long Pond Rd

Western Mtn Connector

Mill Field

Western Mtn Rd

Gilley Field

SEC 10

LONG POND TRAIL (NPS; WESTERN MTN., P. 467)

NPS rating: easy; cumulative from Long Pond pumping station parking area (50 ft.) to:	⇅	↗	◔
Perpendicular Trail (50 ft.)	0.2 mi.	0 ft.	0:05
Great Notch Trail (500 ft.)	2.9 mi.	450 ft.	1:40

This pleasant footpath starts from the pumping station parking area at the south end of Long Pond. The trail enters the woods just beyond the pumping station and quickly reaches a jct. Here, Cold Brook Trail leaves left. Long Pond Trail continues to follows the west shore of the pond for 1.5 mi., then bears west away from it to contour around the base of the north slope of Mansell Mtn. Turning south, the trail passes through a beautiful birch forest and follows Great Brook for a short distance. The trail then continues to a jct. with Great Notch Trail at a point 1.1 mi. east of Long Pond Fire Rd. and 0.4 mi. north of Great Notch between Mansell Mtn. and Bernard Mtn.

PERPENDICULAR TRAIL (NPS; WESTERN MTN., P. 467)

NPS rating: strenuous; cumulative from Long Pond pumping station parking area (50 ft.) to:	⇅	↗	◔
Start of trail (50 ft.) via Long Pond Trail	0.2 mi.	0 ft.	0:05
Mansell Mtn. summit (938 ft.)	1.2 mi.	890 ft.	1:10

This trail ascends Mansell Mtn. from Long Pond Trail on the west shore of Long Pond. Drive to the pumping station parking area at the south end of Long Pond. From the left (west) side of the pumping station, follow Long Pond Trail. In 250 ft., pass Cold Brook Trail, which departs to the left. Follow the shoreline of the pond to the start of Perpendicular Trail. Perpendicular Trail follows a steep course on excellent terrain up the east slope of Mansell Mtn., switchbacking up the scree fields and talus slopes on what some hikers refer to as the "stairway to heaven." More than 1,000 stone steps, several iron rungs, and one iron ladder mark the route. After a long, rising traverse beneath a cliff face, climb a bouldery defile. At 1.0 mi., reach an outlook with excellent views over Long Pond to the fire tower on Beech Mtn., the bulk of Sargent Mtn., Southwest Harbor, and Northeast Harbor. A short side trail leads 200 ft. to a large ledge overlook with views to Somes Sound, Sargent Mtn., and Cadillac Mtn. On the wooded summit (sign) at 1.2 mi., the trail meets Mansell Mtn. Trail, which ascends 0.9 mi. from Gilley Field. Just ahead on Mansell Mtn. Trail, a side trail leads right to an outlook with views west to Blue Hill and Bartlett Island.

MANSELL MTN. TRAIL (NPS; WESTERN MTN., P. 467)

NPS rating: moderate; cumulative from Gilley Field (150 ft.) to:	⬆⬇	↗	⟳
Razorback Trail (850 ft.)	0.8 mi.	700 ft.	0:45
Mansell Mtn. summit (938 ft.)	1.0 mi.	800 ft.	0:55

This trail leaves from Gilley Field and offers a nice hike up the south slope of Mansell Mtn. The trail climbs gradually from the trailhead to ledges, where there are views of Southwest Harbor, Beech Mtn., Long Pond, and Northeast Harbor. At 0.8 mi., a short but steep 0.1-mi. spur from Razorback Trail enters from the left. From this jct., Mansell Mtn. Trail climbs the final 0.1 mi. to the wooded summit of Mansell Mtn. to meet Perpendicular Trail.

COLD BROOK TRAIL (NPS; WESTERN MTN., P. 467)

NPS rating: easy; from Long Pond pumping station parking area (150 ft.) to:	⬆⬇	↗	⟳
Gilley Field (150 ft.)	0.4 mi.	-100 ft.	0:15

This pretty woods walk on a wide track is an important link between the pumping station parking area at the south end of Long Pond and Gilley Field. The trail is a natural start or finish to a loop hike over Mansell Mtn. and Bernard Mtn.

GILLEY TRAIL (NPS; WESTERN MTN., P. 467)

NPS rating: easy; cumulative from Gilley Field parking area (150 ft.) to:	⬆⬇	↗	⟳
Razorback Trail (200 ft.)	0.1 mi.	50 ft.	0:05
Jct. of Great Notch Trail and Sluiceway Trail (350 ft.)	0.6 mi.	200 ft.	0:20

This trail starts at the Gilley Field parking area at the eastern end of Western Mtn. Rd. It provides access to Mansell Mtn. and Bernard Mtn. via Razorback Trail, Great Notch Trail, and Sluiceway Trail. Gilley Trail starts next to Mansell Mtn. Trail, but instead of climbing the peak, it follows easy grades to the west, passing Razorback Trail in 0.1 mi., then turning north and climbing moderately to its end at the jct. of Great Notch Trail and Sluiceway Trail at 0.6 mi. A short side trail halfway along on the left leads 100 yd. to the Reservoir, a small dammed pond in a scenic glen at the end of a short spur off Western Mtn. Rd.

SEC 10

RAZORBACK TRAIL (NPS; WESTERN MTN., P. 467)

NPS rating: strenuous; from Gilley Field (150 ft.) to:	⇅	↗	⏱
Start of Razorback Trail (200 ft.) via Gilley Trail	0.1 mi.	50 ft.	0:05
from Gilley Field (150 ft.) to:			
Mansell Mtn. summit (938 ft.) via spur and Mansell Mtn. Trail	1.0 mi.	790 ft.	1:10
from Gilley Field (150 ft.) to:			
Great Notch summit (650 ft.) via Great Notch Trail	1.0 mi.	790 ft.	0:55

Razorback Trail diverges right from Gilley Trail at a point 0.1 mi. from the Gilley Field parking area at the east end of Western Mtn. Rd. This trail climbs moderately up the west side of Mansell Mtn., offering views of Great Notch and Bernard Mtn. The upper portion of Razorback Trail climbs a narrow ridge of extensive open ledges (the Razorback) to reach a jct. between the summit of Mansell Mtn. and Great Notch at 0.8 mi. To the right, a spur climbs steeply 0.1 mi. to Mansell Mtn. Trail, which climbs an additional 0.1 mi. to the top of Mansell Mtn. Continue left on Razorback Trail, which leads down to Great Notch and the jct. with Great Notch Trail in 0.2 mi.

SLUICEWAY TRAIL (NPS; WESTERN MTN., P. 467)

NPS rating: strenuous; cumulative from Mill Field parking area (150 ft.) to:	⇅	↗	⏱
Great Notch Trail (350 ft.)	0.4 mi.	200 ft.	0:25
Bernard Mtn. Trail (850 ft.) in Little Notch	0.9 mi.	700 ft.	0:50
Bernard Mtn. summit (1,010 ft.) via Bernard Mtn. Trail	1.1 mi.	860 ft.	1:00

Starting from Mill Field, this trail runs north 0.4 mi. to a jct. with a connector trail that leads a short distance east to the jct. of Great Notch Trail and Gilley Trail. At this jct., Sluiceway Trail swings northwest and climbs rather steeply up a narrow valley to a jct. with Bernard Mtn. Trail in Little Notch at 0.9 mi. To reach the summit of Bernard Mtn., follow Bernard Mtn. Trail left (south) for 0.2 mi.

BERNARD MTN. TRAIL (NPS; WESTERN MTN., P. 467)

NPS rating: strenuous; cumulative from Mill Field parking area (150 ft.) to:	⇅	↗	⏱
West Ledge Trail (900 ft.)	1.0 mi.	50 ft.	0:55
Bernard Mtn. summit (1,010 ft.)	1.5 mi.	860 ft.	1:10
Great Notch (650 ft.)	2.2 mi.	1,000 ft.	1:40

This trail also starts at Mill Field on Western Mtn. Rd. It makes a wide and gradual arc west to the south ridge of Bernard Mtn., then swings north to West Ledge Trail at 1.0 mi. Here, Bernard Mtn. Trail turns right, ascending easily north over several wooded knobs to the summit of Bernard Mtn. at 1.5 mi. Iron posts mark an old fire tower site; just ahead is the summit sign. A short distance beyond, reach an overlook to the left and a register box. Ahead, the trail descends steeply to Little Notch and the jct. with Sluiceway Trail at 1.7 mi. Beyond the jct., Bernard Mtn. Trail continues east, climbing over the low but rugged Knight Nubble (nice view to Southwest Harbor and the islands to the south) before dropping into a wet and mossy notch. Climbing out, the trail then drops steeply into Great Notch at 2.2 mi., where there is a bench and a register box. Here, Great Notch Trail leads north to Long Pond Fire Rd. and south toward Gilley Field, while Razorback Trail leads east to Mansell Mtn. in 0.6 mi.

WEST LEDGE TRAIL (NPS; USGS BARTLETT ISLAND AND SOUTHWEST HARBOR QUADS)

NPS rating: strenuous; from Western Mtn. Rd. (150 ft.) to:	⇅	↗	↺
Bernard Mtn. Trail (800 ft.)	1.1 mi.	650 ft.	0:50

This trail connects the western end of Western Mtn. Rd. to the system of trails on Bernard Mtn. and Mansell Mtn. The views to the west over Seal Cove Pond to Blue Hill Bay and the islands south and west of Mt. Desert Island are spectacular. From the east, at ME 102 in Southwest Harbor, drive west on Seal Cove Rd. for 3.3 mi. (pavement ends at 1.3 mi.). Reset odometer. Turn right (north) on Western Mtn. Rd. Pass Bald Mtn. Rd. on the left at 0.3 mi. At 0.7 mi., Western Mtn. Rd. forks. Take the left fork and proceed to the trailhead at 1.0 mi. There is limited parking on the left. If the few spaces are full, drive an additional 0.3 mi. to the boat launch parking area on Seal Cove Pond.

The trail climbs moderately at first, reaching open ledges very quickly. Beyond, it begins a steady, steep climb over open granite slabs and ledges. From here, the views stretch from Bass Harbor to the Camden Hills. The angle moderates halfway along the ridge, and the trail drops into a shallow ravine, then ascends via steep, rocky terrain. Beyond, it crosses an open slope, then climbs steeply again. From this point on, the trail makes several forays into the woods and then back out into the open on its ascent to the jct. with Bernard Mtn. Trail, which enters from the right at 1.0 mi. From here, Bernard Mtn. Trail climbs easily to the top of the mountain in another 0.5 mi.

SEC
10

GREAT NOTCH TRAIL (NPS; WESTERN MTN., P. 467)

NPS rating: moderate;
cumulative from Long Pond Fire Rd. (150 ft.) to:

	⇅	↗	↻
Long Pond Trail jct. (500 ft.)	1.1 mi.	350 ft.	0:45
Great Notch (650 ft.)	1.5 mi.	500 ft.	1:00
Gilley Trail (350 ft.)	1.9 mi.	500 ft.	1:15
Gilley Field parking area (150 ft.) via Gilley Trail	2.5 mi.	500 ft.	1:30

This wooded trail is the only path providing access to Western Mtn. from the northwest. The trailhead is located on Long Pond Fire Rd., about 0.1 mi. beyond the Pine Hill turnaround and parking area, at a point 1.0 mi. east of its jct. with ME 102 (this jct. is about 1.1 mi. south of the jct. with the road to the Pretty Marsh picnic area).

The trail trends east and rises by easy grades to a jct. with Long Pond Trail, which enters from the left at 1.1 mi. Beyond, Great Notch Trail climbs to Great Notch at 1.5 mi., where Bernard Mtn. Trail leads right toward Bernard Mtn., and Razorback Trail leads left toward Mansell Mtn. Great Notch Trail continues through Great Notch and then on a rough footway of rocks and roots down to Gilley Trail at 1.9 mi., where Great Notch Trail ends. Here, a connector trail leads right (west) a short distance to Sluiceway Trail. Follow Gilley Trail for another 0.6 mi. to the Gilley Field parking area.

SCHOODIC PENINSULA

■ SCHOODIC HEAD (442 FT.)

This prominent hilltop, the highest point on Schoodic Peninsula, provides excellent vistas east over Schoodic Harbor along the Downeast coast to Petit Manan Point and the lighthouse there, north to Winter Harbor and the mountains around Donnell Pond, and west over Frenchman Bay to the mountains on Mt. Desert Island. There are five trails on Schoodic Head: Anvil Trail, Alder Trail, Schoodic Head Trail, East Trail, and Buck Cove Mtn. Trail. A narrow gravel road ascends nearly to the top of Schoodic Head from the west; it leaves the Schoodic Loop Rd. in the area of West Pond.

Schoodic Peninsula

Acadia National Park

186

Winter Harbor

Winter Harbor

Birch Harbor

Birch Harbor

Birch Harbor

Birch Harbor Mtn Path

Birch Harbor Mtn

Lower Harbor Tr

Schoodic Woods

100

300

Frazer Point

Buck Cove Mtn Tr

Bunkers Harbor Path

Frazer Creek Path

Wonsqueak Path

Mtn Brook Path

Bunker Harbor

One-Way

200

Ned Island

Mark Island

Buck Cove Mtn Tr

Buck Cove Mtn

Schoodic Harbor

200

One-Way

East Tr

Schoodic Head

100

Schoodic Head Tr

Anvil Tr

— Hiking trail
-- Bike path

Alder Tr

The Anvil

P

Big Moose Island

P

Little Moose Island

Schoodic Island

True North

16° West

Magnetic Declination 2018

0 mile   ½   1

SEC 10

ANVIL TRAIL (NPS; SCHOODIC PENINSULA, P. 473)

NPS rating: moderate; cumulative from Blueberry Hill Picnic Area (25 ft.) on Schoodic Loop Rd. to:	↔	↗	⟳
The Anvil (190 ft.)	0.3 mi.	165 ft.	0:15
Schoodic Head summit (442 ft.) via Schoodic Head Trail	1.2 mi.	480 ft.	0:45
Buck Cove Mtn. Trail (440 ft.) via Schoodic Head Trail	1.3 mi.	480 ft.	0:50

This trail climbs Schoodic Head via the Anvil, a craggy ledge reached early in the hike. From the Schoodic Woods CG entrance road, drive south on Schoodic Loop Rd. for 4.2 mi. to Blueberry Hill Picnic Area on the right. The small lot provides trailhead parking for both Anvil Trail and Alder Trail. If this lot is full, there is a pullout on the right side of Schoodic Loop Rd. 500 ft. ahead.

From Blueberry Hill Picnic Area, walk right along Schoodic Loop Rd. for 600 ft. to the start of Anvil Trail on the left. Climb a rocky defile to reach the open ledges of the Anvil at 0.3 mi. Just ahead, a short trail leads 100 ft. west to a nice lookout to Schoodic Point and beyond to the peaks on Mt. Desert Island. Ahead on the main trail, descend through rocks and on ladder steps. At the base of the descent on the right is the sharp prow of the Anvil. At 0.5 mi., cross semi-open ledges. At 0.75 mi., the trail swings east along the base of Schoodic Head and soon climbs a short, steep pitch via log and rock steps. Moderate switchbacks ahead lead to semi-open ledges above and the jct. with Schoodic Head Trail, which enters from the left.

From this point, it is 0.1 mi. to the right to the top of Schoodic Head via Schoodic Head Trail. En route, a side path on the left leads 100 yd. to a parking loop at the end of the gravel summit road. East Trail enters from the right a short distance beyond. Pass a small communications tower, then reach the summit of Schoodic Head. The best views are just north at the unsigned jct. with Buck Cove Mtn. Trail.

SEC 10

ALDER TRAIL AND SCHOODIC HEAD TRAIL (NPS; SCHOODIC PENINSULA, P. 473)

NPS rating: easy to moderate; cumulative from Blueberry Hill Picnic Area (25 ft.) on Schoodic Loop Rd. to:	↔	↗	⟳
Schoodic Head Trail (50 ft.) via Alder Trail and gravel road	0.7 mi.	75 ft.	0:20
Anvil Trail (425 ft.)	1.2 mi.	425 ft.	1:00
Schoodic Head summit (442 ft.)	1.3 mi.	450 ft.	1:05
Buck Cove Mtn. Trail (440 ft.)	1.4 mi.	450 ft.	1:10

Combine Alder Trail and Schoodic Head Trail for a pleasant hike to the top of Schoodic Head. Add Anvil Trail to the mix for a nice loop hike. Alder Trail departs just across Schoodic Loop Rd. from Blueberry Hill Picnic Area.

Take the wide, grassy, mostly level path through alders and other shrubby growth to a gravel road at 0.6 mi. Go straight here on the gravel road (sign for Schoodic Head Trail). In another 0.1 mi., Schoodic Head Trail leaves the gravel road on the right and climbs at a moderate grade through spruce woods. Old metal bluebird markers still mark this longtime path. Ahead, the trail becomes steeper, climbing granite staircases and wooden steps to a granite outcrop and cairn. A short trail leads left to ledges and a viewpoint. Continuing on, cross a small stream in a wet area on bog bridges. After climbing a wooden ladder, reach sloping ledges and then the jct. with Anvil Trail on the right. From this point, it is 0.1 mi. to the left to the top of Schoodic Head. En route, a side path on the left leads 100 yd. to a parking loop at the end of the gravel summit road. East Trail enters from the right a short distance beyond. Pass a small communications tower, then reach the summit of Schoodic Head. The best views are just north at the unsigned jct. with Buck Cove Mtn. Trail.

EAST TRAIL (NPS; SCHOODIC PENINSULA, P. 473)

NPS rating: moderate; cumulative from parking turnout on Schoodic Loop Rd. (50 ft.) to:	↕	↗	⟳
Schoodic Head Trail (440 ft.)	0.4 mi.	400 ft.	0:25
Schoodic Head summit (442 ft.) via Schoodic Head Trail	0.5 mi.	400 ft.	0:30
Buck Cove Mtn. Trail (440 ft.) via Schoodic Head Trail	0.5 mi.	400 ft.	0:35

This short but steep trail scrambles up the rocky east face of Schoodic Head. From Blueberry Hill Picnic Area, drive north on Schoodic Loop Rd. for 1.0 mi. to a turnout on the right. Park here. East Trail enters the woods immediately across the road, climbing rocky outcrops. Beyond, the trail ascends gently across ledges to reach a small ravine. Cross the ravine and bear left. Beyond, climb steeply via switchbacks, much of the way on small, loose rocks. The angle eases at ledges with views south and east. Moderate climbing over ledges then leads to the jct. with Schoodic Head Trail. From this point, it is a short distance to the right to the top of Schoodic Head via Schoodic Head Trail.

SEC 10

■ BUCK COVE MTN. (225 FT.)

This low, mostly wooded peak rises to the north of Schoodic Head and just west of Schoodic Harbor. It can be reached from either Schoodic Head or Schoodic Woods CG. A popular way to make a long day hike via Buck Cove Mtn. is to leave a car at Schoodic Woods (at the information center or the trailhead parking lot 0.5 mi. beyond) and either drive a second car to Blueberry Hill Picnic Area or, in season, ride the Island Explorer bus. Then hike Anvil Trail or Alder Trail northbound to join Buck Cove Mtn. Trail near the summit of Schoodic Head. Buck Cove Mtn. Trail is therefore described from Schoodic Head north.

BUCK COVE MTN. TRAIL (NPS; SCHOODIC PENINSULA, P. 473)

NPS rating: moderate; cumulative from Schoodic Head (440 ft.) to:	↕	↗	↺
Buck Cove Mtn. (225 ft.)	1.0 mi.	65 ft.	0:30
Schoodic Woods trailhead parking (230 ft.)	3.2 mi.	380 ft.	1:45

From its start, just north of the summit of Schoodic Head, follow Buck Cove Mtn. Trail down the north slope of Schoodic Head. In 0.5 mi., pass through the old (pre-2015) NPS boundary. Ahead, view windows open up to the east. Cross an old skidder trail and make a long, rising traverse to the semi-open woods on top of Buck Cove Mtn. (no sign in 2017). Beyond, switchback down to cross a marshy flow on bog bridges, then cross a bike path (Schoodic Woods CG is 1.8 mi. west on the bike path). A gentle climb leads to a ridgeline of semi-open woods with nice views south to Schoodic Head and east to Pigeon Hill. Descending the north side of the unnamed knoll, the trail reaches another bike path. Turn left to follow the bike path for a short distance, then take the trail left into the woods. Soon, Buck Cove Mtn. Trail again crosses a bike path (a sign indicates that Schoodic Woods CG is 1.0 mi. west on this bike path), rounds the east side of a hill, then climbs northwest up a narrow valley. Pass next to a cliff wall to reach easy terrain on the south slope of Birch Harbor Mtn. Cross a bike path, crest the wooded high point on Birch Harbor Mtn., and soon recross the bike path. Reach the trailhead parking area at 3.2 mi. from Schoodic Head. The area is at a cul-de-sac 0.5 mi. via road or paved walkway from the Schoodic Woods CG information center, just beyond the group campsites.

SEC 10

ISLE AU HAUT

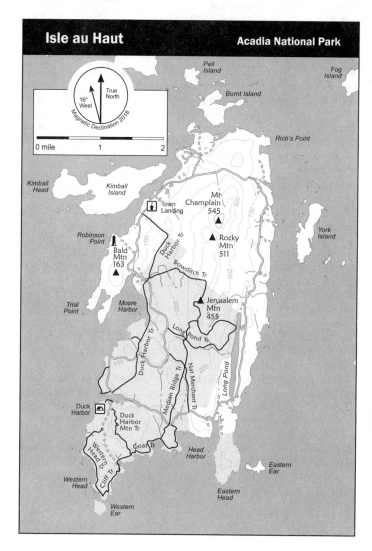

DUCK HARBOR TRAIL (NPS; ISLE AU HAUT, P. 477)

NPS rating: moderate; cumulative from
park ranger station (50 ft.) near town landing to:

	⤒⤓	⟋	⟳
Bowditch Trail (80 ft.)	1.3 mi.	160 ft.	0:45
Duck Harbor and main dirt road (35 ft.)	3.5 mi.	435 ft.	2:00
Duck Harbor CG (5 ft.)	4.2 mi.	435 ft.	2:20

This major north-south connector trail provides access to Duck Harbor
CG and the system of trails on the southern end of Isle au Haut, plus
Bowditch Trail along the way. Duck Harbor Trail begins at the park ranger
station on the northwest side of the island, 0.25 mi. south of the Isle au
Haut town landing via a paved portion of the island's main ring road.
Information, a posted map, potable water, and a toilet are available at the
ranger station.

The trail leaves the ranger station and heads east through the woods for
0.5 mi., then trends southwest over several minor rocky humps. At 1.0 mi.,
turn left at a trail sign. Beyond, cross a brook on a footbridge, then quickly
reach the jct. with Bowditch Trail, which leaves to the left. Bear right to
continue on Duck Harbor Trail. At 1.4 mi., cross the dirt main road. After
crossing a small brook, reach Moore Harbor and follow it closely for the
next 0.3 mi. Ahead, leave the cobble beach, cross a small brook, and pass
an NPS ranger cabin in the woods uphill on the left. Follow the boardwalk
to the right, then trend away from the shoreline and enter thick young
spruce. At 2.5 mi., a short side trail leaves right to Deep Cove; stay straight.
Beyond the Deep Cove side trail, cross a brook, then climb a rise and cross
the main dirt road again. Level off and follow the ridgeline, then scamper
over a rocky knoll. At 3.5 mi., Duck Harbor Trail ends at the main dirt
road on the north side of Duck Harbor.

To reach Duck Harbor CG, continue left (east) on the road for 0.5 mi.
to Western Head Rd. Turn right on Western Head Rd. and follow it for
another 0.25 mi., passing a hand-operated water pump (the water source
for the campground), to a kiosk and toilet. Here, Western Head Rd. bears
uphill to the left (leads to Duck Harbor Mtn. Trail and Western Head
Trail and, at the road's end, to Cliff Trail and Goat Trail). Continue along
the shore to the picnic tables and a kiosk adjacent to the Duck Harbor boat
landing. The five shelters of Duck Harbor CG are just uphill from the
water, each tucked into a mostly secluded spot.

WESTERN HEAD TRAIL (NPS; ISLE AU HAUT, P. 477)

NPS rating: moderate; cumulative from Western Head Rd. at Duck Harbor CG (20 ft.) to: ⇅	↗	⟳
Start of Western Head Trail (80 ft.)	0.5 mi.	60 ft.	0:15
Cliff Trail (35 ft.)	1.9 mi.	175 ft.	1:05

This trail follows the western shore of Western Head and offers spectacular cliff-top views of Isle au Haut Bay, the Gulf of Maine, and Western Ear. Combined with Cliff Trail and Western Head Rd., the trail makes a nice loop around Western Head.

From the kiosk and toilet near the end of the walk into Duck Harbor CG, turn uphill on Western Head Rd., a wide, grassy track. After a shed on the right, bear left at a fork. In 0.1 mi., Duck Harbor Mtn. Trail departs left. At 0.45 mi., Western Head Trail leaves to the right. At 0.8 mi., the trail reaches the western shore of Isle au Haut and turns south along the Gulf of Maine. The view west takes in Vinalhaven and the Camden Hills. Reach a cobble beach and follow it for a stretch as Western Head Trail continues along the coast, ascending and descending between rocky headlands and cobble beaches for most of the next mile. The trail eventually jogs inland, crosses a shallow ravine, passes by low cliff walls with views offshore to Western Ear, and then negotiates a dark, mossy wet area. At 1.9 mi., Western Head Trail ends at the jct. with Cliff Trail and a 0.1-mi. spur out to the gut (channel) separating the main island from Western Ear. From this jct., it is 0.7 mi. north to Western Head Rd., which leads 1.1 mi. back to Duck Harbor CG.

CLIFF TRAIL (NPS; ISLE AU HAUT, P. 477)

NPS rating: moderate; cumulative from Western Head Trail (35 ft.) to: ⇅	↗	⟳
Western Head Rd. (45 ft.)	0.7 mi.	125 ft.	0:25
Goat Trail (45 ft.)	0.8 mi.	125 ft.	0:30

Cliff Trail connects the southern end of Western Head Trail with Western Head Rd. and Goat Trail. From its jct. with Western Head Trail near Western Ear, Cliff Trail heads north through the woods to emerge on a pocket beach. Leave the beach and pass by a cliff wall. Ahead, climb over a low ridge to a rocky beach. Eastern Head is in view to the east. Hike along the margin of the shore, alternating between the woods and the rocks. Cross a gully and make a short, steep climb out. With white cliffs in view ahead, cross another gully, then ascend a steep and rocky section. Descend wooden steps into yet another gully. At 0.7 mi., reach Western

SEC 10

Head Rd. Turn left here, and in another 0.1 mi., reach the jct. with Goat Trail, which leaves right. Straight ahead on Western Head Rd., it is 1.0 mi. to Duck Harbor CG.

GOAT TRAIL (NPS; ISLE AU HAUT, P. 477)

NPS rating: moderate;
from Western Head Rd. (45 ft.) to:

	⇅	↗	↺
Main dirt road near Median Ridge Trail intersection (45 ft.)	2.0 mi.	200 ft.	2:05

Goat Trail connects Western Head Rd. and Cliff Trail with Median Ridge Trail and the main dirt road that rings Isle au Haut. The trail closely follows the craggy shoreline and offers stunning views of Deep Cove, Squeaker Cove, Barred Harbor, Merchant Cove, Head Harbor, and Eastern Head. From Western Head Trail, Goat Trail soon crosses a small brook, then reaches Squeaker Cove and a jct. at 0.3 mi. To the right, a spur leads to a cobble beach. Duck Harbor Mtn. Trail departs to the left. Continuing straight, Goat Trail makes a short climb, drops down to a small brook, then crosses exposed headland. At 0.7 mi., the trail swings inland through a swath of dead and dying spruce and fir, then through a thick understory of young spruce. The big arc of cobble beach at Barred Harbor is reached at 1.0 mi., and just ahead at 1.2 mi., Median Ridge Trail leaves left from the head of the large cove. Goat Trail crosses Merchant Point ahead to reach the head of Merchant Cove at 1.7 mi. At 1.9 mi., a trail sign reads "Merchant Cove." Head inland from this point, cross bog bridges, and reach the main/paved dirt road at 2.0 mi. Turn left and walk the road west for 200 ft. to intersect Median Ridge Trail. From this point, it is 1.1 mi. west via the dirt road to Duck Harbor CG.

MEDIAN RIDGE TRAIL (NPS; ISLE AU HAUT, P. 477)

NPS rating: moderate;
cumulative from Goat Trail (10 ft.) to:

	⇅	↗	↺
Main dirt road (45 ft.)	0.3 mi.	35 ft.	0:10
Long Pond Trail (200 ft.)	1.8 mi.	250 ft.	1:00

Median Ridge Trail connects Goat Trail near Merchant Cove to Long Pond Trail at a point just south of Bowditch Mtn. Median Ridge Trail departs Goat Trail, and in 0.3 mi., crosses the main dirt road. From here, the trail climbs up to a rocky ridge. Ahead, it contours along the east side of the ridge through a semi-open forest of pines. After a short pitch down, the trail continues to contour across the slope, with a rocky knob up to the left. Cross a small stream, the source of Merchant Brook, at 1.2 mi. At

1.3 mi., reach a four-way intersection with Nat Merchant Trail, which goes east and west from this point. Continuing on Median Ridge Trail, gain a ridge at 1.6 mi., then trend easily down, passing a natural rock seat and a view ahead to Bowditch Mtn. Make a moderate descent into a ravine and, immediately after a small stream, turn sharply right to reach the jct. with Long Pond Trail. From this jct., Long Pond Trail makes a loop over Bowditch Mtn., drops down to Long Pond, climbs back to this jct., and heads east to end at the main dirt road, 2.5 mi. south of the Isle au Haut town landing.

NAT MERCHANT TRAIL (NPS; ISLE AU HAUT, P. 477)

NPS rating: moderate; cumulative from main dirt road (205 ft.) to:	↻↑	↗	○
Median Ridge Trail (185 ft.)	0.4 mi.	25 ft.	0:10
Main dirt road (55 ft.)	1.1 mi.	25 ft.	0:35

Nat Merchant Trail cuts across the island from its start on the island's main dirt road 2.9 mi. south of the Isle au Haut town landing, intersects Median Ridge Trail, and ends at the main dirt road 1.2 mi. east of the Western Head Rd. entrance to Duck Harbor CG. From its start, the trail makes a gentle climb to a ridge, then heads along it before trending down to intersect Median Ridge Trail at 0.35 mi. Ahead on Nat Merchant Trail, follow contours through a dark stretch of thick young spruce. Beyond, the trail makes its way down the valley of Merchant Brook, then levels out to cross a wet area. At 1.1 mi., Nat Merchant Trail emerges on the main dirt road. Hikers can hear the ocean at Merchant Cove from this point.

■ BOWDITCH MTN. (425 FT.)

This wooded peak rises roughly in the center of Isle au Haut, just south of Jerusalem Mtn. Long Pond Trail and Bowditch Trail are ascent routes.

LONG POND TRAIL (NPS; ISLE AU HAUT, P. 477)

NPS rating: strenuous; cumulative from main dirt road (140 ft.) to:	↻↑	↗	○
Jct. of Median Ridge Trail and Long Pond Trail (200 ft.)	0.4 mi.	60 ft.	0:15
Bowditch Mtn. high point (400 ft.)	0.9 mi.	260 ft.	0:35
Long Pond (16 ft.)	1.9 mi.	300 ft.	1:10
Complete loop	3.5 mi.	560 ft.	2:05

While Long Pond Trail is relatively easy at the start, the change of elevation is more pronounced on the loop. Despite the strenuous climb of Bowditch Mtn., this trail offers wonderful views of Long Pond, the largest pond on Isle au Haut, as well as access to Bowditch Trail and Median Ridge Trail. Long Pond Trail begins from the main dirt road, 2.5 mi. south of the Isle au Haut town landing. It heads east along the north edge of a cedar swamp and reaches the jct. with Median Ridge Trail (departs to the right) at 0.4 mi.

Turn left to follow the lollipop loop of Long Pond Trail in a clockwise direction. Ascend through a parklike forest of birch and spruce. At 0.9 mi., high on Bowditch Mtn., reach the jct. with Bowditch Trail, which enters from the left. Stay right to remain on Long Pond Trail. The trail drops down the east slope, then levels off and crosses to the next ridge. After a short descent, it follows the long ridge on a contour through semi-open forest. A rocky, washboard stretch of trail leads to a footbridge over a chasm at 1.7 mi. Beyond, descend more steeply via switchbacks to reach the shore of long, narrow, and deep Long Pond at 1.9 mi. After heading south 100 ft. next to the pond, the trail climbs up and away. Cross a rocky ravine at 2.2 mi. Stone walls appear along the trail at 2.4 mi. At a trail sign, old foundation stones and a well are 75 ft. to the left. In the woods at 2.7 mi., cross a boulder field of cobble-sized rocks. Ahead, pass to the right of a bog, and after an easy stretch, make a short, moderate descent to the Long Pond Trail loop jct. at 3.1 mi. From this point, it is 0.4 mi. west to the main dirt road, the original trailhead.

BOWDITCH TRAIL (NPS; ISLE AU HAUT, P. 477)

NPS rating: moderate; from Duck Harbor Trail (80 ft.) to:	⮃	⬈	↻
Long Pond Trail on Bowditch Mtn. (400 ft.)	2.0 mi.	440 ft.	1:30

This trail connects Duck Harbor Trail and Long Pond Trail on Bowditch Mtn. Bowditch Trail diverges from Duck Harbor Trail just 300 ft. east of the main dirt road at a point 1.35 mi. south of the ANP ranger station. Bowditch Trail heads east, skirts a bog to the right, and crosses a marshy area on bog bridges. After a corridor of young spruce, the trail follows more bog bridges, then ascends the west slope of Jerusalem Mtn. At 1.0 mi., it passes a park boundary post. At a high point on the mountain, the old Bowditch Trail goes left into the bushes. The current Bowditch Trail passes another park boundary post at 1.2 mi. Continuing now to the south, it follows the ridgeline, skirts the true summit of Bowditch Mtn., and ends at the intersection with Long Pond Trail.

■ DUCK HARBOR MTN. (309 FT.)

The long, steep, and craggy ridgeline of Duck Harbor Mtn., which links Duck Harbor CG with Goat Trail at Squeaker Cove, presents the most strenuous challenge of any of the locations on Isle au Haut. Duck Harbor Mtn. Trail can be combined with Western Head Rd. for a scenic loop hike, among several other possible combinations.

DUCK HARBOR MTN. TRAIL (NPS; ISLE AU HAUT, P. 477)

NPS rating: strenuous; cumulative from Western Head Rd. at Duck Harbor CG (20 ft.) to:	↧↥	↗	↻
Duck Harbor Mtn. summit (309 ft.)	0.5 mi.	300 ft.	0:25
Goat Trail (15 ft.)	1.2 mi.	400 ft.	0:50

From the kiosk and toilet near the end of the walk into Duck Harbor CG, turn uphill on Western Head Rd., a wide, grassy track. After a shed on the right, bear left at a fork. In 0.1 mi., Duck Harbor Mtn. Trail departs left. Climb steeply over rocks to an outlook to Duck Harbor. At 0.2 mi., reach a rocky knob and more views. After a brief level stretch, climb a second steep pitch, then scramble over more rocky knobs. At 0.4 mi., reach the top of Duck Harbor Mtn. The trail continues east along the spine of the mountain, descends a difficult rock step, climbs down another rock step, then passes through a rock crevice. Ahead, a short pitch leads up to the first of a series of rocky knobs known as the Puddings. After several tricky rock steps, a spur on the right leads to a pinnacle and excellent views east to Eastern Head. Continue down the rocky ridge to meet Goat Trail at Squeaker Cove at 1.1 mi. To the left, Goat Trail wends north 1.7 mi. to Median Ridge Trail and the main dirt road. To the right, Goat Trail joins Western Head Rd. near Cliff Trail in 0.3 mi.

SEC 10

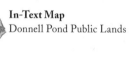

SECTION 11
DOWNEAST

SEC
11

INTRODUCTION

This section, on Maine's Downeast region, includes all of Hancock County, except for Mt. Desert Island and ANP, and all of neighboring Washington County in eastern Maine, a total land area of a little more than 4,000 sq mi. The region extends from the Penobscot River and Penobscot Bay in the west to Chiputneticook Lake, the St. Croix River, and Passamaquoddy Bay (on the New Brunswick, Canada, border) in the east. To the north, the Hancock and Washington county lines meet with the Aroostook and Penobscot county lines in a generally southwest-northeast direction.

The name "Downeast" broadly refers to the Maine coast from Penobscot Bay to the Canadian border and originated in the early sailing days of New England, when ships from Boston sailed east to ports in Maine. With the prevailing winds at their sterns during this leg of the journey, the ships were sailing downwind, hence they were said to be heading "down east." Thanks to its geography, the Downeast region has the honor of seeing first sunrise in the country at West Quoddy Head for a few weeks around the autumn and spring equinoxes.

This section describes 62 trails on 39 mountains. The southern part of the region encompasses the rugged, rocky coastline on the Gulf of Maine and many islands large and small, as well as scattered low craggy hills, wooded bumps, and steep headlands. Amid the extensive wild blueberry barrens that range across the central interior are several jumbles of rugged mountains with peaks reaching to elevations a little higher than 1,000 ft. The northern interior is the lowland home to many large lakes and miles of streams. A number of major rivers have their sources in the here and flow south to meet the Atlantic Ocean. Isolated hills with sweeping southern cliff faces dot the landscape, with the occasional mountain. One lone summit tops out at more than 1,400 ft.

GEOGRAPHY

South of US 1, between Penobscot Bay and Campobello Island in New Brunswick, the Downeast coastline is characterized by a number of wide forested headlands or peninsulas interspersed with a series of large bays and a handful of large spruce-studded islands. East of Penobscot Bay is the Blue Hill Peninsula and Deer Isle, Blue Hill Bay, and Frenchman Bay. At Cape Rosier, Backwoods Mtn. (275 ft.) rises out of the woods near Holbrook Island. Peeking up west of Orcutt Harbor is John B. Mtn. (255 ft.). Low but rugged Pine Hill (150 ft.) looks out over the northern tip of Little Deer Isle just south of Eggemoggin Reach. Blue Hill Mtn. (934 ft.) affords fine views over the village of Blue Hill to its namesake bay.

Beyond Schoodic Peninsula are Gouldsboro Bay and Dyer Neck, then Dyer Bay and Petit Manan Point, followed by Pigeon Hill Bay. North of Sullivan Harbor are Tucker Mtn. (410 ft.) and Baker Hill (381 ft.). The craggy dome of Pigeon Hill (317 ft.) offers a commanding view over Petite Manan National Wildlife Refuge. Narraguagus and Pleasant bays are south of Milbridge, Harrington, and Addison. Jonesport and Beals separate Wohoa and Chandler bays. Englishman Bay is south of Roque Bluffs. Machias Bay is the last great bay before the Bold Coast, a rugged stretch of precipitous headland leading to West Quoddy Head and its lighthouse at Lubec, the easternmost point in the United States. In isolated Lubec, Benny's Mtn. (218 ft.) overlooks Hamilton Cove, and Klondike Mtn. (150 ft.) rises next to South Bay.

The Downeast interior between the Penobscot River and Passamaquoddy Bay is bounded by US 1 in the south and ME 9 in the north. East of Verona Island from Bucksport to ME 193, the blueberry barrens harbor several substantial freshwater lakes and ponds, as well as a jumble of low hills and mountains. Significant here is the 4,500-acre Great Pond Mtn. Wildlands, home to Great Pond Mtn. (1,038 ft.) and its massive south-facing cliffs, Mead Mtn. (660 ft.), Flying Moose Mtn. (910 ft.), Oak Hill (829 ft.), and Flag Hill (946 ft.). Just north is Bald Mtn. (1,261 ft.) in Dedham, its slopes a former ski area. South of ME 9, Blackcap Mtn. (1,018 ft.) and Woodchuck Hill (815 ft.) share a trailhead at Fitts Pond. Eagle Bluff (900 ft.) is a local crag popular with both hikers and rock climbers.

Donnell Pond Public Lands is situated between Franklin and Cherryfield; at more than 15,000 acres, it is the second-largest chunk of publicly owned land in the Downeast region. Trails climb to a small cluster of bare granite summits, including Schoodic Mtn. (1,069 ft.), Black Mtn. (1,094 ft.), Caribou Mtn. (960 ft.), and Tunk Mtn. (1,157 ft.). Donnell Pond, Tunk Lake, and the Hidden Ponds are at the feet of these rugged peaks. Farther Downeast, close to Calais, is the federally owned Moosehorn National Wildlife Refuge, the largest public reserve in the Downeast region, with 29,000 acres of unique wildlife habitat and designated wilderness. Trails lead to the site of an old fire tower atop Bald Mtn. (410 ft.) and to Magurrewock Mtn. (384 ft.), overlooking Magurrewock Marsh. Just east of Moosehorn, Devil's Head (340 ft.) rises precipitously from the banks of the St. Croix River. At Cobscook Bay State Park, tremendous ocean tides range from 12 to 26 feet, some of the greatest in the world. Good lookout points here include Littles Mtn. (210 ft.) and Cunningham Mtn. (150 ft.). Neighboring Bell Mtn. (213 ft.) and Crane Mtn. (269 ft.) loom over Tide Mill Farm on Whiting Bay.

SEC 11

The northern reaches of the Downeast region, from ME 9 north to ME 6 and east to US 1, are dominated by vast swaths of commercial timberland and a string of large lakes. Four major rivers—Machias, Union, Narraguagus, and Pleasant—flow from these woods. Near Bangor, views of ANP abound from the great cliffs of Chick Hill (1,152 ft.) and Little Chick Hill (890 ft.). Bald Bluff Mtn. (1,011 ft.) is the high point in the Amherst Mountains Community Forest. The summits of Lead Mtn. (1,475 ft.), Peaked Mtn. (938 ft.), and Pocomoonshine Mtn. (610 ft.) are all former fire tower sites. Wabassus Mtn. (844 ft.) is a wooded peak just east of Grand Lake Stream. The long ridgeline of Passadumkeag Mtn. (1,463 ft.) in Grand Falls Township, also a former fire tower site, is now home to a windpower project.

ROAD ACCESS

Two major highways cross the Downeast region from west to east. US 1 winds along the coast to connect Bucksport with Calais, providing access to trails along that corridor and to peninsulas to the south. ME 9 slices through the northern interior and links Bangor with Calais, offering access to trails along that corridor and to the north. US 1A is the major route between Bangor and Ellsworth, while ME 3 connects Bucksport to Ellsworth, and ME 46 connects Eddington with Bucksport. A number of trailheads are along these roads. From west to east across Downeast, a number of north-south roads connect ME 9 with US 1. These include ME 180, ME 181, ME 179, ME 193, ME 192, and ME 191. ME 182 links Franklin with Cherryfield. ME 191 and ME 189 both wind eastward to far Downeast trailheads.

CAMPING

Drive-in camping is available at Cobscook Bay and Lamoine state parks. Cobscook has 125 campsites, while Lamoine offers 62; both feature hot showers, restrooms, and picnic facilities. Primitive frontcountry campsites are available in the Machias River Corridor, while backcountry campers will find primitive sites at Donnell Pond and Cutler Coast public reserved lands. Twenty privately operated campgrounds are also available.

SEC 11

GREAT POND MOUNTAIN WILDLANDS

This expansive preserve in Orland is owned by Great Pond Mtn. Conservation Trust and managed for wildlife habitat and low-impact recreation. The Wildlands encompass 4,500 beautiful acres of forests and streams ringed by mountain peaks across two tracts of land.

Miles of old gravel roads wind through the property, remnants of logging in years past, but vehicular access is limited to the southern half of

Valley Rd. and Flag Hill Rd. The Hothole Valley South Gate on US 1/ME 3 is the primary access; it is open from 8:00 A.M. to dusk on weekends only from mid-June through October. Outside of these times, visitors will need to park outside the gate and enter on foot, bicycle, or horseback. Other access points to the Wildlands include Hothole Valley North Gate, Dead River Gate, and Stuart Gross Trailhead (to Great Pond Mtn.).

Complementing the gravel roads is a network of "trails," gravel roads that are closed to vehicles but open to foot travel, bicycles, and horses. A growing system of "paths" for foot travel lead to specific destinations: Great Pond Mtn., which rises to more than 1,000 ft. in the Dead River section, and to Flag Hill, Oak Hill, Flying Moose Mtn., Mead Mtn., and Bump Hill in the Hothole Valley section.

COBSCOOK BAY STATE PARK

This coastal park, which occupies 888 acres on Whiting Bay in Edmunds Township, was carved out of Moosehorn National Wildlife Refuge in 1964 and remains part of the federal refuge by virtue of a long-term, no-cost lease. Tides at Cobscook average 24 ft. and can be as high as 28 ft. when the meteorological conditions are just right. The nutrient-rich waters of the bay support a wide range of sea life and birds, making wildlife watching here a popular activity. In addition, camping, hiking, sea kayaking, and boating are available. Two short hiking trails lead to park high points at Littles Mtn. and Cunningham Mtn.

MOOSEHORN NATIONAL WILDLIFE REFUGE

Moosehorn National Wildlife Refuge is the easternmost such refuge in the United States, part of a vast federal system designed to protect wildlife and its habitats while providing wildlife-related education and recreation opportunities. Established in 1937, the refuge is an important stop for migratory birds on the Atlantic Flyway. MNWR comprises two geographic units: 20,192 acres in Baring Plantation and 8,872 acres in nearby Edmunds. One-third of the refuge is designated wilderness and is part of the National Wilderness Preservation System. Trails lead to Magurrewock Mtn. and Bald Mtn.

SEC 11

DONNELL POND PUBLIC LANDS

This state-owned preserve encompasses 15,479 acres of woods, mountains, lakes, and ponds in Franklin, Sullivan, T9 SD, and T10 SD. Central to the preserve and popular with canoeists, boaters, and campers is the namesake

Donnell Pond and the scenic Schoodic Beach, hemmed in by the walls of Schoodic Mtn. and Black Mtn. To the north of Black Mtn. are the back-country wilds around Rainbow Pond and Caribou Mtn. North of ME 182, the preserve includes many of the north and east shores of pristine Tunk Lake, all of the north and east shores of Spring River Lake, and a number of small remote ponds. Rising high over this northern section is Tunk Mtn. and its great cliffs, as well as several trailless peaks. Donnell Pond PL is home to 20 mi. of hiking trails.

SUGGESTED HIKES
■ Easy
BUMP HILL

LP via Bump Hill Path	0.9 mi.	170 ft.	0:35

This fun loop leads to several rocky lookouts with views to Mead Mtn. and Great Pond Mtn. See Bump Hill Path, p. 496.

BALD MTN. (IN DEDHAM)

RT via Bald Mtn. Trail	1.0 mi.	534 ft.	1:00

Climb over bare granite slabs to ledge outlooks with beautiful views, from Phillips Lake to the mountains of Acadia. See Bald Mtn. Trail, p. 499.

JOHN B. MTN.

LP via John B. Mtn. Trail	1.1 mi.	205 ft.	0:50

Journey through spruce woods to ledges for views over Orcutt Harbor and Eggemoggin Reach. See John B. Mtn. Trail, p. 503.

PINE HILL

RT via Pine Hill Trail	0.2 mi.	50 ft.	0:20

Hike into an old quarry then head to its top for a broad vista of Little Deer Isle, Eggemoggin Reach, Deer Isle, and even the mountains of Acadia. See Pine Hill Trail, p. 504.

EAGLE BLUFF

	⇅	↗	○
RT via Eagle Bluff Trail	1.0 mi.	540 ft.	1:00

From the top of this impressive cliff face, a favorite of local rock climbers, enjoy airy views over Cedar Swamp Pond to Lead Mtn., Chick Hill, and the peaks of Acadia. See Eagle Bluff Trail, p. 508.

SCHOODIC BEACH

	⇅	↗	○
RT via Schoodic Beach Trail	1.0 mi.	100 ft.	0:30

Take a quick walk to a long stretch of sandy beach on the scenic south end of Donnell Pond, where there is swimming and picnicking. See Schoodic Beach Trail, p. 514.

HIDDEN PONDS

	⇅	↗	○
LP via Tunk Mtn. Trail and Hidden Ponds Trail	1.6 mi.	120 ft.	1:00

Hike Tunk Mtn. Trail then make a circuit around two scenic ponds tucked below Tunk Mtn., Salmon Pond and Little Long Pond. See Hidden Ponds Trail, p. 520.

BAKER HILL

	⇅	↗	○
LP via Baker Hill Loop, Boundary Trail, and Cleft Rock Trail	1.2 mi.	0 ft.	0:45

Make a short loop via Baker Hill to ledges with views of Sullivan Harbor, Frenchman Bay, and beyond to the peaks of Acadia. To begin, see Baker Hill Loop, p. 522.

PIGEON HILL

	⇅	↗	○
LP via Historic Trail, Summit Loop Trail, and Silver Mine Trail	1.1 mi.	267 ft.	0:55

SEC
11

The summit ledges of this craggy dome offer extraordinary views over Dyer Bay, Pigeon Hill Bay, and far beyond along this scenic stretch of the Downeast coast. To begin, see Historic Trail, p. 525.

KLONDIKE MTN.

LP via Klondike Mtn. Trail		0.6 mi.	145 ft.	0:25

This little bump in Lubec offers 360-degree views over South Bay and beyond from its bare summit. See Klondike Mtn. Trail, p. 527.

CUNNINGHAM MTN.

LP via Nature Trail		1.4 mi.	60 ft.	0:45

Make a nice circuit through Cobscook Bay State Park to craggy ledges and good views over Broad Cove and Whiting Bay. See Nature Trail, p. 530.

■ **Moderate**
GREAT POND MTN.

RT via Stuart Gross Trail		3.0 mi.	708 ft.	2:20

Climb Great Pond Mtn. Wildlands' namesake mountain to sweeping summit cliffs and broad views that take in Acadia, Blue Hill, Penobscot Bay, and the Camden Hills. See Stuart Gross Trail, p. 494.

BLUE HILL MTN.

LP via Tower Service Trail and Hayes Trail		1.7 mi.	534 ft.	1:40

For extensive views over the village of Blue Hill, the bay beyond, and on to the mountain peaks of Mt. Desert Island, summit this scenic coastal monadnock. To begin, see Tower Service Trail, p. 501.

SCHOODIC MTN.

RT via Schoodic Mtn. Trail		2.6 mi.	819 ft.	2:15

This popular mountain provides good views of Mt. Desert Island and Frenchman Bay, with a pitstop at Donnell Pond's Schoodic Beach. See Schoodic Mtn. Trail, p. 514.

BLACK MTN.

⬤ 🚶 🐕 🍃

	↻↑	↗	⏱
LP via Big Chief Trail, Black Mtn. Summit Trail, and Black Mtn.–Big Chief Connector	2.6 mi.	724 ft.	1:50

Hike to Wizard Pond and on to the pink granite ledges atop Black Mtn. To begin, see Big Chief Trail, p. 516.

TUNK MTN.

⬤ 🚶 🐕 🍃

	↻↑	↗	⏱
RT via Tunk Mtn. Trail	4.1 mi.	850 ft.	3:10

Pass several small ponds en route to the extensive cliffs on Tunk Mtn.'s southwestern ridgeline and nice views over Spring River Lake and Tunk Lake. See Tunk Mtn. Trail, p. 519.

BALD MTN.

⬤ 🚶 🏯

	↻↑	↗	⏱
RT via Headquarters Rd. Trail and Tower Trail	5.4 mi.	200 ft.	3:00

Visit this wooded summit to see the remains of a downed fire tower in the heart of Moosehorn National Wildlife Refuge. To begin, see Headquarters Rd. Trail, p. 532.

■ Strenuous
CARIBOU MTN.

⬤ 🍂 🍃

	↻↑	↗	⏱
LP via Caribou Mtn. Trail and Caribou Loop Trail	7.9 mi.	1,800 ft.	5:05

Tackle this rugged hike through the remote backcountry of Donnell Pond PL, taking in the craggy summit ledges of Caribou Mtn. and Black Mtn. en route. To begin, see Caribou Mtn. Trail, p. 518.

SCHOODIC CONNECTOR

⬤ 🍂

	↻↑	↗	⏱
OW via Schoodic Connector Trail and Schoodic Mtn. Trail	7.8 mi.	1,350 ft.	4:30

SEC 11

This long and interesting trek links five land trust properties with Donnell Pond PL, from the ledges on Baker Hill to the pink granite summit of Schoodic Mtn. To begin, see Schoodic Connector Trail, p. 523.

TRAIL DESCRIPTIONS

GREAT POND MTN. WILDLANDS AND VICINITY

■ GREAT POND MTN. (1,038 FT.)

This mountain, the central natural feature of the Wildlands, is known for the sweeping granite cliffs on its southeast face and for broad views that take in ANP, Blue Hill Mtn., Penobscot Bay, and the Camden Hills.

STUART GROSS TRAIL (GPMCT; USGS ORLAND QUAD, GAZETTEER MAP 23, GPMCT WILDLANDS MAP)

Cumulative from Don Fish Rd. (330 ft.) to:	⇅	↗	⟳
Jct. of Hay Ledges and Dead River Connector trails (480 ft.)	0.3 mi.	150 ft.	0:10
Great Pond Mtn. summit (1,038 ft.)	1.2 mi.	700 ft.	1:00

From US 1/ME 3 in East Orland, 1.5 mi. east of the jct. of ME 15 and US 1/ME 3 in Orland, turn north onto Hatchery Rd. (sign for Craig Brook National Fish Hatchery). At 1.4 mi., pass through the fish hatchery complex. Just beyond, cross a bridge over Craig Brook and turn right, uphill, onto Don Fish Rd. Pass the Dead River Gate on the left and continue to trailhead parking on the right at 2.4 mi. from US 1/ME 3. Stuart Gross Trail starts across the road to the right of the kiosk.

Head up the rock steps and into the woods, bear right, and soon cross a wooden footbridge over a gully. Beyond, climb easily up the slope using switchbacks, pass to the left of several large boulders, then reach a four-way jct. Here, Hay Ledges Trail departs left; Dead River Connector Trail goes straight ahead. To continue to Great Pond Mtn., turn right on Stuart Gross Trail. Ahead on an old jeep road, which is worn down to bare rock, the ascent is easy on the long, gradual west ridge.

View windows begin to open on the right (south) side of the ridge, from the Camden Hills to Blue Hill Mtn. to ANP; Alamoosook Lake lies below. With the summit of Great Pond Mtn. visible ahead, the sidewalk-like trail reenters the woods on the left and continues. After a gullied section, the trail climbs a wide slab past a boulder on the right. With the summit slabs of granite in view ahead, climb a slab, then make a long traverse to the right over sloping slabs—following the blue blazes on the granite. Beyond, the path trends up and left with excellent vistas to the south.

Above, an obscure side trail departs east, trending down and then left to the great cliffs on the south face of the mountain. To reach the true summit, continue left on Stuart Gross Trail and up the wide-open granite slabs. Where the slabs level off, continue ahead and slightly right, down over a rock step and into the woods on the right. Wind around to the right, then bear left (where a muddy track enters from the right). Weave upward through the rocks and ledges. Out into the open again, bear left across a final slab to the wooded summit, marked by a cairn (no sign).

■ MEAD MTN. (660 FT.)

The summit of this mountain is just outside the southwestern boundary of the Hothole Valley section of the Wildlands, but Mead Mtn. Path climbs to ledges high on its eastern flank for a nice view over Hothole Valley to the hills beyond.

MEAD MTN. PATH (GPMCT; USGS ORLAND QUAD, GAZETTEER MAP 23, GPMCT WILDLANDS MAP)

Cumulative from Valley Rd. (150 ft.) to:	⮃	↗	⏱
Start of path (350 ft.) via Mead Mtn. Trail	0.8 mi.	200 ft.	0:25
Path high point (640 ft.)	1.3 mi.	490 ft.	0:50
Mead Mtn. summit ledges (580 ft.)	1.3 mi.	490 ft.	0:55

From Hothole Valley South Gate on US 1/ME 3, travel north on Valley Rd. for 1.3 mi. to Mead Mtn. Trail. on the left. Park on either side of the entrance but please do not block the barrier. Hike Mead Mtn. Trail west, crossing Hopkins Meadow Brook, climbing to a clearing, then bearing right to reach a dead end. The start of Mead Mtn. Path (foot travel only) is on the left. Follow blue diamond markers easily uphill. Ahead, pass three lichen-covered erratics in succession. Beyond, bear right in a small clearing. Cross over a mossy outcrop (cairn) and descend to the right, down a natural rock step, to a viewpoint on the east ledges of the mountain. The view includes Dedham Bald Mtn., Flying Moose Mtn., and Flag and Oak hills. (*Note:* Per GPMCT in late 2017, this trail is being continued as a loop that heads downhill from the outlook through some very rocky terrain, with some rough footing, past the Mitchville Campsite and back to Valley Rd.; look for signs.)

BUMP HILL PATH (GPMCT; USGS ORLAND QUAD, GAZETTEER MAP 23, GPMCT WILDLANDS MAP)

Cumulative from Valley Rd. (150 ft.) to:	⇅	↗	⟳
Start of path (110 ft.) via Hothole Brook Trail	0.6 mi.	-40 ft.	0:15
Bump Hill boulder viewpoints (280 ft.)	0.8 mi.	170 ft.	0:30
Loop jct.	0.9 mi.	170 ft.	0:35

Bump Hill Path offers fine views west to Mead Mtn. and Great Pond Mtn. from three boulder viewpoints that also look out to Flag Hill to the peaks of ANP, and the mountains of Donnell Pond PL.

From Hothole Valley South Gate on US 1/ME 3, travel north on Valley Rd. At 2.3 mi. from the gate, a few yd. down a side drive, there is a toilet and picnic table on the left. At 2.5 mi. from the gate, reach Hothole Brook Trail on the left (kiosk and bench). Turn left here to enter the main parking area for weekend visitors. Please park on the right side of the road.

To access Bump Hill Path, walk west from the parking area through the barrier, following Hothole Brook Trail. Proceed to a bridge over Hothole Brook and on to the end of the road in a large clearing, where there is a nice view of Great Pond Mtn.

Take the wide grassy path on the left. At an old fork, stay right. Pass to the right of a boulder; soon, the path narrows and starts to climb. Reach the loop jct. just ahead. Stay left to hike the loop clockwise. Weave through rocks to a large boulder, then climb on top of it for great views of Mead Mtn. and Great Pond Mtn. From the base of the boulder, continue to the right for a second viewpoint west. Walk through woods to the third boulder and the last view. Continue to the loop jct. and turn left to return to the trailhead.

■ FLYING MOOSE MTN. (910 FT.)

This mountain in the northeast corner of the Wildlands features outstanding views south and west from the sweeping cliffs on its south face. Access the summit via Birches Path, a section of Flying Moose Mtn. Trail, and Flying Moose Mtn. Path.

BIRCHES PATH AND FLYING MOOSE MTN. PATH (GPMCT; USGS ORLAND QUAD, GAZETTEER MAP 23, GPMCT WILDLANDS MAP)

Cumulative from Flag Hill Rd. (650 ft.) to:	⇅	↗	⟳
Flying Moose Mtn. Trail (680 ft.) via Birches Path	0.5 mi.	80 ft.	0:20
Flying Moose Mtn. Path (590 ft.)	0.8 mi.	80 ft.	0:30
Summit cliffs on Flying Moose Mtn. (880 ft.)	1.2 mi.	320 ft.	0:45

From Hothole Valley South Gate on US 1/ME 3, travel north on Valley Rd. for 2.7 mi. to the jct. with Flag Hill Rd. on the right. This point, labeled as the Inner Gate on the Wildlands map (there is no gate, just a barrier), is as far as vehicles may drive north on Valley Rd. Turn right (east) here to continue on Flag Hill Rd. toward the trailhead for Flying Moose Mtn. Drive 0.6 mi. on Flag Hill Rd., passing Hillside Trail on the right halfway along. At the jct. with Flag Hill Trail, continue left on Flag Hill Rd. and proceed to its end, where a barrier marks the start of Mountain View Trail. Park on either side of the barrier. The start of Birches Path is 100 ft. back down Flag Hill Rd. on the east side of the road.

Birches Path heads north on a contour to reach an open slab of mossy granite with nice views west to Great Pond Mtn. Another similar vista is 200 ft. ahead. In 0.5 mi., Birches Path ends at Flying Moose Mtn. Trail. Immediately left at this jct. are two benches a good view west. Turn right at this jct. to continue on Flying Moose Mtn. Trail. Hike over a height-of-land, with Flying Moose Mtn. in view ahead. Just beyond, the trail jogs left and soon reaches a wide road (trail) on the right. This is the unmarked start of Flying Moose Mtn. Path.

Follow the wide path up to an old log yard. Look left for a narrow foot-path (unsigned, but bits of orange flagging marked the start in 2017). Above, climb granite slabs following faded blue blazes on the rock. As the trail gains elevation, big views open up, including the Camden Hills and Blue Hill Mtn. Near the top, the trail bears right to its end at a sweeping cliff face with a panoramic view ranging from the peaks of Donnell Pond PL and Branch Lake to ANP, and closer in, Flag Hill. A sign nearby indicates that this is indeed the end of the trail. Please respect the private property beyond and go no farther.

■ FLAG HILL (946 FT.)

This mountain on the eastern periphery of the Wildlands lies between Oak Hill to the south and Flying Moose Mtn. to the north. Excellent views ranging from ANP to Katahdin are possible from its summit ridge.

FLAG HILL PATH (GPMCT; USGS ORLAND AND BRANCH LAKE QUADS, GAZETTEER MAP 23, GPMCT WILDLANDS MAP)

SEC 11

Cumulative from Flag Hill Rd. (570 ft.) to:

	↥↧	↗	⟳
Oak Hill Path (540 ft.) via Flag Hill Trail	0.4 mi.	-30 ft.	0:10
Flag Hill Path (630 ft.) via Flag Hill Trail	0.8 mi.	60 ft.	0:25
Flag Hill summit (946 ft.) via Flag Hill Path	1.4 mi.	406 ft.	0:55

From Hothole Valley South Gate on US 1/ME 3, travel north on Valley Rd. for 2.7 mi. to the jct. of Flag Hill Rd. on the right. This point, labeled as the Inner Gate on the Wildlands map (there is no gate, just a barrier), is as far as vehicles may drive north on Valley Rd. Turn right (east) here to continue on Flag Hill Rd. Drive 0.6 mi. on Flag Hill Rd to reach the jct. with Flag Hill Trail and parking.

Follow Flag Hill Trail uphill to the jct. with Oak Hill Path on the right. Ahead, Flag Hill Trail narrows and soon reaches the jct. with Flag Hill Path on the left. On Flag Hill Path, climb moderately to the ridge, breaking out onto bare granite slabs with views south to ANP and east to Branch Lake. Follow cairns to the open summit. Just beyond, a short loop trail leads to views north and west all the way to Bigelow, Sugarloaf, and Katahdin.

ESKER PATH (GPMCT; USGS ORLAND AND BRANCH LAKE QUADS, GAZETTEER MAP 23, GPMCT WILDLANDS MAP)

Cumulative from Hothole Valley South Gate (380 ft.) to:	⮁	↗	⏱
Esker Path (390 ft.)	0.1 mi.	10 ft.	0:02
Drumlin Path (400 ft.)	0.8 mi.	25 ft.	0:20
Hillside Trail (330 ft.)	1.2 mi.	25 ft.	0:35

When the South Gate is closed, Esker Path offers a good foot-travel access route into the Wildlands to reach Oak Hill, Flag Hill, Mead Mtn., and more.

From Hothole Valley South Gate on US 1/ME 3, hike north on Valley Rd. for just 0.1 mi. to Esker Path on the right. Leave Valley Rd. and take Esker Path through a cutover area. Cross a wet area on bog bridges, and beyond, follow a small glacial esker through young hardwoods. Cross a brook and then meet Drumlin Path coming in from the left (Drumlin Path connects to Valley Rd. in 0.3 mi.). Pass several large glacial erratics on the left before reaching a viewpoint to Great Pond Mtn. Ahead, contour across the hillside to a second viewpoint and soon reach Hillside Trail, a grassy road, at 1.2 mi. To continue to Oak Hill, turn right and follow Hillside Trail uphill for 0.4 mi. to the jct. with Oak Hill Path.

■ OAK HILL (829 FT.)

This twin-peaked hill straddles the eastern boundary of the Wildlands, with Oak Hill West within the bounds of the preserve. Summit views take in nearby Great Pond Mtn., Craig Pond, and Flag Hill, and range north to Katahdin. Access is via Hillside Trail and Oak Hill Path.

OAK HILL PATH (GPMCT; USGS ORLAND AND BRANCH LAKE QUADS, GAZETTEER MAP 23, GPMCT WILDLANDS MAP)

Cumulative from Valley Rd. (210 ft.) to:	⮁	↗	⏱
Esker Path (330 ft.) via Hillside Trail	0.4 mi.	120 ft.	0:10
Oak Hill Path (570 ft.)	0.8 mi.	450 ft.	0:35
Oak Hill summit (829 ft.)	1.1 mi.	619 ft.	0:50
Flag Hill Rd. (510 ft.)	1.9 mi.	619 ft.	1:15

From Hothole Valley South Gate on US 1/ME 3, travel north on Valley Rd. for 1.1 mi. to the jct. of Hillside Trail on the right. Park on either side of this entrance, marked "Oak Hill."

Hike east on Hillside Trail, and soon cross Hothole Brook. Beyond, bear left and climb gently to a jct. with Esker Path, which enters from the right. Continue to a high point on the west shoulder of Oak Hill, where Oak Hill Path departs to the right. Turn onto Oak Hill Path and climb the slope on switchbacks to reach a grassy meadow on the semi-open summit. The path continues north across the summit plateau on a wide track. Beyond a clearing, begin a steady descent through the woods. Cross Flag Brook, then a small meadow, to reach Flag Hill Trail. Flag Hill Trail leads right to Flag Hill Path, which then climbs to the top of Flag Hill, a total additional distance of 1.0 mi.

■ BALD MTN. (IN DEDHAM; 1,261 FT.)

This mountain in Dedham, also known as Dedham Bald Mtn., is a short hike offering good views for the effort. From the jct. of US 1A and ME 46 in East Holden, proceed south on US 1A and in 100 ft., turn right (south) onto Upper Dedham Rd. In 2.8 mi., turn left onto Bald Mtn. Rd. (fire station on left). Then, at 6.2 mi. from US 1A, where the road bears right, continue straight ahead on Johnson Rd. for 100 ft. Park on ledges to the left.

BALD MTN. TRAIL (NFTM; USGS GREEN LAKE QUAD, GAZETTEER MAP 23)

From Johnson Rd. (700 ft.) to:	⮁	↗	⏱
Bald Mtn. summit (1,234 ft.)	0.5 mi.	534 ft.	0:30

SEC 11

The trail, an old fire tower service road, follows a direct route through open fields and over bare granite ledges to the top of the peak, where there are a number of communications towers. From here, good views are possible to the north and northwest, while the nearby ledges on the north side of the mountain look out over Phillips Lake. The east side offers views of the mountains on Mt. Desert Island, Blue Hill Mtn., and the Camden Hills.

BLUE HILL PENINSULA–DEER ISLE

■ BLUE HILL MTN. (934 FT.)

This coastal monadnock rises prominently just north of the picturesque village of Blue Hill and affords excellent views of Blue Hill Bay and beyond, from the mountains of ANP on Mt. Desert Island to the Camden Hills. The village and Blue Hill Heritage Trust (BHHT) jointly manage nearly 500 acres of conservation land on the mountain, where there is a network of six hiking trails.

OSGOOD TRAIL (BHHT; USGS BLUE HILL QUAD, GAZETTEER MAP 15, BHHT BLUE HILL MTN. MAP)

Cumulative from Mountain Rd. (340 ft.) to:	⇅	↗	⟳
South Face Trail (600 ft.)	0.3 mi.	260 ft.	0:25
Becton Trail (860 ft.)	0.7 mi.	520 ft.	0:40
Blue Hill Mtn. summit (934 ft.) and Hayes Trail	0.9 mi.	574 ft.	0:45

From the jct. of ME 15 and ME 172/176 in the center of Blue Hill, drive north on ME 15 (Pleasant St.) for 0.9 mi. Turn right onto Mountain Rd. and proceed 0.5 mi. to the trailhead for Osgood Trail (sign). Park along the road on the right.

On the opposite (north) side of Mountain Rd., follow the wide, well-used trail into the woods to an information kiosk. Bear right and switchback easily up the mountain following blue blazes. The way becomes steeper as the trail climbs rock steps to a jct. with South Face Trail on the right (contours 0.25 mi. east across the south face of the mountain to connect with Hayes Trail). Continue straight ahead on Osgood Trail. Soon after a rough section of terrain (rocks and roots), the trail breaks out onto open slabs with views to the south. Ahead, it meets Becton Trail in a small clearing. Here, Osgood Trail turns right, climbs a short section of eroded trail, then wends easily along the summit ridge to the peak in an area of extensive open ledges. There is no summit sign, only chunks of concrete that mark its former base. The concrete stanchions of the old fire tower (removed in 2005) remain just below (big views southward), and a communications tower is to the left. Here also is the jct. with Hayes Trail, which enters from the east.

TOWER SERVICE TRAIL (BHHT; USGS BLUE HILL QUAD, GAZETTEER MAP 15, BHHT BLUE HILL MTN. MAP)

Cumulative from Mountain Rd. (400 ft.) to:	⬆⬇	↗	◔
Hayes Trail, lower jct. (540 ft.)	0.3 mi.	140 ft.	0:10
Hayes Trail, upper jct. (900 ft.)	1.0 mi.	500 ft.	0:45
Blue Hill summit (934 ft.) via Hayes Trail	1.1 mi.	534 ft.	0:50

The trailhead for Tower Service Trail (sign, kiosk) is on Mountain Rd., 0.5 mi. east of the trailhead for Osgood Trail and 0.4 mi. west of the jct. of Mountain Rd. and ME 172. There is a large dirt parking lot on the south side of the road.

Tower Service Trail begins on the north side of Mountain Rd. at a sign for the Morse Farm on Blue Hill Mtn. Follow a grassy track across a large hay field with wonderful views ahead to the mountain and its communications tower. At the top of the field, reach the lower jct. with Hayes Trail, which departs left up a long set of rock steps. Here also are a map post and two granite benches.

Tower Service Trail follows a narrow jeep track originally built to service the summit tower, which provides for a more gradual ascent., From the jct. with Hayes Trail, Tower Service Trail bears right on the jeep track, which winds gradually up the hill. Above, traverse west along a contour, then climb more steeply to the summit ridge. Ahead, reach the upper jct. with Hayes Trail, which enters from the left. From here, Hayes Trail continues easily west, passes behind the communications tower (no trespassing), and in another 0.1 mi., reaches the summit ledges.

HAYES TRAIL (BHHT; USGS BLUE HILL QUAD, GAZETTEER MAP 15, BHHT BLUE HILL MTN. MAP)

Cumulative from Mountain Rd. (400 ft.) to:	⬆⬇	↗	◔
Start of trail via Tower Service Trail (540 ft.)	0.3 mi.	140 ft.	0:10
South Face Trail (650 ft.)	0.4 mi.	250 ft.	0:15
Larry's Summit Loop, lower jct. (875 ft.)	0.5 mi.	475 ft.	0:25
Tower Service Trail, upper jct. (900 ft.)	0.6 mi.	500 ft.	0:30
Blue Hill Mtn. summit (934 ft.)	0.7 mi.	534 ft.	0:35

SEC 11

Hayes Trail starts from the top of the hay field, 0.3 mi. from Mountain Rd., via Tower Service Trail. Bear left and climb a long set of rock stairs to reach the jct. with South Face Trail, which heads straight across the south face of Blue Hill Mtn. to join Osgood Trail in 0.25 mi. Turn right here to continue on Hayes Trail, which climbs rocky terrain at a moderate grade via switchbacks. Ahead, make a long traverse west over ledges past a rock face, then turn uphill on a steep, rocky scramble to a shelf just below the summit communications tower. Here, at the lower jct. with Larry's Summit Loop, are excellent views southward. From the open ledges, enter the woods beyond and negotiate a stretch of boardwalk to reach the upper jct. with Tower Service Trail, which enters from the right. Turn left to continue easily along the summit on Hayes Trail. Pass a side path on the left to the fenced-in tower complex (no trespassing), then join a wide track that soon turns sharply left. Just ahead, the trail emerges from the woods at the upper jct. of Larry's Summit Loop and quickly reaches the unsigned summit of Blue Hill Mtn.

LARRY'S SUMMIT LOOP (BHHT; USGS BLUE HILL QUAD, GAZETTEER MAP 15, BHHT BLUE HILL MTN. MAP)

This short 0.2-mi. loop starts on the spectacular open ledges high on the south face of Blue Hill Mtn., at a point 0.5 mi. from Mountain Rd. via Tower Service and Hayes trails. From Hayes Trail, Larry's Summit Loop bears left across the rock shelf, dips into trees, then returns to open ledges. After reentering the trees, the trail crosses a gully to the next ledge viewpoint. Here, the trail bears right and up to reach a map post at the upper jct. with Hayes Trail. Turn left here and walk about 100 ft. to the unsigned summit of Blue Hill Mtn.

SOUTH FACE TRAIL (BHHT; USGS BLUE HILL QUAD, GAZETTEER MAP 15, BHHT BLUE HILL MTN. MAP)

This short 0.25-mi. connector links Hayes Trail and Osgood Trail, allowing the opportunity for a loop hike over the summit and eliminating the need to walk along Mountain Rd. The trail crosses the south face of the mountain and offers excellent views.

BECTON TRAIL (BHHT; USGS BLUE HILL QUAD, GAZETTEER MAP 15, BHHT BLUE HILL MTN. MAP)

Cumulative from Turkey Farm Rd. (360 ft.) to:	⇅	↗	↺
Osgood Trail (860 ft.)	2.2 mi.	500 ft.	1:20
Blue Hill Mtn. summit (934 ft.) via Osgood Trail	2.4 mi.	574 ft.	1:25

SEC 11

From the center of the village of Blue Hill at the intersection of ME 15 and ME 172/176 (Main St.), drive east on ME 172/176. In 0.2 mi., at the Y-jct. of ME 172 and ME 176, bear left uphill on ME 172. At 1.4 mi., pass Mountain Rd. (trailheads for Hayes Trail and Osgood Trail are west along this road) on the left. Continue on ME 172, and at 2.2 mi., turn left on Turkey Farm Rd. Proceed west to the trailhead parking lot on the left at 2.9 mi.

Follow the trail westward over bog bridges into the forest, winding gradually downhill before leveling off. Beyond the bog bridges, climb easily, then more moderately, up the north slope of the mountain. A long switchback leads to views north to Great Pond Mtn. High on the west ridge, Becton Trail ends at the jct. with Osgood Trail, which continues left to reach the summit of Blue Hill Mtn.

■ JOHN B. MTN. (255 FT.)

This little hill in Brooksville lies in the heart of 38 undeveloped acres, just west of Orcutt Harbor and north of Eggemoggin Reach and East Penobscot Bay, and provides good views from numerous outlooks. Hikers are urged to stay on the trail to protect the fragile mountaintop ecosystem. BHHT manages the preserve.

From the jct. of ME 15 and ME 172/176 in Blue Hill, drive west on ME 15/172/176. In 0.75 mi., ME 172 turns south (to the right); go straight here remain on ME 15/176 and drive 4.25 mi. to Grays Corner. Turn left (south) onto ME 15/175 and go 2.7 mi. to Black Corner, then turn right onto ME 175 and drive 0.6 mi. to Brooksville. At this jct. of ME 175 and ME 176, stay straight on ME 176 and drive 3.9 mi. to Breezemere Rd. on the left. Drive 0.8 mi. on Breezemere Rd. to trailhead parking on the right (sign, kiosk).

JOHN B. MTN. TRAIL (BHHT; USGS CAPE ROSIER QUAD, GAZETTEER MAP 15, BHHT JOHN B. MTN. MAP)

Cumulative from Breezemere Rd. (50 ft.) to:	↥↧	↗	↻
John B. Mtn. summit at loop jct. (255 ft.)	0.4 mi.	205 ft.	0:20
Complete loop	1.1 mi.	205 ft.	0:50

From the parking area, walk right, behind a cemetery. Switchback up the hillside at a moderate grade, passing rock ledges on the left. Climb a short step next to a knotted-rope handrail. On the ridge above, pass a mailbox on the right and, immediately ahead, reach a jct. To the left, a short side path leads 0.1 mi. south over the summit to loop past several outlooks with nice views to Orcutt Harbor, Deer Isle, and Isle au Haut. Returning to John B. Mtn. Trail, turn left and quickly reach another jct. Both forks descend to rejoin at the base of the mountain, but the trail to the left is more scenic. Going left from the jct., the trail leads to open ledges with a log bench and more nice views. Beyond, it descends, at one point over a slab with a knotted rope. Going right from the jct., the trail drops down through pleasant woods. Where the trails merge below, bear left downhill

SEC
11

past a mossy cliff face to reach an old woods road referred to as School-house Rd. Bear left and follow Schoolhouse Rd. along the base of the mountain, passing a large rock face before returning to the trailhead.

■ PINE HILL (150 FT.)

Pine Hill is part of Pine Hill Preserve, a small conservation property on Little Deer Isle, protected by Island Heritage Trust. An interesting quarry is carved out of the hill's south wall.

PINE HILL TRAIL (IHT; USGS SARGENTVILLE QUAD, GAZETTEER MAP 15, IHT PINE HILL PRESERVE MAP)

From Blastow Cove Rd. (100 ft.) to:	⮃	↗	↺
Pine Hill summit (150 ft.)	0.2 mi.	50 ft.	0:10

From the jct. of ME 15 and ME 175 in Sargentville, head west on ME 15 toward Deer Isle. Cross over Eggemoggin Reach via the Deer Isle–Sedgwick Bridge. Soon after the bridge, reach the Deer Isle–Stonington Visitor Center on the right. Turn right here (Eggemoggin Rd.), bear right at the post office, and quickly reach Blastow Rd. on the left (Saunders Memorial Congregational Church on corner). Turn onto Blastow Rd. and drive 0.2 mi. south to trailhead parking for Pine Hill on the right.

Beyond the wooden gate, the trail follows the grassy Old Quarry Rd. to a clearing at the base of the defunct quarry, with its scree piles and cliff face. Bear right on a trail into the woods (pass a mailbox), then scramble up the rocky edge of the quarry wall. From the top of the cliffs are fine views over Deer Isle and Eggemoggin Reach that range from the Deer Isle–Sedgwick Bridge to the peaks of ANP.

■ BACKWOODS MTN. (275 FT.)

This mountain is in Holbrook Island Sanctuary State Park, which occupies 1,230 acres on the north end of the Cape Rosier peninsula in Brooksville, including the namesake 115-acre Holbrook Island. There are two trails on the flanks of Backwoods Mtn. (also referred to locally as Bakeman Mtn.) Summit and Mountain Loop.

SEC 11

SUMMIT TRAIL (MBPL; USGS CAPE ROSIER QUAD, GAZETTEER MAP 15, MBPL HOLBROOK ISLAND SANCTUARY MAP)

Cumulative from Back Rd. (175 ft.) to:	⮃	↗	↺
Mountain Loop Trail (165 ft.)	0.1 mi.	-10 ft.	0:05
Backwoods Mtn. summit (330 ft.)	0.5 mi.	165 ft.	0:20

From the center of Brooksville at the jct. of ME 175 and ME 176, proceed west on ME 176. In 4.4 mi., turn left on Cape Rosier Rd. and continue an additional 1.7 mi. to Back Rd. and the entrance to Holbrook Island Sanctuary on the right. Turn into the park and drive 0.6 mi. to the trailhead for Summit Trail on the left (sign). Parking for Mountain Loop Trail is just 0.1 mi. farther ahead, also on the left.

Following orange blazes, cross a narrow power-line corridor, then walk easily to the jct. with Mountain Loop Trail. Turn left here, and in 250 ft., at the next jct., where Mountain Loop Trail continues straight ahead, turn right on Summit Trail. Follow the wide trail easily through pines and young forest growth. It dips slightly before rising to the base of Backwoods Mtn. amid a jumble of mossy boulders. Switchback up the slope over several short, steep pitches and some rocky, eroded trail. Soon after the angle eases, turn sharply right and reach a bench on an outcrop with northwest views through the trees to several islands in Penobscot Bay and beyond to the harbor at Castine. Continuing on, quickly reach the wooded summit of Backwoods Mtn. and a USGS marker on an outcrop just to the left of the trail. A short distance beyond, the trail ends.

MOUNTAIN LOOP TRAIL (MBPL; USGS CAPE ROSIER QUAD, GAZETTEER MAP 15, MBPL HOLBROOK ISLAND SANCTUARY MAP)

Cumulative from Back Rd. (150 ft.) to:	⇅	↗	○
Summit Trail (165 ft.)	0.2 mi.	15 ft.	0:05
Complete loop	1.4 mi.	115 ft.	0:20

See driving directions for Summit Trail above.

Follow the wide, orange-blazed trail into woods and soon pass under a power line. Ahead, reach the Mountain Loop jct. and turn left. In 50 ft., Summit Trail enters from the left to merge with Mountain Loop Trail. Continue straight ahead, and in 250 ft., Summit Trail departs right for the top of Backwoods Mtn. Continue on the level path along the base of the mountain. The trail eventually swings south and trends easily over the east shoulder. Descending, it swings west, passing below the steep, rocky slopes of the peak rising up to the right. Bearing north again, it climbs easily over the west shoulder and then descends to reach the original loop jct. Turn left here to return to the Back Rd. trailhead.

SEC 11

EASTERN ME 9 CORRIDOR

■ BLACKCAP MTN. (1,018 FT.)

This mountain ridge in East Eddington, which rises steeply above Fitts Pond, has several communications towers on its summit. Limited views are possible on the steep ascent, looking eastward over Fitts Pond to the hills beyond. Combine Blue Trail and Blue & White Trail for a hike to the summit.

From the jct. of ME 9 and ME 46 in East Eddington, drive south on ME 46 for 0.6 mi. Alternatively, from the jct. of US 1A and ME 46 in East Holden, drive north on ME 46 for 4.4 mi. Either way, turn east on Blackcap Rd. at a sign for Katahdin Area Council–Camp Roosevelt. Follow the dirt Blackcap Rd. for 0.5 mi., then turn left on Camp Roosevelt Rd. Soon, pass through the wooden entrance arch of the Boy Scout camp and reach a large open area at 1.5 mi. from ME 46. To the left is Maggie's Way, which leads 0.2 mi. to the Peter G. Vigue Scout Center. On the right is a boat launch on Fitts Pond. Park on the right, just before the trailhead kiosk.

The trails to Blackcap Mtn. and Woodchuck Hill emanate from Camp Roosevelt, an 1,800-acre facility that has served as the Boy Scouts of America, Katahdin Area Council's base camp for outdoor education since 1921. Visitors are asked to check in at the Vigue Scout Center to alert camp managers of their presence on the property. For more information, please call 207-866-2241.

BLUE TRAIL AND BLUE & WHITE TRAIL
(NFTM; USGS CHEMO POND QUAD, GAZETTEER MAP 23)

Cumulative from trailhead kiosk at Fitts Pond boat launch (300 ft.) to:	↕	↗	○
Blue & White Trail (300 ft.) via Blue Trail	0.4 mi.	0 ft.	0:15
Blackcap Mtn. summit ridge (1,000 ft.) via Blue & White Trail	1.1 mi.	800 ft.	1:00

Blue Trail leaves to the left of the trailhead kiosk and quickly crosses a brook on a wooden bridge. It soon bears left and follows the western shore of Fitts Pond. At 0.4 mi., reach a jct. with Blue & White Trail. Turn right and follow Blue & White Trail, climbing steadily. Cross a jeep track. Beyond, climb steeply up the hillside. After a scramble up rock slabs, the angle eases, and views to the east begin to open up. Proceed easily up the ridgeline through the predominantly spruce forest. The summit towers soon come into sight. Just ahead, with a long rock wall to the left, climb up to the summit ridge and the towers and access road. An obscure trail heads to the true summit, which is south along the ridge and wooded with no views.

■ WOODCHUCK HILL (815 FT.)

This mountain in East Eddington affords nice views over Snowshoe Pond, Fitts Pond, and Blackcap Mtn. To reach the trailhead, follow the driving directions and visitor check-in protocols for Blackcap Mtn.

WOODCHUCK HILL TRAILS (NFTM; USGS CHEMO POND QUAD, GAZETTEER MAP 23)

Cumulative from trailhead at Fitts Pond boat launch (300 ft.) to:	⮂	↗	⏱
Woodchuck Hill summit (815 ft.)	1.5 mi.	515 ft.	1:00
Road jct. near Little Burnt Pond (390 ft.)	2.2 mi.	515 ft.	1:20
Complete loop	3.8 mi.	515 ft.	2:10

The trails on Woodchuck Hill have no official names. From parking adjacent to the Fitts Pond boat launch, proceed on foot through Camp Roosevelt. Pass Maggie's Way on the left to reach a fork, where there is an information kiosk and camp map. Bear left at the fork, and just ahead, bear left onto Tonini Rd. (sign for Pamola Campsite). Ahead, walk up the gravel road past Gary Robbins Lane and then Paul's St. Pass Twin Rocks Campsite on the right. Just beyond, the gravel road bears right. On the left, look for a sign (Pamola) and a large boulder with blue and yellow paint blazes on it. The old jeep track that leaves left is the start of the trail to Woodchuck Hill.

From this point on, there is no signage on the trail, only painted blazes. The trail rises gently over a low ridge and drops down to some ledges at the northwest corner of Snowshoe Pond. It then crosses the pond's outlet and soon crosses Bangor Water Works Rd. (gated at its entrance from ME 9 in East Eddington and also at Little Burnt Pond).

The summit loop begins at the road crossing. The trail proceeds straight ahead through a logged area directly to the steep hillside, where it ascends in many short switchbacks. The views from the ledges are to the west. In one spot, a short 6-ft. ladder leads to a higher shelf and a 4-ft. ladder with a rope handrail reaches another shelf. Once off the face, the trail levels out as it crosses sloping ledges in semi-open spruce woods to reach the top of Woodchuck Hill and cairn. Views are accessible by walking east to the obvious ledges.

To descend via the same route, stand at the cairn and look west to see the lodge at the scout camp. The trail blazes, painted on rocks and trees, are in front of you.

To continue on the loop, stand at the cairn looking at the scout camp and then turn to the east about 45 degrees; on a rock ten feet away is the first blue blaze. The blazes go straight down a narrow, steep wooded ridgeline to the Bangor Water Works Rd. at the gate near Little Burnt Pond. At the road, turn north (right) and walk about 400 yd. to the trail crossing at the foot of Snowshoe Pond. From there, return to the Fitts Pond parking area using the same trail as on the ascent.

■ EAGLE BLUFF (900 FT.)

The impressive south-facing granite cliffs of Eagle Bluff in Clifton have long attracted technical rock climbers; a short but highly rewarding trail to the top makes it a great spot for hikers, too. In 2014, the Clifton Climbers Alliance purchased 165 acres on Eagle Bluff to protect public access. From the jct. of ME 9 and ME 180 in Clifton, drive south on ME 180 for 2.5 mi. to a small, unsigned trailhead parking lot on the left.

EAGLE BLUFF TRAIL (NFTM; USGS CHEMO POND AND HOPKINS POND QUADS, GAZETTEER MAPS 23 AND 24)

From ME 180 (360 ft.) to:	⇅	↗	↻
Eagle Bluff summit cliffs (900 ft.)	0.5 mi.	540 ft.	0:30

Facing the woods, with your back to the road, start out on the trail from the left corner of the dirt parking lot. In 75 ft., another trail from the road enters from the left. Immediately ahead on the right is an information kiosk. Beyond, occasional pieces of orange flagging mark the trail, which climbs gradually to a fork. A well-trodden climber's path goes right; stay left to continue to Eagle Bluff. Cross an overgrown skidder trail, then climb moderately among scattered boulders. Ahead, stay straight where a narrow climber's path leaves right. Where the angle eases, proceed easily along the southwest ridge. A spur leads right 40 ft. to an outlook. Just past a huge boulder on the right, climb left and up to open ledges along the top of the cliff face. On top of Eagle Bluff are airy views over Cedar Swamp Pond to Lead Mtn. and the peaks of ANP. To the west are several wind towers, Woodchuck Hill, and Blackcap Mtn. The foot trail reenters the woods then emerges to end at a final ledge and a view north to the granite faces of Chick Hill and Little Chick Hill.

■ LITTLE PEAKED MTN. (AKA LITTLE CHICK HILL; 890 FT.)

Little Peaked Mtn., also known as Little Chick Hill, lies just west of Peaked Mtn. (see below) and features spectacular cliffs and fine views. From the jct. of ME 9 and ME 180 in Clifton, drive east on ME 9 for 3.5 mi. Turn left (north) onto paved Chick Hill Rd. and proceed 0.7 mi. to where the pavement ends. At this point, a large dirt parking lot is on the left; to the right, a gravel road leads uphill past an obvious telephone pole. The parking lot is the trailhead for Little Peaked Mtn. and Peaked Mtn.

LITTLE PEAKED MTN. TRAIL (NFTM; USGS HOPKINS POND QUAD, GAZETTEER MAPS 23 AND 24)

From trailhead parking lot (334 ft.) to:	⇅	↗	○
Little Peaked Mtn. summit (905 ft.)	0.5 mi.	571 ft.	0:30

To start up Little Peaked Mtn., walk back to the pavement. With the paved road to the right and the gravel road going uphill to the left, head straight into the woods on an unmarked old jeep track. In 200 ft., reach a fork and bear left. In 700 ft., the eroded old woods road narrows to a footpath. Ahead, a faint trail enters from the left; farther on, cross an overgrown skidder trail. Climbing occasionally on bedrock trail at a moderate grade, reach another faint trail on the right; stay left. Above, emerge into the open at the base of huge granite slabs. Along a short cliff wall on the right, the angle eases. With sweeping cliffs on the right, ascend easily up a long granite ridge. At the final summit outcrop, bear right into the woods. Reach a jct. with a trail entering from the left (take note of this jct. for the return hike). Turn right here to quickly finish the climb atop the south-facing cliffs with spectacular views east to Peaked Mtn. and south to the mountains of Donnell Pond PL. Eagle Bluff, Woodchuck Hill, Blackcap Mtn. and Blue Hill Mtn. are in view to the southwest.

■ PEAKED MTN. (AKA CHICK HILL; 1,152 FT.)

Peaked Mtn., commonly called Chick Hill, straddles the Clifton–Amherst line about 18 mi. east of Bangor. The sweeping granite cliffs on the south face of the mountain can be seen from miles around and offer long views that include the peaks of ANP to the south and Katahdin in the north.

PEAKED MTN. TRAIL (NFTM; USGS HOPKINS POND QUAD, GAZETTEER MAPS 23 AND 24)

From trailhead parking lot (334 ft.) to:	⇅	↗	○
Peaked Mtn. summit (1,152 ft.)	1.1 mi.	818 ft.	1:00

From the start of the trail to Little Peaked Mtn. (see above), turn left to follow the gravel road uphill. Ahead, at a height-of-land, the road turns sharply right. Continue to utility pole 18 (marked in silver numbers) on the right. Just beyond, enter the woods on the right and follow an obscure jeep track for 250 ft. On the foot trail beyond, climb at a moderate to steep grade on mossy slabs of rock to emerge into the open. The path then climbs slabs through an open corridor in the woods. In a small clearing just above,

SEC 11

where a faint trail continues ahead and up, bear right to reach the open slabs above the south face of Chick Hill. Continue up to the left toward the obvious communications tower. Reach the summit at the base of the former fire tower (removed in 1993), where only the concrete stanchions and steel base remain. In view are Lead Mtn., the peaks of Donnell Pond PL and ANP, Blue Hill Mtn., and the hills around Lucerne. The cliff face of Fletcher Bluff is around the corner to the east.

■ BALD BLUFF MTN. (1,011 FT.)

The Amherst Mountains Community Forest in Amherst is a 4,974-acre tract of rugged forestland encompassing six remote ponds, miles of streams, significant wetlands, and a jumble of granite ledges, hills, and mountains, including Bald Bluff Mtn. The preserve is owned by the Maine Bureau of Parks and Lands and managed jointly with the town of Amherst. Bald Bluff Mtn. offers fine views of the lower Penobscot River watershed from its summit ledges.

From the jct. of ME 9 and ME 180 in Clifton, travel west on ME 9 for 8.9 mi. to a snowplow turnout on the right. Just ahead on the left is a blue and white MBPL sign that reads "Amherst." Turn left (north) off ME 9 at the sign and follow the old road, which soon turns to gravel. At 3.0 mi. from ME 9, bear left (gated road on right). At a jct. at 4.8 mi., turn left. Reach the signed trailhead on the right at 6.0 mi.; parking is 300 ft. farther on the right, in a rocky, grassy area at the end of the improved gravel road.

BALD BLUFF MTN. TRAIL (MBPL; USGS HORSEBACK QUAD, GAZETTEER MAP 24, MTF AMHERST MOUNTAINS COMMUNITY FOREST-BALD BLUFF MAP)

Cumulative from trailhead (600 ft.) to:	⇅	↗	↻
Loop jct. (800 ft.)	0.4 mi.	200 ft.	0:20
Bald Bluff Mtn. summit (1,011 ft.) via right loop	1.5 mi.	450 ft.	1:00
Complete loop	2.6 mi.	450 ft.	1:30

From the parking area, walk back to the trailhead sign and enter the woods on the left. The trail rises steadily then eases off to join an old tote road, which it follows for 100 ft. to a jct. This is the start of the lollipop part of the loop, described counterclockwise; bear right here. The old tote road rises at a moderate to steep grade then ends at a large double-trunk oak tree. Now a footpath, Bald Bluff Mtn. Trail turns left onto a ledge then a short distance ahead turns right. Look for blazes on the rocks, as huckle-berry bushes obscure the treadway in places. The trail continues over ledges with good views south and southwest. At 0.7 mi., the trail drops steeply for a short distance then follows a rolling route across the hill through large spruce, hemlock, and pine.

At 1.0 mi., the trail turns left uphill and levels off; crosses a dry, mossy creek bed; and begins a steep climb over ledges to a nice viewpoint looking west and south. At 1.4 mi., the trail makes a gentle U-turn then follows open, mossy ledges across the summit of Bald Bluff Mtn. (Keep an eye out for blazes and small cairns on this stretch, as many animal trails cross the trail through here.) The trail soon reenters the woods and descends at an easy grade. At 2.0 mi., bear left at a fork, ignoring the pink ribbons and an old blaze on the right fork. The trail morphs into an old tote road and fol-lows this to the orginal loop jct. Turn right here to return to the trailhead.

■ LEAD MTN. (AKA HUMPBACK; 1,475 FT.)

Lead Mtn., also known as Humpback, is located in T28 MD in Hancock County, just west of the Washington County line. From the jct. of ME 9 and ME 193 in T22 MD, drive east toward Beddington. In 0.5 mi., cross into Washington County. At 1.0 mi., turn left (north) at the sign for the Maine Forest Service Forest Protection Division, Beddington Ranger Sta-tion. (*Note:* This point is 0.1 mi. west of the bridge over the Narraguagus River on ME 9.) Reset odometer. Proceed on CC Rd. (also called 30-00-0 Rd.), passing a snowmobile trail on the left at the MFS station. Just beyond, turn left onto a gravel road (sign for cell tower), which leads 1.7 mi. to a cul-de-sac turnaround and parking.

LEAD MTN. TRAIL
(NFTM; USGS LEAD MTN. QUAD, GAZETTEER MAPS 24, 25)

From parking area (695 ft.) to:	↥↧	↗	↺
Lead Mtn. summit (1,475 ft.)	1.0 mi.	780 ft.	0:55

The trail to Lead Mtn. starts in the upper right corner of the parking area. Follow a jeep track into the woods. On a telephone pole, a yellow sign with an arrow indicates this is the way to the cell tower (on top of the mountain). In 100 ft., pass around a yellow gate. Follow the old road to a fork; go right here, following the telephone poles. Climb on the old road, surfaced with loose gravel.

SEC 11

Ahead, an ATV trail leads up to the right. Follow this to the old fire warden cabin on the right. Soon after the cabin, the logging road/ATV track narrows to a jeep track. Follow this easily up to a saddle. Beyond, climb steadily to the summit. Here are a former fire tower site, a fenced-in communications tower, and the broad summit plateau. There are no views from the top of the mountain.

■ PEAKED MTN. (IN WASHINGTON COUNTY; 938 FT.)

Peaked Mtn. in T30 MD BPP in Washington County rises just north of ME 9, less than 30 mi. east of a mountain with the same name in Clifton. On the north side of ME 9 at a point 9.2 mi. east of the Narraguagus River, a gravel road (marked by two yellow posts) leaves the north side of the highway. At 0.1 mi. from ME 9, the road passes a private camp. Take a right fork at 0.3 mi., and park on the right 0.7 mi. from the highway.

PEAKED MTN. TRAIL
(NFTM; USGS PEAKED MTN. QUAD, GAZETTEER MAP 25)

From parking area on tote road (565 ft.) to:	⇕	↗	↻
Peaked Mtn. summit (938 ft.)	0.6 mi.	373 ft.	0:30

Follow the tote road a short distance ahead to the former fire warden's cabin, now a private camp. Pass in front of the camp and then between the camp and a shed. Angle across the small opening beyond, and look for small hiker sign on a tree. This sign and a log across the path with a cutout section in it marks the start of the trail. Follow the old tote road, which, like many former fire warden trails in Maine, is quickly reverting back to the forest. Occasional white marker plates with a stick-figure hiker mark the path, which heads on a general compass course of 330 degrees. Ahead, walk easily around a beech blowdown near a mossy ledge, then regain the path. Above, large rock ledges are to the left. Beyond, hike around the back side of the large ledges to the summit of Peaked Mtn., marked by the four stanchions of the former fire tower and a granite bench. The wooded peak offers no views.

DONNELL POND PUBLIC LANDS AND VICINITY
■ SCHOODIC MTN. (1,069 FT.)

This attractive mountain in T9 SD in the southwest corner of the preserve offers fine views of Frenchman Bay and the mountains of ANP from the extensive ledges on its mostly bare granite summit. Two trails ascend the peak from the east: Schoodic Mtn. Trail and Schoodic Beach Trail.

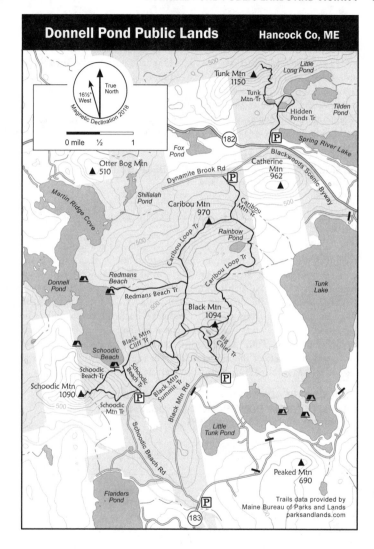

Donnell Pond Public Lands   Hancock Co, ME

True North

16½° West

Magnetic Declination 2018

0 mile   ½   1

Little Long Pond

Tunk Mtn
1150

Tunk Mtn Tr

Tilden Pond

Hidden Ponds Tr

P

182

Spring River Lake

Blackwoods Scenic Byway

Fox Pond

Otter Bog Mtn
▲ 510

Dynamite Brook Rd

P

Catherine Mtn
962
▲

Shillalah Pond

Caribou Mtn
970
▲

Caribou Mtn Tr

Martin Ridge Cove

500

Rainbow Pond

Caribou Loop Tr

Caribou Loop Tr

Tunk Lake

Redmans Beach

Donnell Pond

Redmans Beach Tr

500

Black Mtn
1094
▲

Schoodic Beach

Black Mtn Cliff Tr

Big Chief Tr

Schoodic Beach Tr

Schoodic Beach Tr

Black Mtn Summit Tr

P

Schoodic Mtn
1090
▲

P

Black Mtn Rd

500

Schoodic Mtn Tr

Little Tunk Pond

Schoodic Beach Rd

Peaked Mtn
690
▲

Flanders Pond

P

183

Trails data provided by
Maine Bureau of Parks and Lands
parksandlands.com

SEC
11

The main trailhead for Schoodic Mtn. (and Black Mtn.) is at the end of Schoodic Beach Rd. From the jct. of US 1 and ME 3 in Ellsworth, travel 13.4 mi. east on US 1 to ME 183 in East Sullivan. Turn left (north) on ME 183 (Tunk Lake Rd.) and drive 4.3 mi. to Donnell Pond Rd. on the left (blue and white sign), just after crossing an old railroad bed (now the Downeast Sunrise Trail). Turn left here, and soon pass Black Mtn. Rd. on the right at 0.3 mi. (leads 2.0 mi. to Big Chief Trail on Black Mtn.). Continue left on Donnell Pond Rd. for an additional 1.6 mi. to its end at the Schoodic Beach parking lot, where there is an information kiosk and pit toilet.

SCHOODIC MTN. TRAIL
(MBPL; DONNELL POND PUBLIC LANDS, P. 513)

Cumulative from Schoodic Beach parking lot (250 ft.) to:	⇅	↗	○
Schoodic Beach Trail (720 ft.)	0.8 mi.	470 ft.	0:35
Schoodic Mtn. summit (1,069 ft.)	1.2 mi.	819 ft.	1:05

This direct route to the top of Schoodic Mtn. leaves the left end of the parking lot, to the right of the pit toilet. Descend briefly, then climb, gradually at first and then steadily, passing several huge boulders with overhangs. Reach the top of a cliff and good views east to Black Mtn. Beyond, the trail levels out, then climbs gradually to a jct. with Schoodic Beach Trail, which enters from the right (this trail leads 0.5 mi. to Schoodic Beach on Donnell Pond). For the summit of Schoodic Mtn., continue left on Schoodic Mtn. Trail. Ahead, climb moderately on bedrock trail, traverse the south side of the mountain, and finish by following cairns over extensive ledges to reach the summit towers at 1.2 mi.

SCHOODIC BEACH TRAIL
(MBPL; DONNELL POND PUBLIC LANDS, P. 513)

Cumulative from Schoodic Beach parking lot (250 ft.) to:	⇅	↗	○
Schoodic Beach on Donnell Pond (150 ft.)	0.5 mi.	-100 ft.	0:15
Schoodic Mtn. Trail (720 ft.)	1.0 mi.	570 ft.	0:50
Schoodic Mtn. summit (1,069 ft.)	1.4 mi.	919 ft.	1:10

Take the wide trail at the far-right end of the parking lot just beyond the information kiosk. Follow this 0.5 mi. to Schoodic Beach on Donnell Pond. Just before reaching the pond, arrive at a jct. on the left and a privy; this is the continuation of Schoodic Beach Trail up the mountain. Schoodic Beach, perhaps the most popular destination of visitors to Donnell Pond

PL, is 250 ft. ahead and well worth a visit. Along the beach's sandy expanse are picnic tables, additional privies, individual and group campsites, and excellent swimming.

To continue on Schoodic Beach Trail and ascend Schoodic Mtn., return from the beach and turn right at the jct. (privy) to follow an old jeep road along the base of the mountain. Ahead, turn sharply left to begin a steep ascent on rough terrain. Above, the climbing moderates on switchbacks. At the crest in a small clearing, reach the jct. with Schoodic Mtn. Trail, which enters from the left. Turn right here to follow Schoodic Mtn. Trail to the top of Schoodic Mtn. in 0.4 mi.

■ BLACK MTN. (1,094 FT.)

This mountain in T10 SD rises east of Donnell Pond and offers good views in all directions from its broad open summit. Black Mtn. can be climbed from Schoodic Beach parking lot via Black Mtn. Summit Trail or from Schoodic Beach via Black Mtn. Cliff Trail. Black Mtn. can also be reached from Caribou Mtn. in the north via Caribou Mtn. and Caribou Loop trails.

BLACK MTN. SUMMIT TRAIL
(MBPL; DONNELL POND PUBLIC LANDS, P. 513)

Cumulative from Schoodic Beach parking lot (250 ft.) to:	↿⇂	↗	↻
Black Mtn. Cliff Trail (950 ft.)	1.2 mi.	700 ft.	0:60
Caribou Loop Trail, west jct. (1,050 ft.)	1.8 mi.	800 ft.	1:20
Black Mtn.–Big Chief Connector to Big Chief Trail (900 ft.)	2.0 mi.	800 ft.	1:30
Black Mtn. summit (1,094 ft.) and Caribou Loop Trail, east jct.	2.3 mi.	1,000 ft.	1:40

Black Mtn. Summit Trail leaves from the right end of the Schoodic Beach parking lot (see directions to Schoodic Mtn.). Go past the kiosk, cross a small brook, and head right, uphill. Follow a mostly level woods road over many bog bridges to the base of the mountain. The trail then turns left (north) and climbs steeply on switchbacks and rock steps, weaving between ledges to reach the top of the ridge and a jct. with Black Mtn. Cliff Trail at 1.2 mi. (Black Mtn. Cliff Trail descends from here to Schoodic Beach on Donnell Pond.)

Bear right to continue on Black Mtn. Summit Trail. Proceed easily through the woods, and at 1.8 mi., reach the west jct. of Caribou Loop

SEC 11

Trail (leads toward Redman Beach on Donnell Pond and beyond to Caribou Mtn.) near the heavily wooded western summit of Black Mtn. Continuing to the right on Black Mtn. Summit Trail, descend, steeply at times, to a notch at 2.0 mi. and a jct. with Black Mtn.–Big Chief Connector (leads 0.4 mi. over a knob to Big Chief Trail, then another 0.7 mi. down to Black Mtn. Rd.). Bear left at this jct. and soon break out onto open ledges, following cairns to reach the summit of Black Mtn. at 2.3 mi. (large cairn and sign), the east jct. of Caribou Loop Trail, and the jct. with Big Chief Trail.

BLACK MTN. CLIFF TRAIL
(DONNELL POND PUBLIC LANDS, P. 513)

Cumulative from Schoodic Beach parking lot (250 ft.) to:	↥↧	↗	↻
Start of trail at Schoodic Beach (150 ft.) via Schoodic Beach Trail	0.5 mi.	-100 ft.	0:15
Black Mtn. Summit Trail (900 ft.)	1.2 mi.	750 ft.	1:00
Black Mtn. summit (1,094 ft.) via Black Mtn. Summit Trail	2.3 mi.	944 ft.	1:30

Black Mtn. Cliff Trail diverges right (east) from Schoodic Beach Trail just before reaching Donnell Pond, at a point 0.5 mi. from Schoodic Beach parking lot. It then crosses a stream in a ravine on a wooden footbridge and, beyond, climbs gently to cross three small brooks in succession. The trail merges with a jeep track and proceeds easily to cross another brook. Ahead, it begins a steady, steep ascent using switchbacks. Cross a brook on a short footbridge and continue to climb moderately to gain the ridge. Traverse to the right (southeast) along the top of the cliffs, passing a number of outlooks with views to Donnell Pond and Schoodic Mtn. Reach a jct. with Black Mtn. Summit Trail on the left at 1.2 mi. The summit of Black Mtn. is 1.1 mi. ahead via this trail.

BIG CHIEF TRAIL
(MBPL; DONNELL POND PUBLIC LANDS, P. 513)

Cumulative from Black Mtn. Rd. (370 ft.) to:	↥↧	↗	↻
Black Mtn.–Big Chief Connector to Black Mtn. Summit Trail (930 ft.)	0.7 mi.	560 ft.	0:35
Black Mtn. summit (1,094 ft.) at jct. of Black Mtn. Summit Trail and Caribou Loop Trail	1.2 mi.	724 ft.	1:00

This trail climbs to the peak of Black Mtn. via Wizard Pond. The extensive open ledges on the southeastern ridge offer excellent views east over Tunk Lake. From the jct. with Schoodic Beach Rd., drive on Black Mtn.

Rd. for 2.1 mi. to a small parking area on the right. Just ahead on the left side of the road is a sign for Big Chief Trail.

Follow the well-worn Big Chief Trail into the woods and ascend steadily, passing a number of large glacial erratics. Beyond a high cliff wall in the woods off to the right, climb a short, steep pitch via several switchbacks to a viewpoint on the right. Then weave through rocks as the forest cover begins to thin out. After a level open area, bear right at a large cairn, and drop down slightly to another view eastward. Follow cairns over bedrock trail to the jct. with Black Mtn.–Big Chief Connector (leads 0.4 mi. northwest to join Black Mtn. Summit Trail in a col between the east and west summits of Black Mtn.). Bear right to continue on Big Chief Trail, crossing huge open slabs of granite. Ahead, bear sharply right (watch for double blaze) before dropping into a depression. Here, cross the outlet of Wizard Pond, then climb steeply over ledges to the open summit of the east peak of Black Mtn. and the jct. with Black Mtn. Summit and Caribou Loop trails.

BLACK MTN.–BIG CHIEF CONNECTOR
(MBPL; DONNELL POND PUBLIC LANDS, P. 513)

This short 0.4-mi. trail connects Black Mtn. Summit Trail with Big Chief Trail high on Black Mtn., 0.5 mi. west of its east summit. From the jct. with Black Mtn. Summit Trail, climb a knoll via rock steps, then cross an expanse of bedrock. Beyond an overlook (sign and cairn), crest a knob. Ahead, drop into a gully, then follow a series of cairns to join Big Chief Trail, 0.7 mi. from Black Mtn. Rd.

■ CARIBOU MTN. (960 FT.)

This mountain in T10 SD lies to the north of Black Mtn. in the heart of the backcountry of Donnell Pond PL. From the north, reach Caribou Mtn. from Dynamite Brook Rd. via Caribou Mtn. Trail; from the south, take a longer hike from Black Mtn. on Caribou Loop Trail, which makes a nearly 6-mi. loop over Caribou Mtn.

CARIBOU LOOP TRAIL
(MBPL; DONNELL POND PUBLIC LANDS, P. 513)

Cumulative from Black Mtn. summit (1,094 ft.) to:	⇅	↗	↻
Rainbow Pond outlet (330 ft.)	2.1 mi.	-764 ft.	1:15
Caribou Mtn. Trail (850 ft.)	2.8 mi.	520 ft.	1:55
Caribou Mtn. wooded summit (970 ft.)	3.2 mi.	640 ft.	2:10
Redman Beach Trail (450 ft.)	4.7 mi.	640 ft.	3:00
Black Mtn. Summit Trail (1,050 ft.)	5.6 mi.	1,240 ft.	3:45

Caribou Loop Trail is described in a counterclockwise direction from the summit of Black Mtn. Much of this route lies within the 1,940-acre Donnell Pond Ecological Reserve, designated to protect and study the unique natural areas and plants found here. Hikers are asked to please stay on the trail to minimize damage to plants and soils.

Leaving the summit, follow cairns and blue blazes along the ridge, trending gradually downhill. At the bottom of the initial descent, pass an unmaintained side trail leading right in the direction of Tunk Lake. Continuing ahead on Caribou Loop Trail, pass beneath a cliff face on the left, cross a brook, and continue to descend gradually. Make an arc around a bog area on the left (west), crossing several outlet streams en route. Descend into a drainage and cross the outlet of Rainbow Pond at 2.1 mi.

Beyond, begin the ascent of Caribou Mtn. Pass to the right of a large, square-edged boulder and, above, weave between boulders, climbing steadily. Break out onto open ledges and climb a slab up to the right to reach a viewpoint looking to Tunk Lake, Rainbow Pond, and Black Mtn. Here, Caribou Mtn. Trail enters from the right (north). (This trail leads 1.0 mi. to Dynamite Brook Rd.) Stay on Caribou Loop Trail.

Traverse the semi-open south face of the mountain on slabs and ledges, pass numerous viewpoints, and ascend to a parklike meadow at 3.2 mi. on the wooded summit. Continuing on, descend gradually on the long west ridge. Near the end of the ridge at a large open slab (great views), turn sharply left and make a steep descent, switchbacking between ledges. Pass under a rock roof, go over a knob, and reach a jct. at 4.7 mi. Here, Redman Beach Trail leads right (west) 1.4 mi. to the beach on the east shore of Donnell Pond (water access only).

Continue ahead, descend to a notch, and then begin to climb the north side of Black Mtn. Ascend steadily, passing through a stand of old-growth spruce to gain the level ridge top high on the west peak of Black Mtn. Soon, reach the jct. with Black Mtn. Summit Trail at 5.6 mi., 0.5 mi. left (east) of the east peak of Black Mtn.

CARIBOU MTN. TRAIL
(MBPL; DONNELL POND PUBLIC LANDS, P. 513)

Cumulative from Dynamite Brook Rd. (410 ft.) to:	⮃	⬈	◷
Caribou Loop Trail (850 ft.)	0.9 mi.	440 ft.	0:40
High point on Caribou Mtn. (970 ft.) via Caribou Loop Trail	1.4 mi.	560 ft.	1:00

From the jct. of US 1 and ME 182 in Hancock, travel north on ME 182 (Blackwoods Scenic Byway) for 14.5 mi. to reach Dynamite Brook Rd. on the right (sign: Caribou Loop Connector Trailhead). (Trailhead parking for Tunk Mtn. trails is 100 yd. ahead to the left on ME 182.) Turn right on Dynamite Brook Rd. and drive 0.8 mi. to a small parking area on the left. Caribou Mtn. Trail starts 500 ft. farther along on the road, turning left into the woods (sign) just before a bridge.

Follow the wide, blue-blazed trail gradually uphill, then ascend moderately before leveling off at a jct. Here, an informal trail diverges left to Catherine Mtn., reaching its summit in 0.7 mi. Caribou Mtn. Trail continues easily ahead to a sag between Catherine Mtn. and Caribou Mtn. Beyond, the trail climbs steadily, sometimes on rough, rocky terrain, to gain the east ridge of the mountain. Pass through a cleft in the rock, then crest the summit ridge and reach a jct. with Caribou Loop Trail on an open slab. Here, the broad vista includes Tunk Lake, Black Mtn., and Schoodic Mtn. To the right on Caribou Loop Trail are more lookout points with good views, as well as the wooded summit of Caribou Mtn.; to the left, Caribou Loop Trail descends to Rainbow Pond before climbing to the east peak of Black Mtn.

■ TUNK MTN. (1,157 FT.)

This mountain offers excellent views to the south and east from its extensive summit ledges. A loop trail offers access to several remote ponds at its base.

TUNK MTN. TRAIL
(MBPL; DONNELL POND PUBLIC LANDS, P. 513)

Cumulative from ME 182 (250 ft.) to:	↕	↗	↻
Hidden Ponds Trail, lower jct. (310 ft.)	0.6 mi.	60 ft.	0:15
Hidden Ponds Trail, upper jct. at Salmon Pond (325 ft.)	0.7 mi.	75 ft.	0:20
High point on Tunk Mtn. (1,100 ft.)	2.0 mi.	850 ft.	1:30
End of trail at viewpoint to north (1,050 ft.)	2.1 mi.	850 ft.	1:35

To reach the Tunk Mtn. trailhead, follow directions for Caribou Mtn. Trail. Continue east on ME 182 from the jct. with Dynamite Brook Rd. for 100 yd. to trailhead parking on the left for Tuck Mtn. and Hidden Ponds trails. There is a vault toilet and an information kiosk. Much of Tunk Mtn. Trail (and Hidden Ponds Trail) lies within the 4,274-acre Spring Lake Ecological Reserve, designated to protect and study the unique natural areas and plants found here. Hikers are asked to please stay on the trail to minimize damage to plants and soils.

Tunk Mtn. Trail begins to the right of the kiosk, descends wooden steps, and enters the woods. The wide and well-worn trail, an old woods road, leads past an informal trail on the left. Continue to follow blue blazes to the jct. with Hidden Ponds Trail on the right. (This 1.0-mi. trail makes a loop around Salmon Pond, rejoining Tunk Mtn. Trail 0.1 mi. north.) Ahead, reach Salmon Pond and the upper jct. of Hidden Ponds Trail. Bear left to climb a rise then drop down to Mud Pond. Hike along the pond and cross its inlet on the west shore. Soon after, leave Mud Pond and begin climbing steeply over a winding staircase of rock steps. Ascend at a moderate grade via switchbacks to cross a semi-open area with views south. Beyond, enter thick woods at a cairn, traverse west across the mountain, then climb easily to a spur trail on the right, which leads 100 yd. to a series of huge, sloping ledges and wonderful views south to the Gulf of Maine, Catherine Mtn., Caribou Mtn., Spring River Lake, and the "hidden" ponds of Mud and Salmon below.

Beyond, after a long switchback and a stretch of moderate to steep climbing, ascend three steel rungs in the rock. The view south gets more expansive as the trail gains elevation, and now includes Black Mtn., Schoodic Mtn., and Tunk Lake. At a sign for Monument Vista, a spur trail leads 200 ft. down to the right to another excellent vista and a plaque honoring the family of Harold Pierce, who donated the land on Tunk Mtn. to the state of Maine in 1994. Continuing on, the trail climbs slabs to emerge on the summit ledges. Follow blazes and cairns from this point to the ridge crest on the northeast shoulder of Tunk Mtn. Here, the trail, now on The Nature Conservancy's 9,000-acre Spring River Preserve, avoids the true summit, crosses the ridge, drops into a gully, and ends atop a sweeping granite slab with great views to the north.

HIDDEN PONDS TRAIL
(MBPL; DONNELL POND PUBLIC LANDS, P. 513)

Cumulative from Tunk Mtn. Trail, upper jct. (325 ft.) to:	⇅	↗	↻
Spur to Salmon Pond (325 ft.)	0.1 mi.	0 ft.	0:05
Little Long Pond (250 ft.)	0.4 mi.	-75 ft.	0:15
Salmon Pond (300 ft.)	0.8 mi.	50 ft.	0:25
Tunk Mtn. Trail, lower jct. (310 ft.)	1.0 mi.	60 ft.	0:30

This short loop trail, which diverges from Tunk Mtn. Trail to visit two remote ponds, Salmon and Little Long, makes a good alternative route on the descent from Tunk Mtn.

The loop is described from its upper jct. with Tunk Mtn. Trail., 0.7 mi. from ME 182. Hidden Ponds Trail follows the north shore of Salmon

Pond to a spur on the right, which leads 75 ft. to the pond's shore. Beyond, the main trail bears away from Salmon Pond and soon joins the course of a stream leading to Little Long Pond. An informal trail leads along that pond's south shore, but Hidden Ponds Trail bears sharply uphill to the right. After a huge erratic, traverse mossy ledges to a second view of Little Long Pond. Finally, bear away from the pond and hike south, contouring across the hillside to Salmon Pond, where there are good views of Tunk Mtn. Ahead, pass an informal trail on the left; bear right to continue through the woods above Salmon Pond to rejoin Tunk Mtn. Trail. Turn left to reach the trailhead on ME 182 in 0.6 mi.

■ CATHERINE MTN. (942 FT.)

This mountain in T10 SD lies east of Caribou Mtn., just outside the boundary of Donnell PL. To reach the trailhead, drive east on ME 182 from the main Tunk Mtn. trailhead. At 1.0 mi., a dirt road on the right leads 100 ft. to a grassy parking area and the start of an unmaintained trail.

CATHERINE MTN. TRAIL
(NFTM; USGS TUNK LAKE QUAD, GAZETTEER MAPS 24 AND 25)

From ME 182 (450 ft.) to:	⇅	↗	↻
Catherine Mtn. high point (900 ft.)	0.7 mi.	450 ft.	0:35

A woods road to the right (west) is the start of the hike. Follow the road on the level. Beyond, ascend steeply up the east ridge of the mountain. After the angle eases, pass a spur on the right leading 100 yd. to an overlook and views to the north and east. Just ahead, a short side trail on the left leads to views of Tunk Lake and Black Mtn. Ahead on the main trail, cross a town line (orange blazes) and pass several areas of mined rocks. Continue along the cliff edge with good views to Tunk Lake. Pass the upper jct. of the summit loop on the left. Ahead, traverse easily, passing beneath the true summit at about 0.7 mi. From here, retrace your steps, or continue to the upper end of the summit loop trail and swing back just below the face to rejoin the trail for the descent. (*Note:* Beyond this upper jct., an unmaintained trail descends to join Caribou Mtn. Trail in 0.7 mi. This trail leads out to Dynamite Brook Rd.)

SEC 11

FRENCHMAN BAY CONSERVANCY
■ TUCKER MTN. (410 FT.)

A 121-acre public conservation easement on Tucker Mtn. in Sullivan, managed by Frenchman Bay Conservancy, protects its summit and eastern and northern slopes. The mountain's upper ledges have good views south to the peaks of ANP on Mt. Desert Island.

TUCKER MTN. TRAIL (FBC; USGS SULLIVAN QUAD, GAZETTEER MAP 24, FBC TUCKER MTN. MAP)

From US 1 (30 ft.) to:	⇅	⬈	○
Tucker Mtn. summit (410 ft.)	0.6 mi.	380 ft.	0:30

From the Hancock-Sullivan Bridge in Sullivan, travel east on US 1 for 2.5 mi. to a Maine Dept. of Transportation rest area (toilet) on the right on the wooded shore of Long Cove.

To start the hike, walk west along the rest area parking lot, then cross US 1. The trail, an old paved section of US 1, parallels US 1 east through the woods, with blue diamond markers showing the way. In 500 ft., the trail bears left off the old roadway, climbing moderately and sometimes steeply over the south slope. Orange diamond markers with black arrows mark the ascent trail. At the semi-open ledges above, views are to the south. Ahead, turn away from the south slope to join a jeep track and pass an old privy in the woods to the right. Just beyond, a short summit loop leads to the summit, where there is a picnic table and a survey marker.

■ BAKER HILL (381 FT.)

A 58-acre preserve, managed by Frenchman Bay Conservancy, protects the scenic southern slopes of Baker Hill in Sullivan. About 1.5 mi. of trails loop through the property, leading to ledges with views over Sullivan Harbor to Frenchman Bay, and beyond to the peaks of ANP on Mt. Desert Island. Combine the short Baker Hill Loop, Boundary Trail, and a section of Cleft Rock Trail for a nice loop hike.

BAKER HILL LOOP, BOUNDARY TRAIL, AND CLEFT ROCK TRAIL (FBC; USGS SULLIVAN QUAD, GAZETTEER MAP 24, FBC LONG LEDGES & BAKER HILL PRESERVES MAP)

Cumulative from Punkinville Rd. (160 ft.) to:	⇅	⬈	○
Ledges overlook (320 ft.)	0.4 mi.	160 ft.	0:15
Boundary Trail (350 ft.)	0.6 mi.	220 ft.	0:25
Cleft Rock Trail (270 ft.)	0.8 mi.	220 ft.	0:30
Close of loop at T jct. (190 ft.)	1.2 mi.	240 ft.	0:35

From the jct. of US 1 and ME 200 in Sullivan, travel east on US 1 for 1.5 mi. Turn left (north) onto Punkinville Rd. and go 0.2 mi. to trailhead parking on the left (sign). Baker Hill Loop leaves left of the kiosk and quickly reaches a T jct. Turn left here to hike the loop clockwise. Just beyond, where an unmarked trail leaves left, bear sharply right. At the next fork, stay left to climb the outer loop for the best views. Small blue triangles mark the trail. Views west are limited at first, but open up nicely once the upper cliff edge is reached. Beyond a short connector trail that enters from the right, the trail crosses an open slab with excellent views. Once over the wooded summit of Baker Hill, the trail trends mildly down to reach the jct. with Boundary Trail and Baker Hill Trail (leads north into Long Ledges Preserve). Turn right (east) on Boundary Trail and follow red blazes along the property line between the two preserves. At the next jct., bear right on Cleft Rock Trail, climb through a shallow ravine, and then make a moderate descent to the base of Baker Hill. At the original T jct., turn left to return to the trailhead.

SCHOODIC CONNECTOR TRAIL (FBC; USGS SULLIVAN QUAD, GAZETTEER MAP 24, FBC SCHOODIC CONNECTOR TRAILS MAP)

Cumulative from trailhead at Baker Hill Preserve (160 ft.) to:	↓↑	↗	↻
Baker Hill Trail (350 ft.) via Baker Hill Loop	0.4 mi.	190 ft.	0:15
West Loop Trail (290 ft.)	0.9 mi.	190 ft.	0:25
Schoodic Connector Trail (290 ft.)	1.4 mi.	230 ft.	0:40
Spur to parking on Schoodic Bog Rd. (270 ft.)	3.7 mi.	380 ft.	2:00
Downeast Sunrise Trail (190 ft.)	4.9 mi.	480 ft.	2:40
Schoodic Mtn. summit (1,069 ft.)	6.6 mi.	1,350 ft.	3:50
Schoodic Beach parking lot (250 ft.)	7.8 mi.	1,350 ft.	4:30

The Schoodic Connector Trail links 6.6 mi. of foot trails between Punkinville Rd. near US 1 in Sullivan and Schoodic Mtn. in Donnell Pond PL, making the route one of the longest hikes in the Downeast. The conservation lands across which the trail extends were assembled between 2005 and 2015 by Frenchman Bay Conservancy and include Baker Hill, Long Ledges, Long Ledges II, Dutchman, and Schoodic Bog preserves. Beyond Schoodic Bog Preserve, the trail crosses the state-owned, multiuse Downeast Sunrise Trail before climbing Schoodic Mtn. on privately owned land.

Schoodic Connector Trail is most commonly hiked from south to north, saving the climb up Schoodic Mtn. for last. The southern trailhead for the Schoodic Connector Trail is at Baker Hill Preserve. From the jct. of US 1

SEC 11

and ME 200 in Sullivan, travel east on US 1 for 1.5 mi. Turn left (north) onto Punkinville Rd. and go 0.2 mi. to trailhead parking on the left (sign).

To begin the Schoodic Connector Trail route, enter the woods to the left of the trailhead kiosk and quickly reach a T jct. Turn left here to follow Baker Hill Loop to the cliffs above, where there are good views west and south. At 0.6 mi., on the north side of Baker Hill, reach a jct. with Boundary Trail on the right. Ignore this and go straight ahead into Long Ledges Preserve, following Baker Hill Trail. At the next jct. at 0.9 mi., bear left on West Loop Trail and follow it over ledges through semi-open forest.

At 1.4 mi., reach the jct. with Schoodic Connector Trail. Turn left on Schoodic Connector Trail and climb to a ridge top west of Long Pond. Cross the boundary line of Long Ledges II Preserve and enjoy glimpses of Long Pond below on the right through the trees. Follow the ridge past a few erratics and then descend. Beyond a grove of mature spruce and pine, cross Long Pond Brook on a footbridge to enter Dutchman Preserve. Climb the hillside immediately beyond at a moderate grade, then traverse the west slope of Long Pond Hill. Eventually, the trail makes an arc around a red maple swamp before crossing a gravel road. Just ahead, bear left on the same gravel road and follow it east. At the next trail sign, turn left off the gravel road to reach a boundary line for Schoodic Bog Preserve. At 3.7 mi., reach a jct. To the left, Schoodic Connector Trail continues; to the right a spur leads 0.25 mi. to a trailhead parking lot on Schoodic Bog Rd. (To reach this alternate parking area, follow driving directions for Baker Hill Preserve. Continue on Punkinville Rd. for another 1.9 mi., then turn left on Punkin Ledge Rd. Follow it for 0.8 mi. to Schoodic Bog Rd. Turn left on this road to reach the trailhead in another 0.1 mi.) Continue north on Schoodic Connector Trail and soon reach a bench on the right with a good view of Schoodic Mtn. Shortly after, turn left on a gravel road. Ahead, views open up to the right over Schoodic Bog. A beaver flowage beyond blocks the road, necessitating a jog left into the woods on a footpath. Cross Johnny's Brook, then rejoin the gravel road.

At 4.9 mi., cross Downeast Sunrise Trail and enter private property. Follow blue flagging along a jeep trail to a T jct.; turn right here on another jeep trail, which leads east along the base of Schoodic Mtn. Go straight at the next jct., then cross a power-line corridor. At a cairn on the left (be watching for this), leave the jeep trail and follow a footpath as it angles up the slope. The path soon joins an eroded ATV trail and turns left, uphill. Follow the rough, rocky trail until the angle eases at an open ledge of bedrock. Soon after, crest the west ridge of Schoodic Mtn. and turn right (east). Take the bedrock trail into the open, then follow cairns and orange flagging. Good views abound, taking in the hills around Bangor, Blue Hill

Mtn., the Camden Hills, the mountains of ANP, Frenchman Bay, Schoodic Bog, and Flanders Pond.

Reach the summit of Schoodic Mtn. and its fenced-in communications tower at 6.6 mi. Grand views here include Chick Hill, Lead Mtn., Donnell Pond, Tunk Mtn., Caribou Mtn., Catherine Mtn., the twin peaks and cliffs of Black Mtn., Pigeon Hill, and Schoodic Head. Also at the summit is the jct. with Schoodic Mtn. Trail, which leads to Schoodic Beach parking lot in 1.2 mi. Alternatively, it is 1.4 mi. to Schoodic Beach parking lot via Schoodic Beach on Donnell Pond using the Schoodic Mtn. and Schoodic Beach trails.

To spot a car at Schoodic Beach parking lot in Donnell Pond PL, follow driving directions for Schoodic Mtn.

DOWNEAST COASTAL CONSERVANCY

■ PIGEON HILL (317 FT.)

Pigeon Hill in Steuben, the highest point along the coast in Washington County, is part of Pigeon Hill Preserve, a stunning 170-acre property protected by Downeast Coastal Conservancy. A network of five trails traces the eastern and southern slopes of the hill.

The summit ledges of Pigeon Hill offer extraordinary panoramic views over Dyer and Pigeon Hill bays west to Blue Hill Mtn. and Mt. Desert Island, south to the lighthouse on Petit Manan Point and the islands of the Greater Pleasant Bay archipelago, and north to the peaks of Donnell Pond PL. Historic Trail is the traditional route to the peak, but hikers can also combine Silver Mine and Summit Loop trails to reach the top. Ledge Woods Trail offers a meandering descent route.

From the jct. of US 1 and ME 186 (West Bay Rd.) in Gouldsboro, drive east on US 1 for 10.8 mi. to Steuben. Here, turn right (south) on Pigeon Hill Rd. and drive 4.6 mi. to Pigeon Hill Preserve and trailhead parking on the right (sign), opposite an old cemetery.

HISTORIC TRAIL (DCC; USGS PETIT MANAN POINT QUAD, GAZETTEER MAP 17, DCC PIGEON HILL PRESERVE MAP)

Cumulative from Pigeon Hill Rd.

(50 ft.) to:	⇅	↗	⟳
Silver Mine Trail (80 ft.)	100 ft.	30 ft.	0:01
Jct. of Summit Loop Trail and Silver Mine Trail (220 ft.)	0.3 mi.	170 ft.	0:15
Pigeon Hill summit (317 ft.)	0.4 mi.	267 ft.	0:20

SEC 11

Enter the woods at the trailhead kiosk and proceed 100 ft. to a map stand at a jct., where Silver Mine Trail (yellow blazes) departs to the right. Stay left to follow Historic Trail and its blue blazes. Pass the interpretive signs ("Jack Pine Woodlands" and "Big Maple") before reaching the upper jct. with Silver Mine Trail, which enters from the right, and Summit Loop Trail, which leaves to the left.

Continue straight ahead on Historic Trail and climb to ledges with views south and east. Above, the vista widens at a rock bench. Continue in the open to the summit, where a sign notes that Pigeon Hill played an important role in the Eastern Oblique Arc survey triangulation of the eastern United States from New Orleans, Louisiana, to Calais, Maine, between 1833 and 1898.

SILVER MINE TRAIL AND SUMMIT LOOP TRAIL (DCC; USGS PETIT MANAN POINT QUAD, GAZETTEER MAP 17, DCC PIGEON HILL PRESERVE MAP)

Cumulative from Pigeon Hill Rd. (50 ft.) to:	⬍	↗	↻
Start of Silver Mine Trail (80 ft.) via Historic Trail	100 ft.	30 ft.	0:01
Jct. of Historic Trail and Summit Loop Trail (220 ft.)	0.4 mi.	170 ft.	0:15
Ledge Woods Trail, lower jct. (200 ft.)	0.5 mi.	170 ft.	0:20
Ledge Woods Trail, upper jct. (270 ft.)	0.6 mi.	240 ft.	0:30
Pigeon Hill summit (317 ft.) via Summit Loop Trail	0.7 mi.	287 ft.	0:35

Silver Mine and Summit Loop trails, both blazed in yellow, can be combined for an ascent of Pigeon Hill. Take Historic Trail 100 ft. to a jct. with Silver Mine Trail. Turn right on Silver Mine Trail and ascend to an overlook on the right. Ahead, pass through semi-open forest to reach a granite bench with views south and east. Soon after, reach the tailings from an old silver mine and the interpretive sign "Silver Mine." The trail then bears left past cliffs and a talus slope to a jct. with Historic Trail, which turns right, taking a direct route to the top of Pigeon Hill. Continue straight ahead on Summit Loop Trail to contour around the east and then south side of the hill, passing the lower and upper jct. with Ledge Woods Trail en route. Above, views open up west to Mt. Desert Island and north to Schoodic Mtn. and Black Mtn. The summit is just ahead.

LEDGE WOODS TRAIL (DCC; USGS PETIT MANAN POINT QUAD, GAZETTEER MAP 17, DCC PIGEON HILL PRESERVE MAP)

Cumulative from Pigeon Hill summit (317 ft.) to:	⥮	↗	⟳
Start of Ledge Woods Trail (270 ft.) via Summit Loop Trail	0.1 mi.	-47 ft.	0:03
Glacial Erratic Spur (140 ft.)	0.6 mi.	-175 ft.	0:15
Summit Loop Trail (200 ft.)	0.7 mi.	100 ft.	0:25
Pigeon Hill Rd. (50 ft.) via Summit Loop and Silver Mine trails	1.2 mi.	100 ft.	0:40
Pigeon Hill Rd. (50 ft.) via Summit Loop and Historic trails	1.1 mi.	100 ft.	0:35

Ledge Woods Trail is described here as a descent route from the summit of Pigeon Hill. Depart the top of the hill via Summit Loop Trail, descending open ledges to reach the jct. with Ledge Woods Trail in the semi-open woods below. Turn right on the red-blazed Ledge Woods Trail and continue to descend the southern slope of the hill to the jct. with Glacial Erratic Spur, a white-blazed trail leading 0.2 mi. to the so-called Lonely Boulder, a huge erratic in the woods that is well worth a visit. Beyond the spur, Ledge Woods Trail drops down to a 100-ft. contour before climbing back to end at a jct. with Summit Loop Trail. To the right, it is a little more than 1 mi. to the base of Pigeon Hill via Summit Loop Trail and either Historic Trail or Silver Mine Trail.

■ KLONDIKE MTN. (150 FT.)

Owned and managed by DCC, the 46-acre Klondike Mtn. Preserve in Lubec is home to the namesake mountain as well as some 3,600 feet of saltwater shorefront on South Bay. Summit views from Klondike Mtn. range nearly 360 degrees and include Fowler's Mill Pond and the old mill pond dam, plus South Bay.

KLONDIKE MTN. TRAIL (DCC; USGS WEST LUBEC QUAD, GAZETTEER MAP 27, DCC KLONDIKE MTN. MAP)

Cumulative from North Lubec Rd. (100 ft.) to:	⥮	↗	⟳
Fowler's Mill Pond Trail (45 ft.)	0.3 mi.	-55 ft.	0:08
Klondike Mtn., south summit (150 ft.)	0.4 mi.	105 ft.	0:15
Complete loop	0.6 mi.	145 ft.	0:25

SEC 11

From the jct. of US 1 and ME 189 in Whiting, proceed east on ME 189 for 8.9 mi. Turn left (north) on North Lubec Rd. and drive 1.1 mi. to a grassy trailhead parking lot on the left (sign), where there is a register box, a posted map, and picnic tables.

The trail crosses a meadow (formerly a cow pasture) and passes right of an old orchard. Enter the woods beyond and take the wide path downhill to another old pasture. Follow blue diamond markers to a jct., where the end of the Klondike Mtn. Trail loop enters from the right. Continue straight ahead along the woods line, enter the woods, and soon reach a jct. with Fowler's Mill Pond Trail, which departs to the left. Turn right here and quickly come to a spur on the left leading to an overlook. Climb the steep slope beyond to emerge on the mostly open south summit of Klondike Mtn. Beyond, drop into a notch, then scramble up to an overlook and a bench on the north summit. Descend a steep rock staircase, then eventually level out along the base of the mountain (a very short and somewhat easier path on the right bypasses the rock staircase and rejoins the main trail just below). Hike through woods on a rock rib before closing the loop in the meadow. Turn left to return to the trailhead.

LUBEC

■ BENNY'S MTN. (218 FT.)

Maine Coast Heritage Trust owns and manages the 1,225-acre Hamilton Cove Preserve in Lubec. This rugged property encompasses 1.5 mi. of cobble beaches, steep cliffs, and rocky promontories on the Gulf of Maine, while inland, Benny's Mtn. offers far-reaching views ranging from Carrying Place Cove and the town of Lubec to Grand Manan Island in Canada. Benny's Mtn. is shown as Porcupine Hill on some maps.

BENNY'S MTN. TRAIL (MCHT; USGS WEST LUBEC QUAD, GAZETTEER MAP 27, MCHT HAMILTON COVE PRESERVE MAP)

Cumulative from Boot Cove Rd.

(50 ft.) to:	⇅	↗	↻
Start of summit loop (180 ft.)	1.1 mi.	-55 ft.	0:08
Complete loop	2.4 mi.	145 ft.	0:25

From the jct. on ME 189 and South Lubec Rd., 1.2 mi. west of downtown Lubec (sign for Quoddy Head State Park), drive south on South Lubec Rd. for 2.7 mi. to a fork. Here, turn right on Boot Cove Rd. and proceed 2.5 mi. to trailhead parking for Hamilton Cove Preserve on the left.

Benny's Mtn. Trail is an in-and-out route with a lollipop loop around the summit. From the parking area, walk east 250 ft. to an information kiosk in a small meadow (posted map). Here, Main Trail leaves left, the trail to the beach at Hamilton Cove goes straight, and Meadow Trail and Benny's Mtn. Trail head to the right. In another 75 ft., Meadow Trail breaks off left, while Benny's Mtn. Trail continues right to cross Boot Cove Rd. The wide, grassy trail crosses an alder grassland and multiple sections of bog bridging, bears sharply left at a signpost, goes up stone steps to a low ridge, then crosses a bridge over a small stream. A gentle ascent leads to the base of the wooded, rocky knob of Benny's Mtn. and the summit loop jct. Go straight to walk the loop clockwise. Climb around and up the final knob on rocky steps to several good viewpoints. Descend via rock steps through large boulders to close the loop. Turn left to return to the trailhead.

COBSCOOK BAY STATE PARK AND VICINITY

■ LITTLES MTN. (210 FT.)

A 65-foot steel fire tower, erected in 1963, adorns this wooded bump in the northern section of the park. The tower is closed to public, and there is no access to the ladder rungs. The summit offers limited views east to Whiting Bay.

LITTLES MTN. TRAIL (MBPL; USGS WHITING QUAD, GAZETTEER MAP 27, MBPL COBSCOOK BAY STATE PARK GUIDE & MAP)

Cumulative from state park entrance station (90 ft.) to:	Distance	Elevation gain	Time
South Edmunds Rd. (90 ft.)	0.2 mi.	0 ft.	0:05
Littles Mtn. summit (210 ft.)	0.4 mi.	120 ft.	0:15

From the jct. of US 1 and ME 198 in Whiting, drive north for 4.2 mi. Turn right (east) on South Edmunds Rd. and proceed 0.5 mi. to Burnt Cove Rd. on the right and the entrance to Cobscook Bay State Park. The entrance station is 0.1 mi. ahead on this road. Trailhead parking for both Littles Mtn. and Cunningham Mtn. is to the right (west), in front of the kiosk. A toilet is nearby.

Littles Mtn. Trail starts directly across the road on the opposite side of the entrance station. Walk through the woods, and at 0.1 mi., cross South Edmunds Rd. Watch for the sign (Firetower Trail–0.2 to top). Follow the wide old road on a short but steep and rocky 0.2-mi. climb to the summit tower.

■ CUNNINGHAM MTN. (150 FT.)

The ledges on this mountaintop on the western side of the Cobscook State Park offer fine views to Burnt Cove, Broad Cove, and Whiting Bay, as well as the fire tower atop Littles Mtn.

NATURE TRAIL (MBPL; USGS WHITING QUAD, GAZETTEER MAP 27)

Cumulative from park entrance station (90 ft.) to:	↟↡	↗	◷
Cunningham Mtn. summit (150 ft.)	0.9 mi.	60 ft.	0:30
Complete loop via Burnt Cove Rd.	1.4 mi.	60 ft.	0:45

Refer to Littles Mtn. Trail for directions to trailhead parking.

Nature Trail leaves to the left of the kiosk at the entrance station, heading gently downhill to Burnt Cove Brook and the remains of a log bridge. Bear left and soon pass a big white pine. Ahead, the trail follows the brook, sometimes above it and other times beside it. Beyond a ravine, cross a plank bridge next to a tidal flat on Burnt Cove and quickly reach a jct. Bear left (the trail straight ahead leads 0.3 mi. along Burnt Cove to the state park campground) to climb on eroded trail through cedars.

At the jct. (sign: Scenic Overlook) turn right on the summit spur trail. Scramble on rocky and sometimes steep trail to reach the summit and an overlook a few steps to the right. Beyond, descend stone stairs to reach a second overlook on large open ledges. To continue, retrace your steps to the jct. and the main part of Nature Trail, then turn right to reach Burnt Cove Rd. and the trail's end. From here, it is 0.4 mi. north via this park road back to the entrance station and trailhead.

■ BELL MTN. (213 FT.) AND CRANE MTN. (269 FT.)

These two low mountains in Edmunds Township are located in close proximity to each other on lands that are part of Tide Mill Farm. A conservation easement on the 1,523-acre active saltwater farm held by the Maine Dept. of Inland Fisheries & Wildlife protects the farm's ecology while ensuring public access to nonfarmstead portions of the property. Both mountains offer short, easy loop hikes.

SEC 11

BELL MTN. TRAIL (DIFW; USGS WHITING QUAD, GAZETTEER MAP 27, COBSCOOK TRAILS: TRAIL MAP & GUIDE)

Cumulative from Bell Mtn. parking area (90 ft.) to:	↟↡	↗	◷
Bell Mtn. summit (213 ft.)	0.3 mi.	123 ft.	0:15
Complete loop	0.7 mi.	123 ft.	0:25

From the jct. of US 1 and ME 189 in Whiting, drive north on US 1 for 2.5 mi. Turn left (west) on Bell Mtn. Rd. and drive 0.3 mi. to a grassy semicircular parking area on the left (sign). Avoid the wide, grassy road entering the woods to the left of the trailhead sign. Look farther left, toward the mountain, for the signed opening in the woods on the southeastern edge of the parking lot.

Enter the woods and immediately bear left at the loop jct. to ascend the mountain in a clockwise direction. The white-blazed trail climbs rock steps and weaves between rocks, making a rising traverse on the mountain's eastern slope. There are limited view windows through the trees along here. Cresting the ridge of the heavily forested peak, proceed easily to the summit ledges and a partially obscured view over Tide Mill Farm below and farther to Whiting Bay. Descend a fractured cliff face, then contour along the western side of the peak to close the loop.

CRANE MTN. TRAIL
(DIFW; USGS WHITING QUAD, GAZETTEER MAP 27)

Cumulative from Crane Mtn. parking area (210 ft.) to:	⇅	↗	↻
Crane Mtn. summit (269 ft.)	0.3 mi.	59 ft.	0:15
Complete loop	0.7 mi.	59 ft.	0:25

Follow directions to Bell Mtn. then continue on Bell Mtn. Rd. for an additional 0.7 mi. Bear right to quickly reach a dead end and a grassy parking area (sign). To hike the mountain in a clockwise direction, take the trail to the left of the parking area sign. Climb through thick spruce and fir on the west side of the mountain to reach a viewpoint on the left and, just ahead, a large open ledge with views north to the wetlands along Crane Mill Brook. Ahead, walk easily through mature spruce, circling around the peak to the south. Make a descending traverse, bear west around the mountain, and negotiate a mossy ledge to complete the loop a few yd. east of the sign.

MOOSEHORN NATIONAL WILDLIFE REFUGE
■ BALD MTN. (IN BARING PLANTATION; 410 FT.)

This Bald Mtn., one of eighteen so-named in Maine, is in the Baring Division of MNWR. From US 1/ME 9, at a point 0.5 mi. west of the International Ave. Bridge on the outskirts of downtown Calais, and 2.0 mi. east of the jct. of US 1/ME 9 and ME 191, turn south onto Charlotte Rd. Drive 2.4 mi. to Headquarters Rd. on the right and a sign for Moosehorn National Wildlife Refuge. From the refuge entrance, proceed west on Headquarters Rd. for 0.5 mi. to the headquarters complex. Trailhead

SEC 11

parking is on the left. The main foot trail into the refuge (a gravel road at this point) starts to the left of the flagpole (sign: Headquarters Rd. Trail).

HEADQUARTERS RD. TRAIL AND TOWER TRAIL (MNWR; USGS MEDDYBEMPS LAKE EAST QUAD, GAZETTEER MAP 36, U.S. FISH AND WILDLIFE SERVICE MNWR BARING DIVISION MAP)

Cumulative from MNWR headquarters (210 ft.) to:	⇅	↗	⟳
Tower Trail (270 ft.)	2.1 mi.	60 ft.	1:05
Bald Mtn. summit (410 ft.)	2.7 mi.	200 ft.	1:30

From the MNWR headquarters, head west on Headquarters Rd. Trail, one of many refuge road "trails" that are closed to all but official vehicles. Pass Barn Meadow Rd. on the right, then Mile Bridge Rd. on the left. Ahead, where Two Mile Rd. leads sharply left, continue straight on Headquarters Rd. Trail to Mullen Meadow to enter a federally designated wilderness area. Just past the wetlands of Mullen Meadow on the right, Headquarters Rd. Trail passes a jct. with Conic Rd. Trail, then bears left and narrows to a footpath marked with blue blazes.

Following the route of an old road, the trail traverses Bertrand E. Smith Natural Area, 160 acres set aside in the late 1940s to preserve a representative sample of old-growth white pine. Soon, reach a jct. with Tower Trail on left. Take the white-blazed Tower Trail east, at a moderate and then more gradual grade, to the wooded summit of Bald Mtn. Here are the downed remains of the old 100-ft. wooden fire tower (erected in 1937). There are no views, but the concrete stanchions, bolts, cables and other detritus from the fire tower and fire warden camp make for interesting sleuthing.

■ MAGURREWOCK MTN. (384 FT.)

This low mountain in Calais is just inside the northern boundary of MNWR, Baring Division. The trailhead is on Ice House Rd. on the south side of US 1/ME 9, 2.8 mi. east of the jct. of US 1/ME 9 and ME 191, and 0.7 mi. west of the International Ave. Bridge to Canada on the outskirts of downtown Calais. Park outside the gate on the shoulder of US 1.

MAGURREWOCK MTN. TRAIL
(MNWR; USGS CALAIS QUAD, GAZETTEER MAP 36)

From US 1 (75 ft.) to:	⇅	↗	⟳
Magurrewock Mtn. summit (384 ft.)	1.0 mi.	309 ft.	0:35

From the information kiosk, follow Ice House Rd. (part of the East Coast Greenway, a 3,000-mi. multiuse recreation trail from Calais, Maine, to Key West, Florida), with Middle Magurrewock Marsh on the right. At 0.4 mi. from US 1, the unsigned trail leaves Ice House Rd. on the left. (At this jct., a small sign reads "Moosehorn National Wildlife Refuge Auto Tour Route 4.1 mi.," and another small sign reads "Mature Forest.") Follow the wide, grassy jeep track on an easy grade. The trail trends east before swinging back west to reach the wooded summit at 1.0 mi., where there are three small communications towers. A path in front of the leftmost (westernmost) tower leads 50 ft. to ledges and a narrow view west over Magurrewock Marsh to the St. Croix River and into New Brunswick, Canada.

DOWNEAST LAKES

■ WABASSUS MTN. (844 FT.)

This mountain in T43 MD BPP in Washington County is in the Downeast Lakes Community Forest, a 55,578-acre parcel of conservation land protected by Downeast Lakes Land Trust.

From the jct. of ME 9 and ME 193 in Beddington, drive east on ME 9 for 14.6 mi. to Machias River Rd. on the left, marked by a blue and white MBPL sign. Turn here to enter the state-owned Machias River Corridor Public Lands. Drive north on Machias River Rd. (also referred to and sometimes signed as CCC Rd.). At 8.7 mi. from ME 9, turn right to cross a bridge over the Machias River. Immediately after the bridge, turn left to continue north on Little River Rd. At 13.0 mi., pass a Downeast Lakes Land Trust sign on the right. At 15.5 mi., turn left onto a road signed "60-00-0" and "Reggie's Way." At 17.6 mi., the road forks; bear right on Wabassus Mtn. Rd. At 18.3 mi. from ME 9, reach small, grassy trailhead parking area on the left (no sign).

WABASSUS MTN. TRAIL (DLLT; USGS GRAND LAKE STREAM QUAD, GAZETTEER MAP 35, DLLT WABASSUS MTN. TRAIL MAP)

From Wabassus Mtn. Rd. (360 ft.) to:	⇅	↗	↺
Wabassus Mtn. summit (844 ft.) and complete summit loop	0.9 mi.	484 ft.	0:40

SEC 11

From the parking area, walk ahead on Wabassus Mtn. Rd. for 200 ft. The trail (signed) begins on the right just before a stream/culvert. In 50 ft., pass a trail register. Follow blue and silver trail markers through a hemlock grove along the course of the stream. Ahead, bear right to cross the stream on a short footbridge. Faded yellow blazes also mark the lightly used trail.

Climb to a saddle then bear right up the southeast ridge to reach the jct. with the summit loop. Bear left to follow the short loop clockwise. The wooded summit is just ahead, marked by a rock with a yellow blaze in a small clearing. There are limited views through the trees here and ahead along the loop. Close the loop and descend left to the trailhead.

■ POCOMOONSHINE MTN. (610 FT.)

This mountain in Princeton, rising nearly 500 ft. above Pocomoonshine Lake, is the former site of a Maine Forest Service fire tower. On US 1, 2.3 mi. south of Princeton, and 10.5 mi. north of the jct. of US 1 and ME 9 in Baileyville, turn southwest onto South Princeton Rd. Drive 0.9 mi., then turn right onto Pokey Rd. (unsigned). Follow this gravel road (parallels the power line for much of the way) for 4.0 mi. to a high point on the south side of Pocomoonshine Mtn. and the start of a narrow gravel road, the former MFS fire tower road. Park on the shoulder of the gravel road.

POCOMOONSHINE MTN. TRAIL
(NFTM; USGS PRINCETON QUAD, GAZETTEER MAP 36)

From parking along Pokey Rd. (248 ft.) to:	⇅	↗	↻
Pocomoonshine Mtn. summit (613 ft.)	0.4 mi.	365 ft.	0:25

At the start, the route follows the old MFS road across the power-line clearing and uphill into the woods. Ahead, stay right (straight) at a fork. Above, the gravel road levels off. At 0.4 mi., look for an old jeep track on the left. (The gravel road leads straight 200 ft. to a dead-end overlook with views south to Pocomoonshine Lake; in dry conditions and with care, visitors can drive to this point.) Climb the old jeep track to the ridge crest at 0.6 mi. Ahead, just before the jeep track begins to descend, look left into the thick woods to see the concrete stanchions of the old fire tower (removed in the 1970s) on the summit. There are no views when the trees are leafed out.

CALAIS

■ DEVIL'S HEAD (340 FT.)

Devil's Head Conservation Area, a 315-acre property owned and managed by the city of Calais, preserves the dramatic granite headland known as Devil's Head, as well as cobble beaches and upland forests on the U.S. side of the international St. Croix River estuary. Devil's Head Trail makes a loop over this escarpment on the St. Croix River, offering several good views across into New Brunswick, Canada. Devil's Head is a variant of "D'Orville's Head," which refers to Sieur d'Orville, an early settler on nearby St. Croix Island, which was established in 1604 as the first French colony in the New World.

DEVIL'S HEAD TRAIL
(CC; USGS DEVILS HEAD QUAD, GAZETTEER MAP 37, MTF DEVIL'S HEAD CONSERVATION AREA MAP)

Cumulative from western Devil's Head trailhead (80 ft.) to:	⇅	↗	↺
Devil's Head summit (348 ft.)	1.0 mi.	268 ft.	0:40
Eastern trailhead parking near St. Croix River (30 ft.)	1.5 mi.	268 ft.	0:55

From the jct. of US 1 and ME 9, at the turn for the Ferry Point International Bridge to New Brunswick, Canada, in the center of downtown Calais, drive south on US 1 for 6.2 mi. to a prominent green and gold sign on the left for Devil's Head Conservation Area. On the edge of the large parking lot is an information kiosk and a pit toilet. Continue through the lot to the gravel road, and drive 0.3 mi. to the start of Devil's Head Trail on the right. Another pit toilet is just beyond the trail start. Parking is farther ahead on the left.

Cross a low wet area to reach the base of the climb. Ascend gradually to a fork (old trail) and bear right. Contour at first, then climb via switchbacks and rock steps. Where the old trail enters from the left, go right and up. Ahead, undulating trail leads to a limited view to the southwest. Cross a faint old woods road, then climb gradually to the east to reach a clearing. Bear left up rock steps to enjoy a view to the south, which includes the St. Croix River, St. Croix Island, and Passamaquoddy Bay. Continue upward to reach the ridge crest in a mossy area with a partial view of the St. Croix River.

At 1.0 mi., there is a window view looking east. Proceed easily along the summit of Devil's Head, then trend downward to reach a jct. with an old trail on the right. Avoid this by continuing straight ahead. Below, the old trail enters from the right. Pass through a pretty grove of birch, and where the angle eases ahead, contour east. Wend down to a grassy opening and proceed to the easterly trailhead parking area. The start at the westerly Devil's Head trailhead is 0.7 mi. to the left back along the gravel road.

SEC 11

Just ahead on the road's lower loop is a toilet on the left and an interpretive sign on the right that describes some of the area's fascinating history. Stone steps lead from the sign 150 ft. to the shore of the St. Croix River and a dramatic view downriver past Devil's Head to St. Croix Island.

GRAND FALLS TOWNSHIP

■ PASSADUMKEAG MTN. (1,463 FT.)

Passadumkeag Mtn., in Grand Falls Township, just over the Hancock County line in Penobscot County, rises well above the relatively level countryside and extends in a gradual east-west arc for about 5 mi. The mountain is the site of a fourteen-turbine windpower project. The approach is from the west. From the jct. of US 2 and Greenfield Rd. in Costigan, proceed east on Greenfield Rd. The road turns to an excellent dirt road at 11.7 mi. and passes a major power line that begins to follow the north (left) side of road at 13.0 mi. The road goes through an open gate at 13.9 mi., and at 18.1 mi., the major power line leaves the north side (left) of the road at a locked gate on a side road that follows underneath the power line. Park in any of the areas off the road near the gate.

PASSADUMKEAG MTN. TRAIL (NFTM; USGS BRANDY POND AND SAPONAC QUADS, GAZETTEER MAP 34)

From gate on Greenfield Rd. (450 ft.) to:	⤴	↗	⏱
Passadumkeag Mtn. summit (1,463 ft.)	2.1 mi.	1,013 ft.	1:30

Follow the side road from the gate, walking north toward Passadumkeag Mtn., which is visible ahead. At 1.25 mi., pass the old fire warden's camp and a tiny pond on the right. Continue to the next jct. at 1.6 mi., and take the road to the left (the road to the right goes to a wind turbine tower in view) to a cabin on the left side of the road at 1.9 mi. The old fire tower, once on the top of the mountain, now rests on its side behind the cabin. For a 180-degree view from the summit, ranging from Katahdin west to Mt. Washington and south to the peaks of ANP, continue on the road, passing a tower on the right and then another on the left, where the road surface becomes grass. Proceed to a clearing just before the wind turbine tower at 2.1 mi.

SECTION 12
AROOSTOOK COUNTY

In-Text Maps

INTRODUCTION

This section covers the entire sprawling 6,830 square-mi. Aroostook County: Maine's largest, an area larger than Connecticut and Rhode Island combined. Often called the "Crown of Maine" for its geographic expanse across the northern part of the state, the county ranges 120 mi. from north to south between Madawaska and Molunkus Township, and 104 mi. from east to west between T11 R17 WELS and Easton. The county is bounded to the west by the Canadian province of Quebec and on the north and east by New Brunswick, Canada. The St. Francis River and St. John River form part of the northern boundary. To the south are the counties of Somerset, Piscataquis, Penobscot, and Washington. This section describes 23 trails on 15 mountains.

GEOGRAPHY

Aroostook County is known for its wealth of forestland, lakes, ponds, rivers, hills, and mountains. The county is 89 percent forested, and much of this is commercial timberland. Extensive farmland lies along the US 1 corridor in the east near the Canadian border and upward into the St. John River valley. The Fish River, Allagash River, and St. John River flow northward through Aroostook, and the northern portion of the famous 92-mile-long AWW is here. Long Lake, Square Lake, Cross Lake, Eagle Lake, and Scopan Lake are in the northeast. Just to the south, the Aroostook River flows east into Canada.

The mountains of Aroostook County are widely scattered and often remote, some requiring considerable driving over gravel logging roads to reach. They generally range in elevation from 1,500 ft. to around 2,000 ft., but several are near 1,000 ft. There are no ranges or compact mountain areas except for the cluster of peaks in the nearly 22,000-acre Deboullie Public Lands, east of the Allagash River and west of St. Froid Lake in the north-central region of the county.

A number of mountains are in close proximity to US 1 in the eastern region of Aroostook County. The hills west of Bridgewater include Number Nine Mtn. (1,638 ft.). In the town of Mars Hill, close to the international border at New Brunswick, is the county's best-known mountain, solitary Mars Hill (1,748 ft.), which rises prominently from the level country around its base. Just south of the city of Presque Isle is Aroostook State Park, Maine's oldest, where the twin-peaked Quaggy Jo Mtn. (1,213 ft.) looms over Echo Lake. Popular Quaggy Jo may be the most climbed mountain in the county.

West of Presque Isle, Scopan Mtn. (1,440 ft.) rises east of Scopan Lake amid the 16,700-acre Scopan Public Lands. Northwest of Scopan is the craggy bump of Haystack Mtn. (1,142 ft.). Hedgehog Mtn. (1,594 ft.) is hemmed between ME 11 and St. Froid Lake. Continuing west, Deboullie Public Lands occupies the entire unorganized township of T13 R12 WELS. Rising from the rugged terrain dotted by pristine ponds are Deboullie Mtn. (1,981 ft.), Black Mtn. (1,910 ft.), Whitman Mtn. (1,810 ft.), and Gardner Mtn. (1,839 ft.). The famed 92-mile-long AWW slices through the vast forestland of west-central Aroostook County and extends far south into Piscataquis County, close to the northern end of BSP. Two mountains are found in the wild and scenic Allagash River corridor: Round Pond Mtn. (1,505 ft.) in Aroostook and Allagash Mtn. (1,770 ft.) in Piscataquis. West of the town of Ashland and just north of the Piscataquis County line are Round Mtn. (2,150 ft.) and Horseshoe Mtn. (2,084 ft.). An old fire tower tops Oak Hill (1,099 ft.), which is just east of the Penobscot County line.

Half of the Aroostook County mountains lie within the boundaries of North Maine Woods, a large block of forestland, most of which is privately owned and cooperatively managed for renewable forest resources while providing outdoor recreational opportunities for the public. Visitors must register at a checkpoint and pay camping and day-use fees to enter the area. See p. xxvi for information on access to the lands managed by NMW.

The International Appalachian Trail (IAT) threads its way across Aroostook County en route from KWWNM through New Brunswick and Quebec to its North American terminus at Crow Head in Newfoundland, a total distance of 1,900 mi. The IAT enters Aroostook north of Patten and leaves the United States northeast of Mars Hill. The section of the IAT leading to the summit of Mars Hill is described in this guide.

ROAD ACCESS

Trailheads are scattered far and wide across the great expanse of Aroostook County. I-95 is the primary highway access to the county from the south. From I-95, ME 11 connects Sherman Station to Fort Kent. From the terminus of I-95 in Houlton, US 1 heads north along the eastern margin of the county parallel to the Canadian border as far as Van Buren. ME 163 is a major connector between Presque Isle and Ashland. ME 11 at Ashland and ME 163 at St. Francis are jumping-off points for entry into NMW, where travel to remote trailheads is over long distances on active gravel logging roads.

SEC 12

CAMPING

Aroostook State Park features 30 drive-in campsites, showers, restrooms, trailhead parking, and other amenities, including swimming and picnicking at Echo Lake. The park also features a backcountry shelter on Quaggy Jo Mtn. Deboullie PL has 30 primitive campsites, most of them drive-in, but a few are in the backcountry and accessed by an extensive trail system. There are at least 40 NMW-authorized campsites scattered throughout Aroostook County, not including those accessible from the St. John River. A handful of state campsites are available on the water approaches to Round Pond Mtn. and Allagash Mtn. in the AWW. Several primitive water-access campsites are in Scopan PL. There are six privately operated campgrounds in eastern Aroostook County.

AROOSTOOK STATE PARK

This park, just south of Presque Isle proper, was established as Maine's first state park on 100 acres of land donated by local citizens. Subsequent donations have increased the size of the park to its present 900 acres, which encompass the surprisingly rugged peaks of Quaggy Jo Mtn. and much of the west shore of Echo Lake. The park offers year-round recreation, including hiking, camping, swimming, boating, and picnicking.

From a point on US 1 that is 4 mi. south of Presque Isle and 10.7 mi. north of Mars Hill, turn west onto Spragueville Rd. (sign for state park). At 1.0 mi. from US 1, turn left onto State Park Rd. and proceed to the park entrance station (entry fee). The day-use parking area is a short distance beyond. The park is open all year. Camping is available at 30 drive-in sites (restrooms, showers, potable water).

DEBOULLIE PUBLIC LANDS

Located in T15 R9 WELS, in the vast forestland south of St. Francis and northwest of Portage, Deboullie PL is one of the most remote properties in the Maine public lands system. Deboullie is an adaptation of the French word *déboulier*, which translates to "tumble down," a reference to the many rock slides, or talus fields, found in the area. The 21,871 acres encompassed by Deboullie include seventeen scenic ponds and a cluster of low, rugged mountains. Deboullie Mtn. is the highest of the group at 1,981 ft., and the old fire tower on top offers expansive views. Neighboring Black Mtn. is nearly as high (1,910 ft.). Incorporated in Deboullie PL is a 6,903-acre ecological reserve that protects the shorelines of eleven remote ponds. A 30-mi. network of hiking trails meander through the rugged backcountry.

Remote campsites are on Deboullie Pond and Gardner Pond. Frontcountry campsites are on or near Pushineer Pond, Deboullie Pond, Togue Pond, Crater Pond, Denny Pond, Upper Pond, and Perch Pond. All campsites are primitive and include only a fire ring, picnic table, and privy.

ALLAGASH WILDERNESS WATERWAY

The AWW is a magnificent 92-mile corridor of lakes, ponds, rivers, and streams, meandering northward through the heart of Maine's vast industrial forestland from Telos Lake in Piscataquis County to the town of Allagash in Aroostook County, where the Allagash River joins the St. John River. The Maine legislature established the AWW in 1966 to preserve, protect, and enhance the unique wilderness character of the Allagash River region. The waterway received enhanced protection in 1970 when the U.S. Dept. of the Interior designated AWW as the first state-administered component of the National Wild and Scenic River system. A paddling trip along the AWW is the canoe trip of a lifetime and a Maine classic. Some 80 primitive campsites are along the route. Road access to the AWW is over long distances on gravel logging roads. Two mountains with hiking trails are found amid the beauty of the AWW: Round Pond Mtn. and Allagash Mtn.

SUGGESTED HIKES

■ Easy

HAYSTACK MTN.

	�啠	↗	○
RT via Cpl. Dustin J. Libby Summit Trail	0.5 mi.	280 ft.	0:25

Make this short but steep climb for broad views ranging across Maine's North Woods as far as Katahdin. A memorial bench on top makes a great spot for a break. See Cpl. Dustin J. Libby Summit Trail, p. 549.

HEDGEHOG MTN.

	↺	↗	○
RT via Hedgehog Mtn. Trail	1.2 mi.	540 ft.	0:55

Hike to the open ledges on this summit for a panorama that includes Portage Lake, Fish River, St. Froid Lake, the rugged peaks of Deboullie PL, and Katahdin. See Hedgehog Mtn. Trail, p. 550.

CRATER POND

		↻	↗	○
OW via Crater Trail		2.0 mi.	325 ft.	1:10

Circle pretty Crater Pond and enjoy views at several craggy lookouts on this pleasant ridge walk. See Crater Trail, p. 557.

■ Moderate

QUAGGY JO MTN.

	↻	↗	○
LP via South Peak Trail, Ridge Trail, and North Peak Trail 2.2 mi.	825 ft.	1:40

Make a scenic loop over twin summits for good views over Echo Lake, to the hills and farmland beyond. To begin, see South Peak Trail, p. 544.

MARS HILL

		↻	↗	○
RT via IAT		2.4 mi.	1,100 ft.	1:45

Hike a section of the IAT for extensive views southwest to Katahdin and east into Canada, as well as a close-up look at Maine's first windpower project. See IAT, p. 546.

SCOPAN MTN.

		↻	↗	○
RT via Scopan Mtn. Trail		3.8 mi.	700 ft.	2:15

This pleasant loop hike reaches two lookouts with nice views, first to the east and then to the west, over the vast, forested landscape of eastern Aroostook County. See Scopan Mtn. Trail, p. 548.

DEBOULLIE POND

		↻	↗	○
LP via Deboullie Loop Trail		5.7 mi.	340 ft.	3:00

Make a wonderful loop around this big, beautiful pond for great views of Deboullie Mtn. and Black Mtn., passing ice caves and a small beach along the way. See Deboullie Loop Trail, p. 554.

ALLAGASH MTN.

RT via Allagash Mtn. Trail	2.8 mi.	730 ft.	1:45

From the summit's renovated fire tower, drink in outstanding views of uberscenic Allagash Lake, the Allagash River region, and far beyond. Trailhead access is by foot via an old woods road or by canoe or kayak. See Allagash Mtn. Trail, p. 561.

■ Strenuous
DEBOULLIE MTN. AND BLACK MTN.

LP via Black Mtn. Trail, Tower Trail, and Deboullie Loop Trail	5.8 mi.	1,250 ft.	3:30

Hike the premiere summits in this wild and remote region. Enjoy a handful of craggy outlooks and an old fire tower on Deboullie Mtn. then circle back along pristine Deboullie Pond. To begin, see Black Mtn. Trail, p. 553.

GARDNER MTN. AND GARDNER POND

LP via Gardner Loop Trail	8.3 mi.	1,750 ft.	5:00

Explore the bumpy ridgeline of Gardner Mtn. and loop around the clear waters of Gardner Pond for a look at the talus slopes and cliff faces on the mountain's north side. See Gardner Loop Trail, p. 558.

SEC 12

TRAIL DESCRIPTIONS

AROOSTOOK STATE PARK

■ QUAGGY JO MTN. (1,213 FT.)

This mountain rises abruptly west of Echo Lake and is the central natural feature of Aroostook State Park. Quaggy Jo is a shortened version of its Wabanaki name, QuaQuaJo, which translates to "twin-peaked." A four-trail network on the mountain offers 3.25 mi. of hiking. Day-use parking is a short distance beyond the park entrance station, on the left just above Echo Lake.

For visitors planning to hike the entire 3-mi. loop over Quaggy Jo Mtn. (includes South Peak Trail, Ridge Trail, and North Peak Trail), park officials highly recommend doing so in a clockwise direction, starting with South Peak Trail.

SOUTH PEAK TRAIL (MBPL; USGS ECHO LAKE QUAD, GAZETTEER MAP 65, MBPL AROOSTOOK STATE PARK: HIKING AND CROSS-COUNTRY SKI TRAILS MAP)

From campground at site 18 (640 ft.) to:	⮃	↗	◷
Quaggy Jo Mtn., South Peak (1,215 ft.)	0.5 mi.	575 ft.	0:35

South Peak Trail starts from the campground at site 18 (sign). From the day-use parking lot, walk west on the park road through the campground to the outer edge of the lower loop. The trail starts out on a cross-country ski trail, following blue blazes. In 350 ft., Notch Trail departs to the right (leads 0.25 mi. to the Quaggy Jo ridgeline north of and below South Peak). At 0.15 mi., begin a steep ascent. At 0.25 mi., scramble on slabby rock up the left side of a rock face. At 0.35 mi., negotiate a wide and steep path of loose rock, and soon after, weave up a rock face (nice views back to Echo Lake). At 0.45 mi., Ridge Trail leaves to the right. Towers are in view ahead. Continue on up, pass to the right of the towers, and at the sign "South Peak," bear right and descend to the lookout platform for a wonderful view to the west, as well as to Quaggy Jo's North Peak and the city of Presque Isle.

RIDGE TRAIL (MBPL; USGS ECHO LAKE QUAD, GAZETTEER MAP 65, MBPL AROOSTOOK STATE PARK: HIKING AND CROSS-COUNTRY SKI TRAILS MAP)

From South Peak Trail (1,200 ft.) to:	⮃	↗	◷
Quaggy Jo Mtn., North Peak (1,141 ft.)	1.0 mi.	250 ft.	0:40

SEC 12

Ridge Trail heads north from the jct. with South Peak Trail just below the top of South Peak. Descend moderately at first along the north ridge of South Peak, then more steeply over a short pitch of loose rocks. The path levels out at 0.2 mi. and reaches the jct. with Notch Trail on the right at 0.3 mi. Beyond, climb at an easy grade to join a grassy jeep track at a signpost at 0.6 mi.; go right to stay on Ridge Trail. Proceed easily on the wide track to an Adirondack-style shelter and picnic table on the right at 0.75 mi. This vantage point on the ridge offers a nice view east over Echo Lake and south to Mars Hill. From the shelter, descend easily, then ascend on the wide track to reach the jct. with North Peak Trail, which enters from the right at 0.95 mi. Continue straight ahead, pass a viewpoint on the left, and arrive at the top of North Peak at 1.0 mi., where there is a good view of Echo Lake and Presque Isle.

NORTH PEAK TRAIL (MBPL; USGS ECHO LAKE QUAD, GAZETTEER MAP 65, MBPL AROOSTOOK STATE PARK: HIKING AND CROSS-COUNTRY SKI TRAILS MAP)

From Ridge Trail (1,125 ft.) to:	⇅	↗	↻
Campground near playground (575 ft.)	0.65 mi.	-550 ft.	0:20

From the jct. with Ridge Trail just below the top of North Peak, descend easily at first and then steeply. At 0.25 mi., the grade eases. Soon after, cross a cross-country ski trail at an angle. Ahead, follow a series of boardwalks. At 0.45 mi., a spur on the left leads to the day-use parking area above Echo Lake. Break here to end the hike, or continue on a long, easy contour to end at the campground just above the playground.

NOTCH TRAIL (MBPL; USGS ECHO LAKE QUAD, GAZETTEER MAP 65, MBPL AROOSTOOK STATE PARK: HIKING AND CROSS-COUNTRY SKI TRAILS MAP)

This short connector trail extends from near the start of South Peak Trail to a notch north of and below South Peak and gains 235 ft. of elevation. At 350 ft., begin climbing rock steps through a ravine. Ahead, cross two footbridges over an intermittent stream. At 0.25 mi., join Ridge Trail.

US 1 CORRIDOR

■ MARS HILL (1,748 FT.)

This monadnock rises abruptly in the eastern section of the namesake town of Mars Hill, in an almost-level area of farms and woodland. The mountain extends in a north-south direction for about 3 mi. and parallels the

Canadian border, which is just to the east. It is the site of the first large-scale windpower project in New England, with 28 turbines lining the long ridge top.

To reach the trailhead from the jct. of US 1A and US 1 in Mars Hill, take US 1A north for 0.3 mi. Turn right (east) onto Boynton Rd., and go 1.3 mi. to a T intersection. Turn right onto Country Club Rd., and take the first left (Graves Rd.) to the Bigrock Mtn. ski area. Park in the gravel/unimproved parking lot at the base of the South Star Triple Chairlift (south of the base lodge).

IAT NORTHBOUND TO MARS HILL
(IAT; USGS MARS HILL QUAD, GAZETTEER MAP 59, IAT/SIA
INTERNATIONAL APPALACHIAN TRAIL: MAINE SECTION MAP)

From Bigrock Mtn. ski area parking lot (650 ft.) to:	⇅	↗	↺
Mars Hill south summit (1,748 ft.) via IAT and multiuse trail	1.2 mi.	1,100 ft.	1:10

The trail is marked with light-blue blazes and IAT markers as far as the summit. Begin climbing up the ski trail (Outer Orbit) to the right (south) of the chairlift, past the ski area maintenance building. Follow this trail to the top terminal of the chairlift, then proceed to another ski trail (the Hooch) that merges in 150 ft. to the left (north) of the ski lift terminal. Follow this trail to a fairly large clearing, just below a noticeably steeper section of the ski trail. At this point, look to the left (northeast) for a trail marker and an opening in the woods for the first in a series of four switchbacks. The switchbacks are all marked and serve to reduce the steepness of the ski trail, while giving hikers more of a backcountry feel during the ascent, since each one enters and exits on the ski trail. Use the ski trail for short segments while progressing to each subsequent switchback. After the final switchback, proceed on the ski trail to a footpath on the right (east) side of the ski trail. This path intersects with a gravel multiuse trail near the base of one of the wind towers.

Follow the multiuse trail to the right (south) to reach the summit of Mars Hill, where there is a lean-to. Views extend across forests and farmland in all directions, ranging as far southwest as Katahdin and east into New Brunswick across the St. John River valley.

Return to the trailhead via the ascent route, or follow the multiuse trail northward to the top terminal of the North Star Double Chairlift and then descend via the ski trail to the left (south) of the lift. Use caution on this route because the ski area access road is steep and consists of loose gravel and rocks. An alternative route for ascent or descent uses the access road.

(*Note:* The IAT continues northward along the ridgeline of Mars Hill toward ft. Fairfield and the Canadian border.)

■ NUMBER NINE MTN. (1,638 FT.)

NUMBER NINE MTN. TRAIL
(NFTM; USGS NUMBER NINE LAKE QUAD, GAZETTEER MAP 59)

From parking area and boat launch (1,100 ft.) to:	⇅	↗	↺
Number Nine Mtn. summit (1,638 ft.)	1.5 mi.	540 ft.	1:00

This peak is west of Bridgewater in a small group of mountains clustered around Number Nine Lake. In Bridgewater, from the jct. of US 1 and Bootfoot Rd., turn west onto Bootfoot Rd. (paved) and continue for 3.1 mi. to a T intersection. Turn right onto the unmarked gravel road (Number Nine Lake Rd.). Pass Whitney Brook Rd. on the right at 4.5 mi. At 11.4 mi., bear left at the fork and go uphill to reach the Number Nine Lake parking lot and boat launch site at 12.1 mi. (*Note:* Number Nine Lake Rd. follows a power line for about the first 10 mi. Where the power line leaves the road on the left at 11.4 mi., proceed directly to Number Nine Lake.) No camping is allowed in the area of the boat launch (posted sign).

From the boat launch and parking area, the trail follows a camp road across a bridge over the outlet stream and south along the east side of the lake. At 0.4 mi., pass a gravel road on the left. At 0.5 mi., the route departs on a left fork through a yellow gate and starts climbing on what appears to be a gravel road at the start, but is paved. At 1.1 mi., pass through a second yellow gate. The trail extends to a communications tower and small building owned by Fraser Company. The actual summit is beyond the tower and has some open ledges. Even though no access to the tower is available, there are views from the summit ledges. (*Note:* A 250-megawatt wind farm with as many as 119 turbines is planned for the mountains around Number Nine Lake. As of 2017, it was not known how this project will affect access and the route on Number Nine Mtn.)

ME 163 CORRIDOR

■ SCOPAN MTN. (1,450 FT.)

This long and bumpy ridge in T11 R4 WELS between Presque Isle and Ashland rises east of Scopan Lake amid the 16,700-acre Scopan PL unit.

From the jct. of US 1 and State St. in downtown Presque Isle, turn west on State St. and drive across the bridge over Presque Isle Stream to ME 163 in 0.2 mi. Turn left on ME 163 and drive west for 7.1 mi. to West

SEC
12

Chapman Rd. in Mapleton. Reset odometer. Turn south on West Chapman Rd. and drive 6.9 mi. to a fork (road turns to gravel at 6.0 mi.). Stay right at the fork, and at 8.8 mi., take a right turn (small sign). At the next fork at 9.1 mi., stay right, and at 10.7 mi. from ME 163, turn left into the trailhead parking lot (kiosk, pit toilet).

SCOPAN MTN. TRAIL (MBPL; USGS SCOPAN LAKE EAST QUAD, GAZETTEER MAPS 64 AND 58, MTF SCOPAN MTN. TRAIL MAP)

Cumulative from trailhead parking (785 ft.) to:	⮃	↗	◷
Scopan Mtn. summit (1,450 ft.), first viewpoint	2.0 mi.	665 ft.	1:20
Complete loop	3.8 mi.	700 ft.	2:15

Scopan Mtn. Trail makes a nice circuit hike over the northern portion of the mountain from the base of its eastern slope. The trail leaves to the left of the trailhead kiosk and follows blue blazes north on the level to a fork at 0.1 mi. To follow the loop counterclockwise as described, go right here. Ahead, cross a wet section on several sets of bog bridges, then trend west and begin climbing. At 1.0 mi., the trail joins an old forest road. Follow the wide track up a shallow ravine. Reach a level shelf, then veer left and up to a winding rock staircase. Beyond it, traverse north across the mountainside on an undulating route, passing a low, mossy rock wall on the left at 1.6 mi. At 1.9 mi., after a moderate pitch via a rock staircase, arrive at a view window to the east. A short, steep pitch via a couple of switchbacks leads to the summit ridge, where there's a log bench and a view east over Alder Lake to Quaggy Jo Mtn. and Presque Isle.

Swing around the wooded summit and start down the ridge. At several large, bucked-up logs at 2.25 mi. is a view that includes Peaked Mtn. and a jumble of hills to the southwest. Continue the descent, cross an old forest road in a saddle, and then wend easily along the rolling ridge to a knob on the east side of the mountain at 2.9 mi. Begin a steady descent, then contour southwest into a ravine. Pass below a mossy cliff face before angling down the slope to the mountain's base. Close the loop and turn right to return to the trailhead.

■ HAYSTACK MTN. (1,275 FT.)

Haystack Mtn., the remains of an extinct volcano, is on the north side of ME 163 in Castle Hill, east of Ashland and west of Presque Isle. The Maine Bureau of Parks and Lands owns and manages the 215-acre property encompassing the mountain. In 2011, the summit trail was named in honor of Marine corporal Dustin J. Libby of Castle Hill, who was killed in action in Iraq in 2006. The town of Castle Hill maintains the trail.

The trailhead, a well-marked parking lot and picnic area at a height-of-land on the north side of ME 163, is accessed by a short gravel driveway. From the jct. of ME 11 and ME 163 in Ashland, drive 9.3 mi. east on ME 163. Alternatively, from the jct. of US 1 and State St. in downtown Presque Isle, turn west on State St. and drive across the bridge over Presque Isle Stream to ME 163 in 0.2 mi. Turn left on ME 163 and drive west for 11.0 mi. No water or toilets are available. Camping and overnight parking are not allowed.

CPL. DUSTIN J. LIBBY SUMMIT TRAIL
(TCH; USGS MAPLETON QUAD, GAZETTEER MAP 64,
MTF HAYSTACK MTN. TRAIL: CASTLE HILL MAP)

From ME 163 parking area (995 ft.) to:	⇅	↗	↻
Haystack Mtn. summit (1,275 ft.)	0.25 mi.	280 ft.	0:15

The trail starts to the left of the information kiosk at the north end of the parking lot. Well-graded at the start, it becomes rougher as it climbs moderately and then steeply to an unmarked jct. at the base of the open ledges on the upper mountain. Here, the trail bears left and up. (To the right, a rocky scramble up a gully leads to an exposed ledge face that hikers must scale to reach the summit. MBPL does not recommend this route, even though it is shown on MBPL's map as part of a Haystack loop.) Beyond, the trail ascends on more rugged terrain, then makes a short climb over ledges before swinging around to the top.

The grassy, rocky summit offers a panoramic view that includes Katahdin to the southwest, Mapleton farmland to the south and east, Scopan Mtn. and Scopan Lake immediately to the south, Quaggy Jo Mtn. and Mars Hill to the south-southeast, and Round Mtn. in the heart of NMW to the west. The bench dedicated to Corporal Libby is a fine spot for a break.

ME 11 CORRIDOR

■ HEDGEHOG MTN. (1,594 FT.)

Hedgehog Mountain in T15 R6 WELS rises just west of St. Froid Lake. The trailhead is on the west side of ME 11, 3.5 mi. south of Winterville and 12.9 mi. north of Portage (jct. of ME 11 and West St.). Parking is at a well-marked highway rest area, where there are picnic shelters, a spring, and a vault toilet, but no camping or overnight parking. A trail to the top of the mountain is maintained by Hedgehog Mtn. Land Trust.

SEC 12

HEDGEHOG MTN. TRAIL
(HMLT; USGS WINTERVILLE QUAD, GAZETTEER MAP 63, MTF HEDGEHOG MTN. TRAIL: WINTERVILLE MAP)

From picnic area and parking on ME 11 (1,050 ft.) to:	⇅	↗	⟳
Hedgehog Mtn. summit (1,594 ft.)	0.6 mi.	540 ft.	0:35

The trail leaves from the southwest corner of the picnic area. Look right into the woods to see a small blue sign with a white arrow posted to a tree. Walk to the arrow and then bear left up the now obvious trail. The moss-covered concrete spring will be immediately on your left. The trail soon passes between the old fire warden's cabin and a white building. Beyond, it climbs steadily up the south ridge to a picnic table on the summit, where there was once a fire tower (removed in 1978). From the open ledges are fine views of Portage Lake, Fish River, and St. Froid Lake to the south and west. Deboullie Mtn. and Black Mtn. are visible to the west. Katahdin is in view far to the south.

■ OAK HILL (1,099 FT.)
Oak Hill is located in T8 R5 WELS just west of ME 11. From the jct. of ME 11 and ME 212 at Knowles Corner in Moro Plantation, drive north on ME 11 for 10.6 mi. (or 1.8 mi. north of the jct. of ME 11 and Grand Lake Rd. [left] and St. Croix Rd. [right]). Turn left (west) off ME 11 onto a gravel road. Immediately take the right fork (sign for Irving Maine Woodlands, Camp Violette Rd.; also shown as Unnamed 3 Rd. on Gazetteer map 58). Drive 1.3 mi., then take a right turn (north). Continue for 0.5 mi., where the road turns sharply left (west). In another 0.3 mi., a road leaves to the right; stay straight. The trailhead is just 0.2 mi. ahead, at a high point on the road (2.3 mi. from ME 11). There is a small cairn (may be obscured) on the south (left) side of the road. The roadbed is wide enough for parking.

OAK HILL TOWER TRAIL
(NFTM; USGS UMCOLCUS LAKE QUAD, GAZETTEER MAP 58)

From gravel road (950 ft.) to:	⇅	↗	⟳
Oak Hill summit (1,099 ft.)	0.15 mi.	250 ft.	0:15

The path is flagged with colored surveyor's tape and has a worn tread. Local hikers have, over time, marked the entrance liberally with flagging, but this may or may not be evident. From the road, the trail disappears into the thick woods. Once into the woods, the treadway is more defined. The concrete stanchions of the base of the fire tower are about 200 yd. up the hillside to the south via a fairly steep climb. The summit is heavily wooded with large oak trees. The cabless tower (1924) offers a 360-degree view.

DEBOULLIE PUBLIC LANDS

Access to Deboullie PL from the north or the east is by active gravel logging roads and involves considerable driving distances. En route, visitors will pass through an NMW checkpoint and must pay day-use and camping fees.

The shortest route to Deboullie is from the north at St. Francis. From the jct. of US 1 and ME 161 in Fort Kent, drive west on ME 161 for 17 mi. to the tiny village of St. Francis (town office and post office). From there, drive an additional 6.0 mi. to Chamberlain's Market on the left at the jct. of ME 161 and St. Francis Rd. Reset odometer. Turn left (south) on the unsigned St. Francis Rd., and at a fork in 0.3 mi., stay straight. At 0.4 mi., reach the NMW St. Francis Checkpoint (fee). At 7.0 mi., Hewes Brook Rd. joins from the left; continue straight. Cross a bridge at 7.3 mi. Gardner

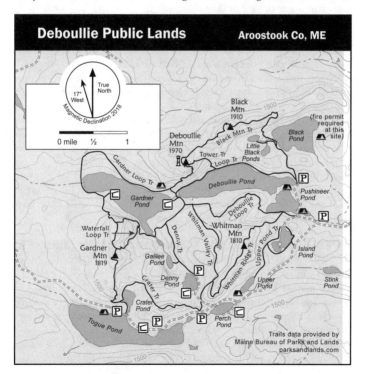

SEC
12

Brook Rd. enters from the left at 8.2 mi.; continue straight. At 8.7 mi. from ME 161, turn left on an unsigned gravel road (small signs for Deboullie PL and Red River Camps).

Enter Deboullie PL just ahead at 8.9 mi. (blue and white sign). Stay straight at all jct. At 15.2 mi., on the left is the Togue Pond trailhead and parking for Gardner Loop Trail and Crater Trail. On the left at 16.5 mi. is the Whitman Mtn. trailhead (east end of Crater Trail, Whitman Ridge Trail, and access to Whitman Valley Trail). Denny Pond Rd. leaves to the left at 16.7 mi. (access to Denny Pond Trail is 0.5 mi. north on this road). At 17.1 mi., a road to Perch Pond goes right; bear left here. Reach a T intersection at 18.9 mi. Here, T15 R9/Red River Rd. enters from the right (access route from Portage). Turn left, and in another 0.2 mi., bear right at a fork (left goes to southeast end of Deboullie Loop Trail and on to Red River Camps). Drive 0.8 mi., passing the outlet of Pushineer Pond and then Deboullie East campsites and a boat launch and parking area to the hiker parking at the end of the road.

Alternative access is from the east in Portage. From the jct. of ME 11 and West Rd. (opposite Coffin's General Store and the Portage post office and next to Dean's Motor Lodge and Restaurant), turn left (west) on West Rd. and drive along the south end of Portage Lake. Just beyond the lake, at 1.0 mi., turn left on Rocky Brook Rd. and drive through an active commercial wood yard (Maine Woods Company). At the next jct., ahead at 1.8 mi., stay straight. Reach the NMW Fish River Checkpoint (fee) at 5.3 mi. At 7.1 mi., leave Rocky Brook Rd. and turn right onto Hewes Brook Rd. Cross a one-lane bridge over the Fish River at 10.4 mi. At 12.4 mi., a road on the left leads to Fish River Lake; stay straight on Hewes Brook Rd. At 19.9 mi., just after crossing the Red River, leave Hewes Brook Rd. and turn left onto T15 R9/Red River Camps Rd. At 27.4 mi., enter Deboullie PL (blue and white sign). To the right, it is 1.0 mi. to the trailhead at the end of the road (just beyond the Deboullie Pond boat launch and parking, and Deboullie East campsites).

■ DEBOULLIE MTN. (1,981 FT.) AND BLACK MTN. (1,910 FT.)

Deboullie Mtn. rises steeply above the western end of Deboullie Pond. Visitors can enjoy a fine view of the prominent peak and tower from the eastern end of the pond. Reach the peak via Deboullie Loop Trail and Tower Trail or via Black Mtn. Trail. The 48-ft. fire tower on the summit affords excellent views that extend south to Katahdin, southeast to Haystack Mtn., and southwest to Horseshoe Mtn.

Black Mtn. is just northeast of Deboullie Mtn., connected by a long ridge. The approach to the wooded peak via Black Mtn. Trail passes by the two Little Black Ponds (North and South) and Black Pond and features numerous outlooks with good views to the south and north. Continue over Deboullie Mtn. and return to the trailhead via the north shore of Deboullie Pond for a fine loop hike.

BLACK MTN. TRAIL (MBPL; DEBOULLIE PUBLIC LANDS, P. 551)

Cumulative from Deboullie Pond hiker parking area at end of road (1,150 ft.) to:	⮃	↗	⏱
Little Black Ponds Trail (1,290 ft.)	0.6 mi.	150 ft.	0:25
Black Mtn. summit (1,910 ft.)	2.3 mi.	850 ft.	1:35
Deboullie Mtn. summit and fire tower (1,981 ft.)	3.7 mi.	1,250 ft.	2:30
Gardner Pond Trail (1,240 ft.)	4.4 mi.	1,250 ft.	2:50

Black Mtn. Trail connects the east and west ends of Deboullie Pond via an ascent over the long, undulating ridgeline of Black Mtn. and Deboullie Mtn. At the trailhead parking lot at the end of the road a short distance beyond the Deboullie Pond boat launch and campsites at Deboullie East, there is a sign for Deboullie Mtn. Trail, Black Ponds, and Deboullie Tower. Deboullie Loop Trail enters the woods on the left; follow this to quickly connect to Black Mtn. Trail.

At a jct. in 0.1 mi. (sign), Black Mtn. Trail goes right, while Deboullie Loop Trail goes straight ahead; turn right to continue on Black Mtn. Trail, which wends easily north on an old jeep track. Climb a rocky stretch, then descend to a jct. Black Pond is through the woods to the right. Here, the 0.5-mi. Little Black Ponds Trail leads west to North Little Black Pond and South Little Black Pond.

From the jct., Black Mtn. Trail quickly passes a side trail on the right that leads 50 ft. to Black Pond. It then swings around the west side of the pond before climbing in earnest via rock steps. The ascent is steady at a moderate to steep grade. More rock steps lead to a shallow notch at 1.2 mi. The trail bears right to gain a shelf above, then drops to Black Mtn. Overlook, which offers fine vistas south over Black Pond. Beyond, climb a short, steep pitch, then descend to a shelf and follow a route west across the ridgeline of Black Mtn. At 1.7 mi., reach Four Ponds Overlook immediately to the left. From here, Deboullie, Black, Pushineer, and Island ponds are all in view. At 2.2 mi., climb rock steps to reach the wooded high point on Black Mtn.

Ahead, descend the western ridge to Fifth Pelletier Brook Lake Overlook on the right at 2.4 mi. After a contour, regain the ridge, then descend toward Deboullie Mtn. Pass an unsigned outlook to the north at 2.8 mi. and make a moderate descent before meandering easily along the ridge. Reach a saddle at the base of Deboullie, then join an old jeep track up and west for a short stretch. On foot trail again, circle around the rugged upper rocks of Deboullie. At 3.6 mi., a view on the right looks out over Gardner Pond to the Gardner Mtn. rock slide. At 3.7 mi., reach the summit of Deboullie Mtn. and its 48-foot fire tower (erected in 1929). Here also are a picnic table, the old fire warden's cabin, a privy, and another outbuilding. To the south, Tower Trail leaves to the left side of the clearing.

To continue on Black Mtn. Trail from the top of Deboullie Mtn., looking south, return to the right edge of the clearing where the path entered. Turn left on an unsigned trail. Soon, begin a very steep descent on narrow trail down the south side of the mountain. At 3.9 mi., the angle eases, and at 4.0 mi., reach the base of a talus slope and proceed along its base. Turn away from the slope at 4.2 mi. and begin a mostly steady descent to reach a T jct. with Gardner Loop Trail at 4.4 mi. To the right, this trail leads west around Gardner Pond. To the left, Gardner Pond Trail connects with Deboullie Loop Trail near the western end of Deboullie Pond.

DEBOULLIE LOOP TRAIL (MBPL; DEBOULLIE PUBLIC LANDS, P. 551)

Cumulative from Deboullie Pond hiker parking area at end of road (1,150 ft.) to:	�??↕	↗	○
Tower Trail (1,140 ft.)	1.4 mi.	50 ft.	0:40
Gardner Loop Trail (1,140 ft.)	2.2 mi.	50 ft.	1:10
Whitman Valley Trail (1,180 ft.)	2.7 mi.	90 ft.	1:25
Whitman Ridge Trail (1,150 ft.)	4.7 mi.	340 ft.	2:30
Access road to Red River Camps (1,180 ft.)	4.9 mi.	340 ft.	2:35
Complete loop via access roads	5.7 mi.	340 ft.	3:00

At the trailhead parking lot at the end of the road a short distance beyond the Deboullie Pond boat launch and campsites at Deboullie East, there is a sign for Deboullie Mtn. Trail, Black Ponds, and Deboullie Tower; Deboullie Loop Trail enters the woods on the left. At a jct. in 0.1 mi. (sign), Black Mtn. Trail goes right, while Deboullie Loop Trail goes straight ahead.

Continue on Deboullie Loop Trail through the woods well away from Deboullie Pond, then return to the shore. At 0.5 mi., a side trail on the right leads 40 ft. to the pond. Soon after, pass a sign on the right: "Ice Caves." (In the narrow, shaded rock crevices here, ice and snow can remain year-round.) At 1.2 mi., reach a talus slope. Cross the slope above the pond and enjoy good views ahead to the Deboullie Mtn. fire tower and Gardner Mtn. Reenter the woods and reach the jct. with Tower Trail on the right at 1.4 mi. There is a picnic table at this jct.

From the jct., Deboullie Loop Trail follows fairly close to the pond. At 2.0 mi., pass through a section of large, mossy boulders, and at 2.2 mi., arrive at an unsigned jct. To the right, Gardner Loop Trail heads west to meet the west end of Black Mtn. Trail, and then continues around Gardner Pond. To the left, Deboullie Loop Trail and Gardner Loop Trail coincide for the next 0.3 mi. Turn left and soon cross the outlet of Gardner Pond. Just beyond, reach Gardner Portage Trail; this 0.1-mi. trail connects Deboullie Pond and Gardner Pond. From the jct., Deboullie Pond and Deboullie West campsite are 100 ft. left (east); Gardner Pond and Gardner East Shelter are 0.1 mi. to the right (west).

From the jct., continue ahead on Deboullie Loop Trail, following an old woods road. Ahead, bear left onto a footpath, and reach another old road at a jct. at 2.5 mi. Here, Gardner Loop Trail turns right, while Deboullie Loop Trail heads left. Go left on Deboullie Loop Trail. In another 0.2 mi., Whitman Valley Trail departs on the right. After this jct., Deboullie Loop Trail crosses a stream and follows the old woods road. At 3.0 mi., the trail diverges right off the old road and, ahead, bears left along the base of a large, mossy cliff wall. Climb the left side of the wall via steps, iron rungs, and roots, then make a rising traverse across the slope. Reach a high point and follow a contour, now high above Deboullie Pond. Beyond, descend steeply off the ridge and follow a contour again.

At 3.8 mi., arrive at a bench next to a boulder with a view to the north across Deboullie Pond to the talus slope on Black Mtn. Wend through mossy boulders, then make a long descent to Pushineer Pond, cross a streamlet, and reach the south shore at 4.5 mi. Follow the shore east to the jct. with Whitman Ridge Trail, which enters from the right at 4.7 mi. From here, follow the old woods road out to the access road that leads to Red River Camps, where Deboullie Loop Trail ends at 4.9 mi.

To return to the Deboullie Pond trailhead, turn left and walk downhill past a privy to a road jct. Turn left and walk north past campsites and a boat launch at the outlet of Pushineer Pond and on to Deboullie Pond. It is 0.75 mi. on the road from the end of Deboullie Loop Trail to Deboullie Pond trailhead.

TOWER TRAIL (MBPL; DEBOULLIE PUBLIC LANDS, P. 551)

Cumulative from Deboullie Pond hiker parking area at end of road (1,140 ft.) to:	⇅	↗	⟳
Tower Trail (1,140 ft.) via Deboullie Loop Trail	1.4 mi.	50 ft.	0:40
Deboullie Mtn. summit and fire tower (1,981 ft.)	2.1 mi.	890 ft.	1:30

SEC 12

Tower Trail climbs from the north shore of Deboullie Pond to the summit fire tower on Deboullie Mtn. Tower Trail leaves from Deboullie Loop Trail at a point 1.4 mi. west of the Deboullie Pond trailhead.

From Deboullie Pond, Tower Trail ascends a rock staircase. Beyond, the trail crosses a footbridge, then climbs more rock steps. The grade is moderate all the way to the ridge, which is gained at 0.4 mi. Walk easily west, then make a steep, rocky climb, winding up the slope on switchbacks. At the base of another rock staircase, a view window yields a look to the northeast. Just above, the angle eases, and the trail climbs the final rock staircase to the summit fire tower in a small clearing atop Deboullie Mtn.

■ WHITMAN MTN. (1,810 FT.)

Located in the southeast corner of Deboullie PL, the wooded ridge of Whitman Mtn. extends from Perch Pond northeast to Pushineer Pond. Several outlooks on the mountain offer views of Deboullie Pond, Deboullie Mtn., and Black Mtn. Whitman Ridge Trail traverses the ridge. Combine Whitman Ridge Trail with Whitman Valley Trail and a section of Deboullie Loop Trail for a good loop hike.

WHITMAN RIDGE TRAIL (MBPL; DEBOULLIE PUBLIC LANDS, P. 551)

Cumulative from Whitman Mtn. trailhead (1,250 ft.) to:	↑↓	↗	⟳
Whitman Valley Trail (1,500 ft.)	0.5 mi.	250 ft.	0:20
Whitman Mtn. summit (1,810 ft.)	1.8 mi.	550 ft.	1:10
Deboullie Loop Trail (1,150 ft.)	2.7 mi.	550 ft.	1:40

From the Whitman Mtn. trailhead on the Deboullie access road, the trail heads north, and in 0.2 mi., crosses Denny Pond Rd. Beyond, the trail is an old woods road that wends easily up to a jct. at 0.5 mi. Here, Whitman Valley Trail goes straight, while Whitman Ridge Trail continues to the right, up rock steps. After a short, moderate climb, the trail turns right onto an old woods road. In another 0.1 mi., it bears left off the road onto a footpath. At 0.75 mi., make a moderate climb up rock stairs, and then head south along the edge of the ridge. Reach Perch Pond Overlook and a bench on the right at 0.8 mi. Crest the ridge of Whitman Mtn. at 1.0 mi. in a small open area.

Follow the undulating ridge northeast, crossing the wooded high point on Whitman Mtn. at 1.8 mi., where there is a bench with a view west to the talus slope of Gardner Mtn. above Gardner Pond. Descend beyond the bench. At 2.2 mi., a viewpoint on the left looks north to Deboullie Mtn., its tower, and Black Mtn. Descend steep switchbacks to a bench with a similar view of the Deboullie tower as before. Continue the descent of Whitman Mtn. and reach the jct. with Deboullie Loop Trail at 2.7 mi. To the left, Deboullie Loop Trail leads 2.0 mi. to Whitman Valley Trail, a good option for a loop hike. To the right, Deboullie Loop Trail leads 0.2 mi. to its end at the access road to Red River Camps.

WHITMAN VALLEY TRAIL
(MBPL; DEBOULLIE PUBLIC LANDS, P. 551)

From Deboullie Loop Trail (1,180 ft.) to:	↕	↗	↻
Whitman Ridge Trail (1,500 ft.)	1.5 mi.	320 ft.	0:55

This trail extends from Deboullie Loop Trail near the west end of Deboullie Pond south to Whitman Ridge Trail, 0.5 mi. north of the Whitman Mtn. trailhead on the Deboullie access road. From Deboullie Loop Trail, follow Whitman Valley Trail south on an easy grade along a brook. At 0.4 mi., bear right away from the brook and soon pass a swampy area on the left. At 0.8 mi., with a beaver bog on the left, swing away west to the base of a mossy cliff face. Hike along the cliff base, sometimes under overhanging rock, for the next 0.3 mi. Eventually, trend away from the cliff to join an old woods road. Turn right and head gradually downhill to the jct. of Whitman Ridge Trail at 1.5 mi. The Whitman Mtn. trailhead on the Deboullie access road is 0.5 mi. straight ahead.

CRATER TRAIL (MBPL; DEBOULLIE PUBLIC LANDS, P. 551)

Cumulative from Whitman Mtn. trailhead (1,250 ft.) to:	↕	↗	↻
High point on ridge (1,578 ft.)	0.5 mi.	325 ft.	0:25
Gardner Loop Trail (1,240 ft.)	1.7 mi.	325 ft.	1:00
Togue Pond trailhead (1,200 ft.)	2.0 mi.	325 ft.	1:10

Crater Trail climbs west to several craggy outlooks before continuing on to circle pretty Crater Pond. The trail begins as a wide, grassy path at the Whitman Mtn. trailhead. It enters the woods at a point 25 ft. left of the kiosk and Whitman Ridge Trail. On the level at first, the trail climbs gradually, then moderately, and then steeply on switchbacks to the ridge above, where there is a view north to Denny Pond, the cliffs around Denny Pond and Galilee Pond, and the Deboullie Mtn. fire tower. Ahead, descend to a notch, then ascend via two log staircases to a bench at 0.5 mi., where there is a nice view south to Togue Pond. Climb to the apex of the ridge, then descend to a saddle. Beyond, follow the undulating ridge, then descend a short, steep pitch. Cross a streamlet, then climb up and left along the base of a great cliff face. Cross another small stream, and just after, pass beneath a mossy cliff wall. At 1.6 mi., the trail passes below a huge vertical cliff wall. Reach Crater Pond and thread through the mossy boulders along the west shore. Impressive cliffs and talus fields are in view up to the right. Soon, bear right away from the pond to reach Gardner Loop Trail at 1.9 mi. Turn left to reach the Togue Pond trailhead on the Deboullie access road in another 0.3 mi.

SEC
12

■ GARDNER MTN. (1,839 FT.)

The wooded south-north ridge of this mountain extends from Togue Pond to Gardner Pond in the south-central section of Deboullie PL. Rugged cliffs and talus slopes characterize the peak's north side, which faces wild and scenic Gardner Pond. Gardner Loop Trail makes a circuit over the mountain and around the pond.

GARDNER LOOP TRAIL (MBPL; DEBOULLIE PUBLIC LANDS, P. 551)

Cumulative from Togue Pond trailhead (1,200 ft.) to:	↻	↗	○
Gardner Mtn., north summit (1,839 ft.)	1.8 mi.	750 ft.	1:20
Side trail to Gardner Point Shelter on Gardner Pond (1,135 ft.)	2.6 mi.	750 ft.	1:40
Deboullie Loop Trail (1,140 ft.)	5.4 mi.	1,000 ft.	3:15
Complete loop (via left fork of Waterfall Loop on Gardner Mtn.)	8.9 mi.	1,650 ft.	5:20
from Togue Pond trailhead (1,200 ft.) to:			
Complete loop (via right fork of Waterfall Loop on Gardner Mtn.)	9.3 mi.	1,750 ft.	5:35

From the Togue Pond trailhead on the Deboullie access road, follow an old woods road north. At 0.15 mi., turn left off the road onto a foot trail. At 0.25 mi., Crater Trail departs to the right. Stay left on Gardner Loop Trail and climb gradually to the base of Gardner Mtn. The steep climbing begins at 0.4 mi., with the trail switchbacking up the slope, eventually passing to the right of a rock wall. Beyond, the angle eases, and the trail arrives at a view on the right at 0.6 mi. that looks east over Crater Pond. Continue on to reach a bench and a view that includes Togue Pond as well as Crater Pond. Climb ahead, then descend a steep slope. Proceed at an easy to moderate grade up the ridge, hike a very brief stretch on an old woods road, and then turn left to pass beneath a mossy cliff face. Ahead, wind up the west side of the peak to reach the wooded south summit of Gardner Mtn. at 1.4 mi. Descend the north side to reach the jct. with the end of Gardner Loop Trail, which enters from the right at 1.5 mi. Cross the saddle separating the two peaks and climb to the wooded north summit of Gardner Mtn., which is reached at 1.8 mi. Cross the ridge to the next jct. at 2.0 mi., where a spur from the other end of Gardner Loop Trail enters from the right. Bear left here to continue on Gardner Loop Trail in a clockwise direction.

Make a moderate descent off the north side of the mountain. From a shelf partway down, there are nice views of Gardner Pond below. Reach the base of the mountain and a jct. at 2.6 mi., where a spur on the right leads 0.15 mi. to the Gardner Point Shelter on Gardner Pond, where there is an excellent view of the Gardner Mtn. rock slide.

From the shelter jct., the trail soon reaches the shore of Gardner Pond and a huge grove of old-growth cedars. Ahead, it crosses a small stream on the west side of the pond, bears left away from the pond, and crosses a footbridge. It then returns to the pond and turns left to cross an earthen berm through a cedar swamp. The trail then bears away from Gardner Pond and makes a moderate to steep ascent to a high point on the north side of the pond at 3.8 mi. Ahead, the trail follows an undulating route across the steep slope of the hillside before descending a rock staircase. It skirts a beaver pond and continues down to the north shore of Gardner Pond. The trail then climbs a mossy gully of rocks to reach a jct. where a side trail on the right leads 150 ft. to nice views south over Gardner Pond to the great cliffs and talus slopes on the north face of Gardner Mtn.

At 5.3 mi., Black Mtn. Trail from the top of Deboullie Mtn. enters from the left. In another 0.1 mi., Gardner Pond Trail merges with Deboullie Loop Trail, which enters from the left. The two trails coincide for the next 0.3 mi., crossing Gardner Portage Trail just ahead (this canoe carry trail connects Gardner Pond and Deboullie Pond). At a jct. at 5.7 mi., Deboullie Loop Trail leaves to the left. Turn right to continue on Gardner Loop Trail. Ahead, where the trail joins an old woods road, turn left. At 6.1 mi., Denny Trail departs to the right. Go straight on Gardner Loop Trail and descend toward an arm of Gardner Pond. Cross an inlet, then turn north along the west side of the arm to reach a jct. at 6.8 mi.

The forks left and right from this jct. form the "Waterfall Loop," as noted on the MBPL map. Options here: Turn left uphill to climb past a seasonal waterfall to reach the saddle between the two summits of Gardner Mtn. in 0.6 mi., then head south to return to the Togue Pond trailhead in another 1.5 mi. Alternatively from this jct., continue along Gardner Pond, then climb steeply 0.5 mi. to the west via boulder fields and rock faces to the north summit of Gardner Mtn. at a point 1.9 mi. from the Togue Pond trailhead.

DENNY TRAIL (MBPL; DEBOULLIE PUBLIC LANDS, P. 551)

From Gardner Pond Trail (1,220 ft.) to:	⇅	↗	⏱
Denny Pond trailhead (1,280 ft.)	1.1 mi.	80 ft.	0:35

Denny Trail leaves from Gardner Loop Trail at a point 0.4 mi. west of its jct. with Deboullie Loop Trail and 0.7 mi. from the jct. with Gardner Portage Trail, which connects Deboullie Pond and Gardner Pond. Denny Trail follows an old woods road on a contour through a narrow valley. At

SEC 12

0.7 mi., a side trail to the right leads to Galilee Pond, set in a wild amphitheater of great cliffs. Denny Pond is reached at 1.0 mi., and the end of the trail is just ahead at a campsite at 1.1 mi. From here, it is 0.5 mi. south via Denny Pond Rd. to the Deboullie access road.

ALLAGASH WILDERNESS WATERWAY

■ ROUND POND MTN. (1,505 FT.)

The trailhead for Round Pond Mtn. is on the eastern shore of Round Pond in the 20,000-acre Round Pond Public Lands in the heart of the 92-mile AWW in T13 R12 WELS. The trailhead is accessible only by canoe or kayak. The mountain is most often climbed by paddlers on the Allagash River, but day hikers can make the climb as well.

The nearest boat launch site is on Blanchette-Maibec Rd. at Henderson Brook Bridge, about 2.5 mi. west of the trailhead. This put-in site is just north of the bridge on a sheltered part of the riverbank. Designated parking is at a site away from the water at Henderson Brook Bridge.

Vehicle access to Henderson Brook Bridge is by Blanchette-Maibec Rd. and, from the east, either by Rocky Brook Rd. from Portage (through NMW Fish River Checkpoint) or by Realty Rd. from Ashland (through NMW Six Mile Checkpoint). Access from the north is by Michaud Farm Rd. from Allagash (through NMW Allagash Checkpoint). A day-use fee is charged to pass through all NMW checkpoints. Travel distances over gravel-surfaced industrial logging roads are considerable, and camping is recommended for hikers desiring to paddle and hike Round Pond Mtn. (NMW daily camping fees apply). Campsites at Round Pond include Tower Trail, Round Pond Rips, Squirrel Pocket, Back Channel, Inlet, and Outlet. Paddlers and campers on the AWW are subject to the special rules governing this Wilderness river corridor.

ROUND POND MTN. TRAIL (MBPL; USGS ROUND POND AND FIVE FINGER BROOK QUADS, GAZETTEER MAP 62, NMW MAP OF MAINE NORTH WOODS, MTF ROUND POND MTN. TRAIL MAP)

From Tower Trail campsite and trailhead on Round Pond (781 ft.) to:	⇅	↗	↻
Round Pond Mtn. summit (1,505 ft.)	2.5 mi.	730 ft.	1:40

From the boat launch site, paddle downriver to Round Pond, then head northeast across the pond to Tower Trail campsite (sign), located on the eastern shore of the pond. Round Pond Mtn. Trail leaves the campsite and climbs more than 700 ft. in 2.5 mi. to reach the summit of Round Pond Mtn. Although the trail is steep in several places, and rocks and roots make for rough footing, the pleasant forest and the solitude of the location make the effort worthwhile. A decommissioned Maine Forest Service fire tower (erected in 1946) is on the summit. MBPL advises hikers not to climb the tower, given its poor condition.

■ ALLAGASH MTN. (1,770 FT.)

Allagash Mtn. rises above the southwest end of 4,210-acre Allagash Lake in T7 R14 WELS in Piscataquis County. The lake is part of the AWW system and is the headwater for the Allagash River. There is no direct vehicle access to Allagash Lake. Access by canoe or kayak is possible from either the upper part of Allagash Stream or Johnson Pond west of the lake. Access by foot is possible from the south via Carry Trail, a former road that leads 1.0 mi. from a gate to Carry Trail Campsite and the ranger station at the southwest corner of the lake, where the trailhead is located. Driving access to the gate is from Ledge Rd.

A number of driving routes are possible to reach the Allagash Lake area; all involve considerable driving time over gravel logging roads. Telos Rd. to Grande Marche Rd. to Ledge Rd. is one option, but there are several others. Because of the travel time and distances, camping is recommended. Visitors must pay day-use and camping fees when passing through any NMW checkpoint en route to Allagash Lake.

ALLAGASH MTN. TRAIL (MBPL; USGS ALLAGASH LAKE QUAD, GAZETTEER MAP 55, NMW MAP OF NORTH MAINE WOODS, MTF ALLAGASH MTN. MAP)

From ranger station on Allagash Lake (1,040 ft.) to:	⇅	⟋	○
Allagash Mtn. summit (1,770 ft.)	1.4 mi.	730 ft.	1:05

The trail to Allagash Mtn. leaves to the right of the ranger station and at 0.1 mi. starts to ascend through mixed forest. The climbing is moderate over a series of stepped rises. At 0.3 mi., the trail begins a steady ascent, reaching the summit of Allagash Mtn. at 0.7 mi. The renovated fire tower provides outstanding views of the remote Allagash River region, including Chamberlain Lake, Eagle Lake, and Churchill Lake to the east; the forestland of the upper St. John River watershed to the west, and the lands of the upper Penobscot River watershed to the south.

NORTH MAINE WOODS

■ ROUND MTN. (2,150 FT.)

Round Mtn. is in T11 R8 WELS, west of Ashland, south of Realty Rd., and just north of Jack Mtn. Rd. Round Mtn. is the northernmost of three adjacent peaks—Round, Middle, and Peaked—that extend northeast to

SEC 12

southwest. Peaked Mtn. (2,260 ft.) is the highest of the three, but there is no trail to its summit.

Round Mtn. is reached from Ashland by traveling west on Realty Rd. A day-use fee is charged to pass through the NMW Six Mile Checkpoint. Just beyond the checkpoint, bear left on Pinkham Rd. and continue southwest, crossing the Machias River at 8.7 mi. Turn right onto Jack Mtn. Rd. at 8.8 mi. This road passes Week's Brook Campsite at 12.2 mi. At 16.4 mi., turn right turn onto a logging road with a sign for Week's Pond. Follow this road to where the forest canopy covers the roadway just before the descent to Round Mtn. Pond. Ample parking is located at 20.2 mi.

ROUND MTN. TRAIL
(NFTM; USGS ROUND MTN. QUAD, GAZETTEER MAP 63)

From parking area (1,313 ft.) to:	᠓	↗	⟳
Round Mtn. summit and fire tower (2,150 ft.)	1.5 mi.	840 ft.	1:10

The unmarked trail follows the canopied road down toward Round Mtn. Pond and stays above but in view of the pond on the west side. Midway along the west shore is an angler's carry and boat access to the pond. About 200 yd. beyond, take the old road to the left (southwest), climbing gently uphill. The road soon passes a camp driveway on the right (the green-roofed camp is partially visible through the trees). Continue southwest and gently uphill on the old road.

The next landmark is a camp with the sign Round Mtn. Lodge. This is the site of the old fire warden's cabin that has been incorporated into one of the two buildings. The old fire warden's trail leaves the camp lot near the covered spring. Look for yellow, orange, and pink flagging tape on trees along the route, which leads generally straight up the steep mountainside (no switchbacks) in typical fire-warden-trail style. The trail is overgrown but shows some evidence of the old tread on the ground, and it's easy to follow the colored tape. Round Mtn. Trail ends at the old fire tower (1918), which is still standing but has no cab. The fire tower offers an excellent 360-degree view of Katahdin to the south-southwest, Mt. Chase to the south-southeast, Horseshoe Mtn. to the west, Haystack Mtn. to the east, and Deboullie Mtn. to the north.

■ HORSESHOE MTN. (2,084 FT.)

This mountain in T11 R10 WELS is part of the Rocky Brook Mountains, which rise just to the north of the Aroostook County–Piscataquis County line, southeast of the Musquacook lakes and southwest of Big Machias

Lake. (*Note:* Horseshoe Mtn. is shown as Rocky Brook Mtn. on Gazetteer map 62.)

HORSESHOE MTN. TRAIL (NFTM; USGS MOOSELEUK LAKE AND FIFTH MUSQUACOOK LAKE QUADS, GAZETTEER MAP 62, NMW MAP OF NORTH MAINE WOODS)

From Realty Rd. (1,050 ft.) to:	⇅	↗	↻
Horseshoe Mtn. summit (2,084 ft.)	1.3 mi.	1,040 ft.	1:10

From Ashland, travel west on Realty Rd. to reach the trailhead. A day-use fee is charged to pass through the NMW Six Mile Checkpoint. The trailhead is 26.6 mi. west of the checkpoint, or 2.4 mi. east of the campsite on Upper McNally Pond (the closest NMW-authorized campsite). The trailhead is on the south side of Realty Rd., on the east side of the Rocky Brook Mountains. Ample parking is located just off the road. There are no signs for the trail.

The trail (a woods road) enters the woods going west and almost immediately takes a left (south). (Continuing straight ahead leads quickly back to Realty Rd.) At 1.0 mi., continue south through a jct. with a road running east, and soon pass an old overgrown road on the right (goes up through a cut in the bank and ends at an old camp). The trail (still a woods road) goes down and up twice, and as it begins to go down a third time, Horseshoe Mtn. and the tower become visible.

Continue to the base of the steep-sided mountain and a fork. Bear left at the fork and proceed downhill for about 100 yd. to a low point and an intermittent stream. Just before the stream are pruned trees with colored surveyor's tape and the flagged trail. The path has been kept open and the tread is visible, particularly on its upper portions. The path, marked with colored flagging tape, generally follows the watercourse for a few hundred yd., then moves left to go straight and steeply to a sag just below the summit. Beyond, the trail climbs the last few hundred yd. to the fire tower.

The steel fire tower is in excellent condition but has no cab. A fine 360-degree view are possible from the tower. Katahdin and Traveler Mtn. are visible to the south-southwest, Mt. Chase to the southeast, Round Mtn. to the east, Priestly Mtn. to the west, and Deboullie Mtn. to the north.

SEC 12

APPENDIX A

HELPFUL INFORMATION AND CONTACTS

Organization	Office	Phone Number
Appalachian Mountain Club (AMC)	Main Office	800-372-1758 (membership); 617-523-0636 (general info); 603-466-2727 (reservations)
AMC Cold River Camp		603-694-3291
AMC Echo Lake Camp		207-244-3747
AMC Maine Woods Initiative		207-695-3085
AMC Maine Chapter		
AMC Four Thousand Footer Club		
Acadia National Park	Headquarters	
Allagash Wilderness Waterway		207-941-4014
Appalachian Trail Conservancy (ATC)	Main Office	304-535-6331
ATC New England Regional Office		413-528-8002
Baxter State Park	Headquarters	207-723-5140
Belgrade Regional Conservation Alliance		207-495-6039
Bethel Conservation Commission		207-824-2669
Blue Hill Heritage Trust		207-374-5118
Camden Snow Bowl		207-236-3438
Chatham Trails Association		

Address or Location	Website, Email
10 City Square, Boston, MA 02129	outdoors.org, AMCmembership@outdoors.org, AMCinformation@outdoors.org, AMClodging@outdoors.org
32 AMC Rd., N. Chatham, NH 03813	amccoldrivercamp.org, crcmanagers@gmail.com
P.O. Box 102, Southwest Harbor, ME 04660	amcecholakecamp.org, managers@amcecholakecamp.org
P.O. Box 310, Greenville, ME 04441	outdoors.org/lodging-camping/maine-lodges, AMClodging@outdoors.org
	amcmaine.org
P.O. Box 444, Exeter, NH 03833	amc4000footer.org, savage@amc4000footer.org
P.O. Box 177, ME 233 McFarland Hill, Bar Harbor, ME 04609	nps.gov/acad
Bureau of Parks and Lands, Northern Region Hdqtrs., 106 Hogan Rd., Bangor, ME 04401	parksandlands.com
P.O. Box 807, 799 Washington St., Harpers Ferry, WV 25425	appalachiantrail.org, info@appalachiantrail.org
P.O. Box 264, Kellogg Conservation Center, South Egremont, MA 01258	appalachiantrail.org, atc-nero@appalachiantrail.org
64 Balsam Dr., Millinocket, ME 04462	baxterstatepark.org
P.O. Box 250, 137 Main St., Belgrade Lakes, ME 04918	belgradelakes.org, brca@belgradelakes.org
P.O. Box 1660, 9 Main St., Bethel, ME 04217	bethelmaine.org, info@bethelmaine.org
P.O. Box 222, 157 Hinckley Ridge Rd., Blue Hill, ME 04614	bluehillheritagetrust.org, info@bluehillheritagetrust.org
P.O. Box 1207, 20 Barnestown Rd., Camden, ME 04843	camdensnowbowl.com, info@camdensnowbowl.com
	chathamtrails.org, president@chathamtrails.org

Organization	Office	Phone Number
City of Calais	Manager	207-454-2521 x10
Clifton Climbers Alliance		
Coastal Mountains Land Trust		207-236-7091
Downeast Coastal Conservancy		207-255-4500
Forest Society of Maine		207-945-9200
Francis Small Heritage Trust		207-221-0853
Freeport Conservation Trust		207-865-3985
Frenchman Bay Conservancy		207-422-2328
Friends of Burnt Meadow Mtn.		
Friends of Libby Hill/ Gray Community Endowment		
Garmin International		913-397-8200
Georges River Land Trust		207-594-5166
Great Pond Mountain Conservation Trust		207-469-6929
Great Works Regional Land Trust		207-646-3604
Greater Lovell Land Trust		207-925-1056
Hebron Academy	Outdoor Education Coordinator	207-966-5223
Hedgehog Mtn. Land Trust		
High Peaks Alliance		
International Appalachian Trail	Maine Chapter	
Island Heritage Trust		207-348-2455
Katahdin Wilderness Camps		207- 837-1599
Katahdin Woods and Waters National Monument		207-456-6001
Kennebec Estuary Land Trust		207-442-8400

Address or Location	Website, Email
P.O. Box 413, Calais, ME 04619	calaismaine.org, manager@calaismaine.org
P.O. Box 1876, Bangor, ME 04401	cliftonclimbersalliance.org, info@cliftonclimbersalliance.org
101 Mt. Battie St., Camden, ME 04843	coastalmountains.org, info@coastalmountains.org
P.O. Box 760, Machias, ME 04654	downeastcoastalconservancy.org, info@downeastcoastalconservancy.org
115 Franklin St., 3rd Floor, Bangor, Maine 04401	fsmaine.org, info@fsmaine.org
P.O. Box 414, Limerick, ME 04048	fsht.org, mail@fsht.org
P.O. Box 433, Freeport, ME 04032	freeportconservationtrust.org, info@freeportconservationtrust.org
P.O. Box 150, 71 Tidal Falls Rd., Hancock, ME 04640	frenchmanbay.org, info@frenchmanbay.org
	friendsofburntmeadowmountains.com, friendsofbumm@gmail.com
P.O. Box 1376, Gray, ME 04039	libbyhill.org, libbyhilltrails@gmail.com
	garmin.com/en-US
8 North Main St., Suite 200, Rockland, ME 04841	georgesriver.org
P.O. Box 266, Orland, ME 04472	greatpondtrust.org, info@greatpondtrust.org
P.O. Box 151, South Berwick, ME 03908	greatworkslandtrust.org, info@gwrlt.org
208 Main St., Lovell, ME 04051	gllt.org, info@gllt.org
P.O. Box 309, Hebron, ME 04238	hebronacademy.org
P.O. Box 250, Eagle Lake, ME 04788	
P.O. Box 98, Strong, ME 04983	highpeaksalliance.org, highpeaksallianceinfo@gmail.com
P.O. Box 916, Gardiner, ME 04345	internationalatmaine.org, info@internationalatmaine.org
P.O. Box 42, 420 Sunset Rd., Deer Isle, ME 04627	islandheritagetrust.org, iht@islandheritagetrust.org
Box 314, Millinocket, ME 04462	katahdinlakewildernesscamps.com, truenorth@KatahdinLakeWildernessCamps.com
P.O. Box 446, Patten, ME 04765	nps.gov/kaww, lunksoos@gmail.com
P.O. Box 1128, 92 Front St., 2nd Fl., Bath, ME 04530	kennebecestuary.org, info@kennebecestuary.org

Organization	Office	Phone Number
Kennebec Land Trust		207-377-2848
Land & Garden Preserve		207-276-3727
Leave No Trace Center for Outdoor Ethics		800-332-4100
Loon Echo Land Trust		207-647-4352
Mahoosuc Land Trust		207-824-3806
Maine Appalachian Trail Club		
Maine Appalachian Trail Land Trust		207-808-2073
Maine Audubon	Headquarters	207-781-2330
Maine Campground Owners Association		207-782-5874
Maine Coast Heritage Trust		207-729-7366
Maine Dept. of Agriculture, Conservation and Forestry, Bureau of Parks and Lands	Headquarters	207-287-3821
Maine Dept. of Inland Fisheries and Wildlife	Headquarters	207-287-8000
Maine Forest Service (MFS)	Headquarters	207-287-2791
MFS Campfire Permits	Ashland office Augusta office Old Town office	207-435-7963 207-624-3700 207-827-1800
Maine Huts & Trails		207-265-2400
Maine Land Trust Network	c/o Maine Coast Heritage Trust	207-729-7366
Maine Outdoor Adventure Club		207-775-6622
Maine State Park Campground Reservations		800-332-1501 (in Maine), 207-624-9950 (outside of Maine)
Maine State Police		911 (emergency), 207-624-7200
Maine Trail Finder	c/o Center for Community GIS	207-778-0900
McPherson Timberlands		207-947-6970
Midcoast Conservancy		207-389-5150
Moosehorn National Wildlife Refuge		207-454-7161

Address or Location	Website, Email
P.O. Box 231, 331 Main St., Winthrop, ME 04364	tklt.org, tkerchner@tklt.org
P.O. Box 208, Seal Harbor, ME 04675	gardenpreserve.org, info@gardenpreserve.org
P.O. Box 997, Boulder, CO 80306	lnt.org, info@lnt.org
8 Depot St., Ste. 4, Bridgton, ME 04009	loonecholandtrust.org, info@lelt.org
P.O. Box 981, 162 North Rd., Bethel, ME 04217	mahoosuc.org, info@mahoosuc.org
P.O. Box 283, Augusta, ME 04332	matc.org, info@matc.org
P.O. Box 761, Portland, ME 04104	matlt.org, srucker@matlt.org
20 Gilsland Farm Rd., Falmouth, ME 04105	maineaudubon.org, info@maineaudubon.org
10 Falcon Rd., Suite 1, Lewiston, ME 04240	campmaine.com
1 Bowdoin Mill Island, Suite 201, Topsham, ME 04086	mcht.org, info@mcht.org
22 State House Station, 18 Elkins Ln. (AMHI Campus), Augusta, ME 04333	maine.gov/dacf/parks
41 State House Station, 284 State St., Augusta, ME 04333	maine.gov/ifw
22 State House Station, 18 Elkins Ln. (AMHI Campus), Augusta, ME 04333	maine.gov/dacf/mfs

496C N. Main St., Kingfield, ME 04947	mainehuts.org
1 Bowdoin Mill Island, Ste. 201, Topsham, ME 04086	mltn.org
P.O. Box 11251, Portland, ME 04104	moac.org, info@moac.org
	maine.gov/dacf/parks/camping/reservations
	campground.reservations@maine.gov
	maine.gov/dps/msp
155 Main Street #2B, Farmington, ME 04938	community-gis.org, info@community-gis.org
1182 Odlin Rd., Hermon, ME 04401	mcphersontimberlands.com, timber@mcphersontimberlands.com
290 Atlantic Hwy., Edgecomb, ME 04556	midcoastconservancy.org, news@midcoastconservancy.org
103 Headquarters Rd., Baring, ME 04694	fws.gov/refuge/moosehorn, fw5rw_mhnwr@fws.gov

Organization	Office	Phone Number
Mt. Agamenticus Conservation Program		207-361-1102
Mt. Cutler Preservation Trust		207-625-4043
The Nature Conservancy	Maine Field Office	207-729-5181
Northeast Harbor Village Improvement Society		
North Maine Woods	Main Office	207-435-6213
Recreation.gov		877-444-6777 (reservations), 888-448-1474 (customer service)
Royal River Conservation Trust		207-847-9399
Rumford Water District	Superintendent	207-364-8531
Spencer Pond Camps		207-745-1599
Sugarloaf Mtn. Ski Resort	Marketing Director	207-237-6887
Town of Carrabassett Valley		207-235-2645
Town of Castle Hill		207-764-3754
Town of Freeport		207-865-4743
Town of Hiram		207-625-4663
Town of Leeds		207-524-5171
Town of Sebago		207-787-2457
United State Geological Survey	Headquarters	888-ASK-USGS
Waldo County Trails Coalition		
White Mountain National Forest	Headquarters	603-536-6100
	Androscoggin Ranger District	603-466-2713
	Saco Ranger District	603-447-5448
Woodstock Conservation Commission		207-875-2773

Address or Location	Website, Email
186 York St., York, ME 03909	agamenticus.org, robin@agamenticus.org
1539 Pequawket Trail, Hiram, ME 04041	
14 Maine St., Suite 401, Brunswick, ME 04011	nature.org, naturemaine@tnc.org
P.O. Box 722, Northeast Harbor, ME 04662	
P.O. Box 425, 92 Main St., Ashland, ME 04732	northmainewoods.org, info@northmainewoods.org
	recreation.gov
P.O. Box 90, 325 Main St., Yarmouth, ME 04096	rrct.org, info@rrct.org
25 Spruce St., Rumford, ME 04276	rumfordwaterdistrict.org
806 Spencer Pond Rd., Beaver Cover, ME 04441	spencerpond.com, spc@spencerpond.com
5092 Access Rd., Bigelow, ME 04947	sugarloaf.com
1001 Carriage Rd., Carrabassett Valley, ME 04947	carrabassettvalley.org, townofcv@roadrunner.com
P.O. Box 500, Mapleton, ME 04757	
30 Main St., Freeport, ME 04032	freeportmaine.com, info@freeportmaine.com
25 Allard Circle, Hiram, ME 04041	townofhiram.org
P.O. Box 206, 8 Community Dr., Leeds, ME 04263	townofleeds.com, townofleeds@fairpoint.net
406 Bridgton Rd., Sebago, ME 04029	townofsebago.org
12201 Sunrise Valley Dr., Reston, VA 20192	usgs.gov, usgsstore@usgs.gov
P.O. Box 106, Unity, ME 04988	waldotrails.org, info@waldotrails.org
71 White Mountain Dr., Campton, NH 03223	fs.usda.gov/whitemountain
300 Glen Rd., Gorham, NH 03581	
33 Kancamagus Highway, Conway, NH 03818	
P.O. Box 180, Woodstock, ME 04255	woodstockmaine.net

APPENDIX B

NEW ENGLAND 4,000-FOOTERS

AMC's Four Thousand Footer Club was formed in 1957 to bring together hikers who had traveled to some of the less frequently visited sections of the White Mountains. The Four Thousand Footer Committee recognizes three lists of peaks: the White Mountain 4,000-footers, the New England 4,000-footers, and the New England Hundred Highest. Applicants for the White Mountain Four Thousand Footer Club must climb all 48 peaks in New Hampshire. To qualify for membership, a hiker must climb on foot to and from each summit on the list. The official lists of the 4,000-footers, in New Hampshire, Maine, and Vermont are included at the end of this appendix. Criteria for mountains on the official list are (1) each peak must be 4,000 ft. high, and (2) each peak must rise 200 ft. above the low point of its connecting ridge with a higher neighbor. All 67 4,000-footers, are reached by well-defined trails, although the paths to Owl's Head and Mt. Redington, as well as some short spur trails to other summits, are not officially maintained. Applicants for the New England Four Thousand Footer Club must also climb the 14 peaks in Maine and the five in Vermont. Separate awards are given to those who climb all peaks on a list in winter; to qualify as a winter ascent, the hike must not begin before the hour and minute of the beginning of winter (winter solstice) or end after the hour and minute of the end of winter (spring equinox).

If you are interested in becoming a member of one or more of the clubs, please visit amc4000footer.org or send a self-addressed, stamped envelope to the Four Thousand Footer Committee, Appalachian Mountain Club, P.O. Box 444, Exeter, NH 03833, and an information packet, including application forms, will be sent to you. If you are interested in the New England Four Thousand Footer Club or the New England Hundred Highest Club, please specify this in your letter, as these lists are not routinely included in the basic information packet. After climbing each peak, please record the date of the ascent, companions, if any, and other remarks.

On the following lists, elevations have been obtained from the latest USGS maps, some of which are now metric, requiring conversion from meters to feet. Where no exact elevation is given on the map, the elevation has been estimated by adding half the contour interval to the highest contour shown on the map; elevations so obtained are marked on the list with an asterisk (*). The elevations given here for several peaks in the Presidential region differ from those given elsewhere in this book because the Four

Thousand Footer Committee uses the USGS maps as the authority for all elevations, whereas in the rest of the book, the Bradford Washburn map of the Presidential Range supersedes the USGS maps in the area it covers.

4,000-FOOTERS IN MAINE

Mountain	Elevation (feet)	(meters)	Date Climbed
1. Katahdin, Baxter Peak	5,268	1,606	
2. Katahdin, Hamlin Peak	4,756	1,450	
3. Sugarloaf	4,250*	1,295*	
4. Crocker	4,228	1,289	
5. Old Speck	4,170*	1,271*	
6. North Brother	4,151	1,265	
7. Bigelow, West Peak	4,145	1,263	
8. Saddleback	4,120	1,256	
9. Bigelow, Avery Peak	4,090*	1,247*	
10. Abraham	4,050*	1,234*	
11. South Crocker	4,050*	1,234*	
12. Saddleback, the Horn	4,041	1,232	
13. Redington	4,010*	1,222*	
14. Spaulding	4,010*	1,222*	

4,000-FOOTERS IN NEW HAMPSHIRE

Mountain	Elevation (feet)	(meters)	Date Climbed
1. Washington	6,288	1,916.6	
2. Adams	5,774	1,760	
3. Jefferson	5,712	1,741	
4. Monroe	5,384*	1,641*	
5. Madison	5,367	1,636	
6. Lafayette	5,260*	1,603*	

Mountain	Elevation (feet)	(meters)	Date Climbed
7. Lincoln	5,089	1,551	
8. South Twin	4,902	1,494	
9. Carter Dome	4,832	1,473	
10. Moosilauke	4,802	1,464	
11. Eisenhower	4,780*	1,457*	
12. North Twin	4,761	1,451	
13. Carrigain	4,700*	1,433*	
14. Bond	4,698	1,432	
15. Middle Carter	4,610*	1,405*	
16. West Bond	4,540*	1,384*	
17. Garfield	4,500*	1,372*	
18. Liberty	4,459	1,359	
19. South Carter	4,430*	1,350*	
20. Wildcat	4,422	1,348	
21. Hancock	4,420*	1,347*	
22. South Kinsman	4,358	1,328	
23. Field	4,340*	1,323*	
24. Osceola	4,340*	1,323*	
25. Flume	4,328	1,319	
26. South Hancock	4,319	1,316	
27. Pierce (Clinton)	4,310	1,314	
29. Willey	4,285	1,306	
30. Bondcliff	4,265	1,300	
31. Zealand	4,260*	1,298*	
32. North Tripyramid	4,180*	1,274*	
33. Cabot	4,170*	1,271*	
34. East Osceola	4,156	1,267	

Mountain	Elevation (feet)	(meters)	Date Climbed
35. Middle Tripyramid	4,140*	1,262*	
36. Cannon	4,100*	1,250*	
37. Hale	4,054	1,236	
38. Jackson	4,052	1,235	
39. Tom	4,051	1,235	
40. Wildcat D	4,050*	1,234*	
41. Moriah	4,049	1,234	
42. Passaconaway	4,043	1,232	
43. Owl's Head	4,025	1,227	
44. Galehead	4,024	1,227	
45. Whiteface	4,020*	1,225*	
46. Waumbek	4,006	1,221	
47. Isolation	4,004	1,220	
48. Tecumseh	4,003	1,220	

4,000-FOOTERS IN VERMONT

Mountain	Elevation (feet)	(meters)	Date Climbed
1. Mansfield	4,393	1,339	
2. Killington	4,235	1,291	
3. Camel's Hump	4,083	1,244	
4. Ellen	4,083	1,244	
5. Abraham	4,006	1,221	

*No exact elevation is given on the map; therefore, elevation has been estimated by adding half the contour interval to the highest contour shown on the map.

APPENDIX C

NEW ENGLAND HUNDRED HIGHEST

The following list excludes the previously listed New England Four Thousand Footers. Those peaks must also be climbed to achieve the goal of climbing the New England Hundred Highest peaks. Where no exact elevation is on the map, the elevation has been estimated by adding half of the contour interval to the highest contour shown on the map. Elevations so obtained are marked on the list with an asterisk(*).

MAINE

	Mountain	Elevation	Date Climbed
1.	South Brother	3,970	
2.	Snow (Chain of Ponds quad)	3,960*	
3.	Goose Eye	3,870*	
4.	Fort	3,867	
5.	White Cap	3,856	
6.	Unnamed (Boundary Peak)	3,855	
7.	Bigelow, South Horn	3,805	
8.	Coe	3,795	
9.	East Kennebago	3,791	
10.	Baldpate	3,790*	
11.	Snow (Little Kennebago Lake quad)	3,784	
12.	Kennebago Divide (N. Peak)	3,775	
13.	Elephant	3,772	

NEW HAMPSHIRE

Mountain	Elevation	Date Climbed
1. Sandwich	3,980*	
2. The Bulge	3,950*	
3. Nancy	3,926	
4. The Horn	3,905	
5. North Weeks	3,901	
6. South Weeks	3,885	
7. Vose Spur	3,862	
8. East Sleeper	3,860*	
9. Peak Above the Nubble	3,813	
10. Scar Ridge, West Peak	3,774	
11. NE Cannonball	3,769	

VERMONT

Mountain	Elevation	Date Climbed
1. Pico Peak	3,957	
2. Stratton	3,940	
3. Jay Peak	3,858	
4. Equinox	3,850*	
5. Mendon Peak	3,840	
6. Breadloaf	3,835	
7. Wilson	3,790*	
8. Big Jay	3,786	
9. Dorset Peak	3,770*	

INDEX

Trail names in **bold type** indicate a detailed description found in the text.

Where multiple page references appear, bold numbering indicates the main entry or entries for the trail.

[Bracketed information] indicates which of the six maps displays the feature and where, by map section letter and number.